HISTORY OF PORTUGAL

SECOND EDITION

A. H. DE OLIVEIRA MARQUES

History of Portugal

SECOND EDITION

COLUMBIA UNIVERSITY PRESS

New York

1976

Columbia University Press
New York   Guildford, Surrey
Copyright © 1972, 1976 Columbia University Press
Printed in the United States of America
Library of Congress Cataloging in Publication Data
Marques, Antonio Henrique R   de Oliveira.
   History of Portugal.
   Includes bibliographies and index.
   1. Portugal—History. I. Title.
DP538.M37   1976   946.9   76-16780
ISBN 0-231-08353-X

To António José Saraiva
and Vitorino Magalhães Godinho

HISTORY OF PORTUGAL

VOLUME I:

FROM LUSITANIA TO EMPIRE

CONTENTS

THE ROOTS OF A NATION

"If we cast a quick glance at the most general geomorphological features of the Iberian Peninsula, considered as a whole, no particularity seems to justify within it a political fragmentation." [*Se relancearmos no seu conjunto os traços geomorfológicos mais gerais da Península Hispânica, particularidade alguma parece justificar uma fragmentação política dentro dela.*]—Jaime Cortesão, Os Factores Democráticos na Formação de Portugal, *reedited as* Vol. I of his Obras Completas, *2nd edition, Lisbon, 1966, pp. 16–17.*

THE SETTING

Geography

It is impossible to speak of a unity of the Portuguese territory based on natural conditions or of an individuality of Portugal within the whole of the Peninsula. The northwestern part (Minho) is a continuation of Spanish Galicia in orography, climate, and form of agriculture. The northeast (Trás-os-Montes and northern Beira) prolongs the Iberian *Meseta* while the central range (*serra da Estrela* and its extensions) separates northern and southern Portugal as it does northern and southern Castile, the neighboring country. Beira Baixa and Alentejo are similar to the Spanish Extremadura. The southernmost province of Portugal, the Algarve, does not differ from coastal Andalucia. In all cases similarities lie not only in the soil and weather features but also in the ways of life and the general economic conditions. The most original regions in Portugal correspond, as a matter of fact, to a relatively narrow strip of coastal territory (Beira Litoral and Portuguese Estremadura) and to an alluvial plain in the Tejo basin (Ribatejo). Yet the whole would not encompass 25 per cent of the country.

R. Minho

Bragança

R. Lima

Viana do Castelo

Braga

Vila Real

Porto

R. Douro

ATLANTIC
OCEAN

R. Vouga

Aveiro

Viseu

Guarda

R. Mondego

Coimbra

Castelo Branco

SPAIN

Leiria

R. Tejo

Portalegre

Santarém

Lisboa

Évora

Setúbal

R. Sado

R. Guadiana

Beja

Faro

0   50   100   km.

0   50   miles

It is true that the exceptional extension of low tablelands gives some parts of Portugal a peculiar characteristic if compared with the rest of the Iberian Peninsula. However, this fact is more a result of taking the *political unit Portugal* as a term of comparison with that other *political unit, Spain,* than of detaching a geographical unit from the Iberian Peninsula considered as a whole. Peculiar morphological traits, as diversified as the Portuguese ones, are also to be found in Catalonia-Aragon, in Murcia-Valencia, and in Andalucia, to mention only the most striking. In the great variety of Iberia several of its regions are detachable. Portugal—in truth a part of Portugal—is one of them. But to quote Madariaga,* "Spain is one under all her Spains." This fact alone does not make the independence of Portugal an absurdity and does not suggest an Iberian union either. All over Europe, as all over the world, geography and history often contradict each other. The morphological unity of the north European plains was and is broken by frontiers which seem as arbitrary as those of Portugal. The same might be said of many vast regions in Africa and America.

Much more important than a presumed geographic individuality, the geographical situation accounts for many relevant features of the Portuguese history and for the very existence of Portugal as a nation. The westernmost country in continental Europe, Portugal was for many centuries the end of the world. Finisterre, the name of a Galician cape, might as well apply to Cabo da Roca, the "point of Europe." Westward there was nothing, not even some islands. Indeed the Portuguese coast is 848 kilometers (527 miles) long with practically no islands, if one forgets the tiny rocks of the Berlengas, off the town of Peniche. Furthermore, the coastline has very few openings, in spite of the long strips of beach. The number of good inland harbors is only three or four. Although the sea affects most of Portugal in weather conditions and vegetation, there are no gulfs, and the amount of economic life dependent upon the sea is secondary. Beaten by the frequently stormy western winds and possessing a rather narrow platform (30 kilometers or 19 miles), the Portuguese coastline does not seem favorable to maritime adventures. On the contrary, geographical conditions in most of the country would suggest a limited maritime life, with local and short-distance fishing only. Land's end, Portugal's geographical

* *Spain: A Modern History,* 4th printing, New York, 1965, p. 9.

situation, did not exactly favor the development of high cultures and for a long time accounted for her backwardness.

Although Atlantic by position, Portugal is Mediterranean in most of her features. Climate, vegetation, type of economy, ways of living, and soil characteristics are more Greek or Italian than Atlantic Spanish or Atlantic French. Rainfall and temperature are typically Mediterranean, with a dry and hot summer followed by a rainy but mild winter. Most of the country's vegetation shows Mediterranean aspects. Every visitor to Portugal is impressed by the variety of the landscape, but there are no real forests, rather clumps of trees and shrubs, thickets, and other scattered vegetation. Fruit trees play a fundamental role, either alone or associated with crop fields and other cultures. Vineyards are everywhere, and such cereals as wheat, maize, barley, and rye are grown. The soil is generally thin and poor, and the terrain largely mountainous and subject to constant erosion. Less than half of the whole territory is actually cultivated. Soil conditions favor either very small holdings that are cradles of intensely individualistic forms of living and working or vast *latifundia,* poorly exploited and partly abandoned to pasture and wilderness. Cattle grazing is secondary to the raising of sheep, goats, donkeys, and pigs. Manual labor and rudimentary techniques persist everywhere.

The farther south one travels in the country the more one feels the effects of the Mediterranean. Portugal's great variety accounts for the enormous differences between the northern and southern parts. Without forgetting the general Mediterranean traits, geographers have been able to divide the country into two large regions, separated roughly by parallel 40. North and South Portugal are contrasts in climate and in soil. All the other differences in economy, psychology, and history are merely its results: 61.5 per cent of the lowlands, below 200 meters (656 feet), are in the South; 95.4 per cent of the tablelands and mountains above 400 meters (1,312 feet) lie in the North. Weather in most of the North is wet, with a much higher percentage of both rainfall and humidity, in contrast to the four to six months of dry weather in the rainless South. No wonder that two forms of living have emerged from such diversity. Deep and humid valleys in the North have always favored isolation, localism, and dense (as many as 200 inhabitants per square kilometer) but scattered settlements. They have also helped to preserve archaisms and to resist invasions and novelty. The southern and arid plains permitted roads to be opened and people's minds as well. The plains made for easy invasion but also for easy communication. They favored the concentration of few people (as few as 25 inhabitants per square kilometer) in large but widely separated settlements.

The People

Man arrived in the Iberian Peninsula very early in his history. Remains of pre-Abbevillian and Abbevillian cultures—the earliest ones archaeologists have been able to characterize—are plentiful in Iberia from south to north and east to west. This fact proves the existence of human beings of the *Pithecanthropus erectus* group contemporary with the first glaciation ("Günz") or even before, and traces man's life there back at least 500,000 years. Vegetable and grub gatherers mostly, they survived the first, second ("Mindel"), and third ("Riss") glaciations and the corresponding interglacial eras with all their consequent changes in climate. They were still existing in evolved forms of culture (Acheulian) by the dawn of the last ("Würm") glaciation, more than 120,000 years ago. Some other more or less contemporary groups were preferably attached to the forest and its peculiar forms of living. Pre-historians classify them as Clactonians and assign them a long period of activity, some 300,000 years (between 540,000 and 240,000 years ago). Significant changes occurred only when, instead of gathering harvests, men developed killing techniques and depended in their daily lives more and more on hunting. Both the Levalloisians (250,000 to 70,000) and the Mousterians (140,000 to 70,000) were hunters and tended to become chiefly so as time went by. Yet they were not the result of a simple evolution of the *Pithecanthropus erectus* group. They seem to be related to groups of other ethnical origins, namely, the Neanderthal type of man, and gradually emerged more than 100,000 years ago.

These cultures populated the whole of Iberia. The western part, Portugal now, is rich in archaeological evidence. From north to south, Lower Paleolithic cultures have been discovered in abundance, particularly in two large areas, with little communication between them: one covers most of Estremadura and the lower Tagus basin, occasionally stretching south to the Alentejo plains; the other is north of the Douro, mostly in present-day Minho and Galicia.

With the coming of the Upper Paleolithic culture more than 50,000 years ago, we reach firmer ground. Human beings belonging to the basic ethnical sediment we belong to, the *Homo sapiens* group, entered Europe and gradually took it over, killing, expelling, or absorbing the natives. Several subgroups, such as the Combe-Capelle, Cro-Magnon, and Grimaldi types, all associated with one vast culture —the Aurignacian continued by the Solutrian and Magdalenian— spread over almost all the continent. Somewhat later another subgroup, the Chancelade man, appeared differentiated in two basic ethnical types, the dolichocephalic and the brachicephalic. Associated with the Magdalenian culture, the Chancelade man emerged between 50,000 and 10,000 B.C. In features he was not much different from the average contemporary Mediterranean man.

The Epipalaeolithic or Mesolithic cultures were responsible in the Iberian Peninsula for the spreading of a human race whose anatomical traits are still to be found in the vast majority of both Spaniards and Portuguese. From roughly 10,000 through 5,000 B.C. several cultures succeeded to or were contemporary with each other. Among them the Epi-Gravettian, the Azilian, and the Asturian were the most important. At the same time the Capsians from Africa entered the Peninsula. All apparently belonged to the same broad ethnical group, and from their fusion originated a fairly homogeneous human type. Such authors as Pericot even consider them the basic demographical stratum of Spain. The discovery of some two hundred skeletons in the Portuguese area (Muge, in Estremadura) revealed an overwhelming majority of dolichocephalic types. There were a few brachicephalians, too, the first ones known in Europe, probably descendants of the Cro-Magnon man, although shorter.

Pure Neolithic is rare, particularly in Portugal. Bronze cultures appeared probably as early as 3000 B.C., subdivided into four large groups: the Almería culture, which spread in the South and Southeast, including southern Portugal; the Megalithic culture, all over Spain; the Bell-Beakers culture (*vaso campaniforme*), also very widely spread; and finally the El Argar culture, little represented in the western part of the Peninsula.

Ethnically speaking, the whole Bronze Age witnessed the pre-dominance of a similar type of man, dolichocephalian, of average height, probably dark-complexioned, blended with some mesocephalians. Furthermore, of note was the north-south separation of cultures: a southern zone covering Alentejo, Estremadura, and the Algarve, generally associated with other "Spanish" sites, appears divorced from a northern zone, north of the Mondego or the Douro, forming a whole with Galicia. No wonder. The two easiest ways of reaching the western part of the Peninsula are by the Alentejo plains in the South or by crossing the river Minho in the North. These have been for centuries the natural invasion routes. However, when those primitive tribes or clans finally got to the terminus of their travel, the end of the world indeed, enough time had elapsed to obliterate earlier group resemblances, if there had been any, and to make them alien to one another. They were now enemies who looked at each other suspiciously and probably fought fiercely. The best way of achieving a peaceful coexistence was to leave a no man's land between them. As time went by, differences in culture only stressed the enmity.

The "splendor" of the Megalithic culture, its abundance, and its earliest dated forms in the west of Iberia have led several authors to suggest a Peninsular origin, possibly with maritime irradiation from its westernmost region. Of this no complete evidence is available at present. The Megalithic culture does indeed cover a large area of Europe, including the British Isles and Scandinavia, yet nothing supports the assumption of direct sea contacts from Portugal eastward. On the contrary, the Portuguese Megalithic sites lie generally quite far from the coastline, rather suggesting a settlement from the East, disassociated from the sea.

The so-called Bronze III period probably saw the arrival of the first Indo-European peoples. They were the pre-Celts, Ligures, or whatever we care to call them, for only assumptions are possible. Copper mining began with them, and we may assume that Alentejo and the Algarve, where that metal is found, were favorite places for settlement. To admit that metallurgy stood for a certain cultural advancement in the southern regions is hypothetical only.

In the Bronze IV period, associated with Iron I, and Bronze V, associated with Iron II, came the Celts and the Iberians, as well as the first highly civilized maritime peoples, the Phoenicians (before 1000 B.C.) and the Greeks. There is little to say about their contribution to the ethnic composition of the future Portuguese. All of them were similar anthropologically, the so-called Mediterranean type of man. The same is true of other invaders who partly or thoroughly conquered the Iberian Peninsula: the Carthaginians, the Romans, and the Moslems (both Arabs and Berbers).

Phoenician and Greek colonization hardly touched the northern part of present-day Portugal. To the north of Estremadura there is no evidence of the arrival of the Phoenicians and the Greeks, with the exception of some coins which alone do not necessarily account for their presence. In southern Portugal, however, their influence is noticeable: along the coasts of the Algarve and Alentejo and in the Tagus basin convincing remains have been unearthed. The Algarve, an extension of Andalucia, was decisively colonized. Ossonoba, near present Faro, is probably of Phoenician origin. There is enough archaeological evidence of fishing industry devices to suggest that fisheries started playing a major role in the region's economy. The Romans afterward took good care of them.

At the same time, to the north of the Mondego and in Galicia, with occasional infiltrations south, an archaic culture of Iron peoples was emerging. In its homogeneous location it continued the old tradition of backward but individually oriented Northwestern cultures. In Galicia alone more than 5,000 *castros* or small fortified villages on the top of a hill have been discovered. This culture lasted until Roman times.

When the Romans conquered the Iberian Peninsula and civilized it permanently (second century B.C. to first century A.D.), they found in the West several native peoples whom they classified and labeled. To the north of the Douro lived the Gallaeci, subdivided into Lucenses (roughly to the north of the Minho) and Bracari (to the south of the Minho). They were the descendants of the *castros* culture. South of the Douro the Lusitani were dwelling. The Guadiana basin was populated with Celtici. In the southernmost part were the Conii or Cunei. Of these groups, the Gallaeci and the Lusitani were the most important, and only they prevailed in geography and administration. Between Lusitani and Celtici there were no great differences in degree and form of civilization, for the Lusitani were most probably native peoples who had become celticized. The Conii were not numerous.

The Language

The origin of Portuguese is still largely undetermined. Philologists as a rule have paid more attention to language evolution after the twelfth century than to its roots back in the past. Yet there seems to be no doubt that "Portuguese" dialectal differences are to be found as early as the Roman period and in areas where the future nation was to emerge. This, of course, is not peculiar to Portuguese but to almost all the Romance languages.

Of all the reasons philologists offer to explain the differentiation of Vulgar Latin, namely, the relative geographic isolation of groups, the development of separate political units, the variation of cultural and educational circumstances, the period of Romanization, dialectal differences in the language of the colonists, the original linguistic substrata and subsequent linguistic superimposures, the dialectal differences in the language of the colonists must always be emphasized and assigned a major role. Furthermore, as Meyer-Lübke has pointed out, communication forms within the same province or among nearby provinces were of enormous relevance in producing contacts among linguistic groups and standardizing them.

The native languages were of little or no importance in the birth and rise of Portuguese. Their contribution to vocabulary or to syntax was negligible. It was the natives who learned Latin, not the Romans who learned the local languages. Communications, legislation, and the school system relied upon Latin. Natives for some centuries might have spoken an odd dialect of local idioms added to bastardized Latin words and forms. As time passed, that dialect completely disappeared. There is historical evidence that the Roman colonizers took thoughtful and good care of spreading the Latin language and customs among the natives. The outcome was thoroughly successful and permanent.

The impact of legions and auxiliary forces on the language has to be estimated differently in Portugal. After a first and obscure period of military conquest, most of the soldiers left, and western Hispania evolved peacefully during the whole Roman rule. In Lusitania, that is, in southern and central Portugal, no legions were ever stationed. In the Tarraconensis, from which Callaecia or Gallaecia (that is, Galicia) was later dismembered, two legions were settled in the Leon area (Leon derives exactly from Legionem, the legion), remaining there for some time. Military roads connected Legionem with Bracara Augusta (now Braga) and with Aquae Flaviae (today Chaves), the two most important urban centers in southern Gallaecia. It is therefore presumable that the dialectal forms of Vulgar Latin spoken by the legionaries have determined or influenced the rise of Galician-Portuguese.

Yet early medieval Portuguese should not be associated with Galician-Portuguese only. The dialect (or dialects) spoken in Lusitania was just as important. If there were no neighboring legions stationed, there were nuclei of Italian colonists settled in the rising centers of the South. Two colonies, composed partly of citizens from Rome and partly from other Italians, were founded very early in the Roman conquest (first century B.C.) within the boundaries of Lusitania: Pax Iulia (the future Beja) and Scallabis Praesidium Iulium (the future Santarém). Both were administrative centers (capitals of *conventus*) and both were connected by road. That same road went through Ebora Liberalitas Iulia (the future Évora), a Latin *municipium,* and Olisipo Felicitas Iulia (the future Lisbon), a municipium of Roman citizens. There were two other Latin *municipia* in Lusitania, namely, Myrtilis (now Mértola) and Salacia (now Alcácer do Sal). No colonies or municipia were ever founded in Gallaecia. Thus Roman or Italic dialects probably had a major effect on the rise of the southern Portuguese and southern Italian dialects, such as Oscian, have indeed been noticed, but much more has to be done in this field. We also do not know to what extent "Lusitania" was spoken in the eastern part of the province, where Emerita Augusta (today's Mérida), the capital city, with its great cultural and therefore linguistic influence, was located. Other dialects, vulgarly spoken in Baetica, might have had their impact too.

Portuguese, like every Romance language, is not an offspring of Vulgar Latin only. Literary Latin, the written language and therefore the language of administration, also played its role, and not a minor one. It helped keep unity among the several dialects, preventing for many centuries their breaking up into different languages.

The gradual decline of the Roman world, accompanied by the disruption of communications and the virtual disappearance of a central government, brought about dialectal freedom and quick evolution of dialects. The school system and the number of literate persons decreased steadily. Their influence on the people obviously decreased too. By Visigothic times (sixth to eighth centuries) dialects in Spain were rapidly becoming languages.

Neither Suevi nor Visigoths affected the Spanish idioms. About thirty Germanic words were introduced into Portuguese, and most of them came through Lower Latin (and also much later through French) and not by direct contact with the invaders, who generally spoke Latin. Swabian words were unknown. It is true that in the Iberian Peninsula Portuguese was the language least influenced by German.

The Arabs arrived early in the eighth century, and with them came the second and last significant component of the Portuguese language. Some 500 words passed from Arabic into Portuguese. This statement, however, must be explained, considering the minor contact with Arabic words that daily spoken modern Portuguese has. The impact was on noun vocabulary, not on the structure of the language, which remained purely Latin. Since the Moslem civilization in Spain was refined and technically progressive, it is no wonder that most of the nouns of Arabic origin referred to such things as clothing (*alifafes, aljubas, eixarafas*) and furniture (*almadraques, alfambares, almucelas*), agricultural implements and scientific devices (*azenhas, azéquias, noras, alqueires*). Moslem sophistication diminished with the decline of Islam, and new influences of French, Italian, or English origin took its place. Fashions and articles of furniture, once so popular, changed their names simply because they disappeared, displaced by new ones. The same was true of technical and scientific words. In medieval Portuguese there were many Arabic words, indicating the presence of a civilization. In modern Portuguese most of these words are obsolete. From a significant position they dropped to a minor one.

The Moslem conquest was lasting only in central and southern Portugal, in the area to the south of the Douro, where Galician-Portuguese was not spoken. "Lusitanian," which we now might call Mozarabic or the language of the Mozarabs, evolved separately and under different cultural circumstances. We know little of its char-

acteristics as distinct from the other Mozarabic dialects spoken all over
Moslem Spain. But there is no doubt that it possessed individuality,
being different from both Galician-Portuguese and the other Mozara-
bics. Once more the westernmost position of Portugal favored its
isolation and its linguistic archaisms. The Moslem civilization was less
brilliant in western than in eastern Lusitania or in Baetica. No wonder
that Portuguese received considerably fewer Arabic words than Castilian, although many more than Catalan.

By the eleventh and twelfth centuries, when the Mondego and
then the Tagus were definitely crossed by the Christian armies, Galician-Portuguese and Lusitanian-Mozarabic came in direct and permanent contact. From this encounter the language Portuguese was
born. We do not know to what extent the Northern dialect did command the Southern one, or vice versa. There were probably more
Northerners than Southerners, and many representatives of the Mozarabic elite were killed or ran away. On the other hand, the most important urban centers, like Lisbon, Santarém, Évora, Beja, Silves, lay
south. The capital was moved southward to Lisbon by the middle of
the thirteenth century, a fact that probably enhanced the role played
by the Southern dialect. Abundant vernacular sources, including
literary texts, date only from the late thirteenth and the fourteenth
centuries, when more than a century had elapsed since the conquest
and both dialects were starting to fuse into a common language. Nor
are there any relevant Galician sources from the same period to permit
a meaningful comparison. However, the enormous changes Portuguese
underwent from the thirteenth through the fifteenth century were
obviously not the simple result of the natural evolution of a single
dialect.

Modern Portuguese dialects show very clearly the fundamental
North-South division, although they are somewhat more complex because of transitional forms that probably go back to the Reconquista
period. Within the Portuguese language there are, in Portugal, three
great dialectal areas, the North, including Minho and Trás-os-Montes;
the Center, comprising Beira; and the South, which includes the rest
of the country. The Northern dialect accounts for the old Galician-
Portuguese; the Southern is the direct heir of "Mozarabic-Lusitanian."
The Center dialect, although more like the Northern than the

Southern, could be explained by the circumstances of the Moslem-Christian war, which spread Galician-Portuguese south of its original boundaries.

The Administration

The Portuguese borders, as they have existed from the thirteenth century on, are not mere products of the hazards of the Reconquest from the Moslems. Nor are they the fortuitous result of military adventures against Christian neighbors. Their origin and permanent traits have to be sought far back in the past and explained mostly by the Roman, ecclesiastical, and Moslem administration systems.

In the first century ᴾ c. (27) the administrative reforms of Augustus divided the former Hispania Ulterior into two provinces, Lusitania and Baetica, separated roughly by the Guadiana River. Lusitania, with its capital in Emerita, included all the western strip of Spain, from the southern to the northern sea. Shortly afterward, however, between 7 and 2 b.c., the region to the north of the Douro (Gallaecia) was taken from Lusitania and annexed to the Tarraconensis province, the former Hispania Citerior.

For judicial purposes each province was further divided into smaller units called *conventus*. By the first century of our era the conventus system was pretty well fixed. Lusitania comprised three of them, named Pacensis (after its capital city, Pax), Scallabitanus (after Scallabis), and Emeritensis (after Emerita, which was also the capital of the whole province). The first two were separated from each other by the Tagus. An artificial border line, probably based on traditional tribal frontiers, separated the third conventus from the other two. Artificial also, but nonetheless founded upon actual separation of native peoples, was the boundary between northeastern Lusitania and the Tarraconensis. The latter province was divided into a great number of conventus. For our purpose, only the northwestern ones have any interest. They were the Bracarensis (after Bracara), the Lucensis, (after Lucus), and the Asturicensis (after Asturica).

Of these divisions, two stand out: the division between southern and northern Portugal by the Douro line and almost complete coincidence between the area of three adjoining conventus (the Bracarensis, the Scallabitanus, and the Pacensis) and present-day Portugal. There

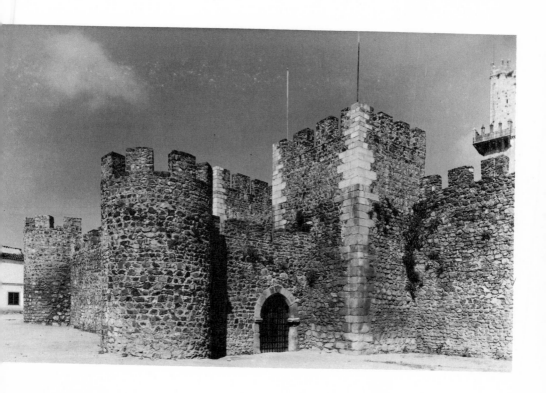

UPPER LEFT: *Roman presence in pre-Portugal: mosaic at Conimbriga (Coimbra), 2nd–4th century* A.D. BELOW: *Moslem presence in pre-Portugal: church of Santa Maria in Beja (Beja), a former mosque, with its minaret on the left, 8th–12th century* A.D. ABOVE: *The Reconquista: castle of Beja, 11th–12th century.*

exist of course minor differences which are indeed dependent on the
Reconquista, as we shall try to explain later. For the moment let us
emphasize only that although the Guadiana formed the main separation of Lusitania and Baetica, some enclaves east of that river administratively belonged to Lusitania. Such was the case of Serpa, nowadays
a part of Portugal.

Later in the history of the Roman Empire there were other administrative reforms. None of them changed the basic conventual division
we have just described. Early in the third century a short-lived An-
toniniana province detached Gallaecia from the Tarraconensis. But
only by the late third century (297?) did Diocletian create Gallaecia
as a separate province with the above-mentioned three conventus of
Bracara, Lucus, and Asturica. The capital was Bracara.

We are much less completely informed of the administrative sub-
division of the province. In each one there were urban nuclei, the
municipia, the *coloniae*, the *praefecturae*, and the *civitates*, as well as
rural areas known as *gentes*, but we have no maps of their boundaries
and no full list of their number. As time went by distinctions between
their political status and their administrative status, which derived
from their origin, were gradually blurred, and civitates prevailed over
all the others as a general name. Coincidence between them and more
modern units is still to be studied.

Some cities emerged as centers of greater political and economic
significance. It was there that Christianity, an essentially urban religion, spread more rapidly. No wonder that they also became important
centers of Christian expansion. By late Roman times most of the cities
were residences of bishops and capitals of religious districts known as
dioceses. In the conventus Pacensis we find evidence of episcopal cities
in Ossonoba and Ebora; in the Scallabitanus, Olisipo; in the Bracarensis, Bracara, and Aquae Flaviae. Dioceses generally coincided with
late Roman municipia but not always. Also there was no coincidence
between episcopal cities and capitals of conventus. Or, if there was
any, the list of the known bishops provides us with some significant
changes in the political role of the Roman cities, probably derived
from economic and social conditions. Scallabis, for instance, seems to
have declined in favor of Olisipo for there was never a bishop resident
in the former capital of the conventus Scallabitanus. The same might

have been true for Pax on behalf of Ebora. In some cases, however, scarcity of sources better accounts for our ignorance in the matter. As a rule, in each province one of the bishops—the one living in its capital city—had a certain pre-eminence but no actual authority. He was called the metropolitan and corresponded to the civil head of the province. The metropolitan of Lusitania lived in Emerita, that of Gallaecia in Bracara.

From the ecclesiastical pattern in western Iberia the significant fact of late Roman times seems to have been the emergence of a new diocese in the South, that of Ossonoba. It provided the basis for a permanent administrative and political new unit in Lusitania.

Suevi and Visigoths brought about minor changes. The *civitas* and its adjoining land, the *territorium,* gradually replaced, for administrative and political purposes, both the conventus and the province. This meant the greater emphasis on the local unit and on the local problems, directly opposed to the existence of an efficient and real centralization. For practical purposes the province (sometimes called duchy, for its head was now a duke, *dux*) ceased to have any real importance. Even its memory faded and left no traces in late medieval times. It was from Visigothic times on that a weak provincial authority left unmolested the conventus unit, not because it any longer played a major role in justice and administration but because it was enforced by the superposition of the episcopal organization.

The conventus, however, was to collapse also. While Christianity expanded, new bishoprics had to be founded within the same conventual area. They, in their turn, became the essential administrative units above the cities and the territories. In Lusitania new dioceses arose, possibly about the sixth and seventh centuries, in Pax, in Conimbria or Colimbria, in Egitania, in Veseo, in Lamecum. North of the Douro bishoprics were founded in Portucale, in Dumio, and in Tude. If, for boundary purposes, the conventus survived, it was simply because the ecclesiastical dioceses were coincident in it and stopped at its borders. But within each conventus new fractures were from now on possible, following the border line of each bishopric. In western Iberia this was particularly true of the dioceses of Tude and Auriense, which comprised the area between the Lima and the northern frontier of the conventus Bracarensis. Part of Tude became "Por-

tuguese" for reasons we shall see. The diocese of Egitania, slightly to
the east of the conventus Scallabitanus, and apparently belonging to
the Emeritensis, was later added to the new country.

The Arab conquest all over the world respected and preserved
the existing administrative units. This was as true for Syria and
Egypt as for Persia. It was also true for the Iberian Peninsula. Only
the identifying names were changed. Emirates were established all
over Islam, each one corresponding to a province or a group of provinces. Below the emirates there were the *kuwar* or districts, corresponding to the former conventus or to the religious dioceses. Lesser
units within each kūra were the *quran* (sing. *qarya*) or local communities. Military reasons led to the rise of other districts or marches,
closer to the frontier, encompassing several kuwar and where the civil
and military powers were unified under a strong command. Part of
Lusitania formed, in late Moslem times, one of such marches, al-
Thaghr al-Adnā, the "Lower" march, with headquarters either in
Mārida (Emerita) or in Baṭalyāws (today's Badajoz). It included the
territory north and northwest of the Guadiana, to the north of Bāja
(Pax).

In western Iberia we find evidence of some five or seven kuwar.
From south to north, they were Ukhshūnuba (Ocsonoba or Ossonoba)
with the capital in Shilb, Bāja (Pax), Yābura (?) (Ebora), al-Ushbūna
(Olisipone or Olisipo), Shantarīn (Scallabis), and possibly Ḳulūmriyya
(Colimbra) and Antāniya (Egitania). In some cases it seems that the
kūra did not coincide with the judicial units, comprising two or more
of the latter. This is why there are doubts of the existence of a kūra
with capital in Yābura, which, nevertheless, was the seat of a *cadī*
(judge), as well as Bāja. Farther south the capital of the Ukhshūnuba
kūra was moved to Shilb, while the judicial seat seems to have been
maintained in the former capital city. By the early eleventh century
the judges of al-Ushbūna and Shantarīn were combined into one,
but we do not know which one prevailed. The same probably happened with the two kuwar for military reasons. North of the Douro,
Moslem authority collapsed by the end of the eighth century, after
some fifty years of troubled and incomplete rule. We know nothing
of the administrative problems of the Moslems, but there is no reason
to believe that their conduct there was any different or that the existing units were erased.

It is easy to realize that the kuwar corresponded to the Roman plus the ecclesiastical division we mentioned before, at least up to the Mondego. To the north it was deemed wiser for military reasons to unify small districts for purposes of better command and defense. Veseo and Lamecum were frontier towns. Their bishops had fled as soon as they could and when they realized some Christian protection was near. The bishops of Egitania and Colimbria behaved the same way. We find them accompanying the kings of Leon in their travels. The hazards of the Reconquista brought the bishops of Veseo and Lamecum back, then forced them to flee once more.

Nothing of the sort happened in the South, where the bishops remained in peaceful and well-organized areas. Still sources are scarce, and of some of them we know practically nothing, not even whether their existence was maintained until the end of the Moslem rule.

We also lack monographs to inform us of the quran and their coincidence with either civitates or territoria. Research in this field will probably bring about striking features of continuity.

Thus, when the Reconquista started and the Christian order gradually encompassed the whole of western Iberia, nothing essential had been changed in the boundaries and administrative habits, which in some cases were almost a thousand years old. No wonder that such a condition would always be kept in mind by kings, lords, bishops, and communities in their efforts to organize, rule, or simply exploit.

Communications and Settlement

The existence of a sparsely populated area between the southern and the northern parts of west Iberia has already been pointed out. The Romans, in their effort to centralize administration and to civilize and pacify the native tribes, built a wide network of roads, permanently connecting areas which until then were more or less isolated. Easy communication became possible among all the provinces and all the conventus. In west Spain Lusitania and Gallaecia were united by two main roads, one connecting Bracara with Olisipo over Portucale, Conimbria, and Scallabis, the other relating Bracara to Emerita through the mountain, over Caurium. Gallaecia, in its southernmost conventus, had Bracara as a good nodal center from which four roads radiated in different directions, northwest (to Iria), northeast (to Asturica), southwest (to Portucale), and southeast (to Aquae Flaviae). In Lusitania, to the south of the Tagus, there were several important roads: one started in front of Olisipo and went to Baetica by way of Pax and Serpa; in Salacia, a branch of the same road headed northeast to Ebora and from there to Emerita. Ebora and Pax were also connected by a direct highway. Another branch of the Olisipo-Baetica road, a little to the south of Salacia, went to Ossonoba, crossing the central part of today's Alentejo. Another road went from Pax to Aesuris in the extreme south, west of the Guadiana; from there, once the river was crossed, there was a direct highway to Hispalis, the capital of Baetica. From Aesuris westward, along the coast, a very much frequented road reached Ossonoba. Two other highways in the north of the conventus Pacensis started in front of Scallabis, heading respectively to Norba and Emerita.

In all this rather complex net of communications, two facts stand out and should be emphasized: first, the existence of two developed areas, one to the north of the Douro, the other to the south of the Tagus basin (thus including the northern bank of the river), separated by a vast region of sparse population and few important settlements; second, the south-north road connection which put those two areas in relatively easy contact.

Jaime Cortesão pointed out the importance of the south-north road to the rise and development of new settlements and to the fostering of a complementary economic life: "Along it and in its encounter with the rivers the most important urban centers of all this area arose, both in Roman and in medieval times." And further, "The Roman road system, as a tool for social organization, implied two consequences of the greatest future reach: one, what we will call the Atlantic-way of settlement (atlantização do povoamento) and, two, its unification by means of a backbone in the sense of the meridians."

The Roman road network was probably expanded after the fourth century. Two of the most important urban centers in Visigothic times, seats of new bishoprics, were relatively far from the main roads we know, Veseo and Lamecum. A third one, Egitania, was indeed connected by road with Emerita, over Norba, but probably had no contacts with the western part of Lusitania. With these exceptions, there is no doubt that all the significant political and economic towns

Lucus

Iria

Auriense

GALLAECIA

Legio

Asturica Aug.

Tudae

† Aquae Flaviae

† Braccara

Portucale

Lameco

Beseo

Conimbria

Egitania

L U S I T A N I A

Norba

Scallabis

Emerita

To Hispalis

† Olisipona

† Ebbora

Salacia

Pax

Serpa

To Hispalis

Myrtilis

To Hispalis

† Ossobona

Aesuris

▬ ▬ ▬ 1
· · · · · · 2
† 3

0   50   100 km.

0   25   50   75
                              miles

in Visigothic and Moslem times were located along the main Roman roads: the capitals of provinces, all the seats of conventus, kūra and judicial units, all the episcopal cities, and even minor urban nuclei and rural centers.

During the Moslem era, the network was slightly improved, particularly in the South, where some new roads were built. Between the Roman and the Moslem itineraries there are minor differences which prove that. Essentially, however, nothing was modified.

There is no evidence from either Roman or early Moslem times that the North was more densely populated than the South, as it is today. On the contrary, more settlements are known to the south of the Tagus than to the north of it. Although practically everything needs to be investigated in this field, it seems that noticeable changes took place only in times of the Reconquista. Such an unbalanced situation accounted for the prosperous trade and artisanship that characterized all territory south of the Peninsula. Whereas both parts were dominantly agrarian in their economic features, there is no doubt of the much greater role played by commerce and navigation in the South. A union of the two areas would therefore bring about a fusion of different but somewhat complementary systems of economy and daily activity. This problem has been emphasized by several historians to explain the viability of Portugal as an economic unit. Without dismissing its importance, we should point out that complementary forms were very often a product of the later Reconquista, when the Moslem South was declining both in resources and in area. They do not date from a time before. The South could live alone with its developed currents of "horizontal" contacts, east-west and west-east. In spite of an existent and possibly intense circulation of people and merchandise along the south-north connection, it was the political-military phenomenon that accounted for the inevitability of a "vertical" axis and created and cemented Portugal.

POLITICAL UNITS

Before the actual formation of Portugal as a separate country in western Iberia, several political units existed in part of her future territory. Of the impact that such realms might have exerted on Portugal's birth and permanence as a nation much has been written. The proof, however, is dubious. Patriotic aims of finding old traditions for new kingdoms have always overcome any serene historical objectivity.

The Kingdom of the Suevi

Among the barbarian peoples who invaded Spain in the beginning of the fifth century, the Suevi or Swaefs played one of the greatest roles. Arriving either by land or by sea, they reached the far Northwest as early as 411, settling down in Gallaecia as *foederati* and gradually emerging in a strong kingdom. Their history is confused and obscure. Documental sources are so meager that any hope of a clearer picture should be abandoned by historians until more progress is achieved in the field of archaeology.

By 419 the Suevi alone were dividing Gallaecia with the natives, after having got rid of the Alani and the Vandals. As usual, they chose the country and turned their backs on the cities, where the Roman population was left undisturbed. Their number was obviously small, and their imprint on the land minimal, for no more than half a dozen Suevi place names are known to have survived. Nevertheless, their combativeness was great, and for a long time they challenged the Visigothic rule in the Peninsula. By the middle of the fifth century, the peak of the Swaef empire in Spain, they controlled Gallaecia, Lusitania, Baetica, and part of the Carthaginensis, and raided the Tarraconensis. Like so many other Barbarian kingdoms, however, their decline was as rapid as their growth. The ebb of the tide brought the Visigoths to the very heart of the Suevi realm: Bracara was stormed and taken (456) and their king Rechiarius made prisoner and killed in Portucale (457). A new dynasty, headed by Maldra (or Masdra), saved the Suevi kingdom from a premature death. Either as a tributary of the Visigoths or coexisting with them in a much reduced area, the realm of the Suevi persisted for more than a hundred years. After a second period of renewed fights with the Visigoths (457–469), who forced them to evacuate Olisipone (469), which they had just conquered in a final push south, complete silence falls on them. Apparently they were able to maintain a frontier line which included

Gallaecia and the two Lusitanian bishoprics of Veseo and Conimbria, later transformed into four. Shortly, they succeeded in keeping the North of present-day Portugal.

We do not even know whether Masdra's dynasty was true Swaef or whether he and his descendants were simply natives (that is, Romans) with some Suevian blood and claiming the Suevian inheritance. This second possibility would much better explain the almost complete lack of Suevi survivals in both Gallaecia and Lusitania. In any case the Roman element quickly took over, and the Christian Roman bishops helped to organize the kingdom. The Suevi were originally heathen. By 448 Rechiarius became a Catholic, thus defying the Visigoths hardened in their Arian faith. By 465 Remismundus or Recchismundus, Masdra's son, was converted to Arianism, probably a condition to keep his kingdom from Visigothic conquest. By the middle of the sixth century, however, the influence and growth of the Catholic faith moved the Suevi leader to a new conversion. A Roman missionary from Pannonia, Martinus (the future St. Martin of Dume), perhaps sent by Constantinople with political-religious aims (Justinian was at the time undertaking the whole conquest of Spain), arrived in Gallaecia (550) and rapidly exerted an enormous influence on the ruling elite, if not on the people. The personal conversion of King Chararicus dates from that same year. However, Martinus' influence in this case has to be minimized for Chararicus' conversion is better explained by contacts with the Frankish monarchy and the prestige of St. Martin of Tours. A second and final conversion, this time shared by king and court, dates only from 559, under Theodemirus. The Visigothic reaction was not immediate, but when it came it was brutal and definitive: by 576 the campaign against the Suevi started. After a short interlude the last Swaef, Andeca, was attacked and defeated in Bracara and Portucale. His kingdom was incorporated into the Visigothic state (585).

For the future Portugal only the ecclesiastical framework of the Suevi is significant. The foundation of new dioceses—Egitania, Lamecum, Portucale, and Tude—has already been mentioned. But Bracara and Lucus seem to have played a much greater role. Their main cities were apparently the two most important or "capital" towns of the kingdom. By the sixth century the acts of the second Bracara council (572) show us two metropolitan centers coinciding with them, each one with a certain number of dependent bishoprics. Bracara headed the dioceses of Dumio, Portucale, Lamecum, Veseo, Conimbria, and Egitania. The division line with Lucus was the river Lima. The interesting fact in this arrangement is that the area of the diocese of Lamecum, Veseo, Conimbria, and Egitania, formerly included in the metropolitan province of Emerita (Lusitania), was now assigned to Bracara (Gallaecia) because of the new political unit. This assignment continued until 660, seventy-five years past the fall of the kingdom in which it had originated. The records containing the list of those seven dioceses under Bracara were much later, in the Reconquista period, used by the bishops of Braga, with the backing of the rulers of Portugal, to claim the ecclesiastical inheritance of the Suevi and thus to unite the whole territory from the Lima to the Tagus.

The Counties of the Reconquista in the North

The Moslems landed in Spain for purposes of conquest in 711. Two years later practically all the Peninsula was under the sway of Islam. Lusitania and Gallaecia also fell in 713. The Christian Reconquista did not begin until the middle of the eighth century, starting not from an indomitable redoubt in the North but as a rebellion strengthened by several migrations of nobles and warriors to the North.

As in so many other military campaigns in history, the holdings grew from a small piece of territory in Asturias to a vast area limited on the south by the Douro basin. It seems that a Berber rebellion left a good number of cities and castles unguarded. This in great part explains the victories of King Alfonso I. Indeed his victories covered all of Gallaecia (which from now on we shall call Galicia in a more vernacular vein) and reached Lusitania south to Veseo (Viseu). The Moslems struck back in several devastating campaigns, mainly those of 764, 791, 794, and 840. For more than a century most of Galicia was, if not a battlefield, at least a very unsafe frontier land, rather disorganized, with half-deserted and half-burned cities, impoverished and sparsely populated, with all its bishops (that is, most of its real authority) fleeing to the king's court and there remaining for a long time. South Galicia particularly, between the rivers Minho and Douro, suffered from such a condition.

It was not until the middle of the ninth century that conditions

R. Minho

R. Lima

• Braga PORTUGAL

• Vimaranis

• Portucale

R. Douro

L E O N

COIMBRA

Coimbra • R. Mondego •

M O S L E M   S P A I N

| 0 | 50 | 100 | km. |

| 0 | 25 | 50 | 75 | miles |

there improved and were thought favorable enough for a general reorganization and new settlement. Two ancient towns, one in the South, Portucale, the other in the North, Chaves (the Roman Flaviae), became important centers of administration. Counts appointed by the king settled there and directed the populating tasks. Vimara or Vimarano Peres, whom King Alfonso III entrusted with the government (*tenentia*) of Portucale, should not be omitted from any historical description of the origins of Portugal. By the end of the century the country was no longer considered a frontier. This was now the case of the regions south of the Douro, where the Christian hosts were busy conquering such important towns as Coimbra (the old Conimbria or Colimbria, the Arab Ḳulūmriyya) in 878, Viseu, Lamego (the ancient Lamecum), and Idanha (Roman Egitania, Arab Antāniyya). Their reorganization began shortly after, at least up to the river Mondego. By the late ninth century all the bishops south of the Minho were back in their dioceses, with the exception of those of Braga and Idanha.

Christian optimism was nonetheless premature. The Moslems returned, bringing with them new destruction and disorganization. Sporadic raids, in one of which the king of Leon, Ordoño III, raided Lisbon in 955, were followed by a systematic campaign in the late tenth century. Al-Mansūr placed the frontier in the Douro again, although ravaging all of Galicia in his victorious attacks. It took the Christians seventy years more to come back to the Mondego. Only in 1057 was Lamego definitely reconquered, then Viseu in 1058, and Coimbra in 1063 or 1064. To evaluate the dismaying condition of all that territory, it is enough to consider the dates when the bishropics were restored: in 1070, Braga; in 1080, Coimbra; in 1114, Portucale; in the middle of the twelfth century, Lamego and Viseu. Dume (ancient Dumio) was never restored, being absorbed by Braga. Idanha was transferred to Guarda, but only in 1199 was a new bishop appointed.

Within the kingdom of Asturias (or Leon, as it was known after the tenth century) the great units for administration purposes were Asturias proper, Leon, Galicia, and Castile. They were called *terrae*, sometimes *provinciae*, and their government entrusted to a count (*comes*), often called *dux*. The old Roman and Visigothic tradition was therefore continued and enforced. There were, of course, many other counts (*comites*), who administered smaller units, also named *terrae* or *territoria*. It is this double sense, a broader one and a stricter one, of the words *terra* and *comes* that often makes the historical analysis confusing. *Dux* and province were always applied to the governor of the larger unit and to the larger unit itself.

From time to time royal wills and internal dissensions made Galicia "independent." This happened under Ordoño II, from 910 to 914, who was king of Galicia before being king of all Leon. It happened again with Sancho Ordoñez, his son, from 926 through 929, and then with Ordoño IV in 958 to 961. From 926 to 930 Galicia was further dismembered, in two parts, the southern part being assigned to Ramiro Ordoñez, who was "King of Portugal" before inheriting the whole of his father's realm as Ramiro II (930–950). The last royal division that gave Galicia political individuality was made in 1065, when, at the death of Fernando I, the country was given to one of his sons, Garcia. He ruled from 1065 to 1071.

Such short periods of separation were meaningless. They were normal events in most feudal monarchies and generally brought about no permanent aims of autonomy; nor were they a result of any local efforts tending toward independence.

Late in the ninth century the territory south of the Lima and north of the Douro, being sufficiently reorganized and too important to be kept united to the rest of Galicia, was detached from it and entrusted to a new governor. This person appears with the title of *dux* at least from the middle of the tenth century on. Its seat was Portucale, one of the first towns to be repopulated and probably the largest of all. And its name gradually became Portucale too, the word appearing for the first time in this broader sense by 938. The land (called *terra* or province) of Portucale—*Portugal* in the spoken dialect—was divided further into small counties also called *terrae* or *territoria*.

One of the first governors appointed to the new unit, if not the first of all, was a Castilian noble, Diogo Fernandes. He married Onega Lucides, daughter of Lucidio Vimaranes and granddaughter of the famous Vimara Peres, both of whom had been counts. We ignore the extension of their territories, however, which were probably limited to the smaller *terrae*. Diogo Fernandes died before December of 928. His daughter Mumadona Dias had in 926 married Count Hermenegildo (or Mendo) Gonçalves, the son of a Galician count named Gonçalo. All three appear only as comites, but Diogo and Hermenegildo at least seem to have ruled over more than just a small *terra*.

The line of known duces started with Hermenegildo's son Gonçalo Mendes, who inherited the province in 950 and died before 999. After him, a dynasty of five or six governors maintained Portugal united as a true fief in the same family until the mid-eleventh century. The governors were Mendo Gonçalves, Tuta or Toda, Alvito Nunes (possibly), Nuno Alvites, Mendo Nunes, and Nuno Mendes.

The role played by Portugal and her leaders in the Leonese monarchy was not minor. Her duces interfered several times in the political affairs of the realm. Bermudo II (984–999) was put on the throne by the Portuguese party. His son Alfonso V (999–1038) was brought up in Portugal under the care of Mendo Gonçalves, who took over the regency during the king's minority (999–1008) and married his daughter to Alfonso. Later on, Nuno Mendes, Mendo Gonçalves' grandson, threatened the authority of King Garcia of Galicia. He finally rebelled openly. Garcia was able to crush the rebellion in 1071, thus putting an end to the ducal dynasty.

South of the Douro the conquered territories formed another province called Coimbra, logically continuing the old administrative tradition. It seems, however, that hereditary transmission in the government was never regular here, although the same family kept it for quite a long time. Counts Hermenegildo, Aires Mendes, Ximeno Dias, and Gonçalo Monis were relatives. Count Gonçalo Monis was succeeded as governor (*tenens*) of Coimbra by his son Múnio Gonçalves, whose power was quickly reduced to nothing when all the lands south of the Douro were lost to the Moslems again. Then the Christians returned, but the small area they were able to control for some time was placed under the authority of the Portuguese duces. It was the so-called *terra* of Santa Maria (nowadays Feira).

Portugal's growth and increasing strength were obvious problems to the Leonese King Fernando I and his centralizing policy. As far as we know, he deprived Mendo Nunes of the province's government, substituting for the dux several minor and temporary officers (called

0   50   100
                 km.

0   50
               miles

C H R I S T I A N

P O R T U G A L

Šantarīn •

BALĀTA

Šintara •
                  • Al-Ušbūna
Al-Qibdāq • • Al-Maʿdin

• Šaṭūbr
                    • Yābura

• Al-Qaṣr Abu-Danis

Yālbaš •   • Baṭalyāws
         Qāya •

         • Julumāniya
         • Talānna

• Maura

• Bāja
       • Šīrba

• Marajīq   • Mārtula

• Al-Mudūra(?)

• Al-Juza(?)

   Šilb •   Šanbrās(?)
      • Al-ʿAliyaa   •   Qastālla
Šāqriš • Halq al-Zāwiya(?)   Ṭabīra
              • Uhšūnuba
      Šānta Mariya

infanzones, maiorini, vicarii, and *economi*) who were directly appointed by him and depended on his authority. Reference to them appears from 1050 on. Fernando also detached from Portugal for administrative purposes the *terra* of Santa Maria. He included it in the new province of Coimbra that he again created and gave (1064) to the Mozarab Sesnando Davides, a wealthy native landowner. Sesnando ruled as a dux or *alvazil* or *praeses* from that date until his death in 1091. Having no sons, he was succeeded by his son-in-law Martim Monis. It was apparently the rise of a new dynasty south of the Douro. The political evolution of Portugal cut this dynasty short at its birth.

Thus, for almost two hundred years, the whole or a great part of northern Portugal was kept united under the same family, with a rudimentary central government, a "ducal" court established north of the Douro (in Portucale, in Vimaranis or Guimarães, in Braga), and with common problems consequently arising. Little is known of the social and economic history of this true fief. Because it was still a part of the Leonese kingdom and strongly related to her political affairs, it is not our concern to study it here in detail. But there is no doubt that a principle of unity was achieved and a permanent separation from the rest of Galicia enforced. In feudal times this meant much more than the old Roman or even Visigothic administrative unit. It meant the beginning of autonomy, the first continuous assertion of political individuality facing the kingdom of Leon.

The Moslem "Taifa" Kingdoms in the South

Geographic and economic conditions always kept the country south of the Tagus basin closely tied to the rest of the Peninsula. Isolationism was unknown, and localisms hardly rose to general elements of cohesion and autonomy. Nonetheless, southwestern Iberia played its role, and not a minor one, in the history of Moslem Spain. Local rebellions spread from time to time to large areas and produced sporadic political units. We know little of the deep roots such kingdoms might have had, but we should not omit an account of their existence for it may help explain the future united Portugal.

The Moslems called all the country west and northwest of the Guadiana al-Gharb al-Andalus (the West of Andalus), and this corresponded roughly to Roman and Visigothic Lusitania. Their actual

rule over that area was soon reduced to the territories south of the
Mondego and then, gradually, narrowed more and more southwards.
Al-Gharb lost in meaning until it became only the final strip of
land which is now the Portuguese province of the Algarve.

By the ninth century, however, Gharb al-Andalus was a flourishing and extensive region, comprising more than one kūra and including several large cities. There in 868 a rich landowner of Mārida,
'Abd al-Raḥmān ben Marwān ben Yūnūs, revolted against the emir
of Kūrtuba (Cordoba), Muhāmmad I. He was nicknamed Ibn al-Jillīki
(the Galician), because he belonged to a native Spanish family from
the North which had passed over to Islam and had become muwallad
(converted). For a short time he was able to control most of al-Gharb
centered about Mārida. Defeated by the emir's armies and forced to
live in Cordoba, he escaped in 875, returned to his town, and revolted again. Then, backed by Alfonso III of Asturias, he held out
until 877. Exiled to the Asturias, he came back in 885 and rebelled
for the third time. First in Antāniya (Idanha), then in Baṭalyāws
(Badajoz), al-Jillīki seceded from the Cordoba princes and founded a
semi-independent state, which lasted until 930. In theory, the state
paid allegiance to the emir. His son, who succeeded him around 912,
was forced to surrender to the caliph's power. His state had comprised
all or almost all of al-Gharb.

In the eleventh century the central authority of the Cordoba caliphate collapsed. In its place there appeared all over Moslem Spain
small kingdoms called taifas (from the Arabic tawa'if, party or banner).
From 1012 through 1094 six of those kingdoms rose and fell in al-
Gharb al-Andalus.

The first successful rebellion (1012) happened in Wālba (Huelva),
where the Bahri Dynasty was able to rule until 1052. One of the
smallest taifas, it controlled nonetheless a strip of coastline which
originally included Ukhshūnuba, now better known as Shanta Marīya.
By 1026 its westernmost part seceded in its turn and formed the still
smaller principality of the Banū-Hārun. Located in Shanta Marīya,
the Banū-Hārun, another native family of landowners, held on until
1052. If nothing else, their name at least survived (instead of Shanta
Marīya) in the present capital of the Algarve, Faro (> Hārun).

In the Guadiana Valley, Mārtula (Mértola) with Bāja (Beja) and probably the whole of the Bāja kūra, formed another taifa under Ibn Tayfūr. Data are very scarce concerning this kingdom, but it seems that Bāja was later taken by the governor of Shilb (Silves) under the authority of the king of Ishbīliya (Seville), thus leaving Mārtula isolated and hastening its fall around 1044. Shilb seceded also but not until 1048. There the Banū Muzayn held power until 1063.

The two important taifas in al-Gharb were, however, Ishbīliya (Seville) and Baṭalyāws (Badajoz). Rebelling against the caliph as early as 1023, the Banū 'Abbād stretched their territory eastward and westward, absorbing some of their neighbors and threatening the might of them all. In the West Abū 'Amr 'Abbād ben Muḥammad, nicknamed al-Mu'taḍid (1042–69), successively conquered Mārtula (1044), Wālba (1052), Shanta Marīya (1052), and Shilb (1063), preventing his northern neighbor from expanding to the south. His heir al-Mu'tamid (1069–91) conquered Kūrṭuba (Cordoba) and Ṭulāyṭula (Toledo), thus completely encircling the kingdom of Baṭalyāws south and east.

Baṭalyāws was the largest kingdom of all, encompassing most of the ancient Lusitania, with the seat in Baṭalyāws, a new military town which more and more was substituting Mārida (Merida). Under the Banū al-Afṭas it lasted from 1022 through 1094, being one of the last kingdoms to fall. Its origin was the Lower March of al-Andalus, a successor of Lusitania, corresponding to the kuwar of Mārida, Baṭalyāws, Yābura, al-Ushbūna, Shantarīn, and Kulūmriyya. Bāja also belonged for a while to the Banū al-Afṭas. They encouraged culture, especially Muḥammad ben 'Abd Allāh al-Muzaffar (1045–63), who was a writer himself and one of the most gifted men of his time. A continuous conflict with the taifa of Ishbīliya weakened Baṭalyāws to the benefit of the Christian advance. All the northern part of the kingdom fell before the Christian armies of Fernando I, including Kulūmriyya. Under Umar al-Mutawakkil (1067–94) Kūriyya (Coria) surrendered also (1079), and the Tagus valley was quickly reached. The Christian advance appeared so dangerous that al-Mutawakkil took the risk of begging the Almoravids for help. In this he was joined by his foe of Ishbīliya. The Almoravids had built up an imposing empire in north Africa. Although their menace to the independence of the small taifa kingdoms was naturally felt, the Spanish Moslems had no choice. The

Almoravids landed in Spain. They did push the Christians back but decided to reunify the Peninsula under themselves. In vain did the king of Baṭalyāws ask the Christians for help, surrendering to them Shantarīn and al-Ushbūna (1093). The Almoravid power was too strong to be resisted, and the whole of al-Gharb fell into their hands (1094–95). Shortly after, those two cities were recovered (al-Ushbūna in 1094, Shantarīn in 1110) and the Moslem frontier was pushed north again to the Mondego basin.

The taifa kingdoms did not last long enough to impose a unification pattern on southwest Iberia. Furthermore, their ties with the rest of Moslem Spain were left unbroken, within an easy system of communications and developed economic relations. They never felt self-sufficient or isolated from the rest of the world. Their rulers never assumed the title of caliph, not even that of king (*malik*); they always acted as theoretical representatives of a fictitious supreme authority. Localisms, however, increased and expanded under their existence. If they were not mighty enough to crystallize into final independence, they certainly helped to throw off a yoke from then on unbearable. Conscious of their own petty interests and oppressed by a tougher and tighter military system, the local units of al-Gharb were the best allies of the northern Christians to accomplish the Reconquista.

THE FORMATION OF PORTUGAL

THE CHRISTIAN NORTH

From County to Kingdom

It has been taken for granted that feudalism never existed in the Iberian Peninsula, with the exception of Catalonia, where French influence was more strongly felt than elsewhere. Most Spanish and Portuguese historians have emphatically denied the existence of feudal structures in their respective countries while emphasizing the historical role of the small freeholders and the decisive strength of central authority. The Reconquista, they argue, prevented feudalism from evolving fully and limited it to rudimentary forms.

This school of thought corresponded to an epoch when feudalism was viewed only from a juridical or political standpoint, and when French feudalism was accepted as paramount. Feudal structures and the Carolingian Empire were considered inseparable, one resulting from the other. Modern thinking, however, tends to reject this view, holding that feudalism arose essentially from the Roman economic and social structures and was a logical consequence wherever the Roman Empire had existed or exerted its influence in the West.

Feudal structures in western Iberia will be studied in some detail in Chapter 2. For the moment, let us consider only those aspects that account for the formation of Portugal.

Comparisons between feudal France and Portugal, or France and Leon, or France and Navarre, seem irrelevant. Medieval France in the eleventh through the thirteenth centuries was a very large country, with a total area of 170,000 square miles, whereas Portugal jumped from 13,000 square miles (in 1096) to 34,000 in 1250, Leon with Galicia from 30,000 square miles in the late eleventh century to 45,000 in 1230 (the date of final union with Castile), and Castile from 40,000 square miles in the late eleventh century to 50,000 in 1230. Navarre never exceeded 6,000 square miles after the eleventh century; and Aragon and Catalonia (that is, the Corona de Aragon states) reached 40,000 by the middle of the thirteenth century. Separated, their areas were reduced to 6,000 square miles (Aragon at the end of the eleventh century) and 12,000 (Catalonia at the same time). Consequently, feudal comparisons would be more legitimate between any of the Iberian kingdoms and the French feudal units such as Aquitaine (30,000 square miles), Burgundy (17,000), Brittany (13,500), Gascony (11,000), or Normandy (10,000).

The myth of a united Spanish kingdom always hovered over the petty kingdoms which actually existed in the Peninsula. Well aware of this ideal, the kings of Leon as theoretical heirs to the Visigothic rulers took over the title of emperor, which they used, although sporadically, from the early tenth century on. Alfonso VI (1072–1109) and his grandson Alfonso VII (1126–57) tried to impose their suzerain authority on all the rulers of Spain. As "emperors" they could and should have kings as vassals. And it is the relationship between such "kings" and their "emperor" that needs to be analyzed first. For Portugal such a relationship is very revealing and helps explain her birth as an independent country.

By the late eleventh century, preceding the general movement of the eastern crusades, there arrived in the Iberian Peninsula, for the purpose of fighting the infidel and helping the Christian princes against the Almoravid threat, several contingents of French knights and some footmen also. Most of the knights and their leaders were recruited, as is well known, among the second-born sons, who lacked estates and power. One of them was Raymond, Count of Amous, the fourth son of Guillaume I the Great (nicknamed *Tête-hardie*, "Bold Head"), count of Burgundy (1059–87). His appanage county was a very small and unimportant piece of territory in the Jura area. He came the first time in 1086 or 1087 under the command of Eude I, Duke of Burgundy

(1079–1102), and then a second time for good, in 1090. This time, the purpose of his coming was not military, or at least not primarily so. He was called as a bridegroom to Urraca, the only legitimate daughter and heiress of "emperor" Alfonso VI, King of Leon, Castile, Galicia, and Portugal, and Constance, Duke Eude's aunt. The marriage had been arranged or sponsored by Constance and the influential French order of Cluny, whose abbot, Hugue, was also Queen Constance's uncle.

Raymond did marry Urraca in 1090 or 1091. Because he was expecting to be king with his wife, he was granted the government (*tenencia*) of Galicia in 1093. He seems to have got a certain amount of glory when he campaigned in the Tagus basin and entered in triumph Santarém and Lisbon, which the Moslem king of Badajoz had surrendered to the Christians for their promise of help against the Almoravids. Probably for this reason he was also granted the government of Portugal (between Minho and Douro) plus that of Coimbra (south of the Douro) in 1094. It was too vast a territory to be given to one person, even to a son-in-law who was expected to inherit the crown; and it did not last long because in 1096, or early 1097, Alfonso VI decided to give Portugal and Coimbra to his new son-in-law Henri. This man was a cousin of Raymond's, brother to two dukes of Burgundy—Hugue I, who had resigned and become a monk of Cluny after a brief rule of three years (1076–79), and Eude I. He was a fourth son, too, and apparently without an appanage. As Alfonso had no more legitimate daughters—in any case the Church would forbid a marriage between direct cousins—Henri was forced to accept Tarasia (or Theresia), a bastard child, although the emperor's favorite daughter. However, either as a tacit compensation or as an established condition, he was granted the whole territory south of the Minho as a fief in the French way. While the original document is lost, roughly contemporary charters refer to the grant as being "iure hereditario" or "pro sua hereditas," and to Henri as "tenente."

The expressions seem contradictory; a "tenens" (governor or simply holder) was in theory not supposed to transmit his government to his heirs. Yet this had happened several times in Leon, even if the actual permission had never been issued. The counts of Castile, at least after the mid-tenth century, had ruled their land hereditarily. Count Fernán González (930–70), the first of the dynasty, married his daughter Urraca to two kings of Leon, Ordoño III and Ordoño IV. By 1028 young Count Garcia Sánchez of Castile was due to marry Sancha, daughter to King Alfonso V and sister to the king-child Bermudo III. As a sort of dowry, he was granted the hereditary tenancy of the Pisuerga and Cea districts. Principles of heredity were from time to time asserted, and after the tenth century the general tendency was for county government to be kept in the same family. Also, in 1089, the famous Cid, Rodrigo Díaz, was promised all the lands he could take from the Moslems in the East, "iure hereditario." Finally it is interesting to note that some sixty years earlier, Henri's grandfather, Duke Robert I, had been granted Burgundy by his brother, King Henri I of France, not in appanage but in full property, "pro sua hereditate," too.

Henri was bound by the usual vassality ties to his suzerain: he was expected to be faithful and loyal and to give him aid and advice whenever necessary. This he seems to have done, at least until Alfonso's death (1109). He confirmed imperial charters, which proves he was summoned to and attended Alfonso's councils (*curiae*). He helped his father-in-law in military campaigns. His presence in Alfonso's court was relatively frequent. In brief, he behaved as a feudal lord should.

At the end of his life Alfonso VI cherished the idea of transmitting the crown to his only son, Sancho, an illegitimate offspring of his concubine Zaida, daughter of the last Moslem king of Seville, al-Mu'tamid. The child was probably born around 1099, when Alfonso was almost sixty. Raymond and Urraca, rightly alarmed at the prospect, sought all the support they could to preserve their rights. A pact was therefore signed with Henri (1106?), by which he pledged all his backing to Raymond's claims as heir to the throne, in exchange for the hereditary government of Toledo and its former *taifa* kingdom, with one-third of all the city's treasures. Should Raymond be prevented from handing him Toledo, Galicia would suffice.

There was little time for Henri and Raymond to consolidate their alliance. Raymond died in 1107, Sancho was killed in 1108, and Alfonso VI died in 1109. Urraca inherited the crown but, being a woman, not the title of empress. Her second marriage with Alfonso I of Aragon (1109) brought about a state of civil war, which lasted almost until her death, in 1126. Aragonese, Leonese, Castilian, and Galician nobles vainly and senselessly fought among themselves for years. Before his death Alfonso VI had invested the tenancy of Galicia in both Urraca and her son Alfonso Raimundez, who was to rule alone were his mother married again. Young Alfonso was still a child, but the Galician nobles promptly backed his claims, giving them much greater freedom of movement.

These circumstances are important in explaining Portugal's definitive separation from Leon. Count Henri, very cleverly, never committed himself entirely to any of the parties, rather leaning to the successive winning sides and maintaining his complete freedom of action, very close to a state of independence. From 1109 to his death, probably in 1112, he ceased to perform his feudal duties, while never rebelling openly. After his death, his widow Tarasia inherited both the government and her husband's policy. She was good at intrigue and used it several times. She managed to keep relatively independent, but not as successfully as Henri, for she had to attend her sister's summons at Oviedo (1115) and to promise her fealty (1121). Her army was even attacked by Urraca's armies and badly beaten. In the end, however, by her submission, she not only kept all of Portugal but added to her rule several new fiefs, both in land and in rent, in Galicia, Leon, and Castile.

Urraca's death put Alfonso VII (Alfonso Raimundez) on the throne (1126). He quickly reminded his aunt of her feudal tenures, forcing her to submission after a brief campaign (1127). For the first time her son Afonso Henriques, a young man of eighteen, appeared in history. Besieged in Guimarães by his cousin's armies, he was bound to surrender and to make vassality promises. Around himself he gathered a group of nobles who opposed Tarasia's rule, and her favorite's, the Galician count Fernando Pérez de Trava. A rebellion inside Portugal gave Afonso Henriques an easy victory in 1128 at the battle of São Mamede (near Guimarães). Tarasia and Pérez de Trava fled to Galicia never to come back again. There Tarasia died in 1130.

From 1128 to 1137, Afonso Henriques was in almost constant rebellion against his cousin Alfonso VII. What Afonso Henriques probably wanted was territorial expansion of his fief, based on promises and claims, more or less fictitious or fallacious, dating from Urraca's times. Furthermore he was clearly aiming at the title of king.

In Spain of the eleventh and twelfth centuries, *rex* (king), *regnum*

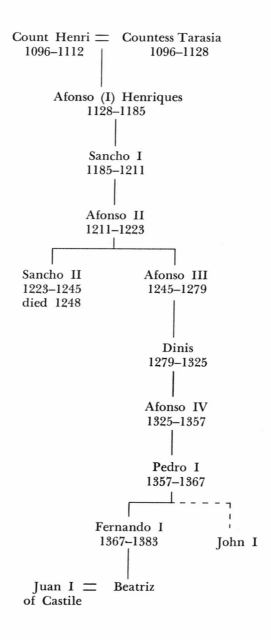

Count Henri = Countess Tarasia
1096–1112   1096–1128

Afonso (I) Henriques
1128–1185

Sancho I
1185–1211

Afonso II
1211–1223

Sancho II   Afonso III
1223–1245   1245–1279
died 1248

Dinis
1279–1325

Afonso IV
1325–1357

Pedro I
1357–1367

Fernando I
1367–1383   John I

Juan I = Beatriz
of Castile

(kingdom), and *regnare* (to reign) had different meanings. *Regnare* was a general word for ruling. Not only kings (*reges*) *regnabant* but also dukes, counts, and so forth. Henri, for instance, appears frequently in the documents as *regnante* (that is, ruling) in Portugal. *Regnum* had a much more precise meaning. It meant a fully independent state, not a feudal parcel, with possible subordination to an emperor (or to the Pope) only. *Rex* or its feminine *regina* were simply titles, but corresponding to very high positions, because only holders of kingdoms (*regna*), their wives, and their children were entitled to use them. Thus Alfonso VI was rex (and furthermore emperor) because his father had been a rex too and because he was the actual ruler of an independent state. Urraca, his daughter, was a regina for the same reasons and so was Tarasia, being the daughter of a rex, although she did not rule over a kingdom herself. Afonso Henriques, however, was no rex because his father was a count and his mother held no *regnum* at all. Theoretically he was not even a count, for he had rebelled against his mother, the legal *comitissa-regina,* without permission of his lord the king; and, worse than that, he had taken arms against the king himself. Legally he was nothing but a rebel, committing the feudal crime of felony.

It is interesting to note that in all charters and diplomas he always presented himself as *infans* (that is, belonging to the royal family) or *princeps* (a general meaningless title). He might have been called a *dux,* which was traditional and meaningful. But as dux he would be inferior in hierarchy to all the great rulers of the Iberian Peninsula, a choice which he obviously rejected.

To aim at the title *rex* was not foolish or unprecedented. Before 1028 the Castilian nobles asked from the King of Leon permission for their count Garcia Sánchez to take the title of rex, as he was going to marry the king's daughter. After 1035 Ramiro Sánchez, who was the illegitimate son of Sancho of Navarre, became rex in Aragon. His son, however, who had no right to the title (for his father was subject to the King of Leon's suzerainty), assumed it nonetheless and so did all his successors. By 1128–37 there existed in Christian Spain, besides the king-emperor of Leon and Castile, two other ruling reges, those of Aragon and Navarre. Afonso Henriques, whose state was larger than either of theirs, could perfectly well aim at the same title. Rex did not imply independence in the sense of breaking the feudal ties completely. Furthermore, Alfonso VII of Leon and Castile had been solemnly proclaimed "emperor" in 1135 at the *cortes* of Leon. An emperor could and should have kings as vassals. It only enhanced his prestige and power. This explains why Alfonso VII did not react too strongly against the idea. Yet he would not accept a rebel as king. Submission, loyalty, and friendship were obvious prerequisites.

In 1137 peace was first made. An agreement or pact signed at Tuy laid down some typical feudal clauses. Afonso Henriques promised his lord fealty (*ut sit . . . fidelis bona fide*), safety, military aid, and counsel. But dissension broke out again. In 1140 Afonso Henriques invaded Galicia while Alfonso VII invaded Portugal. It seems that by that time Afonso was already presenting himself as rex, perhaps after his first important victory against the Moslems a year before. It was only in 1143 that a permanent peace settlement was arranged with the intervention of a papal legate, Cardinal Guido da Vico, deacon of St. Cosma e Damiano. The treaty or pact is lost. It apparently granted Afonso Henriques the title of king while maintaining all the clauses of military help whenever necessary. It was not independence, but it was an enormous step toward it.

Afonso Henriques' external policy was now at stake in Italy. His purpose was to obtain formal papal recognition of both his title and his kingdom (as regnum). In a typically feudal way he commended Portugal to the Holy See and considered himself, with all his successors, a liege vassal of the Pope's. He also promised to pay a small tribute of four gold ounces yearly. This feudal submission was another act of felony against his real lord, the emperor of Leon. Afonso Henriques had no right to dispose of Portugal as a true "alodial" kingdom. He knew it, and so did the Leonese ambassadors who later on would plead against him before the Pope. The Pope knew it too and answered clearly and rightfully (1144). It was Rome's policy in Spain to promote a political union under a supreme leadership which might render easier the fight against Islam rather than to support attempts at secession. Furthermore, Alfonso VII was a favorite son of the Papacy and had been granted the "Golden Rose." Therefore, while praising Afonso Henriques and his action, and accepting the tribute, Pope Lucius II called him only *dux portugalensis* and Portugal only a *terra*.

It was to take Afonso Henriques thirty-five years to change the Pope's mind. It was to cost him important privileges for the Church, and also four times more, because the yearly tribute was raised from four ounces to two marks (sixteen ounces), with an important sum paid in advance. For this price Pope Alexander III solemnly recognized Afonso as king and his state as a kingdom in 1179. Much had changed, too, in the Leonese monarchy. After the death of Alfonso VII in 1157, his two sons Fernando and Sancho divided the kingdom. Fernando inherited Leon and Galicia as Fernando II, and Sancho kept Castile as Sancho III. The two kingdoms remained separated until 1230. The title of emperor was dropped. There was no reason for Afonso Henriques or his successors to feel bound to a theoretical vassality act made to an emperor. No wonder that the king of Portugal after 1157 felt he had the same rights and duties as both the king of Leon and the King of Castile. The year 1157 was for Portugal almost as important as 1143, a further step on the road toward final separation.

The struggle for an autonomous Portugal was closely connected with certain problems of ecclesiastical administration. It was accompanied by the fight between the archbishops of Braga and those of Toledo and by the attempt to create a Portuguese metropolitan province to coincide with the political frontiers of Portugal. The archbishop of Toledo, to whom the Pope had granted primacy over all Spain (going back to the united Visigothic state) by the late eleventh century, met the strong resistance of Braga, conscious of his privileges and traditions as metropolitan of Galicia (up to the Douro). The long struggle had its heroes and its desperadoes. Bishop Pedro of Braga, for instance, put himself and his diocese under antipope Clement III (1091) rather than submit to the authority of his Toledan rival. When Henri of Burgundy was given Portugal, he immediately understood the importance of Braga's claims and promptly supported them. He succeeded (1100) in obtaining from Pope Paschal II a sentence favorable to his archbishop. Some years later, Archbishop Geraldo went a step further, his primacy over not only the ancient Galician dioceses but also those of Coimbra, Viseu, and Lamego being acknowledged by the same Pope (1103). The old Suevian tradition was thus restored.

Internal quarrels between Braga and Coimbra, Countess Tarasia's weak government, and finally the fatal step of Braga's archbishop,

Maurice Burdin, taking sides with Emperor Henry V and accepting the election as antipope of Gregorius VIII (1118), compromised the whole situation. Braga lost its primacy over the bishoprics south of the Douro. The old metropolis of Merida was restored but given to Braga's rival, Compostela, with authority over the dioceses that once had belonged to it.

It took several years to go back to Geraldo's achievements. With Afonso Henriques all the dioceses of Portugal were again united under Braga. The conquest of Lisbon and of Alentejo posed the whole problem again because new bishoprics were restored which had never belonged to Braga. Neither the Portuguese kings nor the Portuguese bishops were ever able, in medieval times, to settle the question as they wished. Practically, however, Braga maintained its supremacy over all Portugal, and theoretical obedience to Santiago de Compostela never threatened Portugal's independence. The same was true in Galicia and Leon, where part of the dioceses accepted Braga as primate.

The quarrels with the Pope and with the neighboring bishoprics were succeeded by new quarrels between those who opposed the king on one side and the Portuguese church on the other. Individually considered, such quarrels now seem insignificant and trivial. They began with a conflict over privileges or royal grants or jurisdiction. They evolved and ended according to the whims and circumstances of a monarch, a bishop, and a period of time. There were periods of violence and intransigence, and the conflicts were finally solved by compromise. In a broader context, however, the conflicts between king and clergy meant much more. They corresponded in Portugal to the bitter struggles between king and nobility which tore apart so many countries in medieval Europe. They were deadly struggles between the two greatest owners of Portugal for the real control of power and permanent influence. The final medieval solution looked like a compromise, an equilibrium between Church and State. When analyzed, however, it meant the triumph of the state. It represented the end of the first round in a match that still goes on and may be deemed one of the great constants in Portuguese history.

Although there were precedents, the main events in the struggle occurred under Sancho I (1185–1211), with the king opposing the bishops of Porto and Coimbra. A part of the clergy sided with Sancho, and so did the burghers of Porto rebelling against their feudal lord. Sancho was excommunicated, but when death approached he asked for forgiveness and favored the clergy with generous grants (1211). His son Afonso II went much farther and succeeded in arousing most of the clergy against him and his supporters, who again included citizens from the towns (Coimbra, for instance). He died excommunicated (1223). Sancho II attacked and was attacked by the prelates of Braga, Coimbra, and Porto, the most powerful in the realm. So bitter was the struggle that any compromise was thought impossible, thus costing Sancho his throne. Backed by other members of the clergy, those three bishops obtained from Pope Innocent IV the deposition of the Portuguese king (1245). His brother Afonso, who was then living in France (he was the Count of Boulogne, having married Countess Mathilde in 1238), accepted the government after signing a solemn pact of agreement with the clergy (Paris, 1245). After a brief civil war he took over the kingdom, expelled Sancho, and became king when Sancho died childless in Toledo (1248). As a monarch, however, Afonso III showed himself to be the most bitter foe of those who had enthroned him. Again the fight found the king and the great majority of the clergy opposed. Again the king was excommunicated, and surrendered with the approach of death (1279). It was only under his heir and successor, Dinis, that a concordat was agreed upon and solemnly signed (1289).

The role played by both nobility and people was a comparatively moderate and minor one. They acted more like allies than representatives of a cause. It is true that we know much less of the political fights with the nobles and with the citizens than of those with the clergy. Afonso II, Sancho II, Afonso III, all of them had their foes among the nobles, and opposition of interests often led to active conflict. The civil war between the two brothers (Sancho and Afonso) had aspects of a feudal conflict. But on the whole, the pattern of political Portugal was shaped almost entirely by king and clergy with the help of their faithful partisans.

The Picture of the North

For about eighty years (mid-eleventh to mid-twelfth century) there were no enduring territorial changes in Portugal. With an area of roughly 13,000 square miles, Portugal was a very small country in twentieth-century terms, but a rather sizable one in twelfth-century Europe. It was matched by other kingdoms such as Aragon, Navarre, most of the *taifas,* Jerusalem, and Denmark. Although divided from Galicia, with which it shared many geographical conditions, it was a surprisingly homogeneous country in climate, vegetation, soil characteristics, types and forms of human settlement, landownership, and religious, political, and administrative traditions. Its people spoke the same language. It covered the whole northern part of present-day Portugal and was remarkable in its almost complete unity. It was a logical, a viable state, with enough cohesion to endure and to resist external menaces. Because of this and because of its expanding possibilities, it was a country with a future, even by medieval standards.

Density of population was certainly high. The core of the country, that is, the area between the rivers Lima and Ave (present district of Braga), had 667 parishes by the end of the eleventh century, or more than six parishes per each ten square miles. The country between the Lima and the Minho undoubtedly had the same dense population. South of the Ave and north of the Douro basin, population density was probably still higher, as it has always been.

Conditions were different elsewhere. The southern part of Portugal was frontier land, sparsely settled by colonists. Trás-os-Montes, the eastern part, was also sparsely populated because soil and weather conditions are not as propitious as in Minho. A modern historian who has carefully analyzed the demographic situation of the bishopric of Braga at that time has estimated its population at 100,000 inhabitants. If to this number we add another 100,000 for the bishopric of Porto, a roughly similar number for the northernmost territory, and as much for all the rest of Portugal, a hypothetical 400,000 would be reached. For the total area, there would be an estimated average density of 45 inhabitants per square mile.

Most of the settlement was dispersed as required by soil and climatic conditions. Despite all the raids, military campaigns, and destruction, the population had never been driven from their traditional homes so favorable was geography to the multiplication of small farms, houses, and clearings. There were few urban centers but a very large number of villae and other rural forms of land exploitation. Braga was the great city in the north of Portugal. It had lost a part of its population and was reduced in area in comparison with Roman times, but this was generally true in all of Europe. Nevertheless it still had some 14 hectares within its powerful walls dating from early Reconquista times. It was a large town with four parishes and a number of inhabitants, probably not much under 5,000. Still a nodal point for communications, Braga possessed minimum conditions for prosperity and for political and religious leadership of the country. Its large cathedral, started in the late eleventh or early twelfth century, corresponded to the town's size and importance.

Close to Braga in size was Coimbra, the "capital" of the South. Its walls encompassed some 12 hectares, which gave Coimbra a similar if not larger population, because Moslem towns were generally greater in density while smaller in area. Like Braga, Coimbra had traditions of religious and political leadership. Its geographical location was a distinctly favorable feature as soon as the Reconquista started again and more southern lands were captured.

Portucale (Porto) was third in size but much smaller than the other two. Its area was only a little more than 6 hectares. Close to it in size, probably, was Chaves, another city of long tradition. All the remnant "centers" were only villages or seats of villae but we could hardly call them towns, even in medieval phraseology. This was true of Guimarães (Latin *Vimaranis*), the villa of Vimara, a tiny burgh less than a hectare in area, walled late in the tenth century as a protection against the Normans. It was then a part-time residence of Henri, Tarasia, and Afonso Henriques. Guimarães' growth, like that of other burghs (such as Constantim de Panoias, Mesão Frio, Vila Nova de Gaia, Castro Laboreiro, and even Porto, or the religious burghs around fortified monasteries, such as Arouca, Lorvão, and Tarouca), was a late eleventh-century phenomenon, and by 1096 Count Henri still felt it necessary to grant a special borough charter, giving privileges to all those who had populated it or who were willing to do so.

There are no reasons to believe that the demographic revolution did not happen in Portugal as it did all over Europe in the eleventh, twelfth, and thirteenth centuries. The borough charters show us new or almost new settlement in such places as S. João da Pesqueira, Ansiães, Freixo, and Ponte de Lima. Semi-deserted areas in Beira and

UPPER LEFT: *Economic life, 12th century.* BELOW: *Coimbra Cathedral (Coimbra), 12th century.* ABOVE: *Count Henri of Burgundy: Santiago de Compostela cathedral (Spain), Tombo A, fol. 39, 12th–13th century.*

Trás-os-Montes, which had never been populated before, were now occupied by small groups of settlers, as the charters granted particularly by King Sancho I (1185–1211) clearly show. Most of the growth, however, affected the existing rural units and should be checked there. The breaking down of the old Roman villa was accelerated. Halves, thirds, or still smaller fractions arose to allow an increasing number of second-born sons a way of living, that is, a way of getting a revenue. Within each villa, the smaller units (*casais*, the Portuguese equivalent of *mansi*) assigned to one family were parceled out for all practical purposes among the surviving heirs, even if they remained united for tax contribution. Alodial holdings became smaller and in many cases economically absurd. Local migrations from area to area, from the country to the towns, had started. Land reclamation, either by wood clearing or by waste cultivation, helped solve the problem. It was by that time that new villae, more in the sense of new hamlets or villages than in the sense of the old Roman exploitation form, were founded here and there. A map of the surviving *Vila Nova, Aldeia Nova,* and similar place names clearly shows that such a movement primarily affected Minho and the Douro valley: of 124 northern Vilas Novas, 75 lie north of the Douro or bordering the river, with the exclusion of Trás-os-Montes; the favorite area for the Aldeias Novas was the present district of Porto, where 43 out of a total of 74 for the whole North are to be found. Corresponding figures and ratios appear for the other place names. In the whole South, once the Mondego is crossed, only 22 Vilas Novas and 12 Aldeias Novas exist, or 15 percent and 14 percent, respectively, of the total. The movement was therefore a result of internal needs in growth, mainly directed toward pacified and long-stabilized provinces, rather than a consequence of the Reconquista with the purpose of filling the blanks caused by war and destruction.

There are virtually no monographs available on landownership and forms of agrarian exploitation in eleventh- and twelfth-century Portugal. By the tenth century many ancient villae were still in the hands of a single owner, but the process of disintegration was being accelerated, and the situation seemed very different a century or two later. Vast latifundia were then practically nonexistent, partly as a consequence of the climate and soil conditions. Neverthless there were villae as large as 600 hectares in area: Creixomil, for instance, in the present-day *concelho* (municipality) of Guimarães. Other villages like Vila do Conde (550 hectares) or Abação (525 hectares) were rare. More common were the middle-sized villae like Fromariz (100 hectares) and Quintela (60 hectares). The majority were probably still smaller. In each villa the original system of economic and social organization assigned a great part (not continuous but distributed among the many possible types of land—grain fields, vineyards, orchards, pastures, woods, etc.) to the owner, who directly exploited it. This land was the *palatium* (*paço* in Portuguese), which also comprised the owner's house, the workers' houses, the stables, the barns, and a church. The remainder was divided into shares granted at quit claim to several types of tenants: they were the *casales* (*casais*), *quintanae* (*quintãs* or *quintas*), or *villares* (*vilares*), roughly similar to the Western European *mansi*. Each casal or quinta was further divided into *glebas*, strips of land not continuous in area. Thus the unity of the casal had no parallel in continuity of land.

Theoretically, each casal provided enough food for a family, but its area changed very much from villa to villa. Of the ones mentioned above, Quintela, the smallest, comprised four casais, an average of less than 10 hectares for each of them. Fromariz' seven casais afforded about the same area to each one. Abação had some thirty casais in a similar average. Creixomil encompassed some fifty-four casais, each one probably smaller than 10 hectares. The gradual breakdown of the villa resulted in the practical autonomy of each casal. In most cases, however, the traditional unity was officially kept, both for purposes of central administration and for taxation. Succession or necessity might lead to the partition of a villa but the unit was not dismembered, co-owners taking the place of sole proprietors and sharing among them everything. The same happened within each casal. Migration south prevented a dangerous situation which might have ruined the existing system and made it economically impossible.

Most of the land belonged to the Church. The Christian Reconquest had respected property tradition, whenever it existed, and transferred to the bishops and to the newly created monasteries all the wealth belonging to the Moslem mosques. Huge grants by generous monarchs matched death legacies by kings, nobles, and even villeins.

During the tenth century and immediately following centuries, the Church increased this patrimony with numerous purchases. Little wonder that by the early thirteenth century its property far exceeded the property of the other population groups.

The see and chapter of Braga came first in the list of the great religious landowners. The Coimbra and Porto cathedrals possessed a lesser but still imposing share of property. Among the religious orders the Benedictines were first in wealth and power, with the monasteries of Arouca, Paço de Sousa, Tibães, and many others, most of them north of the Douro. The Cluniacs, who arrived by the late eleventh century, held some minor houses, and their wealth and power were always very much reduced. The Cistercians, however, who appeared in Portugal by the middle of the twelfth century, enjoyed for a long time the highest favor from royalty and society. They almost completely stopped Benedictine influence southward, even absorbing some Benedictine monasteries, like Lorvão. S. João de Tarouca in the North and Alcobaça in the Center were the wealthiest of all. The canons of St. Augustine (the Portuguese correspondent to Prémontré) owned the famous church of Santa Cruz, in Coimbra, richly endowed. The military orders got extensive donations in the South, but their economic power north of the Mondego was small. Franciscans and Dominicans arrived in the early thirteenth century and quickly challenged all the other orders and cathedrals in wealth and power.

The growth of Church revenues reached such proportions by the early 1200's as to frighten and threaten the royal authority. Afonso II (1211–23) was the first monarch who dared to defy the Church, enacting a prohibition against any further buying of land by religious institutions but allowing nonetheless private acquisitions by clergymen. The attempt failed, but Sancho II carried on his father's policy, not only enforcing Afonso's first laws but enacting new ones, such as forbidding private purchase by clerics and even donations and legacies to the Church. Sancho's deposition (1245) was partly a result of measures like these.

The king came immediately after the Church in landed property. His patrimony was acquired by confiscation of both Moslem state and other lands whose owners had disappeared or had been killed. The king's wealth also included rents and tributes from his new subjects.

But Spanish kings were quick to give away what they had obtained by right of conquest. Grants to their relatives, to the nobility in general, to the clergy, to valiant fighters and followers quickly reduced that patrimony and often endangered the king's position regarding his subjects. In Portugal all the royal patrimony was transferred by the Leonese kings to Count Henri and his successors.

A third share was almost all in the hands of the nobles. It was a minor part, but still a considerable one. Acquired either by king's donation or by right of conquest, later increased by usurpation of royal tenancies into alodial property, the lands of the nobles were spread all over Portugal too. It was again under Afonso II that measures challenging the power of the nobility were first envisaged. He ordered all the property titles and privileges resulting from royal grant to be presented to him and confirmed by his chancellery. This measure had to be followed by an organized system of inquiries (*inquirições*) which he also determined in 1220. Royal commissions were sent to the Minho, where usurpations and property confusion were greater than anywhere else, to find out about the nature and juridical condition of landownership and more particularly the rights held by the Crown (*direitos reais*) in property, revenues, and religious patronates. The king's death (1223) and the coming to the throne of young Sancho II prevented such measures from being enforced. Furthermore, royal authority was still too weak and too decentralized to curb abuses efficiently and permanently. Much smaller in area and in revenue was a fourth and last share, composed of alodial lands belonging to small freeholders and common lands exploited by agrarian or urban communities.

Examining the number of available documents from 950 through the early twelfth century, one gets the impression that landownership remained remarkably stable at least until the 1060's. It seems that only a very small percentage of the lands changed owners at that time. A new situation arose by the late eleventh century, a little before Portugal was granted to Henri of Burgundy. This may well correspond to a new dynamic era on the threshold of a period of expansion. Much more research, however, is required in this field.

The social structure resulted from the typical feudal forms of landownership and land revenues. Within their estates (generally

called *coutos* if belonging to the Church or *honras—honores—*if to
the nobles) the lords were the highest authority for all practical purposes, even if the king maintained the rights of supreme justice (expressed in the sole right of death penalty and cutting off of limbs)
which he always tried to enforce. There lived here a population composed mainly of serfs, bound to the land they tilled by tradition and
custom, prevented from leaving it but also from being expelled from
it, and forced to pay their lord a rent proportional to the annual production, to which labor services and other tributes should be added.
There were several categories of serfdom which have been analyzed
and classified, but these actually meant little to the real situation of
the worker. It is true that the social mobility caused by the Reconquista prevented a complete stagnation of that class and helped free
many serfs who voluntarily quit their lords either with the lords' permission or simply by escaping.

Around the central household (*paço* or *solar*) there lived another
type of serf whose ties with his lord were more personal and whose
duties were more related to domestic or artisan tasks. They held no
land at all, being nourished, clothed, and lodged directly by the lord.
There were also grades labeling and classifying them. A part of the
paço was composed of land. Although its cultivation was assured
mainly by the corvées of the serfs (two or three days' labor), the lord
had nevertheless his own farmers, surveyors, and humbler people too.
The king was a lord like any other lord, and the social and economic
situation of the persons living on his lands (*reguengos*) did not seem
to be better than those on the lands of other lords.

Beside the serfs there were other farmers or laborers (*coloni*), as
well as craftsmen and house servants, who theoretically could dispose
of their persons and goods, move from their lands, and leave their
lords freely. Their ties were based on a lease contract or on the contract of hired laborers, and their economic situation was essentially
different from that of the serfs. They could always be "fired" or evicted
with relative ease from the lands they were holding. Their only real
advantage came when they were able to get a piece of property of their
own or to move within the area of the *concelhos* (the Portuguese communal precincts) where their social and economic promotion was possible. Precisely because of that, their number grew as a consequence of

the Reconquista and especially after the twelfth century. North of the Douro, however, they were still a minority by the thirteenth century. Documentation refers to them by various names, according to their wealth and dependency on a lord. The two basic types were *foreiros,* if they held a piece of land they exploited according to a quit-rent lease, and *herdadores* (inheritors), when they possessed a land of their own. The wealthiest of these herdadores generally lived within the area of a concelho, where they were the notables. If they had enough revenues to own a horse and to go to war on horseback (with all the appropriate weapons), they were called *cavaleiros-vilãos* (knights-villeins). All the others fell within the military category of *peões* (footmen).

Slavery never disappeared completely during the Middle Ages, and the number of Moslem captives depended on the intensity and violence of the military campaigns. A growth in their numbers seems well documented for the twelfth and thirteenth centuries. The increase corresponded to the great wars and conquests initiated by the 1130's and concluded only a century later.

Social distinctions among the nobles seem nowadays confusing, particularly because a new nobility arose in Portugal during the eleventh and twelfth centuries. Most of the medieval genealogies began in this period. Emigration from other countries (Leon, Castile, France, northern Europe) and social promotion as a reward in war and services were the main reasons for the rise of a new nobility. Very quickly the leading positions in command and wealth fell into the hands of a small number of newcomers and royal favorites, to which a limited percentage of native landowners should be added. They hardly exceeded a hundred people before the thirteenth century. Below these *ricos-homens* there was another stratum of landed aristocracy, probably descending for the most part from ancient families of free men *(ingenui)*. Much larger in number (ten times larger, perhaps) this group or class of *infanções, cavaleiros* (knights), and *escudeiros* (squires) resented the power of the ricos-homens and frequently caused trouble and formed parties. We still lack a monograph to give us a clear picture of such rivalries and struggles, but there is little doubt that political fights in the times of both Afonso II and Sancho II can be explained partly by some opposition of interests within the nobility.

The picture is further complicated by the fact that many small nobles were bound by feudal ties to the ricos-homens, whom they served as vassals, both in the most general sense and in the strict meaning of personal clients.

As a social group the clergy possessed little individuality. Its homogeneity and cohesion were religious and intellectual rather than social or economic. In the upper ranks bishops, abbots, and great masters were feudal lords, acting and reacting as members of the top nobility. Below them a vast number of clergymen ranged downward in the social hierarchy, from lower-nobility levels to conditions of serf-dom. A few were even personal serfs.

The main economic activity and source of wealth was probably stock breeding. A high percentage of the land was assigned to pastures. The deep and humid valleys of Minho and northern Beira were very favorable for cattle raising. Indeed, oxen and kine are constantly men-tioned in tenth-, eleventh-, and twelfth-century documentation as symbols of affluence and well-being. Prices were often evaluated in cattle or their equivalents and so were agrarian measures and tributes. In Trás-os-Montes and parts of Beira sheep and goats took the place of oxen and cows. Horse breeding was next in importance throughout the country.

Agrarian production was not very varied. Grainfields, vineyards, and flax fields predominated, with some orchards and groves mixed in. Among the cereals wheat and millet held first place in Minho; barley and rye were favorites in interior areas. Barley, necessary as fodder, was present almost everywhere. Flax provided the material for one of the few "industrial" activities, the linen production, traditional all over northern Portugal. The making of wine was important too. In the fruit and grove production apples and chestnuts predominated. Fish-ing as an economic activity should not be underestimated. Along the coast there were several small villages depending on fish alone and possessing a number of fishing ships. A royal policy of developing the coastline and preventing the sand dunes from invading cultivated fields had started by the early thirteenth century. Several villages were thus created or their rise fostered along the northern coast.

Most of the Portuguese economy at that time had a purely local character. Each villa or small group of villae tended to be self-sufficient and was generally successful. Economic units and boundaries were defined by the land possessions of each monastery or cathedral, normally scattered over a rather small area. A great part of the local exchange was made in kind. Money was in circulation of course, but it was by no means generalized or exclusive. In most of the tenth through the twelfth centuries leases or sale contracts required payment in kind, often combined with money. Neither Count Henri nor Tarasia felt it necessary to mint coins although they were entitled to do so. Leonese bullion deniers circulated, coupled with Moslem gold dinars and silver dirhams and even Byzantine gold nomismata. Afonso Henriques, whose long and eventful reign brought wealth, the development of trade, and the need for prestige, coined the first Portuguese gold *morabitinos,* which copied their Moslem model both in size and value as well as in name (*morabitino* al-Murābiṭūn, the money of the Almoravids). He also coined bullion deniers (*dinheiros*) and half deniers (*mealhas*). This double coin pattern precisely mirrored the economic integration of Portugal, a compromise between the Southern (Moslem) influence and the Northern (Christian) origin. Portuguese trade was born of the viability of exchange currents with both Leon and Islam (more exactly the kingdom of Badajoz). As a partner, however, it did not have much to offer. It was thus slowly that commerce emerged. By the late eleventh century markets are mentioned in several towns and villages, but the first fairs did not appear until late in the twelfth century, if one ignores the unique instance of the Ponte de Lima Fair, organized before 1125.

Small colonies of merchants were gathered around the castles of Porto, Guimarães, Constantim de Panoias, Mesão Frio, Gaia, and others, as well as around some fortified monasteries. In the "cities" (Braga, Coimbra, Lamego, Viseu, Chaves) merchants were also living. Coimbra possibly played a major role, being closer to the Moslem territory. The only "communal" rebellion we have record of also happened in Coimbra, shortly before 1111, forcing Henri to grant a new and more favorable borough charter. Coimbra, however, was an exception, and no other instances were recorded. This single fact shows clearly the weakness of the bourgeois element and the minor role "burgenses" played in the Portuguese history of that time.

Of an external maritime trade there is little evidence, although the Portuguese coasts and ports were well known both to Normans and to Crusaders, who regularly called on them for various purposes from the ninth century through the mid-1200's. The beginnings of a long-distance trade can be dated as early as 1194 when a Flemish ship, loaded with commercial items, was wrecked on the Portuguese coast. The apparently flourishing trade by the middle of the thirteenth century (see chapter 2) presupposes a long period of preparation and irregular activity, of which we know very little.

For political and administrative purposes Portugal was divided basically into *terras* or *territórios,* the number of which was always changing. As a rule, each *terra* or *território* corresponded to a political unit of feudal suzerainty, to a seigniorie, but this rule had plenty of exceptions. As a rule, also, each *terra* was governed by a *tenente,* of royal nomination or confirmation, who generally was the local lord and suzerain. But often the kings handed several *terras* to a single *tenente* or administrator for the crown. This happened, for instance, in vast regions such as Entre-Lima-e-Minho or Entre-Lima-e-Douro, each one subdivided into numerous *territórios.* North of the Douro there were more than forty, while south of that river their number reached only thirty, roughly up to the Mondego. Their area was quite small in Minho and the lower Douro valley, where the greatest concentration was naturally found. In Trás-os-Montes and most of Beira the *territórios* were vaster and less populated.

For religious purposes the bishoprics were naturally the great units of administration. North of the Lima all the lands belonged to the bishopric of Tuy, in Galicia. Between the Lima and the Ave-Vizela, including all of Trás-os-Montes up to the Douro and two regions which later became Leonese (Baronceli and Aliste), there was the archbishopric of Braga. South of Braga the bishopric of Porto encompassed a relatively small but densely populated countryside corresponding to the lower Douro valley. Coimbra was the next bishopric, spreading until the very end of the Christian conquest and comprising the former bishoprics of Lamego, Viseu, and Idanha, which were not restored until the middle and end of the twelfth century. In area, population, and wealth Coimbra was for a certain time the rival and close competitor of Braga for religious and political supremacy. The bishoprics were divided into archdeaconries, each one corresponding roughly to a *terra.* The smallest religious unit was the parish, also called *freguesia,* a neologism formed after *fregueses (filigreses,* that is, *filii ecclesiae),* the "children" of or dependent on a church. The *freguesia* arose in many cases as a substitute for the old rural *palatium* *(paço)* when its lord was no longer a source of efficient protection or a symbol of wealth and authority for the population living in the villa. Instead, the parish priest (or the abbot of a monastery) became the respected leader of many communities and the one whose influence was never diminished. His area coincided with the old villa and inherited its unifying tradition. Thus the expression, reflecting a new reality, has persisted synonymously with parish.

Central administration belonged to the king surrounded by his advisers, some of them entrusted with well-determined offices: the head of the army *(alferes mor),* the head of the royal household *(mordomo),* and the keeper of the royal seal *(chanceler).* Before the early thirteenth century no systematic register of royal acts was kept. Originals of royal grants were copied two or three times and deposited in the archives of the most important monasteries or cathedrals. Under Afonso II, although he maintained the same principle, registers of royal acts started being used and preserved along with the seal and other insignia of power. The first general laws were also enacted by that monarch. Royal advisers, officers, and members of the royal family formed a small group of people whom the king frequently summoned and heard. It was his *curia* or council. When more important matters required a wider debate, the king might summon a larger number of persons, such as archbishops and bishops, the main abbots, the leaders or the most respected among the nobility, and the great masters of the military orders. From these summonings the principle of general assembly or parliament derived. Until the middle of the thirteenth century, however, these assemblies were very rare. The royal curia also acted as a tribunal, and even judicial attributions were its major role.

THE MOSLEM SOUTH

South of the Mondego Valley the brilliant Moslem civilization continued to exist peacefully and to achieve a certain cultural and economic progress. The Almoravid victory of 1092–94 had brought about

0   100   200 km.

0   50   100   150 miles

C H R I S T I A N   S P A I N

•Saraqūsṭa

Ṭurṭūša•

Sahlat Banī Razīn•

•Qulūmriyya

•Antāniya

•Ṭulayṭula   Al-Būnt•

•Balānsiyya

•Šantarīn

•Dāniyya

Mārida•
•Al-Ušbūna   •Baṭalyāws
Yābura•

Bāja•

•Qurṭuba   Mūrsiyya•

Mārtula•

Qarmūna•

Lābla•   •Išbīliya
Šilb•   •Wālba•
     Mawrūr•   •Garnāṭa

Šanta Mariya
Al-Harun   Rūnda•   •Al-Mariyya

•Mālaqa

•Al-Jazīra

unification once again. Al-Andalus was ruled by strong hands, if not by tolerant and intellectually gifted emirs. Half of Spain was still Moslem. There were no reasons to believe that the other half was lost forever and that Islamic power was doomed to death.

Yūsuf ben Tāshufin's glorious reign (1061–1106) was followed by the weaker but still imposing 'Alī ben Yūsuf's rule (1106–43). Events in Africa, however, forced 'Alī to spend most of his time in Morocco, and thus he relieved the pressure exerted on the Christians. Nonetheless, the Moslems were still able to reconquer Shantarīn (1110) and to threaten the new Christian settlements south of the Mondego.

The fall of Sarakūsta (Zaragoza) to Alfonso I of Aragon (1118) marked the beginning of a change. There was a local rebellion in Kūrtuba (Cordoba) and an Aragonese victory at Cutanda, followed by the loss of several castles and towns. In Morocco a new Mahdī appeared and around him a new party of fanatics, the al-Muwahhidūn (from which, Almohads), that is, the monotheists (or unitary), began disturbing the country (1121). Almoravid rule in Spain had become unbearable by that time, forcing hundreds of Mozarabs to move north.

Leon Urraca's death in 1126 resulted in peace and new possibilities of expansion. By the 1130's the three states of Christian Spain launched an attack on al-Andalus, which, with victories and defeats, was to last for thirty or more years and add new territories to Christendom. This movement was accompanied and actually made easier by the complete breakdown of the Almoravids. In the western part of the Peninsula, Afonso Henriques of Portugal built the strong castle of Leiria (1135) as a powerful defensive and operational base, and some years later he proceeded to a daring but in no way unprecedented raid deep into the heart of Islam. He crossed the Tagus and entered the vast deserted plain of Ribatejo and north Alentejo. Some sixty miles south of the Tagus he possibly reached the old Roman-Moslem highway which easily took him south more than 125 miles from his frontier. At Ourique, a small town by that road, he finally met the Moslem defending army, which he was able to crush with some hundreds of mounted warriors (1139). It was his first great victory, but he could not exploit it. His had been but a raid, unsupported by a supply system and by any reserves. Ourique was too far away to mean anything definitive for the Christian conquest. Afonso Henriques went back home, leaving Moslem life in Alentejo most probably undisturbed.

Shortly after, the second taifa period began. Tā<u>sh</u>ufin ben 'Alī Yūsuf (1143–45) and his successors Ibrāhīm ben Tā<u>sh</u>ufin (1145) and Is<u>h</u>āq ben 'Alī (1145–47) were the last Almoravids. All over Spain a wave of rebellions brought about new political units in sixteen cities. In the western part of the Iberian Peninsula there were units in Mārtula, Yābura and Bāja, and <u>Sh</u>ilb, all by 1144.

This second taifa period is highly interesting because of its connections with social and religious movements. The *sufis* were the soul of most rebellions, and their revolutionary and heretical program shaped the birth and rise of the petty states. Although sufism was essentially a mode of thinking and feeling in the religious domain, a mystical current reacting against the intellectualism and formalism of Islam, its consequences and practical ways of fighting made it socially meaningful and dangerous. By the tenth century sufism had become the mightiest spiritual force among the people. Its role continued during the eleventh and twelfth centuries, with inevitable ups and downs. Craft organizations were particularly permeable to the sufis' teachings, adopting ethics and ceremonials which often converted them into a sort of secret association with subversive goals in mind.

The great leader of the western Iberian insurrection against authority and centralization was a sufi, Abū-l-Ḳāsim al-Ḥusaym ben Ḳaṣī, born in <u>Sh</u>ilb, who had traveled widely and studied all over Spain. His rebellion started in September 1144 in Mārtula, where he was governor, with the support of a great part of the population. He proclaimed himself *imam* and al-Mahdī, and his call to arms was quickly responded to in <u>Sh</u>ilb and Lābla. Another religious and social leader, Abū Muḥāmmad Sidray ben Wazīr, who was governor of most of al-Gharb, including Baṭalyāws, Bāja, and Yābura, rebelled in his native town of Bāja, seceding from the central government (1144). A third insurrectional chief was Abū Walīd Muḥāmmad ben al-Mun<u>dh</u>ir, also from <u>Sh</u>ilb, who, in the same year, took over his native town with Uk<u>h</u><u>sh</u>ūnuba a little later. Both came to Mārtula and acknowledged Ben Ḳaṣī's authority. In exchange, they were confirmed in their governments. Thus al-Gharb formed something like a confederation of three kuwar, under the presidency of Mārtula. We do not know to what extent the rebellion spread to al-Ushbūna and to Shantarīn. Al-Mundhir was able to conquer Wālba and Lābla (1145) but he failed to storm Ishbīliya and Ḳurṭuba. In turn, Sidray entered Baṭalyāws (1145). The whole al-Gharb was lost to the Almoravids. Yet the history of the "confederation" proved to be nothing more than a civil struggle among the three leaders, who alternately ruled in the *taifas'* capital cities.

Both the Christians and the Almohads profited from such political anarchy. Afonso Henriques, evidently well informed of what was going on, advanced with his army and succeeded in capturing Shantarīn (March 1147). Approximately at the same time, the Almohads were successfully engineering the submission of al-Gharb. Mārtula, Shilb, and all the other towns fell into their hands. When, three months later, with the valuable help of a fleet of Crusaders who were heading for Palestine ("second" Crusade), Afonso Henriques decided to besiege al-Ushbūna, the city got no outside help and fell after a three-month resistance (October 1147).

The loss of such important territories did not put an end to the internal dissensions of Islam. By 1150 Ben Ḳaṣī revolted again in Shilb and refused obedience to the Almohads. He was backed by similar rebellions in Ḳādis (Cadiz) and Baṭalyāws. To obtain protection Ben Ḳaṣī repeated the treacherous act of sixty years before, begging an alliance with the Christians on conditions we are now unable to check (1151). In any case he succeeded only in provoking a rebellion of his own people, who killed him and surrendered the town to al-Mundhir (1151). The Almohads restored order once more in 1156, when Sidray, now campaigning on their behalf and under their authority, entered Tabīra (Tavira) on the coast and Shilb. Mārtula did not fall until 1157.

The continuation of the Christian advance was the natural result of all these struggles. After the Tagus, their frontier reached the Sado and Alentejo. Al-Ḳaṣr Abū Dānis (Alcácer do Sal) was conquered in 1160. Radiating from there and from the North, other attacks were made. Bāja fell (1162), apparently stormed by contingents sent by the city of Santarém (Shantarīn) under the leadership of Fernão Gonçalves. A local leader and adventurer, Geraldo Geraldes, nicknamed "O Sem Pavor" (Fearless), took several towns in what is nowadays

Spanish Extremadura and was bold enough to attack and subdue Yābura (Évora) in 1165, S̲h̲īrba (Serpa) in 1166, and even part of Baṭalyāws (Badajoz) by 1168. It seemed that the southern sea would be quickly reached and all of al-Gharb definitely lost. But it was not so. The Almohads and the king of Leon, Fernando II, decided to combine their forces against the aggressive Portuguese who were conquering both in Moslem territory and in areas which the Leonese thought should be theirs. United, they stopped Afonso Henriques in Badajoz, where he was helping Geraldo Geraldes to storm the citadel. Fernando succeeded in making him his prisoner after a riding accident in which the Portuguese king broke his leg. Freed only after promising to surrender all the castles held east of Alentejo and north of the Minho, unable forever after to ride a horse, Afonso returned north never to come back. The Moslems had time now to heal their wounds and build up a new and stronger defensive and offensive apparatus.

The great Almohad offensive, which was destined to be the last important Moslem effort to push the Christians back, began under caliph Abū Ya'qūb Yūsuf I, nicknamed al-S̲h̲ahid (1163–84), and continued with his successor Abū Ya'qūb Yūsuf II, al-Manṣūr (1184–99). In 1178 the Portuguese armies, commanded by Sancho, their future king, had launched a daring raid southward, reaching Andalucia and the outskirts of Is̲h̲bīliya. It was simply a raid, with no important consequences, but this time the Moslems felt strong enough to respond. A great invasion in 1184 took them to the Tagus line again, besieging Santarém. Reversing his earlier alliance, Fernando II of Leon now rushed to help the Portuguese, forcing the Almohads to retreat to Alentejo where some fortified towns had held out. The moving frontier was now south of the Tagus, and there it would remain for almost half a century.

By 1189 the Portuguese attacked again, backed by a new fleet of crusaders who had called at Lisbon ("third" crusade). S̲h̲ilb (Silves) and its neighborhoods were stormed after fierce combat. As a result, caliph al-Manṣūr decided to take revenge. Not only did he recapture S̲h̲ilb after a long siege (1190–91) but he proceeded north, passed the Tagus, and raided Estremadura up to Torres Novas (1190). After the end of two devastating campaigns, the Almohads had placed the border line at the Tagus once more, with the sole exception of Évora, which stood alone in the middle of a Moslem territory.

The Christian reconquest was not resumed until much later, when the Almohad power was clearly declining. At Las Navas de Tolosa (1212) the end of their empire came nearer, when an army of Castilian, Aragonese, Navarrese, and Portuguese contingents completely defeated the Almohad caliph Abū 'Abd Allāh Muḥāmmad, nicknamed al-Nasir (1199–1213).

In spite of this defeat, the Moslems were still strong. In Portugal the only advantage taken during the reign of King Afonso II (1211–23) was the conquest of Alcácer, on the Sado. A fleet of crusaders ("Fifth" Crusade) once again made it possible in 1217. But it was only in the 1220's and 1230's that the breakdown of the Almohad empire brought a new period of continuous advance. Led by young Sancho II (1223–48), but more often by the military orders of Santiago, Calatrava, and Hospital, the Portuguese successively conquered Alentejo (1226–38) and part of eastern Algarve (1234–38). Sancho's brother and heir, Afonso III (1248–79), completed the conquest, capturing the isolated enclave the Moslems were still holding in western Algarve, which included Silves and Faro (1249).

Let us now consider the territorial and cultural features of that South which for so long stopped the Christian advance. Sources are meager, and the interest of historians in that area has also been slight.

By the mid-eleventh century, more than half of present-day Portugal was still Moslem, an area of more than 20,000 square miles. Gradually, the Christian offensive reduced the area: A century later, when the Tagus was definitely reached as a frontier, 14,500 square miles were still left. By the 1230's less than 6,000 belonged to Islam. The remnant left to the Moslems between 1238 and the final conquest of 1249 comprised less than 1,000 square miles.

These figures, however, should not lead us to hasty conclusions as to the number of people living in al-Gharb. Geographical conditions south of the Tagus were and are adverse to a high density of settlement. Most of the country, furthermore, was waste land, the soil being poor and the climate often unfavorable. What gave demographic importance and economic prosperity to al-Gharb was not any balanced population distribution but rather the existence of some large towns and villages, unknown in the North. There lived both the rich owners of grainfields, groves, grazing lands, and the laborers who made them productive. There too lived merchants, craftsmen, sailors, and fishermen. The South was urban in character, but there was little human settlement between the towns.

The main cities were al-Ushbūna and Shantarīn, whose importance constantly decreased as they came nearer and nearer the frontier zone. Next in importance were Shintrā (Sintra), al-Ma'din (Almada), al-Ḳaṣr Abū-Dānīs (Alcácer do Sal), Yālbash (Elvas), Yābura (Évora), Julumāniya (Juromenha), Maura (Moura), Bāja (Beja), Shirba (Serpa), Mārtula (Mértola), Shilb (Silves), al-'Aliyā (Loulé), Shanta Marīya al-Hārun (Santa Maria de Faro), Tabīra (Tavira), and Ḳasṭālla (Cacela). This order is purely geographical and does not correspond to any hierarchy in economic, political, or demographical importance, which is hard to determine. The scarce archaeological evidence available, based mostly on the city walls and fortifications, suggests a priority to al-Ushbūna, Shantarīn, al-Ḳaṣr, Shilb, Yābura, and Mārtula. Bāja's importance seems to have declined, while formerly small villages such as Yālbash and al-Ḳaṣr rose to outstanding positions. This shift was often a result of military needs, but no information is available on possible economic circumstances.

Al-Ushbūna was a large town by western al-Andalus standards. Within its walls it encompassed some 15 hectares, but the actual urban area was larger because of the highly populated suburbs east and west of it. It could not be compared, of course, with great metropolises like Ishbīliya (50 hectares), Balānsiyya (45 hectares), or Mālaḳa (37 hectares), not to mention Ṭulāyṭula or Ḳūrtuba. If the population figure of any of these cities is considered, al-Ushbūna's demographic weight would not be put very much above the 5,000 level. Even so, it was an average town according to general European measurements, somewhat larger than its Christian rivals, Braga and Coimbra. The area of Yābura was some 10 hectares, and Shilb not more than 7. Figures are unavailable for the other towns.

Human density varied greatly from region to region. North of al-Ushbūna the country was well cultivated and populated. Tagus Valley, particularly its eastern basin, had important settlements. The present-day peninsula of Setúbal was another area of human concentration. There were also the vast waste lands of present-day Ribatejo and Alentejo, with some oases especially noticeable east of Yābura and along the Guadiana in the present *concelhos* of Évora, Redondo,

Portel, Reguengos, Alandroal, Vila Viçosa, Borba, Estremoz, and Elvas. Scattered areas of developed settlement existed in present-day Baixo Alentejo, but it was south, in the Algarve, that small rural communities developed similar to that of Christian Minho.

Economic life was, of course, based on agriculture. The South produced cereals, mainly wheat, in abundance, the area of Balāta (between al-Ushbūna and Shantarīn) being famous for its high productivity and considered a true granary. Fruit and olive oil were next in abundance, or even held first place. Olive trees covered the whole country, often intermingled with grain. Present-day Algarve was already one of the great centers for figs and almonds, which were widely exported. Around each town, groves and orchards, accompanied by fertile and green herb gardens, nourished the local population and allowed some exports. The Moslems became famous for their contributions to agricultural techniques and improvements. In addition to minor inventions and improvements, they introduced two major devices, the *nā'ūrah* (Portuguese, *nora*), a bucket wheel to pull water from deep wells, and the *sāniya* (Portuguese, *azenha*), a water wheel similar to the Roman water mill but with a vertical wheel. Both, particularly the *nora,* were responsible for the rural development of certain southern areas. The Moslems also introduced several new plants or implemented their use. They brought or spread a botanical variety of wheat *(trigo mourisco)*, rice, oranges, and saffron, to mention a few.

A relevant part in the economy was played by fish and salt. The Lisbon, Setúbal, and Algarve coastlines, facing south, particularly favored fishing activities. Fisherman went possibly as far as Morocco and the African coast, as well as westward. It is interesting to note that al-Ushbūna was related to sea adventures, presumably by fishermen, and that traditional legends mentioned the discovery of inhabited lands, perhaps the Canary Islands. Salt beds were plentiful along the mouth of the Tagus and the Sado rivers.

Little is known of stockbreeding, but there was a sizable production of milk, butter, and cheese, probably from sheep and goats. An abundance of acorns invited hog-raising, at least among the Christian farmers. Islam, however, strongly discouraged it.

There were copper and silver mines in Alentejo, and tin mines in the Algarve, and some gold was collected in the lower Tagus. Amber was also collected around al-Ushbūna and Shantarīn.

Fishing, salt, and peaceful waters, accompanied by heavy demographic concentration, were obvious causes of a rise in navigation and long-distance maritime trade with the rest of the Moslem countries, of which we know practically nothing. Nonetheless, Idrisi's description suggests a shipbuilding industry fostered by pine groves around al-Ḳaṣr. Apparently the Moslems of al-Gharb were considered dangerous pirates, which determined the conquest by the Christians of such ports as al-Ushbūna, al-Ḳaṣr, and Shilb before the actual control of the hinterland. All this accounts for a relatively strong fleet and some familiarity with the sea and its ways.

Although sources are scarce, the existence of sophisticated land communications and commerce seems too logical to dismiss. The Roman road net was probably kept and repaired, if not enlarged. Plains and some rivers (although navigability was limited by soil and weather conditions) offered easier contacts and easier transport than in the North. Money circulated with abundance, in gold, silver, and copper. During the second taifa period Mārtula had its own mint, where some gold coins were issued.

We know little of crafts. Accounts left to later times suggest an abundance of skilled workers in household needs, such as tailors, carpenters, shoemakers, pottery workers, masons, saddlers, and the like. Some were organized in rudimentary corporations and settled in well-determined streets or areas. Paper was possibly fabricated or more probably imported from east of al-Andalus. The Arabic word for a bundle of paper was *rizma,* from which the Portuguese, as well as the Castilians, formed *resma,* a ream.

The social structure of al-Gharb al-Andalus in the twelfth and thirteenth centuries was not very different from the one in the Christian North. A class of landowners held most of the soil and controlled most of the power. Unlike the northern Portuguese, however, they generally dwelt in the towns or in the large villages, receiving their rents and visiting their estates from time to time, but briefly. It seems that many of them were attracted by court life as it existed around the person of the caliph (living either in Spain or in Africa) or of the taifa kings and emirs. Capital cities continued to mean much in those days and encouraged personal mobility and wide traveling.

The estate corresponding in the South to the villa was called *dai'a* (plural *diyā'*), from which the Portuguese word *aldeia* was formed. The process of conversion of a *dai'a* into a parish in later times was similar to the one that changed the villa into a *freguesia*. Its core, where the noble house was surrounded by the houses of the household and other dependencies, became the *aldeia* proper in Christian times, that is, a village in the modern sense of the word. In each *dai'a* the actual rural exploitation belonged to free peasants (*muzāri'*, plural *muzāri'ūn*), who were bound to the landowner by the payment of a certain rent, which could amount to half of the whole production. In turn, the landowner owed the state (in Islam not separated from the Church) a tithe, related to the religious obligation of the *zakāh* (alms). Theoretically all the lands belonged to the state, which at the time of the conquest had granted them permanently to a warrior and his heirs. A few estates or rather small holdings were left in the hands of Christian farmers. They had to pay a tribute called *kharāj*, which was much higher than the tithe. Later on, when many Christians were converted to Islam and became *muwalladūn* (from which comes the Portuguese word *malados*), their land tax was not reduced and their fiscal situation remained worse than that of the old Moslems. This brought about social restlessness and a well-marked cleavage between them and the Moslems.

A very common practice, more and more frequent as the central authority gradually broke down, led to growth in the area of the *diyā'* and to a decrease in the number of *kharāj* lands. Many freeholders preferred to give up their right to full ownership and to place themselves under the protection and authority of wealthy proprietors of *diyā'*, their taxation being reduced and their security enhanced. Many merchants and top civil servants invested their profits or savings in land, thus converting the towns into large gatherings of absentee owners living from permanent land revenues. Theoretically there was no separate Church in Islam. For practical purposes, however, the state assigned as private revenues of the mosques the rents of a large proportion of both rural and urban property, as well as its actual administration. The mosques, therefore, might be considered landowners too. The state in Moslem countries was extremely wealthy and powerful. Through the caliph and his representatives, it possessed cultivated land, urban property, means of production such as mills,

ovens, and presses, as well as most of the uncultivated land. This role
cannot be forgotten or underestimated in order to explain the changing conditions in the royal power and fortune when the Christian
kings took over everything that belonged to the Moslem State.

The breakdown of the Caliphate twice in a hundred years and the
consequent rise of local units of political administration brought about
autonomous tendencies and regular hereditary governments. In many
cases heredity was maintained and even enforced in Almoravid and
Almohad times as a powerful means of curbing anarchy and resisting
external attacks. Local notables were entrusted with governorship and
succeeded in keeping it within their families for more than a generation. If petty dynasties did not develop, it was simply due to lack of
time. In Shantarīn and al-Kaṣr, for instance, military tenancies were
transmitted from father to son until the Christian conquest. The more
we know of Moslem genealogies the more we are impressed by the
kinship among the several top local officers in al-Gharb al-Andalus. A
small oligarchy seemed to hold power firmly and to swap positions
regularly. We lack monographs about the extent to which such an
oligarchical rule determined social rebellions or even helped welcome
the Christian invaders.

Apparently al-Gharb never formed a united province by itself, except in the time of Ben Kāṣi, who seems to have been appointed
wālī (i.e., delegate of the caliph) of al-Gharb by the Almohad Al-
Qaʻim (1145). This was probably an emergency measure to pacify the
territory and gain some partisans there. Al-Gharb used to constitute,
with Ishbīliya and the whole of the West and Southwest, a military
command depending on a single wālī. The administrative history of
Moslem Spain is, as a matter of fact, still very confusing for the
twelfth and thirteenth centuries. It seems that earlier al-Gharb included only the southernmost kuwar of Bāja and Shilb, plus that of
Lābla, the North (with Yābura, al-Ushbūna, Shantarīn, and Baṭalyāws)
forming the Lower military march with seat in Baṭalyāws. Later on,
the Christian incursions south made it necessary to unite both governments and to stress their military aspect.

The kūra pattern is also confusing. Shantarīn and al-Ushbūna
were certainly united in one single kūra but we do not know which of
the two cities prevailed in the supreme command. Yābura was the seat

of another district, which included a great part of the upper Guadina Valley and adjoined that of Baṭalyāws. To the West, however, boundaries seem to have changed with time, a new *kūra* being created with its capital in Al-Ḵaṣr. To the south, too, limits are far from being determined. Bāja's importance apparently declined while that of its rival Mārtula rose. By the mid-twelfth century Mārtula was obviously a seat of administration. The extreme south constituted another *kūra* with capital in Shilb. As all these cities, with many others, had military governors with the same name (*al-qāʿid*) (Portuguese *alcaide*), it is hard to determine their relative hierarchy. In a military context, the *qāʿīd* was the head of a company of one hundred men. Ten battalions, of ten companies each, were headed by an *amīr*.

Below the *kūra* there was the small rural unit called *qarya* as well as the town (*qasaba* or *madīna*). These words account for the Portuguese *alcaria, alcáçova,* and *almedina.*

For judicial purposes a rough coincidence existed between its units and the *kuwar.* Each town and many large villages had a *qādī* (Port. *alcalde*) or judge of their own. In the smaller communities this officer was instead a *hākim* (*alfaqui* in Portuguese). An important official who practically controlled the economic life of each town was the *muḥtasib* (Port. *almotacé*), who fixed prices, verified weights and measures, established the amount of fines, served as an arbiter in economic disputes, surveyed the city supplies in food and water, and so forth. In theory all these officers were appointed, but the practice made them either hereditary or chosen among a small group of local notables.

Jews and Christians (Mozarabs) were numerous in all of al-Gharb. Their communities were segregated from the rest of the population, and they lived in private ghettos and elected their own leaders. They often dwelt outside the main walls of a city. Whenever their number was vast enough, the Christians were ruled by a count (*comes*, Arabic *kūmis*), who was chosen from among the notables or simply inherited. They held their own councils, adopted their own laws (common law, old Roman, and Visigothic law), and fixed their own fine and taxation system. For purposes of justice they had a judge (*iudex*) who, in smaller communities, substituted for the *comes* too. It was the *comes* or the *iudex* who represented the whole community and who was held responsible by the Moslems for the payment of the per capita tax.

Religiously, the Mozarabs were also quite free or, at least, they were tolerated by Islam. Religious freedom, of course, was uncertain and depended on many local and general conditions. Some large Christian communities even kept their bishop. It seems that such was the case in al-Ushbūna, where the bishop with other Moslem and Christian authorities pleaded for mercy to the attackers and negotiated surrender of their town in 1147. Like so many others of his fellow-believers, he was actually murdered by the Crusaders when plundering and killing got entirely out of control.

Very little is known of the cultural advancement of al-Gharb al-Andalus during the twelfth and thirteenth centuries. At most we know of some poets and writers who were born there, but we are ignorant of the actual conditions and means of all cultural activity. Poetry was cultivated, and we have the word of al-Ḵazwīni (died 1283) who asserted that in Shilb one would meet even ploughmen capable of improvising verse. Lyric ballads and songs known as *muwashshaḥ* and *zajal* were probably introduced from central and eastern Andalus where they were flourishing from the eleventh century on. The quick spread of sufism and the religious upheaval of the mid-twelfth century can be explained in social and economic terms. Nonetheless, they suggest some religious and philosophical culture of urban basis. Schools certainly existed, although we know nothing of the number and location of *madāris* (singular, *madrasa*, Moslem "universities" or high schools). In any case, all that culture was Arabic and relied upon the Islamic faith. The Reconquista completely destroyed it, killing or forcing into exile most of its representatives. The Arabic alphabet, however, had spread even among the Mozarabs, who used to write their Latin dialects in it.

Strangely enough, for a long established and somewhat sophisticated civilization very little is known of art in al-Gharb. Most art historians assume that little was left because little had originally been created. The explanation could be different, although no possible comparison should be drawn between the West of al-Andalus and the center of its flourishing such as Ḵūrṭuba or Ishbīliya. A great number, if not the majority, of Moslem monuments were later "disguised" or transformed by the Christians. This is true particularly of the mosques which were converted into churches. Many are still there, awaiting archaeologists and historians, very much as the seventeenth- or eighteenth-century "redecorated" cathedrals hid their original Romanesque and Gothic features behind the baroque and rococo pastiche. The Mārtula main church, where a *mihrab* was discovered and unearthed, is a good example. Most of the castles and walls built in the eleventh, twelfth, and thirteenth centuries south of the Mondego or the Tagus were products of Moslem masonry and military science. They are still there, repaired and believed to be Christian works. City plans going back to Islamic times survive in a great number of Portuguese towns, such as Lisbon, for instance. General principles of decoration, with a stress on stucco and tile (*azulejo*) elements, were created or developed by this time. Their much later revival, known as the *mudéjar* style, will be studied in another chapter.

THE RECONQUISTA AND THE UNION OF NORTH AND SOUTH

Was the Reconquista a religious war? Can it be compared with the Crusades as so many chroniclers and, later, historians have claimed? Is there any meaning in the coined expression "Western Crusades," a sort of geographical variation of the great movement for the liberation of the Holy Land?

The answer is uncertain and depends on the epoch. Before the twelfth century one hardly finds any similarities between the Reconquista and a holy war of religion. After that time the situation undoubtedly changed, but political prejudices always imparted a peculiar Iberian character.

It seems that Pope Urban II, a Cluniac who was certainly well informed on Spanish affairs, also planned a general crusade to the West with the purpose of delivering the rest of the Peninsula from the Moslem "yoke." With that in mind, he reasonably forbade all the Spaniards to participate in the so-called first crusade. Such a prohibition was maintained until the late twelfth century. Yet the Pontifical hopes of arousing a general crusade and crusade feeling in the Iberian Peninsula hardly corresponded to the traditional attitude toward the Moors. Four centuries of intermittent fighting had only brought

Iberian Moslems and Christians closer together. Commercial and cultural relations were matched by many political alliances and personal contacts. For medieval minds and generalized intolerance, the Spaniards presented a rather surprising example of peaceful coexistence and religious respect.

This attitude gradually changed. The Christians were becoming the masters, and the end of Moslem rule might be envisaged. As a result their former tolerance and respect, based mostly on a necessity to coexist, gave way to persecution and an impatience to finish the conquest. Also the Almoravid and Almohad fanaticism did little to seal good relations and mutual tolerance. As constant losers, the Moslems now fought harder for what was rapidly becoming a struggle for survival. Finally, the foreign influences and "fashions" should not be underestimated. No country of Christian Europe could be unaffected by the successive preachings of a holy war against the infidel. Furthermore, such appeals to war, violence, and hatred were backed by highly efficient weapons, such as the spiritual indulgences and the temporal seizure of tithes and other revenues.

The "third" crusade and the following ones were preached in Portugal too. Several times the Portuguese clergy was forced to contribute to the eastern crusades (in 1215, 1245, 1274, 1312). The Portuguese kings were invited to take the cross and to join their fellow-Christians in expeditions to Palestine. More important, however, was the growing belief that the war against the Moors in Spain could and should be put on the same footing with the war for the liberation of the Holy Land; briefly, that it was a "Western Crusade." As such it benefited from all the usual indulgences granted to the crusaders; it appealed to all the Christian soldiers in Europe; and it accounted for the use of similar means and goals. Thus the Portuguese begged and obtained the crusaders' help six times: in 1147 (conquest of Lisbon); twice in 1189 (conquests of Alvor and Silves); in 1190 (help to Santarém besieged by the Moslems); in 1197 (unsuccessful attack against Silves); and in 1217 (conquest of Alcácer). In the last of these the crusaders were forced to beg the Pope's permission to winter in Portuguese waters and so delay for several months their arrival in Palestine. The permission was granted. In 1151 the English bishop of Lisbon, Gilbert, a former crusader from the expedition of 1147, went to his

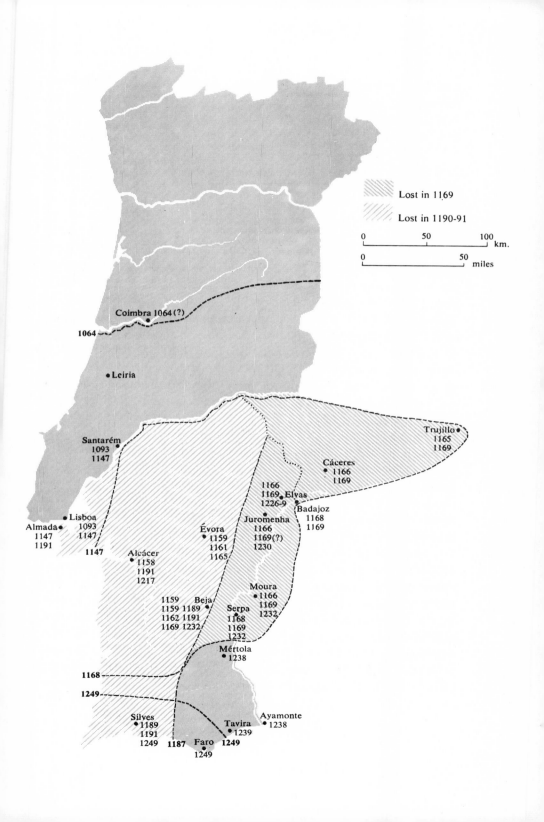

Lost in 1169

Lost in 1190-91

0   50   100 km.

0   50 miles

Coimbra 1064 (?)

1064

● Leiria

Trujillo
1165
1169

Santarém
1093
1147

Cáceres
● 1166
1169

1166
1169 ● Elvas
1226-9   Badajoz

● Lisboa

Almada ●   1093
1147   1147
1191

1147

Évora
● 1159
1161
1165

Juromenha
1166
1169(?)
1230

Badajoz
1168
1169

Alcácer
● 1158
1191
1217

Moura
● 1166
1169
1232

1159   Beja
1159 1189
1162 1191
1169 1232

Serpa
1168
1169
1232

Mértola
● 1238

1168

1249

Silves
● 1189
1191
1249

Tavira
● 1239

Ayamonte
● 1238

1187   Faro   1249
1249

native country to preach the (Western) crusade and get reinforcements in men and weapons. The Portuguese also contributed to several crusades outside their borders: in 1212 (victory of Las Navas de Tolosa); in 1218–19; and, much later, in 1340 (victory of Salado).

Papal bulls and indulgences helped create the ideal of crusade in Portugal: they were granted either to the kings or to the clergy, to the military orders or to private nobles and warriors. One of those bulls, in 1197, even promised the indulgence of Jerusalem in the planned war against Alfonso IX of Leon who was a friend and ally to the Moslems.

The creation in Spain of military-religious orders with the same purposes as those founded in Palestine, or simply the introduction in the Peninsula of the existing ones, greatly helped strengthen the ideal and goals of the crusade. The twelfth century was their century. In Portugal the Knights Templar appeared by 1128. They were followed by the Hospitalers in the middle of the century, and then by the orders of Calatrava and Santiago (both by 1170). All had a clear task to accomplish: expel the Moors, liberate the lands for Christ. The more they grew rich and powerful, the more the ideal of crusade was kept and enforced, for they would be meaningless without it. The Reconquista as a crusade, however, was always imperfect and very different from the eastern wars. In Spain (and thus in Portugal too) the political aspects prevailed, and common movements against the Moslems were rare and difficult. The crusade was felt in a local way. It was always inseparable from the royal interests in each kingdom and strictly depended on them. Indulgences, foreign help, and religious militias served the king of Portugal in the primary task of gaining more lands under his authority. For that, they were precious allies.

More interesting and important seem the military and political aspects of the Reconquista. All over Spain this can be roughly determined by a succession of diagonal lines in the west-east direction. Thus when half of the western coastline (i.e., Portugal) had been gained by the Christian armies (mid-eleventh century, conquest of Coimbra and Montemor-o-Velho, 40° grades N.), Huesca, 42° grades N., was still Moslem. By 1147 when Lisbon (39°) was definitely taken, Tortosa (41°) continued to be Islamic. By 1250, when the Portuguese completed "their" job and incorporated all of the Algarve, the kingdom of

Murcia was not totally conquered. As Moslem Spain was essentially linked to the Mediterranean, the eastern and southeastern coastline and its corresponding hinterland naturally proved more difficult for the Christian armies to conquer than the West.

Within Portugal, the line of cleavage followed the same pattern, at least during most of the eleventh, twelfth, and thirteenth centuries. There were several reasons for this. The fear of Moslem maritime attacks led to the early planning of conquests such as those of Lisbon, Alcácer, and Silves, which were excellent bases for piracy operations. The stopping at rivers which might prove good boundaries for both sides also explains the diagonal lines, as regards the Mondego and the Tagus. Furthermore, it was more difficult for the Christians to conquer the interior regions of al-Gharb, where town concentration was greater and defense better organized and coordinated.

In each Iberian state the lands south of its borders were considered its area of conquest. Boundary details followed the existing Moslem administration pattern which, as we have seen, often went back to the Roman period. Portuguese, Leonese, Castilians, and Aragonese generally accepted such a tacit agreement, which was logical and prevented too much competition. More precise clauses were sometimes written down or orally agreed to. Frequently, however, a state violated the rules and started conquering in its neighbor's area. It would take long to give a complete account of such events regarding Portugal and Leon. What matters is that the conquests never lasted long and that the ups and downs of wars made a more daring or ambitious ruler quickly dispose of illegitimate gains. The Portuguese attack on and loss of Badajoz serves as a good example.

The great exception was the Algarve. Al-Gharb was divided among several *kuwar;* it also belonged to various *taifa* kingdoms. At the time of the Portuguese conquest, the last of them was that of Lābla, whose possessions included the western coastline with S̲h̲anta Marīya and S̲h̲ilb. To get some help, which never became effective, or some money, which he probably received, the King of Lābla ceded his rights to Prince Alfonso, son and heir to Fernando III of Castile and Leon. After some minor hostilities and negotiations between Portugal and her neighbor, war broke out in 1252, when Fernando died and Alfonso inherited the crown as Alfonso X. The war did not last long because

in 1253 Pope Innocent IV succeeded in arranging peace: Afonso III of
Portugal would marry Alfonso's illegitimate daughter, Beatriz, while
temporarily abdicating his suzerain rights over the Algarve (including
all the lands east of the Guadiana) in favor of his father-in-law. Thus
Alfonso X became a vassal of the Portuguese king and the Algarve a
fief held from him. This situation would continue until the first-born
son of Beatriz and Afonso was seven. By 1263, however, five years before young prince Dinis's seventh birthday, an agreement between the
two kings gave the lordship of the Algarve to Dinis. Four years later a
second treaty ratified the existing situation and fixed the border between Portugal and Castile.

In the study of the Reconquista a clear distinction should be
drawn between raids and conquests. Often the Christian monarchs
went deep into the Moslem territory in order to plunder, destroy, and
capture but without any intent of keeping lands. The Moslems did the
same in Christian territory. Such raids explain Ourique (1139) and
several other victories (or defeats). They never lasted for more than a
season, or even less time than that. Then the soldiers wanted to go
back home to take care of the harvests or the vintages. Actual conquests were more carefully planned and executed. They required permanent manpower, economic and political organization, and a suitable defensive system which might stop a Moslem effort of reconquest.
Highly interesting as symbols of lasting conquests (or intended as
such) were the castle lines which in Portugal (as all over Spain) are
seen from North to South, separated from each other sometimes by
hundreds of miles. Such castles were built in strategic positions, often
in half-deserted areas like Leiria, built around 1135. More often, the
conquered place was already fortified or only required some repair.
Whereas most of the towns were strongly walled, some exceptions are
highly interesting to note. Santarém, for instance, one of the key positions to hold the Tagus line, as well as a relatively important town,
was not walled except for its citadel. The Christians probably built
its first wall, but this is not certain.

Offensive and defensive tactics required an organized military
draft. The feudal system provided the king with soldiers as separate
contributions from the various lords. Each military order and each
municipality were also found to furnish a certain number of con-

tingents. The king himself recruited his own forces both from his lands and from alodial holdings. Instead of soldiers he could also gather some money for military expenditures from the payment of the *fossadeira,* a sort of scutage or military tax that gradually freed many farmers from yearly drafting. Knights and riders from the municipalities served as offensive forces, while most of the footmen were especially drafted for defensive purposes. From a strictly political point of view all the Spanish kings considered themselves lawful heirs and descendants of the old Visigothic monarchs. Consequently, every piece of land they could take from the infidel was theirs legitimately. The Reconquista was thus coined as a meaningful word. Permanent war was considered just, until the final goal had been reached. More than a religious conflict, the Reconquista seemed to every one in Christian Europe an affair of inheritance. Even by the eleventh, twelfth, and thirteenth centuries Gothic ancestry was boasted of and tacitly claimed by all the kings. A "Chronicle of the Goths" (*Chronica Gothorum*), beginning with the legendary departure of the Goths "from their land" (*de terra sua*) and continuing with the description of their settling down in Spain, was written and served the purposes of official recording of the truth. The kings of Portugal appeared as legitimate heirs to rule the western part of the Peninsula.

The union of the North with the South brought about, first of all, a population movement. The Christian victory caused a vast migration of Moslems to the area of Spain still unconquered and to Africa. This movement affected most of all the upper classes, but also to a lesser extent merchants, craftsmen, and peasants. The conquest was certainly not welcomed, even by the lower strata of the Moslem population. Past was the time of strict tolerance and mutual respect. The new conditions of Christian-Moslem coexistence were now intolerable for most of the vanquished. If many did not leave, it was simply because they could not afford to do so or because they were afraid of what could happen to them during the trip. Others were too old, too sick, or too humble to quit.

Nonetheless, there was never a demographic vacuum, particularly in the South. Towns and villages might have lost a third or a half of their population, but they were not deserted. The Mozarab element, plus those Moslems who decided to stay or were caught by the speed of the conquest, persisted and preserved life and continuity. Most of the Jews seem to have stayed too. As a matter of fact, a Moslem migration to Granada or to Africa continued all during the late medieval period, which shows that their condition in Christian lands was far from improved through permanent peace. Very many were reduced to slavery, either by right of conquest or because of debt.

In each conquered town the general rule forced the Moslem population to leave its walled precinct within a period of one year and to dwell in the suburbs. This was essentially a measure of security. In the country they were allowed to remain, but their taxation increased, actually becoming worse than that of the Mozarabs in Moslem lands. Every year they had to pay a per capita tax, one-fortieth on all their property, and the tithe on all their production, besides sales taxes and customs taxes and duties. They seem to have lost any property rights, perhaps because all of the alodial landowners left or were killed. Let us not forget that in the South large holdings predominated, thus reducing the actual number of owners. Most of the Moslems, the documents show us, during the late Middle Ages were of low social and professional status; humble craftsmen or peasants, petty peddlers, and the like. Their existence became obscure and their social weight minimal. In a matter of three centuries practically all of them merged with the Christians, leaving very little for the Inquisition to deal with. In many fields, however, their structures persisted and were adopted by the invaders, strongly backed by the Mozarab element and by tradition.

We have little evidence of how quickly and thoroughly the demographic blanks were filled. Documentation is scarce and generally covers a much later period. It is possible that the European trend in the growth of population helped fill the empty houses and the half-deserted fields just by an increase in the birthrate. Migration from the North was the other obvious solution which accounted for a better equilibrium between North and South. Both kings and clergy intensely promoted the coming of new settlers by all the means available: promise of security and privilege, granting or acknowledgment of self-government, light taxation, liberty of serfdom and justice, appeal to foreigners, etc. The Reconquista decisively contributed to a gradual social change through the mobility it implied. All the elements of society went up in their economic and social status. The king, the Church, and the nobility increased their respective patrimony and consequent power; the *coloni* and other dependent cultivators often became small landholders; many serfs became *coloni* or petty craftsmen in a town. A new society was clearly emerging in the twelfth and thirteenth centuries.

Particular problems accompanied the encounter between northern Christians, rough in their culture and manners, arrogant in their victories, suddenly promoted to a social condition they were not prepared for, and southern Mozarabs, more refined in their Arab way of life, urban minded, forced to live with strangers whom they considered themselves superior to. There was the problem of land and house appropriation; there was the problem of social hierarchy; there was the problem of ruling and administration positions. No historian has ever attempted to analyze this contradiction and to show how it was solved. Yet it was from this encounter that Portugal and the Portuguese were born.

North of the Mondego a great part of the lands had been seized by the victorious newcomers in the form of *presúria* (> *prendere,* to take). This was the simple occupation of land considered vacant, and it was accepted as one of the most legitimate property titles. There were several types of *presúrias,* some directed or organized by an authority (king, Church, nobles), some deriving only from an individual act of seizure. We may assume that many, if not the majority, of the alodial lands existing in the North derived from *presúria* acts. South of the Mondego, however, such acts were much rarer. The Reconquista became an organized and centralized affair. Small landholdings gave way to larger units and to latifundia. No royal authority would ever recognize huge land appropriations unless they were accompanied by a gracious donation. Furthermore, many of the regions south of the Tagus did not appeal to private seekers of land. They were vast waste plains or thickets, intermingled with small well-cultivated areas around an urban center, which the king kept for himself.

The action of the religious-military orders also prevented *presúrias.* Most of the war and its glorious victories belonged to the orders of Santiago and Calatrava, to the Templars and Hospitalers. The king's initiatives were secondary. Private enterprises like Gonçalo

Gonçalves' deeds in Alentejo or the incursion of the common of Santarém against Évora were exceptions. The participation of the nobles was also minor. Thus land distribution in the South followed a completely different pattern from that of the North.

For himself (or his protégés) the king kept the essential core of the new conquests: the cities and the towns. No important urban center was ever granted to the religious-military orders. They were all organized in self-governing communities, but their taxes and direct control, as well as vast shares of houses, ovens, presses, and other means of production, belonged to the monarch. Some were later given as appanages to members of the royal family but for their lifetime only. After deducting areas as town districts (*termos*), the king granted almost all the rest in full property to the military orders: the Knights Templar received most of Beira Baixa and a vast territory between the Mondego and the Tagus; the Hospitalers got a relatively small and unimportant share in Alto Alentejo, in the upper Tagus valley and east of the Guadiana; Calatrava (later known as Avis after its main castle) got most of Alto Alentejo; Santiago was given the greatest part of the South, with almost all of Baixo Alentejo, the Setúbal peninsula, and important shares in the Algarve. The non-military orders and the secular Church were also recipients: the Cistercians, for instance, received extensive property in Beira Litoral and Estremadura, as did the Canons of St. Augustine, particularly those from Coimbra (Santa Cruz) and Lisboa (S. Vicente); the Franciscans, the Dominicans, and the cathedrals of each city got extensive shares within and outside each town. From the little we know of the agrarian development of the Moslem South, it seems that the most fertile and productive areas of Alentejo were granted to the friars of Avis. Both size and yield were considered to balance the grants to the Temple, Calatrava, and Santiago. This was an intelligent policy of the first Portuguese kings.

Related to the Reconquista were also the rise and expansion of the municipal organization. In the Moslem towns, where there was a considerable Mozarab population, the law recognized the organization and representativeness of the Christian communities (as well as those of the Jews) through several organs and officers. There was a council of the heads of family or of notables and there were an elected leader and a responsible taxation system. Thus, when the northerners came and conquered the southern towns, they met a traditional self-governing regulation in each of them. There was little need for innovation, and the new authorities simply acknowledged the status quo. With the arrival of newcomers, however, things began to change, both in the social and in the economic spheres. Trade and internal relationships followed different patterns. The population brought with them the usages and the laws from the North. All over the reconquered areas there was an obvious need for new regulations. These, which were granted by kings and lords (Church and nobility), were called *forais*. They rarely created new institutions and were really little concerned about municipal organization. Their main goal was to define and specify taxation and organization of justice.

All during the twelfth and thirteenth centuries *forais* were granted to most of the towns and large villages. Their pattern differed somewhat according to the epoch, the size of the settlement, the purposes of the lord, and the legal preparation of the royal adviser. Some forms were imported from Leon and Castile, others were typically Portuguese. It has been possible to determine some six basic types of *forais* and to establish a sort of "family" tree connecting similar ones within each type. The *forais* should not be confused with communal charters. They did not create communes, the principle of which was very far from the Iberian tradition of community government. Self-rule was accepted, true, but only to a limited extent. In many cases all the officers had to be confirmed by the town's lord, generally the king. Self-administration was greatly reduced by a rigid system of taxation and a limited sphere of local justice. The king had the right to interfere frequently. Few attempts were ever made to secure a greater degree of self-government, which was neither in the Islamic tradition nor in the conditions of life of early Portugal, where a strong central command was required.

Each municipality (*concelho*) possessed its own council of notables or good men (*homens bons*), who generally were small landholders or rich traders. This council elected several officers, whose names and attributes clearly reflected the compromise between the Moslem and the Christian organizations. The two or four *alvasis* (>Arabic *al-wāzir*), also called *alcaldes* (>Arabic *al-qaḍī*) and *juizes* (>Latin *iudices,* the judges), were the supreme representatives and leaders of the community. The *almotacé* (>*al-muḥtasib*), also elected, controlled the economic life of the *concelho,* as he used to do in Moslem times. The king was always represented by another officer, directly appointed by him, sometimes called *alcaide* (>*al-qā'id*) if there was a castle or citadel, sometimes *juiz* if his functions were simply jurisdictional. In some *concelhos* that representative was chosen among the good men. As a rule, however, he was a noble. In most of the North the number of *concelhos* was very small, for the country was already definitely organized according to the feudal tradition, with few individualized groups within the urban centers and with few urban centers. Only the newly formed burghs got some attention and change of situation from their lords. But the nearer we come to the South, the more numerous the *concelhos* are. They corresponded to modern phases of the Reconquest and to the need for attracting settlers by granting them immunities and privileges. Beira and Estremadura, where settlement was somewhat dispersed, show the greatest concentration of *forais* and *concelhos* granted to small villages and nuclei of settlers. It was farther south, however, in Alentejo and the Algarve, that the most powerful *concelhos* existed, in connection with the largest towns and villages.

THE FEUDAL AGE

THE LATE MEDIEVAL STRUCTURES

Late medieval Portugal presents many peculiar characteristics, a consequence of the encounter and fusion of the northern and the southern structures. It put together: (1) pure feudal characteristics typical of and parallel to all of Western Europe, which resulted from the evolution of the late Roman and Barbarian (mainly Visigothic) categories and then from the decline of feudalism itself: (2) twisted feudal elements, a consequence of the needs and particular circumstances of the Reconquista; (3) Mozarab features, with a long tradition of self-development and isolation from Christian Europe; and (4) typical Moslem characteristics, common to the whole world of Islam, which by the twelfth and thirteenth centuries was feudal everywhere or rapidly tending toward feudalism.

Thus feudal Portugal, like feudal Castile, presented highly interesting aspects which can be thoroughly interpreted and understood only by comparison with both the other European countries and the Islamic states. The failure to do so has led almost all the Portuguese historians (and many of their Spanish colleagues) to create an artificial "seignorial non-feudal" Portugal, a sort of *rara avis* of unclear origin and difficult description. Once the idea of a monolithic and geographically restricted feudalism is put aside, the interpretation of medieval and early modern Portugal as a feudal state ceases to be a riddle, although still inevitably posing many problems.

Vassality, as an institution, was well established in Portugal by the thirteenth, fourteenth, and fifteenth centuries. Instead of *fidelis*, so common before, *vassallus* (*vassalo*) came into general use, referring to all the nobles in direct dependency to their king. The small size of the country and the fact that the monarch was one of the largest land-owners explain the relatively large number of direct vassals, who accounted for the monarch's growing strength.

Royal grants in the form of a benefice were called *préstamos* (Latin *prestimonia*). Originally they were not hereditary, but as time went on inheritance became the general and accepted practice although much later than in other feudal countries of Europe. It was roughly by the thirteenth century that fiefs similar to those of France and England appeared in Portugal. Many royal grants began to have the form of *morgadios* or *morgados* (entailed estates), which implied inalienability, indivisibility, and perpetual succession within the same family, generally under the right of primogeniture and male preference. Large estates, small holding houses, offices, and even rents (customs, revenues, tolls, etc.) could be and were given *in prestimonium*.

The word fief (*feu, feodum*) was rare, but it sometimes appeared, as, for instance, in the hereditary grant of the office of admiral to the Genoese Manuel Pessagno (1317). Portuguese fiefs were granted with a remarkable variety of onerous conditions, that is, services. Military or administrative services were not, however, an essential condition for a royal benefice, some type of payment often being substituted for services. In other fiefs, similar to the well-known "free or franc fiefs," almost full property was granted as reward for services. The king, however, kept a certain number of rights, such as the rights of high justice and interference in matters of succession. The word *honra* (Latin *honor*) seems to have been applied to a seigniory of any description, even an alodial one. In medieval Portugal, as in France, a seigniory was *feudum*, a fief. It was usually one of the more important fiefs, especially the older ones, to the north of the Mondego River. Royal grants to the Church were often called *coutos*, a word meaning the complex of privileges and immunities which the estate would enjoy. In all the seigniories immunity was understood to mean prohibition to the entrance of royal officers; the nonexistence of royal taxation; and the exercise, by the lord, of public authority with administrative, judicial, and financial autonomy.

Among the fiefs held by lay vassals and by the king himself there existed parish churches, abbeys, and chapels. Their lords, who often had been the founders of those pious institutions, held the profits of the tithe and the endowments of the Church, and in some cases even the income which came from offerings of the faithful, such as church dues. So profitable did these fiefs (*padroados*) appear to be that they were in high demand and esteem. The Church, of course, tried very hard to abolish them or to reduce their number because of the many abuses connected with them and the considerable impoverishment they caused the priests.

The small size of the country and the peculiar circumstances accompanying Portugal's birth and growth always prevented a thoroughly developed feudal organization. In all the seigniories the king had the last word in the case of high justice. By the thirteenth century he launched a sort of program destined to curb the immunities and the full autonomy of the feudal lords. The confirmation policy of Afonso II was accompanied and followed by successive inquiries (*inquirições*) which lasted until the late fourteenth century but reached their peak under King Dinis (1284, 1301, 1303, and 1307). Possibly influenced, in their developed forms, by the French practice of the *enquêteurs royaux* (Louis IX, 1248), the Portuguese royal inquiries endowed the central administration with a reliable and precise cadastral survey of a great part of the country (most of North Portugal, with Minho, Trás-os-Montes, and Beira). They helped the king by providing a detailed knowledge of property rights and revenues, by establishing his authority firmly, by preventing abuses, and by periodically interfering on behalf of a centralized justice and finance system.

By the fourteenth century other royal acts tended to curb the expansion of the seignorial regime. The king warned the nobility against any abuses of jurisdiction (1317), sent his officers to stop the creation of new *honras* (1321), and forced all the nobles to prove their feudal rights (1325). Under Fernando I the right of feudal justice was denied to all the *honras* created after 1325, with the exception of some dozen lordships. Also, royal grants were often restricted to the legitimate descendants (1384 on), and then to the male descendants only (1389). King John I followed a certain number of rules in his grants, which later (1434) King Duarte enacted as the so-called *lei mental*, according to which all the royal land grants should be transmitted only on the legitimate male line and should not be considered feudal. Because this law applied to the past as well as to the future, many estates went back to the Crown. Some noble families, however, managed to be exempt from it, particularly the powerful house of the Count of Barcelos, King John's illegitimate son, the future Duke of Bragança.

The monarchs themselves threatened their own interests with some very generous grants which circumstances or simply their own irresponsibility had determined. Royal princes, for instance, were granted important appanages, which sometimes made them rivals of the king. This happened under Sancho I. Extensive donations to his children resulted in civil turmoil after his death and in the victory of his first-born son, King Afonso II. Under Dinis (1279–1325) his brother Afonso held a great part of Alentejo, with the inevitable consequence of permanent rivalry between the two. Under John I (1385–1433) appanages became still larger and wealthier. His legitimate sons Pedro, Henrique, João, and Fernando, as well as his bastard child Afonso of Barcelos, were given enormous shares of the Portuguese soil and wealth. The fifteenth century was in Portugal a time of civil unrest partly because of such grants and of the accumulation of landed property in the hands of a single family, the descendants of Afonso of Barcelos (later Bragança).

Grants were made to favorites, both to noblemen and the clergy, in accordance with the appanage policy. King Afonso III (1248–79), Pedro I (1357–67), Fernando I (1367–83), and Afonso V (1438–81) were among the most generous of rulers. By the late fourteenth century the Menezes family and three or four others (including the same Menezes and the Braganças) during the fifteenth century could be compared in wealth, prestige, and military power to some of the typical feudal lords of France or Germany. It is true that their power did not endure and was rather an aberration in a small country like Portugal, a sort of desperate "finale" to the feudal epoch.

The "precarious" land-grant system prevailed in the whole kingdom and affected almost the entire population. Large landowners would grant smaller or larger farms to villeins in the same way they had received them from the king. Some *concelhos* originated in this type of land grant, made to a group of people. They became integrated in the feudal hierarchy, depending upon their lords and not upon the king. In most cases, however, grants were made to individual farmers (*foreiros*) perpetually, under several conditions, such as the payment of a quit rent consisting of a part of the soil production (one-fourth to one-third generally), the share of labor in the lord's demesne, several occasional tributes, and the typical feudal monopolies of the means of production (oven, press, mill, etc.). Other grants, which became more common after the thirteenth and fourteenth centuries, were made temporarily in periods of three, two, or one lifetimes or even for a shorter period. Because conditions for these grants were harder, they were preferred by many lords and particularly by the Church. In all cases, even if the origin of the tenure was not typically feudal, the practical results definitely were.

By the 1200's the population of Portugal probably did not exceed one million inhabitants. From north to south its distribution was most irregular. To the Tagus Valley, with the exception of Braga, Porto, Guimarães (which had grown very much from the twelfth century on), Coimbra, and possibly Bragança, there were no large towns, even by medieval standards. Populations were dense in Minho, the Douro Valley, and Beira Alta, but spread out in numerous and tiny settlements. The great nuclei of population continued to exist in the South, thanks to the Roman and the Moslem traditions: Lisbon, Santarém, Évora, Estremoz, Elvas, Silves, Beja, Faro, Tavira, and several other smaller places. Vast uninhabited areas in between (with the exception of the lower Algarve) gave the country a semi-deserted aspect.

An important development of the thirteenth and following centuries was the coastal settlement. Small fishing villages appeared here and there, some spontaneously, some because of royal or seignorial acts. They were particularly numerous to the north of the Tagus. Their contribution to the country as a whole, however, was minor, and their economic activity was based almost exclusively on fishing. They also played an insignificant role in foreign trade, which was carried on entirely through Lisbon, Porto, and the Algarve. Nonetheless, they helped create a maritime tradition and fishing skills which would prove decisive in the future of Portugal. Let us not forget that such a tradition already existed in the South.

In the North only the town of Porto deserves our attention. Commerce and artisanship worked together in the rise of this city; with its relatively important group of authentic burghers, Porto's development was very close to that of the typical European communes. During the thirteenth and fourteenth centuries the inhabitants of Porto several times rose up in arms against their lord the bishop. In 1354 the town achieved its feudal autonomy and became dependent upon the Crown alone. The part Porto was then playing in Portugal's economy certainly accounted for this situation. Not only did its citizens control most of the significant trade in the North but they also undertook long-distance operations with foreign countries, particularly with England. Although small in area and in population, Porto was a wealthy town, and its affluence was based on "modern" forms of economic expansion.

However, the growth of Lisbon was the outstanding demographic feature in late medieval Portugal. As important as Coimbra, Braga, Évora, or Silves in the twelfth century, Lisbon moved clearly ahead a hundred years later, with four or five times more inhabitants and building space than any other city by the late fourteenth century. In spite of the preference shown by many kings and queens to several other towns and villages (where they would dwell for longer periods than in the capital itself), Lisbon became the center of Portugal's economic, social, political, and cultural life. It often became synonymous with Portugal in the sense that holding Lisbon meant holding the country. Along with this fact there developed another important constant in Portuguese history, namely, the contradiction between the size and the possibilities of the capital city and those of the other settlements in the country. The reasons were manifold: Lisbon was geographically well located, both in terms of an absolute position (an excellent harbor, the best in Portugal, with a hinterland rich in water and food resources, including salt and fish, and rich in quarries and minerals too) and in terms of relative control of the two halves of Portugal. Lisbon also had urban and commercial traditions which contributed to its tremendous rise. It has been a center of piracy, and thus of shipbuilding and navigation. It was well defended, both by land and by sea. It possessed an important Christian nucleus and remained the seat of a bishopric. Possibly it had cultural traditions too. Finally, it had one of the best climates in Portugal. It was "healthy" in a medieval sense (very windy, thus more liable to be free of pestilence and "polluted" air) and beautiful. One of the Crusaders who conquered it in 1147 called it *"aere salubris"* (of healthy air) and praised its buildings, *"artissime conglobata"* (crowded together with the greatest skill).

The development of Lisbon, and other minor towns, obviously accompanied the development of trade, both external and internal. The western coast of the Iberian Peninsula, which in the tenth and eleventh centuries could hardly be considered of any international relevance, was in the 1200's connected with most West European markets. This was basically a consequence of the commercial expansion of Europe, which affected all its parts, even the most remote. It was related to the development of traveling and to the increasing activity of peddlers. The reopening of the western sea route by the Normans and the Crusaders put the Northerners of all countries and the Portuguese in contact with each other. Political ties that brought many Portuguese to France, Flanders, and England included the marriage of Matilde or Teresa, daughter of King Afonso Henriques, to Count Philippe of Flanders in 1184, and then to Duke Eude III of Burgundy in 1194; the embassy sent by John Lackland in 1199 to negotiate his marriage to one of King Sancho's daughters; the marriage of Fernando, son of the same King Sancho I, to Jeanne, Countess of Flanders in 1211(?); and the marriage of Afonso, the future Afonso III to Mahaut, Countess of Boulogne, in the 1230's. Emissaries from the Portuguese monarchs invited and obtained some hundreds of settlers in the same regions and in Germany, who came to Portugal to help populate the newly conquered areas.

Along with political ties came commercial ties. The Portuguese were in the British Isles by the late twelfth century, reaching Dublin, in Ireland. Their main destination was London, where they seem to have had intimate contact with the king and his court. The English monarchs granted them numerous privileges and safe conduct. In exchange, Portuguese merchants settled in Bordeaux and lent them money. There is evidence of the presence of Portuguese merchants as far as Cologne, in Germany, although their most important operational base was in Flanders. By the late thirteenth century the

Portuguese were firmly established all over Western Europe and seemed to control most of the trade with Portugal. In 1293 a compact among Portuguese merchants trading with Flanders, England, and France was approved by King Dinis. It involved an insurance system for all the vessels loading in Portugal or chartered by Portuguese merchants to go abroad. Part of the sum so collected was to be kept in Flanders, but the bulk was to remain in Portugal. By the mid-fourteenth century the number of merchants settled in Flanders and the amount of their trade justified the formation of an official Portuguese factory house (*feitoria*) in Bruges which lasted until the sixteenth century. In 1353 the Portuguese trading in and sailing to England signed a pact or treaty with King Edward III, providing safety to the merchants of both countries for a period of fifty years. This treaty was later officially acknowledged by the King of Portugal, Afonso IV.

Portuguese exports to Western Europe consisted of fruit (figs and raisins); salt; wine; olive oil and honey; some raw materials like tallow, wax, cork, and kermes; leather and skins; and sparto or Spanish grass, apparently much in demand for the making of brooms. From England, Flanders, and France, Portugal received mostly textiles. Their qualities and proveniences changed from the early thirteenth to the fifteenth century, reflecting the evolution of the textile industry in Western Europe. Thus English clothes increased steadily, both in number and in price, while the Flemish and the French ones suffered from their heavy competition. Other merchandise included wood, dyes, and horses.

The number of northern merchants in Portugal seems to have been relatively small in the 1200's and early 1300's, compared with the number of Portuguese abroad. For the Flemish, the English, and the French, Portugal still offered few possibilities and little profit. Furthermore, vast concentrations of commerce monopolies in a few countries were far less developed in the thirteenth century than later. It was still possible for small and "underdeveloped" countries to hold the reins of their own trading activities.

Another area of Portuguese international trade was Spain and the Mediterranean world. Its characteristics, however, were very different from those of the trade with the North. To start with, neither Spain nor any of the other Mediterranean countries needed the typical

Portuguese exports, which were also Mediterranean. Thus trade had to depend on other items, where gold and silver currency would necessarily play a major role. Nonetheless, Portugal could still offer dried fish, honey, wax, leather, skins, wool, and some salt too. In exchange she received spices, sugar, silk and woolen textiles, weapons, grain, and all kinds of household and luxury goods. Yet it was possible for Portugal to hold a position of relative importance within the general framework of the Mediterranean trade. Her role as an intermediary between the northern countries and the south of Europe and Africa accounted for that. The Moslem regions often depended on the Portuguese market (as well as on the Spanish one) to obtain goods from the North. Moslem gold and silver coins were abundant in the Portugal of the 1200's and 1300's and compensated for the lack of Portuguese national gold and silver currency. In spite of all the prohibitions, trade with Islam always flourished during the Middle Ages.

Commercial contacts with Castile were of course favored both by the proximity of the two countries and the intensity of their political relations. Trade with a neighbor was often a mere continuation of trade at home. Local goods of Portugal and Castile were present at most fairs and even in smaller markets. Well aware of the importance of such a trade, the monarchs of the two countries protected it by successive treaties and privileges. Wheat from Andalucia and Spanish Extremadura helped prevent and lesson dearth in Portugal. Castilian clothes were popular among the Portuguese gentry and people. Seville was familiar with the coming and settling down of Portuguese merchants. With Galicia and the northern coast of Spain, too, maritime contracts were many and active, Galician and Basque sailors and merchants coming down the Portuguese coastline and carrying Portuguese goods to the North, while Portuguese sailors and merchants similarly were present in the Galician and northern Spanish towns. With Aragon and Catalonia political alliances provided perhaps the best stimuli to a trade intensification. Catalans and Aragonese, as well as Castilians, were among the most numerous foreigners living in Portugal.

Trade with the Italian cities and kingdoms developed somewhat later. Then, very quickly, the Italians took it almost entirely into their hands. From the 1270's on, coinciding with the first maritime voyages to Flanders, the Italian merchants (most of them from Genoa, Florence, Milan, Piacenza, and Venice) settled down in Lisbon and in other Portuguese ports, binding Portugal to their complex network of international contacts and settlements. They added Portugal to their regular ports of call on voyages to England and Flanders. They not only controlled trade between Italy and Portugal but also much of the Portuguese Mediterranean traffic, still acting as intermediaries with the northern countries of Europe and gradually pushing the Portuguese out. Their skill and wealth brought the Italian merchants royal protection and favor. They competed with the Jews in money lending and in political influence. It was they who improved the Portuguese fleet, and their impact on naval techniques may have had some significance on Portugal's expansion in the fifteenth century.

The decisive step in the history of the internal traffic was the introduction of the market principle during the twelfth and thirteenth centuries. For the ideal of self-sufficiency, expressed by a systematic storage of most of the production and by the nonexistence of a regular buy-and-sell system, the new market principle was gradually substituted. At the beginning only surpluses were sent to be changed into money; later on production itself was conditioned by the placing in market and the circulation of goods. This new system involved an organized exchange between the country and the town. In other words, each demesne started sending most of its production to the closest town. A generalized monetary economy naturally came into existence. This is not to say that the market principle completely destroyed the old feudal forms of self-sufficiency. Such was not the case, not even in more modern times. But what matters is that after the twelfth century the market gradually became the usual form of dominial organization and that one of the features of this activity consisted now in producing for a local market.

An analysis of the *forais* clearly shows the generalization of the market principle. All Portugal proved amenable to it. In the larger or more developed centers the amount of trade even justified the existence of two types of customs duties, one on the loads carried by horses and mules, the other on those carried by donkeys. Lisbon,

Coimbra, Santarém, Porto, and some other towns had, of course, the first type. In the less important towns duties were levied on each kind of goods, regardless of its weight.

Besides the markets (called *açougues* and *fangas* in medieval Portuguese), which were closely supervised by an *almotacé,* fairs broadened the means for internal circulation of merchandise. It is true that the Portuguese fairs never played a role similar to those in Flanders or in France, nor did they originate any new urban centers. Portugal's eccentric location prevented their being international meeting places, despite the few Castilian or Italian merchants who might attend them now and then. Nevertheless, fairs did account for development of the internal trade. Their great epoch in Portugal was the thirteenth century, when 43 of the known 95 fairs were established. In the fourteenth century 26 more appeared, and 23 in the fifteenth century. The reign of Dinis (1279–1325) particularly was marked by a high concentration of charters of fairs—48, or more than half of the total—which accounted for a great epoch in the history of internal trade. A special kind of fair was the so-called *feiras francas* (free fairs), where the merchants paid no duties or taxes. Very rare in the thirteenth and fourteenth centuries, they became somewhat more common in the following century.

Industrial activity, on the other hand, did not match the flourishing trade. Except for some cheap textiles, destined for local consumption, some wooden and clay household and rural implements, goldsmithery, shipbuilding and cooperage and barrels, soap, and a few more items, there was no industrial transformation of raw materials in Portugal. When the sources mention craftsmen, they generally refer to barbers, blacksmiths, tailors, shoemakers, masons, carpenters, pottery workers and tilemakers, bakers, peddlers, butchers, fishermen, and the like. Yet it was not for lack of real artisans that a corporative system did not arise in Portugal before the late Middle Ages. It was rather because of strong interference and control by the king and the rigidly organized municipalities, along with the role always played by the farmers. The craftsmen, however, did have their rudimentary forms of association, as expressed by the religious brotherhoods and fraternities. Late in the fourteenth century the sketch of a corporative system made a timid appearance in Lisbon. Not before the end of the 1400's, however, was any well-organized group of corporations to be found.

With the expansion of internal and international trade came new problems concerning prices and currency. As they did all over Europe, prices went up in Portugal from the beginning of the thirteenth to the mid-fourteenth century. A good example of this rise is shown by the price changes of wheat, a bushel (*alqueire*) of which cost about 1 soldo in the early 1200's, more than double that amount by 1264, between 6 and 8 soldos in the 1270's, between 10 and 12 in 1317, and between 11 and 13 in the early 1360's. By the middle of the thirteenth century the first general price listing with the purpose of preventing a rise was ordered by the king for the North (1253). Almost all available goods were listed, revealing a highly complex and sophisticated market, in both national and imported items. Only grain and other agricultural products were omitted, possibly to protect the interests of the great landowners (including the king) against those of the merchants. After 1253 several other local price fixings were ordered but always by the municipalities. The most unstable epochs were in the third quarter of the thirteenth and the second quarter of the fourteenth centuries.

The Portuguese currency of the time was based almost exclusively on the bullion dinheiro (denier), twelve of which made one soldo (shilling). Counting by libras (pounds), each one equal to twenty soldos, was a novel practice of the thirteenth century which began spreading in Portugal by the early 1240's and then became general when the Count of Boulogne, coming from France and imparting French influences, ascended the throne as Afonso III (1248). The libra-soldo-dinheiro system was in fact a very old one, having originated in the Carolingian Empire. Gradually all of Europe accepted it. In Portugal the last gold morabitinos were minted under Afonso III but in small quantity, and soon they were discontinued. Moslem and other foreign gold and silver coins completely supplanted any Portuguese coinages for more than a century. It was only in the second half of the fourteenth century, and for a brief period (1357–83), that King Pedro I and King Fernando I tried to reintroduce their own gold and silver coins (dobras, torneses, etc.), copying the Spanish and the French models both in name and in value. These coins were soon debased and became rare and then obsolete.

One of the medieval ways of getting money was by debasing it. New coins were minted with the same official value but with less gold or silver. When both administration and the way of living became more complex, deficit budgets made their appearance and extra money was required. With no more booty to collect from the Moslems, Afonso III and his successors faced a problem with which most European kings were only too familiar. He debased the currency three or four times, with and without his people's consent. His son Dinis, more fortunate, experienced an epoch of prosperity which did not force him to such extremes. Afonso IV, however, had to debase again and again.

The gradual complexity in life and politics made it necessary to create new offices in government and administration. Ruling the country was no longer like ruling the household of the king. Thus a man like the butler or steward (*mordomo-mor*), who was a sort of prime minister because he was in charge of the royal household, declined in importance in favor of the keeper of the royal seal, the chancellor (*chanceler*). From the late thirteenth century this man was the true head of the government. Under his orders a growing number of clerks, notaries, and scribes formed a permanent staff, located in Lisbon, and originating a larger and larger chancellery for the enactment of all kinds of royal documents. Only the chancellor and a few scribes followed the king in his travels around the country. After the second half of the fourteenth century the importance of the chancellor suffered from competition with another civil servant, the *escrivão da puridade* (private scribe or secretary), who assisted the king in most intimate matters and immediate decisions. Below the chancellor were the *livradores de desembargos* ("deliverers of dispatches"), sort of under-secretaries of state who informed the chancellor and the king of what was going on and presented matters to be decided. They were legists, trained in the practice of civil or canon law, and very often with a university degree.

For attention to judicial matters (because one of the king's main tasks was the administering of justice) there existed permanent magistrates living in the court who were called *sobrejuizes* ("superjudges") and later *ouvidores* ("hearers"). By the early fourteenth century dispensing justice in Portugal was complex enough to justify the specialization of the *ouvidores'* functions. Three kinds of magistrates or officials thus came into existence: those concerned with civil jurisdiction, those concerned with crime, and those who took care of any matter concerning the royal treasury and the royal estates and revenues. The third group, known as *vedores da fazenda,* acted as finance ministers. For practical purposes of the administration of justice these three main types of civil servants, all appointed by the king, formed three mixed courts: one court settled permanently in Santarém (and later in Lisbon), dealing mostly with civil law (Casa do Cível); a second one accompanied the king all over the country; and a third one was concerned only with the royal property. A special magistrate was in charge of the police (*corregedor da Corte*).

Local administration became more complex also. The number of local magistrates, elected by the council of notables in each municipality, was doubled or tripled and their functions were restricted and specialized. Two of these magistrates dealt only with matters in which the Jews had a part. Two others busied themselves with orphans and tutorships. A *procurador* served as public attorney. Local finance was supervised by a treasurer. Archives were created. Still more important were the changes introduced in the system of relationships between the central and the local administrations. To achieve centralization was the supreme goal of each monarch; to defend the rights of self-rule (as limited as they might be) the supreme goal of each municipality. The conflict, which was particularly fierce during medieval times, always ended with victory for the king.

The *alcaides,* or royal representatives, were assisted after the middle of the thirteenth century by some new officials appointed by the king to make sure that justice was well administered and order enforced. These were the *meirinhos-mores,* a sort of bailiff, who went from place to place instead of being settled in a town or a village. Then the *corregedores* appeared, in the fourteenth century, also to enforce justice, law, and order. The *juizes de fora,* or "judges from the outside," were sent whenever necessary to judge on all matters that required less commitment and less prejudice than the local judges could give. Under Afonso IV even the local judges had to be confirmed by the king, and the administration of justice was firmly monopolized by the Crown. The king's reforms and new regulations were decisive. He ordered the local election of new magistrates—the *vereadores*—who would assist the judges in all matters of justice. He also appointed a new judge to supervise wills and legacies.

In the history of the medieval parliaments one of the top places undoubtedly belongs to the representative assemblies of the Iberian Peninsula. Not only did they appear very early in the political evolution of Europe but they also played a highly significant role in the political life of the Iberian kingdoms. By the late twelfth century the *cortes* in Castile already included representatives of the people, besides the members of the clergy and the nobility who used to assist the king whenever he required their advice. In Portugal, however, there is no clear evidence of such participation before 1254, in the *cortes* of Leiria. The summoning of popular representatives (that is, delegates of the notables, mostly landowners and sometimes *concelhos* only), although it showed the greater importance the "third order" had in the life of the country, should be understood mainly as a royal expedient to secure an extra taxation. This, as a rule, was the major reason for assembling the people, at least during the 1200's and early 1300's. It helps explain why under King Dinis, whose treasury seemed in an enviable situation, the *cortes* seldom met.

The framework for administration and justice encompassed several sources of law. Canon law, for instance, which applied to numerous affairs in the daily life of the Portuguese (such as marriage, kindred relationships, pious donations, wills, usury, and interest), comprised five main corpuses of law: the *Decree* of Gratian, the *Decretals* of Pope Gregory IX, the *Liber Sextus* of Pope Boniface VIII, the *Clementinae* of Pope Clemens V, and the *Extravagants* of Pope John XXII. They were taught and interpreted at the University. Revival of the Roman law, by the twelfth century, reached Portugal very soon, in the middle or late 1100's, but its practical applications were long in being made. In much greater favor were the several Castilian codices of law, which in themselves transmitted a vast share of Roman law: for instance, the *Fuero Real,* translated into Portuguese between 1273 and 1282, and the *Partidas,* translated by the same time and in use by the fourteenth century.

Native Portuguese legislation included the general laws enacted by each king after the early thirteenth century; the *forais* or local characters, very numerous, coupled with local traditions and customs; the concordats with the Church; customs and regulations followed in court; and even the authority of some learned legists. The first, incomplete, corpus of all these acts appeared in the late 1300's (*Livro das Leis e Posturas*). It was followed by two other important collections: one organized under King Duarte (*Ordenações de D. Duarte*); the other, the largest of all, under King Afonso V (*Ordenações Afonsinas*).

There is some evidence of the existence of schools in the Portuguese cathedrals, at least since the eleventh century. Although their only purpose was to prepare future clergymen, their role in the general framework of public education should not be forgotten. Besides these episcopal schools there were classrooms in many monasteries, for instance in Alcobaça and Santa Cruz of Coimbra, the most famous of all. In both types of schools the subjects taught were similar, and they were the same in Portugal as in any other country of Europe: grammar (that is, the reading and writing of Latin), dialectic (logic), and, of course, everything related to the Christian faith and liturgy. In 1288 a group of clergymen, headed by the priors of Alcobaça, Santa Cruz of Coimbra, and S. Vicente of Lisbon, asked Pope Nicholas IV to confirm the creation of a university, which they had agreed with the king to establish in Lisbon. Suggested by the Church and also financially supported by it, the university was intended to be a sort of a high school for future clergymen. Only gradually did the lay people begin to study in it.

Compared with the burgeoning of universities in Italy, France, and England, the Portuguese university appeared rather late. Even in Castile and Aragon universities had been created long before. However, compared with other marginal countries of Europe (like Scandinavia, Scotland, the Slav states) or with Germany, Portugal was much ahead in establishing universities, thus asserting a relatively developed cultural life for that time. It is true that conditions for its prosperity were never very favorable, at least until the fifteenth century. The university had little prestige either in Portugal or abroad. It did not prevent the migration of students to Oxford, Paris, Salamanca, or Bologna, nor did the quality of its teachers ever appeal to the foreign students. Its faculty never numbered more than twenty and was limited to five at the beginning of the fourteenth century. For local purposes, however, the university was certainly useful, preparing clergymen, lawyers, notaries, and a few doctors.

Much more important than the "official" culture, transmitted by the schools and the university, was the one that nobles, clerics, and even commoners obtained elsewhere. Learned tutors were present in every manorial house, often imported from abroad. Learned priests and friars were daily companions of most courts, both lay and ecclesiastical. It is well known that the royal courts, at least after Sancho I (1185–1211), welcomed minstrels who toured the country, or came from abroad, and were an intense focus of culture, especially poetry and music.

The origins of this "troubadour" culture have been widely debated. The French influence, introduced directly from France or via Catalonia and the Aragonese court, was probably decisive. Afonso III, who had lived in France, is the best example, but the French tradition was present from the time of Count Henri, being nourished by political and religious contacts of all sorts. There seems to be no doubt, however, that the Moslem background and tradition in the South—which in turn influenced France—caused the Portuguese troubadours and their poetical expression to become extremely original and to create a typical Portuguese form of literature. Their great epoch was the century between 1250 and 1350, but evidence of much earlier compositions suggests a long period of incubation going back to the twelfth century or even before. From the surviving poems, generally classified into three major types—*cantigas de amigo* or love songs addressed by a female to a male lover; *cantigas de amor* or love songs sung by a man; and *cantigas de escárnio* or songs of mockery, criticizing or making fun of somebody or something—a sort of cosmopolitan ambiance can be detected, wherein Galician, Leonese, and Castilian authors competed with the native Portuguese. The troubadour culture, however, was not restricted to Portugal but spread to the Castilian

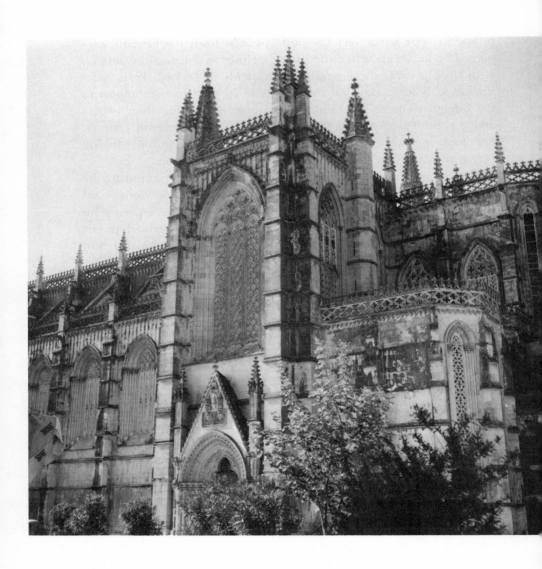

ABOVE: *Monastery of Batalha (Leiria), late 14th–15th century.* UPPER RIGHT:
*King John I: Anonymous, 15th century, Museu Nacional de Arte Antiga,
Lisbon.* BELOW: *Portuguese medieval knight, 14th–15th century: Biblioteca
Nacional, Lisbon, Códice Alcobacense nº 48, fol. 6 v.*

royal and seignorial courts as well, where Portuguese poets vied with their foreign colleagues.

The troubadours were generally nobles. They composed, or at least wrote the words for, the songs which the minstrels—villeins, Moors, Jews, and some lower nobles also—then sang. Their public was also mostly the noblemen. Kings and other members of the royal family shared this gift for poetical composition: for example, Sancho I and especially Dinis, to whom 130 songs are credited.

The language of all these poems was Portuguese or, more accurately, Galician-Portuguese, for the two were united at the time. So strong was the association between this west Iberian Romance language and poetry, and so rooted was its area of expression, that Leonese and Castilian troubadours wrote in it instead of in their own dialects. The best example was the famous King Alfonso X of Castile (1252–84) and his celebrated *Cantigas de Santa Maria*. Some authors claim that Galician-Portuguese was considered to be more appropriate (in inflection and vocabulary) and sweeter in sound than either Leonese or Castilian, a highly doubtful claim.

In any case this cultural development decisively improved Portuguese as a language, making it fit for a national role. By the middle of the thirteenth century Portuguese was already being used as the language of many public as well as private documents. Late in that century it was officially adopted as the written language instead of Latin, and it quickly replaced Latin even in many ecclesiastical deeds. This early achievement of a vernacular language in Europe shows clearly how mature Portuguese had become, in a relatively short period of time.

Compared with poetry other literary forms were not well developed. In literary prose the Portuguese were far behind the Castilians or the Aragonese, historiography making a very poor show before the fifteenth century. The only great achievement was a kind of Arthurian romance called *Amadis de Gaula* (fourteenth century) although its Portuguese authorship is debated.

A large part, if not most, of the immense booty accumulated by kings and lords during the Reconquista was invested in religious buildings. This fact explains the tremendous number of cathedrals, abbeys, parish churches, and small chapels built in a relatively poor

country of Europe, as Portugal was. It also explains why a great period of building activity coincided with the hundred years from the
mid-twelfth to the mid-thirteenth century. Interestingly enough, most
of the monuments of that time reveal the military character of the
Reconquista and the need for defense. They are bulky, solid edifices,
provided with crenels and, like castles, possessing few openings. As a
matter of fact they were often used as castles.

From an artistic point of view this period presented highly interesting features: the Romanesque style waned, and a new style,
Gothic, took its place. In art it was a response to the changed conditions of economy and society. New styles, however, need time to
overcome tradition and prejudice. Although accepted in France by
the mid-1100's, Gothic did not reach the faraway countries of Europe
immediately. When the style became accepted in Portugal, most
cathedrals and other religious buildings had been under construction
for many years. It was no easy task to change architects, foremen, and
skilled artisans, even if bishops and abbots accepted the new building
fashions. As a result the buildings were compromise, hybrid structures, with Gothic chapels and decorations added but with an essentially Romanesque structure. Pure Gothic came late to Portugal, and
still later would it vie with Romanesque, both in number of buildings
and in grandeur.

Each of the nine dioceses wanted a magnificent cathedral of its
own, larger and more beautiful than its rival. The model for most of
them was the huge cathedral of Santiago de Compostela, in Galicia
(almost 300 feet long, 65 feet wide, and 66 feet high), a pilgrimage
church in the purest Romanesque shape, in process of being built from
1078 to 1130. Braga was the first Portuguese cathedral to be built,
early in the twelfth century. Although intended to be the metropolitan
church of the country, and adequate in size (205 feet long, 54 feet
wide), it was never vaulted, the roof being made of wood. One can
imagine that the cost of completing it was far too high for the meager
resources of Portugal before resumption of the Reconquista. Later
on, when money became plentiful, Braga was already a bit neglected
and too far from the scene of operations. Other cathedrals inherited
most of the interest and also most of the funds. This was obviously
true of Coimbra (223 feet long, 85 feet wide) and Lisbon (180 feet

long, 69 feet wide), both erected in the second half of the twelfth
century. The remaining six cathedrals (Porto, Viseu, Lamego, Guarda,
Évora, and Silves) were much smaller. Porto, Lamego, and Guarda
were entirely Romanesque, and Viseu added to a Romanesque structure a late Gothic vaulting; Évora, a remarkable building, was a
definite compromise between the two styles; and Silves, conquered
much later, was a pure Gothic monument.

Many other smaller but often charming Romanesque churches
and monasteries were built in the eleventh, twelfth, and early thirteenth centuries, mostly north of the river Mondego. In many of these
churches, particularly in the large ones, French architects and artisans
labored, bringing to their work forms and local aspects of the French
monuments. Besides the influence of the cathedral of Santiago de
Compostela, there was the foreign influence of the abbeys of Cluny
and Clairvaux in France, duly transmitted by the Cluniac and Cistercian monks who came to Portugal. The best examples of this influence are the Cistercian abbeys. The main church and monastery of
that order at Alcobaça, erected from 1172 to 1252, was a huge building, 328 feet long, 64 feet wide, 66 feet high. Still a Romanesque conception in area, volume, and general structure, it nonetheless exhibited a Gothic vaulting and arch type. Simple and austere in its
decoration, Alcobaça perfectly satisfied the religious-aesthetic ideals
of the Cistercians, who were opposed to the pompous and richly
decorated churches of their time.

The other religious and religious-military orders also had their
churches and monasteries in twelfth- and thirteenth-century Portugal.
The Canons of St. Augustine built in Coimbra another jewel of the
Romanesque art, the church of Santa Cruz (1131–54), and in Lisbon
the church of S. Vicente, which has not survived. Late in the twelfth
century the Templars started their magnificent church at Tomar in
the tradition of the "round churches" of the Middle East.

If the dioceses, the Benedictines and their followers (Cluniacs
and Cistercians), and the military orders were generally associated
with the Romanesque or with a hybrid Romanesque-Gothic style of
architecture, the new religious orders (Franciscans, Dominicans, and
others), founded in and after the thirteenth century, built their
churches and monasteries within the framework of the new style.

Being essentially urban in their way of life and in their goals, it was no wonder that the majority of their monuments were built in that part of Portugal whose towns were more numerous and more populated—the South. For this reason and because the advent of the new style coincided with the reconquest of most of Alentejo and the Algarve, Portugal became divided roughly into two areas, according to the artistic style predominating: the North, Romanesque; the South, Gothic. Exceptions were, naturally, churches already constructed in the South (very few, actually) and the new ones built in the North after the thirteenth century (also few, if compared with existing ones).

The largest and most important churches in the thirteenth century were the two Franciscan temples of S. Francisco and Santa Clara in Santarém, of Santa Clara in Coimbra, and of S. Francisco in Lisbon, which has not survived. Much later, after the 1390's and during the fifteenth century, vaster and more sophisticated temples were erected. The largest of all was the monastery of Batalha, in upper Estremadura, built after 1388, to fulfill the promise made to God by John I on the eve of the Battle of Aljubarrota (1385). He and his successors, until John II, took good care of the new monument, supplying endless sums for its completion (which never occurred) and embellishment. The monastery of Batalha is indeed the most perfect example of Gothic architecture and decoration in Portugal and one of the finest in Europe. Very long (263 feet), wide (72 feet), and high (106.5 feet), Batalha benefited from the skill and the efforts of the best architects, sculptors, and decorators, both Portuguese and foreign. Besides this monument, numerous churches and monasteries were built all over the country, but especially in the South, such as Carmo in Lisbon (236 by 72 feet), S. Francisco in Évora (180 by 65.6 feet), and Graça in Santarém (177 by 115 feet).

Civil monuments were fewer, and they have been more damaged by time. No communal life in Portugal ever matched that of the West European city states in their proud display of town halls and other public utility monuments. In Portugal most public acts took place within the churches. The only really important examples of non-religious architecture (although numerous fountains, houses, aqueducts, pillories and the like could be appointed) were the castles and the town walls. Again the Reconquista played a decisive role in the building and preservation of such fortifications. The Moslem war science and the experience of the natives themselves definitely overcame any foreign influences. The Portuguese castles can be compared only with those of Spain and of the Moslem world. The great epoch of Portugal coincided with the offensive and defensive wars of the twelfth and thirteenth century, although many fortifications could naturally be traced back to the distant past. Under King Dinis (1279–1325) many castles were repaired and several walls built anew, as urban life flourished. Later on, both Fernando I (1367–83) and John I (1385–1433) took good care of castles and other fortifications. The many residential castles and palaces, especially those built during the fifteenth century, gave evidence of the prosperity of a few noble families scattered throughout Portugal.

Sculpture and painting developed according to the principles referred to. In the North the local material, granite, prevented a sophisticated elaboration of sculptural effects. In the South, however, softer materials allowed the Portuguese and imported artists to create many refined forms, both in decorative sculpture and in independent statues. The surviving instances from the thirteenth, fourteenth, and fifteenth centuries clearly show the relatively high level of development sculpture had reached. Painting, in contrast, seems to have been largely neglected, possibly because neither Moorish nor southern skill was available after the many centuries of Moslem occupation.

THE CRISIS

No evidence of a general crisis in Portugal is available before the middle of the fourteenth century. Studies on price behavior or on town population, however, might show a different picture and force us to go back to earlier times to determine the seeds of the crisis. In 1340 prices of industrial products continued high, and comparisons were made with happier periods when prices were lower. Social problems, nonetheless, seemed to worry the king and his advisers, possibly because they were found to be new and disrupting. According to a famous law enacted in that year, the aristocracy was spending too much and heading toward ruin. On the other hand, the bourgeoisie flourished, vying with the nobility for all the signs of hierarchy and affluence. Real estate no longer provided a sufficient source of top revenues and could not cope with profits from trade and artisanship. Obviously the nobility struggled with a problem of adjustment. Unable to face the new realities, to invest in trade and in other profitable activities, the nobles seemed to be attached to and longing for a period of easy prosperity, resulting from the Reconquista. The same law of 1340 also revealed a certain restlessness within the ranks of the lower classes, expressed by the breakdown of feudal stability and the rise of a mobile labor class.

Accounts of the Black Death of 1348 give a much clearer picture of what was going on. We still do not know to what extent the plague represented a cause or simply an accelerating factor. The itinerary of the plague is not known. It probably began in Lisbon, having arrived by way of the sea, as it did all over Europe. From late September to Christmas the country was ravaged by the plague, which killed an undetermined number of persons, perhaps one-third or more of the whole population. Its consequences were, first of all, demographic. The pestilence decimated the towns primarily: Lisbon, Coimbra, Santarém, Silves, and Bragança among others. Monasteries all over the country lost a great many of their members. The countryside was also affected. Although population figures are not available, there is enough evidence to prove that no province was spared.

After this first impact, the demographic effects of the plague were felt in migratory movements. People from the countryside attempted to move to the cities, and people from smaller towns decided to look for a better life in Lisbon, or Porto, or Évora. Again figures are unavailable, but certain actions, such as the building of new walls around the leading urban centers, a typical occurrence in the reign of Fernando I (1367–83), make it clear that, in spite of the plague, there might have been a steady population increase in the towns in the 1350's, 1360's, and 1370's. In Lisbon, for instance, the wall built in 1373–75 encompassed 103 hectares, six times more than the twelfth-century area and twice that of the late thirteenth-century city. As often happened in Europe, the new walling was a prophecy of the continuation of the growing trend, and vast open spaces were enclosed within the walled precinct. As often happened also, the fore-

cast was wrong; the demographic crisis resulted finally in a readjustment of the population between the cities and the countryside and a
stoppage in the flow of immigrants. New plagues, which occurred in
1356, 1384, 1415, 1423, 1432, 1435, 1437–38, 1458, and later, killed
more people and weakened several generations. The late fourteenth
and all the first half of the fifteenth century brought about no increase and even a decrease in the number of inhabitants. From the
north to the south of Portugal there are numerous references to lack
of population.

The social aspects of the crisis seem clear. The towns were affected
by an increasing number of migrants looking for work and for better
conditions of life. After the first years of a high demand for urban
labor, the economic and social readjustment brought unemployment
or unfavorable conditions for most of those who were constantly
coming into the city. Badly equipped for the needs of commerce and
craftsmanship, most of the newcomers led a miserable existence, which
contributed to the rise of a typical modern proletariat. Social discontent and rioting were the natural consequences. What happened
in Lisbon was typical: social grievances brought on the riots of 1371,
the revolution of 1383–85, and the rebellions of 1438–41 and 1449,
to mention only the best-known events. Porto also rebelled in the mid-
fourteenth century. Social unrest provided enough soldiers and adventurers for the several wars with Castile in 1369–97, the fifteenth-century expansion in north Africa, and the great voyages of discovery.

In the countryside there was the same lack of labor. All over
Portugal numerous agricultural units, villages, and small towns were
half deserted or thoroughly unproductive. The number and geography
of the *fogos-mortos* (abandoned households) have still to be analyzed
and estimated. Noble landowners, monasteries, and rich farmers looked
in vain for laborers. If a great number were dead, many others simply
refused to work under the existing circumstances and moved to and
fro, wherever they thought they would be offered better payment. The
landowners appealed to the king, who was facing similar problems
himself. The result of their appeal was a series of acts between 1349
and 1401 that forced rural and non-rural laborers to work for the
same salaries and in the same way and place they always had. A
system of passports was created to prevent open housing, and workers

were apportioned among the proprietors. The Law of 1375 (known as Lei das Sesmarias) went farther in binding the workers to their traditional professions, preventing labor freedom, keeping wages low, and harassing the idle and the vagrant. In spite of this and other local regulations, enacted in the late fourteenth and early fifteenth century, the trend toward labor freedom, or at least greater labor freedom, continued. One hundred years later, a significant, if not a decisive, part of all labor was entirely free, and employment based on revocable and temporary hiring contracts.

Another aspect of the fourteenth-century crisis was noted in agricultural production and the landscape. Unproductive lands became excellent game preserves and pastures. The number and regulation of the game preserves are well documented up to the 1400's. Those soils where the yield was particularly low were the first to be abandoned to pasture. In Alentejo and elsewhere sheep raising increased considerably. We lack records of the details of transformation in wool production and trade and a possible growth in the revenues of the military orders, which owned large tracts devoted to sheep raising. A more extensive use of the fallow system made unproductive for immediate crops a high proportion of the soil but provided enough nourishment for cattle and other stock animals.

The results of these changes were multiple. There is no evidence of a shortage of grain, for instance, before the mid-fourteenth century. Then, gradually, it became a subject of general concern. The number of wheat crises grew in the 1400's. The towns, particularly Lisbon, as well as some country regions (the Algarve is the best example) periodically suffered famine or extreme shortage of bread. All over Portugal harvests decreased in this period. The decline in population obviously accounted for it: there were fewer hands for rural labor, fewer people to feed in the countryside, and plenty of fields uncultivated. On the other hand, the greater demand for surpluses in the towns might have stimulated production. Thus reasons for the constant shortage should be sought rather in a persisting maladjustment between production and consumption, an anachronic system of geographical and social distribution which could no longer cope with the great changes felt by the whole country. The decline in the crop output was probably accompanied and even provoked by an increase in some other agricultural products, such as wine and olive oil. There is evidence that the area devoted to vineyards grew in this period, including many fields formerly sown with wheat or barley. Vineyards, like olive trees, require much less care and therefore less labor, while giving a fair profit. By this time too wine exports from Portugal were playing an important role in the country's economy.

To meet the grain shortage and the grain demands in the growing cities, a regulated policy of ever-increasing imports from abroad came into existence. Long-distance trade contacts were developed with England, northern France, southern Italy, and even the German world, as well as with northern Africa and Spain. In the history of Portuguese foreign trade during the fifteenth century, grain supply was often of major importance, determining trade currents and trade items. The Portuguese, however, were reluctant to admit that the deficit was permanent. Several efforts were made to utilize the soil in a better way. Small-scale reclamations of land were also tried in a vain attempt to correct the waste caused by the "laziness" or "unconcern" of man. Some authors blamed the one-or-two-live quit-rent leases which, they argued, gave no incentive to adequate care of the land.

The general trend was toward contraction, particularly in the fifteenth century. Prices, as a rule, went down after a period of high levels preceding the inevitable adjustment. Except in times of shortage, the price of wheat and other cereals, for instance, dropped or remained constant until the 1470's.

Besides the possible impact of lease forms on the agricultural crisis, landownership itself played a significant part. The Black Death and the many other plagues which ravaged Portugal as well as all of Europe after the mid-fourteenth century, stressing the anguish of imminent death as never before, brought about tremendous social and economic changes. Free landholders, both of villein and noble descent, left their goods to the religious orders, to the parish churches, and to the cathedrals, in a desperate attempt to buy salvation. Such legacies were theoretically forbidden by the law, but no authority would curb them in this troubled period, when the Final Judgment was expected at any moment and when court members and state officials themselves (including the king and the royal family) were trying to appease God's wrath and to save their own souls. If we accept the complaints made in *cortes* and in many contemporary statements, Church property had increased so much immediately after 1348 that it was feared that in a short time "all of Portugal would be in the hands of the Church." This, of course, was an exaggeration, but it reflected the extent of the land mobility and the general concern of many citizens. Royal prohibitions, moreover, were timid and ineffective, and private donations, coupled with frequent purchases of land, continued to increase the wealth of the Church, at least to the end of the century.

The consequences were many. The clergy was not properly equipped to deal effectively with the sudden concentration of property. Many lands were left unexploited, disorganized, unproductive or less productive than before. Taxation by the crown or the municipalities naturally ceased, the Church being privileged and its lands tax-free. Royal or municipal revenues consequently suffered. In order to reorganize vast areas of once productive soil, the Church preferred to insist on the system of one-to-three-live quit-rent leases, which were recommended by the canon law. There were, however, some advantages: with time substantial land grants and land purchasing permitted a better organization of the exploitation itself, in a large-scale sense. They also encouraged the Church to attempt a reconstitution of the old property boundaries, reuniting small units which the population growth had determined.

The impact of the crisis on currency was perhaps greater than on anything else. After the 1350's devaluation of money never stopped until 1435. This may seem irrelevant because medieval coins were constantly debased before and after the crisis of the fourteenth century, yet the amount of the debasement itself should be kept in mind. In 1325, when Afonso IV ascended to the throne, one mark (230 grams) of silver was worth 19 Portuguese libras (1 libra = 20 soldos = 240 dinheiros). In 1435–36 that same mark was worth 25,000 libras. It is true that galloping inflation only started in 1369 and was caused partly by the military adventures of Fernando I and the war of independence under John I. By the end of the century, however, the war was practically over, and in the worst period of inflation, 1409 on, Portugal was enjoying peace and tranquility. Obviously, the causes lay elsewhere: in the deep extension of the crisis, in the lack of gold and silver, in the transitional phases of the economic and social adjustment. Several attempts to counteract inflation failed. Late in the fourteenth century, a new coin, the real (plural reais, later réis), copied from Castile, was substituted for the traditional dinheiro and its multiples, by then completely debased. In 1435–36 King Duarte succeeded in stabilizing the currency, although the trend toward devaluation persisted. To avoid complete economic paralysis payments in the early fifteenth century were often made in foreign currencies or simply in kind. National coins were refused, and the king had to impose their acceptance. The impact of the monetary crisis on the rents and the well-being of the population is still unknown, but it certainly brought about a sharp decline in many revenues and a general state of discontent and uneasiness.

Little is known also of the great social transformations which resulted from the crisis or arose with it. As a whole, it seems that the great beneficiary was the middle class of the urban nuclei. Traders, former craftsmen, small landholders, and the like saw their profits greatly increased and invested them in fruitful undertakings. They competed with the foreign traders (although they were never able to pass them) in long-distance enterprises, the bulk of which had developed with the export of products like wine, salt, and olive oil. They practically controlled the local trade, which was increasing too with the town market's imposing its needs on the countryside in growing demands. Many of them invested their profits in land, buying either alodial holdings or simply foros (quit-rent leases), which placed them within the category of rich farmers in need of labor and therefore compelling labor to work according to the fixed low wages. They took over power or consolidated it in some important concelhos, in Lisbon, but they were never able to control the local administration in most of the country. This was firmly in the hands of the old knights-villein, who also benefited from the crisis, which often freed them from the pressures and abuses of the local feudal lords.

For the lower social groups of proletarians, poor people, and beggars, this middle class represented a natural enemy, one whose oppression was directly and more openly felt. For the nobility, too, the increasing number and the affluence of the bourgeoisie were subjects of scandal and an obvious menace to their traditional prerogatives. The aristocrats were in process of competing with the middle class for economic power. They were also vying with the bourgeoisie in owning money and spending it. If this competition was to endure, radical changes would have to take place in the form of getting revenues and investing them. Thus their grievances against the middle class were very widely felt and, in a different way, as strong as those of the poor. Social cleavages, however, were much more complex. Within the middle class itself there were at least two social groups: the wealthiest, a few people well placed in commanding economic positions, owned capital and estates and were already proud of a name and even of a small lineage; a much larger group of bourgeois were in direct contact with the lower strata of labor. What the first ones wanted was political power and promotion to the honors and offices of the nobility. What the second ones primarily wished for was development of their sources of income and their business enterprises. The king was also a beneficiary of all this turmoil. Siding with either group, but more often with the upper bourgeoisie and the lower people, he achieved greater centralization and political control.

The revolution of 1383–85 was only the foremost example, the symbol, of all these transformations. Yet some other less violent manifestations in the second half of the fourteenth and most of the fifteenth century deserve our attention and should not be forgotten. One of the political results of the crisis was to tighten the ties between king and country. The new epoch required constant consultation with the people, as it required a larger and larger grant of funds by the people to their monarch. Social instability brought about disorder, restlessness, and therefore a general claim for justice. Summoning the *cortes* became a matter of course for all the rulers, from Afonso IV to Afonso V, over a period of one hundred years. John I was "elected" in *cortes* and became dependent on them for quite a while. He was even asked to assemble them every year, which he actually never did. In any case, the *cortes* did meet frequently in the late 1300's and early 1400's.

There was an upsurge of devotion, and new forms of piety developed. People wanted closer contact with God, with the Virgin Mary, and with the saints, and expressed their desire in many new ways. The cult of the Holy Ghost, adapted to the strong popular taste and daily life requirements, became a favorite one during the fourteenth and fifteenth centuries. The same was true of the cult of St. Francis and of the Franciscans, his interpreters in the search for greater love and a mystical way of life. The devotion to Mary was now overemphasized. A typical medieval prayer, the "Salve Regina," with its mystical flavor and its romantic-dramatic expressions, symbolized the new times. Processions of flagellants also appeared, although rare and in a more moderate form. The religious associative movement increased, with the foundation of new brotherhoods and charity fraternities. Charity and general concern with the poor were given much greater expression. Numerous hospitals, shelters, leprosariums, and the like were created all over Portugal. The number of pilgrimages increased also, such as those to Nossa Senhora das Virtudes (Our Lady of the Virtues), Nossa Senhora da Nazaré (Our Lady of Nazaré), and Senhora do Cabo (Our Lady of Cabo).

The impact of this crisis on literature was in Portugal almost completely negative. The second half of the fourteenth and most of the fifteenth century were extremely poor in both poetry and prose. The troubadour period was over. Even if we admit that much has been lost and much is still unknown, there is no doubt of a tremendous decline in Portuguese poetry and prose. After a relatively important period, which had ended by the early fourteenth century, the number of original manuscripts declined. Even copies of old or contemporary foreign works, so abundant up to that time, became rarer. Of 330 medieval codices belonging to the library of the monastery of Alcobaça, one of the most important cultural centers in the country, 26 were made in the twelfth century, about 228 in the thirteenth and early fourteenth century, whereas only 40 date from the late fourteenth and only 36 from the fifteenth century, before 1475. Thus in 150 years 228 books were produced, and in the following 125 years the output was only 76. In the period of decline there were some masterpieces, with a practical and didactical purpose. They included *Livro da Montaria* ("Book on Hunting") by King John, dating from 1415–30; his son King Duarte's *Livro da Ensinança de Bem Cavalgar Toda Sela* ("Book of Teaching How to Ride Well Any Saddle") and *Leal Conselheiro* ("Loyal Counselor"), a treatise on morals and how to live virtuously, both dating from between 1420 and 1430, and some other works dealing with falconry and horse veterinary practice. The greatest achievements in literature, however, were in the historical field, but not before the 1430's: Fernão Lopes' masterpieces, *Crónica del-rei D. Pedro, Crónica del-rei D. Fernando,* and *Crónica del-rei D. João,* all written between 1430 and 1450. He represented the beginning of a school that would flourish in the late fifteenth and sixteenth centuries.

A study of the themes of original Portuguese manuscripts dating from the period of crisis, as well as of those imported from abroad and copied or translated in Portugal, does not show a particular fondness for the macabre or for the subject of death, at least before the very late fifteenth century. The typical instances of new literary forms are rather to be found in the religious productions. Here mysticism was undoubtedly rampant. Translated into Portuguese were numerous well-known treatises of the time, such as "The Book of Joseph of Arimathea" (*Joseph d'Arimathie,* by Robert de Boron), "Tundale's Vision," Isaac of Nineveh's "On Contempt of the World," Jacob of Benavente's "Garden of Consolation," Fray Robert's "Dangerous Castle," and "The Delightful Wood," some dating from well before the crisis but better understood and sometimes readapted at that time. Original Portuguese manuscripts were the *Horto do Esposo* ("The Husband's Garden"), written in the first half of the fifteenth century, and the *Diálogo de Robim e do Teólogo* ("Dialogue between Robin and the Theologian"). Included among the mystical works also were the religious poems of Fr. André Dias (1348?–1440), in which an appeal to concrete experience was made and the verb "to feel" constantly appeared.

Teaching also was affected by the cultural decline of that period. The example of the University is clear. Its difficulties increased, including its economic problems. After the 1340's the number of foreign teachers increased but there was little continuity or efficiency. Salaries paid to local teachers became smaller. Many students preferred to go abroad, which does not speak well for the quality of the teaching. Both Afonso IV and Fernando I tried to reform the studies and combat the evil, apparently with little result. Successive moves from Lisbon to Coimbra (1308), Coimbra to Lisbon (1338), Lisbon to Coimbra (1354), and Coimbra to Lisbon again (1377), although with different motives or pretexts, indicate the uneasiness and instability

that brought about decline. By 1377 Fernando I decided to create a
new university and to transfer it to Lisbon once more. There is no
evidence, however, that conditions improved in the new University.
During the fifteenth century the University had little influence and
impact on the cultural life of the country. Its teachers were obscure
and played a minor role in letters, arts, and science. The best-trained
theologians, doctors, lawyers, and statesmen studied abroad, in France,
Italy, England, or Germany.

Little is known of the impact of the crisis on art. Apparently there
was an artistic vacuum from the mid-fourteenth century to the 1390's.
Very few monuments were built in this period, in contrast to the preceding epoch and to the 1400's. There were no good Portuguese schools
of art, and the schools that did exist had little spirit of invention and
were impermeable to the changes in mentality and life. This situation
probably accounts for the lack of contemporary European themes in
art. The classical motives of the fourteenth- and fifteenth-century
sculpture and architecture were also few in Portugal at this time. The
theme of death, for instance, was treated hardly at all.

THE POLITICAL EVOLUTION

The reign of Afonso III (1248–79) was still a relatively troubled
one in internal affairs. Two (actually three) nations—the Christian,
the Mozarab, the Moslem—had to be converted into a homogeneous,
Portuguese national entity. Such an achievement would hardly be
possible in one generation; as a matter of fact, it took at least one
hundred years to produce a real "Portugal," to fuse North and South
into a feasible country. A succession of three able leaders, each of
them with long reigns, undoubtedly helped to cement that difficult
union. The hundred-year period which started with the accession of
Afonso III and ended with the Black Death was therefore one of the
crucial epochs in Portuguese history. When the crisis came, it met a
well-organized state, fairly centralized around its monarch and economically harmonious.

The rise of Lisbon as the "capital" of the new country meant
much in that fusion. Afonso III apparently liked the town, improved

its dwelling conditions, and started buying property, both houses and shops, thus enlarging the royal share which dated from the time of the conquest. As a matter of fact, his attempt to "buy" the town, a purpose his son and successor Dinis carried on, put him at odds with its people, who complained against his cupidity and consequent abuses of authority. In the end, however, the king stood out as the firm holder of a great part of the town and its best natural protector. In its turn, Lisbon almost always backed the central government and gave the king its full support in times of crisis. After all, centralization meant to Lisbon increasing privilege, strength, and prosperity.

The moving of the central administration to Lisbon had other consequences. It enhanced the role of the South in the Portuguese framework and its cultural and economic values throughout the country. Many Portuguese monarchs after Afonso III preferred to live in other towns and villages rather than in Lisbon, although they never overturned Lisbon's position as the seat of the government. Yet such towns or villages generally lay in Estremadura or south of the Tagus, never in the North. In spite of the fact that medieval monarchs constantly wandered from place to place, the royal presence was undoubtedly felt in the South more than elsewhere. And as the South belonged mostly to the religious-military orders and to the king himself, royal policy was directed toward a close union between king and orders, in prospect of their final nationalization in the late fifteenth century.

Afonso's firm control of the country, in spite of the resentments a three-year civil war left, was partly due to a great stability in government offices. His main adviser and close friend, Estêvão Eanes, held the office of chancellor for thirty-four years, that is, through the whole of the monarch's reign and three more years under that of his son Dinis. Another of Afonso's favorites, João Peres de Aboim, held several offices continuously for a similar period of time. Afonso's constancy, if it encouraged abuses in power and rapacious practices from his favorites, also helped to form cadres of administration, to enforce principles and methods of policy, and to assure the stability of a party of faithful.

Subjugation of both clergy and nobility was approached in different ways. With the Church, the combat was direct and frontal. As has been mentioned before (chapter 1), Afonso opposed first the

Bishop of Porto, then all the other prelates with the exception of that of Évora who controlled the "deep South." Against the nobility (and part of the clergy too) he preferred to dispatch committees of inquiry to find out about any abuses or violations of Crown property and justice in the North. The methods of inquiry were stricter than in his father's time and ruthless too. Whereas little is known of their effectiveness, the nobles posed no particular problems in Afonso's reign. Furthermore, to the inquiries he added several general laws curbing the privileges of the aristocracy and providing for more justice and protection for the people. He was successful in obtaining support of his policy from a large part of the population, as was clear in his fight against the clergy and Rome.

Another important achievement of Afonso's was the final step toward full independence. The union of Leon and Castile (1230) gave Portugal the problem of the restoration of a mighty neighbor, to which some ties of vassality still existed. Success of negotiations with Castile on the subject of the Algarve and peaceful and friendly relations between the Portuguese and the Castilian monarchs favored the final settlement of a matter that was more formal than real. In the early 1270's Afonso III succeeded in getting from Alfonso X of Castile perpetual abolishment of all the feudal duties (military help and assistance) which theoretically Portugal was still obliged to pay.

Civil strife began after Afonso's death in 1279. He had married twice, the first time to Mahaut or Mathilde, Countess of Boulogne, the second time to Beatriz of Guillén, an illegitimate daughter of the King of Castile, Alfonso X. However, at the time of his second marriage (in 1253), Mahaut, whom he had abandoned when he accepted the Portuguese inheritance, was still alive (she died in 1258). Papal annulment of Afonso's first marriage and forgiveness for his second were not given until 1263, when three children had already been born, one of them Dinis, the heir to the throne. A quarrel with his younger brother, Afonso (1263–1312)—who was the first-born son after the Papal dispensation and therefore, he claimed, the lawful heir—developed when Dinis was proclaimed king. Such was the pretext for quite a number of rebellions. What we do not know are the deeper reasons for the conflict and its possible social motivations, considering the relative ease Afonso had in recruiting followers and the number of rebellions he led: 1281, 1287 (this time allied to a Castilian party in civil strife with its king too), and 1299. Furthermore, the spirit of civil, or feudal, war did not die with Afonso's submission. There were other revolts in the fourteenth and fifteenth centuries: in 1321–22, 1323, 1324, 1326, 1355, 1383–85, 1438–41, and 1449. No historian has ever attempted to find a common denominator for all those rebellions or to try to explain them by other than superficial motives or pretexts. Apparently, they corresponded in Portugal, although in a much less degree, to the typical feudal conflicts which tore apart other European countries, especially in the late Middle Ages. One interesting fact is that they took place between the king and his close relatives (brothers or sons), who always were the greatest menace to his centralized and authoritarian policy. The rebellions in the last years of Dinis's rule, for instance, which opposed the king (accused of preferring an illegitimate son to the heir of the throne for purposes of succession) to his son and heir Afonso, saw a temporary "coalition" between the latter and his mother, Queen Isabel, whom the Church later canonized. Another interesting aspect to stress is that such revolts always failed to rally the great majority of the other nobles, who either sided with their lord the monarch or simply awaited the final verdict. The only exception was the 1383–85 movement.

Internal dissensions were followed by war with Castile (1295–97), after a period of peace since 1200. Portugal joined forces with Aragon and both supported one of Castile's civil war parties and pretender to the throne, whose accession would again divide Leon from Castile. The final result was a compromise, which territorially benefited the Portuguese, granting them a district in Beira between the rivers Coa and Águeda, and rectifying the border in Alentejo (Treaty of Alcañices, 1297). This new boundary was to be maintained to the present.

From 1297 through 1320 a period of internal and external peace marked the peak of Dinis's reign and probably the apogee of the Portuguese Middle Ages. Civil quarrels had been appeased. With the clergy Dinis signed a concordat in 1289, which put an end to a long round of disputes. In 1288 the first Portuguese University had been created in Lisbon. Portuguese became the official language of the country. Dinis's court appeared as a center of culture, the king himself being a gifted poet. The country was prospering by the development of trade and crafts. Lisbon's tremendous growth during his father's and his own age converted it into an international town, in close contact with many foreign countries and several colonies of aliens. Dinis was also concerned with the defense of the country. He supported and partly financed the building of new castles and walls (Lisbon's riverside wall, for instance) around the growing cities and the repair of numerous other fortifications. His was an epoch of great building activity, with impact on civil and religious construction too. To organize a fleet, he hired Genoese sailors and a Genoese expert, Manuel Pessagno, whom he granted the perpetual and hereditary office of admiral. One of his greatest achievements, however, consisted in preventing the enormous wealth of the Knights Templar, disbanded in 1312, from either leaving the country or being assigned to any other military order. He succeeded in creating a new and national order, that of Our Lord Jesus Christ (1317), to whom all the belongings of the Templars were transferred. This independent order was to become one of the best weapons in the hands of the royal power.

Times became more difficult under Afonso IV (1325–57), Dinis's son and successor. The great crisis of the fourteenth century was approaching, and all its political, economic, and social elements began to make themselves felt, if only in a preliminary way, by the 1320's and 1330's. Also, Afonso was probably not so gifted an administrator and so tactful a diplomat as his father had been. After a brief civil war at the beginning of his reign, there was a conflict with Castile which passed through successive phases of "cold" and "hot" war. Represented by either their kings or their feudal lords, both countries actively and continuously interfered or tried to interfere in each other's affairs. Made more intense and confusing by the great European quarrel, the Hundred Years War, this conflict was to be a permanent feature in the political history of Portugal and Castile until the early fifteenth century.

As usual, weddings played their role: Afonso IV married his eldest daughter Maria to Alfonso XI of Castile (1328). It was a disgraceful union from the very beginning, which Maria aggravated with complaints addressed to her father. The Portuguese king started backing political opponents to his son-in-law and betrothed his eldest son and heir, Pedro, to Constanza, the daughter of Juan Manuel, one of the leaders of the Castilian opposition (1335–36). War came as an obvious result, with victories, defeats, and destruction for both sides (1336–38). A negotiated peace (in which the Pope and the king of France played their part) brought about concessions by and humiliations to the Castilian monarch (1339). A crusade preached against the Moslems, who were threatening the Christian borders in Spain, introduced a brief honeymoon in the relations between the two rulers. Afonso himself marched on with a powerful army, joined the Castilian forces, and played a decisive role in defeating the infidel at Salado, in Andalucia (1340).

Once the Moslem danger was removed, however, the quarrel between the two continued. Alfonso XI connived with the Pope, and by cunning diplomacy persuaded the Pope to grant the Canary Islands to Castile (chapter 3). In the event of another war, Afonso of Portugal tried to get an ally in Edward III of England to whom he intended to marry his younger daughter Leonor. When negotiations failed, he married her to Pere IV of Aragon (1347), a country which always was a natural ally against the powerful common neighbor. The Black Death, however, dissolved the alliance, carrying away the young bride (1348). Two years later Alfonso XI died in another plague.

A much romanticized love affair became the pretext for Castilian influence in Portugal. Pedro, the heir to the Portuguese throne, fell in love with his wife's maid-in-waiting, Inés de Castro, who belonged to a powerful family of landed aristocrats in Castile. He apparently became a puppet in her hands and, according to the "official" version of the story, in those of her Castilian relatives as well. The aging and proud Afonso IV could not tolerate this, and he ordered Inés to be killed (1355). Consequences of this murder were a brief civil war and (of much greater importance), the rise of a historical drama, which has enraptured chroniclers, fiction writers, and poets for more than five centuries.

The great event in Afonso's reign was undoubtedly the Black Death, which ravaged the country for three months in the fall of 1348. It had terrible consequences and made important changes in economy and society, as we have seen. Politically, too, it gave the central authority a good reason for increasing its power in order to curb injustice and prevent a complete social breakdown. King and upper classes combined to stop the challenge of the daring workers and peasants. In spite of the social and economic changes which gradually overtook the country and which no authority was able to defy, Afonso and his two immediate successors did slow down some threatening convulsions and prevented any open rebellions for more than three decades.

While supporting his nephew Pedro I of Castile in the internal quarrels of the neighboring country, Pedro I of Portugal ruled for ten peaceful years, from 1357 to 1367. He was a typical figure of the late Middle Ages, half crazy and loose in morals, very much concerned with the administration of justice, in close contact with his people, and loved by them in spite of his acts of cruelty and madness. He seems to have done nothing to curb the power of the nobles, but he was feared by them. Against the clergy he took several measures, more personal and whimsical than coherent and reasonable. In 1361 he forbade any Papal letters from being published without his approval (Beneplácito Régio). Although much applauded by the anti-clericals of the nineteenth and twentieth centuries, this measure should be regarded as primarily intending to achieve fair justice in the country, because of the several fake documents with a Papal signature which had appeared on important matters. He also began the process of "nationalizing" the religious-military orders when he conferred upon his illegitimate son João (the future John I) the mastership of Avis (1363).

The peaceful interlude came to an end with Pedro's son, Fernando I (1367–83). Taking advantage of the troubled situation in Castilian political affairs, Fernando claimed the throne for himself as a legitimate grandchild of Sancho IV of Castile, opposing Enrique of Trastámara (Enrique II), who had murdered his half-brother Pedro I (1369). Fernando's allies were Aragon and the Moslem kingdom of Granada. The war (1369–71) was disastrous to the Portuguese, but the peace treaty, negotiated through the efforts of the Pope, brought no particular humiliation to Fernando. Soon, however, he became involved in a second war (1372–73) and then in a third conflict with the neighboring country (1381–82), both times as a minor partner in the somewhat larger Hundred Years War. Giving up his earlier claims to the Castilian throne, he simply backed a new candidate, the English pretender

John of Gaunt, son of Edward III and husband of Constanza, an illegitimate daughter of the late Pedro I of Castile. Enrique of Trastámara, in his turn, had sought and obtained a French alliance and support. Thus the Iberian Peninsula became a new war theater for the conflict between France and England. Aragon played a dubious role, siding either with the English and the Portuguese or with the French and the Castilian. Dubious too was the role of the Portuguese. The first war over, Fernando accepted a sort of alliance with his enemy, pledging himself to marry Enrique's daughter, Leonor, after having made a similar promise to his earlier Aragonese ally. (In the end he married a third Leonor—for this was also the name of the Aragonese princess—of a noble Portuguese family.) After the second war, which brought about a second defeat, he switched alliances again. Then he reverted to England, fought Castile for the third time, and again was beaten. For the third time too he changed allies and became a friend of the Castilians. This political and military turmoil was aggravated by the religious question caused by the Great Schism. Portugal followed the Pope of Rome, Urban VI, in 1378–79, then accepted Clement VII of Avignon in 1379–81, for such was the side taken by Castile. When the English alliance was renewed, Fernando preferred Rome again (1381–82). Defeat brought him back to the Avignon Party (1382–83).

Both war and schism had a tremendous impact on Portugal. The Castilians ravaged and plundered a considerable part of the country. During the second war Enrique II reached Lisbon and occupied most of the city, burning, destroying, and sacking what he could. The English "allies" were hardly any better. Portugal was treated as a conquered country and the Portuguese fleet was almost completely annihilated. Social problems, which Afonso IV and Pedro I had succeeded in containing, gave rise now to a general state of discontent, particularly among the merchants and the lower classes. The *cortes* demonstrated clearly how restlessness was growing and how widely it spread. Only the nobility gained some advantage from the wars and presumably supported Fernando's ambitions or even fostered them. The Menezes and the Castro families rose to power, with privilege unheard of. The Jews were protected by the king and seemed to have played a major financial role. The schism divided the clergy and the faithful, creating hatreds as well as irregularities of all kinds.

To the unpopularity of his policy, which was, as a matter of fact, the result of a desperate attempt by the traditional landed aristocracy to hold on to power and privilege, Fernando added a most unpopular marriage when he made Leonor Teles de Menezes his queen. This lady and her party apparently made themselves hated by the people. For most Portuguese she stood for the interests of the landed nobility and summed up all the bad advice the king was supposed to have followed. Nonetheless, both king and "government" tried hard to curb abuses and to legislate on public defense, and on economic and social problems. Many castles were repaired and new walls built around such main cities as Lisbon, Porto, and Évora. Laws on agriculture and stock breeding attempted to protect the feudal economy and the traditional society and to adjust them to the conditions originating in the crisis. It is true that such laws were designed less for the people than for the immediate interests of the great landowners. Commercial navigation was also defended. Yet, on the whole, the peaceful measures undertaken by Fernando seem to have failed in the framework of the general disruption caused by war and bad administration, against a background of international crisis. His sixteen years of rule were remembered, not for his protection of the people as a "good king," but rather for his inability to render them peace, justice, and prosperity.

The first open social riots had already started when Fernando married Leonor Teles (1372). They broke out again when he died in 1383. Having no male heir, Fernando's throne was duly inherited by his only daughter, Beatriz, whom he had married to Juan I, King of Castile, after his third defeat. Wedding clauses clearly entrusted the regency and the government of the realm to the queen-mother Leonor Teles until a son or a daughter was born to Beatriz. Whatever the circumstances, the two kingdoms were to live permanently separated.

Political maneuvering and ambition prevented any peaceful solution. Juan I of Castile decided to invade Portugal and to take over power. He was probably moved to this violent step by the growing opposition which he found in Portugal against Leonor Teles and her lover, Count João Fernandez Andeiro, a Galician nobleman. Andeiro and Leonor, probably supported by most of the landed aristocracy, had against them the middle and lower ranks of the bourgeoisie under the leadership of the Master of Avis, João, an illegitimate son of King Pedro I. Apparently João first invited the Castilian monarch to enter

Portugal, rather than to accept a dangerous situation for his followers and himself. Later on, however, this situation changed. Hatred for Castile and the Castilians (the memory of their devastations was still very fresh in everyone's mind) forced the Master of Avis to lead a rebellion against both groups, Leonor Teles–Andeiro and Juan I–Beatriz. He himself killed Andeiro, compelled Queen Leonor to flee for her life and join forces with Juan I, and proclaimed himself regent and defender of the realm (*regedor e defensor do Reino*). He sent ambassadors to England for the purpose of renewing the political alliance against Castile. He also started to organize resistance.

The war went through three main phases. In the first phase (January–October 1384) Juan I invaded Portugal, reached Lisbon, and vainly besieged it for four months; meanwhile the Portuguese under Nuno Álvares Pereira, an illegitimate son of the Master of the Hospitallers, beat the Castilians at Atoleiros, in the South (Alentejo). In the second phase (May–October 1385) Juan I invaded Portugal again but was badly defeated at Aljubarrota (in northern Estremadura) by a much smaller but better organized Portuguese army, where the English archers and, possibly, advisers played a significant role. Elsewhere the Portuguese also beat the Castilians in less important battles (Trancoso, Valverde). In the third and last phase (July 1386–November 1387) a formal treaty between Portugal and England brought the Duke of Lancaster to the Iberian Peninsula as a pretender to the Castilian crown. The war theater moved outside the Portuguese borders. A first truce was signed in 1387. Unimportant skirmishes still occurred in 1396–97, followed by a ten-year truce, which was successively renewed. A peace treaty, however, was not signed until 1432.

Meanwhile, the Master of Avis had had himself proclaimed king as John I (1385). He summoned the *cortes* to Coimbra and succeeded in getting rid of two other pretenders (João and Dinis, illegitimate sons of King Pedro I and Inés de Castro, who claimed their father had married her in secret) with the help of a famous legist, João Afonso das Regras, whom he appointed his first chancellor. Foreign recognition came easily. As a regent João had once more switched from the Pope of Avignon to the Pope of Rome, who quickly canceled his vows as a clergyman and approved his marriage with Philippa of Lancaster, a daughter of John of Gaunt.

Both the rebellion and the war with Castile rank with the decisive events in all of Portuguese history. They were the great test of its independence and they brought a noticeable change in the social structure of the country. Schematically, the rebellion opposed the landed aristocracy to the rest of the nation, with its core of action formed by a middle class of bourgeois and artisans. Actually, things were much more complex and our knowledge of the class motivation and issues is still very imperfect. The upper bourgeoisie, with the help of many civil servants and wealthy Jews, sided with Leonor Teles and Beatriz, at least in the beginning. Later on, possibly afraid of the Castilians, they seem to have changed their minds and thrown most of their support to João, Master of Avis. The lower strata of the nobility and the second-born sons, eager to get lands and positions which belonged to the powerful feudal lords, sided with João too. For different motives the middle bourgeoisie and the craftsmen, who wanted a greater participation in the local administration (especially in Lisbon) and in general economic affairs, chose the Master of Avis as their leader against the defenders of the old order. The lower classes, also, ready to support anyone who might give them some hope of a better living, or simply because of despair and the appeal of the leaders, went along with the heads of the movement and actively cooperated in shouting, killing, and plundering. Briefly, the Portuguese movement, with some minor variations only, was in the pattern of other European revolutions of the time. It was one more classical example of the late fourteenth-century social and economic crisis. Again, the lack of comparative monographs on the revolutions in the other countries prevents any fruitful and soundly interpretative explanation.

Victory for the Master of Avis resulted in a new dynasty and a new ruling class. John I (1385–1433) surrounded himself with skilled legists and bureaucrats, and looked for support among the traders, both Portuguese and foreign. He promoted to important positions, politically and socially, people of "lower condition," from the bourgeoisie, the lower aristocracy, and even the artisans. Important changes in local administration took place, craftsmen defying the overwhelming strength of the rural landowners. However, John I could not prevent the rise of a new and strong landed nobility, partly a result of the concentration of estates among a very few. The leader

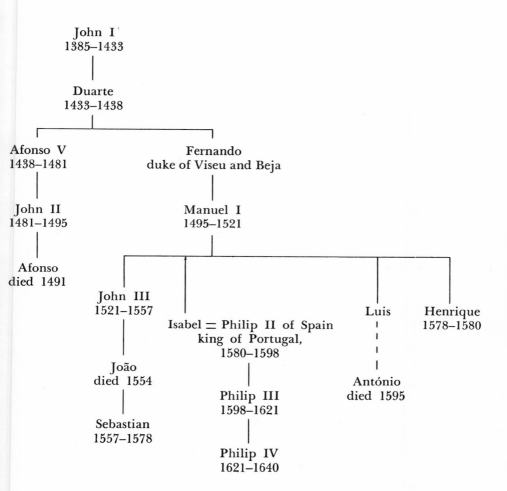

of this new class of feudal lords was Nuno Álvares Pereira, the former war hero, whom he appointed as his constable. When Nuno Álvares retired to a monastery (under what circumstances and pressures we do not know), his son-in-law, Afonso, an illegitimate son of the king himself, took over as the head of the challenging and arrogant new aristocracy. To counterbalance his power, John I (and after him his son Duarte) generously endowed his family: two of John's sons (Pedro and Henry, the future "Navigator") were made dukes and two others received the direction of the wealthy religious-military orders (João as Master of Santiago, Fernando as Master of Avis). Henry was also made the Master of the richest order of all, that of Cristo. It was only the king's personal authority with his children and his tremendous prestige that prevented any open challenge to his power during his lifetime.

After 1411 John I associated his eldest son, Duarte, with the throne. Both organized a plan of military expansion in North Africa as a way of canalizing turbulent energies and securing good profits for the nobility and the bourgeoisie. The African expedition, as a matter of fact, was a very complex affair, involving several different social forces, motivations, and goals (see chapter 3). Politically, it had the advantage of keeping the nobility busy outside the Portuguese borders. It also provided some hope for relieving the great economic crisis and for distracting attention from the internal situation, which was far from good.

The conquest of Granada seems to have been the first considered goal, later abandoned because of Castilian pressures. The epoch was fertile in adventurous expeditions, often with little or no economic and political motivation at all. Uneasy conditions at home obviously encouraged people to think of quitting and looking for something better, even when that "better" was undetermined. The late fourteenth and the early fifteenth centuries were typical epochs of political adventures, rather anarchical in organization and goals, often far distant from the original mother country. Only in this sense was it an epoch of expansion, as shown by the Catalans, the French, and the Italians in Greece and the Middle East, and by the late Crusades and the crusading movement.

Under the command of the king, the constable, and most of the nobility, the Portuguese attacked Ceuta, in Morocco, and easily captured it (1415). Then they went back home, loaded with booty and leaving behind a strong garrison. They soon realized that Ceuta alone was useless and that they must conquer more towns and hinterland in Morocco. Two parties appeared accordingly, an expansionist party under Prince Henry, the Duke of Viseu, the other under Prince Pedro, the Duke of Coimbra. The feudal lords were also divided, but the majority backed the expansionist policy, directed toward Morocco or toward Granada. Old King John I, who was prudent and tired, curbed any attempts to pursue the war in Africa until he died. Instead he devoted a part of his time to literature and to the writing of a book on hunting. His court became a cultural center, somewhat similar to that of Dinis's epoch, though with less variety of themes and less freedom of expression.

The new monarch, Duarte (1433–38), hesitated for a while but finally yielded to the war party. A second expedition was prepared which attacked Tangiers but utterly failed (1437). Almost surrounded by the Moors, the Portuguese were allowed only to embark, leaving hostages, one of them Prince Fernando, the Master of Avis, who died in captivity. In spite of all his efforts, Prince Henry and his group could not persuade Duarte to organize a new expedition. The king died soon and his eldest son, Afonso V, a child of six, ascended the throne. Duarte had appointed his wife, Queen Leonor of Aragon, as sole regent. The queen was supported by most of the war party, headed by Henry and his half brother, Count Afonso of Barcelos, the son-in-law of Nuno Álvares Pereira. Against her, Pedro, the Duke of Coimbra, rebelled with the backing of his brother João, Master of Santiago, and apparently a large part of the bourgeoisie and the lower classes of Lisbon and other cities. The clergy seemed divided too, although a majority supported Queen Leonor. It seemed to be a repetition of the 1383–85 movement, although with fewer patriotic goals and less definite issues. But while in 1383–85 almost all the significant landed nobility formed a united group, personal interests and hatreds divided them now. While in 1383–85 almost all the people looked united and ready to fight for a well-determined cause, their support to Pedro and João had now much of a demagogical adherence. The revolution of 1383–85 was in essence a social movement with a political coloration;

the rebellion of 1438–41 was in essence a feudal quarrel with a social coloration. Again, comparisons with other feudal quarrels throughout Europe, so typical in the wane of the Middle Ages, would probably prove fruitful.

Prince Pedro won, after a brief civil war and a compromise with his half brother, which gave the latter the title of Duke of Bragança and new privileges. Obviously Pedro remained too weak to enforce his authority permanently. His undisputed regency lasted for seven years (1441–48), a troubled period of political unrest and interference in the internal politics of Castile. Finally Afonso V, being of age, dispensed with his services and promptly accepted his uncle Afonso's advice and influence. The defeated party was again in power, and for a long time. With it the last phase of feudal Portugal began. Pedro, forced to rebellion, rose in arms against his king. He was defeated and killed at Alfarrobeira (Estremadura) with most of his followers (1449).

BEGINNING OF THE EXPANSION

EQUIPMENT AND NEEDS

Three inventions in the art of navigation were decisive for the great discoveries. All three were known by the early fourteenth century, more than a hundred years before the voyages actually began. Most important was the invention of the central rudder fixed to the stern-post of the keel, instead of the traditional oar-like lateral rudders. Credited to the Baltic world, where it first appeared in the mid-1200's, the central rudder was known in Spain as early as 1282 (if not before), and was used by the Cantabrian ships. The compass, another innovation of the same period, came from China through the Arabs. A third invention of the thirteenth century, the portolan chart, was derived from direct observation by means of the compass and led to the possibility of plotting a course over a considerable expanse of sea, in contrast to the traditional coastwise navigation. Italian seamen were using sophisticated portolan charts by the early 1300's, with the characteristic compass roses and the consequent representation of lines of direction (rhumb).

These three devices, combined with a refinement in the arts of sailing and shipbuilding, afforded immense opportunities. The triangular or lateen sail, a Greek or Syrian invention of the early Middle Ages, made it possible to navigate even the broader ships with relative ease. Moreover, the Mediterranean seamen knew how to sail close-hauled or obliquely. They had little need, however, to develop or perfect this technique as navigation was mostly coastwise, distances short, and winds generally favorable. In the Atlantic area, both northerners and southerners were gradually increasing the size of their ships, while making them lighter and easier to maneuver. The Cantabrians were considered experts in shipbuilding, and by the 1300's they were exporting ships to several European countries.

Inventions and technological refinements being related to large areas, not to countries, it is hard to determine what role Portugal actually played in all this naval revolution. There is no doubt, however, that her geographical location and cultural features definitely favored the introduction of new processes from the Atlantic, the Christian Mediterranean, and the Moslem Mediterranean areas. We also know that the South of Portugal, with its Moslem and Mozarab tradition, was decisive in fostering long-distance navigation and in absorbing the manifold influences. A great variety of ships, mostly for fishing, betrayed their Moslem origin, both in name and in features. Among them, the *caravo* or *caravela* (> Arabic *karib*), similar to the dhow used by the Arabs in the Indian Ocean, was to be paramount. The Portuguese gradually improved it and by the first half of the fifteenth century a new type of ship had come into existence, which was ideal for long-distance voyages far from the coastline. This caravel of the 1400's, which actually continued to evolve until the sixteenth century, possessed a wide hull displacing little water, with three masts hoisting triangular sails, hung from very long spars. This permitted great mobility in maneuvering and in taking a rhumb which could form an angle of more than 50° with the direction of the wind. The average tonnage did not exceed fifty. A ship with these characteristics and equipped for voyages of discovery required more than twenty men as crew.

Between such practical achievements, resulting from the experience and the skill of seamen, and the theoretical knowledge shared by scholars and statesmen, the gulf was immense. A vast corpus of astronomical and mathematical science had slowly emerged from long centuries of Moslem, Jewish, and Christian study, essentially based upon the attainments of the Roman world. The Moslems were the creators of an extensive and complex terminology, which covered all the fields of science. They had kept alive the Greek doctrine of the sphericity of the earth. They evaluated the length of a degree of the meridian with remarkable accuracy, thus estimating the circumference of the earth as 20,400 miles, not too far from the actual 25,000. They improved the ancient astrolabe. A great part of these theoretical achievements had taken place in Moslem Spain. When the Christians conquered it, many Arab treatises began to be translated into Latin, and a school of translators arose in Toledo. Moslem and Jewish astronomers also composed the so-called Toledan tables, containing a great number of important mathematical observations, with nautical application. By the late thirteenth century, King Alfonso X of Castile ordered a sort of astronomical encyclopaedia from a group of Christian and Jewish scholars (*Libros del Saber de Astronomia*). Several other treatises were prepared in the Iberian Peninsula, particularly Catalonia.

Geographical knowledge was shared, to some extent, by scientists, seamen, and traders. The West African coast was known beyond Cape Bojador (26.5° N), as a Catalan atlas of 1375–80 clearly shows. The same source gives plain evidence that both the Canary and the Madeira islands had been visited by Westerners. The interior of north Africa was described as far as the south Sahara, with plenty of detail on its oases, caravan routes, and native kingdoms. Such information, which derived from scattered sources, transmitted in different periods of time, was mostly gathered from the hinterland and related through and to the Moslem cultural area.

Theoretically, however, Western man knew still more. The anonymous *Libro del Conoscimiento,* written in Spain in the mid-fourteenth century, makes it clear that the Gulf of Guinea and the notion of a change of direction in the African coast were known at the time. The Arab geographers even mentioned the eastern coast of Africa to the Cape of Good Hope.

To the northwest and west, geography was less precise. Christian scholars, like St. Isidor of Seville, reported the existence of the Fortunate, Gorgades, and Hesperides isles, the latter two populated with fabulous monsters. Now and then, a piece of land appeared in the fourteenth- and early fifteenth-century navigation maps that roughly coincided with Iceland and vaguely transmitted the echo of the Norse discovery and settlement. If the Vinland map is authentic, it also represented Greenland and the coast of America or simply New-foundland. West of the European coast, there appeared some forms of isles: the Antilia or "Island of the Seven Cities," Saint Brendan's isles, Brasil, Satanazes, a chain of eight or nine smaller islands extending north-south, and others. Together, they blended a great deal of imagination with the tradition of ancient discoveries, which probably went back to the sources of Plato's description of Atlantic islands and of a western continent. The name "Seven Cities" derived from the legendary seven bishops who had fled the Arab invasion of Spain in the eighth century and founded seven dioceses in an island discovered somewhere in the Atlantic. The name St. Brendan was associated with a legendary travel undertaken by an Irish saint before the tenth century, perhaps a consequence of the Norse expeditions to Iceland and Greenland.

More than any others, however, the Arabs and some of their historically recorded voyages in the Atlantic accounted for the presumed existence of land to the west. Before the twelfth century, some "Adventurers" (as they are mentioned in the Arab historiography) left Lisbon, discovered a number of inhabited islands (probably the Canary Islands), and went back home. Other Arab or Negro travelers, in the framework of the Moslem culture area, seem to have reached the island of Sal, in the Cape Verde archipelago, which they regularly visited for some time in order to load salt. Possibly the Moslems of the Iberian Peninsula or Morocco also discovered (or rediscovered) Madeira and the Azores, but both archipelagoes lay too far from the coast and roused little economic interest in a permanent settlement. The historian Leo Wiener even contended that the Islamized Negroes from the Sudan discovered America and left proof of their deed in many aspects of agriculture, industry, political and social organization, religious customs and practices, and even terminology, of the pre-Colombian civilizations of America.

All such islands and lands, both real and imaginary, had a tremendous impact on the Portuguese voyages of the fourteenth and fifteenth centuries. They provided a strong stimulus and a definite goal for many travels of discovery, while filling people's minds with precise (so it was believed) and rich descriptions of new lands. They appealed to everyone, whether learned and aristocrat, or ignorant and villein. And they would persist in many place names of existing islands and continents and of those discovered anew.

The other side of the picture consisted in the appalling stories related to such lands and surrounding seas. Tales of all kinds of monsters, dangers, and obstacles were associated with the Atlantic Ocean and widely believed. Transmitted or coined by the Arabs, the legend of the Sea of Darkness described an ocean populated with numerous monstrous beings and engulfed in permanent darkness, where all the ships would be wrecked by huge waves or violent winds. All kinds of superstitions slowed down curiosity and lust for wealth. For a long time, the medieval Portuguese, like the medieval European in general, hesitated between the desire to go farther west and south and the fear of never returning. It was necessary that the pressure of a number of powerful forces overcome that fear and force him to set out.

Asia and its mysteries provided another source of appeal. From Asia came the much desired spices, as well as dyestuffs, ivory, precious stones, and all kinds of sophisticated commodities. Medieval geography had Asia starting at the Nile, not at the Red Sea, thus including in it most of modern Ethiopia. It also greatly enlarged the sense of the word "India," a part of which encompassed present northeast Africa. There were several "Indias" and in one of them a great Christian emperor ruled over a vast territory, densely populated. Immensely rich and powerful, he was known as Prester John, for he was at the same time a priest and a king. All kinds of monsters, mythical figures, and landscapes were a part of his Empire. This myth of Prester John was to prove of enormous importance in understanding the goals of Portuguese expansion and the ways in which it was directed. It is now realized that the medieval concept of Prester John (whose name actually derived from žan hoy, "my lord," the way the Ethiopians addressed their king) fused and confused several traditions and information related to three differently located nuclei of Christians, as well as to several political entities and realities: the Monophysite-Christian kingdom of Abyssinia or Aksum, the Nestorian-Christian communities in Central Asia, and the Nestorian groups in India. The Mongol emperors, who attacked "heathen" and Moslem realms all over Asia, were often associated and identified with such a myth, which explains the successive Western attempts to contact them. By the fifteenth century, more precise evidence of Prester John and his identification with the sovereign of Ethiopia was available, after some direct contacts attempted and achieved by both sides. The means of reaching Ethiopia by the west or the southwest, however, remained the object of much controversy, and very little continued to be known of Prester John's real power and wealth.

Most of all this geographical knowledge was transmitted to the Portuguese, not only by the commercial and political currents connecting them with the rest of Europe, but also by the Portuguese ambassadors, travelers, and pilgrims who returned home. Of particular importance were Prince Pedro's voyages through several countries and courts of western and central Europe (1425–28), and perhaps Prince Afonso's pilgrimage to the Holy Land in 1410(?), as well as the embassies sent to the councils of Pisa (1409), Constance (1414–17), Basel (1433–37), and Ferrara-Florence (1438–39).

To embark on extensive and systematic voyages of discovery and exploration naturally required skilled and abundant manpower, both for manning the ships and for general leadership and planning. This is what first tends to puzzle many historians when they analyze the demographic, social, and economic potentialities of the Portuguese in the 1400's. As a matter of fact, one of the important points to note is that for a long time the Portuguese voyages were neither extensive nor systematic and not carried on with continuity. For much more than a century, fishermen from the south of Portugal, carelessly but daringly, through several generations, went farther and farther in their search for fish, whales, and booty. In the Moslem tradition, they frequently reached African waters and often chased small Moslem (and Christian) boats. They did not shun some possible landings in enemy area if they knew the danger was minimal and the profit worthwhile. Slowly but gradually, they perfected their sailing methods and their ships. Slowly but gradually, their skill, transmitted from father to son, improved. When at the dawn of the fifteenth century other circumstances permitted a greater consciousness of what could be achieved, and when enterprising merchants, noble lords, and the king himself required trained crews for their new undertakings, they found them ready and in sufficient number to be diverted from pure fishing tasks to more complex efforts.

The role played by piracy should also be considered. Obviously, by the very nature of piracy, historical records on its activities must be scarce. However, there is enough evidence of a developed piracy along the Portuguese coast during the late Middle Ages. Portuguese, Moslem, and foreign pirates took part in it. They may have looked for permanent operational bases in some of the Canary Islands or even in the Madeira archipelago, so close to the African coast. In their own interest, they disguised their hiding places with all kinds of misinformation.

Technological advance and skilled manpower were, nevertheless, insufficient to back a continuous effort at systematic discovery and exploration of the unknown world. There had been, in the thirteenth and fourteenth centuries, several voyages of discovery, but no continuity or persistence in their resumption, as we shall see. Much deeper and stronger pressures had to intervene. A favorable combination of conditions, in short a favorable conjuncture, had to exist. It made its appearance by the first half of the fifteenth century.

Europe was short of gold. All over the continent the gold output had steadily decreased from the mid-1300's on, while purchases in the East had gone up almost as steadily. The gold shortage prevented commerce from flourishing and spurred on traders and businessmen to control of the gold mines outside the continent. Coin debasements had reached levels unheard of. In Portugal, as was shown in chapter 2, this "hunger" for gold (as well as for silver) was felt particularly in the first third of the fifteenth century, when a mark (230 g) of gold rose from 250 libras (late 1300's) to 251,000 libras (in 1433). Now, the West knew very well that gold was available somewhere in Africa, south of the Sahara, because the Arab and Arab-controlled caravans brought it to the Moslem world. To get it, two ways seemed possible: either to secure control of some north African entrepôts—which partly explains the Portuguese attacks in Morocco—or to attempt direct contact with the peoples south of Islam—which partly accounts for the Portuguese voyages of discovery. In fact, no country of Western Europe was closer to the actual sources of gold than Portugal.

The currency debasement had another consequence as well: it reduced the revenues both of the king and of the feudal lords at a time when their expenditures were increasing. In spite of all the rent and tax adjustments attempted and achieved by the royal ad-

visers and legislators, the nobility—particularly in its lower ranks—
were impoverished and trying hard to overcome that impoverishment. Conquest, privateering, and plundering were obvious solutions.

To what extent did a systematic enlargement of the fishing areas
influence the voyages of discovery in the early fifteenth century? We
still do not know. Many of the fishing expeditions were in the hands
of the king, of rich bourgeois, and of feudal lords, whose advisers
might well have planned a permanent widening of the "territorial"
waters. Morocco and the northwest African coast seemed the obvious
targets. Much more research is also required on the fish and whale
migrations, which might have forced the sailing ships to follow them.

Other motivations, though debatable, may have played a minor
role: for instance, the grain shortage, which directed attention to the
bountiful Moroccan harvests; or the rising sugar plantations in Portugal, producing their first profits and suggesting the conquest of some
rich sugar fields in Morocco; or the search for slaves, "fashionable"
again in the late Middle Ages, rediscovered as a profitable undertaking both for home labor and for export; or the need for dyestuffs
and shellac for the textile industry; or the prospect of finding skins
and leather, supposed to be abundant in north Africa.

Morocco, like every Moslem country, strongly appealed to the
medieval Portuguese (as it did to the Castilians), her wealth and
fertility having been grossly exaggerated. This point has to be fully
understood to realize the goals and future disappointments of the
fifteenth-century expansion.

Economic and social reasons, however, are generally insufficient
for a thorough comprehension of any medieval enterprise. They provide the basis, the reasonable platform for action, but they omit the
colorful wrapper that each man requires to rationalize his own actions
and to convince others of a noble and idealistic undertaking. In the
case of the fifteenth-century expansion, that cover was made of a double
religious texture: the fight against the infidel and the salvation of
souls.

In the 1100's, the ideal of crusade had captivated the Iberian
Peninsula and gradually entered the minds of kings and warriors. The
common fight against the Almohads in the early thirteenth century,
the enterprise which carried Afonso IV and a Portuguese army to

Salado in 1340, looked very much like a crusade, though with an Iberian color and flavor. In the early 1400's the Portuguese had thought of conquering Granada; instead, they launched their attacks on Ceuta and Tangiers. Being now more familiar with learning and with the study of the past, the Iberian elites could perfectly well say not only that the conquest of any Moslem lands was a crusade per se but also that in conquering Morocco they were simply pushing back the Infidel and recovering lands which had once been Christian. A crusade, incidentally, involved several aspects, could be expressed in several ways, and aimed at several goals: it defended Christendom against any possible threats by non-Christians; it attacked the Infidel with the purpose of annihilation and prevented him from spreading his "error" among others; it secured the Christians economic bases for the prosperity of all Christendom; it saved the souls of the unbelievers. Open war, treason, piracy, raiding and plundering, reducing to captivity, all could be considered crusading tasks and justified as such. Political expansion and imperialism, like captivity, was considered a legitimate means to convert the unbeliever. Thus, no wonder that the Church approved Portuguese expansion and gave it the warmest blessing. Successive Papal bulls, cunningly negotiated by the Portuguese representatives in Italy, backed the Portuguese military projects or attainments, labeled them holy "crusades," invited all the Christian rulers to help, and granted indulgences and even a share from church revenues—an always coveted aim. Neither the Church nor the Portuguese were being hypocritical, because Medieval Christianity encompassed all such methods and many others which our own twentieth-century prejudices generally consider cruel, inhuman, and purely materialistic.

Another point that needs a careful analysis is the participation of foreigners and of foreign interests. The Italians controlled a large part of the Portuguese long-distance trade, especially trade directed toward the Mediterranean. They were interested, therefore, in attaining a certain number of commercial goals which might have played a minor role for the Portuguese. As the Italians were wealthier, were more skilled and cunning in commercial practices, and possessed an international network of relationships, they were ideally placed to guide and canalize many undertakings toward their objectives. Their part in the Portuguese expansion started as early as the mid-1300 s, in the first great voyage we have the record of. Later on, they were often present. They also came as adventurers, skilled advisors, and trained seamen, actually participating in the travels themselves. It was they, along with the Catalans, who probably taught the Portuguese how to use a portolan and a compass. It was also they who, from a-shore, pressured many Portuguese captains, sailors, and even more powerful lords to launch this or that expedition with this or that pre-cise purpose.

Along with the Italians came many others: Basques, Castilians, Catalans, North Europeans, and of course Moslems. Their contribu-tion to the Portuguese voyages and methods should neither be forgot-ten nor overrated.

Local Portuguese interests also played a part. Fishermen and traders from the Algarve did not necessarily agree with the goals and methods of Lisboners or other more northern-located Portuguese. The municipalities, with their own selfish and narrow-minded objectives, often contributed to odd and apparently unexplained occurrences, slowdowns or hasty undertakings. The same happened with feudal lords (as a class and individually), with the religious orders, and with the king. Nothing similar to a "national" enterprise took place before the late fifteenth century, when most of the expansion was sort of "nationalized" and "monopolized" by the Crown. It is rather as a summing up of individual or of small-group initiatives that the Portu-guese expansion must be studied in its earlier phase. This does not exclude the more important and often decisive role played by some people or by some communities.

This whole question brings about the much-debated problem of leadership. Who was the actual leader of the discoveries? What part did a man like Prince Henry ("Henry the Navigator") actually play?

Among the appanages John I granted his sons, Henry's share was neither the biggest nor the richest. He was made lord, then Duke of Viseu. He was also lord of several other places in Central Portugal. When Ceuta fell to the Portuguese, the king entrusted it to Prince Henry as a sort of governor-general, in charge of its supply and de-fense. Some years later he was given the perpetual governorship of the Algarve, an understandable appointment for someone officially concerned with the fate of the African town. As such, he moved his usual residence and household from Viseu to Lagos, at the time the largest city in the Algarve. (The much-celebrated Vila do Infante which he founded near the Cape of Sagres was of minor importance in the history of the Portuguese discoveries.) In 1420 he was granted the government of the military order of Christ, which provided him with a permanent military force, along with further revenues in money and in kind. During most of his lifetime, his main concern and ambition seem to have centered on Morocco (as well as Granada) and on a systematic plan of military conquests over there. Accordingly, he backed the defense of Ceuta against Moslem attempts to recover it; he played the major role in forcing the unsuccessful expedition against Tangiers, he strongly pledged himself to retain Ceuta even at the cost of abandoning his brother Fernando to permanent captivity and final death. Prince Henry supported the "war-party" against his brother Pedro, contributing to the latter's defeat and death, and he probably was behind every later attempt to conquer fortresses and towns in North Africa. In 1458, old and tired, he still took part in the conquest of Ksar es Seghir (Alcácer Ceguer). To the end he was military and expansionist, but he cared more for Morocco than for the voyages of discovery. Conquering North Africa and "recovering" it for Christendom was definitely his cherished goal.

Apart from Morocco he never traveled anywhere, in contrast to some members of his family (two brothers and a nephew), who were familiar with Europe and its problems. Nevertheless, like many aristocrats of his time, he seemed interested in astrology and astronomy, mathematics and nautical science. He gathered around him a few scholars, in addition to Jewish doctors and Italian experts on trade. As a typical prince of the late Middle Ages and early Renaissance, he welcomed foreigners, listened to them, and displayed his generosity in gifts and awards. A scholar and a scientist himself (for he was learned and talented), he seems also to have been a model lord, always surrounded by faithful clients and praised by them. Late in his life, the interesting and unexpected results of the discoveries probably developed and stimulted his desire for a greater knowledge and more precise achievements.

The voyages of discovery, if they may have interested Prince

Henry (as they certainly did, but to a minor extent), were nonetheless primarily regarded as a way of increasing his patrimony and rents, which his political and military undertakings, along with opulent household, constantly depleted. He was always short of money: apparently, neither his duchy nor his governorships produced a sufficient income. In revenues, the Order of Christ came after the orders of Santiago and Avis. Thus, he tried very hard not only to get new lordships and revenues but also to improve and render more profitable the ones he already possessed. Interestingly enough, many of those efforts were related to fishing and maritime activities, including piracy and privateering. As governor of the Algarve and Ceuta, where sailing and fishing played a major economic role, Henry was well aware of the profits to be had from the sea, if well exploited. Thus he secured the monopoly of tuna fishing in the whole "kingdom" of the Algarve; he obtained the tithe on all the fish caught by the fishermen of Monte Gordo; he got privileges and revenues on the catching of porpoises and croakers. He controlled most of the fish supply to Ceuta. Later on, Henry also secured the coral-fishing monopoly. Other economic profits were extracted from milling privileges, the dye industry and soap production. As we shall see, he took good care to exploit economically the newly discovered lands, both in agricultural production and in the slave trade. He also managed to get a sort of "subsidy," or annual allowance, from the Crown.

Gradually, Henry became deeply related to seafare, and to sea people. Many of his knights and squires owned ships or controlled maritime activities as well. All of them were entirely dependent upon him as their feudal lord and commander-in-chief. He had little trouble in making himself obeyed whenever he wished. He was in a unique position for launching a vast plan of maritime expansion, once he decided to do so. Yet there is no trace of such a plan for many years. It seems fairly well established that of all the known voyages ordered between 1415 and 1460 (when Henry died) only about one-third were due to his initiatives. The other two-thirds were directed by the king (John I, Duarte, Afonso V), the regent Pedro, the feudal lords, private merchants, and landowners. The same was true of the economic exploration of newly discovered lands. Without obliterating Prince Henry's part, this fact reduces his leadership to a more human and medieval dimension.

THE VOYAGES OF DISCOVERY

Records of the fourteenth- and early fifteenth-century voyages of discovery are rare and scattered. In the late 1200's a Genoese expedition departed from Italy heading for the West African coast, passed the latitude of the Canary Islands, and disappeared without further notice. Early in the fourteenth century a second Genoese voyage reached the same islands: its leader, a certain Lancellotto Malocelli, apparently occupied one or several of them for some years and then returned home, leaving his presence forever commemorated in the island of Lanzarote, named after him and later translated into Castilian. By the middle of the century, Italian merchants in Lisbon succeeded in convincing King Afonso IV to subsidize (and possibly organize) a three-ship expedition to the Canaries: its captains were Italians, Castilians, Portuguese, and Aragonese-Catalans. The expedition visited all thirteen Canary Islands and probably the archipelago of Madeira as well. For the first time in cartography, a famous Catalan portolan chart of 1339 correctly reported most of the isles which actually exist in both groups, with many of their modern names.

The Canaries were inhabited by savage tribes living in a sort of Neolithic stage of culture. The archipelago was rich in economic possibilities, which explains the Portuguese and Castilian efforts to rule the islands, bountiful with cheap slaves, dyestuffs, and fish. The Italians, of course, were too far away to compete seriously with either Portugal or Castile. The long contest for final control lasted for more than a hundred years, both kingdoms organizing and sending successive expeditions which failed to achieve a complete victory. It was too early for an enduring attempt at expansion: local and international events were then playing a major role in the history of the Iberian Peninsula, preventing any good chances of political organization and economic exploitation. Furthermore, the natives fiercely fought for their freedom. The French had their share too in trying to subdue the

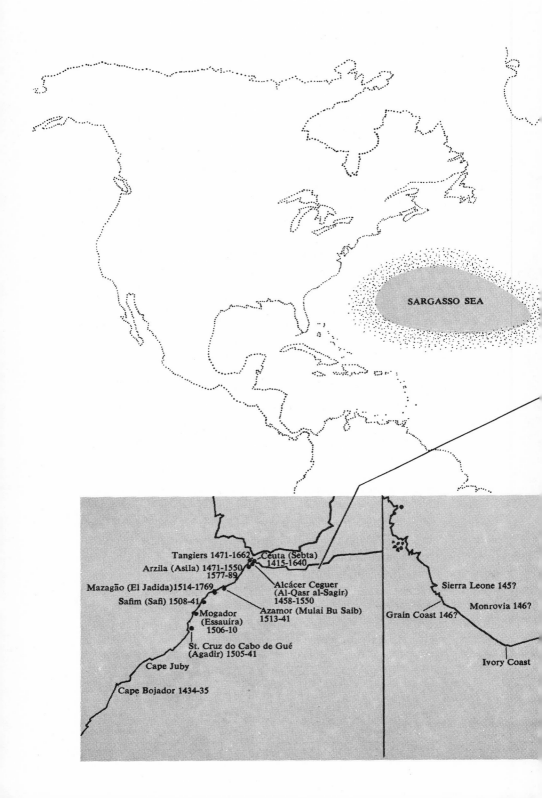

SARGASSO SEA

Tangiers 1471-1662   Ceuta (Sebta)
                     1415-1640
Arzila (Asila) 1471-1550
              1577-89
Mazagão (El Jadida)1514-1769
                              Alcácer Ceguer
Safim (Safi) 1508-41   (Al-Qasr al-Sagir)
                              1458-1550
              Mogador   Azamor (Mulai Bu Saib)
              (Essauira)   1513-41
              1506-10
         St. Cruz do Cabo de Gué
         (Agadir) 1505-41
    Cape Juby

  Cape Bojador 1434-35

Sierra Leone 145?

Monrovia 146?

Grain Coast 146?

Ivory Coast

Lisbon
Lagos

‘zoreš Is. 1427-52

Madeira Is. 1419-20

anary Islands

Rio de Oro 1436

•Wadan 1487-1513

Cape Blanc 1441

pe Verde Is.
145?-6?

Cape Verde 1444
•Cantor
Salum River 1446
Geba River 1456

Bijagós Is.

Gwato 1486

Biafra 1472?

Fernão do Pó 1472?•

St. Thomas 1472?•

1474-75

Congo River 1482-83

Mombaça 1505• •Malindi 1498

Zanzibar 1503

Kilwa 1502•

•Ascension Is. 1501-02

Moçambique 1507•

St. Helena   *1483*
1501-2

Zambezi River 1498

Sofala 1505

Madagascar 1500

S. Jorge da Mina 1482

xim 1503

Samma 1526

1486

Natal 1497

Cape of Good Hope 1488   1488

archipelago, some of the islands being granted as fiefs by the King of
Castile to French knights. In 1436, Pope Eugene IV formally acknowledged the Castilian rights, but the Portuguese refused to give up and
continued the struggle till 1480.

Things worked out differently with Madeira. It seems that the
Portuguese did not pay too much attention to those uninhabited
islands until the early fifteenth century. By 1417, however, the Castilians sent an important expedition to the isle of Porto Santo. This
time the Portuguese responded quickly and decisively: in 1419 and
1420, two expeditions left from the Algarve and occupied Madeira
and Porto Santo for good. It was the real beginning of the great
Portuguese expansion overseas. Interestingly enough, they translated
the Italian or Catalan names of the isles into Portuguese, which proves
they did not feel like real discoverers but simply like settlers: thus
Legname became *Madeira* (wood); *Porto Santo* (holy port) was kept,
for it has the same form in both languages; *Deserte* became *Desertas*
(deserted or waste).

The next step was somewhat more difficult. By the 1420's the
Portuguese were thoroughly familiar with the west Moroccan coast,
which they used to follow to parallel 26° or 25°N. They were also
familiar with the Atlantic around both the Canary and the Madeira
archipelagoes. Whenever they sailed a little farther west, they knew
they had trouble in getting favorable winds to take them back home,
unless they rhumbed northwest and then caught the trade winds
blowing from the west. They might also try to avoid the Castilian
piracy, very active in the Canaries. In one of those detours, by 1427,
a pilot named Diogo de Silves (another Algarvian) perceived the
island of Santa Maria, then that of São Miguel, and possibly five more
of the Azores in a single round-the-island exploration, for all of them
can be discerned from any one. In naming them, either the discoverers
or someone back in Portugal compromised between the legendary
terminology and the right to Christianize newly found lands. Indeed,
the existing portolan charts were much less clear and precise in reporting the Azores than in describing both Madeira and the Canaries.
Thus, of the first group of seven, only one island retained its carto-
graphical name: São Jorge, translated from San Zorzo or San Giorgio
(incidentally, St. George was Portugal's official patron-saint from the

late fourteenth century on, by English or/and Italian influence; it would have been "rude" to change his name). Santa Maria, São Miguel, Terceira (the popular name for the "third" island found or located in the archipelago instead of its officially given name of Nosso Senhor Jesus Cristo, Our Lord Jesus Christ), Pico (the "peak," another popular name for the very high volcano existing there, instead of the official name of São Luis), and Faial (i.e., the beech grove, first called São Dinis), all derive from Portuguese discovery and occupation. The seventh island, Graciosa ("gracious"), was possibly named after another Italian term which appears in the old portolan charts, though it may also signify that the isle was found "gracious" by its discoverers or early inhabitants. Azores itself is another riddle. Açores in Portuguese, it means "goshawks," a kind of falcon. Were there many falcons in those islands when the Portuguese arrived? Or was the name simply translated and adapted from the Arab Rāca, bird of prey, which the Moslem geographer and historian Idrisi had used in the twelfth century for the name of a legendary island in the Atlantic?

The discovery of the west African coast was the main goal of the early fifteenth-century voyages. Somewhere south there existed the famous "gold river" and the gold mines which supplied all of Islam. In 1346 a Catalan ship had sailed south looking for the "rio de l'or" which was thought to be one of the arms of the Nile. Several ships were sent by the Portuguese in the 1420's and early 1430's. The whole coastline was well known by then to parallel 26°N approximately. From Cape Não on, it is a desolate and dangerous area, with nothing in sight but scarped cliffs and sand dunes. The roaring of the waves against the reefs can be heard from afar. When the west winds blow, the waves on the coast may be more than fifty feet high. From October to April extremely thick fogs are usual. For a medieval sailor, with a long training of listening to all kinds of fabulous tales about the Sea of Darkness and the end of the world, that dangerous and deserted coastline undoubtedly heralded the limit of all possible navigation. The long promontory of Cape Bojador, protruding deeply into the sea, clearly showed where the boundary was. Who would dare to sail beyond? Sent by Prince Henry, Gil Eanes was brave enough and skillful enough to make it. If our sources tell the truth, fifteen times he tried and fifteen times he failed! In any case, the usual medieval exaggeration clearly shows how difficult the undertaking seemed to everybody and how important the passage of Cape Bojador was in the history of the discoveries. In 1434 Gil Eanes finally sailed around the famous cape, went on for a number of miles, and returned back with the news that for purposes of navigation the world did not end there. As a convincing proof, he brought with him some wild roses plucked beyond the Bojador promontory. As a matter of fact, historians still argue whether the fifteenth-century Cape Bojador did correspond to the modern cape with that name (26.5°N, in present Spanish Sahara) or rather to Cape Juby, several miles north.

After that, the discovery of the West African coast proceeded more rapidly. In the following year, Gil Eanes, along with Afonso Gonçalves Baldaia, passed the tropic of Cancer (23.5°N) and reached what they supposed to be and therefore named Rio do Ouro (Gold River, now Rio de Oro in the Spanish Sahara). There they got the first samples of what they were primarily looking for: gold. The voyages were beginning to bring about enough profit and to appeal to a great number of people. Undertakings became more numerous, and expeditions started leaving Portugal year after year.

In 1441, Cape Blanc (Port. cabo Branco), in present-day Mauritania (21°N), was reached by Nuno Tristão. This same navigator, apparently a very skilled seaman, discovered at least 10 degrees more of coast southward, in successive voyages during the next five years. He was probably the first to get to the mouth of the Senegal, then to the Gambia or the Salum rivers. Other navigators discovered Cape Verde (Green cape), at 14.5° N, and Red Cape, which they named cabo dos Mastros (Cape of the Masts), in present-day Senegal.

The rhythm of discovery did not slow down in the 1450's. Along the coastline, pilot Diogo Gomes and several others (including two Italians in the service of Prince Henry) reached Guinea and Sierra Leone (Port. Serra Leoa, "the mountain of the lioness"). Early in the following decade, or perhaps earlier, Pedro de Sintra went as far as the latitude of what is now Monrovia (6.5°N) where the coastline was curving unmistakably eastward.

Thus, in less than thirty years, 20 degrees of the earth had been discovered, baptized, and carefully reported. The Portuguese were on the verge of entering the wide Gulf of Guinea which for a long time they declared to be the "southern sea," i.e., the end of Africa. Off the coast, the Cape Verde archipelago was also explored in the 1450's and early 1460's. The island of Sal (salt) was known and appeared on the maps: the Portuguese duly kept its name. The other islands were generally named after the saint of the day in which they were found: Santo Antão, São Vicente, São Nicolau, Santa Luzia, São Cristóvão (later changed to Boavista), Santiago (or São Jacobo), São Filipe (later changed to Fogo, "fire," because of its volcano).

In the North Atlantic as well the Portuguese seamen were attempting new discoveries, in the search for the legendary lands indicated on the maps or told of by tradition. Very little is known of their voyages westward, for no islands actually existed and therefore few records were ever kept. The sea, as such, was unimportant, and only the appearance of land deserved attention. According to the scarce evidence we possess, some historians admit that by the middle of the century the Portuguese had reached or at least caught sight of some of the Antilles, northeast Brazil and northeast America (Newfoundland and Greenland). In one of those travels, they discovered the two westernmost islands of the Azores, invisible from the rest of the group. They kept one of their legendary names (Corvo, "crow," for Corvi Marini), but rechristened the other Flores ("flowers"), a name which entirely suits that pretty island.

In any case, they certainly arrived at the Sargasso Sea (Mar dos Sargaços) and gathered enough data and experience to draw a very complete and precise map of the Atlantic winds and currents, which would be used by all the future navigators.

THE FIRST RESULTS

For a number of years, neither Madeira nor the Azores received any permanent colonization. From time to time Portuguese and also Castilian ships visited both archipelagoes, Madeira particularly, looking for some raw materials they might easily load. One such was the much-appreciated "dragon's blood," a red-colored resin extracted from the dragon-tree (a tree of the lily family) and used in the textile industry for dyeing. All the islands were also rich in wood. By the

1420's, the fear of a Castilian take-over led the Portuguese to decide on Madeira's permanent occupation. Less than a hundred people, under the leadership of the three presumed "discoverers" (João Gonçalves Zarco, Tristão Vaz Teixeira and Bartolomeo Pallastrello, an Italian), landed in the two islands of Madeira and Porto Santo for good. They were probably recruited in the lands which belonged to Prince Henry and to the order of Christ. The majority seem to have come from the Algarve. The social and economic structure of the mainland was introduced in the new islands without any major changes. All three leaders belonged to the lower ranks of the nobility —two of them were squires of Prince Henry's, the third was an Italian nobleman—and the same was true for about fourteen others. The rest were plebians (including some outcasts), socially and economically dependent upon them. Zarco had a certain preeminence within the whole group and was in charge of directing the settlement. Either on his own initiative or simply following instructions, he divided the archipelago in three sections: one for himself comprising half of Madeira, the other two for each of his companions, one encompassing the remnant of that island, the third one limited to Porto Santo. The Desertas were never populated. Division of Madeira followed a mere conventional line, diagonally drawn from the extreme northwest to the extreme southwest. In each share, the "lord" was entitled to grant lands, either in a quit-rent lease system or in full property. Effective occupation and cultivation by a certain deadline were required.

It took more than one generation to achieve a thorough organization of Madeira from an administrative point of view. The islands first depended upon the Crown. In 1433, King Duarte donated them as a sort of a fief to his brother Henry, though only for the duration of Henry's life, keeping for himself only the tithe on all the fish caught. According to the Iberian feudal custom, the monarch did not give up his rights to coin minting and inflicting supreme penalties. Spiritually, the isles were given to the order of Christ, a sophistical form of granting all their ecclesiastical revenues to Henry too.

As lord of Madeira, Henry created a system of three perpetual and hereditary captaincies, which he entrusted to the three existing local "lords," accepting their original allotment. The captains, or captains-donataries, were to exert jurisdiction in Henry's name; they could grant lands to settlers, and they were given the monopoly of the means of production (mills and common ovens) and the sale of salt, as well as the tenth on the tithe belonging to the lord. This system was inspired by the one adopted by the Italian republics in the Eastern Mediterranean settlements after the Crusades, and also by the Catalans and the French in that same area. Far from merely imitating, however, the Portuguese (and the Castilians after them) related the European institutions to the new conditions they found in the discovered lands, thus setting up a highly original structure of colonial administration.

In 1451, Funchal and Machico, the two main villages on the island of Madeira, and seats of administration for the two captaincies, were raised to the status of *vila* (small town) and granted a royal charter (*foral*). Shortly before his death, Henry persuaded King Afonso V to transfer his lordship over the islands to Fernando, the king's younger brother. Fernando's fief, however, included the right of transmission to his eldest son.

From an economic point of view, the islands presented advantages but equally great obstacles to a harmonious development. They were covered with thick vegetation which needed to be cleared over vast areas to allow crops and plantations. Though bountifully supplied with water, they required an elaborate system of canals and irrigation, as well as of drainage. They were very mountainous and therefore not suitable for widespread agriculture without a sustained effort to level the slopes into terraces. Barren of cattle and other tame beasts, the islands provided enough fish but lacked meat. It was these and other barriers that prevented rapid development of Madeira (and of all the other islands) as a profitable colony of settlement.

Nevertheless, there were lucrative enterprises from the very beginning. Some good wood of cedar and yew proved an immediate source of income. Dragon's blood, woad, and other dyestuffs could be counted among the settlers' first exports. (In 1439 a royal charter exempted from customs duties all the merchandise sent from Madeira to the mainland. This privilege was renewed, at least till 1449.) Fish provided a basis for local nourishment. Then, a persistent and well-directed effort—where the traditional Moslem and Mozarab skill was probably present—gradually created a network of sluices (*levadas*) which permitted a great leap forward in agriculture.

From about 1450 to about 1470, Madeira was a large grain producer (some 3,000 to 3,500 tons a year), more than half of its wheat being exported to Portugal both for local needs and for the supply of Ceuta and the overseas expeditions. Catalan and Italian merchants controlled part of this wheat trade. The island was covered with water mills and hand-mills, the monopoly of which (along with that of public ovens) belonged to the captains. With a virgin soil, still enhanced by the ashes of the great clearing fires, the yield was so great that prices had to be kept artificially high. Cattle were abundant, wine and sugar were beginning their "triumphant career." In 1452 Prince Henry had signed a contract with a man called Diogo de Teive for the setting up of a sugar mill and plantation complex. Four years later the first sugar from Madeira was exported to England. Slowly, attracted by the prospect of good profits, a relatively large number of foreign and Portuguese traders came to the island and settled down there: Jews and Genoese were among the prominent, though the Portuguese never gave up their part in the sugar trade, still less in sugar production. In the 1460's, sugar was decisively speeding up the island's economy and living standards. Instead of the usual once-a-year ship to Portugal, Funchal became a frequent port of call for Portuguese and foreign vessels in direct connection with the markets of Western Europe. The population went up, to over two thousand people in the 1460's, including the first slaves brought from the Canary Islands, Morocco, and north-central Africa to work in the plantations.

Of social interest was the rapid evolution of a number of the earlier settlers (where, in spite of social differentiation, no great economic inequalities existed) into a much wealthier group of landed absentees, who preferred to live in Funchal or Machico, handing over their agricultural tasks to tenants or managers. The development of wheat and, later on, sugar and wine production and exports, quickly raised a class of rich landowners, most of them with aristocratic names and lineages. Thus in Madeira, as in Portugal, the feudal structure was typical of the late Middle Ages.

The colonization of the Azores started much later and produced its first important results much later too. Early in the 1430's, sheep and other domestic animals were left in the islands of Santa Maria and São Miguel preliminary to permanent occupation. However, it was only in 1439 that a royal charter authorized Prince Henry to start the settlement, which actually began in the early 1440's. Like Madeira, the whole archipelago had been granted to Henry and to the order of Christ. Unlike Madeira, however, Henry's lordship did not go undisputed. His brother Pedro, who was regent at the time, decided to compete in the profitable undertaking. He took São Miguel for himself and apparently ordered the island's settlement. Santa Maria was granted by Henry to Gonçalo Velho, according to the captaincy system. As in Madeira, exemption of all customs duties on the merchandise exported to the mainland became a keystone in building up the island's economy. Furthermore, in 1447, Prince Pedro enhanced São Miguel's possibilities by renewing that exemption and making it perpetual, a privilege which greatly accounted for its future prosperity. Yet his political disgrace and subsequent death (1449) for a time jeopardized the effective colonization of São Miguel. As in Madeira, also, all the islands—except Corvo, granted as a fief to the Duke of Bragança—were later given by the king to his younger brother Fernando, shortly before Henry's death.

It was only in the 1460's that the Azores definitely became an object of interest. In addition to Santa Maria and São Miguel, Terceira, Graciosa, Faial, and Pico were populated and granted to captains-donataries, one for the latter two, one for Graciosa, and one for Terceira (later divided in two shares, following another diagonal straight line which separated the island in two halves). Captains and settlers were given privileges, lands, and revenues in much the same way as in Madeira. Yet it became clear that the recruiting of settlers would not be easy. Prince Henry was forced to grant two of the most important captaincies to foreigners (both from Flanders), who brought with them a considerable number of fellow-countrymen. In the social structure, however, differences were few.

As in Madeira, wood and dyestuffs held first place in the economic development of the Azores for a while. Again, fish played a decisive role in local supply. Cattle and wheat would become the major sources

ABOVE: *Landing at Arzila, Morocco: 15th-century tapestry, church of Pastrana (Spain).* UPPER RIGHT: *Henry the Navigator: Anonymous, "Panels" of St. Vicente de Fora, 1470's, Museu Nacional de Arte Antiga, Lisbon.* BELOW: *View of Tangiers, late 16th century.*

TINGIS. LVSITANIS. TANGIARA.

of profit and export, but only after the 1470's. Sugar production never developed, because of the unfavorable climate; consequently few slaves were ever introduced.

The West African coast did not become profitable until the 1440's, and for a time slaves proved more abundant, easier to get, and more profitable than gold. It must be recalled that the Canary Islands, long before West Africa, provided the first important source of slavery, and that the Castilians, the French and the Italians, before the Portuguese, had indulged in the slave trade profitably. Like all the others the Portuguese raided the Canaries and brought many of them as slaves to Madeira. Competition, however, prevented Portugal from using the Canary archipelago as a permanent slave market. By the 1460's, when the demand for cheap labor increased in Madeira, with the development of the sugar plantations, Castile was actively defending her rights to the exclusive ownership and economic exploitation of the islands. Piracy was rampant in the waters around the Canaries. Furthermore, the inhabitants fiercely resisted captivity and seemed to be better fighters than workers. The Portuguese made use of them against the Castilian attempts at occupation.

Abduction to slavery was also possible along the Moroccan coastline but presented a number of dangers. The Moslems were excellent warriors and possessed a good military organization. Productive slavery required the complete control of a vast hinterland, which the Portuguese never managed to secure. Further south, when black Africa was reached and the level of civilization was found to be more primitive, a profitable slave trade seemed in prospect. The first black Africans were brought in 1441 by Antão Gonçalves, who raided the coast in the North Mauritania area (about 20°N). Great enthusiasm ensued and three years later a group of people from the Algarve, associated in a sort of temporary company headed by the *almoxarife* (royal controller) of Lagos, equipped six caravels, reached the Mauritanian coast and triumphantly brought back 235 slaves. From then on, the slave trade continued rampant: between 1441 and 1448, at least 1,000 slaves were imported into Portugal; by the 1450's, an average of 700 to 800 slaves yearly entered Europe through the Algarve and Lisbon. The coast of Guinea proved a better slave market than any land reached previously by the Portuguese.

While some captives came as a result of direct incursions inland by the Portuguese, most of them were regularly purchased from Moslem traders and the Negroes themselves. Slaves could be exchanged for cloth and other merchandise, which the Portuguese often acquired from Morocco, again by legal trade. From Portugal, a great number, the majority perhaps, were then profitably sold to Castile, Aragon, and other European countries, only a part being employed in the sugar plantations (as well as in other agricultural or domestic jobs) of Madeira and Portugal. Along with sugar, the slave trade could be considered one of the most profitable of all, appealing to numerous businessmen from all over Europe, Italians particularly.

From Guinea the Portuguese also imported gum arabic, civet cats (from which civet was extracted), red pepper, cotton, ivory, and several other minor items, including parrots. Other lucrative operations involved fish and oil traffic. In addition to fish proper, the Portuguese ships caught whales and sea wolves in the Canarian and North African waters, the skins and oil of which were then sold in Portugal and exported everywhere.

Gold, the much-coveted objective, was first brought to Portugal in 1442, if the chronicles are true. It was exchanged for wheat, which was in great demand by the Africans. This explains why the Portuguese, themselves always short of grain, often brought it from abroad or from Madeira, not for national consumption but for the sake of getting gold. Cloth and clothes, blankets, red coral in the form of beads, and silver were also demanded by the Africans and could be used as a means of exchange for gold. We do not know, not even approximately, how much gold was brought to Europe in those days. The intensity of the traffic, the monopoly of Prince Henry, and the changes which occurred in the Portuguese currency (see chapter 4) suggest that the amount of gold did play a significant role in the country's economy and in achieving the desired aims.

Up to 1443, trade and navigation with Africa were free: anyone might equip a ship and send it to Morocco or to the West African coast for the purpose of regular trading or simply of raiding and pirating. However, one-fifth of all profits belonged to the Crown, in the old tradition of the Reconquista. Only Prince Pedro and Prince Henry had been exempt from this payment, and exclusively in the area of privateering.

In 1443, Prince Henry succeeded in obtaining the monopoly of all the trade carried on with the African coast south of the Bojador. He was even granted the fifth that belonged to the state. By that time, Pedro controlled the government and benefited from all its revenues and privileges; he could afford to be generous with his younger brother, whose support he desperately needed.

Trade monopoly did not signify navigation exclusiveness. Private undertakings continued, although Henry's permission was now necessary. His economic strength and organization were still insufficient for an effective monopoly implying a complete coordination of all the traffic. Instead, he preferred to grant a permit each time he was asked, receiving a carefree part of all the profits. In this way, Henry's monopoly resembled another lordship, similar to the seignorial lands he held at home. Permissions for trade were granted according to two main forms: if private initiatives took over the expenditures of equipment and voyage, Henry would be given 25 per cent of all the profits; but if he was in charge of equipping the ship, the profits would be divided in half. There is little evidence of how the contracts among individuals were arranged, or of how societies were created. In most cases, the merchant seemed to have actually participated in the expedition although some wealthier or better-organized businessmen would send their representatives and stay at home. The same happened, of course, whenever a feudal lord decided to have a share in the African trade. Profits were high, generally above 100 per cent, sometimes rising to 700 per cent. By the late 1440's, the first regular trading post was created in the island of Arguim (20.5°N), not far from the mainland. Using local materials but with tools and manpower brought from Portugal, a Soeiro Mendes de Évora directed the building of a castle or fortress for protection and led the first regular group of settlers, including a priest. The trading post was almost immediately rented to a Portuguese company (possibly with Italian shares too) for ten years. Afterward, general conditions changed. Henry's death (1460) resulted in a new period of commercial freedom (see chapter 5) with the Crown playing a greater and greater role.

In the 1450's a second trading post (and probably a castle too) was founded some miles south of Arguim. Its main purpose was to trade in red pepper, ivory, musk, and parrots. By that time the Crown itself had started a rudimentary organization of overseas trade, appointing some public officials—for instance, a receiver for all the Moors and for all the merchandise arriving from Guinea—and creating a sort of office (Casa de Ceuta) for the general supervision of the overseas lands, particularly Morocco. By 1445 another office was founded in Lagos, specializing in the trade with Arguim. After Henry's death, it was transferred to Lisbon.

Henry's motivations, along with the general ones, have already been discussed in this chapter. It seems doubtful that we can credit him with a well-organized plan for exploring the unknown earth, still less with the objective of reaching Asia and what is now called India. It would be false, however, to say that general conditions at the beginning of the discoveries were the same as when Henry died, in 1460. Much had changed in the interim, as a result of both the conjunctural variations in the world and the discoveries themselves. Henry's views, goals, and knowledge obviously changed too. Late in his life he probably had a much clearer image of the world and of what could be achieved in it than forty years before.

If no precise plan to reach Asia by sea is discernible in the first half of the fifteenth century, there was in contrast a very precise objective in Africa and a very thorough study of its means. Evidence dating from the second decade of the 1400's and continuing for more than a hundred years afterward clearly shows that a plan for conquering Moslem Africa with the final, if distant, objective of recovering Jerusalem was in the minds of many Portuguese leaders, including Kings John I, Duarte, and Afonso V, Prince Henry, and several others. In short, the ideal of crusade directed their efforts for a long time. It was later associated with the prospects of reaching Asia by sea and was fused into a vast enterprise of discovering the world for Christ, but only toward the end of the second half of the century. Until then, the Portuguese policy has to be understood in the general framework of the late crusades, and explained by it.

The Christians had theoretically never accepted the idea of a permanent loss of the Holy Land once ruled by the "ecumenical" Roman Empire. The reconquest of North Africa, following that of the Iberian Peninsula, seemed a natural goal and, at least in theory, belonged to the political objectives of the Iberian monarchs. The kings of both Castile and Portugal felt that same obligation, coupled with and glamorized by the prospect of adding new lands to their realms and new rents to their treasuries.

A nominal bishopric of Morocco had existed for a long time. Early in the fifteenth century, King John I of Portugal succeeded in convincing the Pope to appoint as its bishop a French priest who happened to be the confessor of John's wife, Queen Philippa of Lancaster. After Ceuta's fall to the Portuguese, the same bishop was made the new bishop of Ceuta and given a real diocese to govern. A Portuguese had also been invested with the nominal bishopric of Carthage. Thus, Portugal was already in control of the ecclesiastical administration of a great part of North Africa, in case of a successful war against the Moors.

In 1418, a Papal bull invited every Christian country and all inhabitants to join forces with the King of Portugal against the Infidel, advised the Portuguese clergy to preach a crusade, authorized any territorial conquests, and granted the inevitable indulgences. It was followed by several other bulls aimed at similar objectives. In the same year the Portuguese successfully forced the Moslems to raise their siege of Ceuta, and planned to launch an attack against Gibraltar which never took place.

To the several European attempts of organizing a crusade, the Portuguese monarchs always responded with enthusiasm, both in theory and in practice. Thus in 1437, the crusade was solemnly proclaimed all over Portugal (it actually led to the disaster at Tangiers). Pope Eugene IV spared no effort to stimulate the kings and lords of Europe to fight the Moslems wherever they were to be found. In the 1440's he thought of an alliance with Prester John, who could attack the Mohammedans from the South. He granted Portugal new bulls, full of exhortations and privileges, backing her in Ceuta and in her projects overseas, conceding indulgences to her princes, and so on. At the same time the Pope tried not to commit himself entirely to Portugal, in order to stimulate Castile's interests and benefit from her efforts too. Thus, he refused the Canaries to the King of Portugal and gave them to Castile. In the late 1440's and during the 1450's Castile woke up from a state of indifference and decided to play a role in the discoveries and conquests. Not only did her pirates increasingly harass the Portuguese but a formal concession of the trade with the newly discovered lands was also made to the Duke of Medina-Sidonia, in defiance of the Portuguese monopoly. Shortly after, Africa was officially declared "Castilian conquest," a vain statement in fact, but nonetheless a challenge to the Portuguese policy. The death of King Juan II (1454) solved the problem for Portugal, because the new King of Castile, weak Enrique IV, never seriously continued his father's efforts. At the same time, the Portuguese were busy in Rome trying to secure more Papal privileges. They triumphantly succeeded in 1455: the bull *Romanus Pontifex* definitely endorsed Portugal and Portugal only, sanctioning her monopoly of discovery and conquest, and affirming other important prerogatives. The next year, another bull granted the order of Christ—a national Portuguese order—the spirituality (patronate) of all the lands newly found and to be discovered in the future.

Conquering Africa, therefore, and conquering it in the framework of a crusade, involved much more than Morocco or the whole of North Africa: it also meant the conquest of Negro lands south of the Sahara, in other words, of the whole continent wherever it might end, providing that its inhabitants did not worship Jesus Christ. The Portuguese were completely free to rule in Africa with the full approval of the Holy See: only the kingdom of Prester John was to remain outside their political control.

It has to be remembered that the ways of reaching Prester John from the west and south were still obscure at the time. The river Nile supposedly ran west-east before turning south-north. The Portuguese several times thought they had arrived at it or at least one of its arms. They believed they were much closer to Ethiopia than they actually were. This explains why political targets related to an attack on the Moslem countries "from the back" appeared to the fifteenth-century European statesmen (especially the Pope and the Portuguese leaders) plausible and "just around the corner," thus justifying the continuation of the voyages of discovery and their integration in the general crusade.

THE RENAISSANCE STATE

RECOVERING FROM THE CRISIS

The great demographic depression of the late Middle Ages did not come to an end everywhere at the same time. Local conditions affected the various countries of Europe differently. It seems that in Mediterranean Europe, particularly in Italy, a new trend was in progress much before it reached the rest of the Continent. In Portugal, despite early overseas expansion, one can hardly say that a continuous upsurge in population was already noticeable by the first half of the fifteenth century. With the exception of Madeira, no lands were effectively colonized until the late 1400's or early 1500's—the Azores being a good example of the existing difficulties. There is some evidence of contemporary awareness of the problem.

The population picture changed after 1450. Gradually, stagnation evolved into a steady increase in both the general and the relative number of people. Not only did the towns witness a new epoch of growth—which, incidentally, had already happened after the Black Death—but the countryside also experienced a continuous increase in the number of people. It seems that this new trend characterized the whole of the sixteenth century.

Besides the statistical data in our possession—sparse but revealing—several other clues point in the same direction: the continuous flow of people going overseas and staying there as settlers (see chapter 5); the new migrations from the countryside to the cities and from the mountains to the plains; the expulsion of the Jews and the Moors; the increase in the number of judges and other officials; the administrative and judicial reforms subdividing the number of districts; the creation of new bishoprics and municipalities; the promotion of many *vilas* (small towns) to *cidades* (cities). In 1527–32, the first census in Portuguese history took place by order of King John III. It showed the existence of 280,528 hearths, i.e., a minimum of 1,000,000 and maximum of 1,500,000 persons. These figures corresponded to an average density of 30 to 40 inhabitants per square mile, an estimate similar to that of the other European countries. The distribution among the several provinces matched the medieval pattern and actually was not too different from twentieth-century Portugal: about 20 per cent of the people lived in Entre-Douro-e-Minho, the northernmost and smallest of all the administrative units (13 per cent of Portugal's area), while another 20 per cent sparsely occupied Alentejo and the Algarve, almost half of the total Portuguese territory. Between South and North, the balance definitely leaned toward the latter, a typical modern phenomenon challenged only in our own twentieth century.

Urban life reflected the continuous growth of population, the northern cities starting their upward climb. If there were still more large nuclei in the South than in the North—of towns with more than 500 hearths 29 out of 37 lay on or south of the Tagus basin—it should be noted that the second largest city was no longer Santarém or Évora but rather Porto, with a prominent place being assumed by Guimarães as well. Aveiro and Viana, unimportant villages two hundred years earlier, had become urban centers with more than 900 hearths each. We have the figures for Braga, which clearly show the amount of the increase during this crucial period: 275 hearths in 1477, 492 in 1506, 622 in 1514, 800 in 1527, and 1,724 in 1591. Such figures did not, however, include the large number of clergymen and privileged people.

Lisbon, of course, was far in the lead—a great metropolis by European standards and a huge town for Portugal: 13,010 hearths or between 50,000 and 65,000 inhabitants. Next came Porto with some 3,000 hearths; Évora with 2,800; Santarém with 2,000; Elvas with 1,900; Tavira with 1,500; Guimarães with 1,400; Coimbra and Lagos each with 1,300; and Setúbal, Beja, and Portalegre at the 1,200 level. In most of these towns, new houses and quarters were built outside the walls, as in the thirteenth and early fourteenth centuries. In Lisbon the new quarters built west and north from the late 1400's on finally covered a total surface equivalent to some twenty per cent of the area encompassed by the walls. In the old part of the city, gardens and open areas were reduced or totally disappeared, while the number of stories increased in many of the existing houses. The spirit of the Renaissance had its impact on the growth of many towns, both in the magnificence and general conception of their buildings, and in the planning of the new quarters, with wider and longer streets laid out like a chessboard, large squares beautifully adorned, and the like.

Much impressed by the flow of slaves imported into Portugal, fifteenth- and sixteenth-century chroniclers grossly exaggerated their number, as usually happened in medieval literary "statistics." In truth, there is no reliable source for evaluating the impact of slavery on the growth of population, yet it seems improbable that slaves ever exceeded one-tenth of the total population and usually amounted to a much lower figure. They were seen more in Lisbon than elsewhere because of its urban concentration but probably never numbered beyond 5,000.

The Jews formed a relatively small group, although precise figures are unavailable. Living in the towns and devoted to urban professions, they were organized in communes (*comunas*) as soon as their number exceeded ten families. All over Portugal, but especially in Lisbon, followed by Porto, Lamego, Santarém, Benavente, and Évora, there were communes with their officials modeled after the municipal organization, under the supreme authority of an *arrabi-mor* appointed by the king. Socially the Jews were composed of at least three classes: the wealthy merchants, bankers, financiers, and holders of public offices (a small but economically important group); the artisans or craftsmen (mainly tailors, goldsmiths, blacksmiths, and shoemakers); and the poor and indigent, perhaps a minority. All of them were heavily taxed. Owning their synagogues and relatively free to practice their religion, the Jews had to live in separate quarters (*judarias*), segregated from the Christian areas by walls, fences, and gates which had to be closed at night. In fourteenth- and fifteenth-century Lisbon, three *judarias* existed within the town, covering a total area of 1.5 hectares or 1.4 per cent of the city area.

The Moors, originally a much larger minority, had gradually shrunk to a small group, because of continuous absorption into the Christian community and migration to Moslem countries. Their organization was like that of the Jews but in each town they lived outside the walls, in their *mourarias*. Unlike the Jews, most Moors were peasants or poor artisans, owning their own small farms or serving their Christian masters. A great number inhabited lower Estremadura, around Lisbon, where their presence survived in the place names and in a tradition of skilled herb-garden and orchard farming. Others lived in Alentejo and, of course, in the Algarve.

An interesting feature of this epoch was the arrival of the first Gypsies. Coming from India, they gradually reached the most extreme points of Europe. After crossing Castile, some groups arrived in Portugal by the second half of the fifteenth century. Their nomadic way of living and their skill in all kinds of irregularities (stealing, cheating, witchcraft, fortune-telling) led to an official prohibition against their entry (in 1526, and often renewed), which of course never produced the desired results.

The two main characteristics of Portuguese agriculture in the period from 1450 to 1550 were probably the resumption of land reclamation and the introduction of new cultures, particularly maize. Detailed analyses of the new clearings, so similar to the great expansion of the twelfth and thirteenth centuries, are practically unavailable. However, a close look at late medieval documents, preserved in the archives, shows unmistakably the new trend in agriculture. All over the country, but mostly along the river valleys and on the plains, unused lands were converted into cultivated fields: woods and thickets were burned down and ploughed over, swamps were dried out, and pastures were used for agriculture. Yet it seems probable that few efforts ever passed beyond the limits already reached two or three hundred years before. In studying this late medieval and early modern trend, one is often puzzled when checking place names and trying to analyze "new" settlements by the problem of correct dating, as many of the newly reclaimed areas had been used before and later abandoned.

Legislation provided the framework for well-organized land reclamation. Old and modern laws were accepted, when useful. In
cortes, the representatives of the people often asked for a certain
number of privileges for those who took good care of their lands.
Draft exemption was generally a coveted privilege. The *cortes* also
protested against extension of the seignorial game preserves and succeeded in reducing their areas for agricultural purposes. A good example of some important land reclamation was that of the lower Mondego basin, under the supervision of the Coimbra Cathedral and the
monastery of Santa Cruz, the two largest landowners in that region.
From about 1480 on, more than 10,000 hectares were converted into
arable lands, vineyards, olive groves, orchards, and the like.

In the twelfth and thirteenth centuries, most of the reclaimed
lands had been sown with wheat, rye, and other grain; in the fifteenth
and sixteenth centuries, with vineyards and olive trees, a typical late
medieval trend resulting from the higher profits wine and olive oil
brought to the farmer and the reduction in labor required. Hence
wine and oil production increased while grain output remained
stationary or even declined.

Among the new cultures introduced or extended during that
period, first place undoubtedly belonged to maize. Imported from
America by the Castilians in the late 1400's or early in the sixteenth
century, it was known in Portugal before 1525. Authors have disputed
its focus of irradiation, some ascribing it to the Mondego Valley,
some to the Minho region. In any case, maize quickly attracted Portuguese farmers, generally substituting for the existing millet and
often successfully supplanting wheat in its traditional areas.

The population of Portugal had increased while the areas devoted to wheat and other cereals had remained the same, or had even
declined for other cultures. The obvious result was the need for more
imports and therefore the development of the grain trade. Urbanism
further enhanced the problem of supply and required precise regulation and organization of the grain trade. Until the early sixteenth
century, permission to import grain and customs exemptions on it
had always been temporary, though increasingly frequent: from 1450
to 1500 * special licenses or privileges were granted to the Lisbon

* Specifically, in 1452–55, 1459–61, 1467–68, 1472–73, 1475–78, 1484–88, 1490–91,
and 1494–96.

area, Porto, and the Algarve (Lagos especially). Finally, under Manuel I, an exemption of the tithe on all the grain imported into Lisbon and Setúbal was decreed (1502), to last till the monarch's death (1521). After the great famine of 1521–22, however, his son John III made it permanent (1525) and extended it to the *sisa* (another duty) as well, thus making grain imports practically tax-free. Thus ended a long period of history in which the ideal of agrarian self-sufficiency, symbolized by the production of wheat, gave way to a new commercial era, based upon profitable trade and the consumption needs of the great urban centers.

A consequence in this epoch of the interest in agriculture and land reclamation was inevitably a decline in stockbreeding. Reduction in the number and size of pastures brought about a gradual decrease in the number of sheep and cattle, though this could be fully measured and realized only in the seventeenth and eighteenth centuries. Dairy production declined too, and its effects on the general nourishment still have to be properly analyzed.

There were no great changes in craft activities, which continued to play a minor role in coping with the country's needs. Except for some coarse textile industries (velvet was one exception) and some crafts related to agriculture and to immediate household purposes, only silver and goldsmithery acquired renown. Here and there, attempts to better the quality of national industries met with failure or succeeded only in a special way. Metallurgy possibly prospered, though the best weapons and armor came from abroad. The only important "industries" were shipbuilding and biscuit production, which employed vast numbers of workers and required large capital. Both belonged to the Crown. In shipbuilding the Portuguese were constant innovators; they made significant improvements and became famous for the unrivaled quality of their ships.

The expansion overseas brought a new and decisive element in late Medieval Portuguese trade, namely the introduction of a great variety of exotic, expensive merchandise, unheard of or scarcely existing in Portugal before. Such products as gold, sugar, spices, slaves, wood, ivory and dyestuffs started pouring into the country in greater and greater quantity from the mid-fifteenth century on. They not only became increasingly important in terms of demand and market needs but also superseded all the former exports in economic value. This tremendous change in the type of long-distance trade converted Portugal from a mere producer of raw materials and a very few industrial items to an intermediary between Europe and Africa (or the Atlantic Islands), and later Asia and America as well. This new position was to become a constant in Portugal's history down to the present, explaining what some have called her "parasitary" economic role, yet also providing one of her foremost contributions to the world's economy and progress.

Overseas products, however, did not immediately replace the wine, salt, and fruit which, up to the mid-1400's, composed the basic Portuguese exports. Actually, they never entirely replaced these basic products, although the profit derived from their trade rose to unsuspected levels and gradually placed the overseas products far ahead of any domestic merchandise. Not until the first quarter of the sixteenth century did the new trend come into full force. Even so, salt, wine, and fruit, along with cork, continued to be exported in significant amounts and to bring prosperity to a large number of landowners and traders. In fact, the epoch was one of general expansion for both kinds of commerce, something historians often forget or scarcely understand. Also the overseas trade belonged essentially to a circumscribed number of persons and initiatives: it mattered to the king, to a small group of powerful lords (lay and ecclesiastical alike) and to a few traders, most of them foreign or using foreign investments (see chapter 5). It hardly touched the great majority of people and the long-established trade network based upon the products of the soil.

Imports consisted mainly of textiles, grain, and industrial products, including a great quantity of metal items (copper, tin, etc.), fundamental for the trade with Africa. The metropolitan towns where brokers existed by the end of the fifteenth century and which consequently could be considered the main centers of the Portuguese foreign trade were Lisbon, Porto, Elvas, Évora, Faro, Tavira, and Loulé. The North still played a minor international role compared to the Algarve (devoted to fruit export and trade with Africa, although Lagos was no longer pre-eminent), the Alentejo (important in its relations with Castile), and, of course, Lisbon. No essential changes had occurred in the European areas with which Portugal traded. Wheat came more and more from the Baltic world (through the Hansa, especially Danzig), but also from France (brought by Breton ships), Castile, England, and Sicily. Morocco's role consisted mainly in supplying grain to the Portuguese towns and garrisons there. From Castile, imports arrived either by sea (from Cadiz and other Andalucian ports to the Algarve and Lisbon) or by land (from Andalucia and Extremadura to Alentejo). Textiles and other industrial products were sent from Flanders, England, Germany, and Italy and from Castile and Aragon too.

As for exports, salt (along with cork, wine, and other items) was shipped to the Hanseatic world; wine and fruit to the Low Countries, England, and France. Agents for the Portuguese foreign trade were the trade ports (*feitorias*), in connection with the colonies of residents abroad. The most famous and important of all the Portuguese trade ports, dating from the fourteenth century (see chapter 2), was the one in Flanders, set up first in Bruges and later (in 1488–98) moved to Antwerp when Bruges ceased to be the leading commercial center of Europe. Originally based upon such products as fruit, wine, cork, and hides, the trade port quickly heralded the new possibilities Portugal was offering because of her overseas expansion. Sugar from Madeira and dragon's blood were already playing a significant role by the 1460's. Early in the sixteenth century, the bulk of the trade-port business consisted of spices brought from Africa and India (see chapter 5). The "factor" or trade-port manager, a civil servant appointed and paid by the king, acted as a sort of modern consul, representing the commercial interests of his country but especially of his monarch. By the mid-fifteenth century, the Portuguese factor in Bruges was kept active buying weapons and ammunition, copper, and all kinds of jewelry and clothing for the royal family. Other purchases included furniture, parchment, textiles, and books. Nevertheless, it is interesting to note that most of the textiles imported by the Portuguese from Flanders did not depend upon the Bruges factor but rather upon the private initiatives of Flemish (with other foreign) and Portuguese traders.

Several trade ports were founded in the late 1400's and during the first half of the sixteenth century: in Andalucia, by the 1460's, the Portuguese Crown held a *feitor* who lived in Seville, though the real organization of a trade port there apparently did not take place before 1508. Its factor dwelt either in Malaga or in Cadiz and his main function was to purchase and forward grain for the supply of the Portuguese towns in Morocco. In England and in Venice other trade ports served a similar purpose. They placed the overseas products in the international market and they bought industrial items along with metal both for local Portuguese consumption and for trading in Africa and Asia.

A great number of Portuguese lived abroad permanently, in numerous colonies of residents engaged in trading activities. The greatest concentration was in Bruges, later Antwerp: some thirty families by the middle or end of the fifteenth century, a figure which gradually increased during subsequent decades, and particularly after 1526, when a great number of Jews migrated from Portugal and settled in Antwerp. Besides the Low Countries, there were Portuguese residents in Castile (mostly in Seville); in England (London, Bristol, Southampton); in France, and in Italy (Genoa, Florence, Venice). Foreign factors and subjects living in Portugal—especially in Lisbon but also in the Algarve and in Porto—came from the above-mentioned countries and also from Germany, where few Portuguese ever went. Besides their commercial ties and framework, many of them were organized in religious associations—those of the Flemish or Burgundian subjects, of the English, of the Germans, and so on. Still more numerous were Italians from Genoa, Venice, Florence, and Piacenza; French; Castilians; Aragonese; and Basques.

In the internal trade, medieval principles and ways of exchange were not yet decisively modified, although the trend toward a national market was helped by a stronger monarchy and a more precise customs system. All along the border, a line of customs cities—called "dry ports" (*portos secos*) as opposed to the maritime "wet" ports— gradually emerged, closing the country and helping to form a national economy. In the early sixteenth century, those "ports" were, from North to South, Bragança, Miranda, Freixo, Almeida, Sabugal, Arronches, Elvas, Olivença, Marvão, and Mourão.

The importance of the fairs for internal trade slowly began to wane, but they still played a major role during the first half of the sixteenth century. A few were created in the late 1400's, such as those of Sintra (1460) and Estremoz (1463), while some others were restored. Urban concentration, however, made the local fairs obsolete. At the same time, the development of overseas trade helped concentrate most of the large commerce in the maritime ports, especially in Lisbon. Local markets, consequently, tended to expand. In every town, the number of shops, their concentration and specialization, rose and became more complex. Royal and municipal regulations increased too, for the markets were rapidly becoming favorite sources of revenues for the king, the feudal lords, and the municipalities.

The obstacles that scores of different weights and measures posed to a national traffic had been felt before and forced the central government to encourage the adoption of a common pattern for the whole kingdom. Those efforts failed in the mid-fourteenth century and would fail again and again almost to the present time. Yet some goals were achieved, namely the reduction of weights and measures to a smaller number and the enforcement of a unique standard in certain cases. Both Afonso V (1438–81) and John II (1481–95) to a certain extent succeeded in introducing some order into the confusing system of Portuguese weights and measures, by imposing the standards of only three cities—Santarém, Porto, and Lisbon—on the entire kingdom. But it was under Manuel I (1495–1521) that a more precise and thorough reform was passed: after 1499 the central government decided that all the measures and weights should follow the copper patterns expressly made for the purpose and kept in the capital's city hall. Variety would only be permitted in the very small weights and measures. The new legislative code known as *Ordenações Manuelinas* (first published in 1512) included the reform principles so typical of the Renaissance trend toward centralization.

From a monetary point of view, the epoch 1450–1550 can be roughly divided in two great periods, separated by the reform of 1489. During the first one, the silver and bullion debasement never ceased, a consequence of the lack of silver in Portugal, as in all of Europe. One mark (230 g) of minted silver rose from 800 reais in 1436, to 960 (1441), 1,050 (1445), 1,100 (1451), 1,500 (1460), 1,896 (1472), and 2,280 (1489), a debasement of 185 per cent. Currency reforms (in 1435, 1457, 1472 and 1485), all trying to establish good silver coins, failed, always for the same reasons: lack of the white metal, continuous flow of the silver coins out of the country, hoarding by individuals. However, the discovery after 1450 of new technological processes in extracting silver led to the end of the shortage: from Central Europe, the silver output began its steady increase. All the European currencies were influenced by the change and general stabilization was gradually achieved. The reform of 1489 could thus succeed, and the new silver coins, the vintém (= 20 reais) and later the tostão (from the French teston = 100 reais), generally kept their value for quite a long time.

Gold started to be plentiful as soon as the Portuguese directly controlled its African sources. In 1457, when preparing his great crusade (which would never take place), King Afonso V minted his famous cruzado, a coin of almost pure gold which was destined for more than eighty years of stability followed by a minor debasement only. The cruzado, a symbol of the gold flow to Portugal and Europe during the late fifteenth and early sixteenth century, meant another significant change: the Portuguese gold system, till then still based upon the Moslem-Castilian dobla, began following the Italian pattern of the florin-ducate, a clear symptom of a new economic epoch.

This combined flow of gold and silver explains the remarkably stable period 1489–1539, the real beginning of a new era in the history of Portuguese currency. The value of one mark of minted silver did not suffer great changes: around 2,300 reais in the early 1490's, 2,400 in 1517, 2,500 in 1539—a change of less than 9 per cent, compared with 185 per cent in the preceding fifty-year period. Late in the fifteenth century, Manuel I ordered the fabulous gold portugueses to be minted, $2\frac{1}{4}''$ in diameter and 35 g heavy pure gold coins, equal to ten cruzados; some years later, the silver portugueses or escudos displayed the same wealth: equal to 400 reais, they weighed 39.7 g and were 2'' large. Good propaganda weapons, these coins, along with others, successfully heralded the assumed power and wealth of the Portuguese monarchs, especially in Asia.

As for public finance during the Renaissance period, all over Europe a clear distinction between king and state permitted a greater refinement in the organization of public services, of which finance was probably the most important. In Portugal, the late fifteenth and early sixteenth century saw a significant number of financial reforms. They all tended to improve the existing structures and to provide the state with larger revenues, while attempting to simplify the complex network of local taxes which harassed both internal and external trade. From 1472 on, a general revision of the *forais* (burgh-charters) was undertaken, first as a response to several municipal complaints against exaggerated and illegal taxation, then as a royal attempt to standardize the multiple forms and kinds of local revenues. Effective reform started only under Manuel I, covering approximately the years 1497 to 1520: the new *forais* were now practically restricted to lists of taxes to be paid to the king or the feudal lords in each municipality. Furthermore taxes were rendered more or less uniform, which incidentally reduced the historical interest of the charters for the study of common law and local life. Such a reform, of course, would have been inefficient without the corresponding change in weights and measures previously mentioned.

Equally important for the internal and external trade was the new regulation on the *sisas* (transfer taxes), enacted in 1476, and amended in 1489, 1509, and later. The *Ordenações,* reformed under Manuel I, also included significant changes concerning the payment of land taxes, in an effort at greater standardization and revenue collection. The customs were also reorganized, particularly as they affected overseas revenues (see chapter 5). The abundance of public quittances from the late 1400's clearly shows that an effort was being made for systematic, efficient, and direct control of public finance.

To embody many of the new laws and make them well-known throughout the country, two codes of legislation appeared and were printed: the *Regimentos e Ordenações da Fazenda* ("Regulations and Ordinances of the Treasury") in 1516, along with the *Regimento dos Contadores das Comarcas* ("Regulation for the District Controllers") in 1514. These set the pattern for the mainland. Another innovation, the budget, appeared now and then, after being carefully organized. The first appearance dates from 1473. Public revenues amounted to 47 million reais (about 145,000 gold cruzados) while public expenditure was kept down to 37.6 million reais (some 115,600 cruzados). Overseas revenues were not included here. The huge expenditures for the external policy and armament (wars in Castile and Morocco), the increasing cost of weddings in the royal family and endowments to the nobility (in 1478, for instance, 81 per cent of all the public money went to the royal family and to yearly allowances to vassals), along with the new costs of administration, quickly changed that surplus into an almost permanent deficit. If the commercial and agrarian expansion as well as the population increase and better administration after 1481 substantially increased the public revenues (still 132,000 cruzados in 1477, but 197,000 in 1506, 285,000 in 1518–19, 320,000 in 1526, 388,000 in 1534, and 607,000 in 1557), expenditures went up too but more rapidly. In 1477 the Crown spent 144,000 cruzados, a deficit of 12,000. For the first half of the sixteenth century we lack precise figures, yet the increase in the loans and the public debt (both funded and unfunded) give enough evidence of the treasury's problems. The *cortes* voted several subsidies (called *pedidos,* "demands") to help the Crown finance a number of extraordinary expenditures: 60 million reais for defense in 1478 (more than all the public revenues); 50 million reais for debts from defense in 1483; 20 million for fortification works in North Africa in 1502; 150,000 cruzados in 1525; 100,000 cruzados in 1535; 200,000 in 1544 and so on. In 1500, government bonds (*padrões de juro*) were first issued. A second issue followed in 1528, a third in 1530, and so forth: up to 1554, eight issues in all. Interest dropped from an initial 7 per cent to 6.25 per cent in 1528. Unfunded debt may be said to have started by 1522, in the form of loans incurred by bills of exchange on Antwerp or the Medina del Campo fairs—interest remained at a 20 per cent level until 1544, then rose to 25 per cent. The amount of the funded debt had reached 1,620,500 cruzados in 1534; 1,881,720 in 1557. In the same years, the value of the unfunded debt was 400,000 and almost 2,000,000 cruzados. All these figures give a clear picture of the economic and financial expansion of sixteenth-century Portugal, which can be understood only in an international and imperial context (see chapter 5).

It is well known that the sixteenth and part of the seventeenth century witnessed general European price and salary increases. Rates of increases, however, were greatly dependent upon national and local circumstances. Roughly, one can say that before the 1530's, price increases were moderate to minimal, with no essential changes from the general trend observed after 1475. The great "price revolution" generally took place in the second half of the sixteenth century. Causes for the rise were, among others, the larger amount of gold and silver in circulation, growth of demand (a result of the population increase), war, the geographic expansion, and the creation of new markets. Salaries, however, did not keep pace with the price curve, often tending toward a real decrease.

In Portugal, the few data available at present seem to show an increase in agricultural prices after 1470–80, as all over Europe: in silver grams, wheat prices went up from an average of 1.8 to an average of 2.7 in 1497–1504. This latter figure did not change greatly up to the 1530's, at least on the mainland (the situation in the Azores or Madeira islands was different). From then on, to the middle of the century, wheat prices went up from an average of 30 reais per bushel to double that figure. The same happened with the prices of wine and olive oil.

Thus, in spite of the tremendous flow of gold from Africa in the late fifteenth and sixteenth century (see chapter 5), no "price revolution" took place in Portugal then, a clear sign that most of the gold was rapidly exported abroad and produced a minor impact on the country's internal economy.

As we have seen before (chapter 2), land concentration in the hands of a few characterized the second half of the fourteenth and most of the fifteenth century. Neither John I nor his two immediate successors were able to curb the rising power of a new landed aristocracy, even if they succeeded in forcing quite a number of estates to revert to the Crown. Afonso V's irresponsibility and weakness made him easy prey for the ambitions of the nobles. During his thirty-year personal rule the amount of royal land and royal jurisdiction given away in a feudal form rose to proportions unheard of. A schematic map of seignorial Portugal clearly shows that by the 1470's the royal patrimony was practically reduced to Estremadura and the Algarve with some minor "islands" elsewhere. On behalf of Afonso V one can argue that no different situation had really existed in the thirteenth and fourteenth centuries. The difference, however, lay in the dangerous concentration of land and jurisdiction in a small number of families, in opposition to the earlier feudal mosaic. Furthermore, and following the general European trend, a landslide of new titles (dukes, marquesses, viscounts, barons) revealed the royal preferences and favorites, often promoting obscure noblemen to foremost dignitaries. Under Duarte (1433–38), there were in Portugal only two dukes and six counts; at the death of Afonso V (1481), there were four dukes, three marquesses, twenty-five counts, one viscount, and one baron, thirty-four in all, and an increase in similar proportion in land revenues and privileges. Afonso's son John II was perfectly right in saying that his father had left him king of the roads of Portugal. Land and titles were distributed to no more than fifteen large families or lineages, of which the most powerful were the Braganças (twelve titles: namely two duchies, three marquisates and seven counties), the Meneses (five earldoms), the Coutinhos and the Melos (two earldoms each). Besides these families there was the king's brother, Fernando (died 1470), assumed to be the richest man in Portugal, who accumulated two duchies, the mastership of two religious orders, and numerous other lordships. His patrimony was transmitted to his son Diogo.

To this upper nobility (some five hundred people), a sort of "upper-middle nobility," composed of members of other distinguished lineages, should be added. They were all called royal vassals —vassalos do rei—and, as such, they were given by the Crown a yearly fixed revenue (contia) with no relation whatsoever to their patrimony. The payment of that sum generally assumed the form of a land-grant, and the more vassals the king had the less rent the Crown collected. Moreover, the nobles of contia received a wedding subsidy, which was changed, when the royal treasury was short of funds, into a yearly allowance (tença). This gradually tended to become a fixed and hereditary contribution, heavily weighing on the budget. Other tenças, for no reason whatsoever but royal favoritism, were added to the roll year after year. For his part the vassal always had to be ready to help his king with a fixed number of "lances," a military term which meant both riders and footmen in full armor. In the late fifteenth century the total number of vassals obliged to own a horse and weapons was fixed at the ideal figure of 2,000, i.e., some 6,000–8,000 people, including women and children. Below these, another 2,000 owned weapons although not entitled to any

Crown revenues. This group formed a sort of transition between the upper-middle aristocracy and the lower strata of the gentry (*fidalgos*); they were more numerous, less wealthy in estates, less important in the holding of top administrative and military offices, but more stable in their local influence and in maintaining the economic and social structures. The words *cavaleiro* (knight), *escudeiro* (esquire), or simply *fidalgo* (gentleman) encompassed all those people, including the upper-middle vassals but excluding the upper titled nobility. They seem to correspond to general categories only. *Vassalo,* also, could be applied to lower groups within the aristocracy.

If John II (1481–95) succeeded in crushing the power of some of the most important noble families—namely the Braganças and his cousin Diogo—and in substantially enlarging the royal patrimony at their expense, his successors, Manuel I (1495–1521) and John III (1521–57), were forced to step back and restore most of the confiscations to their former owners. However—and such was actually John II's main purpose—the nobility of the early sixteenth century, if undiminished in privileges and revenues, showed a completely different face, more in agreement with the policy of royal centralization. First, they accepted their subordination to the king and his new absolutist state (the *corregedores,* for instance, were no longer resisted when entering the noble estates); second, to subsist they became more and more dependent on royal appointments and temporary subsidies. As a consequence a large part of the nobility (particularly the highest ranks) migrated from their estates and local courts to the king's court and residence. The monarch himself encouraged such a tendency by granting a *moradia* (another yearly allowance) to all the nobles who, at least theoretically, lived in his court. The number of such subsidies increased from 1,092 under Afonso V to 2,493 under John III (mid-sixteenth century), though with considerably lower levels in between.

Thus, a new court nobility appeared in this period, from which the government regularly chose its foremost home and overseas officers, for diplomacy, army, navy, discovery, and colonization. At the same time, the great majority of the nobles indulged in commercial undertakings of all kinds, competing with the rising bourgeoisie and preventing its full development. Following the example of the king, himself a merchant and a monopoly-owner (see chapter 5), the nobles did not disdain to invest their revenues in transport and economic exploitation. It is true that in most cases they re-invested their profits in land or in nonprofitable activities (buildings, luxury consumption, and so on) instead of becoming true businessmen. Unlike Italy, where the bourgeois rose to nobility, in Portugal it was the nobleman who "climbed down" and took over trade as a means of enriching his household.

The structure of the clergy was less affected during this period, and no important changes took place before the Catholic Reformation of the mid- and late sixteenth century. From a political and economic point of view, the union of the religious-military orders to the Crown was perhaps the only significant fact. Prior to this achievement there had been cases from the fourteenth century onward (see chapter 2) when the mastership of a military order was entrusted to a member of the royal family. Then, between 1418 and 1434, the three foremost masterships—Santiago, Avis, and Christ—passed to the permanent control of secular princes, all of royal lineage. The vast revenues of the orders became a convenient appanage for the heirs to the throne or the members of the royal family, almost always simple teenagers. John II, when he succeeded his father (1481), united the two masterships of Santiago and Avis to the Crown, but he soon gave them up again on behalf of his son Afonso, actually against the advise of the *cortes*. In 1495, ascending to the throne, Manuel I definitely united the mastership of Christ to the Crown. Later, on the death of Prince Jorge (1550), the Pope sanctioned the permanent union of Santiago and Avis to the state patrimony under the fiction of appointing the King of Portugal as their governor. For the first time in Portuguese history, the royal patrimony covered more than half of the country and surpassed, both in extent and revenues, any other. This nationalization of the military orders was accompanied by their secularization: authorized to marry and to own private property, the knights ceased to be churchmen, and knighthood became a simple mark of distinction, a title of honor, a decoration which was greedily coveted by the nobles and only by them.

Although not all the archbishops and bishops belonged to the nobility, the great majority did. Actually, there was a sort of hierarchy in the Portuguese dioceses, the prelates being often "promoted" to a wealthier and more "civilized" bishopric whenever an opening was available and their prestige or royal protection shoved them up. Bishops of a lower social origin were more likely to be found in the least prized dioceses, such as Silves, Guarda, or Lamego. The most coveted ones seemed to be Lisbon and Braga, the two archbishoprics. Several archbishops had been made cardinals in the 1400's; later, and as another example of centralization, royal princes succeeded in almost monopolizing the cardinalship. Thus, Afonso (1509–40), son of Manuel I, became cardinal at the age of eight; his brother Henry (1512–80), the future king, was also appointed cardinal, though at the more reasonable age of thirty-three.

Accumulation of high ecclesiastical dignities, a real plague of fifteenth- and early sixteenth-century Europe, was practically unknown in Portugal before the 1480's: Jorge da Costa, a favorite of King Afonso V whom his son did not dare to touch, was the only scandalous example at this time for he held together the archbishopric of Lisbon with the archbishopric of Braga and the two bishoprics of Évora and Silves, though for a short eight-year period only. Later on, this became somewhat common practice but exclusively within the royal family, bishoprics and archbishoprics being disposed of as true appanages: Afonso, the above-mentioned cardinal, held together Évora, Guarda, Viseu, and Lisbon; Henry kept for himself successively Braga, Évora, and Lisbon. Less important, though affluent, posts were more easily accumulated, such as abbotships, priorates, deaneries, chanter dignities, and many others. We still lack a complete and comprehensive catalogue, which might convey a clear picture of the social and economic role played by Church dignitaries along with the nobility and the royal family.

Most of the monastic orders declined during this period, both in revenues and in increasing relaxation of customs. Only the very wealthy monasteries, such as Alcobaça and Santa Cruz de Coimbra, were able to retain their ancient prestige and popular influence. The granting of commanderies (ecclesiastical benefices composed of Church rents belonging to a church or monastery)—rampant in the late 1400's and early 1500's though with a long tradition—became a favorite way for both the king and the upper clergy to reward services or endow protégés. Thus, a large share of church revenues fell into the hands of Papal, royal, and episcopal clients, a source of luxurious maintenance for the nobility and the top prelates.

Attempts to reform these abuses failed, and a revival of monastic discipline and religious purity was evidenced instead by the creation of new institutes which quickly became favorites among the nobility and the people: the Yeronimites (*jerónimos*), of Italian origin, introduced in Portugal by the early 1400's but blossoming only in the late fifteenth century; the secular canons of St. Salvador de Vilar or the canons of St. John the Evangelist (popularly called *loios*), of Portuguese origin, in the 1400's; the Capuchins, coming from Castile in the late fifteenth century; the Arrábidos, founded by the Duke of Aveiro in 1539; and finally the Jesuits, whose first members arrived in 1540 but whose overwhelming influence was felt only in the second half of the century (see chapter 6).

By the late Middle Ages, the traditional tripartite division of society into clergy, nobility, and people was breaking down and being replaced by a manifold and much more fluid classification. Class transitions assumed a less rigid character, and important subdivisions in each of those three orders started playing a greater social role. Major changes had taken place within the people division, where at least four major categories existed in the late 1400's and early 1500's: the legists, the citizens, the artisans, and all the others.

The legists, aiming at nobility privileges and partly obtaining them, had risen in number as well as in importance. They formed a skilled class of civil servants, magistrates, lawyers and legal advisers, university professors, and the like. Physicians and pharmacists were on the verge of entering this upper group of people. Most of them depended upon salaries paid by the Crown, though still largely benefiting from contributions and services granted by the population, in the form of lodging, nourishment, and so on. The Crown also supervised their qualifications, controlled the exercise of their profession, appointed them for the available jobs or simply nominated them, and so forth. They secured important privileges, such as carrying weapons or riding on horseback and being exempt from general taxation and rough punishment. Indispensable in the rising complexity of public affairs, learned or posing as such, investing their profits in land and in trade, they gradually became as significant as the nobility or the clergy, and as respected. They often married or married their children within the aristocracy. Some were made nobles or even granted titles, such as João Fernandes da Silveira, a royal counselor, scribe, and chancellor who became the first baron of Alvito, in 1475. It has to be remembered that a great number, if not the majority, of bureaucrats belonged to the ecclesiastical status (minor or major orders), enjoying Church privileges and prestige.

The citizens, also called eldermen, honorable people, or "clean" people (*gente limpa*)—because they did no work with their hands—formed a class of landowners and long-distance traders who also invested a part of their profits in land. They controlled the overwhelming majority of the municipal offices, held seats in the *cortes,* and were the only ones listened to by the monarch and the bureaucrats when they complained. The word "bourgeoisie" could also be used when referring to them. Whereas their economic and political strength increased within the country, their share in the external and overseas trade seems to have declined, while that of the foreigners, the Crown, the royal family, the nobility, and the bureaucrats rose. Apparently they were more concerned with land and with investing their profits in its purchase than in actively competing in commercial enterprises.

The whole fifteenth century was a period of struggle between the citizens and the lower class of artisans. If neither obtained a complete victory, it is safe to say that the citizens held on to their positions much better and even got back some of the gains the artisans had secured in the late 1300's. For the artisans, on the contrary, this epoch brought about stagnation and defeat. Their few important privileges of being represented and holding a vote in the municipal assemblies of several cities were gradually lost during the fifteenth century. Only in Lisbon did they manage to retain their conquests, though with reduced strength. John II confirmed their almost total subordination to the citizens in local administration. Manuel I and John III achieved their leveling down and general organization within the narrow framework of the corporative system.

As in Castile, the corporations did not arise in Portugal before the late 1400's, and more as a result of royal imposition and organizaing policy in agreement with the citizens than as a need for common protection and defense against competition. Yet it would be contrary to the facts to assert that the artisans did not benefit from the system or were forced into it. A long tradition of unwritten customs and religious association in brotherhoods had prepared the artisans for the acceptance of permanent regulations. The breakdown of their political power, along with the centralizing spirit of the century, made them ready for stricter royal control and for other class tutelage. In 1487 the king ordered each craft to accept two representatives or deputies (*vedores*) as judges in economic and professional matters. They were to be appointed by the municipalities. This practice had already been followed by some crafts in some towns. Two years later the first craft regulation (*regimento*) was approved for the shoemakers and tanners of Lisbon, containing some relevant rules on working conditions, prices, and hiring of labor. It was quickly followed by many other regulations, which by the early sixteenth century covered almost all artisans in the most important urban centers. In 1539 most crafts in Lisbon were organized into fourteen corporations (*ofícios*), each one assembling a major and leading profession with several others attached to it: barbers and armorers with twenty-eight others; book-sellers and pharmacists with ten others; shoemakers (+3); saddlers (+2); linen weavers (+3); candlers; masons and carpenters (+3); shearers (+1); tailors (+3); coopers; rope-makers (+1); silversmiths (+1); goldsmiths (+4); and potters (+2). Each corporation had its own banner and its saint-protector.

Compulsory *vedores* and generalized *regimentos* had been preceded by the official constitution of professional assemblies of twenty-four or twelve members, which both the king and the municipalities recognized as representing the existing craftsmen. Starting in Lisbon late in the fourteenth century, these assemblies or councils spread to other towns, such as Santarém, Évora, Coimbra, Porto, Guimarães, and Tavira during the 1400's and early 1500's. Although they held some effective political power for a short time, electing their representatives to the municipal councils and intervening in the latter's deliberations, they soon lost it completely. Lisbon was the sole exception, and incurred the anger of the *cortes* (where popular representation was restricted to the landowners and merchants); in 1481–82 the *cortes* bitterly complained of such a "scandal."

Below the artisans there was the vast world of those who owned nothing and who worked for others, as laborers in the fields or hired workers in the towns: the servants, the many salesmen and saleswomen, laundresses, and the like. Their situation hardly changed during this period.

Finally, the growing importation of slaves introduced a new class of people to whom all rights were denied. Young slaves were sold with their mothers but other family ties were hardly kept. The masters, however, had no right to kill their slaves and, in general, slaves seem to have been well treated. Conversion to Christianity might help but not necessarily account for enfranchisement. Freed slaves, moreover, were kept as clients of sorts, utterly dependent on their former masters or on new ones.

For general administrative and judicial purposes, the kingdom of Portugal was divided into six provinces, also called *comarcas:* from north to south, these were Entre-Douro-e-Minho, Trás-os-Montes, Beira, Estremadura, Entre-Tejo-e-Odiana (also called Alentejo), and the Algarve. As the latter held the status of kingdom itself (going back to the thirteenth-century conquest for one of the Moorish *taifas),* the Portuguese monarch entitled himself "king of Portugal and Algarve." The origins of this division could be traced back to a distant past. Yet it was only during the fifteenth century that it became official and permanent, enduring until the great administrative reforms of the nineteenth century. Gradually replacing the complex feudal-military partition into *terras* or *alcaidarias,* coupled with the municipal units, it asserted the new trend toward centralization, standardization, and royal interference. In each of those large *comarcas,* the king was represented by a *corregedor,* whose powers in the judicial and administrative fields never ceased to develop.

Besides the division into *comarcas,* the realm was divided for financial purposes into *almoxarifados,* each one under the authority of an *almoxarife,* who collected the Crown revenues in his district. In the late 1400's and early 1500's the *almoxarifados* numbered 26 or 27: 3 in Entre-Douro-e-Minho, 2 in Trás-os-Montes, 5 in Beira, 7 in Estremadura, 5 in Alentejo, and 4 or 5 in the Algarve. Population growth led to the creation of new units in the mid-sixteenth century— 1, 1, 2, 1 (but another one was suppressed), 2, and 0, respectively—a clear symptom of the greater weight the North was assuming; there were four new districts in the North, only two in the South, with the total number up to 32 or 33.

A third major division concerned mainly the Church, but was often used for civil purposes too. Portugal encompassed nine bishoprics, with no change since the Reconquista. They were Braga, Porto, Lamego, Viseu, Coimbra, Guarda, Lisboa, Évora, and Silves. This ecclesiastical partition no longer corresponded to the social realities of the country. Yet it took a long time to replace it with a new one, better adjusted to sixteenth-century Portugal but still very imperfect: new bishoprics were created in 1545 (Miranda do Douro and Leiria), 1549 (Portalegre), and 1570 (Elvas).

Reforms in government and administration of justice, if not so conspicuous or revolutionary as in many other fields, nonetheless gave clear proof of the new trends in ruling the country. To start with, a reformed code of laws made its appearance (1512–21): the so-called *Ordenações Manuelinas*. It amended and suppressed many of the laws compiled in the *Ordenações Afonsinas,* while introducing the new legislation enacted in the reigns of Afonso V, John II, and Manuel I. Yet, the *Manuelinas* brought something different in the form of writing and publishing the laws: instead of ascribing each one to its author, as traditionally happened, it related most acts to Manuel, as if they were new laws. Hence the *Manuelinas* present the character of a modern code, not a mere compilation of ancient laws.

While not bringing about any essential changes, the *Ordenações Manuelinas* did discriminate and specify both functions and organs in public justice. Inevitably, major innovations were introduced in proceedings. Within the two main courts (Casa do Cível and Casa da Justiça da Corte or Casa da Suplicação), the tendency was for a greater centralization under a stricter control by magistrates closer to the monarch. A new court created by John II, called Mesa or Tribunal do Desembargo do Paço, took special care of petitions for pardon, privileges, freedoms, and legislations. Typical of the Renaissance state, this tribunal offered a good example of an organ for central administration with competency in both judicial and administrative matters. A second new court was the Mesa da Consciência e Ordens (Conscience and Orders Board), instituted in 1532. Its officials

—called ministers or deputies—were both ecclesiastical and lay, though the former predominated. Supposed to function as a sort of moral and religious body to advise the king on all the matters related to his "conscience," this new tribunal quickly became a subtle means of royal interference in ecclesiastical matters, highly disliked and criticized by most clergymen. The king gave it full powers of decision in certain affairs and placed the religious-military orders (which depended upon the Crown) under its supervision. A third court was the Holy Office of the Inquisition, a successful attempt at royal interference in the people's consciences. It will be dealt with later in this chapter.

Local justice was also made more precise by the legislation of the late fifteenth and early sixteenth century. Legal proceedings suffered several changes all aiming at a greater efficiency but also requiring a larger bureaucracy. The number of *juizes de fora* ("judges from the outside"), appointed by the king, increased by about 50 per cent between 1481 and 1521 (also an evidence of the population growth), and their powers were enhanced. In each province, the greater authority assumed by the *corregedores* (particularly after the 1524 *Regimento dos Corregedores*) and their interference in all kinds of deeds, with little respect for the local elected judges, provoked vain protests and clearly meant that new times had come. After 1538, most of the judges began to be paid by the public treasury instead of receiving free lodging and nourishment from the people as before, a permanent source of abuses and complaints.

In government, the rising complexity and number of public affairs led to the creation of a true cabinet composed of six ministers or secretaries: the great chancellor (*chanceler-mor*), in charge of the royal chancellary; the private scribe (*escrivão da puridade*), more intimately related to the king and his decisions; the king's secretary (*secretário d'el-rei*), still closer to the monarch and following him everywhere; the two *corregedores da corte,* resembling attorneys-general or secretaries of justice (one for civil, the other for criminal matters); and the *meirinho mor,* in charge of arresting nobles and controlling the administration of justice in the seignorial lands. Besides these people, the king was still assisted by several other secretaries and a twenty-seven-member council of state, whose functions were mostly honorary, but within which a smaller nine-councillor group was periodically chosen to help the monarch whenever necessary. It is interesting to note that no particular "minister" seems to have ever risen to the prominence of a prime minister, although each king inevitably had his favorites whom he might entrust with the real task of governing.

Around the king and for his special protection, a new organ appeared late in the fifteenth century: the royal guard, formed by more than a hundred men, picked at random from the ranks of nobility or villeiny, chosen for their boldness and bravery rather than for their social condition. It was later subdivided into three smaller specialized bodies.

King Manuel created the first postal system of Portugal (before 1520), an innovation already introduced in France in the reign of Louis XI.

If centralization and enforcement of royal authority hovered over the general government and administration, it is easy to realize that the role played by the *cortes* tended to become less and less relevant. Indeed, if Afonso V still had often to yield to the people's demands and was forced to convene the *cortes* year after year (mostly because he constantly needed money), a completely different situation emerged after his death in 1481. From 1434 to 1481, the *cortes* had assembled every 1.5 to 2 years on the average; from 1481 to 1502, this average went up to 3 years; but from 1502 on, to 1544, the *cortes* were summoned only three times. Gradually, the people gave up their right to control the government or even try to advise on its acts. Gradually, the king forgot the benefits of periodical dialogue with his people. Between the two, contacts ceased to be direct and tended to rely on a developing bureaucracy alone.

A further step in the trend toward centralization and improvement of public services was the decision to reform the hospital service. In Lisbon, the numerous small hospitals, shelters, and charity auberges, dependent upon private subsidies or "foundations," were suppressed (1492) and one large hospital erected in their place. Its organization followed the pattern set up by the Florentine and Sienese hospitals. All the existing funds and rents, plus a generous royal subsidy, became a part of the new hospital budget. Symbolically named All Saints Hospital (Hospital de Todos os Santos), for it assembled all the patron saints of the former hospitals, it provided better lodging and treatment, being supervised by officials appointed by the Crown.

Outside Lisbon, and also there, a new brotherhood of Nossa Senhora da Misericórdia (Our Lady of Mercy) was founded in 1498 under the patronage of queen-mother Leonor. Its purpose was to spread and organize charity all over the country, including an extensive hospital system. Private and royal donations rapidly increased the available funds and converted the *misericórdias* (as each local branch of the brotherhood was called) into a highly efficient and scattered charity network that still exists.

HUMANISM, RENAISSANCE, AND REFORMATION

Humanism in Portugal started later than in Castile but earlier than in many other European countries. Its origin was Italy, and extensive relationships with the Italian city-states, particularly in the economic field, accounted for its quick import and development. Genoese, Florentine, and other Italian merchants lived permanently in Lisbon. Everywhere in Italy, there were traders and emissaries from Portugal. They estimated the prospects of the Italian markets and interviewed Italian bankers and officials. Sometimes residing permanently in Florence, Genoa, and Venice, they served as diplomatic-commercial agents of the Portuguese monarchs and businessmen.

Besides strong economic ties, religious-cultural connections made Italy the country most frequently visited by Portuguese in the fifteenth century, perhaps more than Castile itself. The Pope lived in Italy, and the Papacy constantly required direct contacts with clergymen and bureaucrats from all over Europe. Moreover, the century was one of ecumenical councils where no Catholic country would be absent. Princes of the royal family with their companions traveled to Italy in order to acquire culture and familiarity with the center of Christendom. Pilgrimages to Rome and other Italian shrines (such as Padua, where St. António of Lisbon was buried) appealed to numerous people. The prestige of the Italian universities and professors attracted students to Bologna, Siena, Florence, Padua, and other famous centers. To Portugal came Italian teachers to tutor young noblemen and the king himself. They were welcomed, were well treated, and were given a high salary. Thus, cultural achievements and new currents of thought originating in Italy were sure to be rapidly known and introduced in Portugal. Yet fifteenth-century humanism never flourished in the Iberian Peninsula nor really anywhere outside Italy. It was too early for Gothic Europe to absorb entirely the values of a new epoch. More preparation, more subtle and indirect influences, were required. Fundamentally, circumstances had to change. This needed time.

Indirect influences arrived via France, the Low Countries, England, or Spain, where a good many Portuguese were studying in the mid- and late 1400's—in Paris, Louvain, Oxford, Salamanca, and other places. In Salamanca, some eight hundred students attended classes in the first half of the sixteenth century, mainly in Law and Canons. But it was in France, Paris rather than elsewhere, that the cream of Portuguese humanism was prepared.

Renewed interest in Antiquity appeared in Portugal before the middle of the fifteenth century. A better knowledge of classical Latin was behind translations into Portuguese by Prince Pedro and others of Cicero's *de Officiis, de Senectute,* and *de Amicitia,* and of Pliny the Younger's *Panegyricus Traiano.* In the 1430's and 1440's two Italian scholars arrived in Portugal, invited as masters of the young King Afonso V: Matteo Pisano, who wrote in Latin a *History of the Conquest of Ceuta,* and Stefano of Naples. Late in the same century, a famous Italian humanist, Cataldus Aquila Siculus, tutored Prince Jorge, an illegitimate offspring of John II, as well as several other young nobles. His influence was enormous in setting up new cultural bases and preparing a distinguished generation of Portuguese, who flourished by the time of Manuel I and John III. In the early 1500's prosperity at home and cosmopolitan fashions had led scores of young Portuguese to be educated in the main cultural centers of Europe. Most of them returned to their country and set their imprint on the cultural life of Portugal.

The great epoch of Portuguese humanism corresponded to the

ABOVE: *King Manuel I's third wedding, 1519: school of Cristóvão Lopes, first half 16th century, Museu de Arte Sacra, Lisbon.* UPPER RIGHT: *Religious procession in Lisbon, early 16th century: Anonymous, retable of Saint Auta, Museu Nacional de Arte Antiga, Lisbon.* BELOW: *Monastery of Jerónimos, at Belém (Lisbon), built early 16th century: 19th century engraving by H. Le Keux, London.*

period 1525–50. It can be analyzed according to three fundamental perspectives: the teaching, the literary production, and the international contacts.

Almost all the schools in the medium and upper levels experienced the humanist influence. In the University—first in Lisbon, then in Coimbra—in the many monastical and cathedral schools (Santa Cruz de Coimbra was the best example), in the newly founded colleges, in private tutoring, the number of foreign-trained instructors and the quality of their teaching entirely renovated subjects and programs. Greek and Hebrew appeared among the new subjects taught, while the teaching of Latin experienced the impact of a perfect knowledge of the classic rules and forms. Furthermore, a number of foreign scholars were invited by the king to occupy many of the teaching positions: Nicolas Cleynaerts (Clenardus), born in the Low Countries, and the Scottish George Buchanan were among the most celebrated.

In Paris, King Manuel had tried to buy one of its most famous schools, the Saint Barbara College (Collège de Sainte Barbe). Though negotiations failed, this college became primarily a school for Portuguese students in France, subsidized by their king, who granted it fifty scholarships (1527). In its rectorship, three learned Portuguese humanists of international reputation and belonging to the same family (the Gouveia family) succeeded each other, for thirty-seven years (1520–57): one of them, André de Gouveia, was called by Montaigne "the greatest Principal of France." His methods of teaching and school organization were revolutionary for the time, which explains the several invitations he received to create and reform colleges both in France and abroad. Owing to his efforts, the Collège de Guyenne at Bordeaux, to which he moved in 1534 and which he directed for thirteen years, became the best in France.

In the same epoch, several new colleges were being founded in Portugal. Some continued the old tradition of primarily providing a shelter to needy students or to members of the religious orders who wanted to attend classes within a framework of conventional reclusion. Others, however, a novelty for the time, were designed for young aristocrats or rich bourgeois, thus initiating the modern boarding school system. Most of them tried to copy up-to-date methods of organization and teaching, generally following French or Spanish models. In some—the so-called "major colleges"—courses of university, or even higher, level were offered. They provided a sort of postgraduate studies. Another novelty of most colleges—the so-called "minor colleges"—consisted in offering "secondary" studies, as a better preparation for the university. Humanities and mathematics, in a typical humanistic conception, were taught according to much better processes, and handbooks of international renown were used. This previously nonexistent preparation allowed a complete reorganization of the university system and a considerable raising of its scientific level. Instead of being just a high school for those who wanted to continue elementary studies, the university could now become the center for a greater specialization and learning.

In the 1530's and 1540's more than twenty colleges were created in the main cities of Portugal, but especially in Coimbra. One of the most interesting was that of Braga, founded by Clenardus. It did not last long, but the impact of its teaching and organization methods were to endure. Named Ludus ("the Game"), Clenardus's school sought to replace whipping by persuasion as a means of achieving good learning results. He also introduced new practices in the teaching of languages.

However, the most famous of all the humanistic colleges in Portugal was the Royal College (Colégio Real), also called College of Arts and Humanities (Colégio das Artes e Humanidades), founded and supported by the king in 1547. It followed French patterns, namely the celebrated Collège Royal, instituted in Paris by François I (1530) under Pierre de la Ramée's influence. For the Portuguese Royal College, King John III called André de Gouveia to Portugal and gave him full powers in scheduling the studies and hiring the teachers. Gouveia went back to France and organized a faculty of about ten French, Scottish, and Portuguese professors of grammar, rhetoric, poetry, Latin, Greek, Hebrew, logic, philosophy, and mathematics. With a few more who had already taught in Portugal, the College opened amid the best prospects and greatest praise in February 1548. It was officially connected with the University courses, several of which required compulsory attendance at those offered at the Royal College. Gouveia's sudden death, in June 1548, seriously jeopardized the role assigned to this important school and paved the way for a takeover by the Jesuits.

The reform of the University, permeable as it was to the new tendencies displayed by humanism, should not be envisioned as a typical humanist reform, directed and carried on by scholars, with pure intellectual purposes. Instead, it bore the imprint of the state and pertained to the great efforts of political centralization. As it was, the University of Lisbon, with its low scholastic level and its lack of discipline, showed by both teachers and students, challenged the undisputed authority of the king in his very capital, where quarrels and general restlessness were more likely to exist. The University had ancient privileges which no longer could be tolerated but which seemed hard to revoke. It was a corporative and elective body. It depended upon the Pope and the Church rather than upon the king and the state. A body of conscientious scholars, legists, and canonists, the University knew how to remind the monarch and his advisers of its privileges, and how to have them enforced. Furthermore, the University claimed a cultural "monopoly" in the country, though it seemed unable to keep up with the humanistic culture of its time. A stronghold of scholasticism and medieval prejudice, it reacted against any "modern" tendencies.

The first differences between the University and the royal authority began under Manuel I. As social and economic monographs are lacking for the 1480's and 1490's, we do not know what role its faculty played in the crucial political events of John II's reign and in the Jewish question. Under cover of granting a new building and raising faculty salaries, Manuel imposed on the University a new regulation (between 1499 and 1504), which considerably limited its traditional autonomy, while attempting to curb well-known irregularities. Little was achieved, however, both students and professors resisting or simply ignoring the royal determinations. By 1520, Manuel was seriously thinking of creating a second university in Évora, a possibility already envisioned in the mid-1400's. Lack of qualified personnel prevented him. More determined than his father and more culturally oriented too, John III undertook a complete cultural reform, with the final goal of getting rid of the University of Lisbon and founding a new and more docile school of high studies.

Actually, the teaching quality had sunk to its lowest level, doctoral degrees being sought by Portuguese graduates at Salamanca or somewhere else.

By the 1530's the number of "secondary" and "graduate" courses already offered in Coimbra (attached to the monastery of Santa Cruz and under its supervision) made it absurd not to have a real university in that city. After a long struggle for survival, even the University of Lisbon had to admit that its days were numbered: 1536–37 saw indeed the last school year. Although some of the teachers, the insignia, the archives, and many of the traditions and privileges of the old university were transferred to the new one, the University of Coimbra should be regarded as a new institution. As such, a new sanction by the Pope was thought necessary for the schools of Theology and Canons. Moreover, John did not feel obliged to give the Lisbon faculty automatic teaching assignments in Coimbra, which he reserved mostly for new members. The University of Lisbon had in fact been extinguished and would only be revived in 1911.

Changes in the program of studies affected the whole university structure. Although the five great themes—Theology, Canons, Law, Medicine, and Arts, along with Mathematics—were kept unaltered, the number of courses within each one was considerably increased, in some cases doubled, which meant a corresponding increase in teaching and preparation. The new university clearly copied the pattern of studies set up for Salamanca, from whence most of the new faculty came. Moreover, the new ordinances or bylaws granted to the University of Coimbra stressed its subordination to the royal authority and reduced its traditional relationship to the Pope and the Church. Instead of being a latent focus of political dissent or of ecclesiastical autonomy, the university became an instrument of the state's power. The Rector ceased to be elective and was appointed by the monarch. Furthermore, cultural centralization under royal control was enforced when a law in 1541 forbade Portuguese students from receiving university degrees abroad. This had been previously demanded by the University of Lisbon but never really enforced. The full impact of this measure, however, was thoroughly realized only after the 1560's (see chapter 6).

If in education the impact of humanism brought about improvement and progress, the change was not so clear in literature and general literary production. Late medieval forms, although permeable to humanistic influences, flourished in Portugal under Afonso V, John II, Manuel I, and even John III, a literary and cultural counterpart to the great overseas expansion and its resulting wealth. The courts of John I and Duarte prepared a refined background for later epochs, where the combined influence of feudal competition and royal protection for culture produced the favorable ambience of the late 1400's and early 1500's.

Chronologically, the first literary form to flourish was history. Behind it lay a bureaucratic motivation for accurate recording. John I's revolution, moreover, demanded a convenient justification, and Prince (later king) Duarte ordered archivist Fernão Lopes to write a "truthful" history of his father's epoch and deeds (see chapter 2). Yet Fernão Lopes, still a "medieval man," combined the inevitable praise for the victors with a frank appraisal of events and human beings, which made him amazingly "modern" and scientific. His successors, less rustic and more courtly as true Renaissance men, produced rather elaborate monuments of laudatory rhetoric and other formal gifts, notwithstanding an often invaluable description of facts and details. Gomes Eanes de Zurara (1410?–74?) wrote the only surviving account of the fifteenth-century navigations by a contemporary. Later on, Rui de Pina (1440?–1522), João de Barros (1496–1570), and Damião de Gois (1502–74), three excellent examples of Renaissance formalism, wrote lengthy histories of contemporary events, both at home and overseas.

Under conditions similar to those which in earlier times had originated the poetry of the troubadours, there arose, particularly in the courts of Afonso V and John II, a kind of light poetry traditional in form and full of charm and spontaneity. Verses were compiled by Garcia de Resende (1470?–1536) in the so-called *Cancioneiro Geral* ("General Song-Book"). However, the outstanding representative of this late medieval flourishment was undoubtedly Gil Vicente (1465?–1537?), the creator of Portuguese theater. Influenced by the Castilian author Juan del Encina, yet deeply original in the elaboration of his themes and general conception of his plays, Gil Vicente wrote scores of short, lively, and charming *autos* ("acts"), where he sharply criticized the society of his epoch.

It was only after 1520 that the humanists reacted against what they considered old-fashioned themes and forms, their criticism broadly assailing Portugal's cultural milieu. Italian-influenced authors, such as Bernardim Ribeiro (1482–1552) and Sá de Miranda (1485?–1558), railing against the outdated survival of Gothic times, successfully introduced new metrics, rhyme, and subjects, both in lyric poetry and in theater.

Because of this late triumph of humanism in literary circles, the great names of the Portuguese Renaissance flourished only in the second half of the sixteenth century (see chapter 6). Nonetheless, a numerous groups of grammarians, philologists, jurists, poets, theologians, historians, philosophers, and pedagogues, all deeply imbued with the principles and the ideals of humanism, did arise in the early 1500's, accounting for a very complex and rich literary production. Many were clerics or had professed in a religious order. Most had studied abroad and several never returned to their home country. A great number became professors in the university and the colleges, or tutors to the noble and bourgeois youngsters. Among them, André de Resende (1500–73), a good philologist and poet interested in classical archaeology, and Aires Barbosa (1470?–1540), pedagogue and grammarian, were perhaps the most distinguished.

The key to understanding the rise and development of humanism in Portugal lies in the intensity of the international contacts. A small country, with a spare cultural life of her own, with hardly any possibilities of renewing it, Portugal has always had to depend heavily upon wide international relationships to keep up with currents of thought, absorbing and adapting them to the conditions of the country and often contributing thereby to the intellectual life of the world. The overseas expansion, diverting to Lisbon the attention of all Europe, brought Portugal international publicity and contributed to her cultural development in an intense way. Traders were followed by scholars or simply by curious people who wanted to know more about the fabulous discoveries. Increasing wealth allowed a large migration of students to the main cultural centers of Europe, where they listened to gifted professors and came into contact with different and often higher forms of living and thinking. Some never came back, their names appearing as university professors, tutors, and authors all over Europe. At the same time, a massive importation of foreign scholars—with attractive salaries—for teaching positions also aimed at preparing a larger élite in the future generations. Great names in the history of humanism were invited to come—Erasmus, for one—and even when they refused, for whatever reason, they felt flattered and regarded Portugal sympathetically. Erasmus himself dedicated one of his works—the *Chrysostomi Lucubrationes*—to King John III, in 1527. Two years later, the French mathematician Jean Fernel did the same with his *Cosmotheoria*. In 1531 the Spanish pedagogue Juan Luis Vives dedicated to the monarch his *De tradendis Disciplinis*. Other examples could be mentioned. By attractive gifts of money and other regalia, by scholarships to Portuguese students, by successive invitations to scholars and artists all over Europe, but especially by an intelligent policy of cultural development, the Portuguese rulers of the first half of the sixteenth century—either kings or their advisers—were on the right track to achieve a complete change in the cultural structure of the country, if only that policy could have been maintained.

Contemporary with this great movement, and one of the main reasons for its rise, was the establishment of the printing press. It developed in Portugal rather late, like humanism itself. No printed books survive for the period 1465–72, when tradition reports the first Portuguese press. After a short-lived Jewish press (1487–95), active in the cities of Faro, Lisbon, and Leiria, and publishing religious books in Hebrew only (with one exception), a Portuguese press was started after 1494, by German initiative. German, Italian, and French printers controlled a significant part of the printing business for quite a long time. To the end of the fifteenth century less than twenty different books were printed, a very small number compared with the literary output of most countries in Europe. In the 1500's Portuguese book printing did increase, about a thousand books being published up to 1550, again a small number in comparison with the rest of the Western world. Works on theology and religion formed about 50 per cent of the whole production, less than 10 per cent being devoted to scientific works. Translations were also abundant, as might be expected in a small country like Portugal. Relatively few works were published on Classicism, an understandable phenomenon, because imports from abroad met the demand of the few scholars living in the country. However, many works of Portuguese writers were printed abroad rather than in Portugal. Salamanca, Lyons, Paris, Antwerp, and Venice were the main centers of Portuguese cultural expansion through the printing press, although some thirty other places could be mentioned where works by Portuguese authors were published. It should also not be forgotten that the manuscript book continued to predominate over the printed book until the mid-1500's, the latter being used almost exclusively by the Church, the state, and the university. Most printers depended upon these three institutions and not upon a wide public of private individuals.

The classical period of Renaissance art in Europe exhibited a highly interesting complexity in Portugal. Four different "styles," albeit rarely displayed in a pure form, interacted and blended together with extreme originality in most monuments. These were the late Gothic, the so-called "Manueline," the *Mudéjar,* and finally the Renaissance styles. In each of the four, the main building area—for their highest expression was architecture and the decoration related to it—was the South and the Center of Portugal, the North appearing poorly represented and offering few native artists. Although the Portuguese center of gravity was slowly moving northward, art—generally late in affirming itself in relation to economic and social tendencies—continued to flourish in the old medieval areas of power. Late Gothic showed first as an archaic reaction against the exuberance of fourteenth- and early fifteenth-century forms. In the simple style of early Gothic of the 1200's were the elegant cloister of the monastery of Batalha (built 1448–77), the monastery of Varatojo (Estremadura), and the church of Santiago, in Palmela (south Estremadura). This simplicity and austerity could not last for long and the return to elaborate forms characterized the epochs of John II and Manuel I.

To a Gothic structure, a lavishness of new decorative elements (the great majority of traditional origin but some denoting the influence of the overseas expansion) was added, with some architectural innovations resembling the Baroque: spiral columns, polycentric arches, octagonal towers, a network of complicated ribs on the vaults, flat and spiraled conic spires, and so on. Several church plans followed the German system of the *Hallenkirchen* (salon-churches), although with great originality both in proportions and lighting. Comparisons with the Spanish Isabelino and plateresque styles do show significant similarities but in no way explain the origin of either by the other. This originality of the late Portuguese Gothic led some nineteenth-century art historians to call it Manuelino, though it flourished far beyond the chronological limits of Manuel's reign.

The best example of Manuelino was the monastery of the yeronimites (Jerónimos) in Belém (now a part of Lisbon), started in 1502, a splendorous and elegant masterpiece of architecture and decoration. Significantly, King Manuel ordered it to be built on the beach where Vasco da Gama had departed to discover the maritime route to India and in commemoration of this expedition.

Other examples of Manuelino or pre-Manuelino worth mentioning were the Belém tower (Torre de Belém), built in 1515; the church of Jesus, in Setúbal (finished in 1492); part of the monastery of Batalha; and part of the church and monastery of Christ at Tomar. The French(?) architect Boytac and the Portuguese João de Arruda signed many Manuelino buildings and presumably prepared a good school of later artists.

The Mudéjar style was not so original as the Manuelino because it had its perfect counterpart in Spain, from which it probably came during the fifteenth century. Despite its clear Islamic characteristics, it seems impossible to relate it to a persistence of native Moorish forms, completely hidden for more than two hundred years, or to a revival due to Moslem artists, in an epoch when their presence was of little importance. Typical Mudéjar elements appeared in the materials used (accent on brick and stucco), the decorative forms (geometric motives, tile facings), the wood-carved ceilings, and some others, all arranged upon a basic Gothic or Gothic-Islamic structure. Mudéjar had a tremendous impact on civil architecture, more than on religious buildings. Royal and seignorial residences of the late 1400's and 1500's were lavishly adorned according to its rules. The royal palace of Sintra (west of Lisbon) is perhaps the best surviving example.

A pure Renaissance style arrived late in Portugal and hardly succeeded in ousting the Gothic tradition. By the second half of the sixteenth century it had given way to Mannerism. Introduced or developed by French artists (Nicolas Chantereine, Jean de Rouen, Loguin) it was never fully understood in Portugal, although several seignorial houses and some cathedrals (Leiria, Portalegre, Miranda) tried to copy famous Italian and French models. Many of its elements, however, had been introduced before and survived through the seventeenth century.

Painting developed late in Portugal, possibly as a result of Islamic interdictions, expressed in the lack of artists all over the South. The fifteenth century, so rich throughout Europe, brought to Portugal very little in painting activities. Yet a great school of artists, or one great artist with several disciples, did flourish from the early 1470's to the end of the century. Their origins and the influences they experienced continue to pose a mystery to historians. Among those painters, the name of Nuno Gonçalves survived as one of the ablest and most gifted, praised even by Renaissance followers who generally disdained everything "Gothic." In him, as in all the others, Flemish, Italian, Catalan, and local French schools seem to be simultaneously present.

The Flemish influence on the Portuguese painters, well explained by the intense commercial and political contacts between Portugal and Flanders, as well as the massive importation of works of art from the Low Countries, lasted for a long time and offered a stubborn resistance to the impact of the Renaissance. In the early 1500's, the schools of Lisbon (represented by Jorge Afonso) and Viseu (directed by Vasco Fernandes, nicknamed Grão-Vasco) polarized painting, with a large and varied production of masterpieces. Both gradually absorbed the Italian influences that only after the 1540's or 1550's would completely prevail.

The contribution of Portugal to the Renaissance, however, was not so much in the arts or the humanities, but rather in science. It was in the fields of navigation, astronomy, natural sciences, mathematics and, of course, geography that the Portuguese contribution completely changed the course of science and of learning in general. Furthermore, to a new knowledge of facts the Portuguese added a new method and a new approach, based on experience.

This "revolution of experience" will be studied in more detail in Chapters 5 and 6, for it depended on the overseas expansion and was especially felt after 1550. For the moment, let us consider only some brief aspects of its evolution.

The Portuguese commenced their navigations and first contacted strange peoples and civilizations with medieval equipment and a general approach based on authority. What the classical writers and their commentators down through the centuries had written must be the truth and could not be questioned. If actual observation seemed to prove the contrary, then the observation itself was false, resulting from a trick of the devil or an illness of the body. Such an attitude prevailed for a long time. Even in Portugal, the universities, the books printed, the scholarly culture, continued to teach and to accept the old masters with the old errors, long after everyone, from the humblest sailor to the noblest viceroy, had actually watched and touched a different reality. For a long time, official learning and practical experience coexisted apparently without friction, yet often contradicting each other. A tradition of centuries which created a method and which itself had been strengthened by it could not be shaken off in several decades. The "revolution of experience" definitely was a revolution, and a subversive one. It undermined the very bases of thinking and of acting, and was therefore fought energetically by the defendants of the existing order. It was regarded as heretical, absurd, and immoral. It had its victims and its holocausts.

The Portuguese of the fifteenth and sixteenth centuries proved by experience and scientific deduction that the Atlantic Ocean was navigable and monster-free; that the equatorial world was inhabitable; that it was possible to sail systematically offshore and to become perfectly oriented by watching the sun and the stars; that Africa had a southern end and a seaway existed to India; that the pseudo-Indies discovered by Columbus were in fact a new Continent separating Europe from East Asia and that the three Americas formed a continuous land; that South America had a southern end like Africa and a seaway existed to India westward; that the three great oceans were connected; that the Earth was round and navigable all around. They mapped the contours of the continents and the oceans and for the first time sketched an ecumenical geography of the Earth. They drew the first map of the southern skies. They brought to the knowledge of the Western world a great many unknown civilizations and cultures, while putting many others into permanent contact. They faced and posed the problem of fusing, compromising, or segregating often highly complex cultures (the Indian; the Chinese; the Central, Western and Southern African; the Brazilian) and religions (Buddhism, Brahmanism). They had to find a way of communicating in different languages with entirely new structures and writing signals. They tested numerous new or insufficiently known plants, fruits, and foods, bringing them to Europe. They found and described new animals.

The decisive steps in this immense new world of experience took place before 1550, yet its full scientific description and significant impact on mankind lasted for centuries. And if the Portuguese were helped by innumerable peoples of many countries and traditions, the effort of acquisition was certainly theirs, as theirs was the early consciousness of the new and the challenge to the world that existed.

Although this statement may sound strange, one can say that in Portugal there was no Reformation at all. The modern *Dicionário de História de Portugal,* so concerned with general historical movements, includes no entry under the word *Reforma* (Reformation). No cases of individual Lutheranism, Calvinism, or other religious ideology related to the Reformation were ever recorded within the Portuguese frontiers. At most, some suspected of leaning toward the "heresy" were detected and tried, but no convincing proof of their guilt was ever found. This is all the more strange because the Inquisition was assumed to result from the danger of a Catholic deviation.

Several reasons accounted for this situation. First, the geographic location of Portugal helped prevent an easy importation of German ideologies, filtered as they were by two large, strong, and alert Catholic countries, France and Spain. Lutheranism, however, could have arrived by sea, all the more because frequent contacts bound Portugal to the Hanseatic world. It seems far more important to understand correctly the religious situation of the country and her cultural position in sixteenth-century Europe. No real grievances existed against the moral condition of the clergy, who did not appear more corrupt or unrespected than previously. Abuses and accumulations of ecclesiastical benefices did exist but never played any significant role in calling together the people against the Church. Moreover Portugal, like Spain, felt too many language, racial and cultural affinities with Italy to experience the reactions against the Renaissance, the Latin tradition, and the Papacy which were common in the north of Europe. Generally sentimental and opposed to any kind of puritan movements, the Portuguese, like all the Mediterranean peoples, naturally rejected the basic principles of the Reformation, symbolized by the destruction of the images and the simplification of the Church rituals.

The few "Reformists" or Reformation-oriented Portuguese could only have been some intellectuals, influenced less by direct meditation than by contact with foreigners. They probably existed but were careful to conceal themselves under pious Catholic behavior. Furthermore, the establishment of the Inquisition promptly discouraged such whims by closing the country to uncensored contacts with the foreign world.

Actually, the Inquisition had little to do with the Reformation, at least as a real motive for its foundation. King Manuel had pleaded its establishment to the Pope as early as 1515, two years before Luther's rebellion. His real purpose was to secure one more weapon to achieve centralization and royal control. The Portuguese monarchs wished to be given what Ferdinand and Isabella had obtained from Pope Sixtus IV after 1478, although the circumstances were completely different. Neither Jews nor Moors in Portugal posed a clear menace to the unity of the Faith as might be claimed in Castile. Moreover, the political dangers of the Inquisition had become clear to the Papacy as a powerful instrument in the hands of the Crown. Indeed judges and officials of the Inquisition, although clergymen, were appointed by the king, and their authority and powers, by Papal delegation, were generally independent of the usual Church jurisdiction.

John III and his advisers fought hard for the creation of the Inquisition. Diplomatic maneuvers and intrigue lasted for many years, the Papacy resisting fiercely and the Jews, in the background, bribing both sides to slow down or refuse. Charles V had to intervene on behalf of his brother-in-law, the king of Portugal. The Inquisition was finally "bought" from Rome by John III (1536) but with great restrictions to full freedom of action. Only in 1547 were these restrictions lifted by Pope III and the Inquisition given full powers. In the meantime the first victims had been burned in Évora (1543). For Portugal a new epoch was born.

THE POLITICAL EVOLUTION

The end of Prince Pedro's regency brought about the last great epoch for the feudal aristocracy. To him, young Afonso V preferred his other uncles, Afonso (the Duke of Bragança) and Henry (the Duke of Viseu), the leaders, respectively, of the landed nobility and of the policy of expansion in North Africa. To the end of his long reign (Afonso V died in 1481), he never gave up those two ideals which Afonso and Henry so perfectly represented: the constant strengthening of the noble houses against that of the Crown (a typical feudal point of view which made the king praised, respected, and beloved by his peers, the feudal lords) accompanied by a systematic policy of conquests in Morocco (which again the nobility welcomed as a means of displaying bravery, achieving fame, and obtaining profits). To this policy any other goals were subordinated, at least till the 1470's: the discoveries, for example, considerably slowed down particularly after Henry's death, in 1460.

The monarch's campaigns in North Africa cannot be dissociated from a wider external policy context. Afonso V and the Papacy tried hard to organize a European crusade against the Moslems, namely against the Turks who had conquered Constantinople in 1453. Better yet, the king of Portugal always backed all the Papal dreams and undertook all the efforts to make them come true. The several Papal projects failed, because the time for crusades was over. Afonso V, however, attacked in Africa and secured important victories for his pride and his international prestige, although their real meaning from an economic and political point of view might seem questionable. In 1458 the Portuguese army under the command of the king himself and with the participation of most representatives of the upper classes conquered Al-Kaṣr al-Ṣaghīr (Alcácer Ceguer). To his title of "king of Portugal and Algarve" he proudly added "on this side and the other in Africa," converting the singular "Algarve" into a plural "Algarves": he thus meant, with some exaggeration, to be the sovereign of both parts of the traditional Al-Gharb, "the West" in Arab geographical terminology.

Other expeditions were prepared (in 1460 and in 1463–64) but failed, the second one coming close to disaster. The Portuguese prepared themselves to take Tangiers and avenge the defeat of 1437 and Prince Fernando's martyrdom. They succeeded only in 1471, when Aṣīla (Arzila) fell to them and Tangiers was abandoned by its population. More expeditions were probably envisioned, but the war in Castile forced them to be postponed for a long time.

Intervention in Castilian affairs was nothing new in Portuguese history, having its counterpart in Castilian meddling with Portuguese affairs. As soon as civil dissension plagued either country, the other immediately tried to play some role. This had happened during Pedro's regency and was to happen again and again. Neither monarch would give up some vague idea of uniting the two countries, in the prospect of a still vaguer ideal of "reuniting" the whole Peninsula.

Enrique IV, King of Castile, ruled from 1454 to 1474, partly in a turbulent climate of civil strife. His authority was hardly respected, and his daughter and heiress Juana was rightly or wrongly believed to be the daughter of a nobleman, Beltrán de la Cueva, and was therefore nicknamed the "Beltraneja." Enrique had envisioned several marriages for both his daughter and his willful sister Isabella, in which the widower king of Portugal (Juana's uncle) and his son João (the future John II) were favorite candidates. When he died, the feudal party, hostile to Isabella who meanwhile had married Ferdinand of Aragon and had herself proclaimed queen of Castile, offered the crown of the realm to the Portuguese monarch, provided he married Juana.

Acceptance of the crown meant war. Success in war, however, would mean the union of Portugal and Castile under a Portuguese male. Contrary to what many Spanish historians say, the results would not have been too different from those achieved with the wedding of Isabella and Ferdinand. Instead of Castile plus Aragon, the issue would have been Portugal plus Castile, perhaps a more interesting and less antagonistic union.

Juana's party was small, with many nobles hesitating between prestigious Afonso V and the young but active couple Isabella and Ferdinand who were extremely busy seeking support with promises, bribes, and moral arguments. Afonso invaded Castile (1475), occupied most of León but failed to decisively beat the enemy at Toro (1476). His prestige among the Castilian nobility was lost. He returned to Portugal and tried to provoke French intervention from the north. Chivalrous and utterly incapable of understanding "modern" politics, Afonso decided to travel to France and personally convince King Louis XI of the justness of his cause. Against the advise of most counselors he in fact visited France (1476–77) where he got caught in the final turmoil of the bitter conflict between Louis XI and Charles the Bold, Duke of Burgundy. He played a poor diplomatic role, was politically indoctrinated and then dismissed by both contenders, and finally, in despair, he renounced the throne of Portugal and embarked on a pilgrimage to the Holy Land (1477). Prevented from such an adventure by Louis, he was practically arrested and "deported" to Portugal where he arrived, totally disillusioned, in November 1477. His son John, who had himself been proclaimed king some days before, gave up his new title and convinced Afonso to reassume power.

From 1477 until his death in 1481, Afonso V and his son John were practically co-rulers. More precisely, John was entrusted with complete control of overseas policies (see chapter 5). Negotiations with Castile absorbed most of their efforts during the next two years. The treaty of Alcáçovas (1479) established peace, the king of Portugal renouncing all his rights to the Castilian crown and obtaining, in exchange, several important concessions in Africa.

John II (1481–95) was a typical Renaissance ruler. Unlike his father, he was well suited to his epoch and was a thoroughly "modern" man, "the man" (*el hombre*), as his cousin Isabella of Castile liked to call him. Probably influenced by French and Castilian policies, where centralization under a strong royal authority was being achieved, John embarked on a dangerous fight against the great feudal lords, which he quickly and ruthlessly carried on to final victory. After constraining the nobles to what they thought was a humiliating form of fealty oath, he undertook several measures requested by the people at *cortes* (1481) which directly threatened the nobility in their feudal privileges. Such measures specifically involved the violation of feudal jurisdiction and the cutback of royal grants to the nobles, two fundamental class issues. The upper nobility responded with a widespread conspiracy against the king, where Castilian involvement was not absent. Aware of the main threads, however, John II struck back: the Duke of Bragança, main head of the conspiracy, was briefly tried and beheaded, while the other known or suspected leaders were forced to flee the country to save their lives (1483–84). As a result, the king got rid of the strongest feudal family, whose titles were abolished and whose huge estates suddenly enlarged the Crown patrimony.

After the Braganças, the second feudal lord of the realm, the Duke of Viseu, cousin and brother-in-law to the king, became the obvious target. Foolish enough to lead a second conspiracy, he was stabbed by the king himself (1484), while his followers suffered death at the stake or fled to Castile. Thus, three years after ascending the throne, John II had succeeded in killing or forcing into exile most of the upper feudal lords and in attaching to his patrimony a considerable share of the national territory. Though we still lack developed monographs on the subject, it seems that John's policy sought its greatest support, not among the people, but rather among the lower ranks of the nobility. At the same time, he promoted many legists and civil servants to top positions till then reserved to the upper strata of the aristocracy. Notwithstanding his tremendous achievements, John's victory was not complete. His wife belonged to the Duke of Viseu's family and never ceased to intrigue or rally opposition forces against him. After the death of John's only son, Afonso, in a riding accident (1491), he was forced to declare the queen's younger brother, Manuel, as heir to the throne, a decision which involved the future restoration of the Braganças. The prestige and authority, however, that he had added to the Crown, would never be lost again.

The expulsion of the Jews from Castile and Aragon (1492) posed a serious problem for Portugal. Many Spanish Jews, perhaps a majority, considered Portugal as a peaceful and progressive country, where no persecutions against them had been recorded for a long time. They offered John II a considerable amount of money if he would let them in. For Portugal the situation was difficult: on the one hand, the sudden "invasion" of several thousand skilled and resourceful people, strengthening the Portuguese Jewish colony, posed tremendous problems of an economic, social, religious, and ethnical nature; on the other hand, it seemed regrettable to give up such an important monetary offer. John II compromised: he authorized the Jews' admission at the price of eight cruzados each but refused to let them stay for more than eight months. More than fifty thousand people entered Portugal but most of them had to leave in the allotted time. Once that deadline expired, a great number were reduced to captivity; only some 600 families succeeded in purchasing a permanent residence permit. As they were the wealthiest and the most powerful, their sole presence unbalanced the achieved state of harmonious coexistence with the Christians and led to the ruthless measures of Manuel's reign.

John's external policy involved a great number of issues, mostly related to the overseas expansion (see chapter 5). After a first success obtained with the treaty of 1479, still in his father's lifetime but probably negotiated by him, John went further and managed to get from the Pope the division of the non-Christian world into two hemispheres, one for Portugal, the other for Castile (Papal bull of 1493, followed by the Treaty of Tordesillas, 1494). His daring navigators were on the verge of reaching India by sea when he died (1495). Several years before, he had added to his official titles that of "lord of Guinea" (senhor de Guiné), a meaningful expression of the economic and political significance of the overseas expansion.

Manuel I (1495–1521) inherited a difficult situation. The country had been torn apart by John's fierce and ruthless policy. Peace, centralization, enlargement of the Crown's patrimony, had been achieved at the cost of an almost total annihilation of the feudal party and the confiscation of its property. Manuel's task, the synthesis between Afonso V's debonairness and John's ferocity, would be a reasonable compromise aiming at reuniting the rival factions. In such a hard mission, he had remarkable success. The accomplishments of the overseas expansion provided wealth, positions, or at least hope, for the upper classes. Military commands and conflicts in Asia and Africa gave the nobility an opportunity to affirm themselves without disturbing peace at home and to enrich their households without embezzling the royal patrimony. Furthermore, the nobles felt useful and indeed became useful again as a source of qualified bureaucracy for the higher positions in the colonial administration (see chapter 5).

Manuel's reign seems to have been marked by an excellent administration. The concern for, as well as the number of, reforms in all the fields documents the existence of a small group of cabinet ministers or secretaries, well experienced and really devoted to the task of governing. The king himself apparently knew how to choose them and use them properly. Manuel restored the Braganças and the other banished families to the full ownership of their former dignities, privileges, and patrimony. Being the governor of the order of Christ and benefiting from the first Indian profits, he could afford to be generous and merciful, though he never condemned John's acts and always praised his memory and deeds. For more than a century, and in spite of all their affluence and prestige, the Braganças (like all the other nobles) would pose no particular problem to the royal policy of authority and centralization. The same could be said for the Church. By postponing the summoning of *cortes* and unifying the municipal system, Manuel accomplished the subjugation of the people, which a better administration and the overseas appeal helped him restrain and rule easily.

A more difficult task was presented by the Jewish question. We still lack sources to inform us of the impact of the sudden Jewish immigration of 1492 on the economic, social, and religious situation of the country. Monographs analyzing the years 1492–97 might be revealing on the rivalries that opposed the Spanish-Jewish merchants and capitalists to the Portuguese, the foreign traders (particularly the Italians and the Castilians), and the native Portuguese Jews themselves. Manuel started his rule by freeing the Jews reduced to captivity, a symbolic measure of clemency that should not be taken too seriously. Yet, only a year later, he had decided on their expulsion. His marriage with Isabel, the pious daughter and quasi-heiress to the

Castilian throne, served as a pretext. Isabel and her parents demanded an immediate expulsion of the Jews, following the Castilian example and John II's own initial plans. Actually, other European countries had undertaken a similar measure before. By marrying her, Manuel would come very close to the Castilian and Aragonese thrones, and the union of all the Peninsula appeared likely in the near future. There could be no hesitation. All the Jews were theoretically expelled from December 1496 to October 1497, amid incredible violence, robbery, and confusion. In April 1497 he even determined that all the children under fourteen should be prevented from leaving the country and should be scattered among Portuguese families in order to be raised in the Christian faith. It was clearly an invitation to generalized conversion, a step back in the expulsion policy, perhaps because a great number of Jews had already left and it might seem convenient to let the others stay. This was actually what happened, several thousand Jews accepting baptism rather than lose their property and children. Known as New Christians (cristãos-novos), they were to be left in peace for more than thirty years, by legal decision successively prolonged and due to expire in 1534. Nobody was to inquire about their faith nor were they required to wear any special signs.

The order of expulsion included the free Moslems too. It was a perfunctory measure, for their number was very small, most of them having been completely absorbed by the Portuguese Christian community. They left apparently without violence and without posing any particular problems.

By compromising and quibbling where no compromise was possible, both John and Manuel created a tremendous social and religious problem, the consequences of which would last for centuries. Discontent with the New Christians began immediately among the lower classes and the lower clergy. The first riot occurred in 1504. Two years later a pogrom in Lisbon caused the death of some two thousand ex-Jews. Other riots and illegal discriminatory measures —for legally there was discrimination enough, no New Christians being allowed to hold any honors or public offices, marry within the nobility, etc.—took place here and there for several decades.

Manuel's other (brief) concern was his Castilian policy. The dream of unification haunted the monarchs of Iberia. After the medieval attempts and the campaigns of Afonso V, a peaceful but systematic network of royal weddings was to be woven. Its results were in Manuel's time. The death of Juan, the heir to the Castilian-Aragonese throne, put Princess Isabel, Manuel's wife, in the direct order of succession (1497). Both were accordingly sworn in as heirs to the combined thrones of Castile and Aragon (1498). Two months later, however, Isabel died in labor, and their son, Miguel, followed her shortly after (1500). The dream was over. Manuel married his first wife's younger sister, Maria (between the two existed Juana, the heiress), and much later, her niece Leonor, but with hardly any chances of inheriting the Spanish succession.

In the meantime Vasco da Gama had reached India by sea (1498) and his triumphal return to Portugal (1499), his ships loaded with spices, brought the king immense fame and prestige. Acclaimed as the richest monarch in all Christendom, he added to his titles a new and proud invocation: "Lord of the conquest, navigation and commerce of Ethiopia, Arabia, Persia and India" (1499). From 1500 on, during his lifetime, the Portuguese obtained nothing but victories from Arabia to Malaysia, thoroughly controlling the Indian Ocean. Manuel's titles were fully justified and corresponded to a situation of fact.

In North Africa, the Portuguese tried and to a certain extent succeeded in strengthening their foothold by the conquest of Santa Cruz do Cabo de Gué (near Agadir) in 1505, Mogador (near present-day Essauira) in 1506, Safim (Safi) in 1508, Azamor (present-day Mulai Bu Saib) in 1513, and Mazagão (El-Jadida) in 1514. The Moroccan coast was now almost entirely controlled by the Portuguese, who no longer had to fear Moorish piracy when navigating south. At the same time, the Moslem pressure on the important northern Portuguese strongholds (Ceuta, Tangiers, and Arzila) was considerably relieved. Economic reasons also played a part. However, the constant attacks by the Moors made the Portuguese expansion in North Africa extremely difficult and economically prohibitive. Already in Manuel's lifetime the Portuguese were forced out of Mogador (1510). His son John III, after several decades of difficult maintenance, decided to give up the dreams of controlling Morocco: when Santa Cruz do Cabo de Gué was conquered by the Moslems after a long siege (1540–41), Safim and Azamor were abandoned (1541); some years later, the same happened to Arzila and Alcácer Ceguer (1550). Only Ceuta, Tangiers and Mazagão were kept.

The long reign of John III (1521–57) can be divided in two main periods, with differences occurring in the economic situation, the religious attitude, the cultural policy, and even the psychological mood of the sovereign. The tolerant Renaissance prince, open to international currents of thought, praised by the humanists and eager to welcome them, the true Maecennas, gave way to a fanatic, narrow-minded ruler, entirely in the hands of the Jesuits and the defenders of a strict counter-Reformation policy, arresting and condemning the very ones he had formerly invited, niggardly cutting back funds and subsidies, closing schools and generally isolating himself from any external influences.

If the difficult economic and military background (see chapters 6 and 7) can, to a certain extent, explain the great changes that took place in Portugal after the 1540's, personal reasons may also have influenced the king. All of his nine children died before the age of nineteen, along with five of his brothers and sisters, most of them in the late 1530's and early 1540's. Religion, to the extremes of fanaticism, offered the king and the queen some relief and absolution from the guilt of tolerance toward heretics, Jews, and other "loose" Catholics.

The establishment of the Inquisition, incidentally a project of Manuel's, with political rather than religious purposes, was accepted by the Pope in 1536, but only eleven years later were a number of restrictions lifted to its complete freedom of action. By the same time (1540) the first Jesuits entered the country.

John's external policy ran relatively smoothly, in spite of the increasing French attacks on the Portuguese Atlantic possessions (see chapter 5). The king, as a matter of fact, was becoming less and less interested in general European affairs, absorbed as he was by the great overseas expansion. With his brother-in-law Charles V, an agreement was reached on the Moluccas, in 1529. John had married one of Charles's sisters, Catarina (1525), while Charles had married one of John's sisters, Isabel (1526), thus further enhancing the prospects of a future union of the Spanish and Portuguese crowns.

Portugal's expansion and wealth made her respected by all the European kingdoms. John II, Manuel I, and John III had acquired a certain fame as good administrators and models of strong Renaissance princes. No wonder that international contacts became plentiful, and that cultural, as well as economic, inter-influences served the interests of all.

RISE OF THE EMPIRE

DISCOVERY AND CONQUEST

By the early 1460's the Portuguese had reached the Gulf of Guinea. For a while they believed it was the end of Africa, with the prospect of India "just around the corner." Such a possibility, however, did not speed up their pace of discovery. On the contrary, in the 1460's and 1470's overseas expansion slowed down, dropping to second or third place in the king's concern and in the official policy of the Crown. Expansion in North Africa and the claim to the Castilian throne had undoubted priority.

With Henry's death (1460) his nephew and heir Fernando, the king's brother, took over the leadership. He had been granted the lordship of all the islands and lands discovered. He was the new governor of the Order of Christ, to which he added the mastership of Santiago, a still wealthier order. Supposed to be the richest man in Portugal, he had all the requisites to proceed with the discovery of the world, if only he were interested in it. Obviously, he was not. Like his brother, King Afonso V, Morocco meant everything to him. Until he died, in 1470, only North Africa seems to have appealed to him as worthy of his efforts and his fortune.

The task of discovering new lands was given to a Lisbon merchant as an economic operation. In November 1468, the Crown rented to Fernão Gomes for five years the monopoly of trade with the African coast (with a few exceptions), provided he discovered one hundred leagues of coastline (320 miles) each year. In 1473 this contract was extended for one more year. Indeed, from 1469 to 1474 all the northern coastline of the Gulf of Guinea had been explored, along with the beginning of the eastern part of the Gulf. Foremost were the travels of João de Santarém and Pero Escolar, who reached what is now Ghana (1471); of Fernão do Pó, who arrived at the bight of Biafra, in what is now Nigeria-Cameroon (1472?), and also discovered the island that bears his name but which he called Formosa; of Lopo Gonçalves and Rui de Sequeira, who reached the eastern coastline, at what is now Gabon, about 2°S. (1474–75). Thus the equator had been passed, and by this time the other islands (São Tomé, Principe, Ano Bom) had also been discovered. The Portuguese navigators left traces of their presence all along the coastline in the names of capes, rivers, bays, and mountains. Some have survived to the present day. Aiming at trade and depending on a tradesman, they even called some parts of the coastline according to the main products they found available: Costa da Malagueta (Malaguette or Grain Coast, now Liberia), Costa do Marfim (Ivory Coast), Costa do Ouro (Gold Coast, now Ghana), Costa dos Escravos (Slave Coast, now Togo and Dahomey).

In 1474 young Prince John (the future John II) was put in charge of overseas expansion. To him, rather than to Prince Henry or anyone else, the creation of a comprehensive plan of discovery, with its means and goals, should be credited. He, or his advisers, conceived the project of reaching Asia (present-day India) by sea and subordinated every effort to it, although the situation at home (see chapter 4) prevented resuming the discoveries before the early 1480's. John limited his efforts to the consolidation of Portuguese control in West Africa, both militarily and economically.

The main challenge was posed by Castile. The war between the two countries (1475–79) gave Queen Isabella of Castile a pretext for renewing the claim to suzerainty over the African seas and challenging the Portuguese monopoly. Several fleets sent by the Castilians fought the Portuguese ships in the Gulf of Guinea and indulged in trade with the natives. To maintain its exclusive rights, the Portuguese Crown had to give up its traditional claim to the Canary Islands. By the Treaty of Alcáçovas (1479), ratified in Toledo the

following year and confirmed by the Pope in 1481, Castile acknowledged the Portuguese monopoly to the south of the Canaries. North
of these islands the Portuguese were also recognized as masters in
the Madeira and Azores archipelagoes.

In 1482 John II sent his first expedition of discovery to Africa
under the command of his squire Diogo Cão. It was destined to be
one of the most important of all the expeditions. During the year
and a half he was absent from home, Diogo Cão discovered 13° of
coast south of the equator, covering what is today Gabon, Congo, and
most of Angola (to about 15° S.). On a second trip he went as far as
22°10′S. in today's Southwest Africa, almost reaching the Tropic of
Capricorn (1485–86).

Duly instructed by their masters and scrupulously following the
written regulations they often carried with them, the navigators
checked all passages eastward, maritime or not. Large rivers were
generally explored for a while in the hope of a possible contact with
peoples knowing how to reach Prester John, if not the kingdom of
Prester John itself. This was done also in the Zaire or Congo rivers.
In the first voyage Diogo Cão sent some Portuguese emissaries up the
river with presents to a powerful ruler whom some natives had told
him of. As they failed to return in the time set, he decided to sail
back home, taking with him some hostages but promising to return
soon. On his second voyage he explored the mouth of the Congo,
exchanged the hostages for the Portuguese, and followed the course
of the river for 100 miles (the Ielala waterfalls), where he left traces
of his presence in some inscriptions. He was well received by a Negro
ruler, the so-called king of Congo, and so established a basis for
future relationships.

A practice was begun with Diogo Cão's first journey of bringing
from Portugal some stone pillars with a cross and leaving them with
the royal arms and a chronological inscription at important capes or
rivers as marks of the Portuguese presence. Amazingly, some of those
monuments have survived. They were discovered in the last century
and are now kept in museums. Referring to Diogo Cão's first expedition, the inscription on one of them reads: "In the Era of the World's
creation 6681 years, of the Birth of Our Lord Jesus Christ 1482 years,
the very high, excellent and powerful prince king João II of Portu-

gal ordered this land to be discovered and these monuments (*padrões*) to be put by Diogo Cão, squire in his house."

In 1487 the king sent Bartolomeu Dias, another of his squires, to attempt the discovery of a seaway to India, which was thought to be close. Looking for Prester John had ceased to be the primary goal, and India—real Asian India, source of the spices—was the coveted objective. With three caravels, Bartolomeu Dias navigated south, passed the limit reached by Diogo Cão, and explored the coast of present Southwest Africa and South Africa to the latitude of Table Bay (33° to 34°S.). A storm forced him off the coast. He proceeded south for some days, then turned east, trying to reach land again. He found nothing. Then he turned north, and after a while he was in sight of land (Mossel Bay). He rightly concluded that he had finally reached the end of Africa and that the seaway to India was at last opened (1488). Wanting to be the first to set foot in India, he tried to convince the other ships and the crew in his own to continue the voyage. As everyone else was weary, however, and wished to return home, he managed to continue only to a point close to modern East London, in South Africa. On the way back he explored the whole coast, discovered the two capes that mark the end of Africa (Cape Agulhas and Cape of Good Hope), and called the second one—the impressive one, the one he thought to be southernmost—cabo da Boa Esperança (Cape of Good Hope) in the hope that it would open the way to India. He was back in Lisbon by December 1488 with good news for his king.

At the same time John II dispatched two emissaries to reach Ethiopia (the kingdom of Prester John) by land and to gather information on trade and other matters. It was not the first such attempt or the last, yet its importance surpassed all the others because of the goals attained and the bulk of information received. Disguised as merchants, Pero da Covilhã and Afonso de Paiva left Lisbon in May 1487, traveling together until they reached Aden, via Valencia, Barcelona, Naples, Rhodes, Alexandria, Cairo, and Suez. Afonso de Paiva's fate is obscure. Pero da Covilhã, however, proceeded to India, where he visited Cannanore, Calicut, and Goa, then to Persia and East Africa. Back in Cairo again, he sent John II a detailed report of what he had seen and heard. He finally reached Ethiopia, where he settled down, got married, and died after 1526. In spite of the fact that he never returned to Portugal, Pero da Covilhã's travels were probably decisive in giving the Portuguese the necessary information on trade routes, trade sources, and possible places for settlement. All of this helped prepare Vasco da Gama's expedition and the beginnings of the Portuguese policy in the Indian Ocean.

Along with the discovery of Africa, the Portuguese also tried to navigate westward, searching for new islands and, later on, the eastern point of Asia. Much has been written of these voyages, but many of the authors have substituted imagination for convincing evidence. As the Atlantic Ocean is relatively poor in islands, and as the recording of any trips was generally related to actual discoveries, it is admissible that a number of voyages went unrecorded and became forever lost in time. Yet some evidence does exist and accounts for our suppositions and hypotheses.

In the 1460's, 1470's, and 1480's several royal charters granted rights of lordship to navigators, or confirmed them for their heirs, on islands or lands assumed to have been seen at a distance. In some cases expeditions were launched to look for them. They all failed. However, before 1474, two noblemen, João Vaz Corte Real and Álvaro Martins Homem, seem to have reached Greenland or Newfoundland, which they called Codfish Land (Terra dos Bacalhaus). Others had followed by the 1480's. One of them, Fernão Dulmo, took two caravels and vainly tried to find the "island of the Seven Cities" by 1486 or 1487. In any case, there is no doubt that by the early 1490's the belief in lands existing westward was widespread among the Portuguese, particularly those living in the Azores and Madeira. All kinds of stories circulated, no longer based on the traditional legends but rather on the experience of two or three generations of sailors. The Sargasso Sea, birds that flew from nowhere, pieces of wood found by the seamen on coming ashore, the conviction of many topmen who were sure of having spied land, all accounted for the rumors and the growing interest.

Both the king and his advisers were of course aware of the problem and had studied it. They accepted the sphericity of the earth, therefore assuming that Asia could be reached westward as well as eastward. But in spite of their imprecise knowledge of the ultimate breadth of the Asian continent, which placed China and her adjacent islands much closer to Europe than they actually are, the Portuguese knew that the east route was considerably shorter than the west.

Christopher Columbus had lived several years in Lisbon and in Madeira, where he learned the art of navigation and acquired geographical knowledge. He had even sailed to Guinea once or twice. Daring and ambitious, and encouraged by precedents set by other foreigners who had served under the Portuguese banner, he offered his services to King John II (1483 or 1484). Columbus wanted to reach India sailing westward. His itinerary, possibly the result of a very imprecise geographical idea conceived by the Florentine cosmographer Paolo del Pozzo Toscanelli, supposed a 135° distance between Portugal and the Far East. The distance is actually 217°, and the Portuguese cosmographers of the time were aware of a minimal 183°. They rightly suspected that Diogo Cão had been closer to India than anyone else and insisted on carrying on the east way plan. Columbus's plan was dismissed as lunacy, and the Genoese left Portugal in despair (1485?).

When Columbus himself, returning from America after his first voyage (March 1493), called at Lisbon and paid a visit to the king, John reminded him that the newly discovered lands belonged to the Portuguese Crown, for they lay south of the Canary Islands (treaty of 1479–80). John II immediately dispatched an envoy to the Catholic kings, prepared a fleet under Francisco de Almeida to take possession of the new islands, and acted in bellicose fashion.

Negotiations started immediately. Anxious to avoid war, Isabella and Ferdinand sought Papal backing for their pretensions. Pope Alexander VI, a Spaniard, hastily drafted a bull full of geographical mistakes and utterly inapplicable, dividing the unknown world into two parts, the east for Portugal, the west for Castile, according to a meridian passing 100 leagues (320 miles) west of the Azores or the Cape Verde Islands (the two archipelagoes actually lie some 5 degrees apart). Direct negotiations between the two countries led to a better agreement. By the Treaty of Tordesillas (1494) the earth was divided into two areas of discovery and conquest according to a meridian line passing 370 leagues (1,184 miles) west of the Cape Verde Islands. The western share would belong to Castile, the eastern to Portugal. The

Treaty of Tordesillas prevented a war between the two nations and allowed to each a free area of discovery and conquest. Yet, though it officially lasted until 1750, its detailed clauses were never fulfilled. It did not prevent the Portuguese from expanding in Brazil, much beyond their demarcation line. Elsewhere, the Spanish claimed their rights to the Moluccas in East Asia, clearly located on the Portuguese side, and gave them up only when the Portuguese decided to buy them.

Precise as it was, the 370 leagues detail clearly showed that the Portuguese monarch had some knowledge of lands somewhere in the Atlantic, lying west of the 100-league limit initially proposed by the Pope. Indeed later sources point out that an expedition of discovery was probably sent by the early 1490's, reaching or at least sighting the South American continent. Maps existing in the Lisbon royal palace, and drawn much before 1500, showed lands close to that location. For some reason John II could not immediately send another expedition to explore the route announced by Bartolomeu Dias after his return in 1488. Then the results of Columbus's voyage and the negotiations with Castile prevented any further undertaking before 1494. John died in 1495, after having prepared everything for the decisive fleet that should reach India and having even appointed its supreme commander, the nobleman Vasco da Gama. Wisely, King Manuel carried on his plans as soon as his authority over the realm was firmly established.

Vasco da Gama departed from Lisbon with three vessels and a supply ship, in July 1497. He called at the island of Santiago (islands of Cape Verde) and then sailed directly south in what would be the longest journey far from land made until then. He turned southwest to avoid the wind lulls of the Gulf of Guinea, then east-southeast to reach the African coast again. After ninety days offshore he called at St. Helena Bay, in South Africa (November 1497). The Cape of Good Hope was passed with some difficulty, caused by adverse weather. After having reached the limit of Bartolomeu Dias's navigations, the ships began making their own discoveries: Natal ("Christmas" in Portuguese) on December 25; the Zambezi River in present-day Mozambique a month later; the Island of Mozambique (15°S.) early in March. This was already Moslem territory, and pilots be-

Treaty
of Tordesillas
(1494)

Castilian Portuguese
side side

Papal
Demarcation
Line (1493)

Castilian Portuguese
side side

Treaty of Alcáçovas (1479)

Castilian side
Portuguese side

0   500   1000 Km.

0   500   1000 miles

**Treaty of Tordesillas
as defined by the
treaty of Zaragoza (1529)**

Castilian | Portuguese
side | side

came available. The fleet reached Mombasa, in what is now Kenya, then Malindi (Melinde) a little farther North (April 1498), where friendly relations were established and a famous Arab pilot obtained (Ahmad Ibn Madjid), who led them to India. Pushed by the southwest monsoon the fleet came in sight of India by May 18. Landing took place only four days later. The great feat had been accomplished.

After three months of negotiations Vasco da Gama started on his way back home, his ships loaded with spices and other coveted merchandise. Leaving on August 29, 1498, he arrived in Lisbon after great hardships and the loss of one ship, late in the summer of 1499. The voyage had lasted more than two years, but the results were promising.

A new and much stronger expedition was immediately prepared. Composed of thirteen ships and commanded by Pedro Álvares Cabral, a nobleman, it departed from Lisbon in March 1500. The ships followed the same route as before, but for no apparent reason they sailed southwestward more than Vasco da Gama had done. This led them to the discovery of Brazil,* April 22, 1500, a land which they first called Terra da Vera Cruz (Land of the True Cross). They landed north of present-day Porto Seguro (16°S), met the natives, and explored the coastline for a while. Cabral dispatched one of his ships back to Portugal with the big news, then proceeded to India, where he arrived in August 1500. He returned to Portugal in June or July 1501. Instead of two years, this second voyage had lasted some fifteen months only, while bringing a higher profit than expected and adding a new country to the Portuguese Crown.

Contemporary descriptions show that the discovery of Brazil caused no surprise. Obviously, lands were known to exist somewhere in that area, which explains the 370-league detail in the Tordesillas Treaty. Whether Brazil had actually been visited before, perceived in the distance, or simply conjectured from some signals of land continues to be a matter for argument among historians. So far no totally convincing evidence has been produced by either side.

---

* The Castilian expeditions that explored a part of the northern coast of South America in 1499–1500 did not reach east of present-day French Guiana, assuming they got there. As to the much-praised Amerigo Vespucci, he never discovered anything.

Columbus's challenge stimulated other Portuguese expeditions westward, particularly in the northwest direction. By 1495 Pero de Barcelos and João Fernandes Lavrador (whose last name, or nickname, the "farmer," would later be applied to the Canadian coast) discovered or rediscovered Greenland. In 1500 Gaspar Corte Real reached Newfoundland (previously discovered by Cabot), which he explored in detail. In a second trip a year later he got lost and may have discovered the coast of North America. His brother Miguel, who tried to find him, also disappeared (1502).

Portuguese names on early sixteenth-century maps also suggest the existence of other expeditions that may have reached Florida before 1500. Later voyages discovered or explored some islands or even fragments of the mainland along the North American coast. Their record was vague, and obviously no official attention was ever paid to North America, supposedly within the Spanish boundaries. Only the fishermen came again and again to the waters of Greenland and Canada in search of codfish and whales.

In South America the process of discovery continued. From 1501 on, several Portuguese expeditions (in one of them Amerigo Vespucci participated but not as a commander) searched the Brazilian coastline from north to south and east to west. As early as 1502 what is now Uruguay and Argentina had been reached, to the Rio de la Plata area. However, it was only João Dias de Solis, a Portuguese serving under the Spanish flag, who carefully explored the mouth of that great river, where he died, killed by the natives (1515).

In the South Atlantic waters the few existing islands had been discovered early in the sixteenth century. Both Ascension (Ascensão) and St. Helena (Santa Helena) were found in 1501 or 1502 by the João da Nova fleet, the third fleet the king of Portugal dispatched to India. The fourth fleet to India discovered Trindade (1502), and the eighth, in 1506, Tristão da Cunha, named for its commander. Gough Island, originally named Gonçalo Álvares after its finder, was discovered in 1505. Off the Brazilian coast, Fernão de Noronha or Loronha found an island that he named São João (1502), but it now bears his name.

South of the Rio de la Plata, the American continent definitely fell within the Spanish area, even by the often imprecise sixteenth-century measurements. Such a fact discouraged Portuguese explorers, who were busy enough discovering their own share. Yet it was a Portuguese, Fernão de Magalhães (Magellan), who for the first time reached most of present-day Argentina and Chile, and then sailed the Pacific Ocean. Magellan's intent was not so much to circumnavigate the world as it was to find a seaway to the Moluccas. Both Portugal and Spain claimed the right of possession to that archipelago, an important source of clove and other spices. Serving the king of Spain like so many other Portuguese (and as many Castilians, along with other foreigners, were serving the king of Portugal), Magellan wished to find an adequate solution for his monarch, a way of arriving at the islands without passing "Portuguese waters."

Planned by himself and another Portuguese, the able cosmographer Rui Faleiro, the project was approved by the young King Charles I (future Emperor Charles V) and launched in 1519. Magellan left Spain, sailed southwestward, reached the coast of present-day Argentina and continued south until he discovered the famous strait that still bears his name, that much-desired "southwest passage." With amazing luck he crossed the ocean, which he found so peaceful and storm-free he named it Pacífico (Pacific). He reached the Philippines, where he was killed by natives. His second in command, the Castilian Sebastián del Cano, continued the trip westward and arrived back in Spain by 1522.

Another Portuguese pilot, Estêvão Gomes, who had taken part in Magellan's expedition, was charged by Emperor Charles V with the discovery of a "northwest passage." Leaving Spain in 1525, he failed in his purpose but explored the American coast between Newfoundland and Chesapeake Bay. A Spanish map drawn in 1529 shows that area as "Tiera de Estevã Gomez" and includes a short description of the navigator's achievements. To the northeast the same map shows the "Tiera Nova de Corte Real" and the "Tiera del Labrador," referring to Portuguese voyages and explorers. Much later, in 1542–43, another Portuguese pilot, again sailing under the Spanish flag, reached California for the first time and carefully explored it to San Francisco Bay. His name was João Rodrigues Cabrilho.

The great number of Portuguese taking the lead in these and other Spanish (as well as French and English) voyages shows how skilled in seafare the Portuguese were at the time and how eagerly sought after they were as unrivaled experts in navigation. Much smaller was the foreign contribution to the Portuguese sailing ventures, particularly after the second half of the fifteenth century. Some Spaniards and Italians, however, did help with their learning and practical knowledge. Once in the Indian Ocean, Moslem and Hindu pilots were invaluable in leading the Portuguese wherever they wanted to go.

The fame and originality of the discoveries in Africa and America often cause us to forget that the Indian Ocean and the Asian continent were by the same time almost thoroughly "discovered" and "explored" from a Western point of view. Before the arrival of the Portuguese no detailed maps of Asia were available to Europeans. Italian and other Western tradesmen and missionaries might have known a part of Asia and explored it by land much better than the Portuguese would ever do; yet they were generally unfamilar with the coastline, had never sailed the Indian Ocean by themselves, and offered no help to whoever wished a contour map of Asia for navigation purposes. This the Portuguese did first, with the help of partial Moslem portolan charts, publishing detailed voyage routes and sea charts of all the Indian Ocean.

Off the African coast most of the existing islands were visited by Vasco da Gama during his first trip to India, in 1498–99. Cabral's fleet completed the coastal exploration, discovered more of the smaller islands, and discovered Madagascar, originally called Island of São Lourenco. Discoveries that followed were the Seychelles, first named Almirante (Admiral) Islands (1503); Socotra (1503); the coast of Arabia (1503 on); the Maldive Islands and Ceylon (1505); the Bay of Bengal (1505 on); the Persian Gulf (1507 on); the Nicobar Islands, Sumatra and the Malay Peninsula (1509); and the Red Sea (1513 on).

In the Pacific, the first Portuguese expeditions arrived by 1511, after having explored most of present-day Indonesia, to Timor. Shortly afterward, they may have reached, or seen, the north Australian coast, although they never bothered sailing south along it. Jorge Álvares was the first Westerner to sail to China (1513). Japan much later, in the early 1540's, seems to have been visited by Fernão Mendes Pinto. Thus, with the exception of most of China and Japan, all the Asian coastline had been sailed and described by the Portuguese in a period of about fifteen years (1498–1513).

The economic, political, and religious happenings and conditions that had forced the Portuguese out of Europe promoted voyages of exploration inland where a better knowledge of things and peoples might be obtained. In Africa and Asia (later in America too), gold, spices, and Prester John or someone related to him—Christian communities, for instance—would justify the first travels far from the coast. From the 1440's on there is some scarce evidence of several expeditions in West Africa (Senegal, Sudan), often following the navigable courses of the main rivers (Senegal, Gambia, Cacheu). In the time of John II establishment of a trading post in Wadan, located deep inland, shows that the Portuguese were looking in earnest for the direct sources of gold, even at the cost of hard trips to unknown countries. Timbuktu was reached by them, as well as Mali. In the Congo area most of that kingdom and the northern part of Angola to the south of it had been explored before the middle of the sixteenth century, Baltasar de Castro's and Manuel Pacheco's expeditions in 1520–26 being among the most relevant. In East Africa António Fernandes (1514–15) arrived in what is now Rhodesia, traveling around the important Monomotapa kingdom (in present-day Mozambique).

Official missions to Ethiopia were among the main concerns of the Portuguese until they realized the irrelevance of Prester John to their economic policy of spice and gold control. In response to an Ethiopian embassy to Portugal (1513 or 1514) King Manuel sent Duarte Galvão (who died), then Rodrigo de Lima, to the court of the Negus (1520). He left Massaua on the Red Sea Coast and finally reached his coveted objective, where he first traveled and then settled down for six years of his life. One of his companions, father Francisco Álvares, wrote an impressive description of the expedition and the country, one of the best sources of our knowledge of Ethiopia in those days. (*Verdadera informaçam das terras do Preste Joam.* ["True Information on the lands of Prester John"], printed in 1540 and promptly translated into Castilian, German, French, and Italian.) Other missions followed. One in 1541 was headed by Cristóvão da Gama (Vasco da Gama's son), who met a tragic fate, being killed, with most of his four hundred people, by the invading Moslem Somalis.

In Asia countless expeditions took place, most of them undertaken by private merchants or peddlers looking for profits. Some of them became well known; some left written descriptions of their travels which add a great deal to our knowledge of sixteenth-century Asian geography. Tomé Pires, an able pharmacist in Malacca and well versed in Asian affairs, was chosen by the governor-general of India to head a Portuguese mission to China in 1516. He visited Canton and Peking but was refused an audience by the emperor. Back in Canton, Tomé Pires was arrested and held in captivity for many years. He never left China, where he died around 1540. Before going on his mission he had written a book about Malaysia, Java, and Sumatra, with information on other countries: the *Suma Oriental* ("Sum of the East"), first published in Italy in 1550.

Another explorer was Duarte Barbosa, a clerk in the Cannanore trading post, who traveled in the interior of India from 1501 to 1516–17. His *Livro* ("Book"), published in 1554, described not only India but also Indo-China and China. Domingos Pais and Fernão Nunes, both horse traders, visited the kingdom of Vijayanagar before 1525 and also wrote of their experiences there. António Tenreiro accompanied a Portuguese mission to Persia (1519), and then traveled through Armenia, Syria, Palestine, and Egypt. On a second trip (1528) he was officially dispatched to Portugal by land, crossing all the Middle East and reporting everything he saw and heard in his *Itinerário* ("Itinerary"), first published in 1560. The greatest of all the Portuguese travelers in the first half of the sixteenth century, however, was Fernão Mendes Pinto, an adventurer in search of fortune, who visited Southeast Asia, China, and Japan, traveling extensively for about seventeen years (1537–54). His *Peregrinaçam* ("Pilgrimage"), not published until 1614, combines some imagination and fantasy with a great deal of lively information. He has rightly been called the Portuguese Marco Polo.

In Brazil contacts with the hinterland began shortly after the discovery. The establishment of the captaincies favored the exploration of the interior, generally in search of gold, precious stones, and spices. Captain-Governor Martim Afonso de Sousa ordered two expeditions inland in 1531–32, one departing from Rio de Janeiro (115 leagues inland), the other from São Vicente. Commanded by Pero Lobo and composed of eighty people, this second expedition reached the plateau where São Paulo now lies and continued to the Paraná River, where the whole party was slaughtered by the natives. Other minor journeys inland took place until the middle of the century.

The Portuguese had arrived in India with the main purpose of getting spices and other profitable merchandise. They also posed as crusaders in a permanent fight against the Moslems. They soon realized that to secure control of spice sources and trade in the Indian Ocean they had to destroy the long-established network of Moslem traders and trading places. Furthermore, they found Islam to be one of the leading faiths all over the Asian coastline. Thus spices and war would come together, and any initial peaceful goals were very soon converted into a policy of strategic aggression, sheer destruction, and ultimate conquest.

From 1498 to 1505 the Portuguese simply appraised what they had to do. From some local friendly rajahs they got permission to set up trading posts in Cochin (Port. Cochim), Cannanore (Cananor), Quilon (Coulão), on the west Indian coast, and Meliapore (São Tomé) on the east coast. Yet violence erupted immediately. Local intrigues, where the Moslems always played a prominent part, plus the inevitable distrust and awkwardness of the Portuguese, led Vasco da Gama to bombard Calicut (1498) and to sail back to Europe as an enemy. Pedro Álvares Cabral's fleet, for similar reasons (in spite of an auspicious beginning), repeated the feat (1500). The city was shelled again and again (1503, 1504) until a treaty was imposed by the ever stronger Portuguese.

Sent by King Manuel as a viceroy (*Vice-Rei*), Francisco de Almeida arrived in India in 1505 with a definite program of political action. His instructions included the building of several fortresses at key strategic points (preferably on islands close to the mainland) with competent garrisons, and the permanent stationing of a fleet in the Indian Ocean. He was expected to enforce the Portuguese monopoly of long-distance trade and impose a policy of paid permits (*cartazes*) on all the non-Portuguese trading vessels. Through violence and warlike attitudes he was to remind everyone everywhere of the presence and power of the Portuguese. Yet he was also instructed to have as a policy searching for political and military alliances with the native princes, even with the Moslem ones. Aware of the physical impossibility of conquering too much territory, and actually uninterested in a political empire so far from Europe, the Portuguese aimed only at efficient sea control coupled with political hegemony in the form of areas of influence. Such objectives were generally achieved, though at the cost of tremendous difficulties and an almost permanent state of war. Until the early seventeenth century the Indian Ocean was practically a Portuguese sea.

Francisco de Almeida (1505–9) built fortresses in Kilwa (Quíloa), Sofala, and Mozambique, all on the African coast; in Angediva, Cannanore, and Cochin, on the west coast of India; and in Socotra, off the Arabian Peninsula at the entrance to the Red Sea. Furthermore, he attacked and left in ruins a number of other hostile towns, killing and capturing hundreds of people besides. His successor, Governor-General Afonso de Albuquerque (1509–15), carried on his policy. However, he had a better knowledge of places and peoples (having been in India since 1506 and before, in 1503, and having commanded an expedition to Arabia and built up the fortress of Socotra). A more daring assessor of military forces and a much greater strategic genius, Albuquerque was both the true founder of the Portuguese "empire" in Asia and the best warrant of its permanence. In little more than six years he anchored the Portuguese to the East Indian by conquering Malacca (1511) and so controlling all the maritime traffic with the Pacific; he imposed the Portuguese authority and suzerainty on Hormuz (Ormuz), thus controlling the Persian Gulf (1507 and 1515); and he established a territorial base for the seat of Portuguese administration by conquering Goa (1510). Several petty rulers paid him allegiance and tribute. More fortresses were built, and new trade posts set up. War and destruction ravaged a number of maritime cities, reinforcing Portuguese authority everywhere. Hailed by some as a new Alexander, Albuquerque's main achievement was probably to make the Portuguese the viable successors to the Moslems and to remind the Asian coastal peoples of the presence of the Portuguese as powerful overlords. He failed only in Arabia, where, despite bombardment and destruction, he did not succeed in taking Aden and even had to order the Socotra fortress to be dismantled (1511).

Albuquerque's successors were as a rule less famous than he and have been more blamed for their misdemeanors, cruelties, and deeds of corruption. Yet Portuguese fortune was far from declining; rather it was rising and continued to do so until the middle of the sixteenth century. Colombo, in Ceylon, was taken in 1518, and the island became a pivotal piece in the Portuguese system. Other fortresses were built in Chaul, the Maldive Islands, Pachim (Pacem) in Sumatra, Ternate in the Moluccas, Chale, and other places. Diu, Daman (Damão), and Bassein (Baçaim), all in India, became like Goa true Portuguese cities, and never ceased to grow until the early seventeenth century. In China, finally, the Portuguese got Macao (1557) on a sort of permanent lease, and settled down in colonies of traders in several other Chinese cities. The accompanying map gives clear evidence of the extension of the Portuguese power in Asia through the end of the sixteenth century.

Whereas long-distance trade and the omnipresence of Moslem merchants served as unifying factors in 1500 in Asia, politically the vast continent was divided into a great many small and large units, each one fiercely defending its independence and posing as a rival to the others. In India divisions reached a maximum, Moslem and Hindu states disputing the hegemony of geographical and economic areas. The north and center were Moslem territory, with the western coastline shared by the kingdoms of Gujarat (also called Cambay), Ahmadnagar, and Bijapur. A dozen more kingdoms covered the inland and the eastern coast. Here, however, with the Mughal Empire playing a leading role, the Portuguese impact was hardly felt, and amazingly few references (if any) appear about them in chronicles and other local records. The South of India was relatively unified under the Hindu Empire of Vijayanagar, with some petty tributary states like Calicut, Cochin, Cannanore, and Cranganore. Posing as their friends against the Moslem enemy, the Portuguese achieved most privileges, concessions, and alliances in Vijayanagar, which they never attacked so ruthlessly as the Islamic states.

West of India, the major political forces were Persia (to which

Hormuz was tributary) and Egypt, which fell to the Turks in 1517. Besides these, the coasts of Arabia and East Africa included a great many small sultanates and sheikdoms, all Moslem of course, heavily attacked by the Portuguese in successive raids.

East of India, and skipping the great kingdoms of Pegu and Siam, where the Portuguese never played any significant role, the political breakup was again a fact in Malaysia and Indonesia. The state of Malacca (Moslem) occupied most of the southern Indo-China peninsula, with hegemony over a part of adjacent Sumatra. It fell into Portuguese hands by 1511. In other sultanates the Portuguese constantly meddled with the local problems, trying to impose their suzerainty by intrigue. The only strong country in East Asia was China.

Openly defying the Moslem hegemony and combating the Islamic faith, the Portuguese had to meet as their main enemies in Asia the Egyptians and the Turks, allied to the many smaller Mohammedan kingdoms. Most of the naval and land struggle took place in the western Indian Ocean, between Arabia and India. It helped the Portuguese considerably that none of the major Moslem countries was openly turned toward the sea or based its power upon the sea. Kingdoms like Persia and the Mughal Empire were continental rather than maritime. Only the Egyptians and the Turks were in a situation that required meeting the Portuguese challenge, yet their main strength and interests lay elsewhere, in the Mediterranean, the Red Sea, and Europe.

The most important wars fought by the Portuguese in the first half of the sixteenth century took place in 1508–9 (the battles of Chaul and Diu), 1531–33 (the conquest of Diu), 1538 (first siege of Diu, gallantly held by António da Silveira), and 1546–47 (the second siege of Diu, defended by João de Mascarenhas, rescued by the viceroy João de Castro). All these battles ranged the Portuguese against the same enemies: a coalition of Cambayans, Egyptians, and Turks. Other fiercely fought wars (1510, 1547–48) put the Portuguese at odds with Bijapur, the Moslem state where Goa was located. Calicut always remained a bitter foe, difficult to subject (wars in 1505, 1509, 1510, 1525–26). Elsewhere the Portuguese had to fight in Hormuz (Persia), Malacca, and the Red Sea, where three times they attempted

Basra

Ormuz 1507

Dibba
Suhar 1507
Muscat 1507
Dibai Kuryat 1507
Kalhat 1507

Hugli

Diu 1535
Daman 1538
Baçaim 1533
Bombay 1534
Chaul 1520

GOA (1534)

Goa 1510
Onor 1506
Mangalore
Cannanore 1501-05
Chale 1531 Calicut 1513
Ponani 1507 Cranganore
Cochin 1500-3
Quilon 1503

S. Tomé de Meliapor

Negapatam
Jaffna 1560
Trincomali
Colombo 1518 Batticaloa
Kotte

MELIAPORE (1606)

Aden 1513
Zeila 1516

Socotra 1507

ETHIOPIA (1555)

COCHIN (1558)

Barawa

Malindi 1448
Mombasa 1505

MOÇAMBIQUE (1512)

Zanzibar 1503

Kilwa 1502

Moçambique 1507

Chittagong

• Macao 1557

MACAO (1575)

FUNAY (1588)

TONKIN (1659)

• Martaban

MALACCA (1558)

Achin• •Pasei 1516

•Malacca 1511

Ternate•
Tidore 1521

Macassar 1545•

0   500   1000 Km.

0   500   1000 miles

devastating raids and definitive conquests but met with little success (Albuquerque in 1513, Lopo Soares de Albergaria in 1516, and Estêvão da Gama in 1541, the last one reaching Suez).

ORGANIZATION OF THE EMPIRE

The experimental laboratory for the Portuguese Empire in Asia and America was in the North Atlantic: the Azores and Madeira and later Cape Verde and São Tomé. Despite their small size and sparse population, the methods and forms of settlement that the Portuguese followed there deserve our attention. Those islands were to a considerable extent microcosms of the major continental areas of India and Brazil.

By the second half of the fifteenth century both Madeira and the Azores had become mature colonies of settlement. Replicas in a way of metropolitan Portugal, they presented nonetheless some definite characteristics of their own, along with innovations and failures.

In Madeira increase in population brought about the development of the municipal system; in each of the two captaincies new *concelhos* were rising by the early 1500's. In 1508 Funchal was raised to the category of town and granted a local organization similar to that of Lisbon, a pattern which would be followed again and again all over the Empire. The number of its inhabitants reached some five thousand, which placed Funchal above many important cities on the mainland, such as Leiria, Tomar, and Faro, and equal to Braga, the seat of an archbishopric. In the two islands of Madeira and Porto Santo there lived some twenty thousand people, perhaps one-tenth of them slaves. Justifying a petition to the Pope for the creation of a bishopric in Madeira, the king mentioned the existence of eight important centers of settlement (*vilas*), each one with its own municipal organization. Indeed, Pope Leo X created the bishopric of Funchal in 1514, with jurisdiction over all the overseas territories.

Economically, the two islands produced and exported sugar, the foremost source of wealth in the mid-sixteenth century. The southern coastline of Madeira was covered with plantations, trade being carried on directly with Flanders and other foreign countries. The second economic activity was the production of wine, which would become the major source of wealth by the second half of the sixteenth century.

King Manuel's concern for law enforcement and legislative reforms was felt also in Madeira, where a detailed customs regulation and several administrative and judicial measures were enacted. By the early 1500's the island was unquestionably a minor replica of Portugal itself, resembling Minho or the Algarve. The growth of population on the mainland had the consequences of an increasing immigration, an abundance of free labor, and the resulting decline of slavery. Madeira's growth and development during the sixteenth century were constant, yet never so spectacular as fifty years before. The "new country" for settlement and gigantic economic expansion was then the Azores, neglected previously.

All nine islands in the archipelago, even tiny and remote Flores and Corvo, were populated by the sixteenth century. Competition among the several captains to whom the islands had been granted resulted in increased prosperity. The general growth of population made it easier to recruit settlers in Portugal and to interest them in agriculture, which benefited from an extremely fertile virgin soil. In the mid-1400's not one *vila* (small town) with its *foral* existed in the whole archipelago. By 1500 there were at least five: in the islands of Terceira two, in São Miguel two, and in São Jorge one. Fifty years later the Azores counted two cities (Angra in Terceira and Ponta Delgada in São Miguel) and twelve *vilas,* distributed among São Miguel (five), Terceira (three), São Jorge (three), and Graciosa (one). In São Miguel, the largest island, Vila Franca do Campo, one of the earlier settlements and the seat of administration, declined in favor of Ponta Delgada, better located geographically and economically. A destructive earthquake in 1522 ruined Vila Franca. Founded on flatter soils than Funchal and benefitting from a greater concern for town planning and town building, the two cities of Angra and Ponta Delgada followed a typical Renaissance urban pattern, with a handsome chessboard plan and a rational distribution of the vital centers. They also inherited the Lisbon model for their municipal organization.

In 1534 the Azores seemed important enough for the Pope to

institute the new diocese of Angra, dismembered from that of Funchal and with jurisdiction over the nine islands of the archipelago. Three times as large as Madeira, better favored in ports and places for settlement, less hindered by mountains, and requiring minor works of irrigation, the Azores rapidly became prosperous and economically helpful to the mainland. In the late 1400's wheat became the chief source of revenue. It was exported to Portugal in large quantities and helped to curb the country's permanent deficit in grain. Woad and *urzela* (litmus roccella), first-rate dyestuffs for the industrial countries of Europe, were also widely exported with good profits. Sugar was introduced too as an export, but the profits were small.

In the Cape Verde Islands, discovered in the early 1460's or late 1450's, effective colonization proved more difficult. The archipelago has a mild climate but very little rain, with long periods of drought. Most islands do not appeal to newcomers, the approach being a barren sight. Moreover, cultures—wheat, for instance—considered essential in those days failed in Cape Verde. In Madeira and the Azores the settlers' efforts met with bountiful output, but Cape Verde's soils were not generally as compensating. The archipelago lay too far from Portugal and showed no trace of gold or spices, as did Guinea and India. In short, a permanent settlement required more effort and different forms of adjustment from those that the Portuguese were then prepared to make.

Colonization, however, started in the Cape Verde Islands immediately after discovery. The islands belonged to Prince Fernando, the king's brother. Antonio da Noli, an Italian in the service of Portugal who had probably discovered or visited part of the archipelago, arrived in Santiago with the first settlers (apparently from the Algarve). The setting up of a trade port at Ribeira Grande, on the southern side of the island, favored Cape Verde's location as a safe port of call for the numerous Portuguese ships traveling along the African coast. Slaves imported from Guinea proved more adaptable than the Portuguese. Few white women ever arrived, and the practice of miscegenation developed immediately. In 1466 the settlers, as a privilege, were allowed to trade freely in African slaves and other merchandise. Stock farming and production of dyestuffs developed and brought about a measure of prosperity. Santiago became important as a port of call, with Ribeira Grande gaining some urban features (a migrant population, a hospital, some industrial activities, and so forth), but the growth of an agricultural pattern of settlement was possibly slowed down. The captaincy system was also established; Santiago was divided into two captaincies, and others were successively set up in each island. Conditions were similar to those in Madeira and the Azores.

Besides Santiago, Fogo and Maio had some colonizers but they met with greater difficulties. In Fogo the first settlers, belonging to Prince Fernando's household, had arrived by the 1460's, but most of them left. It was only by 1510, with the establishment of a local captaincy, that there was an effective population. Maio experienced similar problems. The captaincy was sold once; then in an act of royal interference it was divided in two to promote a better settlement. Boavista remained deserted until the sixteenth century, although animals grazed there and a hereditary captain benefited from its profits.

The other six islands (Santo Antão, São Vicente, Santa Luzia, São Nicolau, Sal, and Brava) remained uninhabited until the late seventeenth and eighteenth centuries. Yet they were not utterly unproductive, and the profit from their livestock (in skins, fat, and meat) and salt (in the island of Sal) justified the existence of captains for all of them. Interestingly enough, the captains of the Cape Verde Islands, generally appointed by John II and Manuel I, were often wealthy bureaucrats, some of them later raised to nobility. They realized the economic value of newly colonized lands (for example, Madeira and the Azores) and tried to develop them for their own profit. Yet, unwilling to leave Portugal and direct, with their presence and initiative, the effort of colonization, they helped jeopardize what they were eager to obtain.

In the first half of the sixteenth century only Santiago, and Ribeira Grande within it, could compare at all with Madeira and the Azores in results achieved. Ribeira Grande was raised to *vila* and then, somewhat prematurely, to city (1533) when the bishopric of Cape Verde was created and a first bishop appointed with authority over the overseas territories from Morocco to Guinea. The island (like the whole archipelago) was rich in livestock, particularly goats, horses, mules, and poultry. There was enough maize sown to feed the population and supply the calling ships, with some left to be sent to Portugal. Salt, too, was exported. Sugar cane and cotton had been introduced; and fish, fruit, and herbs completed the economic picture. If Cape Verde did not arouse great enthusiasm among would-be settlers and if its revenues were meager compared with those of other archipelagos, at least it could subsist and be useful as a port of call.

In the Gulf of Guinea, conditions were again different. Located on the equator, São Tomé, Principe (at the time called Santo Antão), Ano Bom, and Fernando Po benefited from an abundant and regular rainfall, coupled with a highly fertile soil. On the other hand, hot climate, excessive humidity, and numerous tropical diseases made for unhealthy living conditions that were hard to cope with and discouraged a permanent European settlement. Yet, as in Cape Verde, arrival of the first colonists followed discovery by only a few years. In the mid-1480's attempts to assemble a permanent group of settlers began in Portugal. They met with failure. In the last years of the century Álvaro de Caminha and António Carneiro, both royal vassals and belonging to the petty nobility, successfully organized the colonization of São Tomé and Principe. Before 1510 Ano Bom also had a small nucleus of colonists, led by Jorge de Melo, another nobleman. These three captains—for the captaincy system was once more set up—gathered together a highly heterogeneous band of colonists, composed of outcasts, some craftsmen and poor people from Portugal, and a number of young Jews ruthlessly taken from their parents and forcibly converted to the Christian faith. For heavier tasks, which Europeans could not perform in the equatorial climate, Negro slaves were imported from the mainland and Fernando Po. As in Cape Verde, few white women ever came to the Gulf of Guinea islands. An interesting native aristocracy of half breeds rapidly emerged and took control of the islands. Actually, social strife was characteristic of São Tomé's history from the very beginning, a rebellion against the great landowners by the mulattoes and slaves occurring as early as 1517.

Administratively, São Tomé developed quickly. The first parish existed by 1504, and twenty years later it had been raised to *vila*. By 1534, when a bishopric had been created with the seat in São Tomé and with jurisdiction over the African coast from Guinea to the Cape of Good Hope, it was promoted to city. The São Tomé captaincy had been abolished in 1522 and the island incorporated into the royal patrimony. The economy of the archipelago was based on cattle and other animals, and on sugar. Another source of prosperity derived from the islands' being supply stations on the Portuguese shipping route from India and later on the slave-trading route between Africa and Brazil.

Fernando Po, because it was inhabited by natives, resisted the Portuguese attempts at settlement and scarcely appealed to the colonists. An effective conquest would take place several centuries later. The remaining Atlantic islands, being too far from the coast and of little importance for navigation, remained deserted.

In Continental Africa settlement was intended only as a means of strengthening a trade port or supporting a vital fortress. At the time it was Portuguese policy to shun any idea of conquest and empire which neither the home resources nor coveted goals of the country seemed to justify. To maintain a trade monopoly, to carry on the fight with Islam, to reach the kingdom of Prester John—such were the acknowledged targets. Christian evangelization was next in importance but was clearly secondary. Conquest, with all its dangers and requirements, might be envisaged from a theoretical point of view but had no practical means of fulfillment. This is why the Portuguese were eager to convert deserted islands into colonies of settlement but paid little or no attention to inhabited ones, such as Fernando Po.

Trade ports and fortresses, however, were necessary for an expanding commerce and had to be established all over the African continent. In the northern hemisphere, besides Arguim (see chapter 3), a group of well-fortified castles, all protecting small trading villages and towns, rose along the Gulf of Guinea. Here, as everywhere in Africa and Asia, the Portuguese only rarely seized the country by force. They always tried a procedure of negotiating with the local rulers first for permission to settle. Once a contract was arranged, men and materials arrived from Portugal, and in a short time a replica of the Portuguese way of life was set up. In the beginning the natives had no reason to regret the Portuguese presence. Between the two sides profitable trade developed, coupled with some learning of more

C luis pir̃ D
sabona a portugal.

C guaspar de lemos D
de santa cruz sjado brasil tornou a portugal
co noua do descobrimeto della

C pero de thaide D
ha tornada se perdeo nos baixos
de s. lazo ca agua salta
ora a palta

C iro diaz D
co a tormenta esqarron
es foy ter a magadaxó sito
do cabo de guarda fuy, cõ
a tornada se emcontrou co
pedra e cabral rodas o

C vasq da thaide D
perdido com a tormenta

C Cabral D

C Nicolao coelso D

C Nuno leytão D

C Simão de miranda D
A bal resou na tormeta cõ pedral e ca
bral, e milagrosamente se salaarão

C Ayres gomez da silua D
perdido com a tormenta.

C Simão de pina D
perdido cõ a tormeta.

C Sancho de thoar D

C bertolameu diaz D
perdido cõ a tormenta

FAR LEFT: *Cabral's armada of 1500: Livro das Armadas (16th century), Academia das Ciências de Lisboa, Lisbon.* ABOVE: *Brazilian Indians, mid-16th century: engraving from the French book,* Une fête brésilienne célebrée à Rouen en 1550. BELOW: *Vasco da Gama: Anonymous, late 16th or early 17th century, Governor's Palace, Goa (India).*

advanced techniques. It was only the slave trade and the Christianization policy that would later jeopardize the entire system. Yet the Portuguese rarely fought any wars or even skirmishes until the middle of the sixteenth century.

The "capital" of all the settlements in the Gulf of Guinea (called Mina and the main source for the gold trade) was São Jorge da Mina (near the present Cape Coast in Ghana), which the Portuguese had started building by 1482 with a force of five hundred armed men and one hundred artisans. Four years later the small colony was granted a town charter and a regular captaincy was established, directly dependent upon the Crown. The captains were appointed for a three-year period. Their authority covered the other Portuguese settlements on the coast and Gulf of Guinea, all founded from 1487 to the early 1500's: Wadan, Cantor, Axim, Samma (Shamá), Gwato (in Benin), and several others, in the present republics of Mali, Senegal, Ghana, and Nigeria. Some were actually abandoned a number of years later.

South of Guinea the other African area of Portuguese expansion was the Congo. Here their experiment was marked by different and highly interesting features. After the two discovery expeditions undertaken by Diogo Cão, the Portuguese sent a mission to the Congo in 1490, ostensibly as a reply to a native request for technological and spiritual assistance. Three ships carried craftsmen, priests, monks, and tools. The alleged purpose was the search for a political alliance with the kindom of the Congo, served by an effective Christian evangelization. The Portuguese believed they were dealing with a more advanced culture and with more sophisticated and powerful rulers than they actually were. The kingdom of the Congo or Manicongo encompassed only a loose confederation of tribes with six provinces, bounded by the Congo River in the north, the Dande in the south, the Cuango River in the east, and the Atlantic ocean in the west. The Congolese, however, even if some of them (particularly their monarch) were genuinely interested in European achievements and wished to raise their own cultural level, were looking only for some military help and profitable commerce. Christianity might appeal to them but only as a means of enhancing their belief in magic and bringing some sort of positive aid to the accomplishment of miracles.

Surprisingly, this mistaken and misleading alliance endured. For more than a century the Congo was a Portuguese protectorate in Africa, although with inevitable ups and downs in effective influence and control. The king, the royal family, and the small ruling elite accepted Christianity or a sort of Christian suzerainty. Nzinga a Nkuwu, the first Christian monarch, was baptized in 1491. He changed his name to João I, like the Portuguese king. His son and heir, Nzinga Mvemba, took for himself the name of the Portuguese crown prince, Afonso. He ruled as Afonso I from 1506 to 1543 and was a loyal friend of the Portuguese, a dramatic figure of African ruler, half-detribalized, half-European and Portuguese-minded, genuinely Catholic, and thoroughly frustrated in his actions and accomplishments. After him a succession of Pedros, Franciscos, Diogos, Afonsos, Bernardos, Henriques, and Álvaros prolonged the Portuguese tradition well into the seventeenth century.

One of the reasons for the Portuguese change of attitude in the Congo was the lack of economic interest the Negro kingdom offered. Except for palm cloth and ivory and, of course, themselves as human labor, the natives had little to give. In a trading empire based on the richest and most prized items the world contained, the poor Congo progressively disenchanted her discoverers. Moreover, the right way to Ethiopia had been found, along with the real Congolese political and military possibilities. Yet Manuel I of Portugal still persisted in sending regular missions to the Congo, reinforcing the alliance. In 1512 a very complete expedition left Europe, equipped with all kinds of technological and spiritual devices, accompanied by careful and extensive instructions. It was a real civilizing mission, that of 1512, which failed in most of its objectives, partly because of the premature death of its leader, Simão da Silva. The Portuguese succeeded in flooding the Congo with priests, traders, and advisers. A caricature state of Portugal was introduced, with even the Portuguese law ordinances presented as Congolese laws: European manners, dress, administrative practices, all were eagerly copied by "João I," "Afonso I," and their courts. A number of young natives went to Portugal to get an education, many returning to the Congo later only to find themselves useless and hopeless in their own country. The most famous of them, Henrique, one of Afonso's sons, spent thirteen years in Europe and was ordained a priest and made a bishop (of Utica, *in partibus infidelium*) and Vicar Apostolic of the Congo. Actually his role was insignificant. He died in the 1530s, almost forgotten, and despised by both whites and blacks.

Slave trade completely changed this ideal pattern of alliance. The islands of São Tomé and Principe gradually became the seat of a profitable human commerce directed toward Europe, America, and the islands themselves. A powerful class of white and mulatto traders emerged, forming a true party that finally controlled Portuguese affairs in the Congo for their own interests. Slaves were recruited everywhere, most of them outside Congo frontiers but many inside also. As their sale brought profit for everyone, it was tolerated by the ruling native minority, often unable to interfere and cope with the busy operations of Portuguese from Portugal, Portuguese from São Tomé, and the local caste of mulattoes and Portuguese-educated Congolese. As the slave demand went up and up, the Congo's human resources were exhausted and traders were forced to look for them further south, in what is now Angola, with important results for the geographic knowledge of that country. By the 1520's and 1530's the region of Andongo, where the Ngola ruled, had become a Portuguese area of expansion. A greater density of population provided good reasons for the traders, some 4,000 to 5,000 slaves from the hinterland of the present Congo and north Angola being shipped each year from Mpinda, on the mouth of the Congo River.

It is hard to say how many Portuguese ever settled in the Congo, but their number probably never exceeded one hundred at any time. Yet the Portuguese brought with them many forms of fortification, housebuilding, and city planning which have survived to the present time, particularly in the Congolese capital, christened São Salvador.

On the eastern coast of Africa settlement was understood in terms of trade relationships with the Indian Ocean. The Portuguese secured native permission to build fortresses in Sofala and Kilwa, both in 1505. In Kilwa, however, there were soon violence and destruction by Viceroy Francisco de Almeida, who imposed a Portuguese protectorate on the native Moslem kingdom. A third fortress had been erected on the island of Mozambique by 1507. Elsewhere trade ports and political suzerainty operated in Zanzibar, Malindi, and Lamu. Kilwa, considered useless, was abandoned in 1512. Sofala and Mozambique, however, became important military strongholds and trade ports, called on by Portuguese ships traveling to and (especially) from India. Each received the status of a captaincy and was directly dependent on the governor of India. Mozambique corresponded to São Jorge da Mina. It quickly became a European town, its houses, churches, and streets following the Portuguese pattern, its administrative system copied from the mainland's *concelhos,* its religious and charitable brotherhoods similar to the ones in Portugal.

The prospect of finding gold favored Sofala's development and led the Portuguese up the Zambezi and other rivers. New trade ports were established in Sena in 1531, then in Tete, Quelimane, and Inhambane to the mid-1540's, with occasional factories on the rivers Pungue and Buzi. Farther south, explorer Lourenço Marques contacted the local chieftains in the area where the present bay of Lourenço Marques is located and succeeded in setting up trade patterns and the basis for a permanent Portuguese establishment.

In spite of these settlements and fortresses the number of Portuguese living in Africa was very small by the middle of the sixteenth century. Excluding the islands, hardly more than two or three hundred whites were scattered around the African coast.

Colonization in India meant little more than strengthening and making permanent the cornerstones of the Portuguese trade monopoly. The idea of conquering India or any other large region in Asia was utterly foreign to the Portuguese rulers. Thus Governor Afonso de Albuquerque's policy of converting Goa into a European town and fostering mixed marriages of Portuguese and Hindus (according to the royal plans) aimed only at strengthening Goa's position as the capital of a trade emporium. Elsewhere Albuquerque simply continued his predecessors' policies—the royal instructions each of them was bound to follow—of putting strongholds in strategic points all over the Indian Ocean and backing them up with permanent fleets as a means of controlling trade and protecting the factories.

Official intermarriages began in Goa by 1509. Each couple was granted an important subsidy or dowry in money, which rapidly increased the number of weddings. In three or four years more than five hundred marriages took place, mostly in Goa, but a few in Cannanore and Cochin also. The marrying Portuguese were generally young artisans and soldiers, with a few lesser nobles too; the Hindu women belonged to the upper castes. This naturally irritated the Hindus, who despised intermarriages and only reluctantly or perforce consented to these unions. Later on, the subsidies were discontinued and the marriage policy was slowed down, but a caste of half breeds had arisen, devoted to the Portuguese and helping to ensure their presence in Goa for centuries.

The administration of Goa followed the pattern of Lisbon. A municipal council was founded and a *câmara* (council) organized with its *vereadores, juizes,* and *procuradores,* ten people in all, presumably elected from among the men who were encouraged to settle down in Goa for good. The captain of Goa, corresponding to the *alcaide* of the Portuguese towns, had the right and the duty to attend the council meetings. Albuquerque's original charter was confirmed by the king in 1516, its privileges being carefully kept by the councilors and successively renewed or confirmed. The town grew in size and in population. Its original native plan underwent many changes, gradually approaching the ideal pattern of the Renaissance cities. Where the governor, the top bureaucrats, and the wealthy traders lived, new and costly buildings appeared. Several monumental churches were also erected. Goa became the seat of a bishopric in 1534, with jurisdiction over Asia and the East African coast. By 1524 a minimum of 450 Portuguese households (about 2,500 people) was counted. By 1540 there were about 1,800 European-descended households, that is, some 10,000 people, besides the pure Hindu, the Moslems, and the slaves, whose number would probably multiply that figure three or four times. The high death rate among the Europeans was constantly offset by arrivals from Portugal. Goa soon became one of the leading Portuguese cities, challenging Lisbon itself.

Elsewhere, patterns tended to be similar. Wherever the Portuguese had effectively conquered a town and dispossessed its rulers, they tried to Europeanize it and convert it into a replica of the places they knew at home. They also promoted a policy of miscegenation, aiming at a quicker growth in population and a stronger, permanent Portuguese presence. Like the Phoenicians and the Greeks of the past, the Portuguese were more interested in weaving a vast web of urban colonies, scattered along the coastline, than in conquering territorial empires.

Comparable to Goa was Malacca, the town the Portuguese promoted to their far-eastern capital. Malacca, too, possessed some hinterland, useful for supplies and a better defensive system. There, also, the intermarriage policy was fostered, and a caste of half breed gradually emerged. Institutions copied the Lisbon-Goa pattern. In some other towns (Cochin, for instance, and later Bassein), where the Portuguese permanence was felt more strongly, European standards were also enforced. This was the exception, however, rather than the rule. In most places the Portuguese hardly changed or tried to change the existing way of life. Confining themselves to their trade ports or their fortresses, and constantly on the move, they accepted local authorities and native traditions, although their presence had some impact on both.

The Crown representative in the Portuguese settlements from Sofala to Macao was the governor-general, appointed by the king for a three-year period and rarely reappointed. Each new governor carried with him three sealed letters (numbered 1, 2, 3) in which the names of his successors in case of emergency were written. This system worked out quite well, making up for the one-and-a-half-year distance to Portugal and to new appointments. When there was pompous lineage or royal favoritism, or when circumstances required someone with greater prestige and authority, the governor-general was turned into a viceroy (*vice-rei*) with almost royal prerogatives. From 1505 to 1550 eleven governors but only four viceroys (Francisco de Almeida, Vasco da Gama, Garcia de Noronha, and João de Castro) ruled over the Portuguese empire in the East. Governors and viceroys appointed local authorities, directed the aggressive and defensive campaigns, supervised the economic policies, and were responsible for the maintenance and enforcement of law.

Brazil was inhabited by natives, an obstacle to permanent settlers. Yet the natives were very primitive, with a tribal organization, many of them cannibals. No possible alliances with local rulers could be envisioned; no respect for native customs or traditions could slow down a European takeover. Furthermore, the Brazilian natives did not point the way toward Prester John or well-known or rumored gold mines. Little effective trade could be carried on with them. For the Portuguese, Brazil offered a similar situation to, and posed the same problems as, the Canary Islands in the early days of their discovery. It was a country to be colonized, yet it posed difficult questions concerning defense and a *modus vivendi* with the natives. Fortunately for the Portuguese, the Indians were relatively few and sparsely distributed. Vast areas of inviting land looked deserted. Although aware of some rudimentary agricultural techniques, most natives were alien to agriculture and to sedentary life, preferring the forest to the open spaces. And being good natured and naive, many welcomed the whites and got along with them.

The Brazilian settlement developed slowly, much as the colonization of the Azores or the Cape Verde Islands. Few Europeans seemed interested in residing there. Yet there were some natural advantages over Africa, the weather being somewhat healthier and the soil more fertile. Moreover, nature offered unsuspected beauties, a fact that appealed to the Portuguese from the very beginning. In the first years after the discovery, Brazil yielded little more than brazilwood, sugar cane, and such exotic animals as monkeys and parrots, which the Portuguese had to pick up in the jungle themselves for the natives ignored trade and its procedures. On such a basis and in contrast to the appealing glitter of the Asian traffic, Brazil obviously attracted few people. The Crown, repeating a proceeding of the mid-1400's, rented the trade monopoly to and from Brazil to a private company of wealthy ex-Jews, headed by Fernão de Loronha. The contract clauses bound Loronha and his partners to the systematic and gradual discovery of the coast. Loronha's pact with the Crown probably lasted until 1512. He was succeeded by another merchant, Jorge Lopes Bixorda, whose activities were ended by 1515 or 1516. In fifteen years the prospects offered by the Brazilian trade had changed radically. The monopoly brought wealth to its owners and called attention to the new country. Settlers arrived, and many people in Portugal were now becoming interested in sharing the profits.

The basis for prosperity had been brazilwood. By 1506-7 a yearly average of 20,000 quintais (hundredweights) was imported and sold with good profit all over Europe. The officially named "land of the True Cross" (Terra da Vera Cruz) became identified with the "land of brazilwood" or, more simply, "land of brazil" (Terra do Brasil). This name, so meaningful also for all those who saw in the new country the actual site of legendary "Brazil," soon replaced the official terminology. Trade ports seem to have been established in Pernambuco (1502?) and Porto Seguro (1503), protected by small fortresses. Other isolated nuclei probably rose in São Vicente (1508?) and Baía de Todos os Santos (1509?). Notice of Brazil economic interest promptly aroused the greed of competitors. Clandestine Spanish and French fleets took their share in the profitable trade. As had happened a hundred years before in Madeira, the Portuguese Crown decided to intervene, fostering colonization and helping in the defense of the new colony. King Manuel decided to dispatch every two years a fleet of some ships, under the leadership of a specially appointed captain or governor, to cruise the coasts of Brazil to and fro. From 1516 to 1530 this system effectively contributed to a better defense of the coastline. Several foreign ships were taken and others discouraged from carrying on their traffic. At the same time the few existing trade ports became real centers of settlement. Organized according to the Portuguese norms, better protected for defense, they were raised to the position of captaincies, with captains appointed by the Crown for a certain period of time. To foster their development, the Crown provided the new settlers with tools, materials, and regular supplies. It also supported the charges of establishing sugar mills and plantation complexes. A sugar plantation was considered the best start of a lucrative settlement. Obviously the examples of Madeira and São Tomé were determinative.

Though documentation does not abound, it seems that captaincies were first created in Pernambuco, Porto Seguro, Rio de Janeiro, and São Vicente. Pernambuco was probably the most important of the four, the one in which King Manuel ordered the setting up of the first sugar mill. The others looked like tiny villages, as a 1527 description of São Vicente clearly shows: a dozen houses, of which only one was made of stone, a lookout tower for defense, some poultry and pigs, some herb gardens. Missionaries who had arrived in Brazil from the very beginning came in larger numbers after 1516. They belonged to the Franciscan and Arrábida orders. The task of converting was relatively easy, the Indians having few religious beliefs.

By the late 1520's the French started actively raiding the Brazilian coasts and "hijacking" as many ships as they could. The cruising Portuguese armadas were no longer sufficient for effective protection. Moreover, the small and scattered captaincies had means only for local defense and did not dream of preventing a full-scale landing and occupation. In Lisbon the government drafted a plan for the systematic colonization of Brazil. Then it dispatched Martim Afonso de Sousa, a nobleman, as captain and governor, with five ships and a total of five hundred men, including crew and settlers. Leaving in December 1530, Martim Afonso de Sousa arrived in Brazil two months later, with full powers to accomplish a triple mission: coastal defense against the French, determination of the exact boundaries of Brazil, and supervision of a permanent settlement from north to south, along the whole coastline.

For this purpose the Crown had divided Brazil into fifteen captaincies (*capitanias*) from the Maranhão basin to Santa Catarina, at 28⅓°S. Each captaincy was to cover fifty leagues of coastline, being separated from the next one by a straight parallel, and theoretically extending westward to the Tordesillas meridian. From north to south these captaincies were Pará, Maranhão, Piauí (a later name), Ceará, Itamaracá, Pernambuco, Baía, Ilhéus, Porto Seguro, Espírito Santo, São Tomé (also called Campo dos Goitacazes), Rio de Janeiro, Santo Amaro, São Vicente, and Santana. For practical purposes, however, this number was reduced to eleven because Pará and Ceará were united under one captain, the same happening to Itamaracá with Santo Amaro and Santana, and to Rio de Janeiro with São Vicente. With some later alterations, deriving more from assembling captaincies or subdividing them than from changing original boundaries, this division would survive to the present and provide the basis for the modern coastal states of Brazil.

Although the original purpose was to make all of them the same size, the inevitable irregularity of the coast resulted in different sizes for each captaincy. Moreover, some lots were from the very beginning smaller than fifty leagues in coastline. Each lot (*capitania, governo*) was granted to a *capitão-donatário* (also called *governador*, governor) whose powers were similar to those of the captains of Madeira, Azores, and Cape Verde. They acted as feudal lords, enjoying full civil and criminal jurisdiction, appointing officers, and requiring homage from them. They could transmit the captaincy to their heirs, without the restrictions determined by the Lei Mental (see chapter 2). The captain was to distribute the land to Catholic settlers, who were obliged to cultivate it in a certain period of time (generally five years), tax-free, except for the tithe to the Order of Christ. The means of production (sugar mills, water mills, ovens, pressers, etc.) belonged to the captain, who could rent them or grant them against the payment of a tribute. The captain also had the right to keep for himself ten to sixteen leagues of land, divided in four or five allotments and rented to other people. Owners of vast areas of uncultivated land could also sublet them to other farmers. This automatically created a four-strata hierarchial society, very much in the feudal manner. Trade pertained both to the settlers in a free system and to the Crown, which owned the brazilwood, slave, spices, and drug monopolies, along with the fifth part of all the ores and precious stones. Depriving settlers of the main and easiest sources of profit, the Crown practically compelled them to develop agriculture and create new sources of revenue. The result was the rise of the sugar industry.

As to the social condition of the donataries, all of them belonged to the aristocracy, although none could be regarded as a first-class noble. Three captains were civil servants in Lisbon, one of them of considerable wealth. Some never went to their captaincies, preferring to endow the necessary capital, send somebody as their lieutenant, and later collect the expected profits. On the whole the social pattern of Brazil copied that of the Atlantic Islands, particularly Cape Verde and São Tomé.

Each captaincy met with a different fate. São Vicente and Pernambuco were fairly successful. The captain of the former was Martim Afonso de Sousa, who left Brazil in 1533 never to return. He later became governor of India and paid little attention to his extensive South American dominions. Yet he appointed some able lieutenants, such as António de Oliveira (1538–44) and Brás Cubas (1544–49) whose efforts were certainly decisive in the progress of São Vicente. In spite of Spanish and Indian attacks, the population of São Vicente increased (more than six hundred Europeans and three thousand slaves, in 1548) and its economic prosperity appealed to new settlers. The neighboring captaincy of Santo Amaro became in effect one of its dependencies. Besides the capital, also called São Vicente, rich in cattle and sugar mills, there was another *vila,* Santos, close to it, and a third developing center at Piratininga, the future São Paulo. All the places were well fortified and organized. In the capital a municipal council had been established as early as 1532. Ten years later a City Hall and three churches had already been built.

Pernambuco (then called Nova Lusitânia) had been given to Duarte Coelho, probably the ablest colonizer of Brazil during the sixteenth century. A fighter, a diplomat, and a gifted administrator, with a good record in India, Duarte Coelho founded Iguaraçú, then Olinda, where he set up his capital. Despite the struggle against the natives Pernambuco prospered and grew year after year. In the mid-1540's, Olinda had four hundred Europeans and five hundred slaves. Iguaraçú had 150 people only. There were five sugar mills, cotton fields, cattle, and many pigs.

The remaining captaincies met with little success. Piauí, Itamaracá, Rio de Janeiro, and Santana were virtually unoccupied. For the exploration of Pará, Maranhão, and Ceará a large expedition of ten ships with more than a thousand people, including a hundred riders, was organized. Its purpose was more the search for gold (which the Spaniards had just found in America) than actual settlement. Having vainly explored the river Maranhão for three years and lost two-thirds of its people, the expedition broke up and the few survivors settled down in the village of Nazaré, which they had founded in the island of Maranhão. In Ilhéus, Porto Seguro, and Espírito Santo settlement continued for many years. In Baía and São Tomé the Indians attacked and destroyed houses and cultures, killing scores of Portuguese and their slaves, including one of the captains. Brazil was indeed difficult to colonize. There were all kinds of obstacles to a smooth way of life. There was the climate, responsible for the death of hundreds. There were innumerable insects and wild beasts, while equatorial and tropical jungles, full of dangers and often impenetrable, prevented moving inland, in search of better places to live.

In spite of all the failures the colonization of Brazil was far from being a disaster. Some two thousand Portuguese, aided by three or four thousand slaves, were permanently settled from Pernambuco to Santos by the late 1540's, a relevant figure if one recalls that in Asia, with all its attractions and several times as large as Brazil, no more than ten thousand Portuguese were to be counted at this time. The Brazilian wood and sugar trade had reached unsuspected levels, competing with Madeira and São Tomé.

We are not familiar with all the details of the economic system adopted by the Crown overseas immediately after Prince Henry's death. It was probably handed over to private enterprisers, provided they paid a 10 to 20 per cent duty to the Crown on all the imported merchandise. Several individuals and temporary companies, where Portuguese capital and merchants generally predominated, took over the exploitation of the profitable commerce with Guinea. African trade, however, did not consist of a single block, permanently in the hands of a single group of people. Rather commerce was divided by geographical tracks, or else by fields, each one comprising a certain number of items. Such regions, or such products, were then rented by the Crown for a certain period of years.

Concerning gold, for instance, there was the Arguim trade, in West Africa; the Cantor and Gambia trade; the Serra Leoa trade; and the Mina trade. The spice and drug traffic was distinct from the fisheries or the commerce in ivory. And the slave trade, of course, was a separate enterprise. The Crown owned a number of monopolies, such as those of the spice trade, the slave trade, and the Mina gold trade. Yet, state monopoly could be expressed in two ways: either direct exploitation by Crown-appointed officials settled in the trade ports or exploitation by special permission granted to individuals. Still, if the gold from Mina, for instance, belonged to the Crown, a great number of people had the right to trade in gold. Captains and soldiers of the fortresses, civil servants, and others were entitled to buy gold to the limit of their salaries or allowances, provided they submitted it to the customs' control and had it coined at the Royal Mint in Lisbon. The coexistence of all these forms, private and state-owned, and the constant change as time passed by, make the analysis of the Portuguese trade in Africa (as later on in Asia and America) particularly complex. Moreover, smuggling and foreign competition often undermined the strictness of the law.

The great epoch for the rented monopolies had begun by 1468, when the Crown (or rather Prince João to whom Afonso V had just granted the African trade) conceded to a Lisbon merchant, Fernão Gomes, the monopoly of every profit in Africa that did not pertain to the state. Others followed, namely, the Florentine merchant Bartolomeo Marchione, who was in control of the African trade by the 1480's and early 1490's. Spanish, German, and French merchants also had their share during Manuel's reign.

Enlargement of the Portuguese undertakings to the Indian Ocean did not bring an immediate change in this state of things. The expeditions of Bartolomeu Dias and Vasco da Gama were partially financed by private capital. Florentines (the Giraldi and the Bardi, for instance), Genoese (the Lomellini among others), and other Italians (the Affaitati from Cremona, as a good example); Germans from Augsburg and Nuremberg (the Fugger, the Welser, the Imhoff); later Castilians from Seville and Burgos; even the French—all competed in the attempts to control the Portuguese trade with India. Among the Portuguese businessmen, the ex-Jews (New Christians) were particularly active because of their capital and their connections abroad.

In the first years after 1498 trade was free, against a 5 per cent customs duty only. Yet profits were becoming so huge and competition so rampant (with an alarming impact on prices) that the Crown decided to interfere. In 1504 state control was imposed on all trade with the East. All merchandise had to be reported to the royal office (Casa da India), which would sell it at a fixed price and give back to each proprietor the corresponding amount of money. Customs duties were raised to 30 per cent. This was not considered enough. In 1506 the king declared an official state monopoly on all imports and sales of spices, silk, and shellac; on the exports of gold, silver, copper, and coral; and on the trade between Goa and the other main factories. Only the Crown could equip and send ships to the Indian Ocean. This system would last until 1570. Again, this did not mean that the Crown handled all the economic matters directly. Contracts were signed with groups of capitalists for the sale and placement of the spices and other products. Crews and colonial civil servants received part of their salaries in import permits of spice bundles, bought at their own expense but transported at the state's expense.

These were the so-called *quintaladas*. High officials might also import merchandise which they shared with the Crown. Everyone was allowed to sell his rights of *quintalada* or simply to rent space aboard a ship to somebody else, a practice that very nearly converted into a merchant every crewman and every civil servant.

From the very beginning of the expansion the major profitable items had been slaves, followed in importance by gold and spices. This trilogy continued to play a decisive role in the economic history of the Portuguese Empire throughout the sixteenth century, although first place passed to spices, followed by gold and slaves. Spices, a general name for a great many products (including sugar) with various uses, had always been rare and expensive, although their use in pre-Renaissance Europe was widespread. Their rarity made them still more appreciated and coveted by merchants because of the huge profits made on their sale. The quest for spices, like the quest for gold and slaves, could affect individuals, societies, and countries.

African spices included red pepper (found in the Gambia and the Gulf of Guinea areas, and black pepper (a variety of the Indian pepper, called *pimenta de rabo*), found in the Gulf of Guinea also. Asian spices (the six major ones were pepper, ginger, cinnamon, clove, mace, and nutmeg) came mostly from the Malabar coast, in India (with Calicut as its foremost commercial entrepôt), Ceylon, the northwest of Sumatra, the Comore Islands of Banda and the Moluccas archipelago, all places to which the Portuguese went and which they controlled.

From the 1450's onward, when the first African red pepper arrived in Lisbon, to the end of the Portuguese dominance in Asia, the spice trade never ceased to grow. In the first decades of the sixteenth century an average of 2,000 quintais of pepper entered Portugal each year from the Gulf of Guinea. At the same time, however, Asia supplied the Portuguese with 40,000 to 50,000 quintais of spices annually (of which a minimum 10,000 were pepper), a figure that rose to 60,000 to 75,000 (one-third pepper) by the 1530's. The spice monopoly gave the Crown a net profit of about 89 per cent, a rate that again explains the appeal of India and the amazing efforts made by the Portuguese to control Asia's maritime commerce.

The gold trade was always related to Africa, although some gold came also from Sumatra. Besides the Mina, the Portuguese tried to dominate the famous Monomotapa gold sources (in present Mozambique and Rhodesia). Their output, however, scarcely paid for the hard labor necessary to get the gold. On the whole, a yearly average amount of 1,500 to 1,900 pounds of gold (700 to 840 kg.) entered Portugal in the first twenty years of the sixteenth century, estimated at 200,000 to 240,000 cruzados each year. Of this total, more than half represented the share of the Mina gold.

The third most profitable item of merchandise, slaves, had its sources all over the coast of Africa, wherever the Portuguese owned trade ports and fortresses. Slaves from Guinea (the broad geographical area) and slaves from the Congo (including Northern Angola) supplied the needs for labor in Europe, the Madeira Islands, Cape Verde, and São Tomé. Later Brazil was to become the main importer of slaves, but only from the mid-1500's onward (see chapter 7). Imprisoned Moors from North Africa, captured in battles, skirmishes, or raids, also accounted for the slave population. Their number, however, was small, most of them being redeemed by their fellow countrymen or exchanged for Portuguese captives in Moslem countries. Asia also supplied the Portuguese with slaves of all races and creeds, but they seem to have been used mostly *in loco,* export to Europe being discouraged by the authorities. Many were resold by the Portuguese to other Asian slave traders. Again we lack precise statistics on the number of slaves bought or captured by the Portuguese until the mid-1500's. A maximum average yearly figure of 750 has been estimated for the period 1450–1500, which gives a total of 41,250. In any case, no fewer than 25,000 slaves were imported into Europe and the Portuguese colonies at that time.

Items other than spices, gold, and slaves included ivory, skins, musk, livestock, and gum from Africa, and a huge variety of beautiful, rare, or exotic merchandise from Asia, in growing demand at the courts and by the bourgeois of Europe. From the Orient came all kinds of soft textiles, such as silks, furniture made of precious woods, many varieties of china and pottery, works of art, and the like. Sugar, which ranked between the latter items and the three main ones, often assumed a more important position than slaves.

Articles in demand by the Africans varied greatly from region to region, according to their cultural advancement. As a rule, textiles occupied first place in the form of colored cloths and garments of all kinds. Glass and coral beads were highly appreciated. Many other manufactured products appealed to the Negroes and to the Moslem traders who often served as their intermediaries. Silver and copper, in the form of bracelets and rings, or as coins, or as industrial items, were other favorites among the Africans.

To India the Portuguese exported metals above all: gold and silver coins, silver and copper in bars or in objects, lead, and mercury, as well as coral. Every ship arriving at the Malabar coast in the years 1510 to 1518 was loaded with an average 50,000 cruzados of such merchandise, which was sold at the trade ports.

State control made Lisbon the compulsory harbor for all the overseas trade. Yet Lisbon, like Portugal, was far from being the final destination of the traded merchandise as well as the origin of all the exports to Africa and India. The commercial routes connected Lisbon with a number of foreign markets, of which Antwerp (and before that, Bruges) was far in the lead. Other destinations were Spain (the fairs of Medina del Campo), Italy, Germany (Augsburg, Nuremberg), then practically all of Europe. Nor should the local Asian trade be forgotten, for the Portuguese replaced the Moslems in many respects, carrying on their initiatives and following their long-established routes. From Morocco to East Africa, from Hormuz to China, a multiple trade, partly controlled by the Crown, partly in the hands of private merchants, put the Portuguese in permanent contact with peoples and economies of all types and in all stages of advancement. Such a trade often had little to do with Europe and its demands, yet it enriched or ruined the daring individuals who undertook it.

By 1515 the spice trade with Portugal reached 1 million cruzados, as much as all the ecclesiastical revenues. It was followed by the metal trade (gold, silver, copper) accounting for 475,000 cruzados. Then came sugar (250,000), brazilwood (50,000), slaves (30,000), and dyestuffs (10,000). Profits on spices and the Mina gold accounted for 40 per cent of the state's revenues. By 1518–19 overseas trade represented 68 per cent of all Portugal's resources, which meant that royalty and its institutions depended mostly on the maritime expansion. Expenditures were also huge. We lack precise budgets for this period, but we know some amounts spent by the Crown between 1522 and 1543: 800,000 cruzados for reinforcements to the regular armadas sent to India; 400,000 cruzados for the maintenance of the fortresses in Morocco; 350,000 paid to Spain for the rights to the Moluccas; 160,000 for the Brazil and Guinea protection fleets. From 1522 to 1551 the Crown lost a yearly average of more than 100,000 cruzados alone on wrecked or captured ships sailing between Lisbon and India or between Lisbon and Flanders.

The first office in charge of African affairs had been the Casa de Ceuta (House of Ceuta), created before 1434 in Lisbon. We know little of its composition and functioning, but the military and economic supply of Portuguese strongholds in Morocco was certainly among its major tasks. By 1445 an economic office in charge of the Arguim trade was established in Lagos, Algarve; another one followed, also in Lagos, for the Guinea trade. In the 1460's both were transferred to Lisbon and fused into a major government bureau, the Casa da Guiné e da Mina. When the Portuguese entered the Indian Ocean, a new office made its appearance, devoted to the Sofala and India affairs. By 1501 these two had been converted into a single government bureau, the Casa da Guiné e Índia (with variant spellings), or simply Casa da Índia.

The Casa da Índia was the center of all overseas commerce and administration. It supervised the exports to India, the disembarkation of oriental merchandise, the distribution of products among interested persons. It controlled all sales in the name of the king. The appointment of colonial officers and the enforcement of general regulations and individual charters had also to be dispatched through the Casa da Índia. The Casa included archives and an accounting and price department, received and registered all letters from overseas, and supervised the equipment, military defense, and supply of ships. In 1520 a bookkeeper was added to its payroll. Thus the Casa combined a modern government bureau with a general trade port. Until 1509, a factor (*feitor*), a treasurer, and three clerks composed the upper staff of the Casa da Índia. As the operations increased and became more complex, a new regulation, enacted in 1509, considerably enlarged the working staff. Besides the factor, who answered to the king only and held full powers over personnel, three treasurers (one for the spices, another for the money, and the third for the Guinea and Mina affairs), and five clerks were created. Furthermore, disputes were settled by a special body, consisting of a judge, a clerk, a bailiff (*meirinho*), and several guards. This same 1509 regulation was used to organize the Casa da Índia quite strictly into separate departments, which later (1530) would become still more precise and more complex.

Besides the Casa da Índia some minor offices were in charge of overseas affairs. For example, the Casa dos Escravos ("House of the Slaves"), founded in 1486, had its own storekeeper (*almoxarife*) and clerk. Despite their autonomy, colonial affairs were never completely separated from home affairs. No separate secretary was appointed to manage them. The old *vedores de fazenda* (secretaries of finance) continued to exert general supervision, although one of them had a more direct contact with everything relating to Africa and India.

THE GREAT PROBLEMS TO SOLVE

For a small country, inhabited by less than two million people, the task of building an empire certainly appears immense. To understand an effort that seems so astonishing today, two main points should be kept in mind.

First, the relationship between great undertakings and the physical dimensions of a nation was not necessarily a direct one in those days. The republics of Venice and Genoa built up economic empires of considerable size from areas smaller than Portugal and inhabited by fewer people. Their merchants were to be found everywhere, and their political alliances were eagerly sought. Later on, in the seventeenth century, Holland ruled a great part of the world, yet the Low Countries were half the size of Portugal and their inhabitants numbered around two million. Within Europe both Aragon and Denmark managed to be mighty powers, their hegemony extending over relatively large and populous areas. Much more important than the size or the number of people was the presence of a strong royal authority, which permitted effective direction and efficient organization; the consequent disengagement from internal political problems;

the national cohesion necessary for common efforts; the economic, social, and other pressures pointing toward expansion; and a number of local conjunctural circumstances, varying with time and country.

Second, Portugal never built a real empire requiring many armed men and extensive military strength until the middle of the sixteenth century. No particular problem was thus posed by lack of manpower. From Brazil to the Moluccas less than forty thousand Portuguese were enough to enforce the economic blockade, protect the trade ports and man the fortresses; intimidate and punish rebels against their supremacy; and colonize four archipelagoes and a long strip of coastline in a new continent. Emigration may have depleted the country of some energetic young people, yet the proportion was small in comparison with the great bloodlettings of the twentieth century.

If the maintenance of the Empire cost little in demographic resources and posed no serious threat to the vitality of the country, a much graver problem arose from lack of *qualified* manpower. It is true that there were enough sailors, soldiers, and peddlers. The problem was to find enough competent pilots, captains, experts in navigation, generals, administrators, able missionaries, economic advisers, and the like. This lack of qualified manpower became a real handicap by the second half of the sixteenth century, when the Portuguese commitments all over the world defied the nation's capacity to cope with them. Yet, from the beginning of the expansion, need had been felt to import foreign personnel. Italians, Castilians, Catalans, Germans, Flemish, Moslems, Jews, all actively participated in the preparation, organization, and management of the Portuguese undertakings. At the same time—a contradiction very typical of Portugal's history to the present—numerous able Portuguese were forced to migrate for economic, religious, political, and personal reasons. The presence of foreign advisers, technicians, and traders on Portuguese soil did not rule out the presence of Portuguese advisers, technicians, and traders in foreign countries. The examples of Ferdinand Magellan and João Dias de Solis serving the king of Spain or of the Portuguese Jewish capitalists settling in Flanders and Germany are typical of this contradiction which Portugal has never been able to resolve.

Another problem arose from the economic and social background of the Portuguese people. The backbone of commercial empires like those of Venice, Genoa, and, later, Holland had always been the existence of a strong middle class of enterprising bourgeois, motivated by the prospect of profit and the reinvestment of that profit in new profitable undertakings. Such a middle class, able to control and carry on expansion, was lacking in Portugal. Instead of private initiatives supported or encouraged by the state, the essence of the Portuguese expansion was a state enterprise, to which private interests or initiatives were applied. There was nothing wrong with this system, if the Crown acted as a true merchant or a private company. Actually, a state enterprise permitted a much quicker search for goals and a much better organization of the necessary means. However, problems arose when the Crown was tempted to substitute a purely mercantile policy for imperialism and sheer political domination, which required expenses disproportionate to possible profits. Moreover, the Crown had a feudal structure based upon privilege that allowed the nobility and the Church to siphon off a good share of the profits for themselves. Lacking a bourgeois mentality, nobles and clerics preferred to invest their new capital in land, in building activities (churches, monasteries, palaces), and in luxuries. As a result, the feudal structure of the country, resting upon the land and depending on agriculture, was not essentially shaken by the expansion and could survive for centuries. As a result, too, the state faced a permanent lack of capital for the maintenance of the empire and had to appeal to foreign money and initiatives, thus further endangering the growth of a native middle class.

A large share of the overseas products increasingly belonged to foreigners through immediate sale, or rentings, or loans. It could have been predicted that the Portuguese would become transporters for others instead of for themselves. Incidentally, this fact should not be exaggerated as many historians tend to do. A considerable part of the profits never passed to foreign hands. There is, however, no doubt that a possible enrichment of Portugal through development of trade and industry was forever jeopardized.

In the eyes of both contemporary and modern observers corruption and administrative confusion played a decisive role in contributing to or even determining the breakdown of the Empire. A subject dear to all historian-moralists or moralist-politicians, corruption allied to internal strife decreed the ultimate fate of the Portuguese in India as early as Albuquerque's time. Historical evidence, however, does not seem to corroborate such a point of view. There was not more corruption in the Portuguese administration overseas than there was at home in Portugal or in any other colonial empire of the same epoch. Corruption has always been a favorite excuse given by contemporaries for failures, mistakes, or simply partial achievements. This often has no basis other than the requirement of an impossible human perfection, constantly demanded by critics. In any case neither corruption nor the inevitable quarrels among the Portuguese ever prevented them from being respected and feared by Asians and Africans.

Race, civilization, and religion posed infinite problems. From Morocco to China, the Portuguese met with people of all races, cultural stages, and beliefs. Their only knowledge and training concerned the North African Moslems, who had roughly the same patterns of race and civilization as they. Difference in faith had always been a motive for slavery. Moslems and Christians enslaved one another whenever war presented them with ransomed captives; yet each side was accustomed to tolerate the other in a free condition. The *mourarias* in the Portuguese towns and the many Moslem free tenants and small landholders in the countryside were a good example of this. Thus the sight of an infidel was not in itself a condition arousing the need for slavery, although it might justify it if circumstances were favorable. On the other hand, conversion to Christianity certainly fostered the grant of freedom but it did not automatically account for it. There had always been Christian slaves among the Christians, as there were Moslem slaves in a Moslem country.

As time passed, with both Moors and Jews being expelled from the Iberian Peninsula, intolerance increased. The era of peaceful coexistence was over and in a much more bitter struggle the partisans of Christ were opposed to the partisans of Mohammed. The latter, moreover, were the guardians of the Asian international trade and therefore the mortal enemies of the Portuguese. This actually never prevented the continuous existence of peaceful commerce between Moslem traders and the Portuguese, particularly in Africa, where nobody disputed the Portuguese maritime supremacy.

In India, as elsewhere in the East, religion first appeared as a confusing issue. Utterly unaware of other organized faiths, the Portuguese at first thought that the Hindus were Christians. In every non-Moslem they saw a Christian, convinced as they were of the existence of large Christian communities in Asia. However, they soon realized their error and started bringing with them more priests and more monks than were usually required. Such missionaries addressed themselves to the non-Moslem rather than the Moslem communities, which the Portuguese well knew were not convertible (as their experience in Morocco had taught them). Both Brahmanists and Buddhists felt the attraction of the new religion, not because it denoted any spiritual superiority but because it was new and active, vehemently preached, and highly appealing to the lower classes and castes. The Christians taught equality and fraternity in contrast to the existing social and economic differences. This practice explains the great number of converts in the first years of the Christian evangelization. Yet it did not take long for the Asians to realize that Christianity stood for as much oppression and discrimination as their former beliefs. To enforce conversions the Portuguese had to enforce discriminatory legislation against non-Christians, a practice generally followed after the mid-1500's.

To achieve conversions the missionaries also realized they had to study the language and the customs of the natives. Therefore, the best accounts of the Asian cultures in the sixteenth century were by the clerics. They also tried to understand the feelings and the mentalities of the people they wanted to convert to Christianity. As a rule, persuasion rather than force was employed. As a rule, also, the missionaries were the ones to realize how complex the Asian cultures were and how deep was the contradiction between these cultures and their own. Better than the conquerors or the administrators, who often saw only sheer military superiority and despised the cultures of weaker peoples, the missionaries assessed the real values, the civilizational achievements, and the general features of the Asian countries. They showed what the West could learn from them and pointed out that in many ways the Asians were more advanced than the Europeans.

Although religion and civilization accounted much more for prejudice than race did, it would be wrong to believe that the Portuguese felt no racial superiority. As historian Charles Boxer rightly puts it, "The most that can truthfully be said is that in this respect they were usually more liberal in practice than were their Dutch, English and French successors." * One might add that in theory, too, the general Portuguese attitude was far from racist oriented. The Crown always maintained that religion, not color, should insure equality with the Portuguese from Europe. Practically, local circumstances determined the real approach. The usual lack of European women fostered an amazing degree of fornication with females of any race, in which everyone indulged, from the governor to the humblest sailor, and including the clerics. The resulting children had the same rights as any illegitimate offspring at home, although they were often despised by Europeans and natives alike. The degree of racial prejudice depended very much on color and on culture. There existed a whole gradation of race acceptance, starting with white Moslems or white Hindus and ending with pitch-black Africans or cannibal Amerindians. One might say that friendly or unfriendly relationships played their role too. The establishment of the Inquisition, with its persecution of Jews and Moors, and the general hardening of the Portuguese policies both at home and throughout the Empire after the mid-1500's clearly introduced an ethnical barrier stricter than before. In this, as in the general attitude toward race, the Portuguese were similar to the Spaniards, the Italians, and all other Mediterranean countries.

The discovery of the Atlantic Ocean, particularly after the passage of the equator, posed a certain number of problems, all difficult of solution. First, there was the question of winds (and of currents also). In the North Atlantic the absence of favorable winds, or of any winds at all, prevented an easy return from the African coast unless the ships sailed northwest in order to catch the trade winds blowing from the west. As we have seen (chapter 3) this led late in the 1420's to the discovery of the Azores, well located as ports of call on the way back. The wind system south of the equator obeyed a symmetrical pattern, a fact which occurred to the Portuguese by the 1480's if not before. Such a discovery enabled them to prepare carefully the best route to and from Asia. Thus Vasco da Gama, in-

* *Four Centuries of Portuguese Expansion, 1415–1825: A Succinct Survey,* 1965, p. 42.

stead of following the southern African coastline, sailed southwestward until he caught the southern trade winds blowing from the west. These took him directly to the tip of Africa. On the way back, however, he sailed near land. Cabral's fleet followed a similar path. From then on, the usual seaway to India followed the same pattern, ports of call being reduced to an indispensable minimum.

Once in the Indian Ocean the way to and from India was determined by the monsoon system. From about May to October the monsoon blows from the southwest; from October to May it blows from the northeast. This enabled the Portuguese to time the arrival and departure of their fleets according to a very regular schedule. Every year a fleet of eight ships on the average left Lisbon in March or April, ready to benefit from the summer monsoon, blowing from Africa and pushing it to India in September. From India the annual fleet departed by late January, arriving in Lisbon in the middle of the summer.

Another problem resulted from the need for more and more offshore travels, where the old methods of approximate directions proved inadequate. It took the Portuguese some time to make use of the skies as a practicable means of determining the latitude. Despite a reference to astronomical observations aboard a ship as early as 1451, it seems that not before the 1460's, and systematically much later only, did the Portuguese regularly estimate their position at sea by watching the sun or the stars. This method required precise knowledge of the deviation (in degrees) of the North Star from the North Pole and of the way to calculate it aboard a moving vessel. For such a purpose navigation rules were prepared, providing the pilots with the different values that should be added to or subtracted from the estimated latitude of the North Star (*Regimentos da Estrela do Norte*). By daylight the navigators simply determined the meridian latitude of the sun, a system which had become widespread by the 1480's. Using the wooden quadrant (*quadrante*), the sextant (*balestilha*), and above all the astrolabe (*astrolábio*), which they developed and perfected, the Portuguese pilots were able to figure out their position at sea with relative precision, although they never succeeded in discovering a satisfactory way of calculating longitude. In the early sixteenth century, the best pilots failed by less than two degrees when estimating latitudes aboard a ship, even in stormy seas. Late in the 1400's the Portuguese also developed the method of the navigation guides (*roteiros*), where the coastline and its adjacent waters were carefully described. The *roteiros* included peculiar signs (trees, mountains, gulfs, rivers, rocks) for purposes of recognizing the coast, as well as soundings, harbors, sandbanks, cliffs, and so forth. A great number of drawings helped the verbal description. *Roteiros* went along with the so-called *livros de marinharia* ("sailing books"), handbooks with everything that a pilot should know.

When the equator was crossed, in the early 1470's, there was a further problem, that of determining a new star, or constellation, which might replace the now invisible North Star. The latitude of the sun in the southern hemisphere also required calculations which could not be found in the existing tables of latitudes. Jewish and Portuguese astronomers were able to provide navigation with accurate means of doing these things, already patent in the great voyages of Vasco da Gama and Álvares Cabral. The Southern Cross was first (summarily) described by the Italian navigator Cadamosto, sailing under the Portuguese flag, in the early 1460's. Gradually the Portuguese discovered the advantages of the new constellation as a substitute for the vanished North Star. A corpus of observations and calculations soon emerged, systematically written down in the so-called *Regimento do Cruzeiro do Sul* (1506).

A great many other problems accompanied, or resulted from, the rise of the Portuguese Empire. Most of them, crucial at first, met with adequate solutions in the second half of the sixteenth century or even later (see chapter 7).

APOGEE AND DECLINE

THE STRUCTURES OF A MODERN STATE

The great demographic push of the late Middle Ages (see chapter 4) continued in most of Europe to the early 1600's, and in the Iberian Peninsula at least to the end of the sixteenth century. Then stagnation, if not actual decline, ensued, although there were changes in regional distribution—namely, migration to the cities.

The inadequate data we have for this period show almost two million people for the mainland by 1640 (compared with a maximum of a million and a half in 1527–32), with probably little change to the end of the century. Some major plagues may have had an impact, but essentially the reversed trend had deeper roots of an economic and social nature, which in turn would later appear as consequences.

Lisbon, with a maximum population of 65,000 by 1527 and 100,000 by 1551, had reached some 165,000 by 1620, less than London, Paris, or Naples but more than any Spanish town (Seville, the largest one, never exceeded 120,000 in this period). It compared roughly in size with Venice and Amsterdam, huge cities for the time. For Portugal the size of Lisbon was really abnormal, too large a head for a small body. The other urban centers of Portugal were much smaller: Porto, Coimbra, Évora, and Elvas had about the same population, between 16,000 and 20,000, by 1620. It seems that the demographic trend favoring the North and the Center against the South continued, gradually moving northward the economic and cultural axis of Portugal. A number of small but active ports, a good many located north of Lisbon, began to challenge the capital's monopoly in foreign trade.

Agriculture in this period followed the trends described in chapter 4. Land reclamation apparently was carried on, although at an inevitably slower pace. We lack enough information on this subject, but a number of clues give us clear evidence of the fact. At popular request many royal hunting preserves were opened to the public (1594). Several measures were taken (in 1576, 1627, 1635) to promote the reclamation of river meadowlands (*lezírias*), marshlands, and fallow grounds. On the other hand, the governments of Cardinal Henry and Philip II tried to plant trees in many areas laid bare by temporary and unauthorized occupation. Vast pine forests were probably planted in this period.

Maize continued to be a successful grain crop. In central and northern Portugal maize seems to have been well known by 1625; its importance continued into the seventeenth and eighteenth centuries. As a nutriment it replaced wheat and rye and often made up for food shortages. Maize probably affected the population rise all over the Northwest to limits unheard of. By considerably reducing the area of marshlands it also brought about, along with many other factors (one of them the demographic trend itself), the decline in cattle breeding and in dairy production. The cultivation of maize, combined with a number of other crops, such as beans and herbs, gradually changed the traditional emphasis on wheat, rye, and barley.

If the area devoted to cultivating maize substantially increased, that of wheat probably declined or stagnated. As a consequence, wheat imports from other countries rose, and Portugal's dependency on foreign wheat became a constant. At the *cortes* of 1581 the king was asked to open the frontier and permit the free trade of grain with Castile. Philip promised to do so, but it was his son who in 1604 franked all the "dry ports" (*portos secos*) between the two countries. After resumption of Portuguese independence, in 1640, wheat had to be sought again in northern Europe.

Other measures for preventing dearth included the writing down of yearly maps with the amount of wheat produced (1632) and the establishment of common granaries (*celeiros comuns*) for grain storage, planned distribution, price fixing, and even rural credit (from the mid-sixteenth century on). The law code of 1603 inflicted heavy penalties on all grain monopolies. Yet, despite all these and other measures, there were bread shortages and actual famines, even if they occurred at a slower rhythm than before (1596–97, 1621, 1627, 1632, 1655, 1659, etc.).

Production of wine and olive oil continued to increase. Early in the seventeenth century economists seemed optimistic about the economic importance of olive oil as a source of wealth for the country. Wine became better and better known abroad, and the bases for the future "Port wine" trade were laid down. From very ancient times wine was exported to England, but it came mostly from the southern areas of Portugal. In the sixteenth century some wine from the Minho Valley began to go to England via the port of Caminha. It was joined by wine of Lamego, from the Douro Valley. After 1650 English firms settled in Porto and began fostering wine production and export.

Cultivation and export of fruit seem also to have been on the rise in this period. By 1635 sweet oranges from China became known in Portugal and were a favorite among all social groups. From Portugal the Chinese type of orange spread all over Europe and the Mediterranean world, its name betraying the Portuguese origin in several languages.

Stockbreeding continued to decline, an obvious consequence of the growth and better distribution of population. Particularly affected was horse raising, of fundamental importance in warfare and the transport network. Several laws were passed to slow down such a decline and to foster horse breeding in large quantities. Under Cardinal Henry and Sebastian some useful and efficient acts (especially the "Regulation" of 1566) brought about a temporary improvement in the supply of horses. Philip II, however, at popular request closed down the stud farms (1581), with harmful consequences for good breeding of Portuguese horses.

The commercial structure of Portugal in the late sixteenth century showed no great changes from that of the early 1500's. External trade depended more on merchandise imported from overseas than on products of the mainland, yet it would be wrong to suppose that the latter did not play a fundamental role in the traffic with Europe. Portugal proper continued to send her wine, fruit, olive oil, and salt—and many other products besides—to northern Europe, to Spain, and to the Mediterranean world. From those countries she imported the same merchandise as ever, although in larger and larger quantities: grain, textiles, metals (copper and silver), industrial items (such as weapons and ammunition), and luxury products. During the sixteenth century trade with Spain gradually rose, particularly in silver imports.

Overseas trade was a world in itself (see chapter 7). Portugal exported to Asia, Africa, and America much the same items she sent to Europe, especially to the settlers in underdeveloped lands. Then she re-exported a great part of the imports from abroad; for instance, silver—perhaps the leading item in her exports—as well as copper, textiles, and luxury objects. So different were the areas she traded with—practically the whole world—that cargoes had to be extremely diversified and complex. From overseas came the main source of Portugal's revenues. The spices from India, the Moluccas, and Ceylon, which reached their top position in the country's imports by the 1550's, gradually declined throughout the late part of the century and the 1600's. Instead, shellac, china, and other items from the Far East (China and Japan), along with sugar, wood, and later tobacco from Brazil and the Atlantic Islands, rose to the top in the list of imports. This evolution depended, of course, not only on the gradual takeover by the Dutch and English in the Indian and Pacific oceans but also on the rise of Brazil as an economic power. Between Brazil and Africa another kind of trade began developing by the mid-sixteenth century and would become one of the most important of all during the seventeenth. This was the slave trade (see chapter 7).

An interesting aspect of trade expansion in this period concerned the cod fisheries in Newfoundland. Portuguese fishermen started visiting American waters by the early sixteenth century, but it was only in the mid-1500's that codfish became a profitable trade item. Fleets were organized, customs duties established, and regulations for the codfish trade set up by the government.

Such a wide-reaching and complex network of trading relations obviously had its weak points but also provided great malleability and capacity for survival. It depended on all sorts of political, military, and economic incidents happening in most of the world. It could be affected even by such small disasters as a shipwreck or lack of wind. But it was not easily destroyed by a conjuncture or a change in structure. In fact, by subtle and gradual transformations it survived the disaster of 1578, the union of Portugal and Spain, the War of Independence, and the loss of the Asian Empire.

Some important crises affected the Portuguese external trade during this period. The international crisis of 1545–52 brought about a clear change in structure: Antwerp ceased to be the final and decisive entrepôt of the Portuguese trade and was replaced by Seville and Amsterdam. State capitalism was slowed down after the closing of the Crown factory at Antwerp. Instead of the traditional trade monopoly, a system of contracts with companies and individuals developed. Then came the crises of 1571–78 and 1595–1600. The Hispanic crisis of 1607 also had a tremendous impact on Portugal. In Lisbon many old firms failed and new ones took their place. Foreign capital changed also. The stress on Italian, Flemish, and German participation faded away or at least accepted the competition of Spanish, English, and French names. Crises had their own "geography" and "itineraries," reaching some cities first and some others much later. This schedule depended, of course, on the intensity of traffic between any two places. Lisbon was very closely connected to Antwerp, to the Azores, and later to Seville and Amsterdam. A part of the network were Medina del Campo (in central Castile) and Madrid. Signals of a crisis could appear in any of these places much before they had reached other inland regions such as Trás-os-Montes or inner Beira.

The dual union with Spain related the Portuguese economic world to the Spanish in a much more intense way, but elsewhere it brought no other peculiar changes to trade. Probably the somewhat more sophisticated commercial life in Philip's monarchy, along with the increasing trend toward economic organization, accounted for the several attempts to establish in Portugal the first great companies or societies for trading activities. State capitalism was clearly being replaced or at least reduced by a much larger share of private initiative and private organization.

The Dutch served as an example in founding trading companies.

In 1587 a short-lived Portuguese Company of the East Indies appeared but aroused little enthusiasm. Of more importance was the Company for Navigation and Trade with India, established 1619 but not chartered until 1628. Despite the participation of more than fifteen traders and the City Hall of Lisbon itself, this company failed too, mostly for lack of capital, a common problem for Spanish-founded companies. It was dissolved in 1633.

The Restoration of 1640 brought no great advantages to external trade. At home the New Christians along with many other businessmen were persecuted by an Inquisition no longer controlled by the strong Madrid government. War with Spain and foreign attacks on the Portuguese Empire and Portuguese ships harassed long-distance trade. The profitable land traffic with Spain disappeared altogether. The Mediterranean was closed to the Portuguese traders.

The government of Portugal succeeded in fostering trade relations with northern Europe, particularly with the Baltic world. Germans, Swedes, and others came to Lisbon in growing numbers. However, the leading fact in Portugal's external trade after 1640 was its gradual surrender to the English interests. The desperate situation of a country fighting for her independence led to the signing of several treaties clearly oppressive to Portuguese commerce. The treaties of 1654 and 1661 with England and of 1661 with Holland gave to both countries freedom of trade with the Portuguese Empire, special privileges to English and Dutch residents in Portugal, and fixed customs duties up to a certain limit. As the English were in Portugal in much greater numbers than the Dutch and as England was on her way up in ruling the seas, they made much better use of their privileges than the Dutch. The political alliance which ratified the treaty of 1661 (marriage of Princess Catarina to Charles II) helped to promote England to the number one position in trade relations with Portugal.

The government of John IV tried again to set up companies of commerce. In 1649 a Company for the Commerce with Brazil was chartered for a period of twenty years. It was given a monopoly of wine, flour, olive oil, and codfish exports to Brazil and of brazilwood imports in Europe. It was also granted the exclusive right and obligation of convoying all merchant ships sailing to and from Brazil.

The government tried to attract capital from the New Christians living outside Portugal but was not particularly successful. The Company languished for several years, being useful only in protecting mercantile ships against the attacks of Dutch, English, and others. In 1662, after several changes it was finally "nationalized" by the Crown, becoming simply a state department called Junta de Comércio, in charge of providing a convoy to the trading vessels.

From a monetary standpoint the period 1539–1641 was remarkably stable. The cornerstone of the Portuguese economic system—the gold cruzado—underwent very few changes in its weight and real value. One mark of minted gold, which cost about 25,000 reais in 1539, went up to 30,000 in 1555, remaining unaltered till 1641. The mark of minted silver varied slightly between 1555 and 1588, but its value in reais only rose from 2,500 in 1539 to 2,800 in 1588. This meant, on the whole, a rise of 20 per cent for gold and 12 per cent for silver in more than a hundred years, a clear proof that the economy of the country (and the empire) was sound and still able to resist the impact of external threats.

To the middle of the sixteenth century, the monetary structure of Portugal depended not only on her overseas possessions (gold arriving from Africa and Asia) but also on Europe (silver coming from Germany by way of Antwerp and Amsterdam). After the 1530's the discovery of silver mines in Spanish America (Peru and Mexico) rapidly changed the economic picture of the world. While German silver output was declining, the expansion of trade and industry required increasing quantities of money. In Portugal, Spanish silver gradually replaced German and became essential to the country's life. Spanish reales came in great quantities to Portugal and were put on a par with the Portuguese silver coins. By the second half of the sixteenth century an intense traffic took place between Seville and Lisbon. Until the late 1620's or early 1630's silver was abundant in Portugal and regularly coined at the Lisbon Mint. Gold was less abundant but also less important. Then things started changing. From 1620 onward American silver output decreased considerably. Consequently, the importance of Seville as a supply market declined too. In Lisbon very little silver was minted until 1640.

The Restoration of Portugal's full independence brought hard times to the Crown and to the country in general. To cope with the huge military expenditures and the decline in overseas revenues there was no other solution but to debase currency again and again: the mark of minted silver went up to 3,400 reais in 1641, 4,000 in 1643, 5,000 in 1663, and 6,000 in 1668, a total of 114 per cent. The mark of gold also rose to 37,400 reais in 1641, 40,960 in 1642, 56,250 in 1642, 75,000 in 1662, and 82,500 in 1668: 175 per cent on the whole. Only peace brought about a stable currency again after 1668.

During the sixteenth century, the increasing Portuguese commitments overseas made public finance more and more dependent upon the situation in Asia, Africa, and America, as well as in the rest of Europe. Revenues and expenditures varied considerably according to some siege in India, some particular output in Brazil, or some economic crisis in Antwerp. But the relative importance of both colonial and foreign traffic changed in the seventeenth century. In 1588 the empire accounted for about 50 per cent of the state income; with the revenues of the customs spread throughout the country, the figure was more than 60 per cent. By 1607 the revenue from the overseas possessions had decreased to some 45 per cent but with the customs the total amount was still 59 per cent. By 1619 the percentages were 48 and 62. From this point on the importance of the empire in the financial structure of Portugal steadily declined, while the maritime traffic with the foreign countries became more important. By the 1650's and the 1660's the structural change had been accomplished. In 1681, with almost 40 per cent of the total revenues, the maritime trade with Europe had become vital to the country.

An analysis of the state budgets—for the mainland alone—shows the tremendous increase in both revenues and expenditures up to the 1620's, a clear evidence of economic and political expansion. After that period, military and economic troubles brought about a decline. Revenues amounted to 607,000 cruzados in 1557, 939,000 in 1588, 1,322,000 in 1607, 1,484,000 in 1619; including overseas figures, the revenues were 1,760,000 cruzados in 1588, 3,344,000 in 1607, 3,488,000 in 1619 but 2,518,000 in 1628. Again we lack precise figures to estimate the expenditures. Successive loans, subsidies, and government bonds, common in Portugal throughout this period, give some idea of the treasury problems. From 1500 to 1554 government bonds (*padrões de juro*) were issued eight times, an average of one issue every seven years. Then the pace became more rapid: nine issues to 1580 (one every 2.6 years), eighteen between 1582 and 1631 (every 2.7 years), fifteen from 1641 to 1664 (every 1.4 years). The *cortes* voted subsidies almost every time they were assembled. Other loans concerned the municipalities (mainly Lisbon), the merchants, and even the clergy. Taxation went up too, particularly after 1580. The budget could still be balanced in 1557, in 1607 (a surplus of 702,000 cruzados), in 1619 (a surplus of 578,000 cruzados), and perhaps in some other years. In 1620, however, there was a deficit of 112,000 cruzados.

Unfunded and funded debts also were substantial: statistics for 1557 show 2,000,000 and 1,881,720 cruzados respectively; for 1588, 178,000 for the funded debt; and for 1607, 412,000 for the funded. The situation was seemingly worse under John III than under Philip III, but we have practically no figures in between. As in Spain, official bankruptcy was decreed at least twice, in 1560 and 1605, when payment of interest by the Casa da India ceased altogether and the unfunded debt was converted into funded. Forced drops in interest took place several times, both before and after the Restoration: in 1563, 1582, 1614, 1620, 1624, 1630, 1650, 1656, and 1672. Financial crises or adjustments should not be confused with economic decline or poor administration. Money seems to have been abundant in Portugal until the 1620's—despite some years of depression. Notwithstanding bankruptcies and the several interest reductions, the state was always able to get the loans it needed, and with relative ease.

The price movement in Portugal reflected the general situation in Europe, characterized by the "price revolution" to the early 1600's and price stagnation (or even decline), with few exceptions, afterward. Thus, by the middle of the sixteenth century, the average price per bushel of wheat was 60 reais. It doubled before the end of the century, hovered around 200 reais by the early 1600's, and reached its maximum in the late 1620's and early 1630's (350 to 400 reais). For the town of Beja, in Alentejo, one of the wheat centers of Portugal, some reliable figures show this tremendous increase: from an average of 30 reais per bushel in 1530 to a maximum of 380 reais in 1636. It is true that wheat prices always fluctuated greatly, in accordance with the highly irregular harvests. In bad years, a bushel of wheat in Lisbon went up in price: to 200 reais in 1594, 480 in 1599, 400 in 1608, 500 in 1611, and 450 in 1614. As the devaluation of the real until 1641 never exceeded 12 per cent, the high prices were actual and had an impact on all social classes.

Prices of other commodities show a similar trend: in Beja one *canada* (= three pints) of wine rose from an average 28 reais in 1589 to 50 reais in 1605, to 66 in 1611, 70 in 1612, and back to 50 in 1618. One arrátel (= sixteen ounces) of mutton, costing 7 reais in 1559, had reached 15 at the beginning of the seventeenth century. After declining a little the price was still between 13 and 15 in the 1620's and 1630's. Olive oil showed a similar rise. We lack precise data for industrial items as well as for salaries and rents, but the little we do have points to an increase in the former and stagnation in the latter. The cost of equipping a fleet to send to India doubled between 1506 and 1620. The value of an average cargo from India to Lisbon went up 2.5 times between 1540 and 1590. Once more Beja is of help: salaries for surgeons, druggists, grammar teachers, doctors, and lawyers remained unchanged between 1581 and 1634.

In the 1630's (or even before) prices dropped again, in Portugal as almost everywhere in Europe, bringing about discontent and uneasiness for producers and traders. A bushel of wheat went down to 150 reais in 1638, then to 120–130 in 1639, and to 100 in 1640. Wine became stabilized at about 40–45 reais the *canada* (1625 to 1650), then 60 reais (1652 to 1665), but as the currency was devaluated 78.5 per cent in the same period, the rise meant in fact a drop.

A correlation between demography and price trends seems clear. Accompanying the great demographic push was the price revolution—a drastic increase in prices. There followed a leveling off of population, then a possible decline, both accompanied by a lower rate of growth in prices, then a price decrease. The price revolution of course had its cycles. Historian Vitorino Godinho has shown that the interruptions in price increases during the sixteenth and early seventeenth centuries meant economic crises, more or less coinciding in Portugal and abroad. In Portugal they occurred in 1533–35, 1544–51, 1576–82, and 1594–1605; and in the 1630's there was another crisis.

Studies of landownership are unavailable for this period. A number of general characteristics, however, suggest the main trends.

After the death of grand-master Jorge (1550), the religious-military orders of Santiago and Avis were united to the Crown. This made John III and his successors the largest landowners in Portugal, a fact of tremendous importance for the strengthening of the royal power. Later on, both the Spanish monarchs and the new kings of an independent Portugal gave up a part of the Crown patrimony by granting new titles and thus securing new followers. In 1640, however, the Duke of Bragança, who was the richest man in the country, became king, which meant a substantial increase in the Crown patrimony. Thus, the king continued to be the first landowner in his realm and an effective brake on the ambitions of nobles and clergymen. This fact also solved the problem of giving appanages to the royal princes. With the property and revenues formerly belonging to the dukes of Bragança, John IV instituted the House of Bragança as a permanent appanage of the Crown prince. With some other lands and revenues—partly from confiscations—a second appanage was established, the so-called Casa do Infantado, granted to the second-born princes.

Along with that belonging to the Crown, land in the hands of the nobles went on increasing, as a great share of the nobility's profits were invested in buying property. Yet the huge latifundium, in the Castilian manner, never existed in Portugal. To begin with, land was scattered about from North to South, rarely forming continuous areas of a single lordship. Then, even when vast tracts of land belonged to the same owner, the general trend was to maintain the traditional quit-rent lease system instead of trying management on a large scale and direct exploitation. King, nobility, and clergy followed this same practice, parceling their properties in small *prazos,* perpetually or temporarily leased to local farmers and petty bourgeois. In the North of Portugal, particularly in Entre-Douro-e-Minho, the tendency was to divide the land into smaller and smaller holdings. The introduction of maize and the rise of a maize–herb garden type of culture fostered individualism and favored smaller property holdings. Population grew and its concentration in the Northwest was more rapid than anywhere else in Portugal. From the seventeenth century onward, Entre-Douro-e-Minho became one of the main regions for emigration overseas, instead of the traditional south.

In Portugal as everywhere in Europe the sixteenth century was characterized by the growth and strengthening of the nobility, particularly of a court nobility. Accepting the principle of an increasing royal centralization and restraining their feudal exuberance, the nobles were kept in most offices of command both at home and overseas and became the instrument of top administration. As a social group based upon privilege, the nobles stood between the king and the people for all practical purposes. They were the intermediaries, the representatives of both sides at any level. Their blood prejudice against trade, profit, and work (in a general sense) faded away: the aristocrat, if not directly handling his affairs, entrusted to a professional businessman the management of his fortune.

By the end of the sixteenth century, the Portuguese aristocracy encompassed some three or four different categories, which were roughly maintained up to the 1700's. At the top level, there was the court nobility or *noblesse d'epée,* composed of most bearers of titles —also called *grandes* from Spanish influence—of high administrative officials and of military and naval commanders. Below came the *noblesse de robe,* which included the members of the courts of justice, lawyers, university professors, and most office-holders in the administration. Finally there was the country gentry, the *fidalgos* living on their rents, only slightly affected by the great structural changes of the century but gradually being impoverished because of the price inflation.

The *noblesse d'epée* grew immensely throughout the late sixteenth and early seventeenth century. To counter the price revolution, the Crown increased their yearly allowances *(tenças).* At the same time the multiplication of offices and commandments both at home and overseas required a growing number of qualified people. A law of 1572 (Regimento dos Filhamentos, "Regulation of Seizures") strengthened the economic and social influence and the participation of the nobles. The number of titles increased: some 25 in 1550–80, 34 in 1590, 46 in 1620, 54 in 1630, 69 in 1640—a rise of 165 per cent in less than a hundred years. This fact partly corresponded to a deliberate policy of the Spanish kings after the establishment of the dual monarchy (1580): by granting titles and privileges, the government hoped to get new supporters and weaken the chances of a Portuguese secession. But it also meant growth in the power of the aristocracy in all its ranks and its numerical enlargement as a social group: in Spain, as in Portugal, the inflation in the number of titles followed much the same trend.

The Portuguese *grandes* were actually neither so affluent nor so numerous as their neighbors in Castile. The situation in Portugal was comparable to that in Aragon, the third great kingdom of the Spanish monarchy. In opulence a Portuguese duke (that of Bragança, the richest of all, with 120,000 ducats of yearly revenue) ranked fifth, after the Castilian dukes of Medina Sidonia (160,000 ducats), Medina Rioseco, Lerma, and Ossuna. The wealthiest Portuguese marquis (that of Vila Real with 34,000 annual ducats) had ten Castilian and Aragonese peers ahead of him. And at the level of count there were eighteen Castilian and Aragonese counts richer than the richest Portuguese one. Obviously, in Portugal less difference in fortune existed among the bearers of titles than in Spain.

The peculiar situation of the country after 1580 led to some interesting changes. Because there was no longer any royal court in Portugal, the court nobility declined in favor of the provincial nobility and the *noblesse de robe*. A great many nobles refused to live in Madrid or retired to their country estates when it gradually became clear that the Portuguese were being discriminated against in favor of the Castilians. Also, the central administration, directed or influenced by the Madrid government, prevailed over the nobles whose participation declined. A patriotic disdain or disregard for the central government often aligned the countryside, where the nobles prevailed, against Lisbon (where the pro-Spanish groups were). As a result provincial localisms developed. When the independence of Portugal was again proclaimed in 1640, the need once again to strengthen the central authority became a major concern to the new government. Moreover, John IV was only the Duke of Bragança, "elected" king by his peers.

Between 1640 and 1670 a radical shuffle of the aristocracy took place with the obvious goal of rebuilding a docile court nobility. A new regulation of court offices (*Regimento dos Ofícios da Casa Real*) was enacted. Half of the existing *grandes* disappeared permanently: 34 titles were dropped, mostly due to treason in favor of .Spain; 34 new ones were created by promoting *nobles de robe* or *fidalgos.* As a consequence there was no final change in the number of title bearers: 69 in 1670 as in 1640. Yet, in spite of this drastic measure, the Bragانças were unable to cut down the influence of the nobles as they wished and reduce them to their former meek obedience. Times were different. In 1670, when peace and prosperity returned to Portugal, power was being shared equally by king and aristocracy.

The great efforts undertaken by the Catholic Church throughout the sixteenth century were aimed at dignifying the clergy and "restoring" it to a condition of purity and efficiency. The Protestant movement was followed by a Catholic Reformation that covered the middle and late 1500's notwithstanding earlier attempts at a partial change. As a result, a new ecclesiastical order gradually emerged, more independent and conscious of itself than ever before, less participatory in the economic and social elements of the other classes. This is not to say that the old identification or parallel between nobility and upper clergy or between lower classes and lower clergy altogether disappeared. Particularly in the former, the same situation persisted, almost as before. The great majority of the bishops and important abbots continued to come from a small number of lineages, where the Meneses, the Noronhas, the Melos, or the Pereiras played a major role. All the inquisitors-general were also nobles. Yet the recruiting of bishops seems to have been somewhat more democratic, drawing from a greater number of monks and friars, where social distinctions were less rigid. From 1550 to about 1670 there were at least 115 aristocrats in a total of 135 bishops (i.e., 85 per cent) with 27 members of one religious order (20 per cent). This latter proportion had been only 3 per cent between 1430 and 1550. Within the lower ranks the change apparently was in the opposite direction: one of the canons of the Council of Trent, enacted in 1564, limited the ordination to those who owned some patrimony or were given ecclesiastical benefices. This measure tended to reduce the so-called Church proletariate, elevating the social and economic status of the clerics.

Other decisions of the council, all enacted in 1564, forbade the accumulation of ecclesiastical dignities and benefices, forced the prelates to live in their dioceses and parishes, established age limits for priests and bishops, and endeavored to cut down abuses of all kinds. For the spiritual and cultural preparation of future clerics, the seminaries were created. To the end of the century seven had been established throughout Portugal and the Azores, besides the existing colleges at Coimbra and Lisbon. In the late 1600's only the dioceses of Porto, Lamego, Elvas, the Algarve, and Angra had been left out.

The relative importance of the Portuguese bishoprics changed only slightly during this period. Évora grew in revenues, if not in charm, and became the wealthiest diocese of them all. It had been converted into an archbishopric in 1540. Lisbon, Braga, and Coimbra were roughly comparable, Braga being the poorest, Lisbon and Coimbra vying for second place. Among the remainder, Guarda rose from one of the last to fifth place by 1632, while Lamego fell from fifth to ninth. The sees of Miranda and the Algarve also grew in importance, with the corresponding decline of Viseu, Porto, and Portalegre. The least-prized ones were of course those of Funchal and Angra in the Azores. Again, it should be emphasized that most of the Portuguese bishops and archbishops could not compare with their Castilian colleagues: the archbishop of Toledo received five times more than the bishop of Évora, and the average Castilian bishop four times more than his Portuguese counterpart.

The Catholic reformation encompassed the monastic orders as well. The reform movement had started much before 1550 (in Portugal it affected the Dominicans, the Carmelites, the Augustinians, and others); but it was systematized and completed only after the Council of Trent. It affected almost all the orders. Reforms included the suppression of commanderies, the prohibition of private property among the friars and monks, the method of recruiting new members, the form of electing the abbots, and emphasis on discipline and obedience. To provide a minimum revenue and a viable organization many monasteries were combined or simply eliminated. Yet, far from declining, the number of orders, monasteries, and monks continued to grow. Each decade brought about the foundation of new religious houses, a result of both the rise in population and the fashionable idea of instituting a monastery. Every new king or queen, each wealthy noble or even bourgeois, wished to have his or her name associated with such a mark of piety. The number of foundations was particularly high up to 1600, when more than a hundred new monasteries appeared, and after 1640. In all, 166 houses were set up between 1550 and 1668, with the largest number belonging to the Franciscans, the Jesuits, the Carmelites, and the Arrábidos. In 1628–30, the total number of monasteries was estimated at 450, with some 7,400 people (4,200 monks and 3,200 nuns). The Franciscans could claim more than a third of the total, followed (but at a great distance) by the Cistercians, the Dominicans, the Jesuits, the Benedictines, and the Augustinians. In 1652, the overall figure was roughly the same in spite of the new foundations.

Several orders had in the meantime been created. The reforms carried on in Spain by St. Teresa de Avila and St. Juan de la Cruz led to the birth of a new branch of the Carmelites, the Barefoot Carmelites. They entered Portugal in 1581. The Carthusians, of a very old foundation, came to Portugal only in 1587 but were never very popular. The Hospitallers of St. João de Deus, a Portuguese saint who spent most of his lifetime in Spain, set up several hospitals of which they were in charge. The so-called nuns of the Conception, the Theatines, the French Capuchins (Barbadinhos and Francesinhas), the English nuns of St. Saviour (Inglesinhas), the Oratorians and the Barefoot Augustinians, all came to Portugal before 1668, but few ever played any significant role in the country's life. Their number was small.

The great order of the late sixteenth and seventeenth centuries was unquestionably that of the Jesuits. They arrived in Portugal in 1540, numbering only three. In 1600 there were already some twenty houses of Jesuits throughout the country with six hundred members including novitiates, hospitals, asylums, schools, and seminaries. There were 650 Jesuits by the middle of the century. They owned a university and several important colleges. Their priests swarmed throughout Portugal and overseas and were among the most popular of all. Their influence increased among the ruling classes, through confessors, chaplains, advisers, and the like. Their affluence challenged that of the other religious orders and made them the subject of envy and attack. The Jesuits created and perfected a special method for spiritual and cultural education. Their main target was the

youth, and in Portugal they almost succeeded in monopolizing regular teaching. They also devoted their energies to attacking heresies
and the Jews. For almost a century they were good allies of the Inquisition and the secular clergy in a sort of a "united front" presided over by the king or the viceroy. Things started changing little
by little as their power and wealth increased, as well as those of the
Inquisition. After the 1620's a hidden struggle opposed Jesuits and
Inquisition. For several reasons, not yet well understood, they chose
the cause of independence and were among the chief supporters of
the Duke of Bragança, proclaimed king as John IV in 1640.

The Inquisition had been established in Portugal by Kings
Manuel I and John III who wanted that new and fashionable tribunal in order to copy the example of Spain and to secure a new
weapon for royal centralization. Yet neither Protestants nor Jews
posed any serious menace to the religious unity of the country. The
Protestants were practically nonexistent. The Jews had been expelled or forced to conversion, and the number of New Christians
steadily declined because of rapid integration or assimilation with
the "Old Christians." In 1542 there were no more than 60,000 New
Christians, in 1604 perhaps half that number. Consequently the Portuguese Inquisition had to find a permanent target in order to justify
its own existence. It was above all a religious institution of course,
considered most holy in goals and procedures. It kept the Catholic
faith in its deeper purity, acting against not only declared apostasies,
heresies, and schisms, but also any presumptions of deviation from
the true faith. Accordingly, it delved into all forms of suspicious
theologies, philosophies, or even literary currents. It also fought what
was considered superstition, witchcraft, idolatry, and all sorts of
pagan practices. As a moral tribunal, it aimed at deviations like
sodomy and bestiality. Yet all these "crimes" were not abundant
enough, particularly in a small country like Portugal, to justify the
powers, the autonomy, and the very existence of the Inquisition. The
New Christians, however, were sufficiently numerous to provide a
good target. By discriminating against them and accusing them of
Judaism, the Inquisition created a true ghetto and kept it alive, instead of extinguishing it.

The integration of the New Christians was thus artificially

stopped and their caste maintained for two hundred years. Yet it would be wrong to regard all the New Christians accused and condemned by the Inquisition as real descendants of Jews. If some were, and if a small minority among them still indulged in Jewish practices (which did not necessarily mean Judaism), many others were simply good Portuguese, perhaps with a slight admixture of Jewish blood, a result of increasing miscegenation. Here, an economic and social element intervened as well. The New Christians formed, in the main, a middle class of merchants and capitalists, with a significant role in the Portuguese and European economies. As such, they were not well accepted by the small "Old Christian" Portuguese bourgeoisie, jealous of their predominance, or by the feudal nobility, also interested in trade activities. The poorer masses saw in them the heirs of the much-hated Jew usurers. In short, the majority of the country harassed the New Christians and welcomed any means of weakening them. In this sense one can say that the Inquisition had behind it the great mass of the people, who applauded the persecutions and eagerly contributed to them. Only the Crown, because of its financial needs, a small intelligentsia of enlightened persons, and the New Christians' own power—the power of money—could defend this middle class against the rigors of the Inquisition.

Thus, the Inquisition appears as a very complex institution, with ideological, economic, and social goals, consciously and unconsciously expressed. Its activity, severity, and coherence changed markedly according to the epochs. Created by the king, it was kept under the direct control of the royal power for a long time, and served its purposes. Cardinal Henry, the king's brother, held the office of inquisitor-general for forty years (1539–80): in the same period he was also the country's regent (1562–68) and finally the king (1578–80). Then, Cardinal Albrecht, governor of Portugal in the name of Philip II (1583–93), became the inquisitor-general (1586–96). After him, Viceroy Pedro de Castilho, bishop of Leiria, who twice ruled Portugal (1605–8; 1612–14), was also appointed inquisitor-general, an office he held from 1605 to 1615. It was only after this time that Inquisition and state were definitely kept apart.

Meanwhile the Inquisition had grown and gradually become a state within a state. Its own bureaucracy was the largest in the country: besides the inquisitor-general there were the General Council of four deputies and the four inquisitorial courts of Lisbon, Évora, Coimbra, and Goa. Each one had its own organization including a central office (*Mesa*), with three inquisitors assisted by several deputies, notaries, minor court officials, prosecuting attorneys, lawyers, wardens, bailiffs, keepers, barbers, doctors, chaplains, solicitors, and janitors. In the seaports there were also the so-called visitors of the ships (*visitadores das naus*), assisted by a scribe, a keeper, and an interpreter, in charge of inspecting all entering ships and confiscating heretical matters. Each important city had its commissioners with the authority to arrest, listen to accusations, interrogate, and so on. Altogether, hundreds of people worked for and were paid by the Inquisition.

There was still another category of clients, the *Familiares*. Belonging to all social groups but especially to the nobility and the bourgeoisie (a *Familiar* had to have some patrimony of his own), they helped the Inquisition everywhere: spying, arresting, denouncing, and informing. To become a *Familiar* was, for the lower classes, a social promotion, because it conferred important privileges, such as being free from taxes or subject only to the Inquisition authority. For the noble it represented a religious honor, a sort of decoration. The total number of *Familiares* varied but generally went beyond a thousand. Spread all over the country, the *Familiares* formed a true political group, strongly backing the Inquisition in its struggle for power and pervading all political, administrative, and economic organs at any level. For instance, they were present at and influenced the decisions taken in *cortes* and in the municipal councils.

The powers bestowed upon the Inquisition were enormous and abnormal. In truth the inquisitor-general depended on the king who appointed him. Yet the monarch's interference stopped here because only the Pope could depose an inquisitor-general. Within the country the inquisitor-general had the quality and the powers of a Papal delegate, including the right of excommunication. He appointed all the other inquisitors and personnel who were responsible only to him. Regulations and procedures were secret to most people. The first Regulation, dated 1552, still had the king's approval. The second (1613) and the third (1640) depended only upon the inquisitor-gen-

ACLAMAÇAÕ DAMAGESTADE DELREI DOM
ÍOAÕ OQUARTO, EM OPRIMEÍRO DE DZENBRO D 1640;

ABOVE: *Revolution in Lisbon, December 1, 1640: Anonymous, mid-17th century, Sociedade Histórica da Independência de Portugal, Lisbon.* UPPER RIGHT: *Poet Luis de Camões: miniature, 1581, Marquis of Rio Maior collection.* BELOW: *View of Lisbon (detail): tile panel, 17th century, Museu Nacional de Arte Antiga, Lisbon.*

OV RETRATO DE LVIZ DE CAMOES OFRESIDO O V REY D LVIZ DE ATHAY DE POR FERNA... TELLES DE MENEZES eral. If many of the rules adopted did not differ from the general legislation, there were still enough changes to make the Inquisition more feared and dramatic than the regular courts and jails. For one thing, every denunciation was accepted, regardless of the denouncer's qualifications. Even anonymous letters could serve. Thus slaves, excommunicated people, thieves, murderers, all could act as denouncers. Furthermore, the prisoners were not told the reasons for their arrest, the names of their denouncers, or the place and time of the crime. They had to "confess" their crimes, often nonexistent. Not only facts but conjecture and hearsay were accepted as criminal evidence. The prisoner could not choose his defender or lawyer, who belonged to the Inquisition's staff. This lawyer, moreover, had no access to the prisoner's criminal files. No appeal was possible, except within the Inquisition itself. The Inquisition procedure contained still other oddities which, together with those mentioned above, could make of an arrest and a trial a tragic absurdity.

Punishments included spiritual penalties, fines, temporary or life imprisonment, confiscations of property, and banishment. Sentences were read and executed in more or less public ceremonies known as autos-da-fé ("acts of the faith"). Some autos-da-fé took place within the Inquisitorial palace or in a monastery. The most famous happened in a public square, with full publicity and the presence of the authorities, including the king and the royal family. These were carefully planned shows, aimed at attracting and moving the masses. The death penalty could not be decreed or executed by the Inquisition; but as the common law punished crimes of heresy (and others) by death at the stake (fire), prisoners convicted of heresy were simply "released" by the Inquisition to Crown justice. After a pretense trial they were immediately executed. From 1543 to 1684 at least 1,379 people were burned at the autos-da-fé, an average of almost ten a year. The total number of condemnations rose to a minimum of 19,247 in the same period, an average of more than 136 each year. Hundreds of people, of course, died in prison where they were often kept indefinitely without trial.

The expansion of long-distance trade favored the growth of a Portuguese merchant class in a permanent struggle with their rivals, the foreign traders, the nobles, and the king himself. In the mid-

1500's the number of wealthy bourgeois in Lisbon had probably reached its peak. There were more than eight hundred "gross traders" in a town of 100,000. These people controlled an important share of the bulky Portuguese external traffic and were strong enough to represent the point of departure for a future commercial nation. Their struggle toward such a goal lasted for a century or more. But their enemies were too strong and were constantly present. To start with, the foreign traders came to Portugal in larger and larger numbers, attracted by the good profits and the royal privileges. They had more money, more resources, and better techniques than the Portuguese. Lack of capital was another problem. The most profitable undertakings always belonged to the Crown, the nobles, or the foreigners. The Portuguese funded little and were not used to reinvest at a rapid pace. They were not enterprising and they got no help from the state; on the contrary, taxation of their profits constantly increased. The numerous petty bourgeois were another obstacle to the rise of a commercial Portugal. They controlled most of the internal trade and were afraid of powerful trusts or big companies which might absorb or destroy them.

Finally, the Inquisition was a permanent menace to daring undertakings and the development of contacts with foreign countries regardless of their religion or politics. Extremely greedy, the Inquisition kept an eye on the world of business and took advantage of every pretext to persecute and confiscate. It must be recalled that many of the wealthy bourgeois were New Christians or related to them in some way.

From the mid-sixteenth century on, the tendency (in Portugal as elsewhere) was to reduce the number of traders in favor of a larger concentration of firms and capital. The Lisbon estimates for 1565 and 1619–20 give us clear proof of this. The forced "loans" of 1626 and 1631 also show how small the group of businessmen had become in comparison with 1552. On the other hand, their economic power had considerably increased.

As mentioned before, the dual union with Spain was favorable to a Portuguese bourgeoisie. The Madrid government was much more conscious of the importance of a middle class in the structure of the realm. Also, it needed money in increasing quantities: only the big businessmen could afford to lend it. With such a policy, the New Christians enjoyed some periods of ease and prosperity, which many took advantage of by leaving the country forever.

The revolution of 1640 brought about a period of decline for the Portuguese bourgeoisie. A good many foreigners—English, Dutch, Germans, French—settled down in Lisbon, well protected by the burdensome treaties of 1641–42, 1654, and 1661. They dealt the Portuguese traders a deadly blow. The Inquisition acted freely and ruined a large number of firms and individual businessmen, preventing the joint initiatives of Portuguese living in Portugal and Portuguese exiles abroad. Despite some wise protests against these actions and attitudes (António Vieira, the writer and missionary, was one of those who strongly supported a policy of tolerance for economic reasons), the Portuguese bourgeoisie declined hopelessly.

Artisans of most crafts remained gathered together in the corporations. In Portugal, as in Spain, the corporative ties developed and strengthened during the seventeenth century, corporations becoming generalized throughout the country and new Casas dos Vinte e Quatro appearing here and there. They controlled most of the industrial activity of Portugal. It is noteworthy that the permanence and strengthening of the corporations in an epoch when they were beginning to fade away in other more progressive countries was a clear sign of the trend toward the maintenance of ancient and obsolete forms, the reaction against innovation, the fear of progress. In their fierce persecution of all those who wanted to escape from regulations and introduce new methods of production, the corporations are strikingly similar to the Universities, the Inquisition, and the Society of Jesus. Artisans were kept firmly "in their place" and even their representation through the corporations was often whittled down. In cortes, many of the people's deputies belonged to the nobility. In the municipal government of Lisbon most of the important administrative jobs were reserved to aristocrats.

The number of slaves imported into Portugal declined during the seventeenth century. At the same time, their process of integration into the white society speeded up, mostly through miscegenation. Slaves became too expensive for simple domestic jobs and were not necessary in the countryside. Fashion and novelty, which had partly determined their importation in the fifteenth and sixteenth century, had changed by the seventeenth. On the other hand, the slave trade to America and the Portuguese African islands became a well-organized and most profitable undertaking. There was little question of diverting some slaves to the mainland. Several royal decrees forbade or made difficult the importation of slaves to Portugal, particularly from India. Moorish slaves were theoretically forbidden. Despite all this, a few thousand blacks, Indians, Moors, and others still lived in Portugal by the middle of the seventeenth century. In Lisbon there were probably some ten thousand by 1620.

In the general administrative divisions of Portugal, only very slight changes took place during the late sixteenth and the seventeenth century. The six provinces (see chapter 4) were now called *províncias* rather than *comarcas*, the latter term being used for the smaller units into which a province was divided for both judicial and financial purposes (thus coinciding with the *almoxarifados*, 27 in number). In 1641 Portugal had, within those six provinces and 27 *comarcas*, 18 towns, 408 *vilas* (i.e., small towns), and 200 *concelhos* (municipalities). The number of ecclesiastical dioceses remained the same, but a new archbishopric (besides those of Braga and Lisbon) was created, that of Évora (1540).

After the great administrative reforms of the early 1500's a period of relative calm followed, encompassing the latter part of John III's rule and the reigns of Sebastian and Henry. The only important achievement before the union with Spain was an act of 1570 setting up two itinerant tribunals of justice, one for the South (the provinces of Alentejo and the Algarve), the other for the North, each one with its permanent body of officials and magistrates. The purpose was to provide a better judicial system for the population.

The administration of the Habsburg kings brought about numerous and substantial reforms, most of which would persist for centuries. Portugal benefited from the highly advanced Spanish bureaucratic pattern, and her government methods were more or less brought up to date. Justice benefited by various improvements. In 1582 the system set up in 1570 was decisively altered: one of the main courts, the Casa do Cível, was permanently transferred to Porto, renamed the Relação da Casa do Porto, and given a completely new organization. At the same time, the other tribunal (Casa da Suplicação) became permanently established in Lisbon, instead of following the itinerant court. A new regulation made the Casa de Suplicação the Supreme Court in the realm while giving it direct jurisdiction over the South of Portugal and the islands of the Azores and Madeira.

Other laws changed the statutes regarding both *desembargadores* (high justice magistrates) and *corregedores,* defining their competence and area of action (1582 and 1592).

The public finance system was entirely changed (Regimento da Fazenda, 1591); the secretaries known as *vedores da fazenda* were abolished and a new council set up instead. The great chancellor (*chanceler-mor*) was given a new regulation too (1589–95).

For the Customs House in Lisbon a modern regulation (*foral*) was drafted (1587), while a new court in charge of economic affairs appeared (1592). This Tribunal do Consulado, in which merchants and legists participated, could take care of disputes among businessmen, problems of money exchange, and other matters of economic interest. It had a very large body of officials, and a special tax was introduced to subsidize its functioning. Later on (1602), Philip III dissolved this tribunal under the pretext that it was useless, while maintaining the very profitable tax.

Under Philip II and Philip III the number of reforms slowed down a little, yet they still showed a deliberate purpose of improving administration and justice. The tribunal known as Mesa da Consciência e Ordens (see chapter 4) received a new and better statute (1607). The central bureau for public finance (Casa dos Contos) underwent important changes, particularly in 1633. Other laws concerned the re-election of judges, the reform of the secretariate of state, and the like.

The city of Lisbon, which had become a large metropolis by European standards, was the object of a vast legislative effort to better its organization. Reforms had already started under Sebastian's rule, with a new regulation for the municipal government. They continued under Philip II and Philip III. Problems of water supply, health, and police in particular were dealt with. The acts of 1605 and 1608 divided the town into ten administrative quarters, changed the police corps entirely, and increased it. Other measures included street pavement, drainage, and the like.

But the main legacy of the Spanish monarchs was unquestionably the new code of legislation known as *Ordenações Filipinas*. After 1512–21, when the *Ordenações Manuelinas* had been enacted (see chapter 4), many important laws successively appeared. These Cardinal-Regent Henry ordered published in a special and bulky volume prepared by Duarte Nunes do Leão and issued in 1569 (*Collecção de Leis Extravagantes*). From 1569 to the 1580's many other laws were enacted. Consequently, Philip's systematic spirit of government led to a new code which included almost all the laws enacted from 1512 to 1595 under a new plan of arrangement and with changes in proceeding. The new Ordenações were ready by 1595 but were published after Philip II's death, in 1603.

In the late sixteenth and the seventeenth centuries government by councils developed, small bodies of more or less competent people, chosen from the ranks of the nobility, the clergy, and the bureaucrats. They advised the king and his ministers on affairs of importance. Later on, after the restoration of independence, they limited and controlled royal power, often seizing power themselves. However, there had always been councillors, whom the monarch listened to whenever necessary. In 1563 Cardinal-Regent Henry created the Council of State (Conselho de Estado), with well-defined functions and statutes granted six years later. The Conselho de Estado was followed by a Council of Finance (Conselho da Fazenda), which Philip II established in 1591 for financial, economic, and mercantile affairs. The same monarch had founded, when he left Lisbon for Madrid (1583), the Council of Portugal (Conselho de Portugal), to assist him in all matters relating to his new kingdom. This council encompassed a secretariate, later (1602) divided into four, then (1607) contracted into two, and finally (1631) fixed at three. It disappeared, of course, with the restoration of the Portuguese kings in 1640.

Then appeared a short-lived Council of India (Conselho da Índia) for overseas affairs. Created in 1604 it disappeared ten years later because of jurisdictional conflicts with other administrative organs.

John IV established three other councils: that of war, for army and navy affairs (Conselho de Guerra, 1640); that of the overseas (Conselho Ultramarino, 1642) for colonial matters, thus restoring the Council of India; and the so-called Junta dos Três Estados (1641) imposed by the *cortes* to supervise the financial administration of the war.

In the executive government, some important changes also took place. The office of private scribe (*escrivão da puridade*) disappeared under Sebastian; arrangement of government affairs into three secretariates resulted. The Spanish administration reduced them to two secretariates, that of state and that of Mercês (Mercies), besides the secretariates established in Madrid within the Council of Portugal. Under John IV things started with one secretariate only, but after a few years the two secretariates of the Spanish period appeared again, and then three—the secretariate of state for the broad lines of domestic, colonial and foreign policy; the secretariate of Mercês e Expediente, for the appointment of the majority of officials, officers and magistrates; and the secretariate of Assinatura (Signature), for the signature of documents coming from any council. From 1662 to 1667, the *escrivão da puridade* was revived by the Count of Castelo-Melhor as a true prime minister, an intermediary between king and secretaries, with powers above that of the Secretary of State.

The role of the *cortes* very much declined during the period we are dealing with. This was nothing new, only the continuation of a much earlier trend in favor of royal centralization. There were *cortes* in 1562–63, 1579, and 1580, but only the first ones meant something in the traditional role assigned to such assemblies. The *cortes* of 1579 and 1580 were summoned to discuss the problem of the succession to the throne. Philip II found it necessary to give the *cortes* a certain appearance of power in order to obtain the support of the Portuguese: he summoned them twice (1581 and 1583). When his son Philip III visited Lisbon, *cortes* were again summoned (1619), more as a session of welcome to the monarch than anything else. After the Restoration their role was for a while somewhat enhanced. Between 1641 and 1668 they met five times, always in Lisbon, playing an important part in the reorganization of the country. But this was actually a mere pause in their decline, which came quickly and decisively shortly afterward.

No great changes affected the University. The main one was to place it under the jurisdiction of the royal tribunal known as Mesa da Consciência e Ordens (1576). The University thus became a state institution. Despite the half a dozen statute alterations between 1559 and 1612 its framework was kept essentially the same up to the eighteenth century. The Statute of 1612, confirmed by John IV in 1653, would undergo no changes whatsoever for more than a hundred years. According to its clauses, the University of Coimbra encompassed four major schools (*Faculdades*)—Theology, Canons, Law, and Medicine—and seven minor schools (*Escolas menores*), for the teaching of mathematics, music, arts, Hebrew, Greek, Latin, and elementary subjects (reading, writing and counting). Consequently, the University included both the upper levels of learning and the secondary, even the primary, studies. For the student it permitted a full curriculum starting with childhood and ending in adulthood.

The Coimbra monopoly in university courses was threatened by the Jesuits, who wanted to control education as much as possible and to whom the University of Coimbra always offered stubborn resistance. In 1559 they succeeded in having their own University, which Cardinal Henry, the inquisitor-general and future regent, founded at Évora and handed them. Nine years later the Pope gave them full control over the new College which was subject only to the jurisdiction of their general. Yet the University of Évora was much smaller than that of Coimbra, and its program offered fewer subjects: only theology, arts, grammar, Biblical studies, casuistry, Latin, and elementary courses. To increase their influence in the upper schools, the Jesuits obtained a rule (1561) that admission into the *Faculdades* of Canons and Law should depend on a degree by the College of Arts, which they directed.

The story of the College of Arts was a sad one. It had started (see chapter 4) as a humanist school, with a very complete nucleus of courses and an excellent team of teachers, many of them foreigners. It quickly became obvious that such a school could evolve into a center of freethinking, a menace to the unity of Faith and the new religious and cultural policy followed by John III. The newly created Inquisition detected in the College of Arts a good victim for its fervor. Several teachers were arrested and persecuted, including Buchanan and Diogo de Teive. Alleged crimes of homosexuality and other immoral acts served as further pretexts. After five years of attack, the College of Arts was "cleansed" of its best and most dangerous elements and became a meek instrument of the Counter-Reformation. John III carried on his new policy by entrusting the College of Arts to the direction of the Jesuits (1555) and united it to the College of Jesus founded by them.

This Jesuit attempt to control education on all levels met, of course, with the resistance of many. The University of Coimbra was one of them. The other religious orders, particularly the Augustinians and the Dominicans, very concerned about education and highly influential too, reacted strongly but in vain. In 1560 the Duke of Bragança, Teodósio, tried to establish a third university at Vila Viçosa, in Alentejo (where his court was) and to place it under Augustinian control. His death shortly afterward jeopardized the whole plan. The *cortes* of 1562 also protested against the growing number and influence of the Jesuits, and against their taking over the College of Arts. Nothing was achieved, however. Jesuits, Inquisition, and Crown were at that time strongly united against heresy, cultural bourgeoning, and deviations from Council of Trent policy. Throughout the country a great many teachers were persecuted, arrested, condemned or forced to leave their chairs. Few innovations in teaching and learning were ever accepted. Universities and colleges became very rigidified, insisting on a scholastic methodology and showing no improvement in their comments to the old masters. They were not permeable to any scientific progress, rejected the cultural advancement which was taking place elsewhere, and offered a century-long example of uselessness and dogmatism. Fruitful and progressive science rose only from the humble and pragmatic achievements of navigators, settlers overseas, travelers, and foreigners.

Some doctors (Amato Lusitano—1511–68, for instance) contributed to medical advancement, while an important corpus of botany and zoology was being built up in Asia, Africa, and America. Working in India, Garcia da Horta (1501–68) related botany to medicine and pharmacology, setting up the basis for tropical medicine. Pedro Nunes (1502–78) gallantly continued and perfected the tradition of scientific seafaring, astronomy, and mathematics. They were few, however, and their experimentalism never went beyond the phase of empiricism to become a true and systematic scientific attitude. Furthermore, they all belonged to a generation which was aging by the middle of the sixteenth century and which had few and inferior successors. The only exception was Francisco Sanches (1551–1623), a predecessor of Descartes in the latter's famous method of doubt (*Tractatus de multum nobili et prima universali scientia quod nihil scitur*, A Treatise on the very noble and high universal sicence of Nescience, 1581).

But Sanches, who taught in several universities, lived in France most of his life.

Within the university framework, the only interesting examples were found in the field of philosophy. At Coimbra, a school of commentators on Aristotle emerged and went on for a good century: the famous group of the Conimbricenses who carried on medieval Aristotelism with no changes in method, complete faithfulness to the master's thought but a perfect and sophisticated way of classifying, describing, and summarizing all the comments and proposed solutions. They were pure scholastics in the sixteenth and seventeenth centuries, wanting to know Aristotle within the entire world of his commentators. Because of this methodological perfection, the works of the Conimbricenses were widely read throughout Europe, particularly in university circles. As a group, the College of Arts published eight volumes of Comments on Aristotle (*Commentarii Collegii Conimbricensis Societatis Iesu*) under the direction of Pedro da Fonseca (1582–99) between 1592 and 1606. Pedro da Fonseca himself (who also taught in Évora) wrote several books on similar subjects, one of which (*Institutionum Dialecticarum Libri Octo*), a sort of textbook, had 34 editions throughout Europe between 1564 and 1625. All these works had a tremendous influence in Portugal and abroad, with many editions in France, Germany, and Italy, praised by men like Descartes and Leibniz.

In Évora,the important name was that of the philosopher Luis de Molina (1535–1600), who was of Spanish birth but lived, worked, and wrote in Portugal most of his life. Molina's *De Concordantia liberi arbitrii cum gratiae donis, divina prescientia et providentia* (1588) brought about a lively polemic of international character on the possibility of reconciling free will and divine prescience. Molinism, a philosophical doctrine derived from Molina's writings, had a great impact on the seventeenth- and even eighteenth-century theological and philosophical world.

Control of culture by the Church and the state was enforced not only through universities and colleges. The introduction of organized censorship became another and still more effective way.

There had been royal control of the press since the 1520's, but it was vague and imprecise. The privileges granted to the printers served as a means of supervising book production. Real censorship was only established with the Inquisition. From 1540 on, a certain number of rules were set up, by which the book stores were periodically inspected by ecclesiastics, as were ships coming from abroad. These rules were gradually made tighter as the Inquisition became stronger and pervaded every aspect of daily life. Not only book shops but also private homes were visited by Inquisition men whenever someone died who was supposed to have owned books and manuscripts.

In 1543 the first *Index* of forbidden works appeared in Italy. It was rapidly followed by a Spanish one (1546) which was the pattern for the first Portuguese roll of *livros defesos* (forbidden books), published in 1547: it contained only 160 foreign titles. Four years later a new *Index* came into existence in Portugal. This time it was printed and encompassed 495 titles, including 13 in Portuguese and Castilian. From then on, to the mid-seventeenth century several lists of forbidden books appeared in Portugal, Spain (which generally set the tone and furnished the basis for the Portuguese ones), and Rome; the latter was valid for all Christendom according to the Council of Trent decisions.

The Portuguese "Indices" of 1561, 1581, and 1624 clearly show not only the development of the printing press but especially the increasing rigor of the censorship: more than 50 titles in Portuguese and Castilian in the first case, 94 titles in the second, and 330 titles in the third—a rise of 88 per cent between 1561 and 1581, of 251 per cent between 1581 and 1624, and of 339 per cent in the whole period. Forbidden works included books considered heretical (or, in general, written, translated, or edited by heretics); books on "lascivious and dishonest things"; books on witchcraft, astrology, and the like. The formula later adopted by the censors forbade all books or parts of books that contained anything against "our holy Faith and good customs." Against "Faith and customs" were the writings of many Portuguese authors, practically all the classics of the Portuguese literature. Writers like Camões, Gil Vicente, Sá de Miranda, António Ferreira, Bernardim Ribeiro, João de Barros, and many others all had their works proscribed or mutilated by the censorship. Books which were not totally forbidden were to be taken by their owners (which few actually did) or by the book sellers to the Inquisition, where the forbidden parts were crossed out or torn up. In their next edition, the text had to appear with the changes determined by the censors. Forbidden books were burned in the autos-da-fé.

The Inquisition did not have a monopoly of censorship. Both the bishops and the king retained their power of controlling literary production as well. The bishops imposed their traditional authority particularly from the seventeenth century on, the king—interested in the political aspects above all—as early as 1576 (effective only in the 1590's). Thus, a complex procedure evolved for the publishing of any manuscript. It was first presented to the Inquisition, then to the "Ordinary" (the bishop of the diocese), finally to the king through the Desembargo do Paço. In each case the manuscript went back and forth to its author and to the censors if there were any changes to be made. The final edition bore the permission of those three authorities and could be removed from the original presentation date by months or years. Censorship varied according to the times, the personality of the censors, and the influences backing the authors. In any case it was always a discouraging element for writers and printers. Along with the Inquisition and the pervasive Jesuit influence, it slowed down literary production, prevented Portugal from accompanying the scientific and cultural progress of Europe at a normal pace, and gave birth to a highly interesting kind of clandestine literature that is still awaiting its historian.

Obviously, the books printed in the late sixteenth and the seventeenth century had to reflect the realities of the nation. Religious literature accounted for the great majority of titles. Other kinds were law studies, poetry, history, and travels, with a very small minority devoted to science. From 1551 to 1599 a little more than a thousand titles were printed in Portugal, an average of twenty books a year. Interestingly enough, this average was more or less the same after the great leap of 1548–51, no increase being noticed in the number of publications. On the contrary, there was a slight backward movement after the late 1560's.

Despite all these barriers to a full cultural development, the Portuguese world in the second half of the sixteenth and the first half of the seventeenth centuries was still vigorous enough to produce a great number of masterworks and cope with the cultural (except scientific) advancement of Europe. The humanist revival yielded some

of its best fruits after 1550, particularly among the men who belonged
to generations brought up before or around the middle of the century.
Luis de Camões (1525?–80) was the greatest of all, a poet of international renown, the author of the Portuguese epic poem "The
Lusiads" (*Os Lusíadas*), published in 1572, and of a most beautiful
corpus of lyric poetry. To his generation belonged poets and prose
writers such as António Ferreira (1528–83?), Diogo Bernardes (1530–
1605), Heitor Pinto (1528–83?), and the aesthete and artist Francisco de
Holanda (1517–89), comparable to the best sixteenth-century Europe
could offer. Later generations produced some good authors such as
historians Diogo do Couto (1542–1616) and Luis de Sousa (1555–1632),
and other prose-writers like Francisco Rodrigues Lobo (1579?–1621),
Francisco Manuel de Melo (1608–66), António das Chagas (1631–82),
and António Vieira (1608–97). Yet there is little doubt that both
number and quality (with the exception of Vieira) somewhat declined
in the seventeenth century and that the flowering caused by the Restoration rapidly became exhausted too.

Quite a different picture prevailed in the arts, where the strictness
of either the Inquisition or other forms of censorship little affected the progress of architecture, or sculpture, or even painting. The
style of the Renaissance which had come to Portugal so late rapidly
evolved to that new way of understanding the classical models, known
as Mannerism. There are few instances of survival of the pure Renaissance style after 1550. The new cathedrals of Leiria, Miranda, and
Portalegre, all started in the 1550's, already show a compromise between Renaissance and Mannerism. The market built at Beja according to the Italian tradition of the *loggie* is one of the few examples of
a style that was dying. Portuguese Mannerism had its main centers
in Lisbon, Évora, Coimbra, and Porto. Italian and Spanish masters
set the tone, as Italian and Spanish monuments were eagerly copied
everywhere. The influence of the Italian architect Serlio pervaded
Portugal throughout the sixteenth and sevententh century. Another
Italian, Filippo Terzi (1520?–97), founded a well-known school of
architecture in Lisbon and directed the building of several important
monuments (S. Vicente de Fora). Among the best examples of this
architecture were the new cathedral in Coimbra, the church of
S. Bento, in Porto, and the church in Graça, in Évora.

The Jesuit conception of religion and its method of gaining souls by appealing to people's attention and imagination also had its impact on the arts, particularly in architecture. Most Jesuit churches (S. Roque, in Lisbon; Espírito Santo, in Évora) had practically no side aisles, many side chapels being reduced to niches in the walls. In this way, the whole church looked like a vast room forcing people's eyes and minds to turn to the pulpit and the main altar. Strongly influenced by the church of Gesù in Rome this kind of temple quickly became a favorite one and was adopted by others than the Jesuits.

Inside the churches a lavish type of decoration developed from the late sixteenth century on. This included fancy tiles (in several colors) and an odd and very Portuguese fabric of carved and gilded wood (*talha*) entirely covering the altarpieces, relief panels, picture frames, cornices, screens, pulpits, choir stalls, organ cases, and the like. There were many instances in which almost all church interior surfaces were completely filled up with both tiles (*azulejos*) and gilt wood. This brought about several results, one of them being the decline of religious painting, replaced by the new and fashionable art forms. Other art works inside the churches encompassed tombs, altars, stone and wooden images, as well as choir stalls.

Civil buildings also became more and more numerous, their artistic expression gaining an increasing value. Military fortresses, for instance, were built all over Portugal and her empire, reflecting many new conceptions in military art. Aqueducts, too, rose in several places (Coimbra, Vila do Conde) showing the growing concern with water supply to the cities. The increasing number of nobles dwelling in towns (particularly in Lisbon) resulted in the building of numerous palaces and mansions. In Lisbon, Philip II ordered a new palace to be constructed. In the noble farms (*quintas*) of the countryside many summer houses displayed their owner's affluence. Other civic buildings were fountains, schools (University of Évora), and hospitals (the Misericórdias).

Painting in the second half of the sixteenth century continued the Renaissance tradition in quality and quantity. However, instead of the all-pervasive Flemish influence, Italian painting more and more gave the tone, without excluding the influence of the new French and Flemish masters. The great name was that of Gregório Lopes (1516–

94), but schools of painting flourished in many small towns (besides
Lisbon), around the courts of bishops and nobles. In the seventeenth
century religious painting declined both in quality and quantity but
the art of portraiture (which had started earlier) rose to some high
levels. Unfortunately, most of those pictures are still in private collections; no complete inventory of them exists, which produces the false
impression that painting thoroughly declined during that period.

IBERIAN UNION

Attempts to unify the Iberian Peninsula can be traced far back
into the past. Up to the fifteenth century, Castile, as the centripetal
force, had always been the leading party in striving for a united Iberia
under her direct suzerainty. Later, however, both Portugal and Aragon
played a role too. The ideal was, as a matter of fact, common to all
the Peninsular monarchies. Despite a separate existence of hundreds of
years, they still looked upon themselves as integral parts of Hispania:
the pagan Hispania of the Romans; the Christian Hispania of the late
Roman Empire; or the Visigothic kingdom, unified for the last time
under the Moslems.

In the late Middle Ages, former localisms raised to the category of
nationalisms began hampering and frustrating attempts at unification.
Local dialects on the way to becoming languages made communication
more difficult; political traditions rejected any easygoing acceptance
of a common leadership, semi-isolated cultural patterns often revealed
themselves more permeable to foreign influences; economic interests
split the Peninsula into well-defined areas, and so forth. Yet the dream
did not die. On the contrary it became a sort of favorite sport within
the royal families of each country, in search of more power and glory.
The rise of central administration was undoubtedly the major factor
in this continuous policy followed by the Iberian monarchs. Each king
wanted for himself a greater name, an array of titles signifying numerous lordships. In the constant strengthening of authority and increase
in force displayed by powerful monarchs like the king of France, the
king of England, or the emperor of Germany, the lords of Castile,
Aragon, and Portugal had impressive models. If such powerful rulers

were able to round off their estates through conquest or peaceful means, carving for themselves new political units, more or less based upon ancient boundaries and remote traditions, why should the Iberian monarchs not do the same? Indeed, international emulation and seignorial grandeur stood behind every attempt to unify Iberia, more than did the ideal of a common fatherland.

The political and economic expansion of both Aragon and Portugal enabled them to play at unification as much as Castile. This explains the intermarriages that resulted in the thwarted attempts of 1474–79 and 1496–1500. In both cases Portugal was to have been the leading party and her male candidate the ruler of Spain. During the sixteenth century, dynastic ties between the Portuguese and the Spanish royal families developed with such an insistence and closeness that final union had to be the inevitable result. Carlos V (in Spain Carlos I) married Isabel, the eldest daughter of Manuel I. At the same time John III married Carlos's youngest sister, Catarina. Some years before, Manuel I had successively married three Spanish princesses: Isabel, her younger sister Maria, and finally Leonor, Catarina's elder sister. Then, Philip II married (1543) Maria, John's surviving first-born daughter, while Philip's sister, Juana, was betrothed to John (1552), heir to the Portuguese throne. From this latter wedding only one child resulted, Sebastian, whose birth (1554) was shortly followed by his father's death, making him the sole survivor of John III's eleven legitimate descendants. Dying in 1557, John III left as successor a weak child of three, whose chances of living were not very good. All of his life he was sickly, both physically and mentally. He abhorred the prospect of marriage. His twenty-year reign was therefore just a long preparation for a change of dynasty.

Yet, the Iberian Union was not simply the whim of a small group of royalty: it also became economically, socially, and culturally viable. As the Portuguese historian Magalhães Godinho put it, the date of 1580 (when Spain conquered Portugal) "is much more a point of arrival than a point of departure . . . it sanctions, dynastically speaking, the turn of structure of the mid-century." Indeed, from the middle of the sixteenth century on, the Portuguese Empire and its general economic organization—with its full impact on Portugal's ultimate destiny—formed a sort of complement to the Spanish Empire (see chapter 7). The traffic with India and the Far East (where the fabulous market of China had been discovered and was in full development) absorbed great quantities of silver, which Europe was no longer able to supply. Thus, the Portuguese became increasingly dependent upon Spanish silver production, burgeoning after the discovery of the silver mines and treasures in Mexico and Peru. Seville, more than Antwerp, was now the main Portuguese trade connection. Also, the regular trade line between Mexico and China (via Manila, in the Philippines) challenged the Portuguese position in the Far East, unless the Portuguese obtained freedom of access and trade within the Spanish colonial possessions. By the second half of the century, the Spanish Empire had reached its zenith and strongly appealed to the Portuguese initiatives, accustomed as they were to different cultures and odd methods of trading, eager to expand their markets everywhere, well aware of the immense possibilities such ties offered them.

At the same time, the direct economic relations between Portugal and Spain were becoming more interdependent, Portuguese traders and ships often serving as intermediaries between Spain and other parts of Europe. Spanish merchants and capitalists controlled part of the Portuguese traffic and held a relevant position in the general affairs undertaken by the Crown. The abolishment of all or part of the customs duties along the border had been a long-cherished dream, particularly among the Portuguese, who badly needed Castilian wheat almost every year. Spaniards and Portuguese also had common enemies, in growing numbers and activities: the French, the English, and later the Dutch. Piracy harassed the ships of both countries, often attacking them on the same maritime routes and requiring the combined action of their fleets. Against Moors and Turks as well, the Portuguese and Spanish exerted joint activities. On the other hand, each country having a huge domain of its own to digest, mutual aggression rarely occurred. Spain and Portugal were natural allies.

Culturally, too, an Iberian union would simply consolidate the increasing process of Castilianization which Portugal had been undergoing for a long time. Castilian influences on culture had always been felt in Portugal, just as Portuguese influences could be observed in Castile. Yet such influences were more or less moderated by the impact of other cultures: French, Aragonese, Italian, Burgundian, even

English, as well as by the vigor of the Portuguese culture itself. While this vigor increased in the sixteenth century to a peak of glorious achievements in the fields of literature, education, and science, it had nonetheless to cope with the impact of the still more vigorous Spanish "Siglo de Oro." When a country like France was culturally influenced by Spain, how could Portugal, with a much weaker cultural texture, resist the impact of her neighbor?

The royal court had always been the center of Portugal's cultural accomplishments. After 1491, the court almost permanently gravitated around a Castilian pole, represented by the queen. And if the four queens who succeeded each other up to 1578 probably learned some Portuguese, there is no doubt that the language usually spoken by them was their native one. In the late fifteenth and during the whole of the sixteenth century, practically every Portuguese author, courtier, and educated man was bilingual or spoke some Castilian. They wrote in Castilian as well as in Portuguese, some being considered nowadays as classical writers of the Spanish literature. Gil Vicente, the creator of the Portuguese theater, wrote about one-fourth of his plays in Castilian only, while another third used both languages. A similar inventory made for all the other great Portuguese authors, including Luis de Camões, would show that a significant proportion of their works were in Castilian rather than Portuguese. As with French later, Castilian had become a fashionable idiom (as well as an international language), a part of everyone's education. We noted earlier (chapter 4) the importance of Spain in the evolution of the Portuguese educational system, the number of Portuguese students in Spanish universities and Spanish teachers in Portugal.

The lower classes, of course, were much less affected by this Castilianization, yet they also felt the impact of popular Spanish romances. Historical ballads and epics were recited everywhere and became a part of daily life. However, as we shall see, such a difference in the degree of Castilianization was significant both in the loss of independence, in 1580, and in its recovery, in 1640. All this is not to say that Spain felt immune to the Portuguese influence. Several Spanish authors were also bilingual and wrote in Portuguese. Numerous translations made the sixteenth-century Portuguese writers known to the Spanish public—but not in the original language. And there were also Portuguese queens in Spain, though for brief periods only, for both the wives of Carlos I and Philip II died young. The impact of their presence could never be felt like that of the Castilian princesses in Portugal. Yet Carlos's wife, Isabel, probably taught Portuguese to his son and spoke with him in her native tongue during his childhood and early youth—a fact of future consequences in Philip's understanding of Portugal.

Sebastian's young age required a regency: his grandmother Catarina ruled from 1557 to 1562; then his great-uncle Henry, the cardinal archbishop of Lisbon and inquisitor-general, from 1562 to 1568. It was the first time that a priest directly governed Portugal, a fact that would be repeated again and again till 1640, so that in forty-one (52.6 per cent) of the seventy-eight years, there was ecclesiastical rule. The regency period, like most of Sebastian's personal reign (1568–78) and like the final years of his grandfather's, meant stability. No structures were altered. No essential reforms were undertaken. The era of change and expansion, so typical of the first half of the century, was over. What mattered now was to maintain and strengthen the existing order, to defend it against all internal and external dangers. This explains why so few innovations characterized the period 1550–80.

A great part of Queen Catarina's and Cardinal Henry's legislative activity, which Sebastian carried on, had a clear religious connotation and referred to ecclesiastical matters: creation of new bishoprics, both at home and overseas; strengthening of the Inquisition and its expansion to India; ratification and enforcement of the decisions of the Council of Trent (Portugal was the only Catholic country not to present any doubts about their applicability); new by-laws granted to the religious-military orders; and so forth. The only important cultural achievement, the establishment of a new university at Évora (1559), had a similar religious flavor: in fact the new school was entirely placed in the hands of the Jesuits, its instructors were clerics, and most of its students were future priests or clerics too.

Military defense deeply concerned the Portuguese rulers. French and English privateering plagued Portuguese waters or prevented a safe maritime route to India and Brazil. Moslem attacks hardened the Moroccan strongholds. Attempts were made not only to convoy the mercantile marine with greater efficiency but also to fortify the coast.

A number of new fortresses were built and others were repaired both in Portugal and in North Africa. The regents succeeded in obtaining Papal bulls that forced the clergy to contribute for defense. It was one advantage of giving supreme power to the Church.

At the age of fourteen, Sebastian took over control of government. If not a king he would probably have been a zealous missionary. Sick in body and in mind, and lost in his dreams of conquest and expansion of the faith, he hardly showed any interest in the tasks of government. To conquer Morocco was his primary ambition, but other projects of imperialism in heathen countries also haunted his imagination. Daring to the limits of insanity he gave no thought to planning, strategy, or retreat, which he simply called fear and cowardice. He despised the old and the prudent, surrounding himself with a bunch of young aristocrats, almost as insane and immature as himself. He would not accept a word of advice nor could he face reality and truth. Only through flattery could one gain access to him. In his first years of rule, he still accepted Catarina's meddling with the problems of administration and general governing. But he soon forgot her advice, fell into the hands of inept favorites, and devoted all his energies to the task of building an empire. Lack of funds deterred his ambitions for some time. The church provided the bulk of the revenues, yet the people were assessed too with some new taxes. Foreign traders loaned a substantial share, Konrad Rott from Augsburg alone contributing about 400,000 cruzados at 8 per cent interest and receiving the exclusive of the pepper sale for three years. Taking advantage of the royal needs, the New Christians "bought" for 240,000 cruzados a Papal bull halting the confiscation of property of those arrested by the Inquisition.

In 1574 Sebastian visited Morocco for the first time; but although he spent some three months there, he was not lucky enough to fight the Moors, as he wished. Back in Portugal he actively prepared a formal expedition, vainly trying to get some support from his uncle Philip II whom he visited at Guadalupe (1576). Then, as a pretext for intervention, he promised to help the former sultan of Berberia, Mulay Muhammad Al-Mutawakkil, who had been dethroned (1575) by his brother Mulay 'Abd-al-Malik. The governor of Arzila (abandoned by John III in 1550), a partisan of Mulay Muhammad's, surrendered the town to Portugal rather than give it to the new sultan (1577). This was considered a good omen.

Despite Sebastian's haste, an army could not leave Portugal before the summer of 1578, and even so it was in a pitiful state of indiscipline and disorganization. Besides the Portuguese main force there were corps of German, Spanish, and Italian mercenaries. Landing in Arzila, the army proceeded south under the king's personal command, which really meant no command at all. Near El-Ksar-el-Kebir (Alcácer Quibir) the Portuguese forces (15,500 infantry and 1,500 cavalry plus some hundreds in charge of the supplies, servants, women, slaves, etc.), with a few of Mulay Muhammad's partisans, were completely defeated by Sultan Mulay 'Abd-al-Malik's army (8,000 infantry and 41,000 cavalry, besides the irregular forces) in the most disastrous battle of Portuguese history. Sebastian was killed and with him the cream of the country's nobility and men-of-arms (some 7,000). The rest were made prisoners. Fewer than a hundred escaped. The whole adventure is estimated to have cost more than one million cruzados, about a half of the state's annual revenues.

Sebastian's death opened the way to the Iberian Union. Cardinal Henry succeeded to the throne, but he was an old gentleman of sixty-six, broken in health and in energy. It seemed evident to all that he would not live very much longer. Thus, several candidates claimed their rights to the Portuguese Crown. They all traced their claims back to Manuel I, for no descendants of John III were left. Manuel's male offspring with descendancy were only two: Luis, who had never married, but who had had an illegitimate son named António; and Duarte, from whose marriage two daughters were born—Maria (wife of the future duke of Parma and governor of the Netherlands, Alessandro Farnese), and Catarina (married to the Duke of Bragança, João). Maria had died in 1577 but left a son, Ranuccio, the future Duke of Parma, heir to Alessandro. Manuel's daughters produced two other candidates: Philip II, King of Spain; and Emanuele Filiberto, Duke of Savoy.

From a strictly legitimate point of view, the lawful heir was Ranuccio. Yet he himself was a child of nine, while his father, governor of the Netherlands, could obviously do nothing against his overlord, the king of Spain. Catarina of Bragança came next and she

posed the most serious menace to Philip's claim, at least from a theoretical point of view. António, the prior of Crato, had the advantage
of being the only living son of one of Manuel's sons. He tried to prove
that his father had legitimized him, and he succeeded in convincing
a great many Portuguese of that. With the people he enjoyed some
popularity. The most viable candidate was of course Philip. If he
lacked legal arguments, he had enough strength and determination
to overrule them. His ambassadors, envoys, and spies, along with his
bribes and powerful forces, did an excellent job of convincing, threatening, and buying the leading elements of the Portuguese society.

Henry's two main concerns were to redeem the thousands of captives arrested in Africa and to appoint a legal successor who might
spare the country a civil war. If he was relatively successful in that
first goal, he completely failed in the latter. Pressured from three sides,
hating António, leaning toward Catarina but fearful of Philip's might,
he summoned the *cortes* (1579–80) but was not cooperative with them
in arriving at any decision, always hesitating and realizing that the
country was hopelessly divided. After finally appointing five governors
to form an interim regency—the archbishop of Lisbon and four nobles,
two of them with jobs in the administration—he died of tuberculosis
on January 31, 1580, leaving a problem difficult of solution.

The majority of the people supported António, because they felt
strongly against a Spanish king and the prior of Crato was the only
candidate brave enough to defy the might of Philip II. He was also a
popular character. The Duke of Bragança, though with the support
of a great many nobles and churchmen, acted very prudently, unwilling to sacrifice his opulent house to the hazards of a more than dubious
political game. He certainly recalled the misfortunes of 1483 (see
chapter 4) and refused to make the same mistake.

Philip benefited from a great number of factors: his power, difficult to challenge by a country whose army had been so completely
annihilated and whose treasure was utterly depleted; his record of wise
administration and of keeping peace at home, two conditions that
Portugal badly needed; his promises to maintain the full sovereignty
of the form of dual monarchy; and, last but not least, his cunning
diplomacy and his monetary arguments within every Portuguese influential circle, cleverly suggesting, convincing, threatening, promising,

and bribing. Nobility and clergy sold out because they found themselves penniless. At the same time they were afraid of a popular reaction headed by António, a disreputable opportunist of dubious morals and character, who had been at odds with both Sebastian and Henry and even sought refuge in Spain, some years before. All over Europe those were times of seignorial reaction and popular turbulence, related to the price revolution and the increasing poverty. For the upper bourgeoisie, too, the Iberian Union meant a strengthening of the state finance system, therefore better protection and defense everywhere. It meant also the opening of new markets and the suppression of the border customs.

Consequently, it did not take Philip II much time to gain the support of the upper clergy, most of the nobility, the intellectuals and bureaucrats, and the merchants. Even the dukes of Bragança were forced to submit and accepted Philip's candidacy. Ironically, it was the Spanish ruling classes who seem to have felt some concern about the union with Portugal. They feared a greater strengthening of the royal power to their detriment. The Spanish merchants, too, may have had second thoughts about the advantages of a sudden and boundless Portuguese competition all over the Spanish Empire. Late in June 1580 the Duke of Alba, Spain's best general with much experience in earlier campaigns, invaded Portugal with a strong army, while the Spanish fleet moved along the coastline. Meanwhile António had himself proclaimed king in Lisbon, Santarém, Setúbal, and other places. A military march took the Spanish army to the Tagus in a few weeks. The Duke of Alba landed in Cascais, fifteen miles west of Lisbon, easily routed at Alcântara the improvised army of seven to eight thousand men António had gathered (August 25) and entered the city that same day. The rest of the country was pacified in a couple of months. António, fleeing for his life, managed to escape to France where he was welcomed and acknowledged as *de jure* king of Portugal. Philip entered Portugal early in December, decided to fix his residence in Lisbon for some time (1581–83), and summoned the *cortes* at Tomar (April 1581) where he was solemnly sworn in and acclaimed King of Portugal with the title of Philip I.

António tried his best to continue the fight with the help of France and England. The Azores, alone in the vast Portuguese Empire, sustained his flag of independence (the island of Fogo, in Cape Verde, also revolted against Philip but for a short time and with no consequences). A first attempt of Spanish conquest defeated (April 1581), it was only in August 1583 that the island of Terceira, last of António's bulwarks, accepted surrender to Philip II. António, fleeing again to France, still managed to foster French and British attacks against Portuguese ships, the Portuguese mainland, and the Portuguese overseas territories. In 1587, Drake paraded in front of Lisbon. In 1589, after the defeat of the Armada, Drake once more attacked the coasts of the Iberian Peninsula, raiding Coruña (in Galicia) and Peniche (in Portuguese Estremadura) and vainly attacking Lisbon. Yet Philip's control of Portugal was so firm that no expected uprising took place on behalf of António. Some years later, his death (in 1595) gave the Spaniards undisputed sovereignty over the country.

Iberian Union did not mean loss of identity for Portugal. Interestingly enough, Philip repeated in relation to Portugal what his grandfather Manuel I had done in relation to Spain in 1499 (see chapter 4). Twenty-five chapters signed by the king at the *cortes* of Tomar provided a great deal of autonomy for the country, despite the fact that foreign policy now became common to Portugal and Spain. Administration remained entirely in the hands of the Portuguese. No Spaniard could ever be appointed for jobs of civil and Church administration, justice, or defense. Viceroys and governors might be Spaniards only if they belonged to the royal family (sons, brothers, or nephews). New legislation depended upon decisions taken in the *cortes,* summoned in Portugal and attended by Portuguese only. The overseas empire continued to be ruled exclusively by Portugal according to the existing laws and regulations. The official language remained Portuguese. Currency continued separate, as well as public revenues and expenditures. The king might not grant places or revenues in Portugal except to Portuguese subjects. In the royal household there was to be no discrimination against the Portuguese. Advantageous innovations included the suppression of customs in the border; a favorable situation for Portugal in the export of wheat from Castile; and the grant of 300,000 cruzados for immediate expenses, part of them for redeeming captives in Morocco. The Portuguese were also allowed to travel to and within the Spanish Empire.

For practical purposes of general administrative supervision and policy, a "Council of Portugal" (Conselho de Portugal) was permanently established to work with the king and follow him everywhere. It was composed of six people, one prelate and five bureaucrats, all Portuguese. Leaving Portugal for good in 1583, Philip II appointed a governor to rule the country in his name. The choice fell upon Archduke Albrecht of Austria, his favorite nephew, a wise and respected young man of twenty-three living in Spain since 1570, made cardinal at the age of eighteen, then Papal legate (1583) and finally inquisitor-general (1586) of Portugal. The specific rules for the government of the country, given by the king to the new governor, stressed and defined the articles sworn to at Tomar. The governor was to meet with the Council of State every week and with three of its members (a sort of government) daily. Administration of justice, matters of defense, overseas affairs, and audiences to the people were carefully regulated. Quick communications with Madrid were provided and matters that required royal attention detailed.

After more than ten years of governmental chaos, misdemeanors, and increasing taxation, these patterns of model administration, which seem to have been sufficiently enforced, along with the wise decision of maintaining Portugal's identity, explain the relative calm that prevailed. For several decades, the country accepted fairly well the loss of total independence. António's several attempts at regaining the throne met with general indifference or the sparse support of the population. Prosperity returned, the treasury became fairly well balanced again, the empire was kept undisturbed. If grievances against Spain continued to exist and if the yearning for a Portuguese king never ceased, there is no doubt that Philip's excellent administration (with few political persecutions) coped with the problem for a long time.

From 1582 to the 1590's a great number of administrative, judicial, and financial reforms took place, carried on by Portuguese officials but clearly inspired on Spanish patterns. They generally improved bureaucracy and government, and met with popular approval. Less popular, particularly in its disastrous consequences, was the Portuguese participation in the Spanish Armada against England, which departed from Lisbon in 1588 (though it should be remembered that the English, under Drake, had threatened Portugal's security a year before): 31 of the 146 main ships, including several of the larger galleons, were Portuguese. Most of them never came back, a serious blow for the Portuguese fleet.

In 1593, Cardinal-Archduke Albrecht was recalled to Madrid by Philip II. Not trusting anyone sufficiently to appoint him for the governorship of Portugal, the king preferred to adopt a collective formula, five governors being chosen to form a regency council, presided over by the archbishop of Lisbon, Miguel de Castro. The other four members carried on leading military and administrative offices. Until 1640 the government of Portugal seesawed between the collective and the individual formulas, according to the circumstances, the reliability of nominees, and the need to weaken or strengthen representative authority. The first council of regents lasted till 1600. In the meantime Philip II had died (1598) and his son Philip III (known as Philip II in Portugal) came to the throne. A weak-minded prince, thoroughly uninterested in state affairs, the very antithesis of his father, Philip III never ruled by himself, but rather entrusted power to favorites. Actually it has to be remembered that delegation of royal power to a prime minister was often a feature of seventeenth-century governments all over Europe. The task of governing was becoming too complex and too specialized for the usually poor preparation and ability of most princes. Moreover, court pomp and etiquette, coupled with absolutist ideologies, pointed to a much more symbolic role for the king, hidden away in a palace, aloof from his people and knowing little of their problems. Yet both Philip III and Philip IV, who came after him, certainly paid little or no attention to public affairs.

In Madrid, the Duke of Lerma, Francisco de Sandoval, started a twenty-year rule (1598–1618), followed by his son, the Duke of Uceda (1618–21). Interested in replacing all of the late king's advisers and influential people, Lerma appointed as governor and viceroy of Portugal one of Philip II's closest confidants and ablest statesmen, Cristóvão de Moura, count and then marquis of Castelo-Rodrigo, a leading personality in winning over Portugal to the cause of Spain. He served two terms (1600–3, 1608–12) and was the best warrant of Portugal's autonomy, struggling for the maintenance of the privileges granted by Philip II and twice leaving the government because the prime-minister had trampled on them. Madrid's policy indeed tended to centralize

administration, gradually reducing the autonomy of the various political units that made up Spain—Portugal as well as Catalonia,
Aragon, Navarre, etc. It was the inevitable result of the impending
hard times, hovering over the Iberian monarchy. Increasing expenditures required a tougher control of the treasury and a better management of the whole financial structure. In 1600 the king dispatched to
Portugal a committee of three members (all Castilians) with the mission of supervising the Casa da India and finance in general. Then in
1602, Castilian ministers were appointed to the Council of Portugal
and to the Finance Council (Conselho da Fazenda), in violation of the
1581 chapters.

These were very unpopular measures. After 1611 taxation increased in the form of compulsory loans paid by the merchants and
the middle class in general. The Madrid government made itself still
more hated by accepting money from the New Christians and letting
them leave the country freely (1604–10). To gain the support of the
aristocracy, Philip III granted some Crown patrimony to the upper
nobles, namely to the Duke of Bragança. Also, the signing of a twelve-
year truce with Holland gave peace to the country and her menaced
overseas territories (see chapter 7) and enhanced her economic prosperity by opening the ports to the Dutch trade (1609). Finally, to
appease discontent, the king decided to visit Portugal, where he spent
some five months of the year 1619. The regency was mostly in the
hands of the clergy, a wise measure to gain their backing: the bishop
of Coimbra (1603–4), the bishop of Leiria (1605–8, 1612–14), the archbishop of Braga (1614–15), and the archbishop of Lisbon (1615–17)
ruled the country as viceroys, further uniting Church and state. From
1617 to 1621 a half-Castilian held the regency, the Duke of Francavila,
Diego de Silva y Mendoza, despite the clamorous protests of the Portuguese.

On the whole, Philip III was still able to keep the situation balanced, although the Spanish administration became increasingly unpopular in Portugal and a new element of resistance was gradually
affecting a great part of the population: Sebastianism. In its late-
sixteenth- and early-seventeenth-century form, Sebastianism was simply
the belief that King Sebastian had not died at Alcácer Quibir and
would soon return to claim the throne that was his. Few people had in

fact seen the royal corpse and still fewer had been able to identify him. So monstrous did the defeat and death of the young monarch seem to everybody, particularly in connection with the loss of Portuguese independence, that the widespread rumor that Sebastian was alive appealed to many, mostly among the lower classes. As to why Sebastian delayed in making his appearance, opinions were divided and different versions circulated: for example, he was in prison, in Morocco or in Spain; or he was ashamed of his defeat and had retired to some obscure place.

Taking advantage of such a belief, several impostors, either by themselves or in the context of a wider conspiracy, rose now and then, claiming they were Sebastian and had come to redeem Portugal. The justices easily unmasked all of them (despite some riots and skirmishes) and accorded them prompt death at the stake. Far from dying, the rumor acquired more and more adherents and became increasingly complex in its formulation. The prophecies of a certain Bandarra, a shoemaker who lived in John III's times and who heralded the future coming of a hidden (*encoberto*) king, redeemer of mankind, were now interpreted as referring to Sebastian and his fate. Incidentally, the epoch was one of strong belief in prophecies, with various similar instances being recorded in neighboring Spain, France, Germany, and elsewhere. In Portugal, however, prophetism gained a new dimension with the peculiar circumstances in which the country was immersed. The Jews and the New Christians, in their turn, enhanced Sebastianism with their Biblical knowledge and typical Hebrew Messianism, exacerbated by the persecutions to which they were subjected. Sebastianism and the belief in the approaching "Fifth Empire" were associated. By the 1620's and 1630's, most people started merging the hidden Sebastian with some more visible body, who was none other than the Duke of Bragança, his lawful heir. And the transference from dream into political reality accompanied the advent of harder times and the need for a radical change. Sebastianism evolved into strict patriotism, and Sebastianists identified themselves with the opponents of the Iberian Union.

Philip III died in 1621. His son and successor, Philip IV, a youth of sixteen, entrusted the premiership to Gaspar Felipe de Guzmán, count (later duke) of Olivares. Realizing the decline of Spain, the new

prime minister attempted a vast plan of reforms, all aimed at strengthening the country's position abroad and enforcing centralization at
home. The twelve-year truce with Holland had expired and neither
side tried to prolong it, the Dutch because they thought of continuing
their expansion overseas at the cost of the Portuguese and Castilians,
the Spaniards because they vainly believed they could gain back their
losses. From 1621 to 1630 the Spanish armies fought in the Netherlands with some success; at sea, however, the Dutch were the masters.
But from 1630 onward the conflict spread all over Europe, in the
framework of the so-called Thirty Years War. France ranged her forces
against Spain; and a succession of disasters dimmed Philip's reign. In
the government of Portugal, Olivares started by again changing the
delegation of power, replacing the viceroy by a collective regency. The
hated Duke of Francavila gave way to three regents, all Portuguese,
presided over by the bishop of Coimbra. Later on, death reduced that
number to two and eventually to one, yet the principle experienced no
change until 1633.

Other early measures of the Olivares regime aimed at correcting
abuses and preventing them for the future: all the owners of Crown
patrimony had to submit their deeds to government confirmation; a
committee was appointed to enforce the payment of debts to the state;
revenues were apportioned according to their sources of collection;
a new system was introduced of partial subsidies by the wealthiest
communities for well-determined objectives; and the like. Such measures, if they were not popular (as correction of abuses never is),
showed at least a genuine interest in good and honest administration. From this point of view, Olivares is much less to blame than
Lerma; the trouble was that Spain's commitments all over the world
were so huge that the only way to cope with them seemed to be despotic rule, which finally resulted in complete disaster.

Overseas, the Dutch (and the English also) began their systematic
attacks on the Portuguese vital centers: Hormuz fell in 1622; Baía in
1624; several strongholds in Ceylon in 1630; Olinda, Recife, and
Mombasa in the same year; São Jorge da Mina in 1637; Arguim in
1638. Other attacks, which the Portuguese were able to repel, affected
Macao, the Cape Verde Islands, Malacca, and Goa. No part of the empire felt safe, and the need for defense everywhere compelled huge ex-

penditures for fortifications, fleets, and armaments. Yet the Portuguese, though badly beaten here and there, were still very far from a complete breakdown. Victories were often recorded: Baía, for instance, was retaken in 1625; the Dutch siege to Malacca was relieved in 1629; Olinda became Portuguese again by 1631; the same happened to Mombasa in 1634. A peace treaty with the English (1635) reduced the enemy to one. If such disasters had occurred under a Portuguese monarch, reactions might have been different, as they were after the recovery of independence. With the situation as it was, the Portuguese tended to blame the Spanish administration for everything that happened, to rely on Madrid for defense, but at the same time to object to increasing taxation and to the necessary army reforms. Olivares again and again forced the Lisbon municipality to subscribe to substantial loans for defense purposes. The whole kingdom had to contribute in 1628, which led to riots in several towns. The rich merchants paid a new subsidy in 1631. In this same year Olivares decreed that every public official should be compelled to pay the treasury, at the time of the appointment, one-half of his annual salary (*meia-anata*). By the same time a state monopoly on salt was established. Three years later a new tax (*real de água*), already existing in Lisbon, was extended to the whole country, while the transfer tax was raised 25 per cent.

Army reforms aimed at unifying the local armies of the several units within the Spanish monarchy. Launched in 1626, this plan was not carried on then, owing to the intense resistance found practically everywhere. Yet Olivares, using surreptitious methods, attempted its enforcement again and again. In 1638 and 1639 cavalry and infantry forces were recruited up to limits unheard of. Paid with Portuguese money, these troops were destined by Olivares for combat somewhere in Europe, where the Portuguese thought their interests were nonexistent. Also, a great number of nobles and clerics were called to Madrid, ostensibly to discuss a new administrative reform. Presumably, Olivares' intent was to deprive Portugal of qualified leadership in case of open rebellion. To increase the malaise, the New Christians were again given an opportunity of freely disposing of their wealth and leaving the country if they wanted to, provided they paid the treasury the huge contribution of 1,500,000 cruzados.

The new changes in the regency reflected Olivares' problems and his authoritarian way of coping with them. Viceroys once more came to Portugal: the archbishop of Lisbon (1633), the count of Basto (1633–34), both Portuguese and little inclined to support the prime minister in all of his acts, then the widow duchess of Mantua, Margherita of Savoy, granddaughter of Philip II and cousin of Philip IV. In direct contact with the Portuguese, all realized the dangers Olivares was incurring by forcing centralization, and how quickly a rebellion might occur.

THE RESTORATION OF INDEPENDENCE AND AFTER

There is little doubt that a spirit of nationalism was behind the restoration of Portugal's total independence after sixty years of dual monarchy. Five centuries of self-government had obviously shaped the nation and strengthened Portugal to the extent of rejecting any form of union with her neighbor. Furthermore, independence had always been defined as a challenge to Castile and a determination not to be confused with that country. Successive and bitter wars occurred between the two countries, the only ones which Portugal actually fought in Europe. Moreover, unlike the union with Aragon, Castile acquired Portugal through conquest. To the majority of the Portuguese and particularly to the popular masses, the Spanish monarchs were nothing but usurpers, the Spaniards enemies, and their partisans sheer traitors. In this sense, one might say that in 1580 the upper classes, far from interpreting the wishes of the people, betrayed them and abandoned them.

Yet nationality does not necessarily account for political independence. History is full of examples of vigorous nations incapable of shaping political units. Within the Iberian Peninsula, the case of Catalonia-Aragon is certainly the most striking one. In 1516, when Castile and Aragon were finally united, Aragon's individuality was comparable to Portugal's. Also, gradual efforts, or tendencies, of Castilianization were felt and resented as much by the Aragonese as by the Portuguese. It is true that Aragon was not a homogeneous nation (as Portugal was, and had been for a long time) but rather a dual or even triple monarchy, including Aragon proper, Catalonia, and Valencia, which made more difficult a unanimous gathering together of forces. It is also true that Aragon never experienced as a separate country that decisive period of rising nationalism and cultural vigorousness that characterized most of the sixteenth century. Nonetheless, the restoration of Portugal's independence, if well justified by her national framework, needs to be explained by a great many other elements.

Cultural Castilianization in Portugal advanced rapidly between 1580 and 1640. Portuguese authors and artists gravitated to the Madrid or Valladolid orbits (wherever the court might be), settled in Spain, accepted Spanish patterns, and wrote more and more in Castilian. Portuguese was considered rustic and vulgar by the cultivated elite of both countries, fit for the marketplace but not for high expressions of poetry or history. Thus, some of Portugal's best contributions to the world of arts and letters enriched the Spanish theater, the Spanish music, or Spanish painting, giving us the wrong impression that a cultural decadence affected the country after 1580. A majority of literary works printed in Portugal during the same period were in Castilian; however, several great Spanish authors had their first editions in Portuguese. The three Philips and some of their appointed governors deprived Portugal (particularly Lisbon) of numerous works of art and literature which they transferred to their palaces in Spain. The lack of a royal court hindered cultural expansion within Portugal, discouraged the flourishing of talents, and made culture local and rural, confining it to small nuclei around bishops and wealthy nobles. Despite its opulence and might, the court of the dukes of Bragança, located in a village (Vila Viçosa, in Alentejo), could never compete with the court of Manuel, John II, or even Sebastian, not to mention the Spanish kings. This gradual loss of a cultural individuality was felt by many Portuguese and resulted in several reactions in favor of the Portuguese language and its expression by means of prose and poetry. Francisco Rodrigues Lobo (1579–1622) and Fr. Luis de Sousa (1555–1632), major authors, clearly showed this attitude. Yet intellectuals who so reacted realized full well that their efforts would be meaningless without the recovery of independence.

From the economic standpoint, things had worsened a great deal since the 1620's or even before. Many of the reasons that had justified the union of the two crowns became obsolete with the changing economic conjuncture. The whole Portuguese Empire was suffering a serious crisis with the victorious attacks of the Dutch and the English. The Cape route, axis of the economic structure, ceased to be the main source of prosperity and revenues. Instead, Portuguese trade between Lisbon and India was reduced to less than one-third after 1595: Asian spices, African gold, and many other commodities were now brought to Europe by Dutch and English ships too. The Portuguese had lost their trade monopoly, which means that everybody's revenues went down—Crown's, nobility's, clergy's, and merchants' as well. Even the Atlantic-based trade, i.e., slaves, sugar, and tobacco, declined with successive foreign attacks on Brazil, the West Indies, West Africa, and the navigation routes.

At the same time, the Spanish Empire was suffering a similar economic crisis, shown by the decrease in the American silver output after 1620. Less and less silver arrived in Spain, and Seville's pivotal role in Portuguese transactions declined too. Also, the Spaniards began strongly responding to the sharing of their empire with the Portuguese. Thousands of Portuguese coming directly from Portugal or from Brazil had gradually settled down in Mexico, Peru, and La Plata, their merchants and capital playing an important economic role. In the 1620's and 1630's both the local Spanish settlers and the Inquisition as a body started persecuting the Portuguese, under the cover of Judaism or other pretexts. By 1635 the Portuguese community in Peru had been practically destroyed. This reaction aroused national feelings in Portugal as well as in Spain, widening the gulf between the two countries.

In Portugal proper the economic situation was far from brilliant. Producers suffered with the fall in the price of wheat, olive oil, coal, and other products. The crisis affected the lower classes, whose poverty clearly increased, as in many other countries of Europe. Rising taxation made things still harder. To explain the difficult times and to appease general discontent, there was the easy and obvious scapegoat: Spain, the source of all evil.

At this time people were rioting all over Europe. In Spain Vizcaya rebelled against the state salt monopoly (1631); then, in Portugal, the masses rose in Alentejo (Évora) and the Algarve (1637), with repercussions in several other places. Although the authorities had no great difficulty in putting down the riots, they showed the upper classes that the whole country would back them if they led a widespread movement against Spain. In June 1640 Catalonia revolted too. This time it was a national Catalan movement with the participation of all social groups, and it took the Madrid government twelve years to win the civil war. It is safe to say that without the Catalan uprising, Portugal's chances of seceding would have been minimal.

Portugal's other ally, France, was deeply interested in weakening Spain at all costs. French secret agents visited Portugal in the 1630's, feeling out public opinion and fostering rebellious tendencies, among both the upper and the lower classes. In 1638, a former French consul in Portugal, Saint-Pé, explicitly promised the Portuguese important French material support in case of a revolt against Spain. Late in that year a conspiracy among the nobles started. Its natural leader would of course have been the Duke of Bragança, João. But his evasive and overcautious attitude often disheartened or exasperated the conspirators, who even thought of a future "republican" government as in Holland. In a bold decision, Olivares, who was well aware of João's potential danger, appointed him military governor of Portugal (1639) in charge of recruiting the forces that would march to the European war. In this way he expected to destroy or neutralize the Duke of Bragança's prestige, making him unpopular with the Portuguese. Later on he planned to send Portuguese troops against the Catalan rebels and force João to accompany the king in a visit to Catalonia.

In November 1640 the conspiracy among the aristocrats had finally obtained the Duke of Bragança's support. On December 1, a group of nobles attacked the royal palace in Lisbon and arrested the Duchess of Mantua. João was acclaimed king as John IV and entered Lisbon some days later. Almost everywhere in Portugal and the overseas empire the news of the change and the oath of allegiance required were well received and obeyed with little question. Only Ceuta remained faithful to the cause of Philip IV. To secede had been a relatively easy task. To enforce secession would require twenty-eight years of fighting and prove a much more difficult undertaking.

It was necessary to justify secession, to show everywhere and to everyone that the new king, far from being a usurper, had only taken

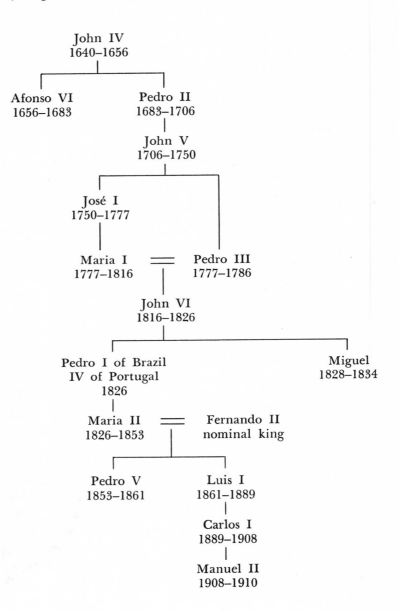

back what legitimately belonged to him. An abundant literature published in Portugal and abroad after 1640 endeavored to prove John's rights. One of the basic arguments was the so-called *cortes* of Lamego decisions, enacted in 1143: according to them (or rather to a forgery made at the monastery of Alcobaça, probably in the second quarter of the seventeenth century, and published in 1632 with patriotic motives) no woman could inherit the crown or transmit succession rights unless she had married a Portuguese nobleman. This automatically excluded Philip II as well as Emanuele Filiberto and Ranuccio, leaving Catarina (married to the Duke of Bragança) as the sole heiress. Consequently, all the Spanish kings had been usurpers and the 1640 movement simply returned the throne to its legitimate owner. Furthermore, the throne had not been vacant in 1580 or in 1640 and there was no ground for an election by the *cortes*. The solution of this problem deprived the people of the importance they might have had if the throne had been declared vacant. Thus nothing was changed in the country's institutions, the aristocracy remaining in firm control of the situation and entirely justified in their revolutionary action.

The *cortes* were actually assembled in 1641 and then, again, three times more during John's lifetime. Their role, however, was more symbolic than real, and their summoning brought no clear changes in government. It is true that they defined an official doctrine, that of power deriving from God through the people and then being transferred by the people to the king. This doctrine, however, was formulated to define tyranny (i. e., when the king governs regardless of justice, the usages and customs of the realm, the natural law and tradition) and to accuse the Spanish monarchs of violating their pact with the people, thus adding one more argument to the legitimate rebellion of the Portuguese. Other matters debated and decided by the 1641 *cortes* confirmed the policy sworn to by Philip II at Tomar sixty years before, particularly that no new taxation could be imposed without common consent. Also, the king committed himself to summon the people whenever grave affairs might endanger the nation's existence.

As in 1580, the Portuguese in 1640 were far from united. The lower classes kept their nationalist faith intact and stuck to John IV, but the nobility, the bureaucrats, the merchants, and the clergy divided their allegiance between the Portuguese and the Spanish king. Upper and lower nobles, often with family ties in Spain, hesitated, and only a portion (from where the revolutionaries had come) definitely sided with the former Duke of Bragança. Many were in a dubious position, others waited for a long time before committing themselves, while some continued to serve Philip and were rewarded with titles and offices (three Portuguese noblemen were governors in the Low Countries and one was viceroy in Sicily after 1640).

Most bureaucrats sided with John IV and became his secretaries and propagandists. Yet a number preferred Spain and aligned as conspirators against the "new order." As to the bourgeoisie, the great majority had no part in the secession movement and were caught unprepared. Their attitude after 1640 was generally one of neutral expectation. Many merchants and capitalists were involved in Spanish affairs and owned some property in Spain or in the Spanish Empire. Another group, however, including a number of New Christians and those with important connections outside the Iberian Peninsula (in Holland and in Germany mainly) supported the revolution and were among its most important financiers. Their economic affairs depended more on the Atlantic traffic (Brazil) and on the trade with western and northern Europe.

The clergy were divided too. Local priests and humbler monks seem to have backed the Duke of Bragança. Within the upper hierarchy, however, things were different. The bishops were hopelessly divided in their political allegiance. The Jesuits supported John IV, a factor of primary importance, both for the national cause and their own future prestige and power. The other orders were not so sure. And the Inquisition remained favorable to Spain, an understandable position if one recalls that the Inquisition had practically governed Portugal during the Iberian Union. John IV followed a very careful policy regarding the Inquisition, conscious of its political and religious importance, yet aware of its unreliability. It is true that the Inquisition, more than anything else, had its own interests as a state within the state, interests which were separate from those of John IV and from those of Philip IV. This makes it very difficult for us to appraise properly the role played by the Inquisition after 1640 and the dubious relationships between it and the Portuguese Crown.

All things considered, the new king of Portugal was certainly not to be envied. His whole reign (1640–56) saw disaster after disaster for the Portuguese Empire, a succession of diplomatic failures in Europe, and a poor economic situation at home, relieved only by a number of military achievements in Portugal that prevented a widespread invasion.

Portugal's desperate efforts in Europe were aimed at making peace with Holland as soon as possible and getting military and diplomatic support from the enemies of Spain. But immediate peace with Holland would prevent the Dutch from pursuing their policy of conquest in Asia and the Atlantic. Despite the cunning activity of the Portuguese diplomats and all their promises of economic compensation, the United Provinces delayed the signing of a peace treaty until 1661. Meanwhile, the Portuguese were being deprived of most of their remaining possessions in the Indian Ocean: Malacca fell in 1641; then Ceylon (1644, 1656); Quilon (1658); Negapatam (1660), and so on. At the same time the Arabs, helped by the British and the Dutch, expelled the Portuguese from Arabia and the Persian Gulf (1650).

In the Atlantic, the situation was at first equally disastrous for the Portuguese, with the loss of part of Angola and São Tomé (1641). Yet recovery became possible because of economic and political conflicts in Holland itself, as well as the attitude taken by the Portuguese settlers in Brazil: the rebellion against the Dutch started here by 1644 and ended in a complete Portuguese victory ten years later. Angola and São Tomé were also regained in 1648. Paradoxically regular economic traffic took place in Europe between the Portuguese and the Dutch after the Restoration, with few interruptions.

England at first posed a less serious problem, mostly due to her internal dissensions. Cromwell's victory, however, led the Portuguese government to a quixotic defense of the royalists. War broke out between 1650 and 1654. The British ships showed a definite superiority on the sea with the consequence that Portugal was forced to sign a treaty of peace opening her empire to the English traffic. The English restoration of 1660 simply confirmed that state of affairs with the marriage of Charles II to Princess Catarina (John's daughter) and the cession, as a dowry, of Bombay and Tangiers to the British.

France's help was mostly verbal and despite all their efforts the Portuguese diplomats were not accepted at the negotiation table in

1648 which put an end to the Thirty Years War. Military reinforcements, however, as well as weapons and supplies, could be obtained
from northern and western Europe, including Sweden.

Another failure was Rome. Pressured by Spain, the Holy See
stubbornly refused recognition of Portugal's secession and denied all
requests to confirm bishops for the vacant bishoprics. In 1668, when
peace was finally reached, twenty of the twenty-eight dioceses in Portugal and overseas had no legal prelate. At home, the new regime
became stable only after stamping out dissension in favor of Spain.
In July 1641 a conspiracy against the king involved some of the best
families in the realm: among others, a duke, a marquis, and three
counts were caught. Members of the bourgeoisie, the top bureaucracy,
and the high clergy also took part in the plot, including an archbishop, two bishops, and the inquisitor-general himself. Other conspiracies, less threatening perhaps but still revealing a certain discontent with the "new order," marred John's reign and showed that
the danger was not over. Also it should not be forgotten that a
number of people—particularly nobles in the upper levels—fled to
Spain or quietly left the country.

John's economic policy was to get money at all costs, mostly to
provide an effective defense. The *cortes* voted subsidies, but the government, acting wisely, tried very hard not to increase taxation. Funds
were often obtained from the merchants who, in exchange, were given
privileges. The New Christians benefited from the abnormal situation
of the kingdom. Both in Portugal and abroad (Holland, Germany, etc.)
Jewish capital helped the cause of independence and helped itself in
fruitful operations. Loans granted by Jewish companies bought ships,
ammunition, and soldiers for defense. From 1649 to 1659 immunity
was conferred on the property of the New Christians sentenced by the
Inquisition. Moreover, the administration of property already confiscated was transferred from the Inquisition to the state. The development of trade with northern Europe and with Brazil, one of the main
goals of John's government, as against the former all-Spain economic
unit, favored numerous merchants and led them to support Portuguese independence.

The war at home mobilized all the efforts Portugal could spare
and absorbed huge sums of money. Worse than that, it prevented the

government from sending help to the often-attacked overseas possessions. But if the core of the empire, at least in Asia, was sacrificed, it
saved the mainland from being overrun by the Spanish forces.

Portugal lacked a modern army; her fortifications were poor,
particularly at the border; her stud farms had been discontinued; her
best leaders fought for Spain somewhere in Europe. From the Portuguese side, this explains why the war was generally confined to limited
border operations, based on the storming of unprotected villages, the
taking of livestock and victuals, the burning down of crops and trees.
From the Spanish side, it has to be remembered that the Thirty Years
War (to 1659 in Spain) and the Catalonian affair (to 1652) delayed
any major offensive. The rebellion of the Duke of Medina Sidonia,
who in 1641 tried to wrest Andalucia from Spain, diverted more troops
from the Portuguese border. The duke was John IV's brother-in-law
and acted in concert with the Portuguese. Some regular battles gave
the victory to the Portuguese armies (Montijo, 1644; Linhas de Elvas,
1659); but as a rule the war had its ups and downs for both contenders,
the Spaniards acting mainly as invaders and the Portuguese as defenders.

John IV died in 1656. His government had been marked by
judiciousness and a series of wise measures in administration. He
abstained (or was prevented) from extreme absolutism and rather
shared the task of governing with a certain number of councils and
high courts, the members of which he appointed but whose decisions
he guided and supervised only in a general way. This put power
directly into the hands of the nobility and the top bureaucracy, from
which the council members were invariably chosen. John's cabinet
was mainly directed by the secretary of state or some favorite of the
king's. The monarch was wise enough to keep his ministers for long
periods of time, thus assuring stability and continuity. No essential
changes took place between 1656 and 1662. The new king, Afonso VI,
a minor, was physically and mentally unfit for governing. A regency
under Queen-Mother Luisa should have ended in 1657 but was indefinitely prolonged. This situation favored the nobles—particularly
a conservative group of nobles—who increased their power considerably.

A succession of disasters and failures characterized the years that followed. In 1657 the Dutch attacked the Portuguese mainland and blockaded Lisbon for three months. In 1659 Portugal did not succeed in being accepted at the negotiations which led to the Peace of the Pyrenees between Spain, the Empire, and France. As a consequence, a treaty in 1661 with Holland and the marriage of Princess Catarina to Charles II of England meant the subservience of the Portuguese interests to those of the other two powers in order to achieve peace and alliances.

Then, the great Spanish offensives started in 1661 and lasted until 1665. Such a situation brought about a growing opposition to Queen-Mother Luisa and her ruling clique: in 1662 a palace *coup d'état* transferred personal power to the king and installed a small group of younger and ambitious nobles. Government by a ministry was imposed on the councils and high courts. One of the leading conspirators, the Count of Castelo Melhor (Luis de Vasconcelos e Sousa), became prime minister with the renewed title of *escrivão da puridade* (private scribe), while António de Sousa de Macedo, an able diplomat, held the secretariate of state. The treaty with Holland was delayed for some years. At home, a new military effort, under a better leadership and a more efficient government, brought about a series of victories for the Portuguese armies. French and German military advisers played their part with remarkable success. Mercenaries had come in considerable numbers. Moreover, Spain was tired of wars and nearly exhausted, while the Portuguese fought for their survival as a nation. Each Spanish offensive was stopped. The decisive battle of Montes Claros (1665) put an end to the war for all practical purposes.

To assure succession to the throne and thus neutralize his enemies (who wanted to replace the king by his brother Pedro), Castelo Melhor married Afonso to a French princess, Marie Françoise of Nemours, better known as Mademoiselle d'Aumale (1666). At the same time, and to secure a better ally in the negotiations with Spain (England, then mediating, wanted a quick settlement at any price), Castelo Melhor signed a treaty of alliance with France (1667). But this group of circumstances brought about his downfall. To start with, poor Afonso VI proved incapable of behaving like a husband, a love affair arising between the new queeen and Prince Pedro. Then, the peace party (war had lasted since 1640), along with British diplomacy, maneuvered against Castelo Melhor. Paradoxically France, not counting much on the alliance with Portugal, preferred the ousting of Sousa de Macedo, a friend of the English. In the background were the nobles aiming at a restoration of their full power. Afonso did not help the situation, surrounding himself with the scum of society, running about the streets at night, and behaving like a brigand and a murderer.

Thus, in September 1667, a second *coup d'état* led by Prince Pedro forced the dismissal of Castelo Melhor and his partisans and finally caused the imprisonment of the king himself. Pedro took the title of Prince Regent (which the *cortes* confirmed some months later), restored the nobles as a class to their former power, and married Marie Françoise (1668) after Afonso's impotence had been proved by a scandalous inquiry.

The conditions for peace were now fulfilled. In Spain, Philip IV died in 1665, his son Carlos II being a child of four. The change of government in Portugal and the diplomatic intervention of England pointed to the establishment of peace, which practically everybody wanted. The peace treaty was signed in 1668: it conferred full independence to Portugal and kept her borders unchanged. Only Ceuta remained in Spanish hands.

CHAPTER SEVEN

THE TRIDIMENSIONAL EMPIRE

THE EAST

The story of the Portuguese Empire in Asia from the mid-1500's to the 1630's was one of remarkable stability. There were few conquests but also few losses. Damão, annexed in 1559, closed out the period of expansion. In Ceylon, full suzerainty over the whole island was achieved in 1580–98 but it involved no territorial conquest and could be considered as a simple police operation. As for losses, it is true that Chale had to be abandoned in the 1570's, as well as the island of Tunata, but neither their political nor their economic significance was great. The only important defeat was the loss of Hormuz (1622), in the Persian Gulf, to the Persians helped by the English. Yet a chain of eleven fortresses still protected the Portuguese interests in its waters and prevented an open challenge to the Portuguese trade monopoly there.

The only possession acquired by means other than military was Macao, in China. The traditional version is that the local Cantonese authorities authorized the Portuguese to settle down in the small fishing village of A-Ma-Kao, as a reward for the help the Portuguese gave them in chasing some pirates. This version is neither confirmed nor rejected by the existing documents, which simply ignore the origins of Macao. In any case the Portuguese established a small trading port and settlement there as early as 1555, which quickly grew and prospered. Macao served as an intermediary between China and Japan and between China and the West. Useful as it was to the Chinese, it is not surprising that they practically leased the town to the Portuguese, who paid them tribute and accepted the interference of Chinese authorities. For three centuries Macao was considered a political part of the Chinese Empire, despite some Portuguese claims to the contrary.

But if the territorial "Empire" was kept intact all those years, it would be wrong to suppose that nothing else had changed. Both Dutch and English had forced their way into the Indian Ocean via the Cape of Good Hope, and the Portuguese could no longer claim full control of the sea traffic as before. The first Dutch ships arrived in the East as early as 1597, led by a Dutch pilot who had served under the Portuguese flag and was familiar with the route to India. Dutch ships returned again and again, avoiding the Portuguese ships whenever possible and establishing their trade ports in places deserted or ignored by the Portuguese. Present-day Indonesia and the Moluccas became their favorite areas of destination. In 1601 the famous Dutch East India Company was founded, and the Dutch presence in the Far East posed a permanent menace to the Portuguese doctrine of "closed seas." The Portuguese backed their claim to exclusive control of Africa and Asia with both political and religious arguments. The Pope had granted them the monopoly of trade and conquest overseas more than a hundred years before. Theirs was also the spiritual exclusive of spreading the Christian faith among the infidels. They had arrived first, destroyed the Moslem power, imposed a certain number of rules on the maritime traffic of the natives, and built a number of fortresses for their enforcement. The Dutch presence not only violated international law but also transferred to the new Christendoms the danger of a confessional deviation. The Dutch were heretics and as such condemned by the Church and all good Catholics. Furthermore they were rebels to their legitimate monarch, the king of Spain and Portugal.

Consequently, the Portuguese tried to rid Asian waters of all Dutch ships, which they regarded as pirates, to forbid the Dutch to trade, and to force abandonment of all dreams of competition. Later on, when such methods proved ineffective, and protestant Holland was being accepted by Catholic Europe, they still relied on legal arguments (Serafim de Freitas' *De justo Imperio Lusitanorum Asiatico*, 1625) in reply to the Dutch doctrine of freedom of the sea defended by the philosopher and jurist Hugo de Groot (*De iure praedae,* 1604–5, partly reprinted in 1618 with the title *Mare Liberum*).

Attacks on Dutch vessels started by 1603, fierce combat lasting for six years, when the truce of 1609 between Spain and Holland allowed the Dutch to trade freely in the Indian Ocean. From then on they had the time and the opportunity to build up their empire in Asia, while the Portuguese monopoly was lost forever.

The British entered the Indian Ocean in 1602, but instead of focusing their attention on the Far East they dared to challenge the Portuguese in the very heart of their empire, India and Persia. Like the Dutch, they took advantage of the natives' desire to throw off the yoke of the Portuguese. By a clever system of alliances—similar to the one the Portuguese had developed against the Moslems a hundred years before—they egged on Persians, Indians, Arabs, and others against the Portuguese, helping them with weapons, ammunition, technicians, etc. Such alliances were able to defeat the Portuguese in some places, particularly in Arabia and Persia.

Other challengers to the Portuguese monopoly followed—notably France and Denmark—though with little success. Up to the 1640's the Portuguese were the leading power in the Indian Ocean. Dutch attacks on Malacca (1616, 1629), on Macao (1622, 1626), and on Goa (several times) were repelled. Successive wars and skirmishes against the natives led invariably to victories for the Portuguese. If Dutch and English were firmly settled down in the Asian world by the 1630's and 1640's, it was more because there seemed to be room for everybody than because the Portuguese had been beaten and replaced by them.

The increased number of attacks and the lack of reinforcements from Europe explain the great Portuguese losses after 1630. Spain was at war everywhere and required Portuguese help. There was not enough money to build, equip, and send ships with armies and ammunition wherever the Portuguese (and Spanish) empires were being attacked: in Brazil, in Africa, in Asia. Little had changed, as a matter of fact, since 1500. There is no evidence of more corruption, more cruelty, less organization, or less bravery. It was simply that the enemies were now too many and as well organized and prepared as the Portuguese or the Spaniards.

In the 1630's most of Ceylon was lost to the Dutch. In 1639 the same Dutch blockaded Goa for several years. After the Restoration of 1640 the losses were more frequent because the government had to organize resistance at home and could hardly send any reinforcements at all. Malacca fell to the Dutch in 1641. A ten-year truce (1641–51) interrupted the process of decline which resumed after 1651: a great many trade ports and fortresses in India fell in 1653; Colombo was lost in 1656; the rest of Ceylon two years later; then Cranganore and Cochin (1662); and finally Bombay, ceded to the English in 1665 as of a dowry for Catherine of Bragança. Meanwhile the Arabs, helped by the British and Dutch, forced the Portuguese out of Arabia and the Persian Gulf (1650). In Indonesia and the Moluccas everything was lost but a part of Timor. In Japan the authorities expelled the Portuguese traders and massacred many Christians and missionaries. By 1665, after twenty-five years of constant losses, the once mighty empire in Asia had been reduced to Goa, Damão, Diu, Bassein, and a few unimportant fortresses in India; to Macao in China; and to half of Timor, in Indonesia.

It must be emphasized that the Lisbon government was forced to make a choice by the 1640's and 1650's, in order to save some important shares of the empire. The choice was to give up Asia in favor of Brazil and her complementary parts in Africa. The Portuguese realized they had not the forces to resist everywhere. Wisely they chose the most promising part, the one where white settlement had spread definitely and permanently, and where profits from trade could compete with declining revenues from the Orient.

In East Africa the Portuguese kept a line of fortresses and trade ports, coupled with some areas of influence, which extended from Lourenço Marques to Ethiopia. Present-day Mozambique continued to be regularly called on by ships to and from India. Expeditions inland, in search of gold, continued. The trade ports of Sena and Tete survived and prospered, helping to maintain the Portuguese presence up the Zambezi River. In 1571 a new attempt to reach the Monomotapa mines completely failed. Without militarily occupying any territories (besides the places conquered or founded up to 1550), the Portuguese constantly increased their supremacy and influence in inland Mozambique, intervening in quarrels among the natives and sometimes sending expeditions for "punishment" or assertion of their presence. The trade in copper and ivory accounted for the setting up of trade ports in Lourenço Marques (Delagoa Bay) in the late sixteenth and early seventeenth centuries. For a few years the Portuguese possessions in East Africa even justified the establishment of a formal government, separated from India, with headquarters in Sofala. It did not last long, however, because Mozambique still depended on India for its survival and would so depend for two centuries more.

To improve settlement and protect commerce, the Crown organized vast land grants, juridically similar to those existing in the Atlantic Islands and Brazil. These were the *prazos*, so called because the land was *emprazada* (quit-rented) by the Crown to donataries in the typical feudal way that existed in Portugal. Yet the Mozambique *prazos* could never compare with the flourishing plantations of Madeira, São Tomé, or Brazil. Trade was much more appealing; and India, with its fabulous riches, was not too far away. Moreover, the natives were ferocious and did not easily accept the presence of the white settlers. The Dutch also attacked Mozambique, and many foreigners disputed the Portuguese monopoly there from the early 1600's onward. In mid-century the several Portuguese possessions north of Cape Delgado fell one by one to the Arabs of Oman, helped by the British: only Mombasa resisted until 1698.

In Ethiopia the Portuguese asserted their influence by means of embassies, military help, and religious missions. The latter, however, despite the geographical knowledge they fostered, brought about the downfall of the Portuguese presence there. As in China and Japan, though to a lesser degree, the Ethiopians had a long tradition of culture and a strongly established religion. The Jesuits and other missionaries had little respect and less tolerance for heretics and schismatics, as they regarded the Ethiopians. Nor would the Catholic Counter-Reformation compromise. Intolerance resulted in a native reaction against the missionaries and all the Portuguese in general. After many fluctuations in the relations between the two countries, the Portuguese were finally expelled in 1634, Ethiopia retreating to a fierce isolationism.

The number of Portuguese living in Asia and East Africa increased up to the 1620's or 1630's, and then started to decline rapidly. Actually, there was considerable variation according to the area. Goa, the capital of the "State of India" (as the Portuguese called their whole network of possessions, from Mozambique to Japan), reached its demographic maximum early in the seventeenth century, when it was equal to, or even surpassed, Lisbon in population. A very large city by European standards, though by no means exceptional in the populous urban East, it had some magnificent buildings, such as the Cathedral, many churches and monasteries, the palace of the viceroys, and other attributes of a sixteenth-century metropolis. It has been called "The Rome of the East." But its population gradually declined and by the 1630's was reduced to half or even less.

Hormuz had some 50,000 inhabitants in the early seventeenth century, of which less than 1,000 were Portuguese. Diu declined from 10,000 people in the mid-sixteenth century to about 3,000 in 1621–33 with 60 Portuguese households. Meliapore was larger, with more than 1,000 Portuguese hearths early in the 1600's. Malacca counted 600 Portuguese households in the 1590's. Macao by 1578 had a total population of 10,000, half of them Christians. Other important nuclei existed in Cochin, Chaul, Ethiopia, etc. In East Africa the whites were very few, under 200 households. But besides these residents and soldiers, settled throughout the empire, there were many others, forming a true diaspora all over Asia. In distant places such as Basra and Baghdad, Lar in Persia, Martabam in present-day Burma, and Bengal, they could be found posing as traders, "tourists," missionaries, mercenaries, and the like. The Mogul fleet in Bengal at one time had 923 Portuguese sailors!

Race relations depended upon many circumstances and were far from adhering to a fixed pattern. The Lisbon government officially decreed that the only bar to Portuguese citizenship should be religion (laws of 1569 and 1572), yet this policy was not implemented throughout Portuguese Asia. Not even within the Church were Christian Asians treated as equal. All the religious orders refused to admit either Indians or half-castes. The secular Church accepted them as priests but generally braked their climb up the hierarchy. One exception was Mateus de Castro, a Brahmin, consecrated bishop of Chrysopolis, in *partibus infidelium,* in 1635. Nevertheless the number of half-breeds constantly increased owing to the lack of European women. Most Portuguese, both settlers and civil servants, had their native concubines, whom they often treated like wives, with numerous children.

Interracial marriages were frequent, yet racial equality did not exist. For practical purposes the population of Portuguese India could be classified in five categories: the European-born Portuguese, or *Reinóis* (singular, *Reinol*); the white Portuguese born in India; those born of a European father and a white Indian mother, called *Castiços;* the half-breeds, or *Mestiços;* and the pure Indians. Among all these castes there was social differentiation and discrimination, even if not always strict or coherent. Slaves, of course, were abundant—of Negro, Moslem, or Indonesian origin.

The governor-general in Goa assisted by a Secretary (Secretário da Índia) ruled the vast Portuguese Empire and areas of influence from East Africa to Japan. The title of viceroy, not often given before the mid-1500's, became customary. From 1550 to 1668 Portuguese Asia was governed by twenty-seven viceroys (appointed for three-year periods) as against thirteen governors. "Governor" was generally restricted to interim, acting governors, who took over government in case of the viceroy's death, deposition, or other event, until the king appointed a new viceroy. Following the trend at home, government by councils was instituted in Portuguese Asia. A Council of State, coinciding with the one in Portugal, was set up in the mid-1500's to assist the viceroy or the governor-general. In the seventeenth century acting governments were often composed of two or more members, instead of an interim governor: this was the situation in 1629, and again in 1651–52, 1665–61, 1661–62, and 1668–71.

The upper aristocracy remained firmly in control of the Indian vice-royalty. Five lineages—the Meneses, the Mascarenhas, the Noronhas, the Castros, and the Coutinhos—occupied half of the forty offices of governor or viceroy from 1550 to 1671. In the 1570's the king found it necessary to subdivide the government of Portuguese Asia in three great areas: one from East Africa to Ceylon, directly administered by the viceroy of India; the second one from Ceylon to Pegú (present-day Burma); and the third one from Pegú to China, each one controlled by a governor, subject to the supreme authority of the viceroy.

Local administration belonged either to the municipal councils elected by the people (as in Portugal) with representatives of the Crown, or to agents of the central government only. It all depended on the number of resident whites or half-breeds and on the capacity to turn the city into a replica of a Portuguese town. Most trade ports and fortress cities were only subject to a sort of military government, with its officers appointed by the viceroy. They were the captain (*capitão*), the factor (*feitor*) with his scribe (*escrivão*) in charge of the economic affairs, the *alcaide-mor* who took care of military affairs, the *alcaide do mar* for military sea matters, the *ouvidor* in charge of justice, and so forth. In places such as Goa, Hormuz, Malacca, Cochin, and Diu there was a customhouse with its judge (*juiz*) and other personnel. In small places many (or even all) of these offices depended upon a single authority, *feitor* and *alcaide-mor* being often united in one person. Goa, Bassein, or Damão, which had hinterlands, were organized into administrative and finance districts called *tanadarias*, going back to the pre-Christian system. Goa, the capital of the Asian Empire, had a very complex network of public bureaus and officials, comparable to that of Lisbon. It possessed, for instance, a gunpowder plant (Casa da Pólvora), a shipyard (*ribeira*), a "secretariate for Finance" (Casa dos Contos), a courthouse (Casa da Relação da India), and the Inquisition. Everywhere native authorities were generally accepted and respected. In Goa, Macao, and Malacca there were municipal councils as in Lisbon, more or less autonomous. The Senado da Câmara (City Hall Senate) was the great council with local administrative powers, from which the ruling officials were chosen. As a rule municipal regulations followed the changes that took place in Lisbon, but there were local characteristics and a local evolution too. This happened particularly in cities like Macao which were far from the authority of supreme Crown representatives. However, no changes could take place without the approval of the Lisbon government. Goa had in Lisbon a permanent attorney or *procurador* to plead its case at court when necessary.

Besides the network of cities, fortresses, and tradeports, the Portuguese Empire in Asia still depended on the government-organized fleets and navigation lines between the main ports. Up to 1570 there were some twenty-seven of these *carreiras,* generally in a monopoly system. They all meant trade as well as supplies, military protection, and privateering. For strict defense of the Portuguese monopoly there were the Hormuz fleet, to patrol the entrance to the Persian Gulf, and the coast of Melindi fleet, which controlled the African coast north of Mozambique to the entrance of the Red Sea. Then, there were regular navigation lines between Goa and Mozambique, Goa and Ceylon, Goa and the Moluccas, Goa and the Indian East Coast, Goa and Bengal, Goa and Malacca, Malacca and Siam, Malacca and Japan, Malacca and Macao, Malacca and present-day Burma (several destinations), Malacca and the Moluccas, Malacca and Timor, Macao and Japan, Macao and Indonesia, Macao and Siam, Macao and Timor. Every ship in these lines had its captain and scribe, appointed by the king or the viceroy. However, the most important line was the yearly one that connected Portugal with Goa (*carreira da Índia*). It encompassed several ships, each one with its own commander (*capitão*) and personnel, the whole under a *capitão-mor*. All these captains served for a limited number of trips and were very well paid as civil servants, in addition to the fabulous profits that each travel might yield.

Each year, the government sent a certain number of ships to India, generally in one fleet. The number varied greatly from 1550 to 1668 but averaged five ships a year up to the 1630's. From then on, the average went down. It must be remembered that tonnage considerably increased throughout this period, which means that trade with the East did not necessarily decline because the number of ships did. Shipwrecks and attacks by enemies and pirates made a trip to India a difficult thing. The percentage of losses in this period generally ranged from 10 to 20 percent, but in some epochs (late sixteenth century, for instance) it reached 40 per cent of the whole navigation.

The trade monopoly with the East had been firmly held by the state for more than half a century. However, the constant violations by individuals and the increased smuggling often made it a fiction, and an expensive one. In 1564 a first experiment in contracts with private groups was attempted. Then, by 1570, the Crown decreed freedom of trade with India, albeit with some exceptions: pepper remained a state monopoly, as well as the export of silver and copper; private purchases in India were confined to Cananore, Chale, Cochin, and Quilon. Although allowing others to share the Asian profits, the state continued to be the main trader and the exclusive one in many areas.

In 1576 the trade system was changed again. Instead of freedom for all, the Crown granted the monopoly of commerce with India to private companies: in the first of those monopolies, given from 1576 to 1578, renewed 1579 to 1581, the Germans Rott and Welser entered with half of the capital, some Portuguese businessmen with the rest. Philip II tried freedom of trade once more (1581–86), with the exception of cinnamon and China silk, which belonged to the Crown, and pepper, the exclusive of which was rented to the Welsers, Fuggers, and others, then to the Portuguese alone. After 1586 contracts were again signed between the state and societies of Portuguese traders, lasting for twelve years. But as the increasing attacks of Dutch and English made it highly problematic for a private group to fulfill the contract clauses with enough profit, the Crown thought it better to take over again and go back to the old monopoly system. This lasted from 1598 to 1642, when freedom was definitely established, with the exception of cinnamon, always in royal hands. Meanwhile, the Dutch and the English had been given freedom of access to India in certain periods.

The spice trade considerably declined after the mid-1500's. In 1547, 36,000 quintais (hundertweights) of pepper arrived in Lisbon: the average yearly quantity exceeded the 30,000 level. From then until 1587 the average figure was about 25,000. Then it went down abruptly, with amazing variations from year to year, not so much because of any actual decline in the cargoes taken in India (which diminished too, but very gradually), but rather because of the dangers during the voyage to Lisbon. In 1607 an optimistic average was still estimated at 20,000 quintais a year. Yet real figures were much below this: averages of 9,000 or 10,000 between 1611 and 1626 and still less afterward. In 1628, for instance, only 1,981 quintais of pepper arrived. Not all the spice trade decreased: clove went down, but cinnamon increased and became *the spice* instead of pepper, replacing the latter in profit, if not in quantity: an average of 4,000 quintais entered the port of Lisbon by 1619.

Other merchandise supplemented the spice-cargoes and gradually made up for them in preserving the profitability of the trips to India: pearls and gems, diamonds, silk from China and Persia, cotton cloth from Cambay and Bengal, indigo from India, china from the Chinese Empire, precious furniture also from China. The trade in diamonds and the trade with China were the two motivations for maintaining such a dangerous and time-consuming seaway after the spice trade definitely turned down.

Historians of the Portuguese presence in India often forget that the amount of trade carried on by the Crown, the civil servants, the soldiers, and a great many individuals did not concern Europe alone. The Portuguese intervened in the local traffic lines and sometimes controlled them thoroughly. From Mozambique to Japan, they had a considerable share of all forms of trade. They carried gold and ivory from East Africa to India and China; pearls from Hormuz and Ceylon to India and Bengal; diamonds from south India and Borneo to north India, Malacca, and Pegú; horses from Arabia and Persia to India; and slaves from East Africa and Madagascar to India. The conquest of a town, the setting up of a trade port, or the building of a fortress were often related to local forms of trade. The Portuguese had to take over most of the supply trade to the coastal towns, because these towns depended on rice, fish, or banana imports to survive. Thus they acted sometimes as absolute lords and owners, and at other times as intermediaries and simple participants. In any case the Portuguese were the ones to teach the Dutch and the English the way to get control of the vital points of the complex Asian trade network.

The Portuguese traffic with Asia suffered two great crises which reduced its importance: one by 1591, when the amount and profit went down one-third; the other by 1650–60, which was the last gasp. It is interesting to note that in spite of all the competition by other countries, Portugal continued to be the main entrepôt for spices and diamonds for most of Europe until about 1650. Payments were made in gold and silver which were abundant in Lisbon and throughout the country.

Many wrong statements have been made about the financial structure of the Portuguese Empire. Based upon the case of Goa and a few others, or upon the usual complaints of prose writers and moralists, Portuguese and non-Portuguese historians emphatically argue that for Portugal Asia started to produce a deficit very early. The facts are not so simple. If Goa, with most of the smaller trade ports in Hindustan, and Ceylon and the Moluccas registered constant deficits in the public accounts, the situation in Hormuz, Diu, Damão, Bassein, Chaul, and Malacca was exactly the opposite. Revenues were derived from property owned by the state; taxes on sales and other property; taxes on the markets, fairs, and customs; and so forth. Expenditures included above all administration (salaries paid to civil and church servants, allowances and gifts to the natives); maintenance of fortresses and weapons, hospitals, churches; and the like.

The budget of 1574 shows that the Asian Empire (including the East African fortresses), far from accruing a deficit, yielded a surplus of more than 80,000 cruzados (more than 40 million reais). In 1607 that surplus had increased to 240,000 cruzados. In the 1620's things began changing, with the growing defense costs.

Public finance in Asia had nothing to do with the official trade system, owned in large part by the state. Revenues and expenditures in connection with the voyages to India depended on other sources and were paid or received in Lisbon or elsewhere in Europe. Revenues came from the direct sale of spices and other merchandise, the taxation on private traders, or the freight of private owners. Expenditures encompassed the equipping of the fleets, the cost and freight of their cargoes (when belonging to the Crown), the constant loss of vessels, and so on. The so-called "Cape Way" (Rota do Cabo), i.e., the trip to India, was almost always profitable, until the conquest of Ceylon by the Dutch in the 1650's. Revenues show an expansion of trade to the early seventeenth century, then a stagnation to the 1620's: 383,000 cruzados in 1587–88, 468,000 in 1607, 468,000 in 1619.

Portuguese Asia had its own currency which blended European and Asian systems. After a first experiment by Governor Afonso de Albuquerque (1509–15) it was only in the mid-century that gold coins were minted by the Portuguese in Goa and Cochin: the so-called golden *pardau-são tomé,* equivalent to the Indian golden pagodes, estimated at 360 Portuguese reais. In silver the Malacca Mint coined the cruzado, equivalent to five Indian *tangas* or five Persian larins, also estimated at 360 Portuguese reais. In the mid-sixteenth century, Goa created its replica, the silver patacão. In copper there were the bazarucos with the value of $1\frac{1}{4}$ real. If gold remained fairly steady until the 1630's, silver, always lacking in India, was debased again and again. The xerafins, which replaced the patacões, appeared in several issues and values. The patacões were reborn in 1630, with another value. Every new coin meant a new debasement: from the mid-1500's to 1630, the mark of silver in Goa went up from some 3,000 reais to almost double.

The Portuguese currency was accepted and could survive because it did little more than adopt the local patterns under a Christian cover. Yet it never replaced for trade purposes, nor predominated over, the numerous native currencies from the various Indian states, Persia, China, and others. Other European coins carried by the Portuguese (the Spanish silver reales above all) made their appearance in the East too.

From a Western and Christian standpoint the expansion of Christianity in Asia, carried on by the Portuguese in the sixteenth and seventeenth centuries, was certainly a most remarkable achievement. Until the mid-1500's, efforts to spread the Gospel among the Asian peoples were limited to a number of fortress cities and trade ports and were not very persistent. It was only the coming of the Jesuits that launched a vast movement of religious expansion, a true crusade with political, economic, and cultural results as well. In this sense, one can say that the spread of Christianity in the East made up for the stagnation of the military conquests and represented a second phase in the history of the Portuguese Empire. The commercial and military empire was thus reinforced and enlarged with a religious one, more enduring and perhaps more expressive of the contacts with civilization.

A simple analysis of the religious-administrative network points up this second Portuguese expansion in Asia. Until the 1550's the diocese of Goa, founded in 1534, had been the only framework in which the missionaries and other clerics endeavored to carry on their task. From then on, to the 1660's, nine other ecclesiastical provinces were established: Ethiopia (1555); Cochin (1558) for all the territory between Cannanore and Ceylon; Malacca (1558) from Pegú to Tonkin with present-day Indonesia; Macao (1575) encompassing most of China; Funay or Japan (1588) with the Japanese islands: Cranganore or Angamale (1600) with part of inland India and a very old tradition independent of the European irruption; Meliapore (1606) from Ceylon to Pegú; Mozambique (1612) with the eastern African coast to Ethiopia; and Tonkin (1659), encompassing most of Indochina and a part of China. It must be remembered that Portugal owned the monopoly (patronate) of religious organization and expansion in Africa and Asia.

FAR LEFT: *Triumphal Arch ("Arco dos Vice-Reis"), 17th century, Goa (India).* ABOVE: *The Portuguese in Japan: Japanese screen, late 16th century, Museu Nacional de Arte Antiga, Lisbon.* BELOW: *Father António Vieira: Anonymous, 17th century, Palácio Nacional da Pena, Sintra (Lisbon).*

The establishment in Rome of the Congregation for Propaganda (1622) first threatened that exclusive. The new Congregation had the right to control territories where the ecclesiastical hierarchy was not definitely organized. In this way, prelates and missionaries could be sent directly by Rome to all those areas which Portugal had neglected. Indochina was one of them. As a matter of fact, Rome had been violating the Portuguese monopoly since 1608, when it allowed the missionaries belonging to mendicant orders to embark to the East from other ports than Lisbon. This concession was later extended to all the orders (1633) and then to any clerics (1673), thus preventing the Portuguese government and Church from having an eye on all the people going to India.

Christian expansion in Asia drew a good many orders: the Franciscans were strong all over India and still had missions in Malacca, Macao, and Japan. The Dominicans were fewer, yet they spread their activity from Mozambique to Japan. The Augustinians sent their people to East Africa, Persia, India, Malacca, and Japan. The Carmelites also contributed a little. But the great order of Catholic propaganda in Asia was undoubtedly that of the Jesuits. Their first arrival in India, in the 1540's, marked the real beginning of missionary activity outside Europe. The Jesuits penetrated lands of diverse beliefs, rapidly setting up missions, novitiates, hospitals, and the like. Their methods were clever and efficient, their enthusiasm stirring, their capacity to endure hardships (including martyrdom) astonishing. In half a century their missions were everywhere in East Africa and Asia, from Mozambique to Japan, reaching central and northern India, and most of China to distant Tibet. In China they had some five hundred missions in the seventeenth century, in Japan more than sixty. By 1623 the Jesuit organization in the East comprised four "provinces": Goa, encompassing East Africa and Ethiopia, India to the north of Goa, and Tibet; Malabar, with India to the south of Goa, Ceylon, Bengal, Malacca, and Indonesia; China, with most of China; and Japan, encompassing Japan, southern China, Indonesia, and the Celebes.

Conversions were achieved quite rapidly, thousands being baptized in a few days. The maps of Christian expansion in Asia registered some 150,000 Christians in China (1635), 300,000 in Japan (1613), more than 200,000 in Ethiopia (in the 1620's), 50,000 in southeast India (1576), 500,000 in Tonkin (by the mid-seventeenth century). In Mozambique there were sixteen parishes organized in 1667. Such figures, heralded throughout Europe, dazzled most people and made them believe that in a few years all Asia would be Christian. However, the conversions actually represented a very small percentage which ceased to grow as soon as the first enthusiasms were followed by the sadder realities of organized Church life. Moreover, the conversions were generally superficial, without any deep change in the traditional beliefs of Hindus or Buddhists. Often, acceptance of Christianity simply meant a way of reacting against an oppressive social or political order. But the European missionaries, pure and learned as they might be, had actually little to offer. From an Asian and non-Christian standpoint they really brought nothing to the peoples they intended to convert. Their civilization was, in many aspects, inferior to the one they found in China, in Japan, or in India. Their religion was intolerant and cruel, and interfered with cherished beliefs and traditions. Furthermore, it was the religion of another race, a race of conquerors and greedy traders. It is true that the missionaries often took the side of the natives against the Portuguese, but such attitudes were dangerous and could not be tolerated by the Church hierarchy.

Thus, from a strictly religious point of view, the missionaries failed. The nuclei of Christians scattered everywhere that the missionaries were so proud of faded away with time and only very few would survive to the nineteenth century. Persecution from local authorities started very quickly and was later reinforced by the Dutch and the English who were Protestants, hated the Catholics, and exhibited few proselytizing tendencies. In Ethiopia, in China, in Japan, the three larger and better organized countries, reaction against the Catholic missionaries brought about bloody persecutions and extensive martyrdom. Japan led the way, with a first "reign of terror" in 1587–98, followed by a second and more decisive bloodbath after 1614. Almost all the missionaries were slaughtered and 3,000 martyrs died between 1597 and 1660. The Jesuit priests were first banned (1587), then the Portuguese (1637). Worse than that, the profitable traffic with Macao was entirely abolished in 1639. Japan thus retreated into isolation for two hundred years.

In Ethiopia there were violent persecutions after 1632, in China after 1664. All these societies reacted not only against an odd religion and change in traditional customs but also against subversive ideas which the Christian missionaries inevitably had to urge upon the converts' minds. The persecutions were thus a result of many causes, a combination of religious, cultural, economic, and political elements. Growing intolerance made it more difficult for the Portuguese to have good relations with the Asian peoples and helped the Dutch and English. In India and elsewhere, late-sixteenth-century Catholicism followed the trends of the Counter-Reformation and hardened its methods. The Inquisition was established for India in 1560 and its ominous activities started shortly afterward (the first auto-da-fé was in 1563). Although monographs on the Goa Inquisition are unavailable, it seems that its persecutions and condemnations were still more violent than in Portugal. The methods were, of course, the same, but instead of the Jews and the New Christians (who also existed in India) most victims came from Hinduism and Buddhism, and particularly from those converts to Christianity who were suspected of backsliding.

Of much more interest was the cultural significance of the missions. They contributed to European knowledge of Asia and to the development of communications between Europe and most of that continent. The Jesuits and other priests settled down deep inland, periodically wrote to their superiors about the missions they were in, studied the native languages, customs, beliefs and histories, prepared dictionaries and other means of communication, and exchanged knowledge, methods, and ideas. They endeavored to understand the complex philosophies of India and China as a way of spreading Christianity with fruitful results. They studied local botany and zoology, transmitted itineraries and trade possibilities, and established regular communications with the Portuguese trade ports and fortresses. Thus, they paved the way for the coming of the Dutch, English, and French, to whom they gave—willingly or unwillingly—a most useful corpus of knowledge.

The Jesuit voyages of the sixteenth and seventeenth century opened up Ethiopia, India, China, and Japan. The lake of Tana, in Ethiopia, was first reached by a Westerner in 1603 (Gaspar Pais). Other missionaries penetrated most of the country, one of them (Pero

Pais) getting to know the springs of the Blue Nile (1618). In India several Jesuit fathers went deep inland, settling down in the Great Moghul Empire. The interior of Bengal was first reached in 1576. An Augustine priest, Sebastião Manrique, traveled extensively in that area (1628–35) and left a highly useful description of his itineraries. From India, the missionaries entered China via Tibet. Bento de Góis passed the Himalayas in 1602 and after a troublesome voyage arrived in China where he died, exhausted. The record of his travels was published some years later. Father António de Andrade was the first European to reach the capital of Tibet, in 1624. Fathers Cabral and Cacela visited Nepal and Bhutan.

In Indochina the Portuguese missionaries also traveled extensively in Cambodia and Cochin China. The first Annamite dictionaries were written by Portuguese Jesuits. In Japan most islands were visited or described by the Jesuit fathers. Everywhere the missions provided schools and hospitals. Although the main purpose and the main subjects concerned religion, instruction included reading, writing, and counting. Schools were free and the most important ones had courses on native languages, for the future missionaries. In the hospitals founded in India and Japan, scientific methods were interchanged between Europeans and Asians. It was also through the Jesuits that the printing press reached Asia. The first press appeared in Goa by 1556; Macao had its own press by 1588 and Japan in 1591. Books were printed, both in Portuguese and in the native languages. The example of Japan is highly revealing of the missionaries' purposes: of 29 existing works, printed up to 1614, 18 were in Japanese (10 using Latin letters, 8 with Japanese characters); 6 in Latin; 2 in Japanese and Portuguese; 1 in Japanese and Latin; and 2 in Japanese, Portuguese, and Latin. Titles included religion above all, but also grammars, dictionaries, and even *Aesop's Fables*!

For international contacts, the language of long-distance trade became Portuguese until the eighteenth century. Not only the natives, but later the Dutch and the English, had to learn Portuguese to be understood by any interpreter. Portuguese words remained in the local languages and dialects, very many having survived to the present. Portuguese in turn received several terms from the Asian languages.

A special kind of literature arose, known as the literature of travels, embracing the great number of itineraries, descriptive letters, reports, diaries, and, of course, historical chronicles. This vast output seems to be "unsurpassed in any language" (John dos Passos). The greatest writers of this genre who lived and worked after 1550 were Diogo do Couto (1542–1616) and Manuel de Faria e Sousa (1590–1649), but the only way of rightly appraising the rich literature inspired by the overseas expansion is to delve into the numerous booklets, descriptive essays, and letters of scores of travelers, some with real literary value. The *Cartas do Japão* (Letters from Japan) aroused great interest, and also the stories of shipwrecks, part of them compiled in the eighteenth century under the title of *História Trágico-Marítima (Tragic History of the Sea)*. Many of these essays and books found translators throughout Europe, and were published in Latin, Italian, Spanish, Dutch, English, German, and French.

The artistic achievements of the Portuguese in Asia must also be emphasized. They blended European and Asian traditions in some remarkable monuments, sculptures, paintings, and objets d'art. Important cities like Goa and Macao became show places of magnificent art. It is true that the Portuguese also destroyed some fine examples of native art—particularly in Goa—which they did not respect or understand, relating them to the abominable heathen practices (as the Spaniards did in America). Yet they replaced monuments with monuments and endowed India and China with some beautiful examples of Renaissance, Mannerist, and Baroque styles. Town-building was one of their main achievements. If in certain cases they accepted the existing patterns of town planning, in many others they were forced to plan and build anew. For that purpose the Renaissance principles of city planning were adopted and blended with local circumstances. Goa (the capital), Bassein, Macao, and others are good examples. Whenever the Portuguese decided to settle down, they immediately tried to create a replica of their native towns or villages. This is clearly shown by most places in ex-Portuguese India (Goa, Damão, and Diu, conquered by India in 1961) where colonization survived for centuries.

Portuguese military buildings were particularly numerous from Mozambique to Macao. Fortresses, towers, and gates still exist in places such as Damão, Diu, Goa, Mombasa, and Ethiopia. Then churches and convents rose everywhere, particularly in Goa (the cathedral, the church of St. Francisco, the church of Graça, the monastery of St. Paulo, etc.), Macao (the church of St. Paulo, the church of the Misericórdia), Damão, and Diu. Other art forms included first-rate giltwood (*talha*); stone and wooden sculpture; painting; tiles and other pottery, including china; goldsmithery; ivory works; textiles; furniture; and tapestry. The so-called Indo-Portuguese art, which flourished throughout the sixteenth, seventeenth, and eighteenth centuries, was a most original and remarkable result of the Portuguese expansion in Asia.

BRAZIL

For more than two centuries the history of Brazil was above all the history of a desperate effort to find gold. Gold and silver had been discovered by the Spaniards in Mexico and Peru. The Portuguese could not get used to the idea that their share of the American world was lacking in precious metals. They tried again and again; they followed all kinds of clues; they suffered unbelievable hardships in order to carry on deep penetration of the jungle, the mountains, and the rivers. Unlike Africa, where until the nineteenth century voyages of exploration inland were always timid or sporadic, Brazil was extensively traveled by Portuguese pioneers throughout the sixteenth and the seventeenth centuries. As a consequence the boundaries of present-day Brazil had been reached and defined as early as 1638. Connected together, the basins of the Amazon and Paraná-Paraguay rivers permitted a sort of circumnavigation of a huge territory and the establishment of contacts with the Spanish neighbors. The limits of Brazil were defined simply by the existence of settled Spaniards, who never proceeded as far east as the Portuguese did west. Thus, gold established the Brazilian borders, if not the structure of the Brazilian economy or society, which rose from sugar and (later) tobacco and cotton.

Explorations inland generally started from existing centers of settlement on the Piratininga plateau located close to the coastline. São Paulo, founded in 1554 by the Jesuit Father Manuel da Nóbrega, and for a long time a frontier town, became perhaps the most important of those centers. Yet there were many others, in São Vicente, in Porto Seguro, in Baía, and in Pernambuco. From any of those the explorers followed the course of the main rivers, whenever they were found navigable: the São Francisco, the Jequitinhonha, the Rio Grande, the Iguaçú, the Uruguay, the Paraná, the Paraguay, and the vast basin of the Amazon. If the rivers, however, did not provide a convenient path, then they walked by land, through the jungle if necessary, following the existing Indian paths or finding themselves new ones. This second "discovery" of Brazil was truly epic, full of unknown heroes and martyrs, and anonymous explorers, though also marked by periodic massacres of natives (who for their part often succeeded in killing and eating their invaders). There were the inevitable hatreds, rivalries, and intrigues among the Portuguese, the constant failures and retreats, but also magnificent results.

In the second half of the sixteenth century the Portuguese reached the springs of the São Francisco and the Jequitinhonha and explored most of their basins. Between the Uruguay-Paraná tracks and the coastline most of what is now Brazil became a familiar territory. A landowner of São Vicente, Brás Cubas, led or organized a famous expedition in 1560–61 (followed by another one in 1561–62) which found the first gold samples. In the North, important expeditions covered most of the hinterland to the Amazon. Paraíba was founded in 1585, then Natal (1597), Ceará (1612), and Belém (1615). They all provided people for more journeys inland.

Principles of organization were set up for many expeditions, according to the Portuguese late medieval and sixteenth-century army group constitution which gave the name *bandeira* ("flag") to a company of 250 people with an insignia of its own (also called *bandeira*). In Brazil this name was given to smaller groups in the late sixteenth century, particularly in the South (in the North, expeditions were called *jornadas,* journeys). *Bandeiras* and *jornadas* could be organized by local magistrates and army officials and even by top administrators, including the governor-general (Governor Francisco de Sousa, 1591–1602, for instance, played a leading role). They searched for gold, silver, precious stones, slaves, etc. In certain cases their purpose could simply be retaliation against attacks by the natives or even military undertakings against the French and the Dutch. Other *bandeiras,* perhaps the most important of all, aimed at a political goal, namely a border definition.

Sixteenth- and seventeenth-century Portuguese maps, copied by the Dutch and cartographers of other countries, tended to represent Brazil as a big island completely surrounded by two vast rivers, the Amazon and the Paraná, both starting at a vast lake. This geographical myth of an "Island Brazil" had a very clear political connotation: it gave the Portuguese Empire in South America a geographical basin and served the purposes of Portuguese versus Spanish imperialism. To "circumnavigate" Brazil with political goals thus became a well-defined target of many expeditions.

Throughout the seventeenth century, the *bandeiras* went farther and farther in their objectives. In 1637–38, Pedro Teixeira explored the Amazon, reaching Peru. António Raposo Tavares, a leading public official of São Paulo, headed several important expeditions from 1627 on. In his last and major one (1648–51), Raposo Tavares departed from São Paulo westward, following the Tietê River to the Paraná; navigating the Paraná, the Ivenheima, the Miranda, and then by land, he reached the Rio Grande or Guapaí, in the Amazon basin. Going down the Mamoré (in present-day Bolivia) and the Madeira he arrived at the main course of the Amazon, which finally took him to Belém. The "circumnavigation" of the pseudo-island had been achieved. Fernão Dias Pais (1638), Luis Pedroso de Barros (1656), and many others left their names in history by the fame of their undertakings.

But in the definitive constitution of Brazil there were threats to the expansion of the Portuguese too. The challenge posed by French and Dutch, as well as the Spanish counter-expansion, prevented the stretching of Brazilian borders northwest and southwest and for a while menaced the existence of Brazil itself. The French were the first to attack South America. In 1555 the Protestant French leader Villegaignon settled down in Guanabara Bay and laid the basis of what they called Antarctic France (France Antarctique). Under Governor-General Mem de Sá, the Portuguese counterattacked from 1560 to 1567 until they finally drove the French out. Other French groups, however, far from discouraged with their first mishap, settled down in the North (Paraíba and Maranhão) where they founded Saint Louis (now São Luis) in 1594. The Portuguese launched several expeditions to fight them, but it was only in 1615 that the French settlers offered their definitive surrender.

The French only succeeded in the Northwest of Brazil, an area which neither Portuguese nor Spaniards were interested in at the moment. There they settled as early as 1626 founding Cayenne (present-day French Guyana). It must be emphasized that the French, unlike the Dutch, were interested in colonization, choosing to settle in places which the Portuguese had left deserted.

The English and Dutch arrived next. The English diverted their energies in attacking ships or in raiding some settlements along the coast (Santos, 1582 and 1591; Baía, 1587; Recife, 1595). The Dutch posed the greatest danger to Portuguese sovereignty in Brazil. They wanted to conquer and get control of towns and areas already prepared by decades of Portuguese settlement—with good prospects of profit in trade and agriculture. Their first attack dated from 1598. Baía, in those days the capital of Brazil, was under their fire for the first time in 1599. But it was only from the 1620's onward that their efforts were rewarded by success and conquest. The Portuguese government—or rather the Madrid government—had little chance of sending important reinforcements. In those days Portugal regarded India as her most valuable possession and diverted all efforts to defending her Asian Empire.

Baía was attacked by Jacob Willekens and Piet Heyn and fell in 1624, yet the Portuguese and the Spaniards were still strong enough to regain it the next year. Then the Dutch, without forgetting Baía, centered their efforts on the Pernambuco area: Olinda fell, then Recife shortly after (1630). Successively enlarging their area of attack, they gained Rio Grande do Norte (1633), Paraíba (1634), most of Pernambuco (1635), Ceará and Sergipe (1637–41), and finally Maranhão (1641). All the Northeast seemed to be lost for the Portuguese cause. A fleet of rescue, sent by the government in 1639 under the command of Viceroy Conde da Torre, suffered a defeat in 1640. Under Governor Johan Maurits van Nassau-Siegen the Dutch tried to organize their new dominions with a brief period of economic and administrative success.

The proclamation of John IV as King of Portugal (1640) posed a very hard problem, both in Brazil and in Asia. After a decade of hesitation, the Crown clearly realized that in order to save Brazil it had to give up India. The economic conjuncture of 1642–44, with a drop in the sugar price in Amsterdam helped to increase the fundamental religious and national discontent against the invaders. The Portuguese settlers themselves decided to take the situation in their hands and make war against the enemy by their own means. In Recife the Portuguese rose in 1645 and defeated the Dutch at Tabocas. Although Baía had again been attacked (1647), the tide was now turning in favor of the Portuguese. The main effort unquestionably belonged to the settlers, but Lisbon sent its help too. Meanwhile, Angola, the most important source of slaves, had been recaptured by the Portuguese. In 1648–49 the Dutch were twice defeated in the first and second battles of Guararapes. Olinda fell (1648), then Recife (1654), with all the territory once lost to the Dutch.

The rise of Brazil in the late sixteenth and seventeenth century is shown by the population increase: 2,000 Portuguese by the 1540's; 25,000 at the end of the century, excluding almost 20,000 civilized natives, 14,000 Negro slaves, and many other half-breeds. Such figures had probably doubled by the middle of the seventeenth century. Emigrants came mostly from Portugal, the Northwest and Beira producing the greatest number. In the South of Brazil (in São Paulo particularly) there were many Spaniards, mostly from Andalucia—some coming directly from Europe, others from Spanish America—and scattered about there were groups of Flemish, Italians, Germans, and English, all Catholics. A number of New Christians arrived too, partly in connection with the sugar trade. The captaincies of Baía and Pernambuco quickly outdistanced the others both in population and in economic importance: 12,000 whites in Baía in 1583 against 8,000 for Pernambuco and 1,500 only for the next important captaincy, that of São Vicente.

A map of the Portuguese colonization of Brazil in that epoch would show only a very narrow fringe of coastal territory effectively conquered. Up to 1650 not even the coastline was thoroughly colonized. Only in the São Paulo and Rio de Janeiro areas did the Portuguese penetration go beyond 250 miles. Brazil presented many difficulties; unlike Mexico and Peru, it lacked any earlier (pre-Portuguese) civilized structure and had to be created anew.

The absence of white women, the conditions of life close to nature in which the settlers found the natives, the rise of slavery, all led to rampant miscegenation, with no parallel anywhere in the Portuguese Empire except perhaps Cape Verde. The crossing of whites and blacks produced the mulattoes, who in a short time became the majority of the Brazilian population. Whites and natives produced the *mamelucos*. This is not to say that race prejudice was absent in the Portuguese colonization of Brazil. Cross-breeding derived from the needs of nature, not from race equality. The whites were always considered superior to the others and held most offices of leadership, although tolerance and respect toward both mulattoes and *mamelucos* reached a higher level in Brazil than probably anywhere else.

The condition of natives and Negroes was always poor, even though the law tried to protect the natives almost immediately. The Christian missionaries found the Amerindian an ideal subject for evangelization. The missionaries succeeded very quickly in their purposes and immediately started to organize small Christian Indian groups and settle them in villages (*aldeias*) and groups of villages (*reduções*) under their direct leadership. The Jesuits were particularly successful in this kind of effort, and the number of Jesuit *aldeias* increased greatly from the late sixteenth century on. Their system was to treat the new converts as adolescents, and only reluctantly did they allow their pupils to work for the white settlers. To defend them from white "corruption" and enslavement the Jesuits went so far as to neglect the teaching of Portuguese, using only the *Tupi* language. From a religious, a humanitarian, and even an ethnological standpoint, the *aldeias* were highly interesting experiments. Yet they had no conditions for survival in a frontier society like Brazil. The settlers complained of being robbed of a labor force which was indispensable for a colonial economy. They often raided the missions, destroying them and enslaving the Indians. Many *bandeiras* had just that purpose. The Jesuits replied by organizing the Amerindians in paramilitary groups and opposing anyone's interference in their *aldeias*. A true Indian resistance to the advance of the settler was thus organized. Gradually the Jesuits, with the native masses as a base, created a state of their own within Brazil, which threatened the very authority of the Crown.

At the top level the Jesuits and other missionaries achieved their purpose, because of the great influence they had in the Court. Successive laws protected the Amerindians for almost two hundred years. Both in Spanish and Portuguese America, Church and state forbade the enslavement of the natives from a relatively early date. In 1570 the Lisbon government forbade it except in case of a "just" war or regarding cannibals. This act was often reaffirmed, particularly in 1609, 1612, 1647, and 1649. The Papal bull of 1639 excommunicated all the Catholics who dared to trade Indians. Despite all these measures, the realities of colonial life were very different. Many of the other laws and local acts changed or reduced the absolute value of theoretical prohibitions. The policy of protection to the Amerindians had its ups and downs according to the extent of Jesuit influence both in Portugal and in Brazil. For short periods the Jesuits were even expelled from São Paulo (1640 to 1653), Santos (1640 to 1642), and Maranhão-Pará (1661–63). Father António Vieira, the leading defender of the rights of Amerindians throughout the seventeenth century, was in disgrace several times and was even arrested. In spite of everything slavery went on.

Yet settlers and missionaries reached a sort of compromise, which incidentally was a thorough contradiction of the nonenslavement policy. This was the importation of Negro labor from Africa. Black slavery was hardly condemned even if men like António Vieira tried to protect the Negroes from their masters' boundless despotism. The settlers, in their turn, quickly realized that the Africans made much better slaves than the natives, being stronger, more disciplined, and more persistent. Imports of slaves from Africa rose from the 1570's onward. Until late in the century most slaves came from the Guinea (Sudan) area. Then Angolan and Congolese slaves became predominant up to about 1660 (when the Dutch occupied Angola, Mozambique replaced it); and afterward they came from both areas. The total number of slaves imported is hard to determine: at least 50,000 came to Brazil from 1570 to 1600, then some 200,000 more between 1600 and 1650, 150,000 between 1650 and 1670. Thus, the yearly average went up from more than 1,600 in the first period to 4,000 in the second and to 7,500 in the third. On the whole, the few existing statistics show some 2,000 to 3,000 Negroes living in Brazil by 1570, and 13,000 to 15,000 by 1600. Conditions of transportation over the ocean were tragic, half of the human cargo often dying during the voyage or shortly after arrival. Slaves had to be baptized before embarkation.

The development of sugar production was the main reason for

the importation of slaves; slavery and sugar plantations were inseparable. Indeed the great culture of sixteenth- and seventeenth-century Brazil, the one that promoted settlement and soil occupation, attracting colonizers from everywhere, was sugar cane. It spread all over Brazil with its main centers at Pernambuco, Baía, and (in the mid-1600's) Rio de Janeiro. Each sugar mill required a minimum of eighty slaves, besides the hundreds who had to work in the fields. The number of mills increased many times from the mid-sixteenth to the late seventeenth century: one mill in 1533; 60 in 1570 (23 in Pernambuco, 18 in Baía); 130 in 1585 (65 in Pernambuco, 45 in Baía, 3 in Rio); 170 in 1612; 346 in 1629 (150 in Pernambuco, 80 in Baía, 60 in Rio); 300 in 1645 (with part of Brazil in Dutch hands); and more than 400 in the late 1600's, a half in Pernambuco, the other half almost evenly divided between Baía and Rio.

Technical innovations, introduced from Peru in 1608–12, fostered both improved quantity and quality. Brazilian sugar was exported, via Lisbon, to most of Europe. The figures show a remarkable expansion of exports: 180,000 arrobas (1 arroba = 30 pounds roughly) in 1560–70, double that in 1580, double that again in 1614 (with still better years in between), more than one million arrobas in the early 1630's, two million and more in 1650–70. The rise of Brazil as the greatest sugar producer in those days completely ruined the suger-based economy of the island of Madeira while replacing the decline of trade with the East. Sugar permitted the Portuguese Crown to give up India without too many economic troubles for the mainland and without too much concern for the future.

Although sugar led the Brazilian economy by far, it was not the colony's only source of revenue. Slaves came next, then brazilwood, the cutting of which continued to make a good profit for Crown, traders, and owners. The expansion of brazilwood trade not only brought about a continuous drop in prices after 1591 but also threatened extinction of the trees themselves. To avoid this the Crown decided to grant the cutting monopoly to the Jesuits who kept it for more than twenty years (1625–49). Until the early seventeenth century the average export figure per year was more than 10,000 quintais (hundertweights). In the mid-century exports had gone down to half of that figure or less.

Other profitable products were cotton and tobacco. Interestingly enough, cotton, which would later bring Brazil a new source of prosperity, was in decline throughout the seventeenth century (because of Venice's competition) after a premature rise in the second half of the sixteenth century. Tobacco, however, continued to develop. The great epoch for tobacco production started after 1650, but it was being produced much before.

Cattle raising should not be forgotten for it was not only profitable but also important in adding new areas of settlement. With oxen necessary for work on the plantations and horses serving for transportation and defense, stockbreeding around the plantations naturally rose and developed rapidly. Throughout the seventeenth century it gradually spread inland, in the São Francisco basin and the São Paulo area, to the vast plateaus of central Brazil. From 1640 on the colony ceased to import meat and leather from Portugal, the Cape Verde Islands, and the Rio de la Plata, and started exporting them. Yet the great epoch of Brazilian cattle breeding did not begin before 1670.

On the whole, Brazil had become a large colony of settlement with a great future for both colonization and trade. The increase in Crown revenues shows this very clearly: 26,400 cruzados in 1588, 84,000 in 1607, 108,800 in 1619, almost double in 1640. It was still less than India, but it was growing much more rapidly. Ordinary expenditures were far less (22,835 cruzados in 1584, 18,744 in 1588, 38,294 in 1607), which presaged a good surplus for the Crown when peace returned in the 1650's. Profits for the government derived from the usual sources. The Crown owned the monopoly of brazilwood trade, as well as that of slaves, spices, and drugs. It gave this up, in Brazil as in India, during the second half of the sixteenth century. After a brief period of trade freedom (with taxes paid to the Crown), the granting of periodical monopolies to private companies or individuals (the *contratos* or *asientos* system) became usual. The slave trade was so organized in 1573 and was never changed from then on, the *contratadores* having to pay the Crown a yearly sum of 22,000 to 80,000 cruzados. Most were Portuguese with a number of New Christians settled outside Portugal. The brazilwood trade varied in system: There were *contratos* (to 1612); then a sort of "régie" (1612–25, 1640–45); then *contratos* again (1625–40, 1645–49). After 1649 the new company for trade with Brazil took over all the commerce in brazilwood.

Sugar trade was free as were cotton, tobacco, and other items, but the exporters had to pay the usual duties. Still more important were the tithes which were paid on every product of the soil to the Order of Christ, i.e., the government. The sugar industry was also taxed in some other minor ways.

Sugar, tobacco, cotton, cattle raising, and the like, which gave strength and prosperity to the colony, favored the rise of the *latifundium* and the growth of a class of rich landowners and planters. Indeed the feudal type of economy that the *donatarias* system had introduced in Brazil only developed throughout the sixteenth and seventeenth centuries. The *sesmarias,* in the old Portuguese way, which the "captains" granted to a settler, became large plantations. But their lords (*senhores de engenho*) directly explored only a portion of them, sub-granting the rest to other settlers, or farmers (*lavradores*), for a number of years. The *senhor de engenho* was a true feudal lord, with a host of relatives, farmers, artisans, clients, and slaves working for him and depending upon him. The *engenho* was a true village, a "villa" in the old terminology, with its big house (seat of the administration), its dependencies, its quarters where the slaves lived, its chapel, and the rest. Like the ancient feudal cells, the plantation tended and tried to be self-sufficient, reducing imports to a minimum but—a less feudal characteristic—striving for a maximum of exports. Smaller landowners based their existence and profits upon other cultures, such as cassava (*mandioca*).

From the standpoint of administration an important change had taken place in the late 1540's: the setting up of a central government for all of Brazil. The failure of many captaincies, the increasing attacks of foreign vessels, particularly French, the example of other Portuguese possessions, the general trend of the whole policy at home, all this led to the act of 1548 which created the general-government for the "State" of Brazil and appointed as first governor-general Tomé de Sousa, a nobleman related to the former captain, Martim Afonso de Sousa. The governor-general would build the new capital of Brazil, Baía; provide for its defense; visit the captaincies (which were not abolished but became subject to his authority); promote the exploration of the country; intervene in economic matters; attend to the good relations with the natives; set up customs houses; serve as a judge in property quarrels.

An auditor-general (*ouvidor geral*) with judicial functions, a purveyor-general (*provedor mor*), a captain-general in charge of defending the coastline (*capitão mor da costa*), a treasurer (*tesoureiro das rendas*), a receiver in charge of the supplies (*almoxarife dos mantimentos*), and a master of fortifications assisted the governor and formed a sort of ministry, with their secretaries, technicians, and artisans. In 1587 a Supreme Court (*Relação*), modeled on that of Lisbon, was set up in Baía acting as a court of appeal for all of Brazil. Several reforms perfected its functioning. Discontinued in 1626, it was again revived in 1652.

Tomé de Sousa arrived in Brazil early in 1549, starting a new epoch for the history of that huge colony. The general government set up the framework for modern Brazil, defining its organization as a nation. It gave Brazil unity, a central bureaucracy, a capital, a leader, continuity in government. Governors of Brazil were generally kept in power for longer periods than in India: Tomé de Sousa and his successor, Duarte da Costa, ruled only four years each, but their successor, Mem de Sá, lasted for fifteen years (1557–72). Later on, Governor Francisco de Sousa ruled Brazil for eleven years (1591–1602). As in India all the governors belonged to the top aristocracy, but not so high as the Indian viceroys of the same period. Unquestionably Brazil was still regarded as inferior to the East politically, economically, and socially. Titles of viceroy were given now and then, but only in special cases and for highly distinguished personalities.

The story of central government had its oddities too: from 1572 to 1577 Brazil was divided into two governments, that of the North with the capital in Baía (to Ilhéus) and that of the South with the capital in Rio. Then in 1621, after the final expulsion of the French from Maranhão, the Madrid-Lisbon government thought it better, for purposes of both defense and exploration, to establish a new "State" with the capital in São Luis, that of Maranhão, stretching from the Amazon River to the Cape of São Roque and encompassing the captaincies of Maranhão, Pará, and Ceará. The first governor was Francisco Coelho de Carvalho, appointed in 1626. This state of Maranhão lasted for a hundred and fifty years (except for a brief extinction in 1652–54) with certain benefits for the development of its territories, where new captaincies were established (Tapuitapera or Cumã; Gurupá or Caetá; Cametá; Cabo Norte; Marajó; Xingú).

The history of the general government in relation to the captaincies shows certain similarities with the history of Europe in the epoch of the strengthening of the royal power. The Crown had purchased or annexed some captaincies in the mid-1500's, such as Baía and Rio de Janeiro, which gave the governor-general a sort of operational basis, a "royal domain" in Brazil. In other cases new Crown captaincies were established, on territories which the former captains had never colonized: Paraíba, in the 1570's and 1580's; Rio Grande do Norte and Sergipe in the late sixteenth century. In Maranhão most of its land belonged to the Crown. But in any case the powers of the hereditary captains gradually declined as Brazil became more and more an object of concern and interest to Portugal. Throughout the seventeenth century the captaincies had practically been converted into provinces for administrative purposes. There were two kinds of captaincies which might be called first class and second class. The latter were subordinated to the former in matters of administration and justice: thus Paraíba and Alagoas depended upon Pernambuco; Rio Grande do Norte, Sergipe and Espírito Santo on Baía; while São Paulo was subject to Rio de Janeiro. At the local administration level the interesting fact was the quick rise and strengthening of the municipalities, whereas in Portugal they were frankly declining by that time. Throughout Brazil successive *câmaras* (city councils) were set up, according to the Portuguese pattern, with similar officials and organs but much greater power and importance. They were ready, if necessary, to fight the viceroy, the central government, or the Jesuits—and they often did. This strength derived from the peculiar conditions characterizing Brazil in those days: a frontier country far from the mainland and far from the capital, based upon the initiatives of her settlers and explorers, with a much higher degree of freedom and individual assertion.

The rise of Brazil was also accompanied by the development of the religious framework. The bishopric of Baía, instituted in 1551, meant that the new colony had reached its religious maturity. In 1575 the South (from Espírito Santo southward) encompassed a new diocese under an Apostolic Administrator, with the see in Rio. Yet the importance of the secular clergy could not compare with that of the religious orders in civilizing and exploring the colony. On the contrary, it often brought about numerous conflicts with everyone, from the central authorities to the natives. Poor in preparation and in morals, the secular clergy sent to Brazil had little qualification for the mission it was supposed to perform. It often indulged in trade activities, slavery, and political intrigue, jealous of the strength and prestige the regular orders showed everywhere, but totally unable to cope with them.

The task of the Jesuits has already been mentioned. In Brazil they were the most numerous and enterprising among all religious orders. From 1540 to 1580 seventeen missionary expeditions of Jesuit priests left Lisbon for Brazil. The overwhelming majority were Portuguese, but some others had their share in the American missions too: Anchieta, for instance, a remarkable Spanish missionary. Many suffered martyrdom, either at the hands of the natives or the French and Dutch Protestants.

A number of the missions they founded became bases for future towns: this was true of São Paulo, Baía, and even Rio de Janeiro. They also contributed to the cultural development of the colony, by establishing schools both for the neophytes and the Portuguese. They tried to set up a University, but here they failed.

Besides the Jesuits, the Franciscans and the Carmelites also played their part in evangelizing Brazil. The Franciscans came after 1580 and were particularly active in the North. They counted more than twenty convents in the mid-1600's. The Carmelites arrived by the same time, but their action was never too noteworthy.

In a frontier land like Brazil culture could not have flourished greatly. Schools were scarce, as was the number of intellectuals and of books available. No printing press existed, no university, no seminary. Under Jesuit control a Royal College for Arts was founded in Baía in the 1570's, the first academic degrees being solemnly conferred in 1575. The Jesuit and Franciscan houses provided the majority of the few existing schools. Sons of planters who wished to study regularly had to go to Portugal. Incidentally the official policy of the Crown was always to centralize learning and force everyone to study in the mother country. From a cultural standpoint the interesting achievements were only the study of the native languages and usages, and the consequent publication of Grammars, Vocabularies, and Catechisms. The same is true of the study of local botanies, zoologies, and geographies. The expeditions inland, the efforts of the missionaries, the tasks of the administrators, brought about some interesting letters, memoirs, reports, and histories. Yet the total scientific and literary production was scarce and poor in quality, especially in comparison with the East. Despite everything, Brazil continued to be a second-class colony and did not attract the attention of India or Japan.

With the arts a similar situation occurred. Smaller and less important churches, monasteries, and civil buildings were built in Portuguese America in those days, compared with the artistic achievements of India or Macao. This explains the relative poverty of present-day Brazil in sixteenth- and seventeenth-century monuments, in contrast to a great part of Spanish America.

THE ATLANTIC ISLANDS AND AFRICA

After John III's policy of abandonment, the Portuguese strongholds in Morocco encompassed only the three fortified towns of Ceuta, Tangiers, and Mazagão. For a while King Sebastian owned Arzila, but Philip II thought it better to give it back to the Moors. Indeed the North African fortresses produced little income but cost a great deal. They had to import almost everything from the mainland or the Portuguese colonies. They were retained more for tradition and prestige than for any effective strategic or political reasons. Moreover, the Moors never stopped besieging all three. Mazagão, for instance, was strongly attacked in 1562. The Portuguese restoration of 1640 resulted in the loss of two of the fortresses: Ceuta did not acknowledge the secession and remained faithful to the Spanish monarch, the peace treaty of 1668 confirming its possession by Spain; Tangiers was given by the Portuguese Crown to England as a part of Princess Catarina's dowry when she married King Charles II (1661). Only Mazagão remained in Portuguese hands.

Strategically located on the natural route to the South and the Southwest, the island of Madeira developed and prospered as the Portuguese Empire grew in extent and economic power. Funchal, the capital of Madeira, was indeed a compulsory port of call for most Portuguese navigation throughout the sixteenth and seventeenth centuries. This circumstance converted Madeira's economy into a very complex one, because the island depended on exports, imports, and re-exports of various kinds. It also made of Funchal a busy harbor and gave the town a cosmopolitanism comparable only to Lisbon and the Portuguese towns in the Far East (Goa, Malacca, and Macao). Madeira naturally grew in population, reaching some 50,000 by 1676, of which one-fifth lived in Funchal. Consequently, the capital of Madeira ranked high among the urban centers of "white" Portugal, surpassed only by some six or seven important cities on the mainland itself.

By the mid-1500's, Madeira's main production was sugar. There were on the island some forty sugar mills, producing a maximum output of 200,000 arrobas (some 6,000,000 pounds) in 1570. Madeira's sugar was sent all over Europe. Its plantations required an extensive labor force, and hundreds of slaves were imported each year from Africa. In 1552 there were more than 3,000 slaves on the island, or close to one-tenth of the total population. A class of wealthy local landowners controlled most of the plantations, with the sugar trade belonging to Portuguese, New Christians, and a few foreigners. Madeira imported textiles and other industrial items, meat, salt, and especially wheat. A century later much had changed in this picture. The competition of Brazilian sugar (the price of which was half that of Madeiran) and a disease in the cane put the production lower and lower: 4,000 arrobas in the 1580's and still less in the following decades. The number of sugar mills contracted to seven or eight (1610), and to five by the end of the seventeenth century. The Madeirans decided to organize sugar purchases in Brazil and sell the sugar again as if it were their own production. This arrangement naturally met with resistance and was forbidden again and again in the 1590's and early 1600's. In the 1630's Madeiran sugar was practically knocked out of the island's economy and taxation. The conquest of Northeast Brazil by the Dutch caused a brief revival between 1640 and 1657, but afterward sugar in Madeira disappeared altogether. With it, slavery declined too. Imports of slaves gradually decreased and the existing ones vanished from the island's demographic features.

Madeira, however, very soon replaced sugar with a new product that prevented drastic structural changes. This was wine. In 1586 the state's revenue from wine did not exceed one-seventh of the revenue from sugar. A century later wine was the essence of Madeira's economy. Its two main exports were wine and a sweet preserve called *casquinha* (made with local and Brazilian sugar). The island's wine was then as famous and widely exported as sugar had once been, reaching the whole of the Portuguese Empire and a good part of Europe. But instead of belonging to predominantly Portuguese firms, the wine trade had fallen into the hands of foreign traders, mostly English. In the same period (late seventeenth century) Madeira imported more or less what it had imported for a long time: wheat, textiles, meat, salt, and codfish. Part of the wheat was reexported to the Portuguese Empire. However, Madeira's affluence considerably declined with the downfall of sugar, and emigration from the island (and from Porto Santo as well) started in those days. Throughout the seventeenth century many Madeirans migrated to Brazil in search of a better way of living.

From an administrative standpoint the great reform accomplished was the introduction of a governor (called governor and captain-general) with authority over the entire archipelago and his capital in Funchal (1586). The hereditary captains continued to exist but subject to the governor. Adopted as a necessary measure for defense, this act also corresponded to a clear policy of converting all captaincies throughout the empire into Crown colonies with temporary appointed governors. Defensive works were also extensively undertaken during the late sixteenth and the seventeenth centuries. Madeira experienced attacks from all the pirates and enemies of Portugal and Spain, namely the French, the English, and the Dutch. Yet they never caused the damage inflicted on other Portuguese territories because of the island's better conditions for defense.

In the Azores the great expansion had ended by the mid-1500's but the archipelago continued to develop its resources and posed no economic difficulties to the crown. The population of the Azores paralleled the growth in Portugal: it rose considerably up to the late sixteenth century, and then less and less, reaching a period of stagnation. As a general port of call for the navigation lines from the Portuguese Empire, the Azores continued to prosper and its trade continued to grow. But at the same time, the islands proved to be profitable agriculturally, with well-managed *quintas* (farms) and plantations, worked by a predominantly white population stratified in a way similar to that of Portugal. Its economy passed through very interesting cycles: in the mid-sixteenth century wheat and woad clearly had the lead followed by sugar cane, wine, and several other products. Azorean wheat reached every part of the Portuguese Atlantic Empire, and above all Portugal itself. Woad arrived in England and other foreign countries in large quantities; output was estimated at 60,000 hundertweights in the late 1500's, and as much as 100,000 in the early seventeenth century. It was this rise in the woad production that caused wheat to suffer a sort of eclipse for more than fifty years, beginning by the 1570's: unheard-of dearths occurred, imports were often necessary, and exports declined greatly. After 1612, however, the woad production dropped (mostly due to the increasing taxes inflicted on it and to the competition of the American indigo) while wheat entered a new period of prosperity: the last serious deficit was in 1613; by 1621 the Azores could produce up to 8,200 moios (492,000 bushels) of wheat annually, with a minimum of 4,000 in bad years. By 1670 both woad and sugar cane had practically disappeared from the island's economy; wine, maize, flax (and flaxseed), and oranges competed for second place after wheat. Maize had been introduced early in the seventeenth century, and its development was bringing about an increase in cattle raising. Fishing (with whale-fishing at the top) figured importantly too.

The sixteenth and seventeenth centuries saw the introduction in the Azores of new products and new techniques in agriculture. In addition to maize and orange trees, sweet potatoes, yams, several other fruits, and pine trees were introduced from Europe or America. Farmers learned how to increase soil fertility by sowing lupine. Still more important was the new method of getting rid of the ashes and pumice stone that spread over the fields after each volcanic eruption (a true plague for the Azores in that epoch as there were violent eruptions in 1563, 1614, 1630, 1649, 1652, and 1659). The new process made use of ditches and canals where the water from streams and rivers passed and where the polluted soil was thrown out. The water carried away most earth, depositing the pumice stone on the bottom of the ditches. On the whole, the Azores provided steady revenue to the Crown, and even extraordinary expenditures could be covered from the islands' own resources and taxation.

Throughout the late sixteenth and seventeenth centuries more and more defensive works became necessary on each island to protect the inhabitants against the increasing attacks of pirates and enemies. French, English, Dutch, and even Moslem vessels often raided Portuguese and Spanish trade ships, daring to storm the towns and villages themselves and landing troops for plundering or destructive purposes. This happened particularly after 1580 when the crowns of Portugal and Spain were united. War also ravaged the Azores, especially Terceira, in 1580–82, because King António was proclaimed and supported by the authorities and people of that island who managed to resist Philip's furious attacks for a while. All these events led to a number of important fortification works all over the archipelago, but particularly concentrated on the two main islands of Terceira and São Miguel. At the same time, Philip II reorganized the island's medieval captaincy system. In 1583 a governor-general to whom the captains were subject was established for all the nine islands with the seat in Angra (Terceira).

The Cape Verde archipelago proved a failure as a colony of settlement, yet its population increased somewhat or remained constant, in relative prosperity because of the islands' location as a necessary port of call for the South Atlantic navigation. Indeed, most ships sailing between Portugal (or Spain) and the Gulf of Guinea, Angola, India, Brazil, or the West Indies stopped in Santiago to get water and supplies. Also the navigation lines directly connecting the Gulf of Guinea with Brazil called at either Ribeira Grande or Praia, both in Santiago. These two cities acted as trade ports, their prosperity depending much more on the number of ship-callings than on their function as centers for agriculture or settlement. The important role played by Cape Verde, which accounted for its survival, also brought about a number of catastrophes. The French, the English, and the Dutch, on their way to raid the Portuguese and Spanish settlements or vessels, called on the archipelago as well, either stealing its cattle or robbing its inhabitants. Several such attacks were followed by almost complete destruction. The French came first, after 1542; the English arrived next, raiding the islands in 1578 (Drake), 1582, 1585

(Drake again), 1598, and subsequently. And finally the Dutch came, after 1598. On their frequent travels to South America they preferred to stop at the island of Maio, which was almost deserted.

To protect Cape Verde, the Crown developed a better defense and management. Fortresses were built or repaired. Government was entirely reformed: above the captains (whose control did not reach beyond their island) a captain-general, later called captain-governor, was created (1587). His authority included not only the ten islands but also the coast of Africa south of Morocco on the Serra Leoa (Sierra Leone). Ribeira Grande was chosen as the seat. The town of Praia, however, had healthier conditions for the Europeans and its climate was better too. From 1612 on both governors and bishops rotated their residence between Ribeira Grande and Praia, which was fortified. In 1652 Praia became the official capital of the colony, resulting in the complete decline of Ribeira Grande. Incidentally the captaincy of Santiago had passed on to the Crown as early as 1564, when the last hereditary captain died.

Besides its function as a supply area for navigation, Cape Verde's main source of wealth depended on cattle and horse raising. Throughout the seventeenth century horses from the archipelago were exported all over the Portuguese Empire and even to the English possessions in the West Indies. A small leather industry also arose with its center in Santiago. Although in short supply salt and maize were also exported. Cape Verde had enough agriculture for its own maintenance, growing corn, sugar cane, cotton, vegetables, and fruit. Fish was abundant too. Most islands had donkeys, goats, and mules. In the late sixteenth and early seventeenth century Santiago was prosperous and covered with small agricultural units in the hands of rich landowners. Social hierarchies had rapidly developed, as well as an increasing miscegenation. The economic development of the other islands, however, stagnated.

Slavery helped Cape Verde's prosperity. Like São Tomé, Cape Verde served as an entrepôt for Negroes from continental Africa who could be bought there more easily than in the mainland. The archipelago's economy also required slave imports from Africa. The slave trade belonged to *contratadores,* who from the late 1580's to 1643 were all Portuguese or New Christians.

Upon the Santiago government depended the several tradeposts that the Portuguese successfully set up along the African coast, from Arguin (in present-day Mauritania) to Sierra Leone. Those places depended on the gold, malaguette, ivory, and slave trade, and they never ceased to prosper and grow more numerous throughout the seventeenth century. Despite Dutch and English competition, new settlements of Portuguese sprang up here and there (Biguba in the mid-1500's; Cacheu in 1587; Farim in 1642; Zinguichor in 1643; and many others), helping to give form to what would later be Portuguese Guinea. At the same time the traditional Portuguese settlements fell to the Dutch: Rufisque, Portudal, and Joal in 1621; Arguin in 1638. The main areas of the new Portuguese penetration were the rivers Casamansa and Geba. A fact that helped European settlement in those areas and contributed to their economic rise was the agreement in 1601 between the Crown and the Jews which gave the latter permission to trade and settle down in Guinea. For the Guinea settlements (called rios de Cacheu) the government established a *capitão e ouvidor*, subordinate to the governor of Cape Verde.

In the Gulf of Guinea the Portuguese had some twelve to fifteen trade ports by the early seventeenth century. In many there were small fortresses for protection. The whole territory under Portuguese control from Cape Palmas (in present-day Liberia) to the Volta River (now Ghana) formed the captaincy of Mina with headquarters in São Jorge da Mina (Elmina). From the Volta River to the Congo, including the Gulf of Guinea islands, the Portuguese possessions were included in the São Tomé captaincy, with the seat in the island and city of São Tomé. For religious purposes the whole area depended on the bishop of São Tomé. Indeed, this isle was the true economic and political center of the Portuguese power north of Angola despite the former prosperity and competition of São Jorge da Mina. Both captaincies were Crown colonies, although the islands of Principe and Ano Bom belonged to hereditary captains subject to the authority of the captain-general and governor of São Tomé. Here there was a municipal organization similar to that of Lisbon, with a city council and a Senate (Senado) of increasing autonomy. In São Tomé and Principe the process of miscegenation had gone very far; the result was a thoroughly Portuguese mulatto population, with its own social hierarchy and a growing rejection of white newcomers from the mainland. The bulk of the clergy was mulatto and even Negro. The number of pure Negroes, however, never ceased to grow, owing to the slave imports from continental Africa. These slaves revolted several times against their lords, irrespective of color: the worst rebellions took place in 1580, 1595, and 1617 and in the intervals a sort of continuous resistance and guerilla type of war gave little security to the plantations. For a while the rebels practically controlled the whole island of São Tomé, with the exception of the city itself and a few miles around.

The Mina had lived on gold and spice (grain) trade, while São Tomé depended on sugar exports. Yet the gold output constantly declined to almost nothing in the early 1600's. The trade ports in continental Africa lingered on, reduced to secondary activities which aroused little interest in Portugal.

Sugar had more importance and lasted longer. In the 1570's São Tomé was a great producer and exporter of very cheap sugar with more than 20,000 arrobas (600,000 pounds) yearly loaded to Europe. There were more than twenty sugar mills and the slave imports went up. The sugar trade was rented by the Crown to *contratores* who paid some 36,000 cruzados each year. In 1602 sugar production had reached 40,000 arrobas, with more than twenty ships sailing from São Tomé to Lisbon loaded with sugar.

In a few years all this had changed. A disease in the sugar cane, the slave rebellions, the attacks by French and Dutch pirates, and Brazilian competition ruined the economy of São Tomé. The 36,000 cruzados were reduced to one-third of that figure by 1610. The number of mills contracted to four or five. From a prosperous plantation colony São Tomé became a mere slave entrepôt where slaves were easier to get than in Angola. It was more because of this and strategic reasons than because of their economic value that the Dutch endeavored to conquer the Portuguese possessions in the Gulf of Guinea. One by one all the trade ports on the mainland fell, in the 1620's and 1630's: São Jorge da Mina surrendered in 1637. The final storming of São Tomé took place in 1641. Yet the Portuguese were not completely annihilated. Inland in São Tomé the Dutch could not go through. Principe and Ano Bom never fell. Lisbon sent two rescue fleets in 1642 and 1643. Both failed. In 1648, however, Salvador Correia de Sá after liberating Angola was able to reconquer the city.

São Tomé's decline continued. By 1661 the economic prostration of the small archipelago had perhaps reached its lowest level. Only the freedom of trade enacted by Lisbon in 1673 could mark the beginning of a new era of prosperity. Another cause for, or result of, the decline was the amazing instability of government. Governors sent by Lisbon never lasted long. They either died or clashed with the local rulers who forced them to leave. Indeed the history of São Tomé throughout the late sixteenth and the seventeenth century was one of permanent conflict between the central government (appointed by Lisbon) and the mulatto ruling groups. The clergy often sided with the latter but at other times followed a policy of their own, contributing another element of dissent and anarchy.

The unsuccessful experiment of a protectorate in the Congo led the Portuguese to try another way in Angola. This area had shown good possibilities for economic profit: the slave trade and the prospect of silver mines inland (in the Cambambe region) appealed to the settlers of São Tomé and forced the Crown to adopt a definite policy of action. Indeed Angola (like the Congo) started as a true colony of São Tomé, whose residents were granted the monopoly of its trade in the 1550's. At the same time (1559), the Lisbon government sent a mission to the Negro ruler of Angola headed by Paulo Dias de Novais and including some Jesuits. After some years there, Paulo Dias returned to Portugal and convinced those responsible for overseas affairs that Angola had good prospects of becoming another Brazil if only the Crown took some interest in it. The fear of attacks by foreigners also forced Lisbon to attempt effective possession of the coast south of the Congo. Finally the Congo itself had been overcome by the Jaga invasion (1569) and the Portuguese endeavored to reconquer the lost territories on behalf of their client, the king of the Congo. An expeditionary force of 600 white soldiers left Lisbon (1571), restored King "Alvaro" to his throne, and built a fortress for future protection. Use of military force was now envisioned to give the Portuguese a firm hold south of the Congo too and prevent possible attacks of both the Jaga and the Teke.

Thus, in 1574 Angola was made into a captaincy (*capitania* or *donataria*) and granted to Paulo Dias de Novais, following some of the rules of the captaincy system in the Atlantic Islands and Brazil. It covered the whole coastline south of the river Dande to 35 leagues south of the river Cuanza, and inland as far as possible. The captain was to provide for the settling of one hundred white families in Angola within six years. He would organize a permanent army of 400 men for defense and build three castles. He would grant the land in *sesmarias* to Portuguese colonizers and might keep a considerable amount for himself. He was given full jurisdiction and authority over the captaincy, the ownership of all the means of production and salt mines, all taxation in his own share and one-third in the rest of the colony, several trade privileges, and so on. Yet his attributions and concessions were not so complete and so feudal as those of the other captains. First of all the grant was not hereditary. Then, only a part remained in the captain's possession as a lordship. For the rest he was no more than a governor of a Crown colony.

Paulo Dias de Novais arrived in Angola in 1575 with 700 people, founded Luanda as his capital (1576), and built the three fortresses as decided. He ruled for fourteen years and fulfilled only some of the clauses in his contract. When he died (1589) the Portuguese were far from being firmly settled in Angola, although they ruled over part of the coastline. The new colony never became what the Portuguese expected nor could it compare with Brazil. The Negroes, who were much more civilized and better organized than the Americans, offered a strong and permanent resistance. The climate killed hundreds of settlers and weakened many others (it seems that of 2,000 soldiers sent to Angola in 1575–94 only 300 survived). The soil was far less fertile than in Brazil. And the slave trade diverted almost everyone from agriculture and made Angola's economy entirely dependent upon continuous raids inland, cheap purchases of human labor from enemy tribes, intrigue and warfare. Also it made Angola a "colony" of, first, São Tomé and, later, Brazil where slave labor was fundamental for the plantations.

Paulo Dias was succeeded by Luis Serrão, but the Negro victory of 1590 forced the Crown to intervene and put an end to the captaincy system. In 1592 Francisco de Almeida was inaugurated as governor of Angola under the direct control of the government. Yet the policy of conquest was enforced, and Angola became a sort of permanent battlefield for the Portuguese. Governor Manuel Cerveira Pereira (1603–07; 1615–17; 1620) was able to make the Portuguese presence firmer than ever, founding Benguela (1617) and assuring control of a vast track of coastline. Inland, too, the Portuguese reached some goals, namely Cambambe (only to find out that the silver mines did not exist); built some castles; and set up some fairs. On the whole however, Portuguese rule in Angola by the early seventeenth century strikingly resembled the Indian and East African trade port system, based on some fortresses and military garrisons but esssentially coastal in nature.

In 1641 the Dutch managed to capture Luanda and thus to control the main source of slaves to Brazil. The Portuguese retreated inland, and for seven years a series of acts of warfare followed by temporary truces marked the history of Angola. From Brazil came two reinforcement expeditions. With the Portuguese close to a complete surrender, the Brazilian settlers sent a third relief expedition under the command of Salvador Correia de Sá, who succeeded in recapturing Luanda and expelling the Dutch from all of Angola (1648).

This Portuguese victory was followed by an active policy of conquest and "punishment" of those who had helped the Dutch. In a few years, Governor Correia de Sá (1648–52) and his successors imposed the Crown's control, if not effective rule, over a great part of the hinterland.

CHAPTER EIGHT

ABSOLUTISM AND ENLIGHTENMENT

THE STRUCTURES

A new population rise followed the demographic stability of the seventeenth century. Especially after 1725, this new trend was felt all over Europe. It derived more from a drop in the death rate than from a rise in the birthrate. With better organization of the system of food distribution, fewer famines and shortages occurred. This was accompanied by increased agricultural and industrial production. As a consequence towns developed, their population and economic activity continuing to grow from then on. For the first time since the Middle Ages most European cities decisively overcame their medieval limits, heralding the tremendous boom of the nineteenth and the twentieth century.

By the middle of the seventeenth century Portugal had some two million people. This basic figure remained fairly constant until 1732 when the first counting of the new century took place. But from then on, the rise was continuous: more than 2,500,000 in 1758, almost 3,000,000 forty years later, some 3,100,000 by 1820. But there was not a corresponding growth in the capital of the country. Lisbon's population in the 1600's, in itself too large for the size of Portugal, stagnated or declined throughout most of the eighteenth century, offset by a better distribution in the countryside: before the great earthquake of 1755, no more than 150,000 people lived within Lisbon's walls; after that Lisbon grew, but slowly, the earthquake being only a minor cause of the slow growth. By 1780 there were still only 150,000 people, some 180,000 at the end of the century, 200,000 in 1820. The number of parishes shows a similar trend: 37 in 1632, 38 in 1741, 40 in 1770, 41 in 1833. If one compares this relatively slow increase with the rise of the great capitals of Europe by the same time, the conclusion is that Lisbon no longer matched the rapid growth of the great metropolises. Instead of being a competitor for the title of "great town," as before, Lisbon declined to the level of a second-class city, just as Portugal's position declined relative to other nations. Comparisons with Spain clearly show this change: while Lisbon in 1620 was the largest city in the Iberian Peninsula, it was overtaken by Madrid through the eighteenth and the early nineteenth century.

The countryside, on the other hand, became better populated and with some prosperous small towns: foremost was Porto, whose population rose to more than 20,000 in 1732 and to more than double in 1787. By 1820 Porto had 50,000 inhabitants. Small ports such as Viana, Faro, and Setúbal competed with Lisbon in absorbing part of the foreign traffic. Porto was a good example of the North's prosperity and economic development in the eighteenth and early nineteenth century, in contrast to the decline of most of the South—a fact that needs to be emphasized in order to understand the Portugal of those days.

From a demographic standpoint, the other interesting aspect was the almost complete absorption of Negroes and Jews into the white Christian population. By 1820 Portugal was practically all-white and all-Catholic, the end of the Inquisition causing no noticeable revival of Judaism. From then on, to the present, no ethnical or religious differentiations troubled Portuguese society.

In the economic sphere the complex structure of this epoch had a common denominator: trade with Brazil (see chapter 9). This trade produced most of the Crown revenues; it determined the coming of foreign vessels to Lisbon and other Portuguese ports as well as a flourishing network of foreign connections; it caused money to be plentiful and stable; it permitted the maintenance of surpluses in the commercial balance; and it allowed bountiful investments in property, building activities, art, and cultural manifestations. Yet the existence of Brazil and her overwhelming influence on the life of Portugal should not make us forget the reality and the growth of a Portuguese European economy, based upon agriculture, trade, and even the beginnings of a local industry.

The constant expansion of olive oil and wine production was fundamental in the upsurge of an agricultural economy. The war of independence had destroyed a great number of olive groves in Alentejo. With the return of peace (1668) trees were planted again and also in Beira Baixa, until then a very sparsely inhabited and unproductive province. Olive oil could be sold profitably to northern Europe, and exports in the late seventeenth century reached one-sixth to one-seventh of all the exports from the ports of Porto and Lisbon. Still more important was the change in landscape and local affluence that the new olive groves brought to Ribatejo, Beira, and part of Alentejo. As to wine, the vineyards expanded to cover extensive areas both in the mainland and in the Atlantic islands. Some unsuitable lands later had to be abandoned. The scattering of vineyards all over the country was comparable to wheat growing in the Middle Ages. The vineyards brought hitherto unknown prosperity to many areas of northern Portugal and supported a rise of population there. A new quality of wine, that of Porto (port-wine), produced along the upper Douro Valley and sold in that city, had its beginnings in the late seventeenth century.

But if wine led to an increase in revenues and population, it also caused the decline of other cultures, less profitable yet highly necessary. This happened with wheat and other crops (except maize) the area of which kept contracting while the population kept growing. The government of Pombal (1750–77) realized that severe measures had to be taken to teach the farmers a lesson. A number of vineyards planted in good soils for wheat were ordered to be uprooted and the fields sown with grain (1765). Yet the incident had few consequences and the grain deficit continued. Some 15–18 per cent of all the grain consumed in Portugal had to be imported from abroad. Only maize expanded its areas of production throughout the North and the North-west.

Among the new cultures introduced from America in the seventeenth century the potato was the most important. It took a long time for the new product to become familiar to farmers and consumers.

Throughout the eighteenth century potatoes began to be planted in large quantities in Northeastern Portugal, making up for grain scarcities. But they were not regularly consumed, being given often to animals rather than to people. Rice, too, had an economic beginning in the late 1700's but no great expansion until the 1840's.

The other enemy of grain production was stock raising, which may have developed throughout the eighteenth century. Cattle, sheep, mules, and pigs yielded excellent profits by supplying the urban centers with meat and the industrial nuclei with leather and wool, and by fostering exports to foreign countries. Indeed both the leather and the textile industries developed in the late 1600's and during most of the 1700's. Beira Baixa and Alentejo produced most of the wool.

Another part of Portugal's production derived from industry, the great innovation of the late seventeenth century. The economic doctrines of mercantilism favored the development of national crafts for export as a way of obtaining gold and balancing external trade. In Portugal a fundamental text for the economic policy of those days appeared in 1675: "Discourse on the Introduction of the Arts in the Realm" (*Discurso sobre a Introducção das Artes no Reyno*) written by Duarte Ribeiro de Macedo, ambassador to Paris and consequently in direct contact with French Colbertism which was then in its beginnings. Ribeiro de Macedo defended industry as being very important for the future of Portugal. His doctrine came at a time of deep economic crisis beginning in 1669 and stimulated several private initiatives which attempted to foster new sources of revenue within the country. The two finance secretaries (*vedores da fazenda*), the Count of Torre (later marquis of Fronteira) and the Count of Ericeira—who was appointed superintendent to the factories and manufactures of the kingdom—sketched out a plan of industrial growth, which included hiring foreign experts and artisans from France, England, Spain, and Venice; lending funds; and granting all sorts of privileges to the new factories. A glass industry was set up in Lisbon (1670–71); textile industries were created in Estremoz (1671–72), Lisbon (1677–79), and the regions of Covilhã, Fundão, and Tomar, in Beira (1671–81); and iron foundries rose in Lisbon, Tomar, and Figueiró dos Vinhos (from 1680 on with some starts before). To protect the new crafts the government enacted a number of laws prohibiting the wearing of several kinds of imported cloths, hats, ribbons, lace, bracelets, and the like (in 1677, 1686, 1688, 1690, 1698). In this way, some treaties of commerce which had been signed with foreign countries were not officially violated. Pottery, tiles, and glass were not to be imported from abroad. Shipbuilding, too, was fostered.

With the end of the economic crisis (1692) and the discovery of gold mines in Brazil (1693–95) harder times arrived for the newborn industries. Prosperity once more derived from the exports of wine, olive oil, sugar, and tobacco, while extra imports could be easily paid for in gold. Trade and agriculture went hand in hand again. The poor quality of many manufactured products, coupled with the prestige of imported goods, pushed the buyers to violate the law and scorn the "made-in-Portugal" items. The policy of "industrialization" had to be abandoned; Ericeira committed suicide and the Marquis of Fronteira completely changed his directives.

When the commercial boom slowed down, after 1712, another attempt to develop the industries took place. French and English capital, artisans, and techniques helped to build up new textile and glass manufactures in Lisbon and other places. A large iron foundry rose in Lisbon too. Other industrial activities included soap, paper, leather, glass, silk, gunpowder, and shipbuilding. But the results were generally poor, mostly because no real crisis had actually occurred. It was only under the government of Pombal that a more fruitful policy could be carried on. For eight years (1769–77), again in a period of depression, the government helped to set up hundreds of small factories for sugar refining, metallurgy, wool and cotton textiles, hats, pottery, clothing, paper, hardware, and glass. Most were established in Lisbon and Porto, but all over the country workshops were to be found, especially close to the sea. Adopting the same methods of protection as before (privileges in the import of raw materials, sales monopoly for a certain period of time, less taxation, and so on), Pombal's policy nonetheless introduced some new principles, such as using foreign immigration, giving up large industrial units, and overcoming (albeit only in a few cases) the corporation system. Only the cotton and silk manufactures, however, survived and prospered. With some exceptions, one can say that these industries had few export goals and simply tried to supply the home market and the colonies. They succeeded for a while, until the Industrial Revolution forced prices lower and lower and ruined most of the Portuguese industrial production, with British manufactures competing even in the Portuguese home markets. By 1805 Portuguese industrial exports to the colonies had gone down one-third, compared with the 1800 level. By 1820 only 27 per cent of the manufactured goods sent to the overseas provinces were of national origin. At home the situation was similar.

Meanwhile some vast "industrial complexes" had arisen in Portugal. The Royal Silk Factory (Real Fábrica das Sedas) in 1776 encompassed not only silk manufactures but also sealing-wax, steel files, lacquer, and stockings in a total of thirty units with more than 3,500 workers. In the same year a very up-to-date wool and cotton plant in Portalegre introduced the first "modern" machines from England. Several types of "jennies," "mule-jennies," and other mechanical devices entered Portugal in the 1770's, 1780's, and afterward. In 1811–13 (after the high point of Portuguese industry in those days had been reached and in a period of real industrial decadence) there were still more than 500 factories throughout the country, but 183 were considered to be outmoded, 8 had closed down, and 6 had just started their activities.

External trade passed through several phases of expansion and contraction with important results for Portugal's economy, one of which has just been mentioned. The great depression of 1669–92 was followed by a period of expansion (1693–1714), Portugal having benefited from the War of the League of Augsburg (1688–97) and the War of the Spanish Succession (1702–13). When the Treaty of Utrecht brought peace to Europe again, trade declined for a while but not to the extent of a crisis. A new recovery followed and, with fluctuations, external trade flourished until the great depression of 1766–79. Another phase of expansion marked the next twenty-five to thirty years. Then came the French Invasion (1807) and the Peninsular war from 1808 to 1814. It brought about a period of depression continuing to 1826, with a deep crisis in 1808–13. All these crises had their counterparts in the international conjuncture. In any of them Portuguese commerce with the foreign countries depended mostly on her colonies. Brazil, Asia, and Africa together supplied three-fourths of Portugal's exports (sugar, tobacco, cotton, slaves, spices, diamonds, currency). And to Brazil, India, and Africa went three-fourths of the country's imports from abroad (see chapter 9).

Yet Portugal alone had much to sell and to purchase. The chief product of the eighteenth century was undoubtedly wine, which brought prosperity to a part of the country but also enchained Portugal to England, her largest wine buyer. Wine meant, for both export needs and English purposes, port wine, i.e., wine produced in the Douro Valley, artificially transformed in the town of Porto, stored there and thence exported (67 per cent of all the Portuguese wine sent to England in 1704–12 was port-wine). The wine was largely in the hands of English merchants and firms, a good many of which were established in Portugal (mainly in Porto). It suddenly increased when the War of the League of Augsburg closed the French ports to the English, compelling them to look for other areas of supply: Portugal and Spain. The Dutch had already been forced to buy southern wines because of France's economic discrimination against them. The figures from 1678 to 1807 show the tremendous rise of wine exports: from a yearly average of 632 barrels (pipas) in 1678–87, to 7,668 in 1688–97, 9,644 in 1708–17, 17,692 in 1718–27, 19,388 in 1758–67, 40,055 in 1788–97, and 44,487 in 1798–1807. After 1807 exports declined drastically, to 26,591 pipas in 1808–17 and 24,985 in 1818–27. But among British wine imports the position of Portugal steadily improved. In 1692 Portuguese and Spanish wines were almost equal in Britain's imports. From 1696 to 1712 wine imported from Portugal rose to ten times the amount from France and one-third more than that from Spain. But wine—Port wine and other kinds—was not sent to Britain alone. Other North European countries such as Holland, Germany, and the Scandinavian countries were recipients too, as well as Brazil and the African possessions.

Portuguese exports also included olive oil, salt, leather, and fruit, sent to northern Europe and to the overseas provinces. In time of war even wool, salted fish, and some other less abundant goods could find buyers abroad.

From Europe Portugal continued to purchase an immense variety of manufactured goods. Textiles always had first place, with England the largest exporter: in 1731 Britain supplied Portugal with four times more fabrics and clothing than her closest competitor, France. Early in the eighteenth century favorable relations between Portugal and England * led to the signing of a famous treaty, the Treaty of Methuen (1703), according to which English woolen cloths and other woolen manufactures would be admitted at all times in Portugal, regardless of the sumptuary Pragmatical Sanctions forbidding them, while all Portuguese wines would enter England paying the same duties as the French ones. This treaty confirmed Portugal's position as a large-scale wine exporter and backed its growth at least to the end of the eighteenth century.

Other fabrics arrived from France (silk and many luxury articles) and from Holland (linen), while manufactured goods of all kinds, made of iron, copper and other metals, were imported from several northern European countries. Wheat and other food items came from France, England, Germany, and Spain. Some iron was imported from northern Spain too. Late in the eighteenth century new economic areas started trading with Portugal: Russia sent iron, wheat, timber, and linen, in exchange for sugar, wine, and fruit; with North America, also, some important commerce began in the late 1700's.

It is interesting to evaluate Portugal's external trade in terms of her trade balance. The great depression of 1669–92 signaled the start of permanent deficits, which increased with the discovery of the gold mines in Brazil and the consequent abundance of money. Only in the 1680's was there a favorable situation owing to the War of the League of Augsburg and Portugal's neutrality. Throughout the first half of the eighteenth century Portugal imported much more than she exported, the difference being paid in gold. The figures for trade with England (by far Portugal's leading partner) show an average yearly deficit for 1705–15 of £389,000, rising to £441,000 (1716–30), £769,000 (1731–50), £825,741 (1750–54), £1,044,081 (1755–59), £1,015,660 (1760) and £1,061,049 (1761). This situation began to change after 1761: Pombal's economic policy led to both an increase in the country's exports and a decline in her imports. The depression

* They were close allies in the War of the Spanish Succession; trade between them had reached a higher level than ever, England seeing in Portugal a very useful buyer for her textiles, Portugal realizing that her industrial policy had failed and seeing the English wine market as a way of developing her external sales and helping to balance her commercial deficit.

of 1766–79 very much reduced trade in both, helping to make sales and purchases more even. After 1761 the figures were £537,415 (1762–66), £250,607 (1767–71), £233,372 (1772–76), and £203,637 (1777–79). In 1780 the miracle happened: for the first time in almost a century Portugal sold to England goods totaling £41,012 more than she bought from England.

This trend continued to 1789: deficits were only £269,745 in 1781–84 and £143,092 in 1785–89. In 1790–92 there were surpluses each year (an average of almost £200,000), then a deficit again in 1793, followed by surpluses in both 1794 and 1795. Clearly things were changing in favor of Portugal. After 1796 we have the total figures for all of the external trade. They show a constant if irregular surplus to 1809 with only two exceptions, in 1797 and 1799. And most probably this had been the situation since 1786.

What had changed? On the one hand, there was the rise of Portuguese industry, as mentioned before; on the other, the increase in the output of certain agricultural products such as cotton and rice for both export and national consumption. Finally, the international situation meant harder times for the North American, the West Indian, and the East Indian trades. Rebellions and wars benefited Portugal for a while and restored to Lisbon some of its former importance as an international entrepôt.

But the war reached Portugal too, and in a catastrophic way. The Napoleonic invasions of 1807–11, the opening of the Brazilian trade to the English, and, still worse, the fabulous rise of the English textile industry brought about an increasing deficit for Portuguese external commerce, with problems difficult to solve. From 1810 on, figures show a return to the old days before 1761. In cruzados the deficit went up from 11 million in 1810 to 79 million in 1811, then 59 and 52 million in 1812–13. Things became better when the war ended, but external trade was still unbalanced at around the 9 million level on the eve of the great revolution of 1820.

Commercial and industrial developments greatly depended upon a conscious economic policy, which was generally followed in the late seventeenth and during all of the eighteenth century. The setting up of chartered companies and monopolies for both trade and industry, which had started before (see chapters 6 and 7), characterized the sev-

eral governments of Portugal in that period. During the depression
of 1669–92 the government chartered three companies for trading in
Cape Verde and Guinea, Brazil (Pará and Maranhão), and India. They
all languished and were finally dissolved when prosperity returned
again. Two other companies for the Gulf of Guinea and Macao trades
appeared early in the eighteenth century, but did not last long. It was
Pombal's administration that more consciously and in the mercantile
field adopted the monopoly principle, entrusting trade to chartered
companies. The Asian, Brazilian, and African commerce was all subject to the monopolistic doctrine: the Company for the Eastern Trade,
1753 to 1760; the Company of Grão Pará and Maranhão, 1755 to 1778;
the General Company of Pernambuco and Paraíba, 1756 to 1780; the
Company for the Trade of the Mujaos and the Macuas (Mozambique),
in the 1760's. (On their rise and failure, see chapter 9.) For Portugal
proper two important companies were set up: the Company for the
Agriculture of the Alto Douro Wines (1756) and the General Company
for the Royal Fisheries in the Kingdom of Algarve (1773). The former
aimed at protecting the good quality of the port wine against an un-
restrained growth of wine production and competition. It gathered together a lobby of large producers from the Douro Valley and exporters from Porto and was granted numerous privileges, for example
on exports to Brazil and elsewhere. The amount of wine produced
annually, as well as price-fixing, was among its goals. Despite strong
opposition of the small producers and traders which led to popular
riots in Porto (1757), the company endured and brought about some
important benefits to the port wine industry. The General Company
for the Royal Fisheries in the Kingdom of Algarve primarily controlled the tuna, corvine, and sardine fisheries in the South and was
also relatively successful.

In the industrial field special charters were granted to the Royal
Factory of Silk and to the National Rope-Factory (Cordoaria Nacional)
which converted the companies into monopolistic organizations. Circumstances permitting, these companies were certainly useful in promoting production and export, and in organizing trade. It was partly
because of them that the Portuguese balance of trade showed a surplus
after 1761. When prosperity returned after the depression of 1766–79,
most were found useless and abolished. But their mission had been

accomplished and Portugal's economic situation was immensely improved. An important measure to foster trade was also the new regime of free circulation of products within the country, which Pombal decreed in 1774.

Until the late seventeenth century, very little gold and silver had been found in Brazil. And as the precious metals from Africa were also scarce, Portugal had to rely almost exclusively on the gold and silver imports from Spain (i.e., from Spanish America, by way of Cadiz) to pay off the deficit of her balance of trade. In Spain, however, the gold and silver outputs went down after the late 1660's, measures being successively adopted to stop the gold flow out of the country. In 1686, money was debased 25 per cent. Largely enchained by the Spanish currency, Portugal had to reform hers too. The mark of gold went up from 82,500 réis (a corruption of the plural reais) to 85,333 (1677), then to 98,700 (1688), while the mark of silver rose from 6,000 to 6,360 réis (1688). By the same time (the acts of 1685–86) new coinage techniques were introduced, with better results in the general aspect of the coins. An outside milled edge prevented clipping, a very widespread practice resulting from the scarcity of money.

Debasement and the reduction of clipping helped to make the situation better for a while. Coins became more abundant and currency imports from Spain went on. But only the discovery of gold mines in Brazil could solve the problem. In 1699 Lisbon received the first 514 kg. of gold, sent directly from Rio. Gold output increased in the following years: almost 2,000 kg. in 1701, more than 4,406 in 1703, 14,500 in 1712. After a decrease in the averages of 1713–19, 25,000 kg. arrived in 1720. However, this was an exceptional year; afterward gold quantities were always below the 20,000 level. In the 1740's and early 1750's averages of 14,000 to 16,000 kg. could still be reached, but then the decline was definite: less than 1,500 kg. in the 1760's, a little more than 1,000 in the 1770's and 1780's. And the curve continued to bend down to almost nothing in the early nineteenth century. It must not be forgotten that the always rampant smuggling would make all these figures much higher.

With so much gold for nearly a century and with a prosperous balance of trade afterward, it is not surprising that currency could remain strong and with very few changes in its value. The mark of gold rose to 102,400 réis in 1722 but suffered no further alterations to 1822. The value of the mark of silver was changed to 7,000 réis in 1734, then to 7,500 in 1747 but that was all. Fabulous coins in weight, width, and design were minted, especially during the reign of John V (1706–50): the dobrão of 24,000 réis, weighing more than fifty grams; the half dobrão of 12,000 réis; the dobra of 12,800 réis; the peça of 6,400; the moeda (4,800); the half peça (3,200); the half moeda (2,400); and the escudo (1,600). In total amounts the gold from Brazil went much beyond all the gold Portugal had ever got from Africa, together with the Spanish gold from America in the sixteenth century. Most of it was sent to England, Holland, Genoa, and other European areas. It stimulated the whole European economy and particularly England's.

Late in the eighteenth century the decline in the gold output plus the expansion of trade and the growth of government duties led to a loan of 12 million cruzados, in 1796–97, at 5 per cent and 6 per cent interest. Government bonds were issued in the value of 50,000 or more réis, which might circulate as currency. Shortly afterward the bonds were imposed as compulsory currency (although with a discount tax), which means that paper money was instituted in Portugal. In 1797–99 bond denominations included 1,200, 2,400, 5,000, 6,400, 10,000, 12,800, 20,000, 50,000, and 100,000 réis. Up to 1807, government bonds totaled 11,356,589,800 réis or 28,391,474 cruzados.

Europe's price trend pointed down during most of the 1600's. The war with Spain (1640–68), however, curbed that trend a little in Portugal and converted the sloop into a plateau with a few rises. When peace returned, the general tendency asserted itself again. Until 1690–93 most prices remained stable or declined, with some exceptions. The commercial expansion of the late seventeenth century brought about a rise to 1712–13, then a new drop or a plateau, to 1728–29. In Lisbon, an almude (16.8 liters) of olive oil, which cost 1,360 réis in 1668, went down to an average of 1,210 réis (1669–78), then up to 1,397 (1679–88), 1,529 (1689–98), 2,088 (1699–1713), and down again to 1,721 (1714–29). Also in Lisbon, an arrátel (one pound) of rice hovered around the 25 réis average till 1690; it went up to 35–40 in 1691–1713, then down again to 30 or less in the following years. Salt, the price of which had not changed for export purposes between 1649 and 1690 (1,490 réis each moio), doubled and tripled in cost afterward, reaching 7,000 réis around 1709, then declining to 3,350 in 1713, and to 3,000 in 1717.

From 1730 on the general trend was up again, to about 1815–17. It corresponded to the great expansion of Europe, to the Industrial Revolution, to the opening of new markets everywhere, to the abundance of gold, to the introduction of paper money. There were of course cycles of decline and depression throughout those eighty-five years, but the tendency to inflation always returned. In Lisbon, one bushel (alqueire) of wheat nearly always rose in cost during that period: from an average of 295 réis in 1728–31, 320 (1732–39), 345 (1747–52), 396 (1757–58), 440 (1767–71), 469 (1772–73), 480 (1789–92), 587 (1793–96), 841 (1800–2), 994 (1808–9), and 1,034 (1810–15).

From 1789 on the rise was drastic; it affected most products, along with many salaries. Olive oil prices in Lisbon rose from 1,410 réis each almude to 2,140 (1735), 2,380 (1742), 2,530 (1771), 2,660 (1789), 3,450 (1793), 4,000 (1797), 4,570 (1800), 5,950 (1805), 6,070 (1812) and 7,600 (1817). As to rice, the 30 réis level was kept stable or slightly increased to the 1770's, then changed upward to a top of 40 (1778), 44 (1785), 49 (1797), 58 (1800), 68 (1801), 75 (1808), and 84 (1812).

Public finance experienced some structural changes: on the one side, revenues and expenditures respectively derived from and were aimed at different points; on the other, reforms of administration brought about a deeper knowledge of the finance system and the beginning of regular budgeting, with a consequent awareness of annual deficits and surpluses. Both revenues and expenditures increased tremendously. An eighteenth-century state spent twice as much as a hundred years before. A despotic state of the late 1700's, with its complex and all-pervasive bureaucratic machine, spent still more. External affairs were extremely costly in periodic wars and continuous diplomatic activity. Revenues, however, never ceased to grow. The eighteenth century was characterized by affluence resulting from several sources, which permitted a rise in taxation and a possibility of meeting the expenses without too many problems. Nonetheless, external and internal debts necessarily rose and bankruptcies took place here and there.

In 1681 Portugal's public revenues including the overseas were no more than 4 million cruzados, a sum much below the high peaks of the early seventeenth century even if one considers the debasement of the currency. Duties on the sea traffic entered with 35 per cent followed by the duties on tobacco, with 17 per cent. Taxation on internal traffic and commerce produced less than 9 per cent. On the whole, almost 40 per cent of the revenues depended upon the sea trade with the rest of Europe.

In 1716 public revenues had risen to more than 9 million cruzados, a figure which was now very close to the prosperity of the old times and twice the 1681 amount (money had again been debased). The intensity of the traffic with Europe, the gold from Brazil, and the rise in taxation at home were responsible for this increase. Duties on sea trade had declined to some 32 per cent but tobacco rose to almost 20 per cent, taxation on internal traffic and commerce to nearly 17 per cent, and the Crown's rights on gold entered with about 9 per cent of the whole amount. Imposed on the meat and the wine sold, the new taxes represented the first violation of the decision taken in *cortes*, in 1641, according to which no taxation whatsoever should be enacted without popular consent. Contrary to popular belief, it must be emphasized that such taxes, along with the rise in the tobacco trade and in other sources of revenue, always produced much more for the state than the Brazilian gold.

Until 1808 total revenues continued to increase: 15 million cruzados yearly on the average for the period 1762 to 1776, 28 million in 1805, with no currency debasement at all. Although less powerful in military resources, the country was undoubtedly richer in the early nineteenth century than ever before. Maritime traffic with Europe based upon metropolitan and colonial merchandise; maritime traffic with America, Asia, and Africa; Brazilian gold; the development of trade and industry at home—all this could bring about a considerable rise in the public revenues and permit a reasonable situation for the public finance.

If expenditures tended to keep pace with revenues, deficits were still not chronic and many administrations could boast a balanced budget. There were some well-known deficits, as in 1769, 1770, and 1771, the last one reaching more than 1½ million cruzados. Nonetheless

Pombal ended his government leaving a surplus of nearly as much in the public treasury.

The old funded and unfunded debts were kept undiminished. The governments of both Pedro II and John V, in the beginning of his reign, were forced to obtain frequent public loans. The end of the war period brought some financial peace to the administration. Despite several loans from individuals and firms public debt was kept at much the same level throughout most of the reigns of John V and José I. After the late 1780's the treasury required more and more money (particularly for the war and for reforms) and had to adopt extraordinary measures for that purpose. Paper money gave the state an extra 12 million cruzados in 1796–97 and more in the following years. Stamped paper was introduced in 1797. But the Peninsular war put an end to the eighteenth-century prosperity. Revenues declined as both external and internal trade was paralyzed for long periods. The Portuguese monopoly of Brazil ended; exports and imports went down. In 1819 the state got only 24 million cruzados, in 1820 less than 20 million. Expenditures in time of peace rose to a yearly average of more than 24 million in 1815–19, having been much higher during the war years. A new loan of 4 million was decided on in 1817.

Financial administrative reform had been accomplished under Pombal. A Royal Treasury (Real Erário) was founded in 1761, with supervision of all public accounts, modern methods of control, and greater centralization and efficiency. Late in the eighteenth century public debt was also reorganized and placed under the direction of a special Junta.

The late seventeenth and the eighteenth century were periods of growing centralization and assertion of the royal power throughout Europe. This was also true in Portugal. Every institution which tended to weaken that power declined and was abolished. This happened with the *cortes*. After a brief interlude in the mid-1600's, they disappeared altogether. Prince Pedro summoned them in 1674 to have his daughter sworn in as heiress to the throne. However, when the *cortes* attempted some interference in royal administration, he disbanded them. They met again in 1679 to discuss the marriage of the princess and then, for the last time, in 1697–98 to have his son John sworn in as future king. Both times the *cortes* were meek servants of the royal wishes. In the first years of his reign John V (1706–50) still mentioned the possibility of summoning the *cortes* but did nothing about it. On the contrary, new taxation was introduced without popular approval. Neither José I nor Maria I nor John VI assembled any *cortes*.

Another symptom of concentration of power was the decline of government by councils. The high point had been reached under John IV and Pedro II, when power was actually shared between the king (with his secretaries) and councils of nobles. Under John V this began to change, government belonging more and more to the cabinet, while the councils' powers faded away. In 1736 a government reform vested more power in the secretaries, whose traditional names were changed with a corresponding assignment of functions: secretary of state of the interior (Reino), secretary of state of foreign affairs and war, and secretary of state of the navy and overseas provinces. The former controlled the cabinet, acting as a true prime minister. This three-man government presided over by the king resisted any enlargement up to the late eighteenth century, when a fourth member was appointed to administer public finance (Fazenda). The council, known as Junta dos Três Estados, was suppressed in 1813. Although several Juntas were set up throughout the late eighteenth and the early nineteenth century for finance, navy, censorship, industry, education, and other matters, their purposes were purely technical or administrative, and their dependency upon the secretaries of state was complete.

For purposes of general administration and justice, the kingdom of Portugal and Algarve was divided, as before, into six provinces subdivided into *comarcas*. The number of the latter, however, greatly increased: 27 in 1641, 44 at the beginning of the nineteenth century. This meant growth of population and also a more complex and perfected system of administration. Between the province and the *comarca* a new unit appeared, the *provedoria,* of which 25 or 26 existed in the late 1700's. Ecclesiastical reforms had also taken place, with the institution of five new bishoprics: Beja in 1770, Penafiel in 1770 (eliminated shortly afterward), Pinhel in 1770, Castelo Branco in 1771, and Aveiro in 1774. This new diocesan division implied a complete reshuffling in the country's ecclesiastical framework, with civil consequences as well.

The most important reforms took place in the areas of justice and finance. In 1760 Pombal created the office of General Intendant of the Court and Kingdom Police, along with complete reform of the police system. This reform not only gave Portugal an efficient and modern police organization to cope effectively with rising crime and banditry, but also instituted an aggressive state police with powers to arrest anyone who dared to oppose or was thought suspect by the government. A fundamental element in the new idea of the eighteenth-century state, the police powers continued to grow: in 1780 the prerogatives of the police were enlarged and in 1801 a Royal Guard of Police was instituted. Intendant Pina Manique, who headed the Police for more than twenty years (1780–1803), became famous for his persecution of liberals and partisans of French and American political ideologies, along with the order and the discipline he managed to impose in the country especially in Lisbon. Yet Pina Manique's actions and competence went much farther than that and brought about some excellent results: public illumination in Lisbon was started in 1780; in the same year, the Intendant founded a Casa Pia (literally, "Pious House") for the sheltering and education of young orphans of poor families. To arrest anyone became much easier after Pombal's laws (1751–53) and up to the liberal revolution of 1820. The whole judicial system was reinforced by increasing the means not only for judging but also for repressing before trial. This repressive policy went along with the concept of state despotism.

Another fundamental reform derived from a law of 1790, which theoretically abolished seignorial justice. In the old *coutos* and *honras,* as well as in the donataries, the lords still possessed some feudal rights concerning jurisdiction and the entrance of royal officials. The reform of 1790 suppressed all those oddities, establishing general law everywhere and unifying the administration of justice.

After the restoration of independence the nobility had been restructured and succeeded in taking over a share of the government responsibilities (see chapter 6). King and councils ruled the country in relative harmony. The "election" of John IV, the regency, then the deposition of his eldest son, Afonso VI, and the passing of both throne and heredity to the latter's brother Pedro, required the support of the nobles and their direct interference in the Crown affairs.

In the late 1600's the great landowners were firmly in control, and the economic prosperity after the depression of 1669–92 gave them the means of enlarging their wealth and consequently their power. As always in Portugal, the nobles competed with the bourgeoisie and the king in trade, thus helping to keep a Portuguese middle class from developing. Until about 1720 this state of things underwent few changes. There was the usual creation of new titles but also the extinction of other ones by death or promotion. By the end of Pedro's rule the number of title-bearers had only increased by three, after the creation of nineteen and the abolition of sixteen. Yet there had been a gradual renewal of the upper and middle nobility, which shows its strength and social resilience. This fact, along with the doctrines and the circumstances of those days, caused the division of the nobility into two large groups: one, tied to the past, seeing themselves in terms of blood and lineage, defending the old methods of government and economic activity, stressing the role of landed property and agriculture; the other, more progressive and open-minded, accepting the promotion to nobility of bureaucrats, men of letters, and even bourgeoisie, caring less for lineage, interested in promoting trade and industry and sharing in the profits. England and Holland set the pattern for this second group, while France and Spain appealed to the first.

John V (1706–50) could enhance the role of the Crown, with an enlarged bureaucracy and intelligentsia. The rise in taxation and the Brazilian gold gave the king the means of controlling the nobles by way of allowances and gifts while asserting his power over everyone. No wonder, then, that the old nobility started its decline and was forced to accept the rising competition of bureaucrats, men of letters, and, later, rich traders. In John's lifetime twenty-four new titles were created but twenty-two others disappeared. After 1720 the number of title grants constantly declined: 5 in 1721–30, 4 in 1731–40, 2 in 1741–50. Several were actually nothing but honorary titles given to widows and ladies of the court with no transmission to their heirs. At the same time a good many nobles, discontent with the "new times" and resentful of their declining role (despite the overseas offices and affluence), left the court and retired to their mansions in the country, which the agricultural development made prosperous. In this way the country gentry strengthened their positions—particularly in the

North—while the *noblesse de robe,* allied to some financiers, the pure bureaucrats, and the intellectuals, rose in Lisbon and in the administration.

The final act in this process of change took place in José's reign (1750–77) and under Pombal's rule. The complexity of the state's functions enhanced the role of the bureaucrats and required special preparation for the administrative offices (including diplomacy) which the nobles no longer had. The economy also needed specialists, i.e., people who would devote all their energies and knowledge to trade, industry, or finance. Trade was officially declared a noble, necessary, and profitable profession (1770), and traders were allowed to institute entailed estates. Regular education became more necessary. The adjustment of the old aristocracy to the new realities would take time; meanwhile their political and economic role constantly deteriorated. The two groups that still maintained a dangerous amount of power and prestige, the country gentry and the nobility engaged in overseas affairs and offices, were persecuted and greatly weakened by Pombal and his new people who ruled the country. In this way a class leveling could be achieved, the ideal of eighteenth-century despotism. The renewal of the aristocracy during José's reign was almost complete: in twenty-seven years of rule, 23 new titles were granted, while 23 existing ones disappeared. It is highly revealing to show this process of renewal by hierarchies: two dukes were created (and two disappeared), seven marquis (against five), twelve counts (against fourteen), two viscounts (against one), and no barons (against one). José I and Pombal instilled new blood in about one-third of the nobility: of some 70 title-bearers in 1750, they renewed 23.

José's death and Pombal's downfall did nothing to change things. On the contrary, the decline of the old, privileged aristocrats was speeded up and the rise of the bourgeoisie (in a general sense) continued as before. In 1790 donataries were abolished and with them the most important functions of administration and jurisdiction reserved to the nobles. Title granting became a simple reward, given to anyone, regardless of lineage. A title inflation resulted, particularly during John's rule (1792–1826). From 70 in 1777, the number of title-bearers went up to 78 (1791), 85 (1801), 104 (1811), and 155 (1825). Thus, in less than fifty years the number of nobles had risen 121 per cent with a positive balance of 85 new titles, almost ten times more than in the century before (1670–1777).

For the clergy the period we are dealing with was one of continuous and rapid decline. Among the lower classes its prestige and its power remained much the same. But among the upper classes, particularly the intellectuals, the bureaucrats, or the nobles, the influence of the clergy waned. New times had come. The spirit of the eighteenth century was one of doubt, impiety, and atheism. The clergy itself became closer to the lay world and abandoned much of its religious discipline and belief. With the strengthening of the royal power and centralization, ecclesiastical privileges and prerogatives were constantly curbed, while the greater influence of the church led to a love of luxury and the good life on the part of its clerics.

Although the number of new religious orders that arose might lead us to believe that faith and sacrifice remained intact, those orders were only a desperate reaction against increasing worldliness. They never had many affiliates and their historical importance was minor. The French Capuchins (called in Portugal Barbadinhos) and the Mercenaries of the late seventeenth century, as well as the Lazarists, the Minims of St. Vincent of Paul, the Ursulines, the Maríans, the Conceptionists, and a few others created in the eighteenth century, never spread widely as did many former orders nor did they exert any influence in the country. Some other orders of Portuguese foundation (the Congregation of Oliveira, the Apostolic Missionaries, the Barefeet Paulists) also met with little enthusiasm.

Among the old orders, too, the growth was small. Only the Barefoot Augustinians had some success and a number of new monasteries. Fewer than ninety new religious houses appeared between 1668 and mid-eighteenth century. After 1782 no more orders were instituted. The religious population of the monasteries declined, many being reduced to a handful of monks or nuns. But at the same time, as their wealth was increasing (a result of the economic expansion of the country and of the Brazilian gold), so was the number of nonreligious dependents in the monasteries. This fact makes it difficult for us to ascertain the exact structure of the regular clergy in the eighteenth and early nineteenth century. We only know that the total number of residents in the monasteries rose: in 1628–30 there were in Portugal some 450 religious houses with 7,400 people living in them; a century later the number of monasteries reached 477 but we do not know their population (probably around the 10,000 level); in 1826 there were 577 monasteries with a total of 12,980 people (7,000 men and 5,980 women), yet the number of monks, friars, and nuns was probably not above 3,500.

In the meantime some hundreds of Jesuits had been expelled from the kingdom (1759) and their society dissolved by Pope Clement XIV. Because they were so wealthy, powerful, and pervasive (see chapters 6 and 7), the Jesuits aroused the antagonism of most people. The other religious orders hated them, and so did most of the upper secular clergy. They had shown themselves unable to keep up with the development of education and science, and their intellectual prestige no longer was what it had been. Their continued strength made them rely too much on the past, with no attention to the birth of new forces. Their diplomatic activity was weak, because they could hardly believe that their might was close to an end. Yet their existence as a state within the state was incompatible with the despotic monarchies of the eighteenth century. Pombal's government ousted the Jesuits, and Pombal's external policy decisively contributed to their expulsion from France (1764) and Spain (1767), and to the dissolution of the order (1773).

A similar thing happened to the Inquisition. The Inquisition was possible as a royal tribunal or when the royal power was not despotic. It had no chances of survival afterward. In Portugal (as in Spain) the Inquisition had become another state within the state, and a formidable one. Throughout the late seventeenth and the first half of the eighteenth century it continued to persecute "Jews," "heretics," and others, i.e., middle-class people with a high percentage of businessmen, traders, and artisans. From 1684 to 1747, 4,672 persons were sentenced and 146 burned at the stake. This meant a little less ferocity than before, because the average number of sentences and deaths per year went down to 74 and 2.3 respectively, whereas it had formerly reached 136 and 10. Yet one must be careful when appraising the action of the Inquisition in terms of averages, because periods of mildness were often followed by periods of unbelievable ferocity. Thus, in 1704–13, 1,392 people were sentenced (139 a year) and 17 executed; in 1724–33,

UPPER LEFT: *Marquis of Pombal: sketch by Joaquim Carneiro da Silva, late 18th century, Museu Nacional de Arte Antiga, Lisbon.* BELOW: *New and old Lisbon, after the 1755 earthquake: adopted plan for the city rebuilding.* ABOVE: *Battle of Buçaco, 1810: contemporary engraving.*

22 people died among 1,070 condemnations; and in 1734–43 the number of executions went up to 51. The last years of the Inquisition as an independent body were terrible: 1,107 sentences in 1750–59 with 18 burnings. But this late ferocity was indeed a death sentence for the Inquisition itself. Like the Jesuits, the Inquisition had been overtaken by the times and was incapable of understanding and adjusting to the changes. In Western Europe in the eighteenth century people might be killed for political reasons but not persecuted for religious or moral reasons. Throughout sophisticated Europe Portugal was despised and looked upon with horror because of the Inquisition. In 1769 Pombal felt strong enough to destroy it as an independent tribunal and converted the Inquisition into a royal court entirely dependent upon the government. As inquisitor-general he appointed his own brother, the layman Paulo de Carvalho. The distinction between Old Christians and New Christians had been abolished (act of 1768, renewed in 1773) and all discrimination based upon blood ceased. Public autos-da-fé disappeared along with the death penalty according to the new regulation of the Inquisition, enacted in 1774 (the last victim had been a Jesuit priest burned in 1761). Instead of a religious body punishing in the name of God, the Inquisition became simply a political tribunal, punishing in the name of the king.

The secular clergy prospered as long as it remained subservient to the king's wishes. John V very much increased the affluence and prestige of the Portuguese Church, by means of gifts to the Pope, who granted him whatever he liked. The archbishop of Lisbon was made a patriarch and a cardinal (1716, 1737). Important privileges and allowances enhanced the wealth and the pomp of the Church in Portugal, particularly around the king. Five new bishoprics were created in 1770–74. Yet all this pomp and affluence brought about worldliness and lack of independence. The clergy became entirely dependent on the royal favor. Cardinals, archbishops, bishops, canons, deans, and others formed a numerous Church aristocracy little different from the upper nobility. High Church offices were reserved to the nobles, as before. Among the 156 bishops active between 1668 and 1820, more than four-fifths belonged to the aristocracy. Indeed the clergy continued to accept and promote the second-born sons of the nobility, who had no property of their own, and to discriminate against those who came from humbler origins.

Little has been done on analysis of the bourgeois groups. Foreign traders, settled in Lisbon and in Porto (particularly after the rise of the wine trade), controlled most, or at least the most profitable, of the trade with Europe. They too helped prevent the development of a Portuguese upper bourgeoisie as well as the establishment of "modern" credit institutions like banks. Some New Christians and some Jews settled far from Portugal dared to vie with the foreign traders, but on the whole the situation for Portuguese big business was not a favorable one throughout the late seventeenth and much of the eighteenth century. Moreover, the few existing large traders focused their attention almost exclusively on overseas affairs, lacking the ability or interest to divert their capital to any foreign traffic.

Nearly all over Portugal was, nonetheless, a petty bourgeoisie of traders and artisans. They controlled practically all the internal currents of traffic as well as coastal maritime trade. They also had a share in the overseas business. Participating in fairs and markets, dealing with all kinds of merchandise and every class of society, linking cities with countryside and peasants with bureaucrats and nobles, retaining many archaic forms of commerce (such as trade in kind as well as in money), the petty bourgeoisie were numerous and active. They had suffered little from the competition of foreigners and continued to multiply as general trade expanded. Opposed to modern initiatives, afraid of bigness, and hostile to all forms of organization, they were generally poor or of only moderate means. They were unenterprising, collectively weak, unaware of themselves as a class, and entirely dependent upon the nobility, the bureaucracy, and the Church, of whom they were the clients.

Throughout the eighteenth century some drastic changes occurred in this picture. An upper bourgeoisie arose because of a number of circumstances in the reign of John V and of José. More allowances for the nobles and more jobs for them in Brazil and India partly diverted the aristocracy from trade. The setting up of the Brazilian trade monopolies, the government policy of fostering companies and protecting investments, the rise of trade with northern Europe, and above all the general expansion of long-distance trade itself (tobacco, cotton, wine, salt, gold, etc.) gave wider scope for the Portuguese, enabling them to develop and strengthen their positions. By the late 1700's the situation of the upper bourgeoisie had very much changed from a hundred years earlier. If the foreigners still controlled most of the external traffic, the rise of trade itself had promoted the Portuguese bourgeoisie to a significant role.

Still more interesting from a social standpoint was the beginning of a practical alliance between the upper and the petty bourgeoisie, i.e., the dissociation between the lower ranks of the traders on one side and the nobility or clergy on the other. Such an alliance meant for the latter (i.e., the petty bourgeoisie) a transference of allegiance; and for the former (i.e., the upper bourgeoisie) a promise of protection. Stronger, backed by the state, and asserting itself for the first time as a class, the upper bourgeoisie was now in a condition of having its own dependents (the petty bourgeoisie). However, this process—the change of dependency from the nobility to the upper bourgeoisie—lasted for a long time and it would be totally wrong to consider it finished or largely accomplished before 1820.

In the early nineteenth century there were in Portugal some 80,000 traders and 130,000 people engaged in some specialized craft (of the latter, 20 per cent lived in Lisbon). The merchant class was asserting itself more and more. The state and the businessmen worked together trying to organize and discipline the mercantile framework (for instance, by fostering larger companies), and to give an efficient form to overseas trade and urban markets. A sort of definition of bourgeois had been achieved, free from the traditional, class connotation. Mostly in Lisbon and Porto a small group of rich traders was definitely made strongly competitive with their foreign colleagues, and desired further power and influence. Some of them had already joined the aristocracy by means of nobilitation, which Prince-Regent John was particularly eager to grant.

A part of this bourgeoisie was not directly engaged in commerce (as we generally understand the word), although its prosperity depended upon sales to the urban centers. This was a group of large or medium landowners, scattered throughout the country, but especially in the South (Alentejo and Estremadura), where holdings were much larger than in the North. Whereas most of those large land-owners continued to be aristocrats (or clergymen), some were not, and their number continued to grow after Pombal's days. Many traders and bureaucrats, following an ancient tradition, liked to buy land, to invest part of their capital in real estate, to which they sometimes retired or where they spent a part of their time. All these landowners had direct contact with the big dealers in the nearest town and in Lisbon, to whom they sold their wheat, their wine, their olive oil, or their wool.

Among the lower classes, the role played by the artisans should be emphasized too. The development of industry accompanied the rise in population and its needs. More craftsmen were necessary, and their number very much increased throughout the eighteenth and the early nineteenth century. Many foreign artisans also came to Portugal and stayed there for good, thus strengthening the workers' ranks. As a social group, however, the artisans were either the clients of the aristocracy or the dependents of the upper bourgeoisie. Some worked for the state, which placed them in the condition of lower civil servants. Slavery gradually disappeared, as the price of slaves rose and the traffic to America went up. Under Pombal, slavery was abolished on the mainland of Portugal (1761).

To conclude this brief analysis of the social groups, a word on the army (including the navy). As a social group, the army started to rise throughout the eighteenth century, when it was organized as a permanent body with definite ranks and promotions. Instead of being just another attribute of the aristocrats, the role of commanding began to require some special qualifications and a proper curriculum. In short, to be an officer became a profession. Officers planned fortifications and public buildings, supervised the setting up of new industries, or studied how to bring water to a city: officers were, in other words, the technicians of those days. In the eighteenth and the early nineteenth century, most officers still belonged to the aristocracy. But some came from humbler origins, namely the bourgeoisie and the bureaucracy. As members of a growing body, whose part in society never stopped developing, army officers began to have a social consciousness of their own and a sense of closeness to other "modern" groups such as the bureaucrats and the traders. Together with the former they represented the elite of that new rising bourgeois class, which would bring such a drastic change to the country as it leaned more heavily upon the money of the traders.

ENLIGHTENMENT

It is customary to draw a parallel between that vast body of principles and actions known as the Enlightenment and the political doctrine of enlightened despotism. Although the latter is often interpreted as a consequence of the former, enlightened despotism can be better explained as the last phase of royal absolutism, more closely related to the great changes Europe experienced in the eighteenth century than to the sole influence of a philosophical attitude.

The new and expanding economic power, the rising complexity of administration, the development of international contacts, required new methods of government and interference in every area of life. Royal absolutism was thus carried to its final consequences, i.e., the doctrine that the king's authority was boundless and that the limits of the state's power were the state itself. Traditional absolutism proclaimed the royal subordination to the usages of the country (common law), to the laws of nature, to the laws of God as interpreted by the Church, and to the laws which the king himself (along with his ancestors) had enacted for the country. Despotism claimed that usages and customs played no part at all; it avowed that the laws of nature were interpreted by the king, that the laws of God were deposited in the king himself with the Church's submission to his will, and finally, that the laws of the realm did not bind the monarch. In this way, enlightened despotism tended to subjugate all social classes to the royal power, to abolish any privileges based upon heredity and tradition, to reject any political and social organs of control over the central administration, and to foster the rise of a national Church independent of Rome. It favored industrialism and new techniques in combating imports from abroad; it supported monopolies and economic protectionism; it developed bureaucracy. In the cultural field it had to adopt secularization by means of direct intervention in the public educational (and cultural) system and a strong state censorship. It also favored public beneficence over religious charity.

Enlightened despotism started in Portugal with José's reign, particularly after 1755. Its chief architect was the Marquis of Pombal, who in part adopted theoretical principles espoused by some Portuguese philosophers and pedagogues who had lived abroad (Verney, Ribeiro Sanches, Sarmento) or by some of his predecessors in government and diplomacy (Luis da Cunha, Alexandre de Gusmão). Pombal's despotism outlived its creator, surviving as the general doctrine of government for more than forty years, up to the liberal revolution of 1820. His successors for practical purposes were several secretaries of state in the reigns of Maria and John, such as José de Seabra da Silva (Secretary of the Interior, 1788–99) and the Count of Linhares, Rodrigo de Sousa Coutinho (Secretary of the Navy, 1795–1803; Secretary of Foreign Affairs and War, 1807–12).

The juridical basis of all enlightened states was reason. Legislation was considered to be no more than a body of wise principles deduced from reason according to human nature. Reason would direct man to discover the law that human nature determines, i.e., natural law. Enacted in 1769, the so-called "Law of the Good Reason" (Lei da Boa Razão) based every law and every custom upon the "good reason," without which attribute it could not be valid. Although the law tried to define what "good reason" was, it opened the door to much imprecision and subjectiveness, giving judges and courts a wide latitude of interpretation and consequently of susceptibility to political pressures. The act of 1769 in effect derogated the laws of the country without building up a new body of legislation. It is true that several attempts to revise the existing Ordenações (which dated from 1603) had taken place throughout the seventeenth and the eighteenth century. In 1778 a committee was formally entrusted with the task of preparing a new code of legislation, but the conflict between absolutism and the rising principles of liberalism prevented its final enactment. The law of 1790, unifying jurisdiction throughout the country, was a further step in leveling feudal privileges down to nothing and in imposing everywhere and on everyone the sole authority of the Crown.

The other vast field where Enlightenment played a decisive role was culture in general and formal education in particular. The backwardness of the Portuguese system of instruction was stressed by all those who made comparisons with advanced European countries. Portuguese who lived abroad or had traveled extensively in Europe were instrumental in defining the many faults and preparing the total revision of the Portuguese system. These *estrangeirados* ("imitative of foreigners"), as they were derogatorily called, were many, and their part in fostering cultural progress was immense. Comparable to the sixteenth-century humanists who studied abroad (see chapter 4), they included diplomats like Luis da Cunha, Alexandre de Gusmão, and Pombal himself, who had been sent as an envoy to Vienna and London; residents in foreign countries like the Jew Castro Sarmento (in England), Father Luis António Verney (in Italy), or Dr. Ribeiro Sanches (doctor in the Russian court, later a resident in France); exiles like Cavaleiro de Oliveira (in London), the Duke of Lafões (in London and all over Europe and the Near East), Father Correia da Serra (in Italy, France, and England), the poet Filinto Elísio (in France), or the scientist Avelar Brotero (in France); army officers like General Gomes Freire de Andrade, educated in Austria and later serving in the French Army of Napoleon; or simple "tourists" like Pina e Proença who accompanied Prince Manuel on a European tour.

Some of these Portuguese scientists and men of letters gave the best or a great part of their efforts to the countries which had welcomed them. Several were famous in international societies and their renown went much beyond Portugal. This was true of Father João Jacinto de Magalhães, known in France where he lived as l'abbé Magellan, one of the men who did so much for the general progress of physics; or the botanist Avelar Brotero, almost as famous as Linnaeus in his lifetime; or Correia da Serra.

The *estrangeirados* were influential in various ways. Many of them, as civil servants, were formally consulted by the government or had enough authority and prestige to give their advice on diplomacy, politics, and education. Luis da Cunha's *Political Testament* (1747–49), for instance, contained a full program on how to rule a country. Castro Sarmento was consulted (1730) on the way to reform the College of Medicine, which actually led to nothing. Ribeiro Sanches, on Pombal's demand, wrote a "Method on how to learn the study of Medicine" (1763). Verney's fundamental "True Method of Study" (1746) covered almost all fields of learning and gave Pombal the basic principles to accomplish his reforms on education.

Other *estrangeirados* returned to Portugal, where action was direct. This was true of the two diplomats Alexandre de Gusmão (appointed the king's private secretary and in effect the prime minister from 1730 to 1750) and Pombal in the field of government, and also of Gomes Freire who spread the doctrines of the French Revolution and died a martyr (1817), and the Duke of Lafões who was both a wealthy and cultivated Maecenas and a member of government. Correia da Serra, whose life was rich in travel and experiences and who fared unevenly in his country's official protection, was one of the first Portuguese diplomatic envoys to the United States, where he was highly respected. (President Jefferson even consulted him on the statutes of the new University of Pennsylvania, and he was offered a chair in that university and the presidency of that of Virginia.) Still others showed their contact with modern ideas by means of their work and literary production: Filinto Elísio and Brotero, among others.

The deep cultural revolution which was taking place in Portugal in those days also meant the replacement of Spanish influence by French, English, Italian, and German influences. After 1640 (and even before) Spain had become the enemy, but its influence declined much more because of Spain's own decline and backwardness. Up to the late seventeenth century Spain was among the leading countries of Europe in most fields of knowledge; afterward Spain, in decline, needed to seek stimuli outside her borders. Thus Portugal, always eager to catch up with the most advanced developments, looked elsewhere, tending to despise whatever came from her neighbor. This permeability to new influences has to be stressed, because it marked the beginning of a new cultural period for Portugal along with a different mentality and a new attitude toward Europe. Beginning with the eighteenth century Portugal realized that her place among the civilized countries of the world and her individuality as a European nation depended upon her reaction against Spain. For the first time in history, though there had been struggles and cultural assertions in the past, the cultural unity of the Iberian Peninsula was severed, and with it the possibility of a political union. Between the two Iberian countries there was now a permanent breach. Portugal began to hate and despise Spain as an obstacle to contact with France and the rest of Europe. Gradually, Portugal became less Iberian and more European. And with this change there also began for Portugal the frustration of loneliness and isolation.

Signs of this cultural breakaway were many. Spanish, which had been Portugal's second language, gave way to French, beginning in the late seventeenth century. The first Portuguese grammar of French appeared in 1679, followed by several others in the early 1700's. In the 1730's the first grammars of Italian and Dutch were published, as well as the first English-Portuguese dictionary. Translations and adaptations of French, English, and Italian authors were made, along with imports of books in those languages and the performance of French and Italian theater. Spanish literature and theater were scorned as being old-fashioned and in poor taste. Latin also declined, a natural consequence of the decline of the Church. In the arts, baroque, considered a Spanish corruption of the pure Classical models, was forsaken for French and Italian classicism.

One of the main arenas where the new "lights" could be discussed was the academies. The first of these appeared in the second half of the seventeenth century, but their practical effect was slight. They multiplied in the early 1700's, not only in Lisbon but also in Brazil and elsewhere. In 1720 King John V instituted the Royal Academy of History, following the example of the French and Italian royal academies; it was, however, quite original in that it specialized in the study of history. The Academy was given a press of its own, revenues, and several privileges such as being free from royal censorship. About half of its fifty members did not belong to the clergy, an important fact in documenting the rise of a lay intelligentsia. Although this Academy did not last long, its efforts led to the publication of several important works: a Genealogical History of the Portuguese Royal Family (*Historia Genealogica da Casa Real Portugueza* by António Caetano de Sousa, 1735–49, actually a history of most noble lineages); the first general bibliography of Portugal (*Bibliotheca Lusitana* by Diogo Barbosa Machado, 1741–59); and the stimulus for the completion of the first comprehensive Dictionary of the Portuguese language (*Vocabulario Portuguez e Latino* by Rafael Bluteau, 1712–28). Another important academy was the Arcadia Lusitana (1756) modeled after the famous Italian Academia dell' Arcadia and devoted to literature. Of private origin (with bourgeois founders) it fought for classicism and defined some literary and aesthetic principles.

The most important of all Portuguese academies and the one where the doctrines of Enlightenment were fully represented was the Royal Academy of Science founded in 1779 by the Duke of Lafões and Father Correia da Serra under royal protection. One of its purposes was to relate the University to the development of economic and scientific research. It first had three sections: for Natural Science, Mathematics, and Literature. It organized a scientific museum and an excellent library with foreign and Portuguese books; participated in or fostered numerous projects of economic, scientific, and health reform; and had contacts with academies and institutions in Europe and America. It defended the economic doctrines of the physiocrats and a complete change in the feudal agrarian regime. To a certain extent it favored freedom of trade and industry against the monopoly system. By 1820 the Royal Academy of Science had published a number of highly important works (many of them reports) on general economy, agriculture, literature, history, and philology, and had become the main center of the country's intellectual advancement.

A very rich cultural life resulted from all this ferment and from the intensity of international contacts. John V and his successors sent many students abroad to Italy and France to become familiar with music and the arts. And the coming of foreigners to Portugal, invited by the king or the nobles, or simply on their own, also helped to spread new fashions and new doctrines in every field of activity.

Interestingly, the eighteenth century in Portugal produced few great names in literature or the arts but a very large group of amateurs turned out little or of poor quality; yet there was a highly cultural ambiance expressed through collective bodies, like the academies. This was first shown by the last two monuments of Portuguese baroque literature, the compilations of poems by many authors known as *A Fenis Renascida* (1716–28) and *Eccos que o Clarim da*

Fama dá: Postilhão de Apollo (1761–62). Plays were also abundant either in the form of comedies, farces, and tragedies (Manuel de Figueiredo), or with musical accompaniment (Antonio José da Silva). Opera was the great theatrical genre of the eighteenth century in Portugal. Translations from the Italian but also recasts into Portuguese and original Portuguese librettos were familiar in Lisbon and Porto to a large audience of nobles and bourgeoisie. Special opera theatres began to be built in the mid-1700's, the most famous and beautiful being the São Carlos Opera House in Lisbon, opened in 1793 after the Scala Theatre in Milan. Many national musicians tried to compete with the Italian and French masters, both in operatic and concerto compositions, sometimes with relative success (Marcos Portugal; Carlos Seixas). Varied talents were given expression at the aristocratic salons (for instance, that of the Marchioness of Alorna), the fashionable picnics, the garden parties, and the popular small theaters and patio performers. Taverns too played a significant role in gathering together literary amateurs or musicians of all kinds. Finally there were the convents, where many nuns spent their time reading, writing or listening, with frequent male visitors including King John V himself. An interesting literary genre arose in these convents, a mixture of vulgar mysticism, baroque trifles, romances, and nostalgia for the outside world.

Journalism and the writing of memoirs provided another kind of literary expression. After some premature attempts in the mid-1600's, the first newspaper with continuity was the *Gazeta de Lisboa,* which started publication in 1715 and lasted for more than a century. It was directed by several talented writers and revealed the growing Portuguese interest in foreign affairs and fashions. Other newspapers appeared throughout the century and in the early 1800's, some devoted to general news, others to literary or economic subjects. State censorship, however, particularly severe after 1750, prevented the development of a free press as it existed in England or in Holland. Among the major writers of this epoch (who all flourished in the late eighteenth or early nineteenth century) mention should be made of Bocage (1765–1805), a preromantic who lived a miserable life and died in poverty; Filinto Elísio (1734–1819), who died an exile in France; Cruz e Silva (1731–99); and Correia Garção (1724–72), all poets and all of bourgeois origin.

The scientific movement was certainly more modest but not less important in revealing a new mentality with international connotations. Mathematics, geometry, biology, chemistry, physics, astronomy, and medicine were of great interest among a part of the intelligentsia, including King John V himself, who protected some European scientists of renown. Many books appeared on science and technology, along with translations and adaptations into Portuguese of foreign treatises and handbooks. Father Bartolomeu de Gusmão invented a flying machine which went up to the ceiling in the ballroom of the royal palace and then, again, in the open air (1709). By the same time an astronomical observatory was set up in the king's palace. In the public squares of Lisbon, as well as in the "laboratories" of those days, a good many naive experiments took place, some of them with commercial purposes, like the optical tube or the magic lantern. New techniques and technological devices were introduced with practical purposes (in engineering, dyeing, and shooting, for instance). Machines of all kinds were imported or copied according to foreign models, often without any results or practical aims. The setting was thus prepared for the great educational reforms which tried to adjust official education in Portugal to the general progress in every field of knowledge, particularly in science. Those reforms brought about a better framework for the development of most sciences, namely medicine, biology, physics, chemistry, and mathematics.

Attempts to set up the basis for progressive education by others than the Jesuits had actually started before. The religious Order of St. Philip Nery (Oratorians) was protected by John V, who granted them a school for teaching humanities according to Roman "modern" methods. The Oratorian Fathers had been among the first to fight Jesuit control of education and denounce its backwardness. But it was only under Pombal that something more radical could be accomplished. Reforms began in 1759 and went on to 1772, covering the primary, secondary, and university levels. The expulsion of the Jesuits served as a pretext because they had in their hands a good share of the teaching system. The act of 1759 created throughout the realm classes of Latin, Greek, Hebrew, and rhetoric for young children, and forbade use of the prevailing Jesuit manuals and methods of teaching. Classes in Latin included regular learning of Portuguese. Teachers were also to give their pupils elementary instruction in handwriting, spelling, arithmetic, catechism, and rules of politeness. In 1761 Pombal instituted a sort of secondary level of learning for the nobles and sons of top bureaucrats by founding the Royal College of the Nobles (Colégio Real dos Nobres). It provided studies of languages (Latin, Greek, French, Italian, and English), humanities (rhetoric, poetry, and history), science (arithmetic, geometry, trigonometry, algebra, optics, astronomy, geography, nautics, military architecture, civil architecture, design, and physics), along with sports (fencing and riding) and dance, to a maximum of one hundred young students. Classes started in 1766 with most of the faculty composed of foreign instructors.

The University system was completely reorganized. In 1759 the University of Évora had been shut down, along with the expulsion of its owners, the Jesuits. Thus, only the University of Coimbra survived. After an inquiry (1770–71) into its conditions that showed the thorough decadence and backwardness of its studies, new statutes were issued in 1772 embodying a modern program of humanities and sciences. Besides the existing schools of Theology, Canons, Law, and Medicine, Pombal created the colleges of Mathematics and Natural Philosophy (i.e., Sciences), providing them with an astronomical observatory, a museum of natural history, laboratories of physics and chemistry, a "theatre for anatomy" (i.e., a laboratory of medicine), a pharmacy, and a botanical garden. The existing schools were thoroughly renovated, with the introduction of new disciplines, such as legal history and ecclesiastical history. Medicine was made much more practical. Pombal (and others afterward) invited a number of foreign teachers (Vandelli, Della Bella), particularly for the newly created colleges.

Cultural reforms and innovations did not stop there. In Porto and Lisbon, schools for nautical studies and design were opened, as well as military classes. A School of Commerce, for young bourgeois, appeared in Lisbon. A Royal Printing Press was set up in 1768. To obtain funds for so many reforms a new tax—the so-called "literary subsidy"—diverted money from wine, brandy, and vinegar taxation.

It must be emphasized that all these important cultural changes did not imply cultural freedom. Censorship ceased to be primarily religious and generally backward in spirit but continued on political grounds. The Real Mesa Censória, created in 1768, transferred to the state full control of books and other publications, while abolishing the existing censorship and making the editing of any book bureaucratically easier. Yet it did not oust religious principles from its rules nor the participation of ecclesiastical representatives in its meetings. As before books were forbidden which defended atheistic or non-Catholic doctrines, or which taught witchcraft or astrology or fostered any superstitions. Obscene publications were also ruled out as were those that attacked the government or might be considered subversive of the existing social order. Control of private libraries did not end either. And the powers of the Real Mesa Censória (later called Junta da Directoria Geral dos Estudos e Escolas) were further extended when the entire administration and direction of primary and secondary education was placed under it.

Notwithstanding the persistence of censorship and the apparent similarity to the old forms, there is no doubt that greater freedom gradually rose from the new cosmopolitan spirit of "reason" and enlightenment. The traditional principles no longer had the universal strength that had imposed them throughout the kingdom. Every intellectual, nobleman, and bureaucrat was in transgression against the rules determined by the Real Mesa Censória, by owning, reading, and disseminating the forbidden books. Many approved works on history, philosophy, physics, medicine, and natural sciences, even if seemingly harmless, actually undermined the bases of the old regime, the inviolability of religious beliefs and the doctrines of despotism, if not of royalty itself. The censorship only repressed what seemed obvious; it allowed free circulation of menaces to the existing order which soon would bring it down.

Pombal's cultural movement did not die with his downfall; on the contrary, his reforms were maintained and enlarged under his followers. The trend toward empiricism and the reaction against the excesses of an empty and suffocating metaphysics (as expressed by the "Jesuit" kind of knowledge) continued: in 1791 the teaching of rational philosophy and morals was deleted from the School of Philosophy courses and replaced by a chair of botany and agriculture. Thus, philosophy (as we call it today) completely disappeared from university studies. More schools for design were set up in Lisbon and

Porto, a much-debated "Academy of the Nude" (Academia do Nú) being founded in Lisbon for the aesthetic study of the human body (1780). Special schools for arithmetic and geometry were also instituted. The most important steps forward in the field of a better and more specialized education were perhaps the creation of a Royal Academy for the Navy (1779), a Military School for young sons of officers (1803), and schools for young girls (1815). At the same time the enlightened principle of spreading culture was furthered when the king's library opened its doors to the public as the first Royal Public Library in Portugal (1796).

The impact of Enlightenment on the arts is not so easy to measure. Until the mid-eighteenth century, baroque (which the *estrangeirados* abhorred as a backward style) entirely ruled Portugal. Churches continued to be built and adorned with splendid examples of gilt wood and tiles (see chapter 6). Countless Romanesque and Gothic interiors experienced the vandalism of an epoch which could not appreciate them and had them covered with new decoration. The gold from Brazil and the wine exported to England had brought prosperity to the kingdom, an incredible number of aristocratic mansions being erected throughout Portugal in the baroque tradition. John V ordered a magnificent library interior for the University of Coimbra (1716–25). But at the same time, Italian and German masters were invited to the country and started building in a less adorned and more classic way. Architect Ludwig built the huge monastery of Mafra (consecrated 1730) and many other sober and elegant buildings. Architect Nazoni was active in the north of Portugal (the church and tower of the Clérigos, in Porto), among others. Of the more useful and practical buildings, a special reference should be made to the long and artistic aqueduct which solved the problem of supplying water to Lisbon (Aqueduto das Águas Livres, opened 1748).

The great event that influenced the arts, however, was the earthquake which destroyed about half of Lisbon on November 1, 1755. The most important part of the capital fell down, including the royal palace, countless churches and monastaries, the main Hospital, the Opera House, and the wealthiest streets and quarters. Instead of having the city rebuilt according to the old plan, Pombal had the rebuilding follow new conceptions in urbanism and architecture.

He chose a very simple yet revolutionary plan that transformed most of Lisbon into a huge chessboard, starting at a vast square opening at the river. In that square, the government offices were built, as well as a triumphal arch and an elegant statue of King José on horseback. All houses were to be similar in both size and height. The city ended at another vast square surrounded with better and more splendid palaces. For the achievement of this ambitious and unique plan, Pombal ordered all ruins to be leveled, including many houses that had not been destroyed. Everything was built anew. Accordingly, Lisbon became a truly "enlightened" city, rationally planned and built, its streets, squares, and houses drawn with a ruler in the most theoretical way an eighteenth-century philosopher could envision. This new city took some decades to be completed, many details being later subject to changes of all kinds. Yet essentially its plan was kept the same, the one which engineer Manuel da Maia and architects Eugénio dos Santos and Carlos Mardel had mapped out and started to make effective.

Besides Lisbon with its new palaces, churches, and fountains, a beautiful royal country house was built at Queluz (near Lisbon) modeled after the French palace of Versailles; a sumptuous palace was built at Ajuda; and many other noble or bourgeois residences displayed throughout the country the "restoration of the arts" defended by the classicists.

Sculpture and painting were less splendorous than architecture, yet some good schools of both arts rose from the late seventeenth to the early nineteenth century. Domingos António de Sequeira, a renowned painter, flourished in the late 1700's and the beginning of the next century. Once again, a good part of the artistic movement rose anonymously, expressed in church and palace decorations but without individualizing itself.

THE DECISIVE EVENTS

The year 1667 inaugurated for Portugal a long period of political stability, which would end only with the French invasions in the early nineteenth century. Three long reigns, to start with, ensured continuity: those of Pedro II (1667 to 1706), John V (1706 to 1750), and José I (1750 to 1777). Maria's relatively brief period of personal rule (1777 to 1792) was followed by another long one, that of her son John VI (1792 to 1826). Royal continuity was matched by secretarial continuity: the most relevant offices in government were kept by the same persons for long periods of time. Thus, Pedro II entrusted power to the first duke of Cadaval, who practically controlled the government until the king's death, assisted by secretaries such as the third count of Ericeira (died 1690) and the second marquis of Fronteira. Under John V, secretaries of state Diogo de Mendonça Corte Real (1706–36) and Cardinal of Mota (1736–47) ruled the country, along with the king's private secretary, Alexandre de Gusmão (1730–50). José I entrusted full powers to Sebastião José de Carvalho e Melo, later Marquis of Pombal, for twenty-seven years (1750–77). Under his successors governmental control was not so concentrated, yet the Viscount of Vila Nova de Cerveira (later Marquis of Ponte de Lima) ruled for twenty-three years (1777–1800), Martinho de Melo e Castro for twenty-five (1770–95), and Miguel Pereira Forjaz for twelve (1808–20), albeit with much less individual power. Governmental stability had its advantages but also its inconveniences: if it permitted reforms, it also favored conservatism and routine. Which of the two prevailed very much depended upon the sovereign's character, the secretary's personality, and, above all, the circumstances of the epoch.

Either as prince-regent or as king after his brother's death (1683), Pedro changed little his methods of government, which he shared with the upper nobility. Cadaval, Ericeira, Fronteira, and other ministers were able statesmen who tried, successfully, to restore Portugal's prosperity and international prestige. For this purpose, and contrary to the traditional policy of the country, they took an active part in European affairs, a way of asserting Portugal's position as an independent country again. Cadaval was a partisan of an alliance with France as the best way of containing Spain's power, a policy generally followed to the beginning of the eighteenth century. France, too, was interested in that alliance for similar reasons. Nonetheless, when Queen Marie-Françoise died (1683), and the king decided to marry again, a German princess was chosen, Marie Sophie of Neuburg, which drew the Portuguese closer to the Austrian court, because the new queen was a daughter of the Elector Palatine.

Despite these and other facts, Portugal's external policy never ceased to be a cautious one. The country did not become involved in the European wars of the late 1600's, particularly the Nine Years War or the War of the League of Augsburg (1688-97), where France had to fight a coalition of powers composed of Germany (the Palatinate playing a large role), England, Holland, Spain, and Savoy.

The succession to the Spanish throne was Portugal's excuse for a change in external policy. Pedro II had been a candidate for that throne, among many others in Europe. Portugal claimed the Rio de la Plata as the southern Brazilian border (see chapter 9)—which Spain would not accept—and wished to secure better protection of her European boundaries by acquiring a certain number of fortified towns in Spain. Hence Portugal intervened after the death of Carlos II of Spain in 1700. Her claims having been rejected by England, Portugal first rallied with France but hesitated to enter a war where France's enemies controlled the sea. Economic reasons—the rising wine exports to England—helped to convince the partisans of a war alliance with France. By the treaty of 1703 Portugal joined the allies (England, Holland, most of Germany, Austria, Savoy) against France and Spain, recognizing Archduke Karl of Austria as the legitimate king of Spain. The treaty of 1703 gave Portugal the boundaries she wished, both in America and in Europe.

From 1704 to 1708 war ravaged a part of Alentejo and Beira but the allied forces generally took the lead, the Marquis of Minas at the head of the Portuguese army conquering Madrid (1706) where Archduke Karl was solemnly proclaimed king. In Catalonia that same general won again at Almanza (1707) and later on, in Aragon, the Portuguese were victorious once more at Zaragoza (1710). Yet, despite all these victories, the Portuguese army had to retreat home when the allied coalition broke down in 1711 in order to avoid the political union of Austria and Spain. An armistice (1712) led to the Treaty of Utrecht, according to which clauses Spain and Portugal simply gave back the fortresses they had captured from each other. In Brazil, however, Portugal obtained some advantages.

Fifty years of peace followed, interrupted only by a brief intervention by King John V (1706-50) in the Mediterranean to help the Pope and Venice fight the Turks. Two fleets were sent, in 1716 and 1717; the second one victoriously engaged in a naval battle off the

Greek coast (Cape Matapan). Useless from a strictly nationalistic stand-point, this intervention showed John's determination to continue his father's policy of interfering in general European affairs. Because of the country's diplomacy in those days, and also because of her econo-mic prosperity, Portugal reaffirmed her place as a respected state, whose independence was undisputed. Nevertheless, the price of that independence more and more was shown to be a commercial and in-dustrial dependence upon England. From the early eighteenth cen-tury on (and incidentally to World War II), Portugal's subordination to England's interests continued to grow.

John's government developed its relations with Rome, partly because of the king's personal devotion, partly because of questions of international prestige. By way of gifts, promises, diplomatic arts, and effective help, John V succeeded in having the archbishops of Lisbon made cardinals and patriarchs, in creating two cathedrals in Lisbon, in increasing the number of ecclesiastical dignitaries and enhancing their privileges, in being granted the title of Most Faithful (Fidelís-simo), and so on. He also pretended to have all Papal nuncios raised to the level of cardinal, which led to a diplomatic quarrel and to a break in diplomatic relations with Rome (1728–32). This incident was also related to problems of state autonomy versus the Church, which John V, a clear predecessor of Pombal in principles of despotism, was not inclined to give up.

John's rule was famous for its tendency to copy Louis XIV and the French court. Brazilian gold and the economic expansion of the country gave the monarch and most nobles the possibility of display-ing wealth as never before. Numerous churches, chapels, palaces, man-sions, and other buildings were erected everywhere. In Mafra, near Lisbon, a huge monastery showed the royal magnificence. John also took good care of arts and letters, spending vast sums acquiring books and building libraries. As in so many eighteenth-century courts, de-bauchery was prevalent. The king—and many nobles—begot children from nuns of various convents, which had become centers of pleasure and brothels for the aristocracy rather than religious houses.

When King John died, his son José I (1750–77) entrusted full power to a former diplomat, Sebastião José de Carvalho e Melo, a representative of the lower aristocracy, whom the monarch successively raised to Count of Oeiras (1759) and to Marquis of Pombal (1770). This principle of entrusting power to a prime minister was nothing new, either in Portugal or abroad, and it had actually become the general rule in seventeenth- and eighteenth-century Europe. Both Pedro II and John V had granted full powers to secretaries of state and to favorites who ruled for longer periods than Pombal. The only difference was that now the prime minister entirely controlled not only government but also the whole country by leveling down all possible opposition, and even the king himself, who had few talents for ruling. In this sense, one might say that Pombal's control of government was the final achievement of a trend which lasted for more than a century, just as despotism was the final phase of royal absolutism. Pombal's rule had the great merit of (unwillingly) preparing the country for the liberal revolution of the nineteenth century. Both the Church and the nobility suffered a deadly blow from which they would never recover. At the same time the bourgeoisie (businessmen and bureaucrats) were given the power they needed to take over administrative and economic control of the country. By subordinating all classes, laws, and institutions to the sole despotism of the king, Pombal prepared the revolution of social equality and the end of all feudal privileges; while by enforcing the state's repressive machine and getting rid of Church interference he prepared the rebellion against lay oppression and thus the revolution of liberty.

The earthquake that occurred on November 1, 1755, destroyed half of Lisbon and a good part of southern Portugal. Some five thousand people died in the capital under the ruins and as many throughout the month due to wounds and heart attacks. The catastrophe enhanced Pombal's prestige because of the strict measures which were immediately adopted in the emergency to restore order, take care of the dead and wounded, and rebuild the city. Several foreign governments helped Portugal with money, tools, and victuals.

After eight years of outraging the nobility and humiliating it in various ways, Pombal's government aroused a wide conspiracy of aristocrats with the aim of getting rid of José and enthroning his heiress Maria. Led by the Duke of Aveiro, an attempt to kill the monarch took place but failed (1758). This gave Pombal the pretext he was waiting for: many people were arrested, including many top aristocrats. Along with the Jesuits, they were all accused of plotting against the king. A mock trial led to death at the stake of one duke (Aveiro), two marquis and one marchioness, one count, and several servants and clients. Other nobles were punished or banished. Most Jesuits were expelled from the country (1759), many others were arrested, and one died at the stake, under the charge of heresy. It is probable that the Jesuits had no direct part in the plot, but their action in creating a general atmosphere of fear and hatred against Pombal (to the point of interpreting the earthquake as God's punishment for his crimes) was undeniable.

The expulsion of the Jesuits had very complex motivations and brought about a whole chain of consequences. Apart from the order's participation or nonparticipation in the plot against the king (a mere pretext) or opposition to Pombal (a more serious reason), there were in the background a series of reasons shared by many people. In Brazil the Jesuits defied the Crown's authority and had built up a state of their own opposing the state's interests (see chapters 7 and 9). In Portugal most learned persons accused them of being responsible for the backward educational system and of rejecting any modernization. Their long-established situation of privilege opposed the general trend toward enlightened despotism. They had gradually risen to positions of command disproportionate to their number and unique among the other religious orders and the secular clergy itself. If Pombal and a great part of the intelligentsia hated them, no less hatred was displayed by many bishops, abbotts of monasteries, and humbler priests or monks. Even among the people they were far from being loved or from having the contacts with the lower classes that other orders had. This explains the drastic attitude Pombal could adopt, the help he got from other clergy and countless persons, and the general support he was given both at home and abroad. Other Catholic countries had similar grievances against the Jesuits. Pombal's measures and intense diplomatic activity had a tremendous impact throughout Europe, leading to the successive expulsion of the Jesuits from France, Spain, and Naples, and finally to the bull of extinction by the Pope himself. Also, the sudden lack of teachers forced the government to a complete educational reform, encompassing all levels.

To the end of his rule, Pombal continued to persecute the nobles, the clergy, and any others who dared to oppose his policy of despotism. At the same time he promoted many bureaucrats, bourgeois, and lower representatives of the Church and the aristocracy to the top hierarchies. Supported by the bourgeoisie, part of the clergy, and the lower nobility, he was able to remain in power to José's death.

His religious policy must also be emphasized. Pombal was a partisan of or looked sympathetically upon both Jansenism and Gallicanism. He might have cherished the idea of fostering a national Portuguese Church. Again, this was nothing new and John V's policy toward Rome could be regarded as a precedent. Some minor quarrels led to the expulsion of the Papal nuncio and the break in diplomatic relations with Rome (1760 to 1769). Pombal tried a common plan with France and Spain to force Pope Clement XIII to abolish the Jesuit order. He did not succeed, but meanwhile Clement XIII died and his successor Clement XIV promptly submitted to the international pressures.

After getting rid of the Jesuits, taming the nobles, and converting the Inquisition into a well-disciplined state tribunal, Pombal ruled despotically for a number of years. Yet both the economic crisis and the international conjuncture brought him no luck and the failure of many goals he was aiming at. Portugal tried to be neutral in the Seven Years War (1756–63). However, a naval battle between English and French ships in Portugal's territorial waters and the advantages that the friendly Portuguese ports offered to the English cause made neutrality a difficult thing. In 1761 the Bourbon sovereigns of France, Spain, Naples, and Parma signed a defensive and offensive alliance known as the Family Pact. Invited to join the allies and to declare war on England (for José I was married to a Bourbon), Portugal refused, and the Spanish and French troops invaded the province of Trás-os-Montes (1762). Portugal had a poor army and was ill-prepared for war. Pombal hired a German prince, Count Wilhelm von Schaumburg-Lippe, as commander-in-chief, in charge of reorganizing the troops. English army corps and Swiss volunteers came too. With this help, the Portuguese were able to resist in the North and force the invaders to retreat. In Beira and Alentejo further invasions were also repelled. The signing of the Paris Peace Treaty (1763) prevented any possible disasters.

One of Pombal's last plans was to force Princess Maria (the throne heiress) to renounce rights to the Crown in behalf of her son José, a disciple of his. Both the minister and the king were well aware of Maria's weakness of mind and lack of determination to carry on the policy of despotism. She was very pious and religiously afraid of the consequences of her father's persecutions. She hated Pombal and showed no sympathy for his work. She and her husband (Prince Pedro, a brother of José's) led the party of all those who were not content. Pombal's plan was denounced and could not be achieved. Shortly afterward the king died (1777) and new people came to power. Until 1786, Maria I ruled together with her husband Pedro III. When the latter died, she governed alone for six more years. Late in 1791 she became insane and when all hopes of recovery were given up, her son John took over the regency (1792). John's older brother, José, had died in 1788.

Most state prisoners were set free, the memory of some of the executed nobles was rehabilitated, Pombal was tried and banished, and many of his partisans stepped down. Yet his work could not be abolished, except in some minor details. Despotism was a fact, the bourgeoisie allied to the new aristocracy ruled the country, the Jesuits were out, and the Inquisition was finished. Thus, Maria's and John's reigns simply continued the new order and in certain cases they helped to enforce it. Two of the three government secretaries were even kept in power. And persecutions of those who resisted state despotism went on, although at a slower pace.

The main change was in external policy. Contrary to Pombal's firm attitudes and clear alliance with England, Maria I and John fostered a dubious diplomacy of compromise with England, France, and Spain. To avoid war, the new government gave up present-day Uruguay, in South America, and ceded to Spain the two islands of Fernando Po and Ano Bom, in the Gulf of Guinea (1778). Then the French Revolution and the war between France and most of Europe made Portugal's external policy an extremely difficult one. Portugal's maneuvers to achieve a triple alliance with Spain and England against revolutionary France led nowhere but to France's systematic hostility. In 1793 the French privateers started attacking the Portuguese ships and convoys. An expeditionary force was sent to Catalonia for a joint Spanish-Portuguese offensive against France. But the war ended with no advantages for either side (1795). In 1796–97, secret negotiations and agreements between France and Spain presaged an invasion and conquest of Portugal. After lengthy diplomatic maneuvering, which brought Portugal neither advantages nor honor, Spain and France renewed their alliance and war was declared upon Portugal (1801). The campaign lasted only three months but was a disastrous one. In Alentejo, the Portuguese army was defeated everywhere. A hasty peace forced the Portuguese to surrender the town of Olivença to Spain and to pay a heavy indemnity. Moreover, Portugal had to close her ports to the English men-of-war from then on.

Portugal's humiliations in the field of external policy were partly compensated by the better situation at home. Commerce and industry showed every sign of prosperity; the balance of trade was revealing a surplus for the first time in decades; the treasury knew some years of relative abundance; arts and letters, and even science, flourished. Socially a state of equilibrium had been reached: old and new nobility accepted each other, the bourgeoisie prospered and the lower classes showed no signs of being worse off than before. The police kept peace at home, fiercely eradicating any symptoms of "Freemasonry," arresting all suspects of "liberalism" and putting them in jail for years. Within the royal court and outside it, French, Spanish, and English styles— rather than groups or parties—were all-important in influencing fashions. Princess Carlota Joaquina, a Spaniard, wife of the Prince-Regent John, set the tone, surrounding herself at the Queluz palace by all those who "opposed" the government, and begetting children of unknown fathers. Queluz had become Portugal's Versailles, in truth a less gay and splendorous one, but nonetheless a good example of the "Old Regime" decadent royal ambiances. As in Spain or France before 1792, and in many other places, the government and the prince-regent himself were characterized by indecision, fear, and awkwardness, controlled only by whims and pressures from favorites, utterly incapable of understanding the great changes that were taking place and of adjusting to them. Such was the inevitable result of boundless despotism when only mediocre despots ruled the country.

From 1801 to 1807 (as before) Portugal's external policy wavered between the pressures of England (whose assistance was indispensable

1st invasion
- French army
- Anglo-Portuguese army

2nd invasion
- French army

3rd invasion
- French army
- ▲▲▲ Allied fortifications
- ✳ battle

0   50   100
km.

0   50
miles

Montalegre   •Chaves

Braga•
•Guimarães

•Porto

Castelo Rodrigo•

Viseu•   Celorico•   •Almeida

✳   •Guarda
Buçaco

Coimbra•

Lavos•

Castelo Branco•

Leiria•   •Alcantara

•Tomar

•Abrantes

✳
Roliça

•Santarém

Vimeiro ✳
▲▲▲▲

•Lisbon

both economically and militarily) and those of France. Partly supported by the latter, Spain tried to be given a free hand and help in
Portugal, which might enable her to invade the country and possibly
to rebuild the Iberian unity lost in 1640. Such was Godoy's policy,
the Spanish court favorite and prime minister.

Late in 1806, Napoleon decreed the continental blockade, according to which no country of continental Europe should trade or maintain any relations with the British Isles. As Portugal showed no haste
in accepting the blockade, Napoleon sent her a clear note (July 1807)
on how to close her ports to the British, to arrest all the British citizens in Portugal, to confiscate all British ships and property, and to
break diplomatic relations with the British government. The Portuguese government realized that either the blockade had to be enforced
and the English take possession of the Portuguese Empire or Portugal
would be conquered by the French and her government forced to flee
to Brazil. This plan dated back to the Seven Years War and was in
the mind of most people when Napoleon started to threaten all of
Europe. The Regency tried its usual maneuvers of compromise and
appeasement. But it was too late and too much for Napoleon's pa-
tience.

In August 1807, the French and Spanish diplomatic envoys in
Lisbon presented to the Portuguese government an ultimatum: either
declare war on England by September 1, or the French and Spanish
armies would invade the country. Late in October, a treaty signed
at Fontainebleau between France and Spain divided Portugal in three
parts: the province of Entre-Douro-e-Minho with capital in Porto
was given to the king of Etruria as the "kingdom of Northern Lusitania"; Alentejo and the Algarve would belong to Godoy and form
the principality of the Algarves; while the rest of Portugal would be
disposed of when general peace came. In mid-November, French
General Junot crossed the Portuguese border with a large army,
starting the invasion. In those days Napoleon was thought to be in-
vincible and his armies spread terror everywhere. The Portuguese
government gave up any hope of opposing the French and gave orders
to stop all resistance and welcome the invaders. In Lisbon, the royal
family, the government, and hundreds of people loaded with riches,
books, and archives, embarked for Brazil late in November (when

Junot was entering the city) arriving in South America early in 1808.
The new capital of the kingdom was established in Rio and for fourteen years Portugal was nothing more than a colony of Brazil (see
chapter 9).

In Portugal a regency of five members and two secretaries had been
set up by the government, presided over by the Marquis of Abrantes.
But Junot immediately ousted it and ruled the country as a conquered land under a foreign military occupation. Some 50,000 French
and Spanish soldiers spread through all the provinces, confiscating,
plundering, robbing, killing, and arresting as they pleased. The Portuguese army was partly disbanded and partly converted into a "Portuguese Legion," sent to Spain and then to France and elsewhere, to
fight under Napoleon. Many nobles and top bureaucrats were sent to
France under various pretexts.

Popular resistance started immediately and a guerrilla war had
its beginnings against the invaders. In June 1808 Prince-Regent John
was acclaimed in the North, a Provisional Junta being established
under the supreme command of the bishop of Porto. The revolution
spread everywhere, stimulated by the retreat of the Spanish troops
and by the news of the rebellions against the French in Spain. Local
juntas rose in many places. Supported by this wide popular movement, the English under Sir Arthur Wellesley (the future Lord Wellington) landed in Galicia (northern Spain) and entered Portugal in
July 1808. Other British troops joined him and together with the
Portuguese forces Wellesley beat Junot twice (the battles of Roliça
and Vimeiro, in upper Estremadura) and forced him to ask for a
truce. In September the French embarked for home, taking with them
most of the loot (a part of it can be admired today in French museums
and archives).

The old Regency appointed by the government was reinstalled,
now under the presidency of the Marquis of Minas. Order could be
more or less restored everywhere, and defense against a new French
attack (which seemed likely) immediately started to be organized under
the command of the English general William Beresford (March 1809).
Beresford was made a field marshal in the Portuguese army and given
full powers. He practically ruled the country until 1820.

The second French invasion had begun in February 1809, under the command of Marshal Soult, the Duke of Dalmatia. The French entered Portugal by Trás-os-Montes and conquered the whole North, to the Douro River. Soult cherished the dream of becoming king of "Northern Lusitania," yet his forces could not stand the Anglo-Portuguese pressure and retreated to Spain in May 1809.

In the Fall of that same year and foreseeing a new French attack, Lord Wellington organized a proper defense for Lisbon. Three fortified lines surrounding the capital to about twenty miles were built and the city became impregnable. Indeed, when Marshal Masséna at the head of a strong army and with the participation of famous French generals like Ney invaded Portugal (July 1810), he stopped at the lines (linhas de Torres Vedras) after a first defeat at Buçaco (in Beira). For five months the two armies watched each other, Masséna waiting for reinforcements, Wellington waiting for the enemy's general fatigue. Early in March 1811, tired of waiting and low in spirits, the French started a retreat. Wellington went after them, beating them again at Redinha, and forced them to cross the border in October. In Spain, the English army, helped by the Portuguese and the Spaniards, continued to push the French, to Toulouse (Spring 1814). Besides restoring Portugal's independence and integrity, the Vienna Congress (1814–15) gave the town of Olivença back to Portugal, but the Spaniards never complied.

Four years of war had left the country in poor condition. The French invasions and occupation devastated a large part of Portugal, particularly to the north of the Tagus. Agriculture, trade, and industry were deeply affected, not to mention the loss in lives, the usual cruelties, and the countless destruction. Both French and English sacked a good many monasteries, churches, palaces, and humbler dwellings, taking home all kinds of precious loot, including paintings, sculptures, furniture, jewelry, books and manuscripts. In a small country like Portugal such losses were deeply felt. Together with the great earthquake, the Peninsular war was responsible for the later absence of monuments, museums, archives, and libraries of countless materials. Moreover, the French invasions left Portugal in a very peculiar political situation. From 1808 to 1821 the country was both an English protectorate and a Brazilian colony. The government was in Rio; in Portugal there was only a regency. Brazil had become a united kingdom with Portugal. Beresford had been given full powers to organize defense, which actually meant supreme rule of the country. British officers served in the Portuguese army, which was becoming entirely English in organization. King John VI (Maria I had died in 1816) showed no wish to return to Europe. The princes were more Brazilian than Portuguese, the eldest one having left Lisbon at the age of nine. The regency kept intact the old methods of governing, showing no disposition whatsoever to adjust to modern ideas. A ferocious persecution of all liberals went on. Throughout the country discontent against the king, the English, and the regency were accompanied by a deplorable economic and financial situation. Revolutionary ferment was everywhere and would soon lead to open rebellion.

"BRAZIL"

BRAZIL, BASIC ELEMENT OF THE PORTUGUESE EMPIRE

From the late 1600's to 1822 Brazil was the essence of the Portuguese Empire. With some exaggeration one might even say that Brazil was the essence of Portugal itself. It was Brazil that partly caused secession from Spain in 1640. It was Brazil that gave Portugal the means to remain independent afterward and that justified the other powers' support of the Portuguese separation. It was Brazil that brought about a new wave of prosperity during the eighteenth century and that made Portugal respected once again among the civilized countries of Europe. This explains a political current of the time, which proposed that Portugal be concerned only with Brazil (and the other overseas provinces) and neglect European affairs. Rule with one's face turned to Brazil and one's back to Europe, as a renowned diplomat advised his king.

The creation of the general-government in the mid-sixteenth century had very much reduced the autonomy of each captaincy and the consequent powers of each captain. By the early 1600's, it seemed possible that the tendency toward centralization and reinforcement of the governor's powers would lead to a unitary Brazil, strongly controlled from Bahia. But the colony was too large to be governed like the mainland; and the growing needs of territorial expansion brought about a political, social, and economic structure altogether opposed to centralization. The tremendous increase in Brazil's potentialities after 1650 broke such a precarious unity and resulted in greater and greater autonomy of the captaincies. The general-government retained its powers of assuring defense but gradually lost many others related to administration, economy, and finance.

This gradual change, which in a way likened eighteenth-century Brazil to the "golden age" before 1549, was accompanied by a series of regulations, acts, and instructions, defining the responsibilities of the governors-general as well as the powers of the other captains (also-called governors). The first and second-class captaincies were maintained, under the official names of general-captaincy (*capitania-geral*) and subaltern-captaincy (*capitania-subalterna*), the latter being dependent upon the former, as before. What changed, however, was both the number and the relationships among the several captaincies. The development of the interior brought about the establishment of new units, such as Minas Gerais (1720), Goiás (1748), Mato Grosso (1748), Rio Grande de São Pedro (1730), and Santa Catarina (1737), all dismembered from São Vicente; and São José do Rio Negro (1757), separated from Pará. São Vicente was under Rio de Janeiro until 1709; then it became a general-captaincy, it was briefly united to Rio de Janeiro (1748–65), and finally regained its individuality as São Paulo, the real name by which it had been known for a long time.

At the same time the Crown endeavored to get back under its direct control all the captaincies which still belonged to the hereditary captains created in the sixteenth century. Some reverted to the Crown by the grant of pensions or titles to the donatorial families, some by confiscations. By 1761 the process was practically completed. Each captaincy became now a purely administrative unit, depending upon the Lisbon government, which appointed the captains or governors for a three-year period.

Paradoxically, this gradual cutback in the effective authority of the governors-general (except, of course, in their own captaincy, that of Baía, with its *capitanias subalternas* too) also saw enhancement of their social and economic prestige and an elevation in their title. In 1720 governors-general of Brazil were made viceroys (*vice-reis*), with a commensurate increase in their salaries. More and more they were chosen from the cream of the Portuguese nobility with experience in colonial affairs in India, Africa, or Brazil, and their hierarchical position in the whole Portuguese Empire administration rose to first place. The Meneses, the Noronhas, the Mascarenhas, and other first-rate lineages were distinguished with several viceroy appointments.

In 1763 the seat of the general-government was moved from Baía to Rio de Janeiro, as the economic and political center of Brazil was also moving southward. This meant that, instead of Baía, the captaincy-general of Rio de Janeiro, a much smaller and poorer one, became the operational basis of the viceroy. Upon it depended the two *subalternas* of Santa Catarina and Rio Grande de São Pedro.

In 1772, with the extinction of the state of Maranhão, the two Brazils became forever united and the administrative changes of a whole century were accomplished. From then on, all of Portuguese America was a single vice-kingdom with the seat in Rio, divided into nine captaincies-general and nine subordinate ones: Grão Pará (with São José do Rio Negro—present-day Amazonas); Maranhão (with Piauí); Pernambuco (with Ceará, Rio Grande do Norte, and Paraíba); Baía (with Sergipe and Espírito Santo); Rio de Janeiro (with Santa Catarina and Rio Grande de São Pedro—present-day Rio Grande do Sul); São Paulo; Minas Gerais; Goiás; and Mato Grosso. A map of Brazil in the early twentieth century shows that, with the exception of the two states of Alagoas (founded 1817) and Paraná (created 1853), all the other units coincide, both in name and in boundaries, with the *capitanias* of 1772.

The ecclesiastical division changed still more, showing the tremendous development of the colony throughout the seventeenth and eighteenth centuries. In the early 1670's only Baía had a bishop, whose authority covered all of Brazil and Maranhão. Then, in 1676–77, three new dioceses appeared, in Rio de Janeiro, Olinda, and Maranhão, the bishop of Baía becoming an archbishop. Early in the eighteenth century the Pope set up a new diocese for Pará (1719), then several others for Mariana (1745), São Paulo (1745), Goiás (1745, first prelate only in 1781), and Cuiabá (1745, first prelate only in 1782), the latter two under the ecclesiastical jurisdiction of a prelate. Maranhão and Pará depended upon Lisbon to the extinction of the "State" of Pará and Maranhão. Thus, in the late eighteenth century, Catholic Brazil encompassed one archbishopric, that of Baía, with direct authority over the captaincies of Sergipe and Baía, and supremacy over all Brazil and in Angola too. The bishop of Pará ruled São José do Rio Negro and Grão Pará; that of Maranhão, Maranhão, Piauí, Ceará, and Rio Grande do Norte; that of Olinda, Paraíba and Pernambuco; that of Rio de Janeiro, Espírito Santo and Rio de Janeiro; that of São Paulo, São Paulo, Santa Catarina, and Rio Grande de São Pedro; and that of Mariana, Minas Gerais. The prelates of Goiás and Cuiabá had jurisdiction over Goiás and Mato Grosso, respectively. The ecclesiastical division did not rigorously coincide with the political one but was quite close to it.

Local administration evolved according to the gradual strengthening of the Crown's power and the decline of municipal prerogatives. It is true that in Brazil, a typical frontier country, local and regional autonomy was not eroded to the extent that it was in Portugal or elsewhere in Europe. Nonetheless, the general trend had its impact on Portuguese America too, the decline of the local *câmaras* (municipal councils) being a fact during the eighteenth and the early nineteenth century.

In 1696 the government altered the election system in Baía, giving the Crown-appointed judges of the Relação the task of scrutinizing the ballots, and the viceroy the final selection of officials among a list of elected people. Other reforms further enhanced the role played by the Crown. Price-fixing, for instance, one of the prerogatives of Baía's *câmara* (as in most big centers) was often discouraged by the central government but only definitely barred in 1751, when a board of inspection composed mainly of Crown bureaucrats was established for that purpose. Inevitably, small cities far from "civilization" had a higher degree of autonomy for carrying on local affairs than the large urban centers in direct contact with Crown representatives.

As in Portugal, the important local offices of Brazil were in the hands of the wealthiest residents. Sugar planters had the lead in a town like Baía. Elsewhere, large cattle-ranchers or tobacco-planters might predominate. A conflict between this landed aristocracy and the growing bourgeoisie of traders and rich craftsman soon developed, with open struggle in a town like Recife, for example. Compromise rather than final victory generally ended such clashes, depending upon the general economic conjuncture and the local social sharing of influences. Available monographs on the social struggles within the *câmaras* are still very few. In Baía, it seems that the landed sugar aristocracy continued to lead the way throughout the eighteenth and the early nineteenth century. Representatives of the crafts, which had been allowed in the mid-1600's, were dropped from the *câmara* as late as 1713, but restrictions on their full participation in local affairs had been imposed much earlier.

The rise of Brazil was also apparent from the increase in her population. With some 50,000 whites and less than 100,000 others (not counting the savage Indians) by the middle of the seventeenth century, Brazil proudly registered more than 1,500,000 people in the 1770's, a more than tenfold increase! Comparatively, Spanish America had less than doubled its total population (Indians included), from some ten million in the mid-seventeenth century to about fifteen million in the late eighteenth century, of which only 20 per cent were whites. British America increased from less than a million (1620) to two million (1763), not counting the Indians, of course. Thus, Brazil in the late seventeenth and the eighteenth century showed the highest rate of increase in all of America, the beginning of a continuous and rapid expansion. Of all these people, a little more than half were probably Black slaves and among the others the number of half-breeds was considerable. The captaincy of Minas Gerais, after the gold rush, had grown to more than 300,000 inhabitants, or 20.5 per cent of the total population of Brazil. Baía followed, with 289,000 (18.5 per cent); then Pernambuco, with 240,000 (15.4 per cent); then Rio de Janeiro, with 216,000 (13.8 per cent). São Paulo had only 117,000, or 7.5 per cent. Together, these five captaincies encompassed 75 per cent of Brazil's population.

A good many cities had come into being. Rio de Janeiro counted 51,000 inhabitants in 1780, having become the third town in the Portuguese Empire, immediately after Lisbon and Baía. Rio had a city plan similar to that of the Portuguese capital, its architecture attempting to copy some of the novelties proudly displayed by "modern" Lisbon—a product of the earthquake. Within Latin America, Brazil now came to be well represented, her two "metropoles"—Baía and Rio—ranking immediately after Mexico City (135,000 in 1749) and equal to Puebla and Lima (both with some 52,000 in the 1790's).

Urban concentration was higher than in Mexico (10 per cent), bureaucracy and general administration reaching from the cities to the
countryside, a general feature of Portugal, Spain, and their Empires.

Most of this growth resulted, of course, from immigration. The
gold rush and further news of Brazil's affluence appealed to thousands
in Portugal, coming from all over but particularly from the North and
from the islands of Madeira and the Azores. During the first two decades of the eighteenth century a maximum of five to six thousand
people may have quit Portugal for Brazil, quite a large exodus for
those days. It must be remembered that in Europe the eighteenth
century meant a general population increase too (see chapter 8).
Few measures were ever adopted to channel the emigration properly,
yet the ever-growing number of able-bodied men who left the country
each year led the government to limit emigration by establishing a
passport system (1720). A substantial number of newcomers arrived
compulsorily: the African slaves, whose numbers never ceased to grow
throughout the eighteenth century. Although global statistics are
poor, an annual average of 20,000 slaves may have arrived during
the peak years of the gold rush.

Last but not least, another proof of Brazil's expansion was found
in the conquest of the new lands in the interior. By comparing maps
of the colony in 1650 and in 1750, one can see the immense addition
of newly settled or explored territory. From south to north, all the
territory of the coastal captaincies to Piauí had been changed into
profitable land. Great shares of Maranhão and Pará were also places
of settlement, including a large part of the Amazon Valley. Inland,
all of Minas Gerais and some good parcels from Goiás and Mato
Grosso had been conquered by the settlers. In all, about a half of
present-day Brazil was explored and her native population subjected
to Portuguese rule. This fact was internationally acknowledged when
the Treaty of Madrid (1750) between Spain and Portugal formally replaced the old and forgotten Tordesillas demarcation of 1494 by a
new border roughly identical to that of present-day Brazil.

This great expansion inland resulted from the successive *bandeiras*
and *entradas* (see chapter 7), which left São Paulo and other centers
under the leadership of many brave and able captains. Fernão Dias
Pais Leme, his son, and his son-in-law Manuel de Borba Gato ex-

plored for seven years (1674–81) the territory of Sabarábuçu (Minas Gerais) looking for precious stones. Luis Castanho de Almeida traveled all over northern Mato Grosso (1671), while Bartolomeu da Silva wandered about in Goiás (1682). Other expeditions departed to fight the Indians or the Spaniards, to relieve besieged garrisons, or to capture fugitive slaves. Clashes with Jesuits often occurred. The settling down of the Portuguese in the interior of Brazil did not mean that a continuous area of settlements with cultivated fields in between had been accomplished. On the contrary, there were a great many "islands" of settlement, in a river valley or around a layer of ore, totally isolated in themselves, surrounded by hostile or poorly known territory and lacking any adequate communications.

Late in the seventeenth century, explorers from São Paulo did find the gold they had been seeking for so long. Ore beds with gold, emeralds, and other precious stones were successively discovered in the last years of the 1600's and to the 1720's. The most important gold mines were located in what is now Minas Gerais ("General Mines"), a name that clearly suggests the importance of that area. But Goiás, Mato Grosso, Baía, and other captaincies soon opened their fabulous interiors to the miners. All over Brazil names of newly founded settlements symbolized the gold rush of the eighteenth century: Ouro Preto (Black Gold, because of its darker color), Ouro Fino, Minas de Santa Isabel, Diamantina, Diamantino, and many others. The gold rush brought thousands of people, mostly from Portugal. A conflict immediately arose between them and the Paulistas, who felt they had a right to make use of the mines which they had discovered by their persistent efforts. A series of skirmishes known as the war of the *Emboabas* killed some hundreds in 1708–9. The Emboabas, who were much more numerous, won, but the real victory belonged to the Crown (to whom both sides had appealed), which profited by the dissension to set up a strict and rigorous control over the mines and their exploitation. Gold thus became the cornerstone of the Brazilian economy throughout the eighteenth century.

It is hard to know how much gold was actually extracted from the Brazilian soil in those days. As always happens, an enormous amount was smuggled and could never be controlled or registered. The most reliable sources have already been mentioned in chapter 8.

Gold shipments started around 1699 and went on increasing to 1720, when a maximum of more than 25,000 kg. arrived in Portugal. In 1725, 20,000 kg. were shipped but from then on quantities slowly but steadily declined. Yet, to the 1760's annual averages of more than 14,000 kg. were recorded. The decline speeded up in the 1770's and 1780's. The ore beds were gradually exhausted; only an insignificant amount appeared in the customs records by the early 1800's, The gold export figures still showed 15.2 per cent of the total Brazilian exports in 1801, but only 5.6 per cent in 1805 and a ridiculous 0.2 per cent in 1816. After 1729, gold was coupled with diamonds, found in great quantities also in Minas Gerais, Mato Grosso, and Baía. The epoch of expansion in diamonds roughly coincided with that of gold, quickly declining by Pombal's time. Gold and diamonds together have been estimated in gold pounds sterling up to the 1740's: totaling £728,000 in 1711–15, their value went up to £1,715,201 in 1721–25, then declined to the 1730's. It increased again to £1,311,175 (1736–40), then to £1,371,680 (1741–45). Summing up, gold and diamonds worth some £7,248,669 entered Lisbon—which means Europe—in thirty-four years.

It took some time to organize an efficient tributary system from the new mines. In the beginning, the general legislation on mining was simply applied. Going back to the Middle Ages, it exacted the payment to the Crown of one-fifth (*quinto*) of all the ores. The problem was how to control the amount of gold actually extracted and to avoid smuggling in large quantities. No wonder that up to 1713 the total amount of gold confiscations by Crown officials almost matched the product from the fifths. On the whole, more than 155 million réis were collected both ways, an annual revenue of about 12 million réis. In 1713 the governor-general wanted to set up royal foundries, in order to prevent gold dust from circulating and thus curb smuggling. The miners vehemently opposed the measure, a compromise being reached between the two: the Crown would receive a fixed yearly revenue of 30 gold arrobas (1 arroba = 32 lb. avoirdupois), later reduced to 25, then increased to 37. In ten-and-a-half years (1714 to 1725), some 312½ arrobas were paid, a total of 1,920 million réis, or 182 million a year. From 1725 to 1735 foundries were at last established, all the gold being carried there, the Crown share (⅕) deducted and the rest given back to its owners in sealed bars. According to this system, 1,068 gold arrobas entered the royal treasury in 1725–35, a total 5,249 million réis, i.e., 524 million per year.

In 1735 a new taxation system was established. Each miner, aged fourteen or more, had to pay a per capita tax of 17 grams of gold a year. Up to 1751 this system reported 2,066 arrobas, or 12,700 million réis (almost 800 million a year). The revenue afterward declined: yearly averages of about 100 arrobas (1751–54), 105 (1755–59), 97 (1760–64), 87 (1765–69), 77 (1770–74), and 73 (1775–77). In 1785 no more than 57 arrobas were paid; in 1808 only 30; in 1819, 7; and in 1820, just 2! The amount of the per capita taxation was gradually reduced, of course.

Sugar ranked in value above gold and diamonds combined for many, many years. In 1670, 2,000,000 arrobas of sugar left Brazil, estimated at more than £2,000,000. The crisis which followed (see chapter 8) brought the Brazilian sugar industry almost to collapse, but the economic recovery afterward restored its importance. Throughout the first half of the eighteenth century more and more sugar was produced and shipped to Europe: 1,600,000 arrobas in 1710, 2,500,000 in 1760. Interestingly enough, England had virtually ceased to be Brazil's main market for sugar—preferring her own, from the West Indies—which hardly affected production, at least in those days. Italy and other Mediterranean countries absorbed most of it, while Portugal and her empire were by no means unimportant buyers. But the decline started because of West Indies competition. With better techniques, which led to a remarkable yield increase—Jamaica in 1788 exported more sugar than all of Brazil—the Central American sugar ousted Brazilian sugar from the European markets. Production went down to 1,500,000 arrobas (1776), a level that could be maintained for a while (particularly because of the Anglo-American war), then to 660,000 (1809), and 460,000 (1812).

Both mining and sugar plantations required cheap and abundant labor. Later on, cotton, tobacco, and other extensive plantations needed this labor too. It is not surprising, then, that slave imports from Africa jumped to figures unheard of before. The 7,500 annual level of the 1660's doubled or even tripled by the late eighteenth century. In 1775, Angola alone exported 13,534 Negroes, but others arrived from Guinea and elsewhere. There are no reliable figures that help us estimate the total slave trade, yet a tentative number of two million for the period 1700–1820 would probably be near the truth.

Below the three mainstays of the Brazilian economy in the eighteenth century—gold and diamonds, sugar, and slaves—there were many other lesser but not insignificant commercial items. Tobacco ranked first, an important merchandise after 1650, with rising quantities and values. In certain areas of Brazil, such as Baía, it even surpassed sugar, and for a long time that captaincy owned its monopoly for export purposes. When restrictions were lifted, tobacco expanded in Pernambuco and elsewhere although it later declined in favor of cotton. Cotton had much less importance in the beginning and valuable exports did not start before the 1780's. From then on, its position never ceased to grow, cotton being shipped to Portugal and then re-exported to England in large quantities. Pernambuco and Maranhão were the main areas of production. In the second half of the eighteenth century the Crown fostered the sowing and export of wheat and rice with great success. By 1781 all the rice consumed in Portugal came from her American colony. Fibers and dyestuffs also increased in the late 1700's, despite the fact that Brazilian indigo could never compete with the West Indian and the Indian, either in production or quality. Cacao became profitable after 1750, exports doubling in both quantity and price in twenty years. Last but not least, hides became another significant export by the late eighteenth century. Cattle grazing had gradually developed all over the colony but most particularly in the southern captaincies and the colony of Sacramento, in what is now Uruguay. Leather became the cheapest and most usual raw material for all purposes, from clothing to housing. In 1777 hides valued at more than £150,000 were exported. Horses, too, were bred in large quantities and shipped alive to the mainland. In the early nineteenth century, exports of hides gradually made up for the loss in the gold output (10.7 per cent in 1801; 13.6 per cent in 1805; 20.8 per cent in 1816).

Summing up, one could say that Brazil's fantastic growth and wealth throughout the eighteenth century depended chiefly on three main items but was supported by a large variety of other products.

The end of the gold and diamond era stimulated cattle grazing and sugar, tobacco, and cotton plantations.

Local manufacturing was not stimulated, except for shipbuilding: during the eighteenth century many of the India ships had been made in Brazil. While fostering agricultural activity, the traditional colonial policy of all countries was to prevent any competition with the mainland. A royal act of 1785 forbade all textile manufacturing in Brazil, except for the production of cheap cotton cloth used by the slaves and for sacks. As a consequence most of the Portuguese craft output went directly to Brazil, which accounted for 96 to 98 per cent of all national industry exports to the overseas territories by the early nineteenth century. Despite this, Portugal's balance of trade with Brazil showed a constant deficit to the end of the Peninsular War.

Part of Brazil's economic—as well as demographic and geographic —development should be credited to the several companies of commerce formed in the 1600's and the 1700's. The Junta do Comércio, a state institution that derived from the mid-seventeenth-century Company for the Brazilian Trade (see chapters 7 and 8), organized ship-convoying to and from Brazil to 1720. The African Company of Cabo Verde and Cachéu (1680) indirectly stimulated trade with America. It was followed by a short-lived Company for Pará and Maranhão (1682), which was granted the slave-trade monopoly with the duty of supplying that region with 10,000 slaves annually and with all kinds of merchandise.

Pombal's government instituted two other companies: one for Pará and Maranhão only (Companhia Geral do Grão-Pará e Maranhão, 1755); the other for Pernambuco and Paraíba (Companhia Geral de Pernambuco e Paraíba, 1759). The former was concerned with both trade and agriculture. With headquarters in Lisbon and a capital of 1,200,000 cruzados, directed by a council of deputies elected from among the largest share-owners, it was given important privileges (such as being exempt from the usual court jurisdiction), although the state had no financial part in it. For twenty years the Company was granted the trade monopoly with Pará and Maranhão, having its own fleet which included men-of-war. It fostered agriculture in that area, especially cotton and rice. North Brazil—particularly Maranhão—developed greatly because of its activity, becoming in

442   "BRAZIL"

twenty years "one of the most dynamic and prosperous" regions
(C. R. Boxer). It is true that the War of American Independence also
had a share in promoting Maranhão's expansion, because it forced
Great Britain to look somewhere else for the cotton which usually
came from North America. By the 1770's the Company owned more
than thirty ships, actively engaged in trading cotton, wood, salt, rice,
and slaves between the Old and the New World. The other Company
was still wealthier, with initial capital of 2 million cruzados and was
granted similar privileges and monopolies for the areas of Pernambuco and Paraíba. Its action fostered agriculture too, particularly
production of sugar and cacao. Thirty ships constantly crossed the
Atlantic, supplying those two captaincies with slaves and other
commodities, while exporting to Europe the bountiful Brazilian outputs. Quoting historian C. R. Boxer again, "the stagnant sugar trade
of Pernambuco-Paraíba experienced a temporary revival."

Private interests and especially the anti-Pombaline reaction of
Maria's government put an end to the chartered companies as such
(1778–79). Nonetheless they continued to exist as private associations,
albeit with much less significance for the development of Brazil.

Brazil's own currency started in this period. As a rule, money was
not very abundant throughout the colony until the early 1700's (the
situation was the same in Portugal's colonies in Africa), although in
some areas—like Baía—it could be plentiful. It all depended on the
amount of trade carried on with Europe.

The sugar crisis of the late seventeenth century, for instance,
depleted Brazil of most of its currency, creating all sorts of problems
for the colony and for the people in general. Besides Portuguese coins,
Spanish currency was legal and often easier to get. Different commodities could be used instead of currency, namely cloth, flour, salted
meat, hides, sugar, and cotton. The gold era, of course, introduced
gold as a standard currency, even when coins were not available.

In 1694, after countless demands and representations, the Crown
established the first Brazilian Mint in Baía. It also functioned, for
short periods, in Rio de Janeiro and Recife, where it minted the
coins necessary for those areas. The Brazilian currency encompassed a
great many denominations, both in gold (1,000, 2,000, and 4,000 réis—
the moeda) and in silver (20, 40, 60, 160, 320—the pataca—and 640

réis). Copper coins appeared only in John V's times, Cape Verde and Angola currency circulating in Portuguese America to that period (5, 10, and 20 réis). From 1702 onward a second permanent Mint was active in Rio de Janeiro. New denominations gradually made their appearance: the gold coin of 6,400 réis; the silver coins of 960 and 80 réis, related to the pataca; and those of 75, 150, 300, and 600 réis, related to the Portuguese tostão (100 réis). Copper coins included 5, 10, 20, 40, and 80 réis. The State of Maranhão received the first local currency only in 1749. To prevent currency exports from the colony, the Brazilian real had a lower value than the Portuguese one. Some of these coins circulated all over the Anglo-Saxon world (including America) up to the late 1700's.

Public finance was gradually organized and improved in revenue collecting, centralization, and accounting methods. Pombal's reforms in the mother country (see chapter 8) affected Brazil too, as they affected the whole Portuguese Empire. Treasury boards (Juntas da Fazenda) appeared for all captaincies-general during the 1760's and the 1770's. Directly subordinated to Lisbon, they exercised collective responsibility and supervision for all royal fiscal arms, including the customs houses.

The Crown's revenues suffered no structural changes by this time, yet new ones appeared, as public expenditure grew larger. The tax on gold and diamond mining, for instance, was certainly the most relevant of all. Between 1699 and 1715 the first import duties were imposed on all items. On slave imports several heavy taxes were also introduced in the same epoch. In the mid- and late 1600's several local excises (on wine, brandy, oil, salt, tobacco, etc.) appeared on imports. Brazil also had to contribute 8 million cruzados to help finance royal marriages between the ruling houses of Portugal and Spain in 1729. Pombal created new taxes and duties (for education and other matters) and his successors did the same in Maria's and John's reigns. Yet royal revenues from Brazil constantly declined from the 1740's on. In the late 1770's they were reduced to about a third of what they had been before.

On the other hand public debt continued to grow: figures from 1762 to 1780 show that the colony's exchequer owed more and more, particularly in 1763–67 and in 1774–78. The budget wavered between surplus and deficit: in 1775 it registered a surplus of 11,762,000 réis, and a deficit of 111,502,000 réis two years later. It was actually more a matter of war and defense than of good or bad administration.

The growth of a landed aristocracy in Brazil had started much before the end of the seventeenth century (see chapters 5 and 7), an obvious consequence of the quasi-feudal structure introduced by the Portuguese settlers and government. Nevertheless, problems of curbing land concentration did not apparently affect the development of the colony before that time. The Crown attempted to restrict the size of land grants and even mentioned expropriating those properties which were kept fallow (in the medieval tradition). Yet large units continued to exist and to grow larger, a serious obstacle to the rise of a middle class and to the advancement of the economy. Throughout the eighteenth century, Brazilian agriculture lagged, especially in contrast to the West Indies and North America, yields being low and progress nil.

Socially speaking, the growth of the latifundium brought about the rise of an upper class of large landowners, mostly white yet frequently mixed with black or Indian blood. In economic and social influence they soon had to compete with a flourishing bourgeoisie of traders in the main ports. By the mid- and late 1700's, this class was doubled by the growing bureaucracy (jurists, lawyers, clerks), the army officers, and several other professions. The process in Brazil thus corresponded to that in Portugal, although with less of a class struggle. Despite some conflicts, expressed in several local riots and town administration, landed proprietors, traders, and civil servants managed to get together within the general framework of being Brazilians. Instead, rising opposition to the mother country and to those Portuguese appointed to offices in Brazil would overcome the social contradictions until the moment of independence.

This group of *crioulos* totally controlled the coastline and the large towns, in spite of often being outnumbered by Negroes and mulattoes. In São Paulo and Rio Grande de São Pedro they formed a majority by the mid-1700's, some with well-known or presumed lineages which could be traced back to the earliest times of settlement.

In the interior, particularly in the mining areas, social realities were different. Blacks and half-breeds predominated, well-established landed families were few, property was more evenly divided and less often entailed. It was the frontier region, unhampered by social barriers and open to social changes. During the gold and diamond rush it was also the country of immigration, constantly flooded with white Portuguese newcomers and black African slaves. Social organization was vague, outlawry rampant. Miscegenation naturally flourished, the ethnical patterns being altered every generation. It did not take much time to give the half-breed the social and political leadership in those areas, again despite their being outnumbered by the Blacks. In Pará and Maranhão the social, and especially the race, picture had some peculiarities. The majority here was formed by the Christian Indians and the *mamelucos* or *caboclos* (half-breed of white and Indian). Up to the 1750's Negroes were few, but a massive import of slaves afterward completely changed Pará and Maranhão's ethnical structure.

The religious orders had a very relevant role in exploring and colonizing Brazil. The natives were relatively easy to convert, compared with the peoples of Africa and Asia. This fact made Brazil a sort of "choice" country for all the missionaries, despite the climate, the hardships geography offered, and the dangers posed by the ferocity of many Indian tribes. However, nowhere was missionary zeal more rewarding than in Portuguese America. Brazil gave to all those who cared for the "salvation" of her inhabitants spiritual solace as well as material affluence.

Among the many orders which exerted influence in Brazil, the Jesuits undoubtedly took the lead. Dominant by the late sixteenth or early seventeenth century, they had built a true kingdom by the middle of the eighteenth. They could be found everywhere, from Amazonia to the River Plate, although their main fiefs lay in the Paraná-Uruguay basins. They owned extensive landholdings, such as sugar plantations and cattle ranches. They were the lords of hundreds or thousands of black slaves and had under their direction armies of thousands of Amerindians, who acted as their clients. In the *reduções* and *aldeias* (see chapter 7) their power tolerated interference from neither settlers nor Crown representatives.

Regarding slavery, the history of the Jesuits in America appears most contradictory. Struggling to absurd limits for freedom for the

Indians, which they finally achieved, harassing the economic expansion of Brazil by resisting the settlers' demands for cheap native labor, incurring the hatred of the whites and the secular clergy itself by their systematic policy of protection for the Amerindian, they yet found few words to condemn the import of slaves from Africa and even favored Negro slavery as a way of diverting attention from their protégés. In a way they can be regarded as responsible for the intensity of the slave trade between the two continents and the replacement of an evil by a still greater one.

From a political standpoint, the Jesuits soon menaced both the policy of centralization carried on by the Crown and the very definition of Brazil's boundaries. They considered the *aldeias* as theirs and would not tolerate their integration into the general economic, political, and administrative framework of eighteenth-century Brazil. In this sense they opposed white settlers, Crown bureaucrats, and even Church representatives, making themselves hated by all three. Aiming only at the spiritual purity of their Indians and regarding the unity of the Order as above the political distinctions of Portugal and Spain, they often challenged the border definition theoretically arranged by the Lisbon or the Madrid courts, which might destroy the unity of their *aldeias* in America. In this sense they certainly fought for more logical and ethnographically correct borders than the two Crowns, borders that were more related to the natives' interests than the arbitrary principles decided by the governments. Yet such a policy could never and would never be tolerated, not in the eighteenth or in any other century down to the present.

In the Amazon basin, Jesuits and Carmelites often clashed, the latter (a smaller and less important order) defending Portuguese expansion there, the former resisting any change of the status quo which united a great many missions under theoretical Spanish control. In Mato Grosso the Spanish Jesuits preferred to burn out several *aldeias* and migrate with their Indian flocks inland, rather than surrender to new authorities when they learned that the Treaty of Madrid gave to Portugal the right bank of the river Guaporé, where they had settled. Later they tried to get back what they had lost, returning to their former places but resisting the Portuguese authorities. At the same time they attempted to attract Indians who lived in Portuguese territory. A hostile situation resulted from all this, involving an open fight between Portugal and Spain. Along the Paraná-Uruguay rivers similar incidents occurred throughout the late seventeenth and most of the eighteenth century. If, in the beginning, the Jesuit *aldeias* gave soldiers and full support to the Spanish against the Portuguese, afterward they opposed both countries and instigated the Guaraní Indians to open rebellion (in 1752 and 1756), which prevented the enforcement of the Treaty of Madrid.

One can rightly say that this war was the last cause for the "final solution" of the Jesuit problem. Pombal, who was then full master in Lisbon, could not tolerate such a defiance of his government's orders. The Jesuits had to be put down. When he found he could accuse them of plotting to kill the king (1758; see chapter 8), he expelled them from Portugal and all her overseas dominions (1759). Two years afterward he declared all Brazilian Indians to be free and strictly forbade any act of enslavement by the settlers. Cheered by most people, the arrest and expulsion of the Jesuits could be carried out with much less trouble than one might believe. In 1760 practically all the Jesuits had left Brazil. Urban and rural properties of the Society passed into the hands of the Crown, some being immediately auctioned off and the rest remaining under royal administration for some years before meeting the same fate. The Indians certainly lost their best friends, while the missionary effort was jeopardized for a good many decades because the other religious orders had neither men nor resources to take over the Jesuits' task. Education also suffered for a while, with the sudden lack of many teachers. Pombal established the Subsídio Literário (1772) to subsidize primary and secondary schooling, but the results came slowly. It was only in 1800 that the new Seminary at Olinda offered the Brazilian students a fine body of disciplines.

Among the other orders, the Carmelites, the Franciscans, and the Benedictines should be mentioned. The latter two tried very hard to replace the Jesuits but with little success.

The secular clergy, more interested in administrative problems (a result of the newly created dioceses) and in providing bureaucratic or teaching personnel to the civilized areas, neglected the missions and became thoroughly integrated in the white society of the *crioulos*.

In Brazil, as elsewhere, the late 1700's and early 1800's brought about the decline of the secular clergy and the religious orders, and of the Church in general.

FROM COLONY TO NATION

Brazil's internal life had gradually become a more independent one, and one more worth recording as well. Each captaincy began experiencing local evolution, not necessarily connected with the general situation affecting the whole colony. This was a natural result of Brazil's rise and expansion in every aspect of activity. The expulsion of the Dutch from the North and the Northeast (see chapter 7) had been very much a Brazilian affair, despite the help the colony got from the motherland. The reconquest of Angola and São Tomé depended mainly upon the initiatives and the interests of Brazilian settlers who could not give up their main source of labor. In the late seventeenth and throughout the eighteenth century Brazil had grown so much and the advance of the Portuguese inland had gone so far that the vague terms of the Tordesillas Treaty (1494) between Portugal and Spain no longer served any purpose. A real border definition, based upon facts rather than theories, was becoming necessary, actually less for the Portuguese than for the Spaniards who witnessed a constant erosion of their own territory.

It was in the North that Brazil's frontiers were first defined. The French had settled down in Cayenne and their attempts to expand southward, to the Amazon, challenged the Portuguese allegation that their border should be much more to the north. To enforce this point of view, King Pedro II ordered a fort built in Macapá, on the northern bank of the river (1687). The French stormed this fort, but the Portuguese were able to regain it shortly afterward (1697). As Portugal's external policy in those days aimed at strengthening an alliance with France, the Lisbon government compromised with Louis XIV. A treaty signed in 1701 gave France all the lands between the Amazon and the Oiapoc. The change of alliances in Europe reversed this. Portugal's entrance in the War of the Spanish Succession on the side of England and Austria against France, and the victory the allied forces achieved, gave back to Portugal the disputed territory (Treaty of Utrecht, 1713). Thus, the final border of Brazil was defined at the Oiapoc River, as it still is. (For a brief period, from 1809 to 1815, the Portuguese occupied French Guiana in response to Napoleon's invasion of Portugal.)

With Spain, problems were somewhat more complex and hard to solve, particularly in the South. The Portuguese had always claimed the Rio de la Plata (River Plate) as their southern border, but had done little or nothing to enforce that claim. Along the river's Uruguay basin, Portuguese and Spanish Indian *aldeias,* directed by the Jesuits, spied on each other but went no further. In 1675 the limits of the newly created diocese of Rio were defined as reaching the River Plate. In 1680 the Portuguese decided to try a definitive occupation of "their" territory, sending an expedition to the South and founding a settlement at Sacramento on the northern branch of the Rio de la Plata, opposite Buenos Aires. This new "colony," as the Portuguese called it, depended on the Rio de Janeiro captaincy. Those were the days before the gold rush, when Portugal depended heavily upon Spanish silver. The founding of Sacramento was an attempt— which failed—to control the silver stream from the Potosí mines in what is now Bolivia. Actually, what the Portuguese got from it derived from cattle raising alone.

The Spaniards immediately realized the danger of a Portuguese fixation; as a result the history of the Sacramento colony consisted mostly of political and/or military strife, with alternate victories for either party. In 1681 the first Spanish raid destroyed the small settlement but the Portuguese returned. In 1704, during the War of the Spanish Succession, the Spaniards attacked and took possession of the colony. The Treaty of Utrecht (1713) restored it to the Portuguese, yet less than twenty-five years later both sides were again engaged in an open war in America (1735–37). Although victory belonged to the Portuguese, it seemed clear that their permanence there would hardly be sustained without a constant struggle involving a continuous flow of money (with little profit). In 1719 the Crown had tried to back Sacramento by setting up new settlements, such as Montevideo, which the Spaniards promptly captured and fortified (1726). Influenced by the able diplomat Alexandre de Gusmão, the Lisbon government compromised and after lengthy negotiations both sides signed the Treaty of Madrid, which gave Sacramento to Spain in exchange for seven Spanish Jesuit mission stations along the River Uruguay (January 1750).

But nothing was settled yet. The colony was not actually evacuated by the Portuguese nor were the Spanish Jesuits willing to surrender to a hated enemy. Moreover, in Portugal Pombal had come to power (1750), and with him a new uncompromising policy. The Treaty of Madrid was unilaterally denounced (1761), and the Seven Years War transposed to the Rio de la Plata region. Once again the Spaniards ousted the Portuguese (1762), but once again international treaties put them back (Treaty of Paris, 1763). Pombal's downfall brought about a reversal in external policy. Maria's government decided to step back and implement the 1750 decisions. Thus, the Treaty of San Ildefonso (1777) definitely put Sacramento in Spanish hands, along with the seven villages that in 1750 had become Portuguese, some months after another Spanish attack had expelled the Portuguese forces from the much-disputed colony. Brazil's southern border was defined as beginning at the Chuí River, and the River Plate estuary could safely remain a Spanish possession. Later attempts to absorb Uruguay (as in 1817, when Montevideo was made the capital of a new province called Província Cisplatina) showed that the problem had not been satisfactorily resolved yet.

The definition of the western border owed much to the Jesuit and Carmelite missions established all over the Amazon basin, but not less to the daring expeditions of seventeenth- and eighteenth-century *bandeirantes*. By the mid-1700's, a series of advance posts had been established, justifying the claims of Portuguese diplomacy and leading to frontier definition in the treaties of Madrid and San Ildefonso. These rounded out the Brazilian territory in close approximation to present-day borders, as the appended map shows more clearly than any literary description.

Internally, social and regional strife characterized many of the captaincies. Frontier regions were more likely to be marred by dissension than the more stable coastal areas. Interestingly enough, the first important rebellions aimed at expelling the Jesuits and counterbalancing their influence among the Indians. The foremost of those

STATE OF THE
MARANHÃO AND GRÃO PARÁ

MARAJÓ

• Belem de Pará

• S. Luis de Maranhão

C. S. Roque

Rio Maranon

Rio Negro

Rio Branco

Rio Solimoes

Rio Javari

Rio Jurua

Rio Purus

Rio Madeira

Rio Amazonas

Rio Tapajos

Rio Xingu

Rio Araguaia

Rio Tocantins

PIAUI

CEARÁ

RIO GRANDE DO NORTE

Rio Jacuariba

PARAIBA

Olinda

• Recife

ITAMARACÁ

• Vitória

PERNAMBUCCO

SERGIPE

BAHIA

Rio São Francisco

Rio Paraguassu

• Cidade do Salvador

B R A S I L

GOIÁS

Rio das Antas

ILHEUS

Rio Pardo

Rio Guapore

• Vila Bela

• Vila de Cuiabá

DE MATO
GROSSO

• Villa Boa

O

Rio Paranaiba

MINAS
GERAIS

Rio Jequitinhonha

PORTO SEGURO

• Porto Seguro

Rio Taquari

Rio Grande

• Villa Rica

ESPIRITO SANTO

• Vitória

SAO PAULO

Rio Tietê

Rio Paranapanema

Rio Paraiba

S T A T E

O F

PART OF THE
SPANISH VICEROYALTY
OF PERU

S. Paulo •

Santos •

• S. Sebastião

• Cabo Frio

Rio de Janeiro

RIO-DE-JANEIRO

Curitiba •

• S. Vicente

Paranagua

Rio Iquaçú

I. S. Catarina

Rio Paraguai

Rio Uruguai

RIO GRANDE
DE S. PEDRO

COLONIA DO
SACRAMENTO

• S. Pedro do Rio Grande

| 0 | 550 | 1100 Km |

| 0 | 350 | 700 miles |

riots took place in Maranhão and Pará (1661, 1684–85). They must be regarded as among the earlier organized resistance movements within the colony against principles and determinations imposed from the outside.

The gold rush brought about the turmoil among miners that has already been mentioned. The Paulistas resisted the overwhelming immigration of Portuguese, whom they scornfully called *emboabas,* a native word for feather-legged chickens, because most immigrants wore long boots. The war of the *emboabas,* actually a succession of skirmishes of little importance, opposed the local settlers to the newcomers, and was the forerunner of a civil war in Brazil (1708 to 1709). Shortly afterward another dissension, this time with a more social coloration, took place in the North, in Pernambuco, between the petty bourgeoisie of traders and craftsmen and the wealthy sugar landowners. The pretext was the bourgeois participation in the municipal assemblies and councils, which the landowners tried to prevent or reduce to a minimum; the deeper reason, however, was the conflict between long-established families of settlers and the prospering Portuguese newcomers. When Recife, the traders' center, was raised to *vila* (1709), thus becoming independent of the old capital, Olinda, the landowners strongly reacted, and an open struggle began. It seems that some landowners even thought of seceding from the motherland. The fight, known as the War of the *Mascates* (i.e., street peddlers of small wares, especially fabrics), lasted until 1711, when the Crown succeeded in restoring order and punishing the rebel landowners. A third rebellion with somewhat more precise goals of autonomy took place in 1720, when Filipe dos Santos Freire led an armed protest in Minas Gerais against the Crown's fiscal policy, represented by the gold foundries. The rebellion of slaves, miners, and landowners was put down by the governor count of Assumar, and its leader executed.

Brazil's general prosperity, along with the wise administrative policy followed by the Crown throughout the eighteenth century, smoothed over rebellious or autonomous tendencies for a long time. But it was obvious that the American revolution and the rise of the new political ideologies would have their impact on the colony sooner or later.

Again Minas Gerais, the most troubled and active of all Brazilian captaincies, led the way. A small intelligentsia had risen there, composed of poets and prose writers quite receptive to modern currents of thought. The decline of gold output brought about a serious crisis for Minas, and discontent grew, mainly against the oppressive fiscal policy. Second Lieutenant (*alferes*) Joaquim José da Silva Xavier, known as *Tiradentes* (lit. "tooth-puller"), because he also practiced dentistry, apparently led a conspiracy against Portugal, vaguely aiming at the secession of Minas under a republican government and at the abolition of slavery (the so-called Inconfidência Mineira). The plot was discovered (1789), its members arrested, and Tiradentes executed (1792). He was the first—and actually one of the few—Brazilian martyrs for the cause of independence.

In 1798 another republican plot, this time in Baía, gathered together some low-class coloreds and slaves. The execution of four of the leaders easily suppressed it.

This brief reference to breakaway movements suggests that Brazil had reached for political maturity and that the question of her independence would just be a matter of years. Demographically, the colony's growth was paralleling that of the motherland: more than 1,500,000 people in the 1770's, 2,500,000 by the end of the century, 3,600,000 in 1819. The large towns were Rio de Janeiro (60,000 in 1808; 130,000 in 1818) and Baía (80,000 in 1819). About a half of Brazil's population were Negroes (mostly slaves), more than one-fourth were half-breeds, and the remainder "whites." It is to the latter that the independence movement must be credited. In 1819 the whites who considered themselves Brazilians by birth or descent—landowners, traders, craftsmen—almost totaled one million people, against some fifty to sixty thousand *Reinóis* (lit., "realmers") or *Marinheiros* (sailors), i.e., immigrant newcomers from Portugal and Portuguese bureaucratic personnel. The white Brazilians (many actually with mixed blood) despised the other groups and naturally aimed at taking power in their own hands. In Brazil, as everywhere in Latin America, autonomy really meant power for the white settlers. They resented the maintenance of colonial status, which prevented them from trading directly with foreign countries; they complained of Lisbon's great distance for the solving of administrative and political matters;

they accused the officials sent from Lisbon of corruption and despotism; and so forth. In short, their grievances were those that every colony close to independence harbors against its mother country.

Culturally, too, some autochthonous forms were in the making. In the early 1700's, several mediocre writers started exalting Brazil's natural beauties. Descriptions of the colony, in its several aspects, became somewhat more common, a growing interest in Brazil arising both in Portugal and abroad. In 1769, Basílio da Gama published *Uraguay*, the first sort of epic ennobling the natives of Brazil. But it was the literary academies, founded during the last quarter of the century, that stimulated the development of a true Brazilian literature and helped shape a national culture in Portuguese America. In Minas Gerais, in those days the wealthiest and most populous region of Brazil, a group of academicians set the style for the country's poetry and prose writing, while indulging in political activities as well: lawyers and jurists like Cláudio Manuel da Costa (1729–89), Tomás António Gonzaga alias Dirceu (1744–1810), Alvarenga Peixoto (1744–93), and Silva Alvarenga (1744–93) became very popular, both in Brazil and in Portugal, where their works were first published. Two clerics, Caldas Barbosa and Santa-Rita Durão, exerted a similar influence with their poems.

In the arts, the eighteenth and early nineteenth century saw the proliferation of monuments in the main cities, a consequence of Brazil's wealth and expansion. Those monuments, as well as the newly founded towns, reflected exuberant baroque and rococo styles, of Portuguese inspiration yet with local features. The well-preserved towns of Ouro Preto, Mariana, and Diamantina are good examples of that fusion. Local architects and sculptors, like the renowned António Francisco Lisboa (1730–1814), nicknamed "Aleijadinho" ("the Little Cripple"), flourished, giving rise to a national art. The cathedral of Baía (of Jesuit origin), the monasteries of St. Bento (in Rio and Olinda), and the churches of St. Francisco (Baía, Olinda, Paraíba, Ouro Preto, Mariana) still exhibit the affluence of the colony in those days, providing good examples of fine architecture and lavish decoration in gilt-wood and tiles.

Brazil's progress toward autonomy did not follow the same pattern as the other American countries. A unique succession of events altered Brazil's condition with a minimum of violence and practically no change of structure.

In November 1807 Napoleon's army invaded and occupied Portugal. King John VI with most of his government and court decided to take refuge in Brazil. He arrived in Baía in January 1808, then in Rio in March. The seat of Portugal's government was thus transferred from Europe to America. In effect, Brazil became the motherland and Portugal the colony.

Brazil's role as the provisional seat of the Portuguese government lasted for thirteen years, a crucial period for both the European and the American parts of the empire. A new nation was gradually rising from the American colony, and John's rule there was concerned with setting up the needed political, administrative, economic, and cultural framework for Brazil's full emergence. In this sense the years 1808–21 meant much more than the countless decades preceding. The Portuguese court spared no efforts to raise the colony to the status of a great empire.

Up to 1811 or 1812 Napoleon's power and potential impressed all of Europe. Nobody could then foresee his rapid decline and downfall. It was thought that Portugal, like Spain, could be invaded again and again, her territory permanently occupied for an unforeseeable period of time. Pessimists could even argue that the country's independence was lost forever. In this sense, Brazil's promotion to motherland was a natural consequence, and John's anti-colonial acts in Rio de Janeiro can hardly be faulted, even from a purely Portuguese standpoint. Yet things started changing after the first five years. The Iberian Peninsula was free from new French attacks. Fernando VII had been restored to the throne of Spain. But neither John VI (his mother, Maria I, old and long insane, had died only in 1816) nor his wife were willing to go back to Portugal, even with Napoleon confined to exile in Saint Helena, peace in Europe restored by the Vienna Congress (1815), and all of Portugal imploring a return to normality. The government in Rio by then forgot that the abnormal situation had passed, that Portugal was the mother country and Brazil the dependent colony, so much so as to impair Portuguese trade, industry, and finance in favor of the old colony. In fact the court oddly became more Brazilian than Portuguese until a revolution forced it to make a decision about allegiance.

One of John's first acts when arriving in Brazil was to open the ports of the country to all friendly nations and to permit international trade to be carried on with all kinds of merchandise, except a few monopolized ones. Confirmed and defined by the treaty of 1810, this act marked the true end of colonial status. Ships no longer had to proceed to Portugal and pay duties there before their cargoes could be forwarded anywhere in the world. As England was then Portugal's foremost buyer and seller, the act of 1808 (suggested or pressured by English interest) benefited her immensely, while dealing a cruel blow to Portugal's trade. Exports to Portugal went down two-thirds by 1813, then increased a little, but never reached the level of 1807. Imports from Portugal followed a similar trend: about half of what they were to 1813, then some high years, but a decline again after 1816. Imports for 1819 were at a level below that of 1806 and the entire decade before.

In this period the government continued to foster trade, both internally and externally. A Junta for Commerce, Agriculture and Navigation was set up in 1808, roads were opened (particularly in the South), and regular postal communications were established or improved. In the industrial field the measures adopted were still more revolutionary. A royal act allowed the creation of manufactures all over Brazil. In the following years rapid development of local industries such as iron foundries, gunpowder, and the polishing of diamonds occurred. By 1820 a small but well-based industrial activity had arisen.

Brazil's bureaucratic machine was also improved and given a proper framework. Tribunals for all causes and appeals were set up in Rio. Inevitably new taxation had to be imposed, copying that of Portugal (the *sisa,* or sales tax, was introduced in 1809), but other more attractive measures were also enacted. The first Portuguese bank was created in Brazil in 1808. A Junta de Fazenda, like the one in Portugal, for supervising finance matters was established. In 1815 the inevitable political-administrative step was taken: Brazil was made a kingdom, with her own royal institutions. Following the British pattern, a United Kingdom of Portugal, Brazil, and Algarve was created. The captaincies were abolished (although not the offices of captain-general and governor) and replaced by provinces (*provincias*) as in Europe. Successive acts tended to get rid of every colonial attribute and to set up in Brazil a replica of independent Portugal.

A number of educational and cultural measures also helped to shape a modern country. No university was established but academies for the Navy, Artillery and Fortifications, and for Fine Arts were instituted. Other acts created studies of Political Economy, Agriculture, Chemistry, and Sciences in Rio and Baía. The government also established a Museum, a national theater, and a National Library, and planted a Botanical Garden. A Royal Printing Press was founded as well as Military Archives. Until then Brazil had had no press of her own. Every book sold in the American colony had to be imported from Portugal or smuggled from other countries. Along with the lack of schools, this policy aimed to tie the colony to the motherland as closely as possible, preventing any dangerous writings and entirely controlling the forms of culture spreading in Portuguese America. With the arrival of the court, all this changed and books began to be printed in Brazil. The *Gazeta do Rio de Janeiro,* founded in 1808, corresponded to the Lisbon *Gazeta* and was the official government newspaper. In London, a group of Brazilian exiles from Portugal (because of the French invasions) started the *Correio Braziliense,* which espoused independence from Portugal and which lasted to the 1820's. Although forbidden in Portuguese lands, that newspaper was smuggled into and widely read both in Portugal and Brazil.

If the transfer of the seat of the Portuguese monarchy from Lisbon to Rio brought about the definite shaping of a new country, buttressing her unity and displaying her maturity as a nation, it could not thoroughly protect Brazil from the revolutionary turmoil caused by the spread of liberal principles. Republicanism and federalism became fashionable ideas, with relevance to Brazil's modernity and extension. All over Latin America, more or less definite movements toward autonomy had started after 1810, most of them with a republican tinge. Most, yet not all. And it was precisely the existence of an active royal family and court in American lands that "monarchized" some of those movements and posed the problem of whether it would be necessary to change the political institutions in order to achieve independence. Interestingly enough, there were negotiations between the La Plata provinces (future Argentina) and Princess (later queen) Carlota Joaquina, John's wife, to put Carlota on the throne of an autonomous South American country. On the republican side, discontent and revolutionary principles led to an open revolution in Brazil in 1817. Sometime before, the fear of political troubles had already compelled the Rio government to ask for troop reinforcements from loyal Portugal. Shortly afterward the royal act of December 1815 made Brazil into a kingdom, with the purpose of overcoming any attempts at secession. Nonetheless, Pernambuco revolted, its governor was forced to flee for his life, and a republic was proclaimed (March 1817). Although victorious for a while—a constitution was even adopted—with the concurrence of some neighboring provinces, the new republic could not resist the assault of the royal batallions sent from Rio. Thirteen people were executed, and through repression in Pernambuco and elsewhere agitation was put down for a time.

Events in Portugal determined the final independence of Brazil. A revolution broke out in August 1820 (see chapter 10), and one of the first acts of the new constitutional government was to demand the return of the king. John VI still tried to compromise by sending his son, Prince Pedro, to Portugal with full powers, but this the new government rejected. Confronted with the dilemma of staying in Brazil and losing Portugal, or going back to Portugal and (probably) losing Brazil, John VI realized that, after all, he was king of Portugal and a Portuguese. Thus he went back with the whole court, disembarking in Lisbon amidst general contentment in July 1821. His son Pedro stayed in Rio as regent of the kingdom, heading a separate cabinet composed of a secretary for the interior and foreign affairs, one for finance, one for war, and another for the navy.

The constitutional movement had been well received in Brazil. A revolution in Pará (January 1821) gave its support to the victorious Portuguese rebellion. Baía and Rio followed, King John being compelled to accept the new state of things (late February) and to appoint a new cabinet. Yet the return of the monarch to Lisbon could not be well accepted. Brazil was now used to having a king and a court of her own, with the full seat of administration established in her own territory. This understandable feeling was further intensified by the awkward attitude of the first Portuguese constitutional parliament.

Elected in late 1820 and up to March of 1821, the first *cortes* was composed of 181 representatives, of which 100 were from Portugal, 65 from Brazil, and 16 from the other overseas provinces. Each Brazilian province was represented according to its population: Minas Gerais had 13 deputies, Pernambuco 9, Baía 8, São Paulo 6, Rio de Janeiro 5, Ceará 5, Alagoas 3, Paraíba 3, Goiás 2, Maranhão 2, Pará 2, Piauí 2, Rio Grande do Norte 2, Espirito Santo 1, Rio Negro 1, and Santa Catarina 1. Up to October 1821, harmony was maintained between the new *cortes* and Brazil. An act of September 29 even improved administration in Portuguese America by uniformalizing the two categories of provinces and placing them under provisional elected juntas of government, assisted by "generals" for military affairs. The offices of captain-general and governor were abolished.

Controlled by the Portuguese bourgeoisie, however, who saw in Brazil's autonomy as a united kingdom the loss of huge profits in trade and industry, the *cortes* soon adopted a policy intending to force Brazil to give up her new privileges and go back to the old situation of colony. In January 1822, the Rio tribunals were abolished (along with the other less important yet exasperating measures), while in Lisbon a campaign against Brazil, deriding her aspirations and her practices made difficult any agreement. Moreover the *cortes* ordered Prince Pedro to come to Europe, in order to complete his education. This, Brazil could not endure, nor could Pedro, an ambitious and gifted young man whom his father had instructed to stay and take over the leadership of any separatist movement. After having decided to stay, defying the resolution taken by the *cortes,* Pedro was proclaimed "Perpetual defender of Brazil" in May 1822. He appointed a new cabinet headed by José Bonifácio de Andrade e Silva, one of the great architects of Brazil's independence. A Brazilian assembly was summoned and the opposition against Portugal became general. When Lisbon outlawed Prince Pedro's decisions, the latter made up his mind and proclaimed the independence of Brazil (Ipiranga, São Paulo, September 7, 1822). A month later, following the example of Mexico, he was acclaimed emperor. All of Brazil welcomed indepen-

ABOVE: *King John VI, by Domingos António de Seqüeira, early 19th century, Museu Nacional de Arte Antiga, Lisbon.* UPPER RIGHT: *Colonial art of Brazil: group of prophets by António Francisco Lisboa (O Aleijadinho), Congonhas do Campo (Minas Gerais), late 18th century.* BELOW: *Life in Colonial Brazil, 18th century.*

dence, although in some areas the presence of strong Portuguese garrisons made impossible an immediate rally to the Ipiranga proclamation. However, desire for a quick compromise came from both the Brazilian and the Portuguese sides. In Portugal the restoration of absolutism (June 1823) gave John VI and his cabinet full powers to solve the problem, while removing the bitterest obstacle to the recognition of Brazil's independence, the bourgeois *cortes*. Negotiations immediately started, private correspondence between Pedro and his father having never been altogether interrupted. Plans were devised to reunite the two crowns in a fictitious way, by proclaiming John VI as emperor of both countries and Pedro as king of Brazil. At the same time, Pedro's rights to the Portuguese Crown as direct heir were never questioned by anyone. Concepts of being a "Portuguese" or a "Brazilian," as something antagonistic, were still far from defined in those days. Two countries, surely, yet a single nation with a single cultural patrimony. Pedro regarded himself both as a Portuguese prince and a Brazilian ruler and in this he saw no contradiction at all.

Desired by most people and with pressure from the English (for whom the independence of Brazil brought immense possibilities of economic and political expansion, while forever weakening Portugal and making her, if possible, still more dependent on Britain), an agreement could rapidly be reached. By the end of 1823 the last Portuguese troops left Brazil. On August 29, 1825, the treaty of Rio acknowledged the separation of Brazil and its creation as an empire. According to its clauses, John IV was proclaimed theoretical co-emperor of the new country in his lifetime. With very little bloodshed and as smoothly as possible (there had been some fighting in Baía and Rio) the largest nation in Latin America had achieved full sovereignty in her territory. For Portugal, too, a new epoch began.

THE SECONDARY ELEMENTS OF THE EMPIRE

Between the end of the seventeenth century and the end of the nineteenth, there were almost no changes in the Portuguese Empire, except for Brazil. In the North Atlantic Ocean there were the three archipelagoes of the Azores, Madeira, and Cape Verde. On the coast of Guinea, the Portuguese owned some small trade ports and fortresses located in the basins of the rivers Cacheu and Geba. Then there were the islands of São Tomé, Príncipe, Fernando Po and Ano Bom in the equatorial waters of the Gulf of Guinea, together with the fortress of Ajudá on the mainland. South of the equator the Portuguese possessed a long strip of coastline (with some hinterland) on the western coast, known as Angola, and another strip on the east coast called Mozambique. In Asia they had the "State of India" including Goa, Damão, and Diu; Macao in China; and Timor in Indonesia. The only diminution was the town and fortress of Mazagão in Morocco and perhaps some area of influence around Ajudá. In effective territorial area as well as in economic and political importance, this empire was incomparably smaller than it is today (1972). The strength and wealth of the Portuguese lay elsewhere, in huge Brazil. Brazil was in fact the empire, and all the rest only secondary parcels, of little interest by themselves.

It is true that previously India had represented a similar pole of attraction. However, while most of the Portuguese possessions were located on the way to India (Brazil included) and thus somewhat benefited from India's glamor, only Madeira and Cape Verde were on the way to Brazil. It is not surprising, therefore, that the Portuguese Empire outside Brazil stagnated and declined (except for some short periods of revival) throughout the late seventeenth, the eighteenth, and the beginnings of the nineteenth century. Several times Lisbon attempted to end stagnation by means of reforms, either economic, political, or administrative. This was the purpose of the chartered companies, especially under Pombal's government. Yet the results were always disappointing, because the essence of the problem had not and could not be touched.

Among the remnants of a glorious past Mazagão was certainly the most useless of all Portuguese dominions. It was costly to the treasury and served no purpose whatsoever. After an uneventful history, Pombal's government rightly appraised the situation and ordered Mazagão to be abandoned when a powerful Moslem army besieged the fortress in 1769. Its inhabitants were transferred to Portugal, and then to Brazil where they founded Vila Nova de Mazagão.

Madeira and the Azores had little of the colonial about them, even in those days. Populated by an almost all-white population, very like the motherland in most institutions, social patterns, and economic circumstances, they were rapidly tending toward the status of distant appendages of Portugal, similar to backward provinces like Trás-os-Montes or Beira Baixa.

Crowded in relation to the possibilities existing at that time, both archipelagoes began shipping emigrants to Brazil and to other parts of the empire. In the eighteenth century many youngsters of military age went to Angola as draftees when a new governor was appointed, and there they died a miserable death. In the mid-1600's, the Azores had less then a hundred thousand people, Madeira more than fifty thousand. A century later resident population had increased some 25 per cent to 50 per cent (Madeira had some 75,000 people in 1748), a large number having emigrated. The government even took care of organizing migration to Brazil, promoting the settlement of couples and giving them land.

Despite this, the two archipelagos developed their economic resources. Madeira depended on maritime traffic and on the export of wine, both of which expanded, with fluctuations, during the late seventeenth and the eighteenth century. In the Azores, the decline of woad and wheat was rapidly matched by the export of oranges, flax, and maize. In the early 1700's a textile factory with French workers was even founded on the island of São Miguel, with a relatively long period of activity and expansion. Whaling started to yield some profit throughout the century, and potatoes from Portugal were introduced. Both archipelagoes showed a surplus in their balance of trade and were able to pay for their own expenditures at no charge to the Crown. Funchal, Angra, and Ponta Delgada became large provincial towns, displaying relative affluence in their baroque palaces and lavishly decorated churches.

Pombal reformed administration by doing away with the donataries and creating a captaincy-general for each archipelago, with captains appointed for a three-year period (1766). Angra, where the bishop lived, was made the capital of the Azores. He also instituted *juizes de fora* for all islands, and *corregedores* for São Miguel and Santa Maria. A further improvement was the introduction of special copper currency for both the Azores and Madeira, thus solving (or trying to solve) the chronic problem of lack of small coins. To foster a better grain supply for the growing towns, local granaries (*celeiros públicos*) were set up in Funchal, Angra, and Ponta Delgada. Pombal's successors enhanced the competence and jurisdiction of the captains (1799), and enforced a number of measures favoring agriculture and the interest of the local landowners. Juntas for the improvement of agriculture were set up in the early 1800's. Among other goals they tried to make use agriculturally of fallow lands, by promoting their division into parcels and leasing them to farmers. This policy, which Pombal had already attempted, went against the century-long interests of poorer farmers and rural workers, who made collective use of fallow lands. Proper silver currency was also introduced, as well as paper money. Foreign traffic stimulated the economy so much that most of the money in circulation consisted of Spanish and Mexican silver coins, as well as currencies from other countries.

The history of Cape Verde and Guinea is tied together. The islands and the coastline depended on each other, particularly in the slave trade, and were put under a single captaincy. Despite the maritime traffic to and from Brazil and the rest of the empire, the archipelago languished throughout the late seventeenth and most of the eighteenth century. There was little commerce, and the lack of exports resulted in a continuous coin drainage and a coin shortage. Cotton cloth served as currency, and all attempts to induce the Lisbon government to mint special coins for Cape Verde failed.

In 1676 a Company for Cachéu and the Rivers of Guinea owned the trade ports on the African mainland but disappeared several years later without too many practical consequences. From 1690 to 1706, Cape Verde and Guinea practically belonged to the newly created Company of Cachéu and Cabo Verde, which was given a trade monopoly in both parts and which succeeded in having a much better monopoly, that of the slave exports to Spanish America. It lasted a little more than six years (1696–1703) and, though never taken too seriously, it brought about a short period of prosperity. When the Company failed, activity in both the archipelago and the mainland lapsed again, despite some attempts to develop agriculture by the introduction of new industrial plants: indigo, roccella (*urzela*),

and senna, as well as coffee (much later). Only roccella became important for any trade purposes, and along with cotton it gave Cape Verde
(or, rather, the British who controlled it) the only profitable exports.
In the mid-1700's, the islands depended mainly on cattle, maize, beans,
and fish (including whales), but the whole economy enjoyed little
prosperity and was much too affected by the highly uncertain rainfall. Droughts were (and are) frequent, and, as population had increased, poverty and famine were the obvious consequences.

In Guinea a small new trade port was founded at Bissau
(1696), with a fortress, a church, and even a hospital. Settlers were
hard to find and the Crown could only "rely" on the outcasts, forcibly
sent overseas every year. The law even fixed their annual quota, not
more than a dozen being assigned to Guinea and Cape Verde every
year. Although this figure was later increased to forty, population
grew only slightly, because of the extremely high death rate. In
Guinea the Portuguese also had to think of the natives, who often
attacked trade ports and fortresses, requiring retaliation and "punishment."

From 1757 to 1777 Cape Verde and Guinea were again granted
to a Company, that of Grão-Pará and Maranhão, followed by a Company for the Trade Exclusive of the Islands of Cabo Verde, Bissau
and Cachéu, until 1786. Both companies, but especially the former,
stimulated the economy of the archipelago for a while. Perhaps on
this account, the number of inhabitants increased again, and for the
first time in two centuries of history, the remaining deserted islands
were gradually populated: Santo Antão, São Vicente, São Nicolau,
and Sal. The island of Brava had already received its first inhabitants
after 1680—when a volcanic eruption in Fogo forced many people
to look for another place, so only small Santa Luzia remained
deserted.

Meanwhile Pombal's reforms had reached Cape Verde too. The
last donataries had sold or were forced to give up their privileges,
and a short-lived captaincy-general was made to encompass all the
islands and Guinea as well. Rule by the chartered companies downgraded the captains' authority to the level prevailing in Guinea.
It was only in 1808 that a new administrative reform restored the
Cape Verde government to its former power. The capital of the

colony had been definitely and officially transferred to Praia, in the island of Santiago (1769), where both the bishop and the main officials had in fact lived for a long time.

Cape Verde, like most Portuguese possessions, experienced the dangers of the several international wars. In 1712 the French attacked and plundered both Ribeira Grande and Praia. In 1798 the French came again and sacked Brava. The English as well tried to gain a footing on several of the islands by both peaceful and military means. They failed in Cape Verde, albeit controlling part of the trade, but they succeeded in Guinea, where they founded a trade port in Bolama, in the last years of the eighteenth century.

In the Gulf of Guinea there was a short-lived Portuguese expansion late in the 1600's. In present-day Dahomey the captain-general of São Tomé, Bernardino Freire de Andrade, ordered a fortress built in 1677–80. This was São João Baptista de Ajudá (which the English called Whydah); it commanded a small network of trade ports along the coast where several missionaries (mostly Capuchins) departed for dangerous but useless missions among the natives. Ajudá depended upon the captaincy of São Tomé and was little more than an operational base for the slave and ivory trade.

The Company of Cachéu and Cabo Verde (1690) also extended its activities to the Gulf of Guinea. It controlled Ajudá and stimulated commerce there, new factories being established at Jaquin (Jaquém), Popó, Apa, Calabar, and Camarão, all on the mainland, with Corisco and Fernando Po on the islands. Tobacco ships from Baía went there to load slaves. The Company also developed trade in Principe, where a fortress was built (1694). A short-lived Company of the Island of Corisco rose and faded away in a few years. When the Company of Cachéu failed (1706), the Portuguese possessions in the Gulf area entered another phase of stagnation and decline. The French sacked Principe and São Tomé, helping the Negroes to revolt once more (1709). São Tomé appeared in those days as one of the most corrupt colonies in the Portuguese Empire. Power belonged to the local "aristocracy" of slave traders and landed mulattoes, who controlled the municipal council (*câmara*) and passed their time quarreling with the island's other force, the clergy. Among bishop, Capuchin friars, and *câmara*, intrigue and open violence were boundless. The Crown-appointed captains could do little or nothing to enforce order and royal decisions. Many were killed or died in mysterious circumstances. No one endured. In the absence of a captain, the *câmara* often held power.

Attempts to remedy both the economy and the administration of São Tomé led nowhere. In 1721 the island was open to foreign trade, but with little result. Only Pombal's government managed to change this state of things slightly. Principe had been bought by the Crown from its hereditary captain (1753). Pombal elevated its main village, Santo António, to a town, and made it the capital of the colony. A new captain-general was appointed with authority over the one in São Tomé. Later on (1770), new government acts reduced the power of São Tomé's *câmara*. This legislation did not heal the wound but lessened its effects. Trade between Brazil and the Gulf of Guinea somewhat expanded in the mid-1700's, which helped provide the central government with more power and the islands' inhabitants with more money. Ajudá got a subsidy from Baía because more than one-third of Brazil's slaves actually came from there. By the end of the century the situation had improved, despite some French attacks on Principe. Meanwhile Portugal had realized the uselessness of some of her possessions in the Gulf of Guinea. Most of the trade ports on the mainland were abandoned and Fernando Po with Ano Bom was ceded to Spain by the Treaty of San Ildefonso (1778). Portugal's efforts could now be concentrated on the two remaining islands, São Tomé and Principe.

Angola's role as Brazil's most important supplier of slaves went on throughout the seventeenth and eighteenth century. As the Portuguese territories in South America grew, Angola's position as a labor reservoir did too. In this sense, one might say that, although a colony of Brazil, Angola was the cornerstone of the Portuguese Empire.

We do not have total figures for slave exports from Angola in this period. The ones we do have, however, give a clear picture of the growing slave trade. By the 1670's, a yearly average of 7,500 Negroes entered Brazil, mostly from Angola but also from other sources. In the early eighteenth century slavery had seemingly declined a little, for statistics from Angola do not register more than an annual average of 4,618 slaves exported in 1710–14. But this number increased rapidly:

6,101 in 1720–24, 10,054 in 1735–39, 12,415 in 1755–59, 14,259 in 1765–69. Thus, the slave trade had practically doubled from the mid-1600's to the mid-1700's. Negroes were shipped from Luanda and from Benguela, in south Angola, the role of which constantly increased throughout the 1700's: exporting one-fifth to one-fourth of Luanda's shipments by mid-century, Benguela supplied 5,739 Negroes out of a total of 13,534 in 1775.

Slave trade was the only form of commerce that showed constant growth in Angola. Trade based on any other commodity was highly irregular, periods of prosperity being followed by longer periods of stagnation and decline. Brazil and Portugal supplied the colony with practically everything it needed, both for trade and survival of the settlers. Textiles, china, enamels, tobacco, metals, knives, brandy, and salt were demanded by the Negro kingdoms of Angola in return for slaves and ivory. Money was always scarce, despite the introduction of a proper copper currency as early as 1694. Small straw rectangles, salt, and shells were used as currency too, even for the payment of troops.

By 1665 Luanda had some 132 white households; all of Angola not more than 326. According to a contemporary chronicler, Luanda by the end of the century possessed some "costly and sumptuous buildings, which greatly ennoble this city," and was a very active seaport with considerable financial resources. Miscegenation was common, soldiers, sailors, and others mating "with black ladies for lack of white ladies." In 1684 all distinction between white and nonwhite soldiers (mulattoes and Negroes) was abolished and nondiscrimination in the lower ranks actually enforced. Officers, of course, were all white. The local *câmara* had a great influence on control and administration of the colony. It held government in its hands thrice (1667–69, 1702, and 1732), when the acting governors died. Like all the other Portuguese and (non-Portuguese) colonies in Africa in those days, Angola's white society was certainly not very reputable, many "notables" being old outcasts or their children. Gypsies were also sent to Angola, which motivated some complaints from the local whites.

In the late 1600's, a series of military campaigns gave the Portuguese a still firmer hold on Angola, both on the coastline and inland. The Negro Kingdom of Ndongo or Andongo was defeated and converted into a protectorate (1671). South, in Benguela, a trade port and a fortress were set up far from the coast, in Caconda (1682), and Benguela began to compete with Luanda. During the eighteenth century several expeditions departed from Luanda and Benguela for trade, military, or purely geographical purposes (to the Kingdom of Cassanje in 1775; to Encoje in 1758–64 and so on). To promote evangelization the Church set up in Luanda a Junta of Missions (1682). Italian Capuchin missionaries led most efforts to Christianize the natives, although with poor results. The climate made difficult any white incursions inland, while the Negroes offered fierce resistance to conversion and to the presence of the whites.

From 1683 to the 1730's there was peace in Angola. The Portuguese had succeeded in imposing their suzerainty, or even full sovereignty, in the areas which they ruled, no Black kingdom posing any special problem of containment. A smallpox epidemic among the Bantu tribes (1685–87) helped to weaken the Negroes and favored the Portuguese take-over. Also, the Portuguese generally respected the existing tribal or royal structure. Provided they got enough slaves to ship to America, and some acceptance of their suzerainty, they did not act too much like masters and were not particularly disliked by the natives. Nevertheless, the Crown gradually tried to give some organization to the colony and increase the ties that linked it to the motherland. In 1651 an *ouvidor-geral* had been created to supervise justice. In 1666 the Crown established a finance purveyor (*provedor*) to rule on matters of finance and war. In 1676 the Crown succeeded in having the see of São Salvador do Congo transferred to Luanda. In 1688 the first secretary for the "kingdom" of Angola was appointed to serve a three-year period and assist the captain-general in recording acts, local laws, and so forth. In 1722 a *juiz de fora* was also appointed, presiding over the municipal government of Luanda. Perhaps still more important was the act of 1721 forbidding the captains-general from taking part in the slave trade as was their custom.

There were some popular riots in Luanda in the late seventeenth century; a successful campaign ousted the English from Cabinda (1723), but little else occurred in the routine history of an underdeveloped colony. Luanda's population stagnated around the level of 150 white men.

Colonial wars started again after 1730. The most important campaigns were in 1744, launched against the Matamba kingdom (the Portuguese reached farther than ever inland), and in 1765, against the Hungus.

When Pombal took over government, he found Angola's trade in a general expansion which dated from the 1720's and which probably led him and his advisers to the erroneous assumption that the colony could be converted into another Brazil. Pombal's great act—which affected not only Angola but most of Portugal's dominions—was to declare freedom of trade for the Portuguese (1755–56), abolishing the Crown monopoly. In the interior of Angola, also, the whites were granted permission (1758) to trade freely, a practice up to then restricted to Blacks and mulattoes. Governor Francisco de Sousa Coutinho (1764–72) tried hard to stimulate agriculture, trade (other than slavery), settlement, and even industry. Roccella and indigo were introduced, mining was set up on a new basis, an iron foundry was established near Luanda, a leather industry was fostered. Sousa Coutinho had a public granary, a customs house, and a hospital built in Luanda. He founded several villages inland, to promote the development of the interior. The slave trade was made a royal monopoly, a way of both encouraging individuals to engage in other activities and giving the central government a good source of profits. At the same time Portuguese explorers reached the river Cuango (Kingdom of Cassanje) and the area known as Encoje, where they founded a settlement. Sousa Coutinho's great plan was to assure land communications between Angola (in West Africa) and Mozambique (in East Africa). He also fortified several trade ports and tried to put an end to English trade competition. In administration the Crown instituted a junta for financial matters.

Pombal's and Sousa Coutinho's efforts in Angola in general failed. After 1766 an economic contraction brought the export level to what it had been in 1720. Most reforms were not enforced because they could not be. Until 1790 a new wave of stagnation and decline covered all of Angola, except for the slave trade with Brazil. Attempts

to control those ports to which foreign vessels came failed too. In
Cabinda the Portuguese were beaten by the French (1783–84). Religious missions faded away. The only important exploration was a
sea expedition to Cabo Negro, in the South, organized by governor
baron of Moçâmedes (1784).

After 1790 another short period of expansion followed. Exports
increased, mining was again fostered, and the first real attempt to
connect Angola and Mozambique by land succeeded, when the mulatto traders (pombeiros) Pedro João Baptista and Amaro José left
Cassanje, reached Tete, and went back home, from 1806 to 1815. Yet
Angola continued to be a colony of Brazil almost until that country's independence in 1822.

The role of the Portuguese East African dominions throughout
this period was a much more insignificant one. By the end of the
1600's there were in the town of Mozambique no more than fifteen
white Portuguese households—which in fact meant fifteen white
males only—and sixteen Goese Indian ones, not counting the clerics,
who were very few, and the garrison soldiers. Scattered about the
whole territory of what is now Mozambique, less than a hundred
whites controlled the few trade ports which claimed Portuguese sovereignty. Mozambique continued to depend upon India, both economically and administratively. There was much more trade and connection between the two than between Mozambique and Lisbon. From
1686 to 1777 an Indian Company from Diu held the exclusive of all
commerce between Diu and Mozambique, a quite profitable one. It
is true that the Crown attempted several times to foster Mozambique's
own economy. Projects to convert the several Portuguese colonies into
other "Brazils" were of course envisaged. If slavery, however, deter-
minatively ruled out such a policy in Angola, in Mozambique the
dependency upon India had a similar, if less forceful, impact.

As early as 1671 the Crown had declared all trade with the town
of Mozambique free for Portuguese citizens, instead of being controlled by the local captain. This freedom was later extended to the
rivers of Sena trade (1680), after a brief Crown monopoly. To foster
commerce in the colony a junta was established (1675), later converted
into a Company for trade, which obtained the exclusive of all commerce with the colony's capital, except the one with Diu (1694). Once

more this Company had more connections with India than with Africa and tried to control trade even with Macao. It failed, as did all colonial Portuguese companies, shortly afterward (1699).

Mozambique was further harassed by foreign attacks and wars with the natives. In 1670 the Arabs from Oman, who had expelled the Portuguese from Arabia (see chapter 7), attacked the capital of Portuguese East Africa. In 1693 black Kaffirs raided many white strongholds and killed a number of people, including some settlers who had recently arrived from Portugal. Three years later the Arabs returned and besieged Mombasa, the northernmost Portuguese fortress in East Africa. After a long siege, Mombasa surrendered (1698) and with it Pate and Zanzibar. Later on, in the 1720's and 1730's, the Dutch and the British often tried to settle down in Lourenço Marques (Delagoa Bay). In the 1740's French piracy in Mozambique waters had its beginnings. The only successful Portuguese counterattack took place against Mombasa—including Pate and Zanzibar—which were regained (1728), but soon lost again forever (1729). Thus the colony lingered on for many decades, internally troubled by the usual quarrels among friars and priests, whose spiritual mission had been entirely forgotten. A law of 1739 regulated the sending of outcasts to the colony, limiting the number who entered each year.

Mozambique was given new life under Pombal's government. The colony was made into a separate captaincy (1752), named "government and general captaincy of Mozambique, Sofala and rivers of Sena." Commerce throughout the new captaincy was declared altogether free for all Portuguese, civil servants being forbidden to trade, and paid in money (1755-61). Lourenço Marques was recaptured, while Governor Baltasar Pereira do Lago (1765–78) fortified Tete, Inhambane, and Mossuril. For the preparation of the local clergy the Church founded a seminary in the city of Mozambique (1761), foreseeing the ordination of mulattoes and Negroes (which actually never happened).

In the late eighteenth and early nineteenth century Mozambique enjoyed a slight expansion, with the development of whaling, the creation of a Junta de Fazenda for finance and trade matters, and the opening of a customs house at Ibo. Coffee was introduced, a future source of wealth. Tete replaced Sena as the most important Portuguese foothold inland. Governor Cavalcanti de Albuquerque (1816–18) did much to foster Mozambique's development. In order to explore the interior and reach Angola by land, an expedition under Lacerda e Almeida left Tete (1798) but went no further than Cazende where its leader died (1799). After the French Revolution, French attacks were launched several times against Mozambique; Lourenço Marques was raided and destroyed in 1796. Even the Austrians tried to settle down in Delagoa Bay.

By the late 1600's the Portuguese power in India was reduced to Diu, Damão, Bassein, and a few other fortified towns in the North, and to Goa, with its dependencies, in the South. Despite its continuous decline and loss of population, Goa, the capital, continued to be too huge a head for so small a body. It still posed as a Lisbon or a Rome in the East, with a great number of administrative, economic, and religious institutions that no longer made any sense. One of them was certainly the Royal *Padroado* or Patronage, which the kings of Portugal had secured from the Papacy in the prime of their expansion and which endowed them with full responsibility and control of the spread of Christianity in Asia (as in their other possessions). After the late seventeenth century the Portuguese clearly had no way of implementing that burdensome duty. Yet they always stuck to the Patronage right and theoretically refused to accept any competition. In Rome, however, several Popes realized the situation and gradually broke the Portuguese monopoly on the grounds of Portugal's manifest incapacity to fulfill it. Throughout the eighteenth century the action of the Congregation for Propaganda (see chapter 7) made itself felt more and more. Italian, Spanish, and French missionaries preached in India, Indochina, China, and elsewhere in the Far East. The Popes appointed Viçars-Apostolic without reference to Lisbon. When Pombal expelled the Jesuits, the main pillar of the *Padroado* in Asia, the few Portuguese instruments to maintain their rights disappeared also. In China, by the early 1800's, there were probably no more than 50,000 Roman Catholics, where a century or so earlier there had perhaps been 300,000. In India the ecclesiastical authority of the *Padroado* began to be denied outside the tiny Portuguese territories in the 1770's, but only in the following century did it almost completely disappear.

Yet Goa's economic force remained disproportionate to its size.

Regardless of their territorial losses and foreign competition, the Portuguese controlled a certain amount of traffic, both within Asia and between Asia and other continents. With a much smaller number of ships and carriers, it was still worthwhile to trade with Goa, and undoubtedly much easier for an immigrant to become rich in India than in Portuguese Africa. Diamonds represented the main source of wealth. They were exchanged for currency and for coral. Along with questions of prestige and a tradition of two centuries, this explains why the Crown never neglected India the way it neglected some other parcels of the Empire, and why a certain policy of revival and reconquest was attempted and enforced from time to time.

The late seventeenth and the first half of the eighteenth century brought about stagnation, decline, and even defeat for Portuguese India. The Arabs sacked Diu (1668) and harassed navigation for a while. Then the Portuguese recovered, but soon the rise of the Maratha power endangered the last bulwarks of the once mighty Empire. After a long period of menaces, humiliations, and open conflicts, the Marathas took possession of Bassein and of all the other northern places, with the exception of Diu and Damão (1739). Shortly afterward they attacked Goa, and only the payment of a tribute could save the "Rome of the East." Chaul, however, had to be abandoned to them. With their fleet destroyed, the Portuguese by 1740 had certainly reached the lowest level of their power in Asia. They recovered, however. In Lisbon there was money and a strong wish for revenge. An expedition of more than two thousand soldiers, with artillery and money, left Portugal, arrived in Goa, and defeated the Maratha army at Bardez. This battle opened a long series of campaigns which lasted into the 1750's, then again from 1779 to 1795. The Portuguese were sometimes beaten, the viceroy—Count of Alva—even being taken prisoner and killed (1756), yet theirs was the final victory. A territory four times larger than their possessions in the south, although half as populous, was attached to Goa, and known as *Novas Conquistas* (New Conquests). This policy of conquest finished the Portuguese expansion in India, giving them the full extent of the territories which they would keep intact to the twentieth century. It also brought much prestige (and wealth) to the generals (i.e., the nobles) who led the armies and conquered the towns.

Meanwhile, several other problems troubled Goa's existence. One was the need to transfer the capital elsewhere, because conditions in Goa had proved unsuitable for the health of Europeans. During the late 1600's and early 1700's there were urban works at Mormugão (south-west of Goa), as a possible substitute. Later on Mormugão was abandoned in favor of Pangim, a village much closer to the city of Goa. Although Pangim became the official capital of Portuguese India in 1760, the actual transfer of many public services, including the viceroy's residence, was delayed for a long time: the customs house was moved only in 1811 and the tribunals in 1818. Pangim was thus built mostly in the late eighteenth and early nineteenth century, at the same time that Lisbon was rising from the ruins of the earthquake. Between the two cities there were naturally many similarities.

Pombal looked at Portuguese India realistically and tried to reduce its swollen size to manageable proportions. First he declared trade to be free to all Portuguese citizens (1755–56) as he had done in other colonies. Then he set up the usual junta for finance affairs; abolished the Tribunal dos Contos and the Relação (supreme court), along with many public offices and dignities; created public granaries; reorganized the municipal system suppressing many of the municipal government's prerogatives; and simplified justice. In short he reduced Goa's position to that of any other Portuguese colony, Brazil excepted. In 1774 the pompous title of viceroy was dropped too, and replaced by that of governor. Finally, he decreed that the Christian natives, regardless of their race and color, should be considered equal and given preference to Portuguese from Portugal for all public offices and even for landownership. This measure, which was effectively implemented, had been preceded by several other acts that paved the way; for example, the acceptance of natives in the religious orders.

Another important measure of Pombal's administration concerning India had to do with the Inquisition. If one considers the population of Goa and its dependencies, one realizes how fierce the Goa Inquisition was throughout the seventeenth and eighteenth centuries. From 1600 to 1773 there were 71 autos-da-fé, with 4,046 sentences, of which 57 meant death by fire. This represented a yearly average of more than 23 sentences, with one killing every three years. The new Crown policy of religious and ethnical enlightenment could not tolerate a tribunal like the Inquisition of Goa, the main victims of which were

Hindu. If in Portugal the Inquisition was converted into a state institution, overseas it had to disappear altogether. One must remember that a period of conquest was underway, and that consolidation of the Portuguese presence in India implied tolerance. Consequently an act of 1774 simply abolished the Inquisition in Goa.

Pombal's policy stimulated a counteraction, in some aspects more severe in Goa than elsewhere. The Inquisition appeared again (1779), albeit in a very moderate way. The Relação was re-established (1778), and some years later the title of viceroy was again being given to the governors of India. Yet Goa's importance within the Empire continued to decline. The Crown spent much more there than it gained. Despite the act of 1774, and a law which created a Legislative Council for Goa (1778), native reaction against the whites persisted, a conspiracy with the purpose of expelling all Europeans being discovered in 1787. From 1801 to 1815 Goa—like Portugal—was practically under British occupation, with all the forts manned by English garrisons. It was then that the useless Inquisition was once more and forever abolished (1812).

In China, the Portuguese kept Macao, not as a Crown colony —as they often liked to pretend—but as a simple favor from the Chinese to whom they were useful as traders; the Chinese always held their rights as actual rulers. Until the nineteenth century, Macao was more like a feudal territory in the Iberian manner than a European colony. Proof of Chinese interference was abundant. In 1688 they established a customs house in Macao, which controlled all trade and imposed duties on every Chinese vessel and on every export in Portuguese ships. On imports brought by the Portuguese duties had to be paid only to the municipal council, unless the goods were re-exported to China. In this case duties were paid at the Chinese customs. In 1689 military honors to Chinese authorities, to Chinese dead, and to celebrate Chinese festivities were sanctioned by local Portuguese law. In 1718 China enacted several laws to harass and limit all foreign commerce, most of which was Portuguese. Then, in 1736, China appointed a special mandarin for Macao, a sort of delegate of the Canton authorities. He acted as the real governor, to whom the Portuguese authorities had to pay homage.

The remaining power belonged to the local municipal council or

Senado which gave Macao the curious aspect of a tiny urban republic.
The Senado was composed of whites, most of them residents for generations, and of half-breeds (Portuguese and Chinese). Indeed, miscegenation characterized Macao's society more than any other Portuguese colony except Cape Verde.

Royal attempts to enforce central authority and curb the power
of the local Senado were many. Concerning the Chinese, nothing
could be achieved until the mid-nineteenth century, despite some
pompous embassies to Peking and a general state of good relationship. Concerning the Senado, however, something more positive was
reached after a long struggle, with temporary victories and defeats for
both sides. In 1738 Lisbon appointed a royal *ouvidor* to take part in
the Senado administration, but had to remove him some years afterward. Pombal's reforms also tried the same, but in vain. In the 1780's
new acts tended to curb the powers of the Senado. Actually, nothing
very essential could be achieved up to the 1830's, and the Senado was
the real authority in Macao. Between it and the Crown-appointed
governor conflicts often arose, the final victory generally belonging
to the Senado.

Economically speaking, Macao brought good profits to the Crown,
despite her gradual decline throughout the eighteenth century. This
fact helps explain the Lisbon government's tolerance of a highly
irregular situation and the maintenance of a rather strange status
quo. Trade between Macao and both Southeast Asia and Goa was free.
Between Macao and Timor, however, trade belonged to the Senado,
and this constituted Macao's main source of profit in those days:
sandalwood, gold, wax, and slaves were the main imports. In each
ship the Senado distributed shares to shareholders.

Macao's population declined until the nineteenth century. In
the late 1600's there were 150 Portuguese households in a total of
19,500 Christians and many more non-Christians. By 1746 only 50
Portuguese residents lived in Macao. Along with a few half-breeds
they formed a local aristocracy who fiercely fought for their privileges,
in particular the exclusion of natives from the Senado administration.
In this they succeeded, despite Pombal's legislation that would force
them to accept total equality with the yellow race.

The easternmost Portuguese possession was Timor and Solor,

the last remnant of the once mighty empire in Indonesia. Both islands were only partly occupied by the Portuguese, who respected the petty native kingdoms and tribal rulers, under the superficial cover of the Portuguese suzerainty. Timor depended on Macao and on the intensity of her trade relations with China. Highly irregular communications made it difficult for the Lisbon government to control Timor. Late in the seventeenth century the village of Lifau was fortified and became Timor's seat of government. António Coelho Guerreiro, a wealthy trader and businessman, went to Timor as the colony's first independent governor, in 1701. He could not do much, but he tried to set up a pattern of relationships with the native rulers, which his followers continued and which became the main basis for the Portuguese permanence there. Timor lingered on, amidst the usual quarrels between governor and friars. The natives rebelled also. In 1742 a Dominican brother led the mutiny. In 1769 the governor had to flee Lifau and take refuge in Dili, which became the new capital. The petty kingdom of Mambara revolted in 1790 and seceded from Portuguese control. The Dutch in Indonesia harassed the Portuguese occupation but, on the whole, Portugal's share was so small that the Dutch saw no particular interest in getting rid of their neighbors. As a matter of fact, their empire was decaying too.

BIBLIOGRAPHY

Introduction: The Roots of a Nation

The Setting, pages 1–5

The best geography of Portugal, rich in historical background and offering a vigorous survey and a detailed scientific observation, is Orlando Ribeiro's *Portugal* (in Spanish), Barcelona, 1955, vol. V of the *Geografía de España y Portugal*, directed by Manuel de Terán. Ribeiro had previously written a summary of Portugal's geographical features, titled *Portugal, o Mediterrâneo e o Atlântico*, 2nd ed., Sá da Costa, Lisbon, 1963 (1st ed. 1941).

Pierre Birot's short manual, *Le Portugal. Étude de géographie régionale*, collection Armand Colin (séction de Géographie) no. 260, Paris, 1950, is perhaps the best available work written by a non-Portuguese. It should be supplemented with another manual-form description, *Géographie de la Péninsule Ibérique*, by Michel Drain, collection "Que sais-je?" no. 1091, P.U.F., Paris, 1964, which permits an integration in the general frame of the Iberian Peninsula. Somewhat outdated, but always worth reading and scientifically based, are Hermann Lautensach's several works on Portugal.

Of the several English works dealing with geographical aspects of the Peninsula as a whole and Portugal alone, I would not wholeheartedly recommend any. Dan Stanislawski's *The Individuality of Portugal, Study in Historical-Political Geography*, University of Texas Press, Austin, 1959, is geographically accurate and detailed as far as description is concerned, but historically poor and prejudiced by the assumed geographical "individuality" of Portugal.

It is Orlando Ribeiro who again presents a worthwhile résumé in his article "Portugal, Formação de" in the *Dicionário de História de Portugal*, directed by Joel Serrão, vol. III, Lisbon, 1966, pp. 432 ff.

All the aforementioned books and articles contain extensive bibliographies.

The People, pages 5–9

The best account of prehistoric cultures in the Iberian Peninsula, with innumerable references to Portugal, is perhaps Luis Pericot García's *La España Primitiva,* Colección Histórica Laye, VI, Barcelona, Editorial Barna, 1950. It contains a bibliography with reference to all the "classics" of Peninsular prehistory, such as Obermaier, Bosch Gimpera, Martín Almagro, Santa-Olalla, H. Breuil, Georg and Vera Leisner, and Mendes Correia. For more detailed aspects see Ramón Menéndez Pidal's *História de España,* t.I., vol. I, Madrid, Espasa Calpe, 1947, and t.I, vol. II, Madrid, 1952, with the collaboration of specialists like Hoyos Sáinz, Martín Almagro, Alberto del Castillo, Maluquer de Motes, Mata Carriazo, and García y Bellido.

Exclusively for Portugal there is nothing general and recommendable, although the number of articles and papers is large. The best and most up-to-date résumés are possibly those published in the *Dicionário de História de Portugal,* directed by Joel Serrão, vols. I, II, and III, Lisbon, Iniciativas Editoriais, 1969 on, under the entries "Paleolítico" (III, 298), "Mesolítico" (III, 43), "Neolítico" (III, 142), "Eneolítico" (II, 33), "Bronze" (I, 386), "Ferro" (II, 223), "Celtas" (I, 549), "Iberos" (II, 463), and "Lusitanos" (II, 830). They all include up-to-date bibliographies and were written by specialists. Orlando Ribeiro's article previously mentioned, "Portugal, Formação de," is also useful. Other Portuguese authors, such as José Leite de Vasconcelos and António Mendes Correia, are outdated.

Glyn Daniel's study, *The Megalith Builders of Western Europe,* Pelican Books, 1963 (1st ed., Hutchinson,1958), helps relate the Peninsular and the general European areas, while Frederick E. Zeuner's *Dating the Past, An Introduction to Geochronology,* 4th ed., New York, Hafner, 1958 (reprint 1964) is always useful for dating and chronological relationships. The same might be said of H. Alimen's *Atlas de Préhistoire,* vol. I, Paris, Editions N. Boubée, 1950.

The Portuguese edition of André Varagnac's *O Homem antes da Escrita (Pré-história)* colecção "Rumos do Mundo," Lisbon, Edições Cosmos, 1963, is useful because it provides complementary notes on the Portuguese prehistoric phenomena and furnishes a valuable and up-to-date bibliography.

The Language, pages 9–13

Among the many general books and articles on historical philology of the Iberian Peninsula, with particular emphasis on its western part, one should mention Ramón Menéndez Pidal's *Orígenes del Español, Estado lingüistico de la Peninsula Ibérica hasta el siglo XI,* 3rd ed., Madrid, 1950, as well as the various articles in the *Enciclopedia Linguística Hispánica,* directed by M. Alvar, A. Badía, R. de Balbín and L. F. Lindley Cintra, vol. I, *Antecedentes, Onomastica,* Consejo Superior de Investigaciones Científicas, Madrid, 1960. Rafael Lapesa's *História de la Lengua Española,* 2nd ed., Madrid, n/d, and Serafim da Silva Neto's *História da Língua Portuguêsa,* Rio de Janeiro, 1952–57, are also useful works for a general background. Special mention should be made of Harri Meier's article, "A formação da língua portuguesa," reedited in his *Ensaios de Filologia Românica,* Revista de Portugal, Lisbon, 1948, pp. 5–30, in which he poses very clearly the problem of relating Portuguese and Latin dialects.

Among the several historical grammars, the *Gramatica Portuguesa,* by Pilar Vázquez Cuesta and Maria Albertina Mendes da Luz, 2nd ed., Biblioteca Románica Hispánica, Ed. Gredos, Madrid, 1961, is worth mention.

The only historian worth mentioning who posed the problem of a dialectical individuality of western Iberia as an important prerequisite for the birth of Portugal was Jaime Cortesão in *Os Factores Democráticos na Formação de Portugal,* reedited as vol. I of his *Obras Completas,* 2nd ed., Lisbon, Portugália, 1966. His arguments were (poorly) questioned by Damião Peres, *Como nasceu Portugal,* 7th ed., Porto, Portucalense Editora, 1970.

In English, there is really nothing worth mentioning on the historical origins of Portuguese. The classics, Edwin Bucher Williams, *From Latin to Portuguese,* Philadelphia, 1938, or William J. Entwistle, *The Spanish Language (together with Portuguese, Catalan and Basque),* 2nd ed., London, 1951, though excellent as historical grammars, practically ignore the linguistical situation of Iberia before the fall of the Roman Empire and hardly refer to the Moslem part of Spain.

The Administration, pages 13–19

The best survey on the Roman administrative pattern for Spain was given by Eugène Albertini, *Les divisions administratives de l'Espagne Romaine,* Paris, E. de Boccard, 1923. Summaries can be found in any history of the Iberian Peninsula, particularly in the *História de España,* directed by Ramón Menéndez Pidal, t. II, *España Romana (218 A. de J.C.–414 de J.C.),* Espasa Calpe S.A., Madrid, 1935; the chapters on administration were written by Manuel Torres. For Visigothic, Suevi, and Moslem times, t. III and V of the same *História de España,* Madrid, 1940–57, offer a general background (chapters respectively by Manuel Torres and E. Lévi-Provençal). This last volume is, in the part written by the latter, an adapted translation (by Emilio García Gómez) of Lévi-Provençal's original French edition, *Histoire de l'Espagne Musulmane,* vol. III, *Le Siècle du Califat de*

Cordoue, Paris, Ed. Maisonneuve, 1953. It is important to supplement and check this work, particularly for later periods of the Moslem rule, with the several entries in the *Encyclopaedia of Islam,* new edition, directed by B. Lewis, Ch. Pellat, and J. Schacht, Leiden-Paris, 1960 ff.

For details on Lusitania a good description is still provided by the classic Cardeal Saraiva (D. Francisco de S. Luis) in his article "Limites da Lusitania Antiga" *(Obras Completas),* vol. 2, Lisbon, Imprensa Nacional, 1873, pp. 67–94). Much better is the one by Claudio Sánchez-Albornoz, "Divisiones tribales y administrativas del solar del reino de Asturias en la época romana" *(Boletin de la Real Academia de la Historia,* t. XCV, I, Madrid, July–September 1929, pp. 315–395).

On the ecclesiastical divisions see Zacarias Garcia Villada, *História eclesiástica de España,* vol. I and II, Madrid, 1929-36; Fortunato de Almeida, *História da Igreja em Portugal,* vol. I, 2nd ed., Coimbra, 1930, and Pierre David, *Etudes historiques sur la Galice et le Portugal du VIe au XIIe siècle,* collection Portugaise, VII, Institut Français au Portugal, Lisbon-Paris, 1947.

On the Moslem divisions and general geography of future Portugal, see the article by David Lopes, "Os arabes nas obras de Alexandre Herculano," *Boletim da Segunda Classe,* Academia Real das Sciencias, Lisbon, vol. III (1909–10) and IV (1910–11).

Jaime Cortesão (in *Os Factores Democráticos na Formação de Portugal*) was the first historian to notice and emphasize the role played by Roman administrative boundaries in the origins of Portugal.

Communications and Settlement, pages 19–23

Besides the descriptions of the road system contained in the aforementioned general histories, a special reference should be made to the excellent maps published by Emil Hübner in his *Inscriptiones Hispaniae Latinae,* vol. II and vol. II, *Supplementum,* of the *Corpus Inscriptionum Latinarum,* Berlin, 1869–92. E. Lévi-Provençal, *Histoire de l'Espagne Musulmane,* t. III, Paris, 1953, includes two maps of Moslem itineraries.

A good survey of the demographic, economic, and social problems in west Iberia before Reconquista times is that by Jaime Cortesão, in his *Os Factores Democráticos na Formação de Portugal (Obras Completas,* vol. I).

The Kingdom of the Suevi, pages 23–25

On the Suevi, all histories are hardly more than surveys, so meagre are the sources. In addition to the few pages devoted to them in the *História de España,* directed by R. Menéndez Pidal, vol. III (by Manuel Torres) there is an up-to-date summary in Lucien Musset, *Les Invasions: les vagues germani-*

ques, col. "Nouvelle Clio," no. 12, Paris, P.U.F., 1965, pp. 108–110 and 294. On their origin and way of getting to Spain, see the interesting and somewhat revolutionary article by Robert L. Reynolds, "Reconsideration on the History of the Suevi," *Revue Belge de Philologie et d'Histoire,* XXXV, no. I (1957), pp. 19–47. Though valuable, the manual by Wilhelm Reinhart, *História General del Reino Hispanico de los Suevos,* Madrid, 1952, should be used with caution, particularly the cultural history.

A solid political and religious description is still to be found in José Leite de Vasconcelos' *Religiões da Lusitania na parte que principalmente se refere a Portugal,* vol. III, Lisbon, Imprensa Nacional, 1913, pp. 545–575. For the religious-administrative aspect, the fundamental work is Pierre David's *Etudes Historiques sur la Galice et le Portugal du VIᵉ au XIIᵉ siècle,* Lisbon-Paris, 1947, pp. 1–118.

The Counties of the Reconquista in the North, pages 25–31

On the political and military aspects of the Reconquista in the eighth to eleventh centuries any good history of Spain may be used. Luis G. de Valdeavellano's *História de España,* vols. I and II, 3rd ed., Madrid, Manuales de la Revista de Occidente, 1963, is possibly the most up-to-date and reliable survey.

The first two centuries of "Portugal" were consciously studied by Luis Gonzaga de Azevedo in his *História de Portugal,* vol. II, Lisbon, Ed. Biblion, 1939. However, it was Paulo Merêa who in several model articles defined the limits and the circumstances of the birth of the new unit. See his latest compilation of writings, *História e Direito (Escritos Dispersos),* vol. I, Coimbra, Acta Universitatis Conimbrigensis, 1967, particularly his "De 'Portucale' (civitas) ao Portugal de D. Henrique" (pp. 177–214).

The Moslem "Taifa" Kingdoms in the South, pages 31–34

There is no general history of the taifa kingdoms. Lévi-Provençal died before finishing his monumental analysis of Spanish Islam which stops in 1031. Reinhart Dozy's *Histoire des Musulmans d'Espagne, jusqu'à la conquête de l'Andalousie par les Almoravides (711–1110),* 4 vols., Leiden, E. J. Brill, 1861 (2nd ed., 1932), with English (*Spanish Islam,* London, 1913), Spanish (1877), and German (1874) translations, is still the classic. In the new edition of *The Encyclopaedia of Islam,* Leiden-London, 1960 on (in progress), there are some good articles such as those on "Aftasids" (I, 242), "al-Andalus" (I, 486), "Badja" (I, 862), "Batalyaws" (I, 1092), "Gharb al-Andalus" (II, 1009). They provide up-to-date bibliography. The article by David Lopes, "Os Arabes nas obras de Alexandre Herculano," *Boletim da*

Segunda Classe, Academia Real das Sciencias, Lisbon, vol. III (1909–10) and IV (1910–11), contains much good information and commentaries. Only on the kingdom of Badajoz, from the first rebellions to the Christian Reconquest, is there a fair monograph, though limited to political history: Matias Ramón Martínez y Martínez, *História del Reino de Badajoz durante la dominación musulmana,* Badajoz, 1904–5.

Antonio Prieto y Vives, *Los Reyes de Taifas, Estudio histórico-numismático de los Musulmanes españoles en el siglo V de la Hégira (XI de J. C.),* Madrid, Junta para Ampliación de Estudios e Investigaciones Científicas, 1926, offers little new, except in numismatics.

Chapter One: The Formation of Portugal

The Christian North, pages 35–59

General histories and surveys are numerous, most of them reliable as to facts and political developments. The best ones are the *História de Portugal,* directed by Damião Peres, vol. I and II, Barcelos, 1928–29; the *História de Portugal* by Fortunato de Almeida, vol. I, Coimbra, 1922; the *História de Portugal* by Luis Gonzaga de Azevedo, vol. III to VI, Lisbon, 1941–44 (ending with Sancho II's reign); and always Alexandre Herculano, *História de Portugal,* 9th ed., 8 vols., Lisbon, n/d (ending with Afonso III). Neither in English nor in any other language is there a highly recommended work.

The grant of Portugal to Henri of Burgundy has been studied by numerous authors: the best ones are Paulo Merêa in defense of the traditional anti-fief thesis ("Sobre as Origens de Portugal," *História e Direito (Escritos Dispersos),* t. I, Coimbra, 1967, 177–311) and Charles Verlinden in a short but clear article demonstrating the feudal character of the *tenencia* ("Quelques aspects de la tenure au Portugal," *Recueils de la Société Jean Bodin,* III, Bruxelles, 1938, 231–243).

On the negotiations with the Holy See, there is an excellent study by Carl Erdmann, *Das Papsttum und Portugal im ersten Jahrhundert der portugiesischen Geschichte,* Abhandlungen der Preussischen Akademie der Wissenschaft, 1928, Phil.-hist. Klasse, 5, Berlin, 1928 (Portuguese translation by J. da Providência Costa, *O Papado e Portugal no primeiro século da História Portuguêsa,* Publicações do Instituto Alemão da Universidade de Coimbra, Coimbra, 1935). *The História da Igreja em Portugal* by Fortunato de Almeida, vol. I, 2nd ed., Coimbra, 1930, gives a good background for understanding the struggle between king and clergy.

Demographic aspects of north Portugal were closely analyzed by Avelino de Jesus da Costa, *O Bispo D. Pedro e a Organização de Diocese de Braga,* vol. I and II, Coimbra, 1959. The *villa* and all the property system had in Alberto Sampaio ("As Villas do Norte de Portugal," *Estudos Historicos e Economicos,* vol. I, Porto, 1923, 1–247) a competent historian. For this and for detailed administrative, social, economic, and even political aspects, the standard work continues to be Henrique da Gama Barros, *História da Administração Publica em Portugal nos seculos XII a XV,* 2nd ed., 11 vols., Lisbon, 1945–51, in spite of Armando Castro's attempt to revamp problems and methods (*A Evolução Económica de Portugal dos séculos XII a XV,* 9 volumes published, Lisbon, 1964 ff.). Jaime Cortesão's often-mentioned survey *Os Factores Democráticos na Formação de Portugal* is still worth reading, especially for the evolution of economy and society. Paulo Merêa's article in the *História de Portugal,* directed by Damião Peres, vol. II, 445–524, is perhaps the best attempt to put together social and administrative problems and facts in a comprehensive and learned way ("Organização Social e Administração Pública").

Most of these works include comprehensive bibliographies on more detailed aspects. Also the *Dicionário de História de Portugal,* directed by Joel Serrão, 4 vols., Lisbon, 1960 ff., is strongly recommended as an aid in updating subjects and bibliography.

The Moslem South, pages 59–73

A fundamental work is the article by David Lopes, "Os Arabes nas obras de Alexandre Herculano," *Boletim da Segunda Classe,* Academia Real das Sciencias, Lisbon, vol. III (1909–10) and IV (1910–11), which simultaneously provides sources, a linguistical analysis, and a political, administrative, and economic survey.

Many elements of interest are found only in the pages of the new edition of *The Encyclopaedia of Islam,* Leiden-London, 1960 on. For the political and military events, Alexandre Herculano's *História de Portugal,* 9th ed., 8 vols., Lisbon n/d, is still basic, complemented (in minor details) by Luis Gonzaga de Azevedo's *História de Portugal,* preface and revision by Domingos Maurício Gomes dos Santos, vols. 3–6, Lisbon, Bíblion, 1939–44.

General comparisons with the rest of the Moslem world are found in any good handbook of Moslem history, such as Philip K. Hitti's *History of the Arabs,* 8th ed., London, Macmillan, 1964 (especially useful for its cultural chapters on Spain); Reuben Levy's *The Social Structure of Islam,* 2nd ed., Cambridge University Press, 1965; and Gustav E. von Grunebaum's several works on medieval Islam.

S. M. Imamuddin's *Some Aspects of the Socio-Economic and Cultural History of Muslim Spain, 711–1492 A.D.,* Medieval Iberian Peninsula Texts and Studies, vol. II, Leiden, E. J. Brill, 1965, is sometimes useful as a catalogue, though its errors in detail and misprints are so numerous that its regular use seems unadvisable.

The Reconquista and the Union of North and South, pages 73–84

There is no general history of the Portuguese Reconquista per se, but several reliable surveys have appeared in general histories of Portugal. Suggested readings are the several chapters in Alexandre Herculano's *História de Portugal;* Luis Gonzaga de Azevedo's *História de Portugal;* Fortunato de Almeida's *História de Portugal;* the *História de Portugal* directed by Damião Peres, vols. I and II; and especially Rui de Azevedo's fine chapter, "Período de formação territorial: expansão pela conquista e sua consolidação pelo povoamento. As terras doadas. Agentes colonizadores" in the *História da Expansão Portuguesa no Mundo,* directed by António Baião, Hernâni Cidade, and Manuel Múrias, vol. I, Lisbon, Atica, 1937, pp. 7–64. This article is followed by several others also worth reading, though not exclusively on the Reconquista. Recommended for updating are the many articles published in the *Dicionário de História de Portugal,* vol. I, II, and III.

Spanish material should not be forgotten. There are good chapters in the general histories of Spain and also an excellent short handbook, *La Reconquista Española y la Repoblación del País,* Conferencias del Curso celebrado en Jaca en Agosto de 1947, Consejo Superior de Investigaciones Científicas, Escuela de Estudios Medievales, XV, Zaragoza, 1951, which is very helpful for comparative purposes.

On the crusade problem, there is a fundamental work by Carl Erdmann, "Der Kreuzzugsgedanke in Portugal," *Historische Zeitschrift,* 141, 1 (1929), 23–53 (*A ideia de cruzada em Portugal,* Portuguese version by A. Pinto de Carvalho, Publicações do Instituto Alemão de Universidade de Coimbra, Coimbra, 1940).

On the *concelhos* and their forais, check, besides the general works mentioned above, Torquato Brochado de Sousa Soares' several articles and books, especially his contribution to the *História da Expansão Portuguesa no Mundo,* vol. I. Entries in the *Dicionário de História de Portugal* again are very useful in bringing doctrine and bibliographies up-to-date.

Chapter Two: The Feudal Age

The Late Medieval Structures, pages 85–108

Besides the general works already mentioned (*História de Portugal,* directed by Damião Peres; *História de Portugal,* by Fortunato de Almeida;

História de Portugal, by Alexandre Herculano; *História da Administração Pública em Portugal,* by Henrique da Gama Barros; *História da Expansão Portuguesa no Mundo,* directed by António Baião, Hernâni Cidade, and Manuel Múrias; *Dicionário de História de Portugal,* directed by Joel Serrão; and *Os Factores Democráticos na Formação de Portugal,* by Jaime Cortesão), several monographs are available on each of the subjects treated.

On the problem of feudalism, the studies by Manuel Paulo Merêa are well documented; Armando Castro presents an economic point of view in *A Evolução Económica de Portugal dos séculos XII a XV,* vol. I, Lisbon, 1964, pp. 50–64, while Charles Verlinden gives convincing evidence of the feudal character of the tenure in his "Quelques aspects de l'histoire de la tenure au Portugal," *Recueils de la Société Jean Bodin,* t. III, Brussels, 1938. General works on feudalism, such as F. L. Ganshof, *Feudalism,* English translation, 3rd ed., 1964, are useful for comparison. Marcelo Caetano's *Lições de História do Direito Português,* Coimbra, 1962, is extremely helpful for a general survey of the medieval institutions. Also helpful for the Spanish counterpart is Luis Garcia de Valdeavellano, *Curso de Historia de las Instituciones Españolas. De los orígenes al final de la Edad Media,* Revista de Occidente, Madrid, 1968.

On demographic and economic history there exist some useful and reliable monographs, such as the classic Alberto Sampaio, *Estudos Históricos e Económicos,* vol. I, Porto, 1923; Virginia Rau, *Subsídios para o estudo das Feiras Medievais Portuguesas,* Lisbon, 1943; Bailey Diffie, *Prelude to Empire: Portugal Overseas before Henry the Navigator,* University of Nebraska Press, 1960; A. H. de Oliveira Marques, *Introdução à História da Agricultura em Portugal: A questão cerealífera durante a Idade Média,* 2nd ed., Lisbon, Cosmos, 1968, as well as his *Ensaios de História Medieval Portuguesa,* Lisbon, Portugália, 1965.

The cultural aspects were competently analyzed by António José Saraiva, *História da Cultura em Portugal,* vol. I–II, Lisbon, Jornal do Foro, 1950–53, and by Manuel Rodrigues Lapa, *Lições de Literatura Portuguesa: Época Medieval,* 4th ed., Coimbra, 1956.

On art, there is a general work, *História da Arte em Portugal,* vol. I–II, Porto, Portucalense, 1942–48, begun by Aarão de Lacerda and continued by several others after his death.

The Crisis, pages 108–118

There is no general account of the crisis of the fourteenth and fifteenth centuries. A first attempt, in the form of a short survey limited to the Black Death and its consequences, was made by a group of teachers and students of the Faculdade de Letras in Lisbon, *Para o estudo da Peste Negra em Portugal,* Centro de Estudos Históricos da Faculdade de Letras de Lisboa, offprint of *Bracara Augusta,* vol. XIV–XV (January–December 1963), no. 1–2 (49–50), pp. 210–239.

A general survey of the fourteenth and fifteenth centuries, with some references to the crisis, can also be found in the *História de Portugal,* directed by Damião Peres, vol. II and III. On the agrarian aspects, see Virginia Rau, *Sesmarias Medievais Portuguesas,* Lisbon, 1946, and A. H. de Oliveira Marques, *Introdução à História da Agricultura em Portugal,* 2nd ed., Lisbon, Cosmos, 1968. On society and some aspects of economy and finance, see A. H. de Oliveira Marques, *Ensaios de História Medieval Portuguesa,* Lisbon, Portugália, 1965.

Extensive research monographs on the social and economic aspects of the revolution of 1383–85 are unavailable. The best surveys were written by António Sérgio, "Sobre a revolução de 1383–85," in his *Ensaios,* vol. VI, Lisbon, 1946, pp. 153–203, and Joel Serrão, *O carácter social da revolução de 1383,* Cadernos da "Seara Nova," Lisbon, 1946. Marcelo Caetano wrote two important monographs on the political aspects: *As Cortes de 1385,* offprint of *Revista Portuguesa de História,* vol. V, Coimbra, 1951, and *O concelho de Lisboa na crise de 1383–85,* offprint of *Anais,* Academia Portuguesa da História, vol. IV, Lisbon, 1953.

On the psychological and religious changes, see A. H. de Oliveira Marques, *Daily Life in Portugal in the Late Middle Ages,* The University of Wisconsin Press, Madison-Milwaukee-London, 1971. On art, only general histories are available, such as the collective *História da Arte em Portugal,* vol. II, Porto, Portucalense, 1948–53. The same is true for culture: see António José Saraiva, *História da Cultura em Portugal,* vol. II, Lisbon, Jornal do Foro, 1953, as well as Manuel Rodrigues Lapa, *Lições de Literatura Portuguesa: Época Medieval,* 4th ed., Coimbra, 1956.

The Political Evolution, pages 118–132

The evolution of the political facts is generally covered by the two main histories already mentioned: the *História de Portugal* directed by Damião Peres, and the *História de Portugal* by Fortunato de Almeida, besides the *Dicionário de História de Portugal* directed by Joel Serrão. To the end of Afonso III's reign, Alexandre Herculano's *História de Portugal* is still the fundamental work. Gama Barros' *História da Administração Publica em Portugal nos séculos XII a XV* is extremely helpful on political theory, military events, foreign alliances, etc.

Some political and biographical aspects of the 1383–85 crisis were studied by Salvador Dias Arnaut, *A Crise Nacional dos fins do século XIV, I, A Sucessão de D. Fernando,* Coimbra, Faculdade de Letras, 1960.

For the international problems related to the Hundred Years War and the English alliance there is an excellent monograph in English by Peter E. Russell, *The English Intervention in Spain and Portugal in the Time of Edward III & Richard II,* Oxford University Press, 1955. Details on the Schism can be found in Júlio César Baptista, "Portugal e o Cisma do Ocidente," *Lusitania Sacra,* vol. I, Lisbon, 1956, pp. 65–203.

Chapter Three: Beginning of the Expansion

Equipment and Needs, pages 133–145

Any further readings on the history of the Portuguese discoveries must include four general works, which contain both original research and vigorous synthesis: Jaime Cortesão, *Os Descobrimentos Portugueses,* vol. I, Lisbon, Arcádia, 1958; Vitorino Magalhães Godinho, *A Economia dos Descobrimentos Henriquinos,* Lisbon, Sá da Costa, 1962 (as an introduction to many other books and articles by the same author and with an excellent critical bibliography); Duarte Leite, *História dos Descobrimentos. Colectânea de esparsos,* 2 vols., Lisbon, Cosmos, 1958–61; and the *História da Expansão Portuguesa no Mundo,* vol. I, Lisbon, Ática, 1937 (some chapters of which are worth reading).

Though any good general histories of technology and science include a survey of the late medieval naval inventions (*A History of Technology,* directed by C. Singer, E. J. Homyard and T. L. Williams, vol. II, Oxford University Press, 1956; and A. C. Crombie, *Medieval and Early Modern Science,* Garden City, New York, 1959), they generally overlook some more detailed aspects which are fundamental in understanding the Portuguese expansion. For this, see, among many others, Luciano Pereira da Silva, *Obras Completas,* 3 vols., Lisbon, Agência Geral das Colónias, 1943–46; Abel Fontoura da Costa, *A Marinharia dos Descobrimentos,* 3rd ed., Lisbon, Agência Geral do Ultramar, 1960; and Luis de Albuquerque, *Introdução à História dos Descobrimentos,* Coimbra, 1962. The latter is also the author of several worthwhile entries in the *Dicionário de História de Portugal,* directed by Joel Serrão, On cartography, the standard work was written by Armando Cortesão, *Cartografia e Cartógrafos Portugueses dos séculos XV e XVI (contribuição para um estudo completo),* 2 vols., Lisbon, Seara Nova, 1935 (summarized and updated in 1960, under the title *Cartografia Portuguesa Antiga*). In English, there is a short but excellent survey by G. R. Crone, *Maps and Their Makers: An Introduction to the History of Cartography,* New York, Capricorn Books, 1966.

On Prester John, see also Denison Ross, "Prester John and the Empire of Ethiopia," Chap. IX of *Travel and Travelers of the Middle Ages,* directed by A. P. Newton, London, 1930.

There is no good biography of Henry the Navigator. Old Major and Beazley are now entirely outdated. Vitorino Nemésio wrote a short book on Henry and his epoch which deserves attention: *Vida e Obra do Infante D. Henrique,* Lisbon, Comissão Executiva do Quinto Centenário da Morte do Infante D. Henrique, 1959. In English, Peter Russell delivered an interesting lecture, *Prince Henry the Navigator,* London, 1960.

The Voyages of Discovery, pages 145–151

In addition to the general works already mentioned, the best general account of the voyages of discovery, chronologically oriented, is Damião Peres' *História dos Descobrimentos Portugueses,* Porto, Portucalense Editora, 1943.

On the expeditions to the Canary Islands, see Florentino Pérez Embid, *Los Descobrimientos en el Atlántico y la Rivalidad Castellano-Portuguesa hasta el Tratado de Tordesillas,* Seville, 1948.

In English, Edgar Prestage's *The Portuguese Pioneers,* London, 1933, is still a reliable handbook, though somewhat dated.

The First Results, pages 151–163

In addition to the general works already mentioned, on the colonization of both Madeira and the Azores, see Vitorino Magalhães Godinho, *A Economia dos Descobrimentos Henriquinos,* Lisbon, Sá da Costa, 1962, also fundamental for the study of all the aspects of the fifteenth- and pre-fifteenth-century expansion. Joel Serrão's short article, "Madeira," in the *Dicionário de História de Portugal,* vol. II, gives an excellent survey of that archipelago. A short survey of the fifteenth-century colonization (particularly the agricultural aspects) is also presented by A. H. de Oliveira Marques, *Introdução à História da Agricultura em Portugal (a questão cerealífera durante a Idade Média),* 2nd ed., Lisbon, Cosmos, 1968. On the same subject, Charles Verlinden wrote an interesting article which deserves mention: "Formes féodales et domaniales de la Colonisation Portugaise dans la zone Atlantique aux XIVe et XVe siècles et spécialement sous Henri le Navigateur," *Revista Portuguesa de História,* vol. IX (1960), pp. 1–44.

Chapter Four: The Renaissance State

Recovering from the Crisis, pages 165–190

Besides the general histories (Fortunato de Almeida, Damião Peres) and the *Dicionário de História de Portugal,* the following works are useful.

For the general economic, administrative, and social patterns, see Henrique da Gama Barros, *História da Administração Pública em Portugal nos séculos XII a XV*, 2nd ed., 11 vols., Lisbon, Sá da Costa, 1945–50. For population, the chapter by Orlando Ribeiro in his geographical survey of Portugal, *Portugal* (vol. V of the *Geografía de España y Portugal*, directed by Manuel de Terán, Barcelona, Teide, 1955) and his article "Cidade" in the *Dicionário de História de Portugal*, vol. I, pp. 574–580, provide the most comprehensive reference to the 1527 census and its general meaning. On agriculture, some details can be gathered in A. H. de Oliveira Marques' *Introdução à História da Agricultura em Portugal: a questão cerealífera durante a Idade Média*, 2nd ed., Lisbon, Cosmos, 1968, as well as in Maria Olímpia da Rocha Gil, *Arroteias no Vale do Mondego durante o século XVI: Ensaio de História Agrária*, Lisbon, Centro de Estudos Históricos, 1965. For the introduction of maize, again Orlando Ribeiro gives a very clear survey in his article "Milho," *Dicionário de História de Portugal*, III, 58–64.

On trade, there are several detailed monographs, such as Anselmo Braamcamp Freire, *Notícias da Feitoria de Flandres*, Lisbon, 1920; A. H. de Oliveira Marques, "Notas para a história da Feitoria Portuguesa na Flandres, no século XV" (his *Ensaios de História Medieval Portuguesa*, Lisbon, Portugália, 1965, pp. 219–267); Manuel Henrique Corte Real, *A Feitoria Portuguesa na Andaluzia (1500–1532)*, Lisbon, Centro de Estudos Históricos, 1967; Virgínia Rau, *A Exploração e o Comércio do Sal de Setúbal*, Lisbon, 1951; A. H. de Oliveira Marques, *Hansa e Portugal na Idade Média*, Lisbon, 1959; Violet M. Shillington and Annie Beatrice W. Chapman, *The Commercial Relations of England and Portugal*, London, 1907.

The best study on currency, devaluations, and the gold-silver flow is now contained in Vitorino Magalhães Godinho's *Os Descobrimentos e a Economia Mundial*, vol. I, Lisbon, Arcádia, 1963 (Part I). The same author wrote a very good survey of public finance in the *Dicionário de História de Portugal*, vol. II, pp. 244–264 (entry "Finanças Públicas e Estrutura do Estado"). More details on legislation, administration, and the bureaucratic reforms are found in Marcelo Caetano, *Lições de História do Direito Português*, Coimbra, Coimbra Editora, 1962. The budget of 1526 was discovered by João Cordeiro Pereira, (see *Diário de Notícias,* March 21, 1969).

On prices, there is little available: see, however, A. H. de Oliveira Marques, *Introdução à História da Agricultura em Portugal*, 2nd ed., Lisbon, Cosmos, 1968; A. de Sousa Silva Costa Lobo, *História da Sociedade em Portugal no século XV*, Lisbon, Imprensa Nacional, 1903, and Vitorino Magalhães Godinho, "A revolução dos preços e as flutuações económicas no século XVI," in his *Ensaios*, vol. II, Lisbon, Sá da Costa, 1968, pp. 155–174.

There is nothing modern nor recommendable on landownership and social structures other than some entries in the *Dicionário de História de Portugal*. On the clergy, see Fortunato de Almeida, *História da Igreja em Portugal*, vol. I and II, 2nd ed., Porto, Portucalense Editora, 1967–68. On the corporations, useful material was collected and published by Franz Paul de Almeida Langhans, *As Corporações dos Ofícios Mecânicos, Subsídios para a sua história*, vol. I, Lisbon, 1943.

On the hospital system and the "misericórdias," there is a good survey in English by A. J. R. Russell-Wood, *Fidalgos and Philanthropists: The Santa Casa da Misericórdia of Bahia, 1550–1755*, University of California Press, 1968 (in chapter I).

The modern work by Frédéric Mauro, *Le XVIᵉ siècle Européen: Aspects Economiques*, col. Nouvelle Clio, no. 32, Paris, Presses Universitaires de France, 1966, correctly appraises Portugal's economy with the international framework of the sixteenth century.

Humanism, Renaissance, and Reformation, pages 190–207

On humanism and the cultural relations with France, Spain, and Italy, several reliable monographs have been published, such as Marcel Bataillon's *Etudes sur le Portugal au temps de l'Humanisme*, Coimbra, Acta Universitatis Conimbrigensis, 1952 (to be accompanied by his masterpiece, *Erasme et l'Espagne, Recherches sur l'histoire spirituelle du XVIᵉ siècle*, Paris, 1937, also with a Spanish translation, 2 vols., México–Buenos Aires, 1950); Manuel Gonçalves Cerejeira, *Clenardo e a Sociedade Portuguesa do seu tempo*, 3rd ed., Coimbra, Coimbra Editora, 1949; Luis de Matos, *Les Portugais à l'Université de Paris entre 1500 et 1550*, Coimbra, 1950, and his *A Corte Literária dos Duques de Bragança no Renascimento*, Lisbon, 1956; Joaquim Veríssimo Serrão, *Portugueses no Estudo de Toulouse*, Coimbra, 1954, and his *Portugueses no Estudo de Salamanca*, vol. I (1250–1550), Lisbon, 1962; *Relazione Storiche fra l'Italia e il Portogallo. Memorie e Documenti*, Rome, Reale Accademia d'Italia, 1940; Pietro Verrua, *Umanisti ed altri "sudiosi viri" italiani e stranieri di qua e di là dalle Alpi e dal Mare*, Geneva, 1924 (chapter XVIII); Joaquim de Carvalho, *Estudos sobre a Cultura Portuguesa do século XV*, Acta Universitatis Conimbrigensis, Coimbra, 1949, and *Estudos sobre a Cultura Portuguesa do século XVI*, 2 vols., Acta Universitatis Conimbrigensis, Coimbra, 1947–48; Mário Brandão, *O Colégio das Artes*, Coimbra, 1933.

The classical work by Teófilo Braga, *História da Universidade de Coimbra*, vol. I (1289–1555), Lisbon, 1892, continues to be a fundamental piece of sound scholarship. Updating, along with some reinterpretation, is possible by reading Mário Brandão and Manuel Lopes de Almeida, *A Universidade de Coimbra: Esboço da sua história*, Coimbra, 1937.

The stimulating and entirely renovating book on the general problems of the Portuguese culture is now António José Saraiva's *História da Cultura em Portugal,* vol. II, Lisbon, Jornal do Foro, 1953. For more literary details see, by the same author and Oscar Lopes, the *História da Literatura Portuguesa,* 2nd ed., Porto, n/d. (1956).

On the printing press, besides the latter, see Francisco Marques de Sousa Viterbo, *O Movimento Topográfico em Portugal no século XVI (Apontamentos para a sua história),* Coimbra, Imprensa da Universidade, 1924; and particularly the *Bibliografia Geral Portuguesa. Século XV,* 2 vols., Lisbon, Academia das Ciências, 1941–42, and António Joaquim Anselmo, *Bibliografia das Obras impressas em Portugal no século XVI,* Lisbon, 1926.

On art, besides the general *História da Arte em Portugal,* vol. II, Porto, Portucalense, 1953, see also Virgílio Correia, *Obras,* vol. III, Coimbra, Acta Universitatis Conimbrigensis, 1953, ad Albrecht Haupt, *Die Baukunst der Renaissance in Portugal,* 2 vols., Frankfurt, 1890–95.

The best account of "experimentalism" and the scientific contribution of the Portuguese is to be found in A. J. Saraiva's *História da Cultura.*

Finally, on religion and the Inquisition, besides the general survey by Fortunato de Almeida, *História da Igreja em Portugal,* 2nd ed., vol. I and II, Porto, Portucalense, 1967–68, see José Sebastião da Silva Dias, *Correntes do Sentimento Religioso em Portugal,* Universidade de Coimbra, Instituto de Estudos Filosóficos, Coimbra, 1960, the classic Alexandre Herculano, *History of the Origin and Establishment of the Inquisition in Portugal,* translated by John C. Branner, Stanford University, 1926, and again (above all) António José Saraiva's *História da Cultura; A Inquisição Portuguesa,* Lisbon, colecção Saber, 1956 and *Inquisição e Cristãos Novos,* 2nd ed., Porto, Inova, 1969.

The numerous and important articles contained in the *Dicionário de História de Portugal,* directed by Joel Serrão, 4 vols., Lisbon, 1960–69, should not be forgotten. See, for instance, the entries "Humanismo," "Luteranismo," "Renascimento," "Santo Ofício," and the biographies of the most distinguished individuals of the time.

The Political Evolution, pages 207–216

The fundamental books are the general histories often mentioned (Fortunato de Almeida, Damião Peres), as well as the *Dicionário de História de Portugal.* The existing biographies on the several monarchs are all of mediocre or no value whatsoever. The best ones are F. A. da Costa Cabral's *D. João II e a Renascença Portuguêsa,* Lisbon, 1914, and Alfredo Pimenta's, *D. João III,* Porto, Tavares Martins, 1936; the latter is very poor in interpretation but useful because of its many notes, references, and quotations.

Chapter Five: Rise of the Empire

Discovery and Conquest, pages 217–238

On the voyages of discovery, the best account is Damião Peres' *História dos Descobrimentos Portugueses,* Porto, Portucalense Editora, 1943. In English, the classical work by Edgar Prestage, *The Portuguese Pioneers,* 2d ed., New York, Barnes & Noble, 1967, continues to be useful.

For the conquests and general expansion in the Indian Ocean, the best survey is still Jaime Cortesão's article "O Império Português no Oriente até 1557," inserted in the *História de Portugal,* directed by Damião Peres, vol. IV, Barcelos, Portucalense Editora, 1932, pp. 9–77.

A brief but excellent summary of the Portuguese discoveries and conquests was written by Charles R. Boxer, *Four Centuries of Portuguese Expansion, 1415–1825; A Succinct Survey,* Johannesburg, Witwatersrand University Press, 1965. This, however, is now superseded by his general work on *The Portuguese Seaborne Empire, 1415–1825,* London, Hutchinson, 1969.

Organization of the Empire, pages 238–263

Besides the general histories and the works mentioned earlier, the reader should especially consult several important articles in the *Dicionário de História de Portugal,* which summarize modern points of view on colonization, trade, and administration: "Madeira," "Oriente," "Complexo Económico-Geográfico," "Especiarias," "Finanças Públicas e Estrutura do Estado," "Índia (Casa da)."

On the Portuguese expansion in Congo and Angola, see David Birmingham, *Trade and Conflict in Angola: The Mbundu and Their Neighbours under the Influence of the Portuguese, 1483–1790,* Oxford, Clarendon Press, 1966. James Duffy's works (*Portuguese Africa,* 1959; *Portugal in Africa,* 1962), though often reliable and providing good surveys, should be approached with care, because of the author's bias against the Portuguese.

Charles R. Boxer wrote a documented study, *Portuguese Society in the Tropics: The Municipal Councils of Goa, Macao, Bahia and Luanda, 1510–1800,* Madison-Milwaukee, University of Wisconsin Press, 1965, fundamental for the study of local administration. He also wrote *Race Relations in the Portuguese Colonial Empire, 1415–1825,* Oxford, Clarendon Press, 1963, important for the study of the colonization methods and problems.

On the beginnings of the colonization of Brazil, the best survey is probably that by Jaime Cortesão, in the first book of *Brasil* (in which Pedro Calmon also collaborated), vol. XXVI of the *História de América y de los Pueblos*

Americanos, directed by Antonio Ballesteros y Beretta, Barcelona, Salvat, 1956.

The economic organization of the Empire was extensively studied by Vitorino Magalhães Godinho in *Os Descobrimentos e a Economia Mundial,* 2 vols., Lisbon, Arcádia, 1963–71.

The Great Problems to Solve, pages 263–270

The sources indicated above and in chapter 3.

Chapter Six: Apogee and Decline

The Structures of a Modern State, pages 271–306

The best survey on the structures of Portugal in 1550–1668 was written by Vitorino Magalhães Godinho for *The New Cambridge Modern History,* vol. V, *The Ascendancy of France, 1648–88,* Cambridge University Press, 1961 (chapter XVI, "Portugal and Her Empire," pp. 384–397). See also several articles of his reprinted in *Ensaios,* vol. II, *Sobre História de Portugal,* Lisbon, Sá da Costa, 1968.

Luis Augusto Rebelo da Silva's *História de Portugal nos seculos XVII e XVIII,* vol. IV and V, Lisbon, Imprensa Nacional, 1869–71, continues to be useful because of the lack of up-to-date monographs. The same is true of his *Memoria sobre a População e a Agricultura de Portugal desde a fundação da Monarchia até 1865,* Lisbon, Imprensa Nacional, 1868.

José Gentil da Silva published two important books on trade: *Stratégie des affaires à Lisbonne entre 1595 et 1607,* Paris, SEVPEN, 1956, and *Marchandises et Finances, Lettres de Lisbonne,* vol. II and III, Paris, SEVPEN, 1959–61. Frédéric Mauro studied the general Atlantic trade in a masterpiece of research and synthesis, *Le Portugal et l'Atlantique au XVIIe siècle, 1570–1670,* Paris, École Pratique des Hautes Etudes, 1960. See also the two works by Hermann Kellenbenz, *Unternehmerkräfte im Hamburger Portugal- und Spanienhandel 1590–1625,* Hamburg, Verlag der Hamburgischen Bücherei, 1954, and *Sephardim an der Unteren Elbe,* Wiesbaden, Franz Steiner Verlag, 1958. Also on trade and on the monetary problems, see again Vitorino Magalhães Godinho, *Os Descobrimentos e a Economia Mundial,* vol. I and II, Lisbon, Arcádia, 1963–70.

A student of ours (Maria Amélia Lança Coelho) was able to collect and publish, as a dissertation, some price data from the Beja region: see "Esboço de um Estudo Económico Administrativo de Beja e seu Termo durante o período Filipino," dissertation deposited at the University of Lisbon, Faculdade de Letras, 1961–62.

On the Church and the clergy, the best source remains Fortunato de

498

Almeida, *História da Igreja em Portugal,* 2nd ed., vol. II, Porto-Lisbon, Livraria Civilização, 1968. António José Saraiva studied the Inquisition in several works of his, the last of which is *Inquisição e Cristãos Novos,* 2nd ed., Porto, Inova, 1969. See also his *História da Cultura em Portugal,* vol. II and III, for cultural problems, as well as his *História da Literatura Portuguesa,* written with Oscar Lopes, 2nd ed., Porto Editora, n/d. For the University, the best source continues to be Teófilo Braga's monumental *Historia da Universidade de Coimbra,* vol. II, Lisbon, Academia Real das Sciencias, 1895. There is a good survey on the arts by Reinaldo dos Santos, *História da Arte em Portugal,* vol. III, Porto, Portucalense edit., 1953, together with the modern work by Robert C. Smith, *The Art of Portugal, 1500–1800,* New York, Meredith Press, 1968.

Finally, the often mentioned *Dicionário de História de Portugal* as well as Fortunato de Almeida's *História de Portugal* (vol. III, IV, and V) and Damião Peres' *História de Portugal* (Barcelos edition, vols. V and VI) continue to be of fundamental use.

Iberian Union, pages 306–322

From a biographical and strictly political standpoint, the best works on the period 1557–80 were written by J. M. Queirós Veloso: *D. Sebastião,* 3rd ed., Lisbon, 1945; *O Reinado do Cardeal D. Henrique,* Lisbon, 1946; and *O Interregno dos Governadores e o breve reinado de D. António,* Lisbon, Academia Portuguesa da História, 1954. On António, see also Joaquim Veríssimo Serrão, *O Reinado de D. António, Prior do Crato,* vol. I, Coimbra, 1956.

After 1580 there are no good monographs available, except for the period 1583–93: Francisco Caeiro, *O Arquiduque Alberto de Áustria,* Lisbon, 1961. The short survey "A Dominação Filipina," written by J. M. Queirós Veloso and Damião Peres for the *História de Portugal,* directed by the latter, vol. V, Porto, Portucalense Editora, 1933, is outdated and incomplete. Spanish works, though they pay little attention to Portuguese affairs, should be consulted, particularly on Lerma's and Olivares' policies (for instance, Gregorio Marañón, *El Conde-Duque de Olivares. La pasión de mandar,* Madrid, 1945). The *História de España,* directed by Ramón Menéndez Pidal, vol. XIX, 1 and 2, Madrid, Espasa, 1958, is extremely useful.

On the economic and social backgrounds, see especially Vitorino Magalhães Godinho, several articles reprinted in his *Ensaios,* vol. II, Lisbon, Sá da Costa, 1968. The cultural aspects can be approached by using António José Saraiva's often-mentioned *História da Cultura em Portugal,* vol. II and III, as well as general histories of the Portuguese and Spanish literatures.

The Restoration of Independence and After, pages 322–333

The fundamental study for this period was written by Vitorino Magalhães Godinho for *The New Cambridge Modern History*, vol. V, *The Ascendancy of France, 1648–88*, Cambridge University Press, 1961 (chapter XVI, "Portugal and Her Empire," pp. 384–397). With some changes, an introductory part relating it to 1580 and a bibliographical orientation, that same study was recently published in Portuguese: "1580 e a Restauração," in V. M. Godinho's *Ensaios*, vol. II, *Sobre História de Portugal*, Lisbon, Sá da Costa, 1968, pp. 257–291.

Chapter Seven: The Tridimensional Empire

The East, pages 335–355

The best surveys continue to be Jaime Cortesão's "O Império Português no Oriente" (though poorer for the period 1580–1640) and "As colónias do Oriente," in the *História de Portugal*, directed by Damião Peres, vol. V, Barcelos, 1933, pp. 319–389, and vol. VI, Barcelos, 1934, pp. 639–672 as well as Charles Boxer's *The Portuguese Seaborne Empire, 1415–1825*, London, Hutchinson, 1969. After 1648, the best survey (for all aspects) was written by Vitorino Magalhães Godinho for *The New Cambridge Modern History*, vol. V, *The Ascendancy of France, 1648–88*, Cambridge University Press, 1961, pp. 384–397 ("Portugal and Her Empire"). The *História da Expansão Portuguesa no Mundo*, directed by António Baião, Hernâni Cidade, and Manuel Múrias, vol. II and III, Lisbon, Ática, 1939–40, contains a few useful articles. In the often-mentioned *Dicionário da História de Portugal*, see, for instance, the entries "Finanças," "Oriente," "Ásia," Índia," "Jesuitas." Some first-rate articles by Vitorino Magalhães Godinho were compiled in his *Ensaios*, vol. II, Lisbon, Sá da Costa, 1968.

On race relations see Charles R. Boxer, *Race Relations in the Portuguese Colonial Empire, 1415–1825*, Oxford, Clarendon Press, 1963. Boxer also wrote a good monograph on some aspects of local administration: *Portuguese Society in the Tropics: The Municipal Councils of Goa, Macao, Bahia, and Luanda, 1510–1800*, Madison and Milwaukee, University of Wisconsin Press, 1965. Because of the lack of monographs on administration subjects, some sources that are still useful are the *Livro das Cidades e Fortalezas que a Coroa de Portugal tem nas partes da Índia*, edited by Francisco Paulo Mendes da Luz, Lisbon, Centro de Estudos Históricos Ultramarinos, 1960. On trade and currency, besides the above-mentioned books, Vitorino Magalhães Godinho, *Os*

Descobrimentos e a Economia Mundial, vol. I and II, Lisbon, Ática, 1963–70. On finance there is some useful material in *Orçamento do Estado da Índia (1574) feito por mandado de Diogo Velho, Vedor da Fazenda da Índia,* edited by Águedo de Oliveira, Lisbon, 1960.

Christian expansion still awaits its historian, but much material has already been gathered by Fortunato de Almeida in his *História da Igreja em Portugal,* 2nd ed., vol. II, Porto, 1968. For the printing press in Japan, see Kiichi Matsuda, *The Relations between Portugal and Japan,* Lisbon, Junta de Investigações do Ultramar, 1965. The expansion of the Portuguese in Asia was studied by David Lopes, *A Expansão da Língua Portuguesa no Oriente nos séculos XVI, XVII e XVIII,* Barcelos, Portucalense, 1936.

On literature, see António José Saraiva and Óscar Lopes, *História da Literatura Portuguesa,* 2nd ed., Porto, n/d. There is a modern edition, by António Sérgio, of the *História Trágico-Marítima,* compiled by Bernardo Gomes de Brito, 3 vols., Lisbon, Editorial Sul, 1955–56.

Macao and the East have been exhaustively studied by Charles R. Boxer: *Fidalgos in the Far East, 1550–1770,* Hague, 1948; *The Christian Century in Japan, 1549–1650,* California and Cambridge University Press, 1951; *The Great Ship from Amacon: Annals of Macao and the old Japan Trade, 1555–1640,* Lisbon, Centro de Estudos Históricos Ultramarinos, 1959. On Ethiopia, see Girma Beshah and Merid Wolde Aregay, *The Question of the Union of the Churches in Luso-Ethiopian Relations (1500–1632),* Lisbon, Junta de Investigações do Ultramar and Centro de Estudos Históricos Ultramarinos, 1964.

Brazil, pages 355–368

The best surveys on the late-sixteenth- and seventeenth-century Brazil were probably those written by Jaime Cortesão: "Colonização dos Portugueses no Brasil (1557–1640)" and "A integração do território do Brasil," in *História de Portugal,* directed by Damião Peres, vol. V, pp. 390–436 and vol. VI, pp. 673–741, Barcelos, 1933–34, as well as his contribution to the "Historia de America y de los Pueblos Americanos," directed by Antonio Ballesteros y Beretta, vol. XXVI, *Brasil,* Barcelona, Salvat, 1956. Among the general histories of Brazil written by Brazilian historians, see Visconde de Porto Seguro (F. A. de Varnhagen), *História Geral do Brasil,* 5th ed., 5 vols., São Paulo, 1956, and Sérgio Buarque de Holanda, "A época colonial" in *História Geral da Civilização Brasileira,* vol. I, São Paulo, 1960. The modern work by Pierre Chaunu, *A América e as Américas,* translated from the French under the direction of Manuel Nunes Dias, Lisbon–Rio de Janeiro, Cosmos, 1969 (the Portuguese edition is preferable to the French original version, *'L'Amérique et les Amériques*, Paris, 1964), is useful, particularly because it compares the Brazilian and the other American nations.

There is a vast bibliography on the *bandeirantes:* the classic work was written by Afonso de E. Taunay, *História Geral das Bandeiras Paulistas*, 11 vols., São Paulo, 1924–50, with a shorter version in the *História das Bandeiras Paulistas*, 2 vols., São Paulo, 1954. See a very complete list of works on the subject in the *Manual Bibliográfico de Estudos Brasileiros*, directed by Rubens Borba de Morais and William Berrien, Rio, 1949, article "Bandeiras" by Alive P. Canabrava, pp. 492–526. In English there is a useful introductory compilation of texts, with notes, edited by Richard M. Morse, *The Bandeirantes. The Historical Role of the Brazilian Pathfinders*, Borzoi Books, New York, Alfred A. Knopf, 1965. Jaime Cortesão wrote extensively on the bandeiras. His best work on the subject was *Rapóso Tavares e a formação territorial do Brasil*, Rio de Janeiro, 1958.

Charles R. Boxer's work is another classic, with a number of excellent monographs on Portuguese America: *Portuguese Society in the Tropics: The Municipal Councils of Goa, Macao, Bahia, and Luanda, 1510–1800*, Madison-Milwaukee, University of Wisconsin Press, 1965; *The Dutch in Brazil, 1624–1654*, London, 1956; *Race Relations in the Portuguese Colonial Empire, 1415–1825*, Oxford, Clarendon Press, 1963; *Salvador de Sá and the Struggle for Brazil and Angola*, Oxford, 1952.

On miscegenation problems see, besides the books mentioned, Gilberto Freyre, *The Masters and the Slaves*, New York, 1946.

Economic problems were studied especially by Frédéric Mauro in a masterpiece, *Le Portugal et l'Atlantique au XVIIᵉ siècle, 1570–1670*, Paris, École Pratique des Hautes Etudes, SEVPEN, 1960. See also Caio Prado Júnior, *História Económica do Brasil*, 3rd ed., São Paulo, 1953, and Roberto Simonsen, *História Económica do Brasil, 1500–1820*, 2 vols., São Paulo, 1939. For social aspects see Caio Prado Júnior, *Formação do Brasil Contemporâneo*, 2nd ed., São Paulo, 1963.

For the history of the Jesuit missions the classic work is that of Serafim Leite, *História da Companhia de Jesus no Brasil*, 10 vols., Lisbon–Rio de Janeiro, 1938–50.

There are some useful chapters and articles on several aspects in the *História da Expansão Portuguesa no Mundo*, vol. III, and the *Dicionário de História de Portugal*, vol. I to IV.

The Atlantic Islands and Africa, pages 368–378

Besides the general histories and the *Dicionário*, so often mentioned, further bibliography covers:

On Morocco, António Manuel Dias Farinha, *História de Mazagão durante o Período Filipino*, Lisbon, 1969. On Madeira, the Azores, Cape Verde, Guinea, São Tomé and Brazil (economic aspects mainly), the best work is Frédéric Mauro's *Le Portugal et l'Atlantique au XVIIe siècle, 1570–1670*, Paris, SEVPEN, 1960. There are some important documents (not studied yet) in João Cabral do Nascimento, *Documentos para a História da Capitania da Madeira*, Lisbon, 1930. A fundamental source on the Atlantic Islands in the late sixteenth century still awaits its historian: the *Saudades da Terra*, by Gaspar Frutuoso, 5 books in 7 volumes, Ponta Delgada, 1922–63.

On Angola there is an acceptable monograph by David Birmingham, *Trade and Conflict in Angola: The Mbundu and Their Neighbours under the Influence of the Portuguese, 1483–1790*, Oxford, Clarendon Press, 1966; also Charles R. Boxer, *Portuguese Society in the Tropics: The Municipal Councils of Goa, Macao, Bahia, and Luanda, 1510–1800*, Madison and Milwaukee, University of Wisconsin Press, 1965.

Chapter Eight: Absolutism and Enlightenment

The Structures, pages 379–406

To about 1730 (or even 1740) the best survey on Portugal's structures is found in Vitorino Magalhães Godinho's article, "Portugal and Her Empire, 1680–1720" for *The New Cambridge Modern History*, vol. VI, *The Rise of Great Britain and Russia, 1688–1725*, Cambridge University Press, 1970, chap. XVI, pp. 509–540.

There is also a fair monograph on the trade relations between England and Portugal: A. D. Francis, *The Methuens and Portugal, 1691–1708*, Cambridge University Press, 1966. A reading of the introductory chapters and conclusions of Albert Silbert's monumental two-volume work *Le Portugal Méditerranéen à la fin de l'Ancien Régime—XVIIIe–début du XIXe siècle*, Paris, SEVPEN, 1966, is very helpful on many subjects, in addition to agriculture and the agrarian structure which is the main purpose of the book. Also important for both the general and the economic-financial aspects (fundamental for the latter) is V. M. Godinho's *Prix et Monnaies au Portugal, 1750–1850*, Paris, SEVPEN, 1955. The economic situation in the mid- and late eighteenth century was analyzed by Jorge B. de Macedo in three books: *A Situação Económica no tempo de Pombal: Alguns aspectos*, Porto, Portugália, 1951; *O Bloqueio Continental: Economia e Guerra Peninsular*, Lisbon, Delfos, 1962; and *Problemas da História da Indústria Portuguesa no século XVIII*, Lisbon, 1963.

On the clergy, see Fortunato de Almeida, *História da Igreja em Portugal*,

2nd ed., vol. II and III, Porto, 1969–70. On the Inquisition see also António José Saraiva, *Inquisição e Cristãos-Novos,* 2nd ed., Porto, Inova, 1969.

A good deal of pertinent information is contained in the various articles of the *Dicionário de História de Portugal,* for instance, "Burguesia," "Nobreza," "Finanças," "Companhias," and "Indústria." Some data can also be be gathered from the general histories previously mentioned.

Enlightenment, pages 406–417

An excellent, if short, survey of the Portuguese Enlightenment was written by António Coimbra Martins for the *Dicionário de História de Portugal,* directed by Joel Serrão, vol. II ("Luzes," pp. 836–856). In the same *Dicionário* there are some other good articles on different aspects of the movement, or on their main representatives, namely on "Estrangeirados" (vol. II, pp. 122–129) by the same author, and on "Absolutismo" (vol. I, pp. 8–14) and "Despotismo" (vol. I, pp. 804–806) both by Jorge Borges de Macedo. They all include good bibliographies.

On law see L. Cabral de Moncada, "O século XVIII na legislação de Pombal" in his *Estudos de História do Direito,* Coimbra, Acta Universitatis Conimbrigensis, 1948, pp. 83–126.

On the foreign influences in Portugal see José Sebastião da Silva Dias, *Portugal e a Cultura Europeia (sécs. XVI a XVIII),* Coimbra, 1953. The academies and the general literary problems can be studied in António José Saraiva and Óscar Lopes, *História da Literatura Portuguesa,* 2nd ed., Porto, Porto Editora, n/d. On theater there is an excellent monograph by Luciana Stegagno Picchio, *Storia del Teatro Portoghese,* Rome, Edizioni dell'Ateneo, 1964. On the printing press and the newspapers see José Tengarrinha, *História da Imprensa Periódica Portuguesa,* Lisbon, Portugália, 1965. The scientific movement can be best studied in the general histories (such as the *História de Portugal,* directed by Damião Peres, vol. VI, Barcelos, Portucalense Editora, 1934, and the *História da Literatura Portuguesa Ilustrada,* directed by A. Forjaz de Sampaio, vol. III, Lisbon, Livraria Bertrand, 1932) which also include good articles on literature and culture in general.

Rómulo de Carvalho wrote an excellent monograph on education: *História da Fundação do Colégio Real dos Nobres de Lisboa, 1761–1772,* Coimbra, Atlântida, 1959. Teófilo Braga's classic *Historia da Universidade de Coimbra,* vol. III and IV, Lisbon, 1892–1902, still renders good service. On the Real Mesa Censória see Maria Adelaide Salvador Marques, *A Real Mesa Censória e a Cultura Nacional,* Coimbra, 1963.

For the arts the two complementary works are Reinaldo dos Santos,

História da Arte em Portugal, vol. III, Porto, Portucalense, 1953, and Robert C. Smith, *The Art of Portugal, 1500–1800,* New York, Meredith Press, 1968. José-Augusto França wrote an outstanding monograph on the rebuilding of Lisbon after the earthquake: *Lisboa Pombalina e o Iluminismo,* Lisbon, Livros Horizonte, 1965. On the artistic movement in the time of João V, see Aires de Carvalho, *D. João V e a arte do seu tempo,* Lisbon, 1962. For the late eighteenth and early nineteenth century see also José-Augusto França, *A Arte em Portugal no século XIX,* vol. I, Lisbon, Livraria Bertrand, 1966.

The Decisive Events, pages 417–430

The *História de Portugal,* directed by Damião Peres, vol. VI, Barcelos, Portucalense Editora, 1934, is practically the only recommended general survey for the political aspects. Fortunato de Almeida's *História* is extremely biased and should not be used. In the *Dicionário de História de Portugal,* directed by Joel Serrão, there are some good articles on the crowned heads and the main ministers, with valuable bibliographies.

No modern biography of Pedro II exists. John V was studied by many historians, yet recommended monographs hardly appear. Among the best, see Eduardo Brazão's five books: *Portugal no Congresso de Utrecht (1712–1715),* Lisbon, 1933; *Relações externas: Reinado de D. João V,* Porto, 1938; *D. João V e a Santa Sé—As Relações Diplomáticas de Portugal com o Governo Pontifício de 1706–1750,* Lisbon, 1937; *D. João V. Subsídios para a História do seu Reinado,* Barcelos, 1945; and *Subsídios para a História do Patriarcado de Lisboa, 1716–1740,* Lisbon, 1945. On José I and the Marquis of Pombal the monographs are countless but extremely partisan. The classic work continues to be Simão José da Luz Soriano, *Historia do Reinado de El-Rei D. José I e da Administração do Marquez de Pombal,* 2 vols., Lisbon, 1867. Jorge Borges de Macedo wrote a short biography of Pombal: "Marquês de Pombal" in *Os Grandes Portugueses,* directed by Hernâni Cidade, vol. II, Lisbon, Arcádia, n/d, pp. 141–152. In English, Marcus Cheke's work, *Dictator of Portugal: A life of the Marquis of Pombal (1699–1782),* London, 1938, gives the essential data. On Maria I there is a poor study by Caetano Beirão, *D. Maria I,* 4th ed., Lisbon, 1944, which makes José Maria Latino Coelho's classic work, *Historia Politica e Militar de Portugal desde os fins do seculo XVIII até 1814,* 3 vols., Lisbon, 1874–91, still a valuable book. On John VI and his time (before 1820) see Simão José da Luz Soriano, *Historia da Guerra Civil e do estabelecimento do Governo Parlamentar em Portugal,* 17 vols., Lisbon, 1867–90; Raul Brandão, *El-Rei Junot,* Lisbon, 1912. A good monograph of the Peninsular war was written by Charles Oman, *A History of the Peninsular War,* 7 vols., Oxford, 1902–30.

Chapter Nine: "Brazil"

Brazil, Basic Element of the Portuguese Empire, pages 431–448

Boxer's books, the general histories of Brazil previously mentioned (see also chapter 7), the *Dicionário de História de Portugal* with its many entries, and the general histories of Portugal give the most important facts and a survey of the evolution toward independence. See also Caio Prado Júnior, *The Colonial Background of Modern Brazil,* trans. by Suzette Macedo, University of California Press, 1967.

For the border definition, see Jaime Cortesão, *Alexandre de Gusmão e o Tratado de Madrid,* 9 vols. Instituto Rio Branco, Rio, 1950–63, as well as his *História do Brasil nos velhos mapas,* Rio de Janeiro, 1966; Luis Ferrand de Almeida, *A Diplomacia Portuguesa e os Limites Meridionais do Brasil,* Faculdade de Letras da Universidade de Coimbra, Coimbra, 1957; and his excellent article on "Sacramento (Colónia do)," with a good bibliography, in the *Dicionário de História de Portugal,* III, 708–714.

On the cultural and artistic movements see, among others, António José Saraiva and Óscar Lopes, *História da Literatura Portuguesa,* Porto, Porto Editora, n/d.; José Veríssimo, *História da Literatura Brasileira,* Rio, 1916; Sílvio Romero, *História da Literatura Brasileira,* 5th ed., Rio, 1953; Germain Bazin, *L'Architecture Religieuse Baroque au Brésil,* 2 vols., Paris, 1956–58; G. Kubler and M. Soria, *Art and Architecture in Spain and Portugal and Their American Dominions,* The Pelican History of Art, Harmondsworth, 1959.

João's court in Brazil has been studied by many authors. The classic work is Manuel de Oliveira Lima's *D. João VI no Brasil,* Rio de Janeiro, 1908.

For the independence movement, where a vast bibliography exists, check from the Portuguese side António Viana, *Apontamentos para a História Diplomática Contemporânea,* vol. II, *A Emancipação do Brasil,* Lisbon, 1922. The classic work is F. A. Varnhagen (Visconde de Porto Seguro), *História da Independência do Brasil,* 3rd ed., São Paulo, 1957.

From Colony to Nation, pages 448–462

The classic work for the history of Brazil in this period is Charles R. Boxer, *The Golden Age of Brazil, 1695–1750,* University of California Press, 1962. See also his *The Portuguese Seaborne Empire, 1415–1825,* London, Hutchinson, 1969. For the period after 1750, see Visconde de Carnaxide, *O Brasil na Administração Pombalina (Economia e Política Externa),* São Paulo, Companhia Editora Nacional, 1940, as well as Jorge de Macedo, *A Situação*

Económica no Tempo de Pombal: Alguns aspectos, Porto, Portugália, 1951, and *F Bloqueio Continental: Economia e Guerra Peninsular,* Lisbon, Delfos, 1962. To the 1730's see also Vitorino Magalhães Godinho's article, "Portugal and Her Empire," for *The New Cambridge Modern History* vol. VI, *The Rise of Great Britain and Russia, 1688–1725,* Cambridge University Press, 1970, Chap. XVI, pp. 509–540.

For general administration there is a solid monograph by Dauril Alden, *Royal Government in Colonial Brazil. With Special Reference to the Administration of the Marquis of Lavradio, Viceroy, 1769–1779,* University of California Press, Berkeley and Los Angeles, 1968. On local administration, see Charles R. Boxer, *Portuguese Society in the Tropics: The Municipal Councils of Goa, Macao, Bahia, and Luanda, 1510–1800,* University of Wisconsin Press, 1965. See also the general histories of Brazil and Portugal already mentioned and the several articles published in the *Dicionário de História de Portugal,* vol. I, II, III, and IV.

The Secondary Elements of the Empire, pages 462–479

For a general survey, see Charles R. Boxer, *The Portuguese Seaborne Empire, 1415–1825,* London, Hutchinson, 1969. The several entries in the *Dicionário de História de Portugal* provide up-to-date knowledge and bibliographies. Damião Peres (editor), *História de Portugal,* vol. VI, gives some facts but is not very good. The same is true for the *História da Expansão Portuguesa no Mundo,* vol. III. Fortunato de Almeida's *História de Portugal* is practically useless for this period. Charles Boxer published another good work on local administration: *Portuguese Society in the Tropics: The Municipal Councils of Goa, Macao, Bahia and Luanda, 1510–1800,* University of Wisconsin Press, 1965.

On Angola see David Birmingham, *Trade and Conflict in Angola: The Mbundu and Their Neighbours under the Influence of the Portuguese, 1483–1790,* Oxford, Clarendon Press, 1966. On Mozambique there is no equivalent except António Alberto de Andrade's *Relações de Moçambique Setecentista,* Lisbon, 1955, and Alexandre Lobato's several monographs (*Colonização Senhorial da Zambézia e outros ensaios,* Lisbon, 1962; *Evolução Administrativa e Económica de Mocambique, 1752–1763,* Lisbon, 1957). In addition E. Axelson, *Portuguese in Southeast Africa, 1600–1700,* Witwatersrand University Press, 1960, may prove valuable. In German, Fritz Hoppe wrote a monograph on *Portugiesisch—Ostafrika in der Zeit des Marquês de Pombal, 1750–1777,* Berlin, 1965. On Mombasa, see Charles R. Boxer and Carlos de Azevedo, *A Fortaleza de Jesus e os Portugueses em Mombaça,* Lisbon, 1960. For India there is a not very good *História da*

Colonização Portuguesa na Índia, by Germano da Silva Correia, Lisbon, 1948–58. On Macao, see Charles R. Boxer, *Fidalgos in the Far East, 1550–1770,* The Hague, 1948. On Timor, see Humberto Leitão, *Os Portugueses em Solor e Timor de 1515 a 1702,* Lisbon, 1948, and *Vinte e oito anos de História de Timor, 1698–1725,* Lisbon, 1952.

HISTORY OF PORTUGAL

VOLUME II:

FROM EMPIRE TO CORPORATE STATE

CONTENTS

CONSTITUTIONAL MONARCHY

OLD STRUCTURES AND NEW ORDER

The opening of Brazilian ports to all nations in 1808 and the commercial treaty with England in 1810 ruined the foundations of the Portuguese economy. In 1820 the balance of trade registered a deficit of 21 million cruzados for Portugal. When the bourgeois dreams of recovering the lost colony were over, and the total autonomy of former Portuguese America was acknowledged by the Treaty of Rio de Janeiro (1825), the shaping of a new economic physiognomy for Portugal had to be realistically envisaged.

For many, the answer lay in an upsurge of agriculture. Father Correia da Serra, expressing the physiocratic view, had stated that "the first step in any nation, to take profit of her advantages, is to know exactly the land she inhabits, what they produce in themselves, what they are capable of." Thus, to exploit the soil and to foster agriculture became for nineteenth-century Portugal the main goal. Skeptical about the possibilities of developing a new empire, both statesmen and economists attempted to look inward, to realize the country's possibilities in the fields of agriculture, stockbreeding, fishing, mining, and (somewhat later) industry. This attitude and program needs to be stressed, because it was the opposite of almost four centuries of colonial exploitation. It went against tradition and habits; in fact, it seemed revolutionary and had to be backed by many other revolutionary structures. Constitutional Portugal was indeed, or tried to be, a revolutionary new order. Starting from chaos, from the lowest point in economic decline, and from political enslavement to England, it fought bravely to raise up a new nation. The very survival of Portugal in the twentieth-century world is proof that this struggle succeeded, although not entirely in the manner desired.

No development of agriculture would be possible—so the physiocrats and the liberals contended—without complete destruction of "feudal" ties, which harassed the farmer and his activities as a producer. In Portugal, as in France during the Revolution and elsewhere in Europe, legislation was enacted for the alleged purpose of "freeing" the field worker and making possible an upsurge in agriculture. Such legislation affected both property in all its forms and rural society in many ways. The ecclesiastical tithe was abolished. The sales tax was reduced by half and maintained only on real estate. All feudal rights such as corvées; exclusives on ovens, presses, wine sales, and the like; and payments of all kinds to the lord or the king or others disappeared. Other seignorial traditions were abolished too, like the game preserves and the stud farms. The so-called Crown patrimony (Bens da Coroa) became the "Nation's patrimony" (Bens Nacionais), and all lands and rights granted to commandatories and donataries were to revert to the state as soon as their present grantees died. Entailed property was also limited to wealthy estates with more than 200,000 réis of annual liquid revenue, and several measures were adopted to ensure their elimination in the near future. The numerous duties of all sorts existing in the borough charters (forais) were also abolished, as well as many internal tolls on trade and circulation, import and export permits, and all hindrances to free commerce. Finally, lands to be cleared or recently cleared were granted freedom of taxation for a period of twenty years. All this legislation was enacted in 1821–23 (by the cortes elected in 1820 and 1821) and later, in 1832 (by Secretary Mousinho da Silveira). In between, conservatives had repealed most of the earlier acts, which had to be renewed when the liberals came to power again.

Another important act eliminated the religious orders (1834), and their property was conveyed out of mortmain and auctioned off. The government also sold much land belonging to the Crown. In this way previously wasted or improperly cultivated land now became productive, owing to the interest of the new proprietors. These lands gave excellent yields in the beginning, because they had been fallow so long. The total suppression of entailed estates in 1863 gave property in Portugal a modern structure and further helped the rise of agriculture. Rural credit was organized, a large company appearing in 1864 for that purpose (Companhia Geral do Crédito Predial Português). Last but not least, the development of transportation and communications after 1840 brought about the beginnings of an adequate substructure for the rise of agriculture.

It took some time for these and other measures to produce their effects on agriculture. The political turmoil and the civil wars of 1832–34 and 1846–47 did nothing to improve clearing of land and agricultural output. Little by little, however, agrarian conditions changed and effective development was noticeable by the second half of the century.

Imports of wheat gradually declined. From 1838 to 1855 Portugal even exported some grain to the overseas territories and to foreign countries. This was mainly a result of two protectionist laws, enacted in 1821 and 1837, which strictly controlled imports, raised the customs duties, and protected national grain production. However, when soil fertility waned, with the number of people increasing, imports became necessary once more. The law of 1837 was repealed (acts of 1856–65). Wheat imports rose from nothing to 31,000 tons (1856–57 to 1862–63), then to 67,000 (1865 to 1888), and to 134,000 (1890 to 1899). A number of agrarian studies and plans appeared, all aimed at solving this problem. They either dealt with grain alone or with the broader question of developing agriculture in general. Partly because of this, some important laws and regulations were enacted from 1889 to 1899 which had significant results for agriculture, particularly the act of 1899 (signed by Secretary Elvino de Brito). By closely controlling imports and again raising customs duties, fixing prices, and fostering grain production, this law succeeded in reducing wheat imports—to an annual average of 88,000 tons for 1899–1913. In the same period the population grew 10 per cent while the cultivated area of the country was enlarged. Indeed, the study of Portugal's empty lands throughout the nineteenth and the early twentieth century is the best proof of the country's development in agriculture and settlement. In 1819 two-thirds of the Portuguese soil lay uncultivated; this had decreased to one-half fifty years later, and to less than 40 per cent in 1902. The law of 1899 encouraged further clearing of the land up to World War I (see chapter 12).

Among the new crop cultures introduced or developed in this period, potatoes and rice were foremost, with important consequences. Potatoes replaced the extensive consumption of turnips and chestnuts in people's diets, particularly in the North and the Northeast. Vast areas of chestnut groves gradually yielded to potato plantations. In many regions of Portugal, fallowing could be partly replaced by potato fields. Rice cultivation spread in the mid-nineteenth century and imports declined. High-tariff legislation (1837) promoted rice fields all over the country. Later on, a reaction against their proliferation (to the detriment of other cultures) and their unhealthfulness prevented larger outputs for a time. At the beginning of the twentieth century, however, rice production was again intensified, gradually becoming a popular food for all Portuguese.

Cork too was extensively developed. After 1822, Catalan immigrants fostered its cultivation by using more advanced techniques for both growing and transforming cork. From 1870 to World War I, cork exports increased 100 per cent, with a corresponding increase in the area in groves. Other more traditional cultures showed a similar expansion. Vineyards, for instance, were extensively planted in Estremadura and Ribatejo. In the North, however, countless vines were destroyed by a disease, phyloxera, after 1872. Areas devoted to almond groves and carob groves increased in the Algarve. Orchards and herb gardens spread, making the general landscape more varied than before. With few exceptions all forms of agriculture made remarkable progress in yield per hectare, a result of better techniques too. In the 1860's the first agrarian machines were introduced although it took a century for them to be adopted countrywide.

To promote agriculture and its modernization, several associations developed: the Sociedades Agrícolas, officially constituted 1844–54; the Associação Central da Agricultura Portuguesa, founded 1860; the Liga Agrária do Norte, appearing in 1889. In addition, many exhibitions and congresses were held in various places.

Redistribution of property was one of the main features of nineteenth-century Portugal, with important consequences, both economic and social. During the Civil War of 1832–34, the Liberals decreed the confiscation of all property belonging to their foes, an act which they called "indemnity." Victory was still far off, but it did not matter. Land and other goods were auctioned off and promptly acquired by the wealthy victors, most of them traders or industrialists. Some months later the liberal government disbanded all religious orders and confiscated their vast property. It also decided to sell off property belonging to the Crown. Some thousands of acres changed owners and cloyed the greedy appetites of the victorious bourgeois. Up to 1836 one-fourth of the nationalized goods had been auctioned off to more than six hundred people; but it took at least a decade to complete the whole transaction, the value of which was estimated at twice the amount of the state's annual revenues. When finished, the sale revealed a new Portugal in landownership. While many estates changed hands with no significant boundary alteration, many others were either parceled off or purchased together by the same buyer. The rich Tejo and Sado meadowlands were acquired for 2,000 contos by a company (Companhia das Lezírias) with several capitalists joining. A class of landed bourgeois rose, strongly supporting the liberals and preventing the return of the old regime.

The development of industry was another feature of constitutional Portugal. Until the 1830's few changes were achieved in this field, partly because power belonged to rural landowners, traders, bureaucrats, or nobles and partly because the political struggles were not favorable to any steady growth of industrial activities. England eagerly assured the supplying of industrial items to Portugal.

After 1834 things changed; for example, a law abolished corporations and other hindrances to the free growth of trade and industry (1834). The junta for commerce, agriculture, factories, and navigation, which controlled the industrial development of the country, disappeared. Industrialists were thus given a free hand to adopt innovations, invest capital, fix prices, and exploit labor as they pleased. Then, in 1836 power was concentrated for a time in the hands of some industrialists, supported by craft workers and other townspeople. The 1837 customs tariff firmly protected existing national industry, while fostering the rise of new activities. For Portugal this marked the beginning of a new epoch.

Pre-capitalistic forms of production and industrial relationships gradually evolved toward fully capitalistic forms. It took a long time, however, for Portuguese industry to overcome the craft tradition, the female handwork at home, the lack of capital, and the scarcity of qualified labor and modern machinery. Some figures may help to show this evolution. Steam engines, for example, were nonexistent for industrial purposes before 1835. In 1840 four were already working, with a total of 79 horsepower. Ten years later almost double the number were working, with ten times more horsepower. In 1881 Portuguese industry employed a total of 9,087 horsepower, which had again increased ten times by the early twentieth century, including a very small percentage from electricity.

Such "leaps" forward, while revealing Portugal's general industrial growth, also show the weakness of its industry compared with that of other countries. Thus Belgium, half the size of Portugal, employed 720,000 horsepower in the early 1900's, against 111,000 for Portugal. Statistics for factories and human labor are also meaningful: there were less than 15,000 workers in 1,031 plants in 1822; 180,000 in 1,350 factories in 1881; some 200,000 in more than 5,000 factories on the eve of World War I. In a population of $5\frac{1}{2}$ million, the number of industrial laborers was certainly minor, particularly since statistics did not distinguish between homeworkers and plant workers. The rate of increase in the number of invention patents also shows the growing interest in industry: 5.1 in 1837–52 (annual average), 14.4 in 1863–67, 27.4 in 1873–77, 60 in 1878–82, 109.5 in 1887–92.

Which were the industries experiencing this growth? Here, too, changes had deeply affected the Portuguese tradition. Before 1820 leather led the way, followed by textiles. Together, they accounted for 80 per cent of the workers and the factories. Sixty years later the leather industry had declined to a second-class level, using no machinery at all. The textile industry had risen to first place, followed by tobacco (which employed 4,000 people and used 30 steam engines), milling, ceramics, cork, and glass. On the eve of World War I textiles accounted for one-fourth of Portuguese industry (50,000 workers). In addition to the other crafts mentioned for 1881, the processing of dairy products and sardine-canning were showing a rapid rise.

From the 1870's on the process of capital accumulation and concentration of firms speeded up. In 1881 there were already some large industrial combines, in tobacco and textile manufactures. Foreign capital (English mostly) began to enter Portugal at a quickening pace: in 1884, some 10 per cent of all the anonymous societies and companies (for both trade and industry) in Portugal were foreign, but their invested capital amounted to about 20 per cent. By 1900 foreign firms had increased to one-sixth of the total (half of them British), and their investments controlled one-fourth of Portugal's trade and industry. In 1891 the tobacco industry was converted into a monopoly, the capital of which belonged predominantly to foreigners. Yet some large Portuguese combines also appeared, the first important Portuguese industrialists or millionaires becoming apparent by the end of the century. The milling industry was one of these, with a virtual monopoly in supplying Lisbon with bread, biscuits, and pastries. In glass and ceramics similar concentrations developed. Two big names related to industry arose in the early 1900's: Narciso Ferreira (Riba d'Ave) in textiles and Alfredo da Silva in the chemical industries. They started dynasties which are still going on.

The economic expansion of Portugal resulted largely from the governmental policy of developing transportation and communications. The building of roads, railroads, harbors, lighthouses, and telegraph connections were the goals of most Portuguese governments, particularly after 1851. Some timid measures of road development had been enacted in 1838 and 1843, when the government entrusted several companies with the building of a number of roads in the northern, central and southern regions. Those firms were authorized to set up toll stations along the new roads for a certain period. In 1844 a Company for Public Works (Companhia das Obras Públicas de Portugal) endeavored to make or repair roads all over the country. At the same time (under Costa Cabral's "strong governments," 1842–46; 1849–51) several bridges were erected—the important suspension bridge over the Douro River, for instance—while work began for the improvement of the Douro sand bar. But it was only under Secretary Fontes Pereira de Melo (Secretary of Finance, 1851–52; Secretary of Public Works, 1852–56; Prime Minister, 1871–77, 1878–79 and 1881–86) that a well-developed policy of public works became a major concern of government. Known as Fontismo (after Fontes), its aim was to modernize Portugal through a program of material improvements, emphasizing transportation and communications, i.e., the infrastructure of trade, industry, and agriculture (areas where the state intervention should be minimal according to the liberal ideology). Fontismo strove hard to give Portugal an honorable place within the civilized world, to "Europeanize" the country and pull her out of a condition of deep backwardness. By means of extensive loans, Secretary Fontes and his successors (especially Emídio Navarro, Secretary of Public Works from 1886 to 1889) could get the necessary credits for their policy of expansion.

Road building led the way: when Fontes took office as the first Secretary of Public Works, in 1852, Portugal had only 218 km. (135.5 miles) of modern, macadamized roads. Four years later, when he left office, there were 678 km. (411 miles) ready and 120 km. under construction. In 1884 such figures had increased more than tenfold (9,155 km. = 5,667 miles), and in 1900 Portugal could boast a road network of 14,230 km. (8,843 miles).

Railroad building also had a spectacular growth. Projects for endowing the country with trains had started in the 1840's, Prime Minister Costa Cabral having commissioned the Companhia das Obras Públicas de Portugal with the building of a first track from Lisbon to the Spanish border. The project failed, however, and it was Fontes who had the credit of providing the country with her first railroads: from 1851 to 1856 several contracts with Portuguese and foreign companies were signed and the first trains were in operation after 1856. The network increased twentyfold from an initial 36 km. (22.3 miles) in 1864, to more than 1,500 in the mid-1880's, 2,288 km. in 1892, 2,381 km. in 1902, 2,974 km. in 1912. In 1894 Portugal held an honorable tenth place among the countries of the world in the extent of railroads for each 100 miles of territory—ranking above Spain, Roumania, Norway, Greece, and other European countries. The situation was roughly the same twenty years later.

Along with roads and railroads went bridge building. At the end of his first term in government, Fontes claimed the construction of seventeen bridges and the beginning of twenty-eight others. The great train bridge over the Douro built by the famous French engineer Eiffel (1875–77) allowed the completion of the railroad from Lisbon to Porto. The same happened with the building of the international bridge over the Minho, which opened direct railroad communications between northern Portugal and Spanish Galicia (1886). For people and carriages a new monumental bridge over the Douro opened in 1886, replacing the suspension work of forty years before.

Gradually, all the provinces of Portugal welcomed the advantages of easy communication: departing from Lisbon by train it became possible to reach Alto Alentejo (1861); Ribatejo (1863); Beira Litoral, Douro, and Baixo Alentejo (1864); Porto and Minho (1877); Beira Alta (1882); Trás-os-Montes (1883); the Algarve (1889); and Beira Baixa (1893). In less than forty years the whole country, even the most distant towns, had been brought closer together. Connections with Spain (i.e., with Europe) started in the 1860's.

Railroads were followed by telegraph (1857), with an almost immediate connection with Spain. In 1864 more than 2,000 km. of telegraph were working, a figure which had jumped four times by World War I. Submarine cable also began in the 1850's (Lisbon-Azores). In 1870 it linked Portugal to England, then to Brazil via Madeira and Cape Verde (1871). Telephone connections entered Portugal very early: Lisbon had its first phones by 1882. Wireless telegraph arrived only at the beginning of the twentieth century.

Harbors and lighthouses were greatly improved. The government had an artificial port made at Leixões in the North, to serve Porto and its hinterland (1884–92). In the port of Lisbon, a development plan was begun in 1887. In the 1890's, efforts to give light to the Portuguese coastline (called the black coast) led to fruitful results with the building of numerous lighthouses.

The post office was thoroughly reformed and improved in the 1850's, and then, several times, up to the end of the century. Postage stamps appeared in 1853, along with a new map of postal districts. The complex and traditional system of weights and measures underwent a complete change, when the government introduced the decimal metric system, effective by 1868 (in currency the decimal system had been established in 1835). It took, of course, generations to get the public used to so different a process of accounting. Post office, telegraphs, and telephones (with the exception of those in Lisbon and Porto) were nationalized from the very beginning. Half of the railroad network belonged to the state too.

In trade, the adoption of the liberal ideology prevented government interference. In the beginning, its main goal was only free exchange inside and outside the country; hence all the measures abolishing local tolls, permits of circulation, municipal monopolies, exclusives and privileges for certain companies, sales taxes, the corporations, and the like. It was, however, possible for the state to endow commerce with a framework that could regulate, organize, and also simplify the free circulation and distribution of products. The first Portuguese code of commerce was soon enacted in 1833, revealing clearly the bourgeois features of the new administration. Its author was Ferreira Borges, one of the main leaders of the liberal revolution. The code lasted until 1888, when the tremendous development of trade, both in Portugal and abroad, required a new one, that of Veiga Beirão. Tribunals of commerce were also established (1834). Lavish legislation starting with Ferreira Borges' code created and regulated economic associations, particularly joint-stock companies, which rapidly became favorites. Quota partnerships officially appeared in 1901. Other important legislation included codes of commercial proceedings (1896, 1905) and a code of commercial failures (1899).

Private associations of all sorts for trade purposes resulted from these laws and the general economic expansion of the country. The big traders of Porto and Lisbon founded their respective commercial associations (Associação Comercial do Porto, 1834; Associação Mercantil de Lisboa, 1834). By 1875 some fifteen commercial associations existed in the main urban centers, with an important impact on the rise of trade, industry, agriculture, and overseas expansion. In 1894 the government authorized a Chamber of Commerce and Industry for Lisbon. Joint-stock companies developed, particularly after 1867, when governmental restrictions on their free constitution were lifted: in 1875, 136 existed throughout the country (29 of them foreign); in 1885, 445 including companies of trade (46 foreign); in 1900 more than six hundred (one-eighth foreign). Half of the foreign companies and capital was British. Up to the end of the nineteenth century, the overwhelming majority of joint-stock companies were in trade, a minimal number only being concerned with industry. After 1900 the proportion drastically changed in favor of industry.

Obviously, a large share of this commercial growth—which brought about the rapid development of Lisbon and Porto—derived from better transportation and communications. Railways and roads made it easier to sell the products of agriculture (and industry), and facilitated rural credit operations and property transactions.

The development of external trade began especially after 1832. Duties on national exports went down from 8 per cent to 1 per cent. The customs tariff of 1837 (Passos Manuel) registered 1,499 different items, rationalizing duties on imports and exports, and trying to protect the national interests against exploitation by foreign powers. With England, Portugal's largest commercial partner, a new treaty of commerce was signed in 1842. It reduced the privileges granted to the British in 1810 and 1831. Other treaties of commerce were later signed with different countries.

Fontism reacted against protectionism. The new customs tariff of 1852 lowered the duties on many imports, particularly raw materials, instrumental for the development of industries and communications. For forty years, and despite some later corrections of the customs tariff, general economic policy tended toward free exchange. Only in 1892, when a serious crisis threatened the country, did a new tariff go back to less liberal principles, on behalf of national and colonial products.

The balance of trade registered a permanent deficit, which substantially increased after 1899: a yearly average of 12,017 contos de réis in 1880–89, 15,244 in 1890–99, 31,033 in 1900–1909. At the beginning of the century Portugal imported (mainly from England) twice as much as she exported. The most important imports included woollen, cotton, and silk fabrics; machinery; raw cotton, wool, and silk; coal; sugar; iron; and codfish. Understandably industrial expansion created the need for more and more raw materials and consequently a worsening balance of trade. The deficit could partly be covered by the foreign exchange credits sent by Portuguese immigrants in Brazil.

The rise to power by the bourgeoisie and the economic expansion of Portugal coincided with the foundation of the first banks. Up to the early nineteenth century, the peculiar economic structure of Portugal, based upon state intervention and foreign domination, had prevented the rise of a banking system. Several attempts since 1800 had failed, except in Brazil (see chapter 9). After the liberal revolution, however, the new economic and social conditions permitted the establishment of the first Portuguese bank, the Bank of Lisbon (1821). With a capital of 5,000 contos, this Bank was granted the monopoly of banknote issues, which it kept to 1835. It was primarily a commercial bank. Up to the 1860's, growth of the banking system was minimal. Three new banks appeared, one of them devoted to the Overseas (Banco Ultramarino, 1865). The important feature of this earlier period was rather the fusion of the Bank of Lisbon with another one, the result being the much more important Bank of Portugal (1846), with a capital of 11,000 contos.

In the 1860's an economic boom stirred the country, a consequence partly of the international conjuncture and partly of the policy known as Fontismo. Transactions on the stock exchange developed and speculation reached a level disproportionate to the country's possibilities. The number of banks increased from four (1863), to twelve (1865), then twenty-six (1874), and finally fifty-one (1875). Their deposits increased from a level of 3,183 contos in 1858, to double that in 1865, again double in 1872, and double once more in 1875 (24,513 contos). But while the total amount of deposits had grown, their concentration in a few large banks very much declined: 79.4 per cent in the five main banks by 1870, 55.2 per cent five years later. When the economic crisis of 1876 shook Portugal, a good many of the smaller and local banks closed their doors. By 1880, when the crisis was over, only forty-four banks survived. The late 1880's were a similar period of expansion: forty-eight banks in 1887–88, then forty-five in 1889–90, and forty-four in 1891. Deposits, which had increased to 55,000 contos in 1889—comparable with the "high" level of 1875—went down again: 48,000 contos in 1890, 39,000 in 1891, and 33,000 in 1892. The great crisis of 1892 reduced the number of banks to less than thirty. Afterward, though deposits went up once more—in 1917 they were double the amount in 1892—banks were roughly the same in number: twenty-eight in 1910, although concentration of deposits in the five largest ones continued to increase.

The history of prices in Portugal was no different from the other countries of Europe during the same period. The long-term price trends showed a decline from about 1817 to the 1840's, then a rise to the mid-1870's, followed by another drop until 1890 and a new rise which would stop only some years after the end of World War I. These rises and falls were usually gentle and gradual, causing no great disturbances from a social standpoint (with a few exceptions) at least to the early twentieth century. In Portugal the price graph for the period 1868–1910 shows very few variations till the rise of 1890, after which there was a plateau with some slight fluctuations to 1904. Beginning with that year there was an almost continuous upward movement, which brought about widespread discontent and revolutionary tendencies.

Money followed a similar trend, with few devaluations and a general stabilizing tendency. Lack of Brazilian gold produced the first change in the value of the money after the mid-1700's: an act of 1822 raised the price of a mark (230 g.) of minted gold from 102,400 to 120,000 réis, a debasement of 17 per cent. This measure again put into practical circulation gold coins, which up to then tended to disappear and be melted. Silver experienced no change, which means that the ratio between the two rose to 1:16 instead of 1:13.5. In 1835 a full monetary reform was accomplished. Silver was debased almost 20 per cent (1 mark = 7,750 réis instead of the former 7,600) but no alteration affected gold. More important was the adoption of the decimal principle in currency: while keeping the real, the law established a new coin denomination system, based upon 1,000 réis—gold coins of 5,000 and 2,500 réis; silver coins of 1,000, 500, 200, and 100 réis; and copper coins of 20, 10, 5, and 3 réis.

In 1847–54 money suffered a new slight debasement: 7 per cent for gold (1 mark = 128,000, later 129,000 réis), 18 per cent for silver (1 mark = 9,180 réis); but up to the beginning of World War I no other important changes affected the currency. Besides the Portuguese gold coins (10,000, 5,000, 2,000 and 1,000 réis), British gold pounds fixed at 4,500 réis had legal tender in Portugal. In silver, a new 50 réis coin appeared, while the 1,000 réis ceased to be minted.

By the end of the century, the gradual disappearance of the Portuguese gold coins, which under Luis I and his successors had no longer been minted (after 1861), coinage of nickel (100 and 50 réis), and the increase in the circulation of paper money were signs of a gradual deterioration of the currency. English gold flooded the country, altogether replacing the Portuguese and being trusted much more than the national bills. Note circulation increased, despite all the efforts to hold it down.

Public finance also received the attention of the liberal governments from the very beginning. It actually became the main source of concern for most administrations throughout the nineteenth and the early twentieth century. The old system of government irresponsibility was over, and with it the confusion between king and Crown. From 1820 on, governments had a parliament to supervise them, an organ to which they periodically rendered accounts. The law of 1832 (Mousinho da Silveira) abolished the royal treasury and organized a public treasury tribunal (Tribunal do Tesouro Público), actually determined by the constitution. This tribunal was to audit all accounts throughout the country and define them as current or not. In each province a receiver-general or collector-general (recebedor geral) centralized revenues and paid expenditures. He had, as his representative in every *comarca,* a delegate *(delegado),* and he could also name deputies wherever he thought advisable. Another body known as Junta do Crédito Público (junta for public credit) was created (later dissolved and created again) for the purpose of receiving an annual endowment fixed by the *cortes* and of spending it on public debt interest and amortization.

Later acts introduced some changes in this system. The public treasury tribunal was dissolved, then reestablished. A law of 1842 set up central coffers in each district for collecting all revenues which had no well-determined local use. According to the same law, the court would appoint a receiver or tax collector for each municipality. The civil-governors of the administrative districts were entrusted with the supervision of tax collecting and its application to the public expenditures. An act of 1849 created the court of accounts (Tribunal de Contas) in charge of fiscalizing all public revenues and expenditures. Other laws (1860, 1870, 1886, etc.) corrected and altered some minor details without essentially changing the basic principles.

No reform, however, could solve one of the major problems of parliamentary Portugal, that of the scarcity of government funds. In truth, this problem was as old as the country itself. The introduction of public control in the state finance system, however, gave wide publicity to what previously had been the concern of only a few. Moreover, the end of Brazil as a colony and the abolition of many feudal taxes reduced the revenues, while the French invasions, the revolution, the Civil wars (that of 1832–34 cost 6,000 contos), and reforms of structure hopelessly increased expenditures. Later on, the very expansion of Portugal brought about new state expenses in all areas. Public works cost money and their eventual profit took some time to be collected. Meanwhile, more expenditures arose to absorb the new revenues. Again, this was (and is) a general concern of all countries, with somewhat graver aspects in a small one, with less maneuverability. Consequently, both the budget deficit and the public debt grew larger and larger, because the increase in expenditures greatly exceeded the increase in revenues.

In 1805 the Crown received 11,200 contos (i.e., 11,200,000,000 réis) in revenue. This figure went down to an average of 5,000–7,000 contos after the French Invasions, while the figure reached almost 15,000 contos in the years of highest expenditures (1828, 1834). Public debt went up to nearly 40,000 contos (annual charge of 1,269), including interest, paper money, promissory notes, and unpaid pensions and salaries. In 1834–43, the average yearly government revenues had gone up to 8,000 contos, but expenditures reached more than 10,000 contos a year. Yet the trend in revenues pointed to better days: the 1842–43 revenues matched the level of 1805, for the first time in almost forty years.

Fontismo along with the general development of the country and the end of the revolutionary period eased the budgetary situation. In the 1850's, revenues permanently surpassed the level of 1805 and jumped forward rapidly: annual averages reached 14,527 contos in 1854–63, 18,560 in 1864–73, 30,323 in 1874–83, 41,332 in 1884–93, 54,104 in 1894–1903, and 67,090 in 1904–10. Thus, at the beginning of the twentieth century Portugal, in terms of taxation, was five times wealthier than at the apogee of her exploitation of Brazil, a clear proof that the country could survive even without colonies (in those days the colonial weight on public revenues was minimal). At the same time, expenditures grew to still higher levels: 17,520 contos (1854–63), 25,220 (1864–73), 34,108 (1874–83), 47,420 (1884–93), 57,372 (1894–1903), and 69,085 (1904–10). The history of deficit was thus the history of constitutional finance, with its most terrible years in the late 1860's and in 1888–91. Afterward, the pressure of public opinion, and particularly the republican threat, led to a more careful management of state finance, which reduced the deficit by reducing expenditures.

The growth of public debt was still more impressive. The government borrowed money from every possible source, both internally and abroad. England, of course, was its main source, and England required prompt and honest payment. Regarding other sources, the usual solution was not to pay and periodically to declare bankruptcy, in the old tradition of the Portuguese Empire. After 1851 the governments elevated the principle of non-amortization to a rule of administration, funded debt increasing to unheard-of proportions (around 38,000 contos in 1835, 93,000 in 1855, 194,000 ten years later, 573,000 in 1890, 797,000 in 1910, some 90 per cent of the total debt).

Among the structural changes which shaped a new Portugal, the reforms in administration are significant. The *cortes* began those reforms in 1822 by regulating elections at the municipal level and adopting new principles for city organization. Then the Constitution set up the bases of administrative reform and the independence of the tribunals. Portugal was thoroughly divided into districts (*distritos*), each one encompassing a number of municipalities (*concelhos*). Administrators-general (*administradores gerais*) appointed by the king represented the government in every district, while the municipalities elected their deputies to an administrative junta (*junta administrativa*), which assisted the administrators. Such principles closely followed the French law, in those days considered the most perfect one, which had a tremendous influence on many new liberal regimes of Europe. The counterrevolution of 1823 ended all that. It was only in 1826 that the liberal restoration began another plan of administrative and judicial changes by entrusting two committees with the task of studying and suggesting practical methods of reform. But again the political evolution of Portugal interrupted this until 1832. In that year, the "provisional government" active in the Azores enacted three laws reforming public finance, civil administration, and judicial administration (Secretary Mousinho da Silveira). They would become the foundations of modern Portugal.

According to the constitutional principles, administrative and judicial functions could not and should not be confused, as before. Thus, the new laws thoroughly changed most of the existing rules on administration, repealing a large part of the *Ordenações* (see chapter 7) and other legislation. Along with the Azores and Madeira Islands, Portugal was divided into provinces *(províncias), comarcas,* and municipalities *(concelhos)*, the first headed by a prefect *(prefeito)*, the second by an under-prefect *(sub-prefeito)*, and the last by a purveyor *(provedor)*, all appointed by the king. Each of these officials would be assisted by collective bodies, indirectly elected by the people: *junta geral de província, junta de comarca,* and *câmara municipal.* In every province a three-member court or council, of royal choice, had consultative as well as substantive powers *(conselho de prefeitura).* A high degree of centralization and extensive powers granted to the representatives of the government characterized the act of 1832.

This law was altered three years later (Rodrigo da Fonseca) although its basic provisions underwent few changes. Provinces disappeared and districts replaced the *comarcas.* Under-prefects were renamed civil-governors *(governadores civis)*, and purveyors, administrators *(administradores dos concelhos)*, the latter being elected by the people and then confirmed by the government. A *conselho de distrito,* with consultative powers, substituted for the *conselho de prefeitura.* Elections for the general junta *(junta geral do distrito)* and the City Council became direct. Below the municipalities the new law acknowledged the existence of parishes *(paróquias)*, with their local juntas— elected by the population—and their commissioners *(comissários de paróquia)*, also directly elected but confirmed by the administrator. The administrative code of 1836—the first one in Portugal—maintained the law of 1835 with minor alterations (Passos Manuel). Both acts tended to lessen centralization and increase local autonomy.

The acts of 1840–42 (administrative code of 1842—Costa Cabral) reacted against decentralization and went back to the principles of 1832. Administrators and *regedores* became once more of governmental choice. The seesaw policy between centralization and decentralization would continue to the present, according to the changes in politics. Thus, after several attempts to correct the legislation of 1840–42, the administrative code of 1878 (Rodrigues Sampaio) granted local autonomy as never before, depriving the government of most powers of inspection and supervision. The code of 1886 (with later alterations) strengthened centralization again (José Luciano de Castro). (The *juntas gerais* of the districts disappeared.) The codes of 1895 and 1896 (João Franco) went along with the same trend toward greater centralization, particularly in regard to the districts and the municipalities. The *juntas gerais* were restored for the Azores and Madeira Islands. With some minor alterations afterward, stability in administration could now be achieved, the new laws enduring for quite a long time.

The judicial organization of Portugal as enacted in 1832–35 (Mousinho da Silveira and others) besides introducing a fundamental principle, that of the jury, divided the country into judicial circles later named districts (*círculos judiciais, distritos de relação*), subdivided into *comarcas,* which encompassed *julgados,* divided in their turn into *freguesias.* In Lisbon a Supreme Court was established, with jurisdiction over all the realm. An attorney-general (*procurador geral da coroa*) assisted it. In each circle there was a court (*tribunal de segunda instância,* later called *relação),* assisted by an attorney (*procurador régio*). The *comarcas* had their own judges and jurors, assisted by an attorney-delegate (*delegado do procurador régio*). Each *julgado* had its judge and its under-delegate (*sub-delegado*). The *freguesias* also possessed their justices of the peace. Up to the *julgado* level, the magistrates were chosen by election. The higher judges were appointed by the government.

In 1836–37 and 1841 this reform underwent some alterations, although its fundamental clauses were kept unchanged. The new civil code (1867) brought about the need for more changes, particularly in proceedings. Thus, the code of civil proceeding (1876, Secretary Barjona de Freitas) simplified and shortened its forms, without jeopardizing precise and good justice. Another important body of law was the Penal Code of 1852, which would last for a long time with only minor changes. Among their achievements, the Liberals had also abolished the death penalty, a quite revolutionary measure in the world of those days (1867, Secretary Barjona de Freitas), and slavery (1869), reforms which had been under way for a long time (see chapter 11).

The most relevant step in this whole field of administration and justice was the enacting of the Civil Code (Código Civil) of 1867, prepared by the Viscount of Seabra and countersigned by the Secretary of Justice, Barjona de Freitas. Highly original in its structure and in many of its articles, this new code, which at last replaced the *Ordenações* of Philip III, introduced some principles "revolutionary" for most Catholic countries in those days, such as lay marriage for non-Catholic couples.

In government, the growing complexity of public affairs led to an increase in secretariates and internal departments. The four portfolios of the early nineteenth century (i.e., interior, foreign affairs and war, navy and overseas, and public finance) rose to six in 1821, when the secretariate of foreign affairs and war was split into two parts, and a new secretariate of ecclesiastical affairs and justice came into existence. In 1852 the secretariate of public works was established and then, for a few months only (1870), that of public instruction, reintroduced in 1890–92. To preside over the ministry there had been assistant secretaries from time to time since the reign of Maria I, yet no permanent prime minister. Maria II's first constitutional government in 1834 introduced the novelty of a president of the council of ministers or prime minister (Presidente do Conselho de Ministros), who was then the Duke of Palmela. Very often, the prime ministers were also entrusted with one or more secretariates, particularly with that of the interior. Other reforms encompassed the army and the navy, public charity, and of course the Overseas territories (see chapter 11).

Throughout Europe, the nineteenth century was one of boundless growth of population. In the towns the number of inhabitants multiplied several times in a hundred years. The countryside, too, showed an increase and a better distribution of its people. Although in a more moderate way, Portugal reflected that trend, a result of a century of peace and prosperity, featured by important achievements in the areas of health and hygiene. Population estimates, roughly to the 1860's, more precisely after 1864—when the government organized the first scientific census—clearly displayed such a growth: 3,100,000 in the 1820's, 3,500,000 in the 1850's, 3,829,618 in 1864, 4,160,315 in 1878, 4,660,095 in 1890, 5,016,267 in 1900, 5,547,708 in 1911. With the inclusion of the Azores and Madeira archipelagoes, these figures would be some 300,000 to 400,000 higher. The rate of growth was particularly impressive after 1878. In a European context Portugal's birth and death rates at the beginning of the twentieth century were below countries like Germany, Spain, and Italy but above Belgium, Switzerland, England, and France.

Lisbon and Porto showed some interesting and peculiar aspects. The capital had some 200,000 people in 1820, a figure that remained static to the 1860's. The great leap forward started then: 227,674 in 1878, 301,206 in 1890, 356,069 in 1900, and 434,436 in 1911. Thus, Lisbon's population doubled in less than fifty years after remaining static for the preceding fifty years. Its parishes also increased from 41 in 1833 to 48 in 1885 when a sort of "Greater Lisbon" made its appearance with the incorporation of vast suburban boroughs. In total area, Lisbon rose from 947 hectares (early nineteenth century) to 1,208 (1852), then to 6,500 (1885), and finally to 8,244 (1895–1903). The area devoted to housing, however, increased much less; it was perhaps twice as great at the beginning of the present century as in 1820.

Porto jumped from 50,000 inhabitants (around 1820), to about 60,000 in 1838, 86,000 in 1864, 105,000 in 1878, 138,000 in 1890, 168,000 in 1900, and 194,000 in 1911. Up to about 1870, Porto's growth was major, the population difference with Lisbon gradually diminishing. Afterward, the trend changed, and by 1910 the capital had 8 per cent of Metropolitan Portugal's population, as against only 6 per cent in 1820. Figures for Porto were, respectively, 3.4 per cent and 1.6 per cent. Together, the two great cities encompassed more than 11 per cent of the country's population in contrast to 8 per cent ninety years before. Such was the result of the urban movement. The other towns registered a more modest increase. Some even declined, particularly in the interior and in the South. The trend in the countryside toward a continuous rise of population in the coastal North and a stagnation or decrease in the rest of the country went on undisturbed, to the late 1800's. Only the laws on agriculture were able to change this tendency afterward and foster a southern rise.

Another important trait of demographical evolution was the increasing emigration to America, particularly to Brazil. Emigrants came mostly from Minho and coastal Beira—and the Azores and Madeira Islands—all places where the number of people had become disproportionate to their conditions of survival with minimal well-being. As in many other countries of Europe, accelerated emigration only started after 1850. The figures for Portugal show an increase of emigrants from a possible 6,000 level in 1855 to about 10,000 in 1886, then double that annual average, to 1900, reaching almost 50,000 in 1911. Clandestine emigration would put these figures still higher. Only a small minority returned home, yet the money from Brazil and elsewhere sent by emigrants to Portugal had an impact on the Portuguese economy, helping to solve the balance of trade deficit: estimates give about 3,000 contos in the 1870's, more than 12,000 in the 1890's, and perhaps 20,000 by 1910—an amount equal to more than one-fourth of the total state revenues!

Among the fundamental changes in structure carried on by the liberal governments after 1820 the religious reform should not be omitted. It brought about serious consequences, which still affect modern Portugal. The *cortes* started by abolishing the Inquisition. This abolition of a centuries-old body with such a tremendous impact on history had undoubtedly a symbolic meaning but very few practical consequences, because the Inquisition had been slowly fading away for years. Much more important was the liberal attitude regarding the regular clergy.

The religious orders still played a significant role in the Portuguese society of that time. They partly controlled charity and education. They owned extensive property, which made them an economic power throughout the country. The religious orders influenced all social classes, especially in the lower ranks of society, and were thus political forces of importance. Under their direct command, thousands of clients lived with them, worked with them, and thoroughly depended upon them. From a strictly religious standpoint, they were soldiers of Christ everywhere, doubling or tripling the presence of the secular clergy, pervading the country in the remotest places, constantly reminding everyone everywhere of the traditional, deeply Catholic, old Portugal, intolerant and superstitious, fanatic and reactionary. The convents had moreover the dubious moral role of welcoming many young ladies whose parents did not want them to marry, and of accepting their forced vows.

Anticlerical feeling had slowly emerged in Portugal, as everywhere, a characteristic of the late eighteenth-century ideologies. The upper classes became increasingly indifferent in matters of religion, to the point of atheism. To many, the clergy was a dangerous symbol of the past, an obstacle to progress. The notorious decadence of the ecclesiastical order, both in the secular and the regular forms, did nothing to contradict this view. Priests, monks, friars, and nuns were gradually playing a less and less relevant role in the fields of education and culture in general. A lay intelligentsia had arisen, composed of nobles, bureaucrats, army and navy officers, traders, and industrialists, which had no need for clerics and often scorned them. Even in charity, state intervention had much reduced the clergy's traditional role.

Victorious Liberalism directed an offensive against the clergy, particularly the religious orders. Tithes were abolished, along with several other taxes, depriving the clerics of their most important source of revenue. Moreover, the constitutional governments imposed on Church property a new burdensome taxation, in some cases as much as 50 per cent of all revenues. Confiscations based upon several pretexts further increased ecclesiastical grievances against the new order. In the political sphere, the Constitutions of both 1822 and 1826 denied the regular clergy's right to representation in the Chambers and to voting in the elections. And it seemed obvious that a free press along with the right to free discussion, would bring about a decline in the clergy's influence on the minds of people by way of the confessionary and the pulpit.

For these and other reasons the great majority of the clergy sided with the absolutist opposition. They backed the restorations of 1823 and 1828; they supported Miguel against Pedro. Yet their integrity as a class was no longer the same during the second restoration and the Civil War. Secular clergy and regular clergy were now divided, because the Constitution of 1826 favored the former against the latter. The bishops had now been granted permanent representation in the upper Chamber, which put them on the same level with the high nobility. And paradoxically, their subordinates at the head of the parishes also started to receive some economic benefits from the triumph of the new order, based upon equality and governmental subsidies, because most of the existing revenues went to the bishops and to the regular clergy. Through this internal division the liberal governments achieved a victory over the clergy, which permitted a relatively easy, yet revolutionary, set of ecclesiastical reforms.

The fact that many monasteries actively supported the defeated side in the Civil War, while many friars and monks took up arms against the "impious and blasphemous" liberals, encouraged them to enforce measures that had been considered for a long time. To start with, the Nuncio was ordered to leave the country and diplomatic relations with Rome were broken, because the Holy See had recognized Miguel's regime. This deprived the Portuguese clergy of a powerful ally and put them at the mercy of their triumphant enemy. The Jesuits, whom the Pope had re-established and Portugal welcomed in 1829, were immediately expelled. All bishops nominated by the "usurper" king were deposed and their sees declared vacant. Ecclesiastical patronates were abolished. A good many monasteries, which their occupants had abandoned in fleeing the invasion, were considered extinct. Monks, friars, and priests suffered all kinds of persecution and discrimination, even open violence and death. A law of 1833 forbade novitiates in any monastery, thus insuring the gradual extinction of the orders. At last, Regent Pedro made up his mind and accepted Secretary Joaquim António de Aguiar's repeated proposal to abolish all monasteries and disband their male population (May 28, 1834). This act affected 401 religious houses (including colleges, hospices, and also twelve convents) all over the country and the Overseas provinces and more than 6,500 people, of whom less than half were actually friars and monks. Many of them left the country, while others retired to the homes of relatives or friends. A goodly number were still young enough to start a new life, which they did, several later rising to positions in administration, education, organized charity, and the world of letters. Many others joined the secular clergy and became priests. The law endowed every ex-monk or ex-friar with an allowance, if he could get no other source of revenue (but it excepted all those who had fought against the liberals). Convents were not dissolved, but lacking any further novitiates, they gradually closed. Property belonging to the monasteries (both male and female) was nationalized. Sacred vessels and apparel were given to the churches.

The dissolution of the religious orders brought no special harm to the country, apart from the losses in artistic monuments, books, and manuscripts which were destroyed or sacked in the confusion. On the contrary, it generally benefited agriculture and landownership, as we have already emphasized. It also gave the nation an important share of wealth in landed property and solid buildings. Socially, it met with little resistance and was applauded or accepted with indifference by most people, including the secular clergy. From a religious standpoint, however, it contributed to a certain decline of faith among the lower classes. And it helped prepare them to accept other influences instead.

The religious orders came back, although in a disguised form. In 1857 some French Sisters of Charity (order of St. Vincent of Paul) were admitted to Portugal for charitable purposes. They had to leave five years later, because of the anticlerical campaign against them which ravaged the country. After the 1850's, Jesuits, Franciscans, Fathers of the Holy Spirit, Benedictines, Brethren of St. John, Sisters of the Poor, Salesians, Lazarists, and scores of others arrived with the professed aim of establishing schools, hospices, hospitals, and the like. A law of 1901 (Hintze Ribeiro's government) practically authorized the coming of any religious order to Portugal provided it pursued educational or charitable goals. In the early twentieth century there were again more than fifty religious congregations or associations in the country with some hundreds of members. They had a growing influence, particularly among the aristocracy.

The reform of the secular clergy had a much more limited impact. According to the Constitution, the priests became civil servants of a sort, paid by the state to perform services for the benefit of the nation. This put the entire clergy under the government's supervision and converted them into docile clients of the ruling groups. Sitting in the upper Chamber, the bishops took an active part in the political life of the country, siding with one or another party but never posing any threat as an ecclesiastical body. After the re-establishment of diplomatic relations with Rome (1842), an agreement signed six years later solved some problems and paved the way to peace and harmony between Church and state (the concordats of 1857 and 1886 concerned the Overseas only), which would last until the Republic. The gradual decadence of the clergy, in spite of its official protection by king and government, could not be denied, and went along with the rise of anticlericalism. The Church, as it became increasingly involved with cultural problems, displayed its reactionary tendency and its inability to cope with the new times. The number of priests declined in proportion to the rise in population. As lay schools increased, the educational role of the Church declined. Yet its seminaries continued to be nuclei of instruction throughout the country and to provide free studies to all classes.

A symbolic aspect of the decline of the Church throughout the nineteenth century was the stagnation and even decrease in the number of dioceses. Despite the fact that Portugal's population almost doubled by 1910, no administrative reform was ever accomplished by the Church; moreover, five existing bishoprics disappeared: Aveiro (1837), Castelo Branco (1831), Leiria (1873), Pinhel (1838), and Portalegre (1833, re-established 1883).

With the triumph of the new order the other pillar of absolutism, the feudal nobility, suffered much less than the clergy. In theory, the official acknowledgment of equality downgraded the aristocrats. The law abolished feudal rights and commanderies (1821–46) and also entailed property (partly in 1832, totally in 1863); deprived the nobles of their usual allowances granted by the king; nationalized Crown property; and so forth. To subsist—and many could not—the nobles had now to rely exclusively upon their own estates and their participation in trade and industry. This moved them closer to the bourgeoisie than ever before. On the other hand, the government policy of granting titles to petty aristocrats, traders, bureaucrats, and soldiers went on at a still more rapid pace. In 1821–30, title-grants had reached 51, but this was small in comparison with the inflation of later decades: 101 in 1831–40, 38 in 1841–50, 112 in 1851–60, 205 in 1861–70, 192 in 1871–80, 152 in 1881–90. Most such titles were not permanent, being granted for one or two lives only. Scores of Brazilians and other foreigners were included, which meant little else than a modern decoration. Viscounts and barons took the lead, with 81 per cent of the total. Up to about 1850, baron-grants surpassed any others, their beneficiaries having become an object of derision for all the other nobles. Partly because of this, titles of viscount went up instead and led the way to the end of the century, with of course a similar result. Besides, the policy of title-granting was so discredited by the end of Luis I's reign that his successors, Carlos I (1889–1908) and Manuel II (1908–10), reduced it to a minimum, granting nobilitation according to the ancient rules.

As a result of all this, by the end of the century the old aristocracy and constitutional aristocracy were so intermingled that it would have been difficult to make a distinction between them on other than historical grounds.

The constitutions of 1822 and 1838 did not provide for a separate representation of the nobility in the Chambers. Yet the constitutions did not endure, and precisely because of that. The landed aristocrats—and almost all the new title-bearers coming from other sources of wealth wanted to buy land—played such an important role in the economic structure of Portugal (at least until the 1870's) that leadership in public affairs naturally had to belong to them, either in part or in whole. This is why the Constitution of 1826, granting the nobility hereditary representation in the upper chamber, could triumph and subsist—despite its several changes—to the end of the monarchy.

Yet the evolution of Portuguese society was somewhat more complex. To a first phase of aristocratic rule, lasting for about half a century (if one omits the rather short periods of 1820–23 and 1836–42, of almost pure bourgeois predominance), a second phase of leadership by nontitular bankers, industrialists, and traders followed. Up to the 1870's, more than one-fourth of the cabinet ministers and 80 per cent of the prime ministers were title-bearers, all of constitutional stock. Afterward, their share of government responsibilities rapidly declined. The Duke of Ávila, Prime Minister in 1877–78, was the last title-bearer to head a government. Up to 1910 the number of cabinet ministers who were title-bearers constantly decreased: 35 per cent of the positions in 1861–70, 17 per cent in 1871–80, 3.2 per cent in 1881–90, 3.4 per cent in 1891–1900, and 2.9 per cent in 1901–10. This decrease in participation of the upper nobility in the tasks of governing was partly replaced by a rising petty aristocracy of ancient lineages but no titles, depending upon government jobs as well as their lands. The proclamation of the Republic in 1910 cut short the rise of this new nobility, without giving it time to assert itself.

The decline of the constitutional nobility after 1870 had its parallel in the legislation. With the complete abolition of entailed property, there was no place for heredity anywhere. The second amendment to the constitution (1885) abolished hereditary peers in the upper House of Parliament, reduced to a hundred the number of nobles and clerics seated there, and instituted elective peers as well. In the 1890's, however, the nobility had still enough strength to strike back and regain some of the lost positions. The third amendment (1896) suppressed elective peerage and allowed the hereditary peers existing in 1885 to go back to their seats, although on a temporary basis. Such was the situation when the Republic was proclaimed.

The bourgeoisie, which had been given a large share in government and administration since Pombal, triumphed in 1820 and then, permanently, in 1834. Few monographs exist concerning its features, evolution, and quantitative aspects. By 1820, the bourgeois groups constituted some 8 per cent of the total population, but the great majority consisted of civil servants (including army and navy officers), teachers, students, lawyers, doctors, and the like. Traders and businessmen accounted for only one-tenth. By 1867 the proportion of bourgeoisie in the country had perhaps doubled, traders and industrialists predominating over civil servants and all the others. Up to the beginning of the twentieth century, both groups continued to grow. An analysis of the general censuses based upon reliable data (from 1864 on) clearly shows the decline of that part of the population engaged in agriculture: 72 per cent in 1864, 61 per cent in 1890 and 1900, 57 per cent in 1911. As the figures for the industrial groups do not reveal more than about 100,000 real proletarians by 1910, the gap may be accounted for by the rise of a bourgeoisie, where traders and industrialists soon led the way.

Lisbon and Porto were the two cities with a particularly high percentage of burghers. In Lisbon government and central administration went hand in hand with army officers, liberal professions, bankers, traders, and a few industrialists. Many large landowners lived in the capital too. In 1880, 568 firms (of which one-sixth were foreign), 192 doctors, and 140 lawyers (including solicitors) were active in Lisbon. Porto had proportionally more trade and more industry but was obviously weaker in all the other fields. Both towns controlled banking, commerce, and industry in the country, the role of capital being successively enhanced by the rising centralization of administration and the general development of Portugal.

The bourgeoisie undoubtedly increased in class-consciousness by the second half of the century. Titles of nobility became less coveted and were even refused by some wealthy bourgeois. Allied to a petty aristocracy, the bourgeois permanently controlled government after the 1870's. No more title-bearers were appointed prime ministers. No member of the high nobility ever presided over the twenty-seven governments which ruled Portugal from 1878 to 1910, and only three or four of the heads of government could be considered nobles of ancient lineage. None of the great statesmen of that period bore a title. At last the bourgeoisie realized its own value and looked down upon nobles and titles. They preferred to become peers, to be granted the title of councillor (*conselheiro*), and to be decorated.

Among the lower groups of society, what must be stressed was the slow and gradual rise of a proletariat. Early in the nineteenth century, the craft workers who owned their shop and tools in the old style of production still made up two-thirds of the whole "industrial population." Workers and apprentices numbered about 36,000. Rural workers, however, who owned nothing, constituted some 70 per cent of the total rural population.

A century later workers in plants with more than ten people—i.e., real proletarians—were no more than 100,000, some 20 per cent of the total number of workers engaged in industry and craft activities. The great majority of the industrial population were still working in small shops with less than ten workers, in craft activities at home, and the like. Women continued to perform a large role, although the proportion in active production had been declining since the 1880's or 1890's: 34.8 per cent in 1890, 29 per cent in 1900, 28.3 per cent in 1911. Child labor was also declining. Yet the Industrial Inquiry of 1881 still showed minors (those less than sixteen years old) to be 6.6 per cent of the total industrial population, and a 1907 estimate showed 7 per cent.

General working conditions seem to have worsened during the nineteenth century. Real salaries decreased, particularly after 1880, with the increase in capital and industrial concentration. The standard of living—of nutrition, lodging, and the like—also worsened. Despite a law of 1891, the workday could not be standardized throughout the country. By 1900 the average pointed to ten hours, but there were many exceptions in excess of this. Neither the government nor the industrialists provided the workers with any legal protection or assistance against accidents, old age, and the like.

The workers responded in the two usual ways: by joining in associations and by striking. Apart from some old and insignificant associations, the first group to engage in class struggle appeared only in 1853, in Lisbon (Centro Promotor do Melhoramento da Classe Laboriosa). It was followed by many other groups with several different goals—the cooperative movement soon rose in Lisbon and Porto, for instance—the whole accompanied by propaganda and social indoctrination in newspapers, pamphlets, and books of all kinds. Mutual benefit societies of workers rose from 65 in 1876 to 590 in 1903. In 1889 the total number of workers' unions of all types reached 392, of which more than 300 were in the districts of Lisbon and Porto. Their combined membership was 138,870. Syndicalism developed from 24 associations in 1876 to 135 in 1903. A Socialist Party appeared in the 1870's.

Up until the Republican revolution, strikes were considered illegal and punishable according to the Penal Code. Nonetheless, they first occurred in the 1870's, and their role in the life of the country began to have a certain importance after the turn of the century. By 1899 more than sixty strikes had affected Portugal, but their number increased to 91 between 1900 and 1910, most of them successful. In 1903 there were three very important strikes, one in Porto (practically a general one), another in Lisbon (exceptionally violent), and the third in Coimbra (where workers and students fought together). At least 8 per cent of the proletariat was mobilized by such strikes. In the South of the country, rural strikes also played a role.

Despite these and other factors of social unrest and industrial growth, the proletariat of Portugal in the early twentieth century was far from posing any threat to the bourgeois leadership. The urban workers were few, illiterate for the most part, and easily maneuvered by bourgeois and noble politicians and philosophers. Both in the towns and in the country, proletarians generally appeared as the humble clients of traders, industrialists, and landowners, with a strong clerical influence to divert them from any widespread rebellion.

Official concern with education began in Pombal's days. The Enlightenment espoused the principle of spreading instruction to the people, but not to everyone. The law of 1772, one of the world's earliest attempts to officially organize primary lay education, led to

establishment of a number of first grades by the end of the eighteenth
century: 720 schools existed by 1779. But such an interesting movement was not carried on as it deserved. Many schools were closed and
few new ones ever opened. Others were entrusted to the Church.

The liberal revolution fostered glamorous principles of giving
education to all citizens—quite logically, because free voting depended
upon it. Thus, in fourteen months, 59 primary schools were opened;
there were improvements in the financial and moral situation of instructors; and freedom of teaching was proclaimed. The Constitution
of 1826 established free primary instruction as a right for every
citizen. The reactions of 1823–26 and 1828–34, however, closed down
schools and persecuted teachers, who were supposed, and rightly so, to
be sympathetic to Liberalism.

After 1834 progress in all the fields of education could be carried
on without interruption. The first task was to set up schools everywhere, to prepare instructors, and to try to overcome the nearly 90
per cent illiteracy. This took time and money, which was often hard
to come by. In 1841, for instance, only about half of the male children
of school age attended school. Nonetheless, the number of official
primary schools steadily increased: one to 120 square kilometers in
1820, one to 40 fifty years later, one to 20 in the early twentieth century. To these, private schools must be added—270 in 1845, 1,500 in
1870—although their growth never matched the rate of increase of
the official schools, which constituted 74.2 per cent of all primary
institutions by 1900. Girls' schools also increased, particularly after
1860. Primary instructors tripled between 1870 and 1910, hand in hand
with the establishment of teachers' colleges after 1860. Accordingly, the
rate of illiteracy gradually declined: 76.0 per cent for those over seven
in 1890, 74.1 per cent in 1900, 69.7 per cent in 1911. These figures
seemed quite high, even for late-nineteenth-century Europe, a fact
which endowed Republican propaganda with one of its best weapons.
Throughout the country 702 parishes (17.5 per cent of the total) still
had no school. Nonetheless, considerable efforts had been undertaken
by the government, especially after 1900. Primary schools included
three years of compulsory attendance, plus a voluntary fourth year.

As in many aspects of administration, one of the great problems
here concerned centralization or decentralization of the primary

system. Should the central government direct everything or should the municipalities control schools? Governments and reforms wavered between these alternatives. In the 1820's the tendency was to centralize education from a bureaucratic standpoint; in the early 1830's decentralization prevailed. The reform of 1836 pointed again toward centralization, which was confirmed by the reform of 1844, but thoroughly changed in 1878–81. After 1890 centralization once more won out. Of course, this question went along with political ideologies, which defended full concentration of power in the hands of the government or else favored greater autonomy to the local institutions.

The ruling classes of Liberalism were actually more concerned with the two upper levels of education, which affected their own children for a long period of time, than with the creation of new primary schools or the sending of more primary teachers throughout the country. One of their major achievements was the thorough reform of secondary studies, according to the French pattern of the lycée (high school). After long planning which had started in 1821, Secretary Passos Manuel instituted a *liceu* in every district capital and two in Lisbon (1836). At the same time a full program of secondary studies was organized, including humanities (history, geography, literature), languages (French, English, and German) and sciences (chemistry, physics, algebra, geometry, natural history), besides the traditional study of classical languages, rhetoric, and philosophy. *Liceus* were thus restricted to urban centers, precisely those places where the ruling bourgeoisie dwelt.

Passos Manuel's reform was too progressive and too ambitious to endure. Thus, Secretary Costa Cabral totally eliminated scientific studies from the lycée program, while limiting the teaching of living languages to the main cities (1844). More progressively he reduced fees to one-fifth. Only in 1860 did the legislators go back to Passos' original ideas although in a moderate way: secondary studies were extended to five years, including physics, chemistry, and natural history (Secretary Fontes Pereira de Melo). Up to the end of the century, several other reforms did little to improve this state of things. They were concerned mainly with the extension of studies (five years, six years), the arrangement of disciplines per year, the examination system, and some further technical points.

In 1894–95, Secretary João Franco approved a new reform and regulation for the high school, which Professor Jaime Moniz had elaborated. It was a model reform, framed by the most advanced principles of pedagogy, insisting on the so-called "class regime" (i.e., the conforming of subjects to a common goal), adding a seventh year to secondary studies and increasing the number of disciplines. Despite some later amendments, Jaime Moniz's reform was to last for a quarter of a century.

The introduction of secondary technical studies resulted from the need to equip Portugal with experts in the industrial and commercial fields (little was achieved in the area of agriculture). Passos Manuel set up the basis for regular technical studies with his Conservatórias de Artes e Ofícios (Conservatories of Arts and Crafts) in Lisbon and Porto (1836). Fontes Pereira de Melo's new Secretariate of Public Works organized a full system of technical studies in three levels: elementary, secondary, and complementary. Industrial schools opened in the 1850's, followed by commercial ones in the 1880's. Secretary Emídio Navarro's reforms were paramount in developing technical studies, reaching much farther than ever before. Yet the proper framework for the modern technical schools resulted much more from a gradual evolution of efforts than from the achievements of a single man. Up to the proclamation of the Republic the decisive steps had been undertaken.

By comparison, the reform of the University was a poor one. Coimbra continued its theoretical monopoly of university studies, but the majority of its teachers could never cope with the tremendous progress which was taking place in the world in all the fields of knowledge. From the very beginning, the Liberals distrusted the University of Coimbra (which they considered a center of tradition and absolutism) and always fought it. The University, in its turn, always slowed down all efforts to create new centers of higher knowledge. Until 1859 Coimbra even supervised general teaching throughout the country. It had few powers to influence any reforms at primary or secondary levels, but it had powers to prevent its own reform. Indeed both Passos Manuel and Costa Cabral included the University in their legislation, yet they were unable to produce in it any revolutionary consequences. It was the teachers of the University itself who prepared the reforms, and they were too timid and too conservative to change structures. Therefore, the only significant alterations in almost a century were the fusion of the two schools of Law and Canons into one—the new School of Law—and the adding of a few scientific disciplines. In spite of some exceptionally good and up-to-date teachers, the University of Coimbra played a poor role in practically every field of knowledge to the twentieth century. Only the School of Law could boast a certain prestige—much more because of its uniqueness in the country than because of any significant advancement in the Law studies—and an always increasing enrollment. It became a real college of administration and "the school" where every noble or wealthy bourgeois wished to send his sons.

The development of upper university studies in nineteenth-century Portugal should rather be referred to the eight other schools which were gradually created in Lisbon and Porto. In 1836–37 Passos Manuel abolished the Colégio dos Nobres (see chapter 8) and the Royal Naval Academy, replacing them by the new Escola Politécnica (Polytechnical School) based upon the French *Écoles Polytechniques*. In Porto he instituted a Polytechnical Academy (Academia Politécnica). Both schools offered a plan of courses in science and prepared future officers for the Army and the Navy. (At the same time a new Military Academy—Escola do Exército—replaced the old Academy of Fortification and enlarged its plan of studies; some years later, a Naval School—Escola Naval—made its appearance too.) The existing schools of surgery in both cities were also converted into Schools of Medicine and Surgery (Escolas Médico-Cirúrgicas), with a much larger group of disciplines. The fifth upper college established by Passos Manuel was the General Conservatory of Dramatic Art (Conservatório Geral de Arte Dramática) of Lisbon which incorporated a recently created school of music with new schools for theater and dancing. Finally he established schools of Fine Arts in both Lisbon and Porto. The last important school founded in the nineteenth century (owing to the initiatives of King Pedro V) was the so-called Upper Institute of Letters (Curso Superior de Letras) for the teaching of humanities, which opened its doors in Lisbon in 1859, and was constantly improved and enlarged thereafter.

Along with several other institutions of culture, such as numerous

ABOVE: *Pedro IV, king of Portugal (Pedro I, emperor of Brazil), by Simpson, 1821–34: Museu Nacional dos Coches, Lisbon.* UPPER RIGHT: *Fontes Pereira de Melo.* BELOW: *Bourgeois architecture and decoration: the Stock Exchange Palace (Palácio da Bolsa), Oporto, 1862–80.*

museums, academies of arts and letters, the Royal Academy of Science, and private associations of all sorts, those schools could prepare a relatively rich elite that flourished in the second half of the century and gave Portugal an honorable place among the civilized countries of the world. Indeed, one of the most interesting features of nineteenth-century Portugal was her cultural development, which probably surpassed the golden age of the 1500's.

This was first of all a result of the opening up of the country. The liberal governments started by abolishing censorship of books and newspapers (1821), by proclaiming and effectively enforcing freedom of speech and press, and by stimulating discussion on all levels and on almost all subjects. As a consequence, the number of publications jumped to unsuspected levels. Newspapers, for instance, of which there were only four in all of Portugal and Brazil in 1820, rose to more than twenty a year later. The reactionary periods of 1823–26 and 1828–33 brought about censorship again and, as might be expected, a decline in publications. The following three decades showed a constant moderate growth in the number of newspapers. After 1860, however, there was a marked upward spurt. In the late 1800's and early 1900's Portugal had a very honorable ranking among nations in both the absolute and the proportionate number of newspapers of all kinds. Similarly with books and pamphlets. Despite some restrictive laws and some (moderate) persecutions of the press, freedom of publishing could be considered complete.

The large number of newspapers and magazines stimulated literary production and were, in turn, stimulated by it. Most great authors started by publishing articles or by serializing their novels in daily issues of newspapers. Freedom of speech and association led to the growth of lecturing and of cultural clubs of all kinds. Parliamentary life contributed to the development of political rhetoric, while the frequent elections favored cultivation of good speech throughout the country. The consequence of all this was a widespread cult for good writing and for lay oratory. The newspapers, magazines, and books of those days display amazingly good style and a general tendency toward rational and clear thinking, if one makes allowance for the inevitable romanticism of the epoch.

Another aspect that helps explain Portugal's cultural expansion was the improved means of communication with Europe, particularly with France. The setting up of railways and the possibility of reaching Paris directly in two or three days brought Portugal closer to the great centers of European culture than ever before. It must be recalled and again emphasized that Portugal looked upon France as her cultural model and strongly reflected every French influence. The growing imports of books and magazines by train—which made them more readily available and also much cheaper—enhanced such a cultural link from the 1870's on. But railways also linked Portugal to other countries of cultural significance, such as Spain, Germany, Belgium, Switzerland, Italy, and England. Nobles and bourgeois had their children learn foreign languages, French above all, but also German and English. Later, they began sending them abroad, to the best schools available.

From a literary and artistic standpoint, the great social, economic, and political changes of the century brought about Romanticism in Portugal as everywhere in the world. The new style exhibited its best elements in the theater and in historical fiction as well as in painting and sculpture, the genres which appealed to and could be easily understood by the bourgeoisie. The legislation of 1836–37 provided the framework for the development of a Portuguese theater, the best representative of which was Almeida Garrett. A national playhouse controlled by the government was built up in Lisbon, while many other theaters, lavishly decorated, rose all over the country to the end of the century, as symbols of the bourgeois urban culture. In a way, they replaced the traditional church and monastery building as a mark of affluence and prestige. Despite Garrett's fine play-writing (*Um Auto de Gil Vicente*, 1838; *O Alfageme de Santarém*, 1842; *Frei Luis de Sousa*, 1844), accompanied by many other Romantic authors, foreign translations soon flooded the stages and were often preferred by the public. Nonetheless, the quality of the Portuguese plays was comparable to the best abroad, particularly by the end of the nineteenth century and the beginning of the twentieth (authors Marcelino Mesquita, 1856–1919; Gervásio Lobato, 1850–1895; João da Câmara, 1852–1908; among many others). Comedies and satires displaying a fine humor—which the public welcomed and showed a preference for —led the way and revealed better talents than drama. This also explains the rise of the musical show (*operette*), where Spanish, French, and Austrian imports competed with some good Portuguese examples. A genuine national genre, the *revista* or musical satire of current events, started in the 1850's with a tremendous success. Both drama and comedy had at their service one or two generations of outstanding actors, who flourished from the 1880's on. On the other hand, a national opera could never develop despite the love for musical drama. Italian, French, and (later) German companies visited Portugal year after year and entirely fashioned the Lisbon and Porto tastes. The same happened with concert music, where the Portuguese contribution was poor.

Historical fiction developed after the publication in Portuguese translation of Walter Scott's works. A periodical magazine, the *Panorama* (first number 1837), published several historical novels serially, which influenced at least one generation of writers and readers. Alexandre Herculano, the greatest Portuguese author of the mid-1800's, was also the main representative of historical fiction, where the Middle Ages had a predominant role (*O Bobo*, 1843; *Eurico, o Presbitero*, 1844; *O Monge de Cister*, 1848). Many others followed him, such as Rebelo da Silva (1822–71), Andrade Corvo (1824–90), and Arnaldo Gama (1828–69). Historical novels continued to appeal to the bourgeois taste well into the twentieth century, with a second remarkable group of authors flourishing in the late 1800's and early 1900's (see chapter 12).

History experienced a tremendous development, with the systematic use of archival sources. When the liberal governments nationalized the monasteries, most of the ecclesiastical archives entered the official depositories, particularly the Lisbon National Archives, where organization and proper classification started. Alexandre Herculano, who had a hand in such a task, showed an incomparable talent for history, the conception of which he entirely remodeled according to the modern principles of his time. Besides many other important works, he began writing a monumental *History of Portugal* (1846–53), which only extended to the late thirteenth century. His work, his strong and austere personality, and his methodology had a formidable impact on his contemporaries and on all the following generations of historians, to the present. History, too, flourished to the beginning of the twentieth century.

The novel developed in Portugal in accordance with the new social conditions and also because of the influence of French and English authors. A first generation of Romantics (Camilo Castelo Branco, 1825–90; Júlio Dinis, 1839–71) supplied the basis for the exceptional realistic novels of Eça de Queirós (1845–1900) and some other lesser-known contemporaries of his. A diplomat, who lived most of his life abroad, Eça introduced in Portugal a sort of international taste and way of writing, although insisting on Portuguese themes and cudgeling the Portuguese bourgeois society with his satire (*O Crime do Padre Amaro*, 1876; *O Primo Basílio*, 1878; *Os Maias*, 1888).

Eça de Queirós belonged to the "generation of 1870," a remarkable group of intellectuals who were in their twenties by that time and who consequently flourished from the late 1870's to the beginning of the twentieth century. They were the result of Portugal's total opening up with the development of communications and the maturity of press freedom. They were the exponents of the new Portugal, European-minded, modern, striving to rise from industrial, commercial, and political underdevelopment to a new society based upon the industrial revolution, the bourgeois leadership, and the parliamentary system. Although these intellectuals often reacted against and strongly criticized those aspects of society, they were its best and most thoroughly integrated representatives. In foreign influences, the generation of 1870 was particularly affected by the French writers Renan (biblical criticism), Michelet ("Germanism"), Victor Hugo (struggle for freedom, progress), and Balzac; these writers, in turn, transmitted and disseminated other influences from Germany and England. The Portuguese generation of 1870 was anticlerical, rationalist, positivist (or at least strong believers in scientism) and generally antimonarchist, some of their members tending toward a Republican system, others even aiming at a vague socialism.

Most of these intellectuals studied at the University of Coimbra. There, the beginnings of their assertion started (1865) with the so-called "Coimbra question" (*questão coimbrã*), which involved two groups of opponents—a younger group of students, led by Antero de Quental, eagerly contesting the prevailing spiritual, social, and literary values of their time, and an older group of intellectuals led by the blind poet Castilho, defending them. Later on, in Lisbon, the former joined together in a private club, which organized a cycle of lectures in a

Casino, on the modern aspects of literature, history, religion, and education. These lectures (conferências do Casino) soon became a daring social and political attack on the existing order, and were cut short by the government, which forbade them (1871).

The generation of 1870 had, as its main representatives, besides Eça de Queirós, Antero de Quental (1842–92, a leading poet and social essayist); Ramalho Ortigão (1836–1915, a social critic and novelist); Teófilo Braga (1843–1924, a productive historian of literature and politician, and the future President of the Republic); Oliveira Martins (1845–95, a penetrating historian, sociologist, and politician); and Guerra Junqueiro (1850–1923, an extremely popular poet, anticlerical and antimonarchical). But it also included artists, scientists, professors, aristocrats, journalists, and many others, who helped raise the level of Portuguese culture to a remarkable height.

In the domain of science, Portugal played a much more modest role. Modern science required more extensive equipment, costly devices which the generally meager budgets of schools and governments were unable to supply. Nonetheless, countless efforts led to the opening of many scientific museums, laboratories, observatories, and botanical gardens, and to a moderate flourishing of science, which, if not inventive, at least managed to keep up with the international scientific movement. Mathematics, geology, chemistry, botany, zoology, and anthropology developed; there was special interest in the soils, the fauna, and the flora of Africa, where the Portuguese had a natural field of research. In medicine, too, the nineteenth century meant great progress for Portugal, especially in the field of tropical diseases.

The art movement is still poorly known, except in the area of painting. Classicism, neo-classicism, and neo-medieval styles (Romanesque and Gothic) had their impact on architecture, as everywhere in the world. The first half of the century saw the completion of Lisbon and the disappearance of the last earthquake ruins. Numerous churches, all alike but all relatively pure in neo-classic forms and sober in decoration, were built in the capital and in other parts of the country. Their internal decoration, particularly in regard to images and pictures, probably deserves something more than the twentieth-century disdain paid to them. More important were the countless bourgeois dwellings, both within the towns and in the countryside, displaying the increasing affluence of their owners. Theaters, statues, railroad stations, city halls, bridges, fountains, hotels, and other lay examples of architecture still await their impartial historian. There were some unique examples of tile coverage of walls and façades. The growth of Lisbon, Porto, and other towns caused widespread building activity, which covered extensive urban areas with typical Portuguese houses and improved city planning. By the end of the nineteenth century, a nationalist reaction against the use of international formulas in architecture led to a Portuguese school which flourished only in the 1900's. It struggled for a "Portuguese house" where tradition and modern conceptions would be harmoniously combined.

Sculpture and painting had some noteworthy representatives. Soares dos Reis (1847–89) was perhaps the leading sculptor of his time. The painters Silva Porto (1850–93), José Malhoa (1854–1933), and Columbano Bordalo Pinheiro (1857–1929) emerge from a large group of excellent artists, who absorbed nationalist tendencies much earlier than the other fields of culture. Most of them preferred rural themes, scorning the cities and their "corrupt" society. Despite its good quality and a certain originality in Portuguese painting, especially in the second half of the nineteenth century, one must acknowledge its inability to follow the advanced international trends of the time. Currents like impressionism, fauvism, and cubism had practically no adherents in Portugal, where conservative tendencies always played the leading role.

THE POLITICAL LIFE

As a system of political, economic, and social doctrines, Liberalism was known in Portugal beginning with the late 1700's. Among the "enlightened" authors of Pombal's and Maria's times (see chapter 8), a certain body of liberal or pre-liberal indoctrination could certainly be detected; yet Enlightenment as such should not be confused with Liberalism, which is often its most complete opposite. Indeed, the Liberals defended a political constitution set up on popular bases; a strong restriction of the royal prerogatives; freedom of religion, press, and speech; freedom of trade and industry; and many other "subversive" doctrines altogether contrary to the fundamental principles of enlightened despotism.

The American Revolution gave reality to many theories of French and English philosophers and essayists. Then, thirteen years later, the French Revolution completed and enlarged the process. By the 1780's and 1790's, to be a Liberal came to have the precise meaning of one defending doctrines which had triumphed somewhere. Consequently, most European governments became increasingly concerned with the Liberal "subversion" and began to adopt severe measures of repression.

In Portugal, Liberalism entered by way of the French and English influences. Although the former have generally deserved the main attention of historians, the English influences should not be neglected. Authors like Jeremy Bentham and Adam Smith were widely quoted and praised. The impact of the American Revolution was felt—mainly via England—but much less than that of the French Revolution.

In the spread of Liberalism, Freemasonry had a leading role. Although known in Portugal from early days, only by the time of Prince John's regency did the number and activity of the Portuguese Freemasons start to trouble the government. In 1801, there were five masonic lodges in Lisbon, with a membership that included nobles, wealthy bourgeois, and some clerics. The first Portuguese grand-master, a nobleman and top bureaucrat, was elected in 1804. Persecutions of all kinds prevented a smooth development of the Masonry. The French Invasions had a new impact, and by 1812 thirteen lodges were active in Lisbon. In Porto, several Freemasons and Masonry sympathizers founded the so-called Sinédrio (1818), a secret society which decisively contributed to subversion and actually organized the Revolution of 1820.

Other vehicles for spreading liberal thought were the exiles (mostly in London and in Paris) during John's regency. They encountered the realities of Liberalism, watched the function of parliamentary institutions, and conceived a whole program of political and economic reforms to be established in their country. Their revolutionary newspapers (*O Correio Braziliense*, London, 1808–22; *O Investigador Portuguez em Inglaterra*, London, 1811–19; *O Portuguez*, London, 1814–23; *Annaes das Sciencias, das Artes e das Letras,* Paris, 1818, among many others) and pamphlets managed to enter Portugal, despite police controls, and were widely read. Some of those exiles returned to Portugal after the Napoleonic wars and became leaders or at least influential figures among those who opposed the existing regime.

The ideology that triumphed in 1820 contained some of the international trends of Liberalism but also a good many national tendencies. It rested upon the right of individual property, from which all the liberties derived: freedom to do everything not forbidden by the law; freedom from arrest without charge or trial except according to the law; freedom to use one's property; freedom of speech and writing without previous censorship (although limited by the church in dogma and morals); equality of rights and laws for all; the end of property confiscations, legal infamy, torture, and other physical penalties; the right of all to compete for public offices; the right of protest, complaint, or petition; inviolability of the mails; abolition of feudal law and rights. It asserted the national sovereignty, the principle of the law as the citizens' will, the tripartite division of powers, and so forth. Portuguese Liberalism also stood for the union of Church and state, and for the hereditary constitutional monarchy.

More peculiar principles, a result of Portugal's own needs, were a certain defense of protectionism and high tariffs against free trade with foreign countries; the development of technology, transport and communications; and an "agrarian reform" tending to get rid of the huge *latifundia* in the hands of the Crown and the religious orders. Portuguese Liberalism also acknowledged the nation as being "the union of all Portuguese in both hemispheres" (which justified its "colonial" policies, both in 1820–25 regarding Brazil, and later on regarding Africa); all Portuguese were granted, at least in theory, equal rights and duties.

It is important to note that the basic principles of Liberalism were retained and enforced in Portugal throughout the whole monarchical period (1820–1910) and even during the Democratic Republic (1910–26). Its various political tendencies did not alter the basic fundamentals defined in 1820–22 and clearly expressed in the first constitution.

Liberalism also triumphed because it posed as a restorer of the old "liberties" of the realm. The preface to the first constitution was quite frank regarding that point. It stated that the *cortes* ". . . intimately convinced that the public disgraces, which so much have oppressed and still oppress her [the Nation], had their origin in the contempt for the citizen's rights and in the oversight of the basic laws of the monarchy; and having also considered, that only by the reestablishment of those laws, enlarged and reformed, the prosperity of the same Nation can be achieved. . . ." In this way, the Liberals altogether condemned that period of history which had preceded them— a vague period because some limited it to Maria's and John's reigns, while others traced it back to the end of the Middle Ages—and presented themselves to the nation as restorers of something destroyed and forgotten, rather than as revolutionaries. The adoption of the traditional word *cortes* was symbolic of this.

The Constitution of 1822 was a long document with 240 articles. It mainly followed the Spanish constitution of 1812, although with some changes and adaptations to the Portuguese case. After a listing of the individual rights and duties—possibly influenced by the French constitution of 1795—it went on to assert the sovereignty of the nation and admit the independence of the three powers—the legislative, the executive, and the judicial. The first belonged to the *cortes* (with one chamber directly elected by all the literate males—friars, servants, and some others being excepted); the second to the king and the government (composed of secretaries of state appointed by him); and the third to the judges. On law-making the king had only the right of "suspensive veto," i.e., the right to return to the *cortes* once any law he did not agree with, explaining the reasons for his discordance. The government was responsible to the *cortes* and could be called by them for explanations or information. The constitution also adopted a sort of federal system for Portugal and Brazil (according to John's decision in 1815), creating a five-member regency and a three-member government to act in Rio de Janeiro. There was still a Council of State, composed of thirteen counselors, of which six were for Portugal, six for the Overseas, and one for both.

This constitution did not endure (see part 3 of this chapter). It was too progressive and too democratic for its time. Suffrage for all male literates might be dangerous for the interests of landowners and big businessmen. It did not satisfy the nobility, or the clergy (neither were given any special prerogatives), or the king, whose powers were reduced to almost nothing. No wonder, then, that it lasted for less than two years in its first phase (October 1822 to June 1824), and then, on a provisional and theoretical basis, from September 1836 to April 1838.

The second Portuguese Constitution bore the name of "Constitutional Charter" (Carta Constitucional) and was generally known as "The Charter." Its name followed the French examples (1814), copied elsewhere in the world (South Germany, Poland, Brazil, and others), and reflected the conservative, strong monarchist reaction against the popular enacting of constitutions. The emperor of Brazil, Pedro I, who was also the heir to the Portuguese throne (see chapter 9), had granted a constitutional charter to Brazil, in 1824. When his father, the king of Portugal, died (1826), he immediately granted one to Portugal (April 29, 1826), which closely followed the Brazilian text (which, in its turn, was influenced by the French model).

The Constitutional Charter had only 145 articles. Individual rights (no mention was made of duties) had now been placed at the end. In addition to those expressed in 1822, they also included the right to public help (beneficence), the right to free primary education, the right to have colleges and schools, and several others. As in the first Constitution, freedom of religion to the Portuguese was not expressly granted but nobody could be persecuted on religious grounds, provided he respected the state's religion and did not offend public morals. Among individual rights included in the Charter were respect for the hereditary nobility and its privileges, and the public debt, an effort to get the support of the aristocrats and the bourgeois.

Moreover, the Constitution of 1826 introduced a number of antidemocratic innovations. The state powers became four, instead of three: the legislative, the moderating (Poder Moderador), the executive, and the judicial. The first one was vested in the cortes composed of two Houses, the Chamber of Deputies (indirectly elected by a limited number of males who owned property) and the Chamber of Peers, appointed by the king for life and with the right of transmission to their heirs—archbishops and bishops also included. The moderating power, which the Charter considered to be "the key of all the political organization," belonged to the king, who, as its head, could appoint the peers, summon the *cortes* and dissolve the Chamber of Deputies, appoint and dismiss the government, suspend magistrates, grant amnesties and pardons, and veto the laws made in *cortes*. The executive power was vested in the king and the government, and the judicial one in the judges and jurors. A Council of State, composed of life-appointed counselors, would assist the king as head of the moderating power.

The Charter of 1826 pleased the nobility and the secular clergy, as well as the landowners and the wealthy bourgeois. It also granted extensive powers to the king. For these reasons, it had all warrants of success and long rule. Indeed, after an initial brief period of almost two years (July 31, 1826, to May 3, 1828), it lasted from 1834 to September 1836, and then, again, from February 1842 to the proclamation of the Republic, on October 5, 1910 (see part 3 of this chapter). In all, seventy-two years.

The third Portuguese Constitution lasted less than four years (April 1838 to February 1842). A compromise between the Constitution of 1822 and the Charter, it was influenced by the Spanish constitution of 1837 and also the Belgian constitution of 1831. It attacked the Charter by reasserting that sovereignty rested upon the nation (not on the king); by suppressing the hereditary Chamber of Peers and replacing it by an elective Chamber of Senators (to which could be chosen only wealthy landowners and bourgeois, archbishops and bishops, top magistrates and full professors, Army and Navy officers of high rank, and ambassadors and ministers); and by accepting direct elections for the Chamber of Deputies, albeit with highly restrictive conditions to qualify as a voter. The moderating power was abolished, but the king kept the right to dissolve the Chambers and veto the laws.

The sixty-eight years of continuous validity of the Charter (1842–1910) depended upon the three amendments, which gave way to a more democratic system and adapted the Constitution to the various changes that had taken place in the country.

Among other things, the first amendment (Acto Adicional), in 1852, made elections to the Chamber of Deputies direct and enlarged the voting capacity, while abolishing the death penalty for political crimes. The second amendment (1885) suppressed the hereditary peers and limited their number to 100, while introducing elective and temporary peers; it also somewhat restricted the moderating power. The third amendment (1896) restored to the king certain prerogatives abolished in 1885, and suppressed the elective peers (although not thoroughly re-establishing the hereditary peerage).

Electoral procedures started within the early months of the Liberal Revolution. The "Instructions" on how to vote and on how the first National Assembly should be constituted were the first Portuguese electoral code. They provided an indirect system, by which all the male heads of family chose a number of electors on the parish-basis, who, in their turn, chose another group of electors on the *comarca* or province basis. The latter would then elect the deputies to the *cortes*. Every head of family could qualify for deputy. National representativeness was one deputy for 30,000 inhabitants. With Brazil and the other Overseas possessions, this brought to the first Parliament 181 representatives: 100 from Portugal proper, 9 from the Azores and Madeira, 7 from the African and Asian territories, and 65 from Brazil. A plurality of votes decided the election of each group of candidates, arranged by provinces.

The adoption of the first Constitution somewhat changed this system. Elections became direct—indeed a more democratic way—but restrictions to deputy qualification were first introduced. To become a representative, one now had to have a "sufficient income." Instead of provinces, the electoral code of June 1822 introduced a larger number of represented units, twenty-six for Portugal instead of six. In all, the number of deputies went down to 118, because Brazil ceased to be represented.

The first elections held after the granting of the Constitutional Charter (1826) clearly reflected the conservative tendencies of the "new order." Up to 1852, with the exception of a brief period (1836–42), all elections were indirect, and the voters' and candidates' qualifications were considerably tightened, on an income basis. To be a voter, one had to have at least 100,000 réis of income, to be a deputy at least 400,000 réis. Such restrictions severely reduced the number of voters. They put parliamentary representation in the hands of the landowners, traders, and industrialists, and parliamentary voting in the hands of a middle class both rural and urban. After the September Revolution (1836), a short interlude of six years made elections direct again but hardly changed the voter and deputy qualifications.

The electoral law of 1852 was a long document which embodied the typical principles of bourgeois parliamentarism. It kept the income qualification for voting and for being elected, but it made elections direct again and altered some other minor points such as the definition of plurality for election purposes (one-fourth or more of the ballots, or else a run-off with victory for any plurality). From 1859 to 1878 plurality gave way to majority in the first round.

Important changes in the electoral system took place with the law of 1878. It greatly enlarged the number of voters, by enfranchising all those who could read and write or had a minimum income of 100,000 réis, or were heads of families. Furthermore, voting age went down from twenty-five to twenty-one. Thus, voting capacity ceased to rest upon money alone and depended now upon literacy or family status. The trend toward a more democratic basis was further enhanced in 1895, when a new law lowered the 100,000 réis basis for the illiterates to about a half (i.e., a minimum 500 réis of taxation, when formerly it was estimated at 1,000). This law particularly increased the number of rural voters, who depended upon local bosses and party structures. Run-offs disappeared in 1884.

Electoral laws were numerous to the end of the monarchy—fifteen such laws in ninety years—but their main concern was generally the circle division throughout the country. Most defended an average two-three deputies for each circle, but several introduced the principle of one deputy to one circle. The total number of deputies did not follow too closely the general growth of population, but as a rule popular representation could be kept the same. In 1820 there were 100 representatives for some three million people (i.e., one/30,000); in 1870 there were roughly the same number for nearly four million people (one/40,000). But the latter figure was afterward maintained by gradually increasing the number of deputies. Total voters went up from 350,000 in 1864 to 500,000 in 1911.

The troubled political life of the country, along with the faculty the king had of dissolving Parliament whenever the government thought it convenient, made it rare to have full four-year or three-year legislatures (determined by the Constitution). After 1834 and to the end of the monarchy, there were forty-three elections for Parliament, which gives an average of one year and eight months per legislature. Elections thus became a usual thing in the political life of the country; moreover, parish and municipal ones happened regularly too. Their organization was an important and expensive undertaking both for the Secretariat of Interior and the political parties.

Which were those parties?

The organization of parties in a modern way came somewhat late in the history of constitutional Portugal. Before the 1860's and 1870's there were currents of opinion, ideological groups, political forces or whatever one wishes to call them, but hardly parties in the sense of duly organized bodies. Until 1834 the two opposing forces were the absolutists, defending the traditional monarchy, and the liberals, fighting for the Constitution. In each group there were different trends, particularly in the latter, where the democrats (sometimes called Vintistas, because they claimed to follow the true doctrine of the Revolution of 1820) opposed the conservatives (who aimed at a compromise between the national traditions and the liberal principles) and the "bourgeois," who leaned toward a middle ground between the two. These three forces within the liberal ideology composed Parliament roughly until the 1840's, although with changed labels and sporadic coalitions. The Democrats, with a part of the bourgeois, triumphed in September 1836 and became known as "Septembrists" (Setembristas). The conservatives, with another part of the center, remained faithful to the Constitutional Charter and were thus called Chartists (Cartistas). A new Center, more related to the Right than to the Left, realigned forces by 1838 under the name of Order Party (Partido Ordeiro).

In the 1840's the Right conquered power and imposed a dictatorship under Secretary Costa Cabral. Opposing this Cabralismo all the other forces rallied together in a "Progressive" coalition, which rose in arms in 1846–47 (being then known as Patuleia) and then, again, in 1851 under the banner of "regenerating" the country. Calling themselves Progressive Regenerators, they preferred the second to the first label and became definitely titled as Regeneradores. It was from this group that the first regular party emerged, always sticking to the same banner and name, and persisting as the strongest and most able party to the beginning of the century.

Cabralism died out without succession. Opposition to the "regenerating" regime, however, soon arose, bringing about a new group known as the Historic Progressives (because they claimed to be the true Progressives), later shortened into "Historics" (Históricos). They encompassed sort of "left-wing" opponents to the ruling party. Regenerators and Historics divided between themselves Parliament seats and governmental tasks for more than fifteen years. Then, a third party, more Left oriented, strove for power in the late 1860's and early 1870's: the Reformists. But the three-party system did not last. In 1876 Historics and Reformists got together and formed the Progressive Party, a true party, with a program and a well-defined structure.

Regenerators and Historics first, Regenerators and Progressists later, a two-party system which tried to follow the English way, rotated in power rather peacefully for almost fifty years, with a few interludes of crisis. Yet this "Rotativism" was soon threatened by the rise of new political forces and the decline of the monarchical regime itself.

In uncompromising opposition the Republican and the Socialist parties emerged, both in the 1870's, the first one with a tremendous appeal to the popular masses, particularly in the towns. But within the monarchical groups, too, new parties were born, fighting for "new life," new principles, and less political corruption. This was the period of dissensions, of rebellion against the party leaders, of assertion of younger people who tried to instill new blood into the veins of a dying body. In the 1880's, dissidents from the Regenerators formed the so-called "Dynastical Left" (Esquerda Dinástica), which did not endure but for a while earned the support of many. Between 1900 and 1910, the two big parties came apart, some six or seven major factions resulting from their breakdown. Besides the two main branches, which claimed "true inheritance" and kept the traditional name of the party, the most prominent new groups were the "Regenerating-Liberal" Party (founded 1901, in power 1906–08) and the "Progressive Dissidents" (founded in 1905). The Catholics, too, emerged as a new political force under the name of the Nationalist Party.

The secret and the religious societies provided the framework for much political activity. Their real influence, however, must still be appraised from a historical standpoint, because gross exaggerations have been stated and written on their impact upon government policies and revolutionary acts. Freemasonry was the most relevant among those societies, its action increasing in the early 1900's and becoming almost thoroughly republican-oriented. Yet to be a Mason was also much of a fad, a virile connotation so to say, and Masonry membership should not necessarily account for revolutionary potentiality. More popular and active was the Carbonary (Carbonária), arising at the beginning of the twentieth century after the Italian model of the mid-1800's. Among the religious associations with semi-secret clauses and the purposes of defending God, the Catholic faith, the Institutions, and the like, against subversion, the Society of Jesus Third Order and its by-products should be emphasized.

It was often hard to discern the precise differences among the several parties. The idea of defining ideologies and currents of action in a written program and of carrying on that program to the end was still far from the party conception. The Regenerating Party, for instance, had no written program up to January 1910, a few months before its end. The Regenerators defended the Charter and its amendments (all enacted by them), and emphasized order under a strong government which might permit free individual initiatives. They also stood for intensive public works supported by the state with public loans, particularly in the field of communications. The Progressive Party defended a constitutional revision and dissented from the Regenerators in other minor points related to finance, economy, and political organization. Yet, by the late nineteenth century, its real differences from the other party were reduced to nothing. The Regenerating-Liberals stood for a strengthening of the king's authority and for a much closer intervention of the state in the country's economic and social life. To a certain extent they represented in Portugal state socialism, in the German manner.

Theoretically, the great parties of the monarchy were organized upon the basis of local, freely elected centers. As a matter of fact, such centers existed only in the towns. Elsewhere, and even in many towns, the party basis was the local boss, who controlled everything and everyone. In this way, and as the Spanish author Luis Araquistain

has put it, "power did not emanate from the people to the parties
and from the latter to the Crown, but from the Crown to the parties
and from the latter to the local organizations of bosses. The people
voted as they were ordered by whoever paid most for votes." In this
way, also, the constitutional regime had much of the character of an
absolute monarchy "which entrusted the parties with power; and the
parties, by cynically manipulating the political machinery, proceeded
to impose that power on a people for the most part ignorant and
indifferent." As public opinion was inconsequential and existed only
in a few towns, the parties were simply groups of clients depending
upon a boss or a leader and eagerly coveting public jobs. Elections
were "made" by the government, which always won them by means
of a network of local authorities. Consequently, instead of the king
choosing the prime minister based on popular voting, it was the king
who had to dissolve the House of Deputies, in order that the government might have a majority in the next House, which it "made."
Premierships changed from one to the other party, whenever the
ruling party, or an agreement between the two, or even the king
thought it convenient. Reasons varied greatly from case to case: often
a simple fatigue of governing brought about the change; at other
times, it was the fear of some responsibility, a parliamentary debate
in either House of Parliament, a press campaign cleverly oriented,
personal matters affecting any cabinet member, or the like.

Governmental instability was not a feature of the constitutional
monarchy in Portugal. But there were times when governments did
not last, as for instance in 1820–22 (a five-month average for each),
1826–28 (a four-month average), 1834–37 (a four-month average) and
1908–10 (a six-month average). But those periods corresponded, for
the first three, to the troubled assertion of the constitutional monarchy, and for the last one, to its final disaggregation. Averages between 1837 and 1908 were much higher, a year and a half to the
"Regeneration" (1851) and more than two years afterward. There
were long-lasting governments, of five and a half years (Fontes Pereira
de Melo, 1871–77); five years (Saldanha, 1851–56); four years and nine
months (Loulé, 1860–65); four years and four months (Hintze Ribeiro,
1900–04); four years and three months (Fontes Pereira de Melo, 1881–
86). Such averages and "long" terms in office were certainly much

below the long periods of rule in the old days of the absolute monarchy. But times had changed, and nowhere did Liberalism represent too much stability, which it understood as stagnation and corruption. In a European context, the Portuguese governments were as stable as any others.

The Portuguese constitutional monarchy like most constitutional monarchies of the world was, and has often been regarded as, a corrupt regime, characterized by fake elections and general bribery in public administration. Parliaments were defined as organs of systematic obstruction to government, as machines of vain oratory, and as arenas of disorder. Indeed, all those things did happen, but it would be a gross exaggeration to reduce constitutionalism to some examples of poor functioning. Elections, for instance, had little meaning in the countryside but undoubtedly represented public opinion in the towns, particularly in Lisbon and Porto. Thus, if majorities were "made" by the government for most of the country, they were not "made" for the big centers, in those places where the commercial and industrial bourgeoisie were concentrated. In Lisbon the governments often lost an election, and this had a far larger impact on politics than the huge majorities obtained elsewhere in the country. Irregularities of all kinds were usual in every election, but in the capital or in Porto things were smoother and few ever dared to try these practices. Freedom of press, which had practically no limits (at least from a political standpoint), helped to build up a civic consciousness in the large centers which it would be wrong to neglect.

In bribery and political corruption, we have no proof that the constitutional regime went farther than any other before or afterward. As usual, corruption became the scapegoat for every sign of Portugal's weakness or backwardness in a European context. The loss of Brazil, the inability to develop the Overseas territories, several humiliations abroad, lack of funds, illiteracy, all seemed to most contemporaries (and to historians who followed them) a result of incompetence, irresponsibility, and political corruption. Actually, what common sense suggests is that daily control of public affairs by the press and Parliament—regardless of their imperfection and faults—made corruption and poor administration more difficult than in the old times of despotism. This suggestion, however, awaits a historian.

MAIN EVENTS

The triumph of Liberalism in Portugal was preceded by an unsuccessful conspiracy, the goals of which seemed to be more political than ideological. The Portuguese felt abandoned by their monarch; they complained about the heavy sums of money shipped yearly to Brazil in the form of rents and taxation along with the commercial decline and the unbalanced budget. In addition the Portuguese resented the British influence in the army and in the regency. In 1817 several persons were arrested on the charge of plotting against Marshal Beresford's life, the government, and the existing institutions. A short trial brought death at the stake to a dozen people, including the alleged leader of the conspiracy, Lieutenant-General Gomes Freire de Andrade. This execution had a deep impact on the rise of a liberal consciousness among the army and the bureaucrats. Far from preventing any future rebellions, it only fostered them: the opponents of the existing regime fully realized the tyranny of its supporters and the impossibility of any change by other than violent means.

It should be emphasized that to a certain extent the regency understood how grave the situation was, and suggested several ways of coping with it. Yet it mainly stressed the economic and financial problems and simply proposed cuts in the expenditures and petty reforms in administration. Far from Portugal, neither the king nor his government were fully aware of the political and economic tensions, while the regency always tended to ignore facts or dilute them in order to please the rulers.

Early in 1820 Liberalism triumphed in Spain. Contacts between the Spaniards and the revolutionary Portuguese intensified. Beresford decided to go to Brazil in order to get more extensive powers both for improving the army and suppressing the liberal danger.

Taking advantage of his absence, the military revolted in Porto (August 24, 1820) and in a few days claimed full sovereignty in the North. A Provisional Junta was formed, presided over by Brigadier-General António da Silveira. Its main goals were to take over the regency and to summon the *cortes* with the aim of adopting a constitution. In Lisbon, the regency tried to resist and denounced the revolutionaries as enemies of the country. However, it could not prevent a second uprising (September 15), this time in Lisbon, which ousted the rulers and set up a provisional government under the presidency of Freire de Andrade (a cleric and a relative of the martyr of 1817). At the same time the northern revolutionaries started a march south. On September 28, North and South fused into a new Provisional Junta, in which Freire de Andrade held the presidency and António da Silveira the vice-presidency. The great names of the revolution, however, were Fernandes Tomás, Ferreira Borges, and Silva Carvalho, all jurists and bureaucrats who together took over the secretariates of interior (Reino) and finance (Fazenda).

The new government did practically nothing but promote elections for the *cortes*. They took place in December, and a majority of bourgeois landowners, traders, and bureaucrats was elected. One of the first measures of the *cortes* was to request King John VI to return to Portugal. They also elected (January 1821) a new government and a new regency (under the presidency of the Count of Sampaio) to rule the country in John's absence, thus putting an end to the Provisional Junta.

John VI arrived in Lisbon in July 1821 after having sworn to uphold the future constitution. Many Liberals viewed him suspiciously and saw in him the natural leader of a conservative and anticonstitutional current of opinion. Yet John VI did not betray his oath right away and quite willingly accepted whatever the *cortes* and the government imposed on him. It is true that he appointed predominantly conservative ministers but on the whole and for two years he behaved well as the first constitutional monarch. The leaders of the absolutist movement were rather to be found in Queen Carlota Joaquina, along with her son, Prince Miguel.

The "Liberals" were far from united. Most jurists and bureaucrats stood for the revolutionary principles based upon the American and French ideologies, wanted the *cortes* elected by all the people regardless of social class, defended the need for a constitution, and required thorough reforms in administration leading to a truly new order. Among them several wings could still be distinguished. By contrast, most of the military, who had led the revolution, aimed at

Houses of Bragança and Bragança–Saxe-Coburg

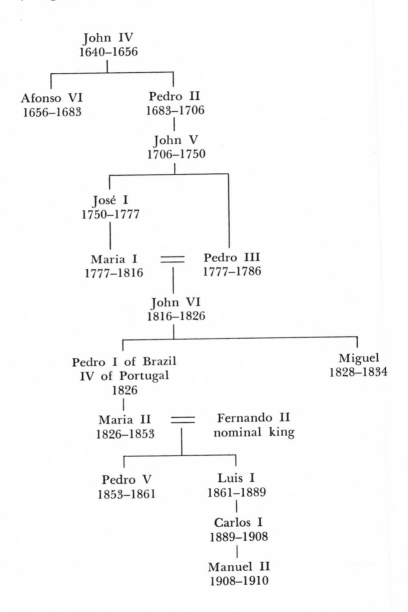

Teófilo Braga	1910–1911
Manuel de Arriaga	1911–1915
Teófilo Braga	1915
Bernardino Machado	1915–1917
Sidónio Pais	1917–1918
Canto e Castro	1918–1919
António José de Almeida	1919–1923
Teixeira Gomes	1923–1925
Bernardino Machado	1925–1926
Mendes Cabeçadas	1926
Gomes da Costa	1926
Óscar Carmona	1926–1951
Oliveira Salazar	1951
Craveiro Lopes	1951–1958
Américo Tomás	1958–1974

much more moderate goals, namely the return of the king, the end of the British influence in the army, and the summoning of the traditional *cortes* with the three-order representation (clergy, nobility, and people). What everybody wanted was to put a full stop to Brazil's total autonomy, and go back to Portugal's former situation of motherland versus colony.

The liberal jurists and bureaucrats took the lead for a while. They controlled the *cortes* and wrote a highly advanced constitution, started the revolutionary work of changing institutions and abolishing privileges, decreed freedom of press, and dissolved the Inquisition. Most government ministers were also bureaucrats. Several top military tried some coups d'état or even armed rebellion, but they failed.

The independence of Brazil (September 1822) inflicted a mortal blow to the liberal *cortes* and made the Liberals highly unpopular. People now realized that one of the main goals of the Revolution, i.e., bringing Brazil back to the condition of a colony, had failed, and they blamed the *cortes* for it. Also, many of the innovations met with the resistance of the great majority of the people, who did not understand them, not to mention the clergy and the nobility. Soon the ruling Liberal Party felt isolated and without support. Queen Carlota Joaquina refused to swear to uphold the constitution, which gave her wide popularity. In Spain, the French army had just intervened to restore absolutism (April 1823).

Under these circumstances it was relatively easy for the anti-Liberal party to rise up in arms at the small town of Vila Franca and proclaim the restoration of absolutism (May 1823). Yet John VI altogether rejected a return to the old regime. He promised instead a new and better constitution to the country, while dissolving the *cortes* to please the victors. In this, he was very wisely trying to prevent future rebellions from the oppressed side.

Although Prince Miguel posed as the head of the anticonstitutional movement known as Vilafrancada, he was no more than a tool in the hands of a vast group of people, in which some of the revolutionaries of 1820 played a major role. However, as in 1820, the counterrevolution could now be defined as a rebellion against something, although rather vague in what it actually wanted. This became clear as time passed and the counterrevolutionaries broke up into an extremist right wing lead by Miguel and his mother and a moderate center wing symbolized by the king and his government. The former started plotting again and revolted once more in April 1824 (Abrilada). John VI sought protection aboard an English man-of-war and from there, backed by England, he forced Miguel into submission. The prince left the country, and the Center Party regained power. Up to the king's death (March 1826), a moderate absolutism ruled Portugal, leaning more toward the Right than toward the Left. No new constitution ever appeared; on the contrary, John VI announced the intention of summoning the *cortes* in the old manner. Numerous liberals fled the country and went to England and France.

John's death posed a difficult problem. His eldest son, Pedro, was the emperor of Brazil. And although nobody had ever questioned his rights to the throne of Portugal, it seemed obvious that neither Brazilians nor British would accept a reunion of the two crowns, even under separate, autonomous conditions. Thus Pedro, acclaimed in Portugal as Pedro IV as soon as his father died, promptly abdicated (a week after John's death was known in Brazil) on behalf of his daughter Maria da Glória—then a child of seven—provided that she marry her uncle Miguel, who would immediately take over the regency of the kingdom. At the same time, Pedro granted Portugal a highly conservative constitution, which had been hastily drafted. He also declared an amnesty. In this way, Pedro IV tried to carry on his father's policy of compromise, to the extent of calling back Miguel, the head of the extremist faction, and of entrusting to him full government powers for at least eleven years.

In Portugal, despite the fact that many people resented Pedro's abrupt decision without previously swearing the traditional oath of fealty to the nation, and disliked the granting of any constitution, this solution was generally accepted. A regency under Princess Isabel Maria had the new queen (called Maria II) and the new constitution sworn to throughout the country, and organized elections to the new *cortes*. In Vienna (where Miguel was living), the prince and future regent accepted his brother's conditions, swore to uphold the constitution and was bethrothed to Maria. Late in 1827 he left Austria and arrived in Portugal, via Paris and London, in February 1828.

By that time the early atmosphere of conciliation had altogether vanished. The Liberals, with a constitution and a parliament again, proclaimed victory and demonstrated in the streets. Most exiles returned home. The absolutists realized that the maintenance of things as they were meant defeat and a return to the hateful constitutional days. They started invoking all kinds of arguments to prove that Pedro had no rights to the throne—because he had proclaimed Brazil's independence and had therefore betrayed Portugal—and consequently could not transmit them to anyone. Miguel, they argued, was the lawful heir and king. Military uprisings and guerrilla warfare occurred here and there, and an actual, albeit brief, civil war ravaged a part of the country with the support of Spain in 1826–27.

The government was weak and did little to contain such violent methods. It obviously showed more sympathy toward the absolutists than toward the liberals. To protect itself and the status quo, it even required Britain to send a troop garrison to Lisbon, which stayed there for some time.

For the second time Miguel swore his faithfulness to both Pedro and Maria, as well as to the constitution. Pressures on him, however, came from every social class, and particularly from his closest advisers, to pass over his oaths and be proclaimed absolute king. The Austrian and Spanish governments were also favorable to the restoration of absolutism. In March 1828, he dissolved the *cortes* and in May he summoned new ones according to the old style. They proclaimed him king (July 1828), which he promptly accepted. The foreign countries had their representatives removed from Portugal until 1829, when most of them—but not the three major powers, England, France, and Austria—formally acknowledged Miguel's kingship.

The liberal opposition responded with a military uprising in Porto and elsewhere, which failed. Other conspiracies also led nowhere. As a consequence, violent persecutions against the liberals featured Miguel's six-year rule. Thousands left the country, thousands were arrested and kept in jail in the worst possible conditions, dozens were executed or murdered. Repression hit every aspect of Portuguese life and surpassed Pombal's despotism fifty years before. Yet the majority of the population applauded such measures, because they regarded the liberals as pure atheists, enemies of the country and guilty of the worst crimes.

Miguel's repressive system at home seemed to herald a bitter civil struggle. The king was unable to surround himself with able and competent ministers, with the result that both his internal and his external policies were awkward and led to disaster. After 1831 he gradually succeeded in alienating all the foreign support he could expect to obtain, even that of reactionary and neighboring Spain (by backing Carlos' claims against his brother, King Fernando VII). The economic and financial situation, far from improving with the definite return to absolutism, became worse.

Meanwhile Emperor-King Pedro dispatched young Maria to Europe. Her presence in England gave the thousands of exiles new hope, while money arriving from Brazil (which that country owed Portugal according to the peace treaty of 1825) helped prepare an expedition which landed in the island of Terceira (Azores) early in 1829. This island had revolted against Miguel and gallantly upheld the liberal cause for more than two years. There, many exiles and local people set up a provisional regency under the leadership of the Marquis of Palmela. Queen Maria went back to Brazil to await better days.

The absolutists vainly tried to subdue Terceira, but the liberals gradually conquered all the other islands of the Azores. In Brazil, circumstances had forced Emperor Pedro I to abdicate on behalf of his son Pedro II (1831), which gave him full freedom of action to try to gain the Portuguese crown. He left Brazil with his wife and daughter Maria and went to England and France, assuming the direct leadership to the liberal cause. The French government, sympathetic to the liberals after the revolution of 1830, raised no obstacles to his organization of a new military expedition with the purpose of liberating Portugal. Arriving at Terceira (March 1832) Pedro replaced Palmela as regent and left for Portugal with his people in June 1832. The expedition was formed by some 7,500 men, including 800 French and English mercenaries and volunteers. Landing in Portugal took place in July, near Porto. Caught by surprise, the absolutist forces which protected the city retreated, and the liberals entered Porto almost without bloodshed four days later.

The civil war had thus started on the mainland. It would last for two years and bring about considerable devastation. It ruined the country's already shaken economy and made liberals and absolutists both dependent upon foreign creditors. English, French, and others had their share of Portugal's wealth, and imposed their control there more than ever before. Foreign help and direct interference in Portugal's affairs featured the troubled history of constitutionalism to the 1840's. Diplomatic envoys often acted as royal advisers.

In the beginning, the civil war seemed a thoroughly unbalanced duel between a handful of liberal exiles aided by France and England and the overwhelming majority of the country, counting upon a large regular army of more than eighty thousand. Yet the liberals had the advantage of fighting for something new and practically unproved, thus pure and with good propaganda possibilities. They could make promises, herald a reign of prosperity and liberty, compare a dubious and corrupt past and present with a future full of glory. Mousinho da Silveira's theoretical legislation had quite an impact on the minds of the absolutist soldiers and other supporters. Moreover, the liberals included the cream of the Portuguese intelligentsia, the ablest lawyers, bureaucrats, doctors, scientists, and writers, with a significant number of young and daring fighters. Their upper-grade military were few, but they had with them some first-class young officers in the making. From the very beginning, military command supremacy belonged to the liberals, who proudly displayed men like Saldanha, Vila Flor, and Sá Nogueira. Also, the liberals were desperately fighting for a return home, for the right to live in their fatherland, while defeat for the absolutists would not necessarily result in death or exile. Freedom was meant for all, while despotism excluded many.

Yet the absolutists did not give up that easily. After their first disorientation, they rallied together and besieged Porto. The siege lasted one year, but the liberals along with the population of the city gallantly held to the end. In June 1833, they decided to try another landing somewhere, which might relieve the absolutist pressure. A maritime expedition composed of some 2,500 men under the command of Vila Flor (now honored with the title of Duke of Terceira) left Porto and in a surprise operation landed in the South, in the Algarve. Some days later the liberal fleet (under the mercenary English commander Napier) completely defeated the absolutist men-of-war. This fact gave the Duke of Terceira and his men new hope, and helped spread the liberal cause throughout the country. The absolutists were now demoralized and desertions occurred in large numbers. Liberal uprisings and guerrilla warfare resulted here and there, particularly in the South. Terceira marched on, reaching the Tagus in less than a month. The absolutists were badly beaten in front of Lisbon and their government decided to evacuate the capital. A day later Lisbon was occupied with little fighting (July 24, 1833). England and France formally recognized Pedro's government.

The main absolutist forces were still besieging Porto, and Miguel himself was with them. The appalling news from the South forced them to lift the siege and march southward in order to recapture the capital. Yet they were beaten again and again, particularly at the battles of Almoster (February 1834) and Asseiceira (May 1834). Late in that month, Miguel and his partisans were compelled to lay down arms. According to the concessions, signed at the village of Évora-Monte (May 26, 1834), a general amnesty was granted, the military were maintained in the patents they had in 1828, and the civil and church servants were indemnified although not kept in their jobs. Miguel was to live outside the country with a yearly allowance of sixty

battle
Liberals' landings,
1832 and 1833
Terceira's way from
Oporto to Lisbon
by sea and land - 1833
Napier's fleet
Miguel's army

0   50   100
                  km.

0   50
                  miles

Pampelido
Oporto

Coimbra

Asseiceira

Almoster

Lisbon
Almada
Setúbal
Évora-Monte
Alcácer do Sal
Évora

Garvão

Messines
Tavira   Alagoa
Loulé
Faro
Olhão
Cabo de São Vicente

contos. He left forever on June 1, but once he arrived in Italy he disavowed his signing of the agreement, therefore losing the right to the allowance.

The end of the civil war did not mean stability at home. The liberals were plagued with internal divisions, and the reintegration of the absolutists in the political family only made things worse. The inevitable persecutions against the defeated side took place, accompanied by confiscations and destruction. The right wing became stronger than ever but the left wing was more aggressive too. The military and all those who had fought for the liberal cause now wanted a reward for their services. The most impetuous and famous army commanders (Saldanha, Terceira, and others) strove for power and considered themselves the natural leaders of the country. Not used to the constitutional practice, most statesmen tended toward a disguised dictatorship which brought them into an almost permanent conflict with the *cortes*. The latter also was riven by the opposition between the upper Chamber of Peers and the lower House of Deputies.

Regent Pedro was the first victim of the new system. He was accused of dictatorial acts and blamed for his lenience regarding Miguel. He quickly became unpopular among the leftists and many of his former partisans. But he died shortly after (September 1834) of tuberculosis. Rather than have a regency, the *cortes* and the government preferred to declare fifteen-year-old Maria II of age. She appointed as premier the conservative Duke of Palmela, who formed a center-right cabinet, supported by the rural landowners, the wealthy traders and bankers, the Church, and most of the old aristocrats.

Until 1836 the conservatives held power. Palmela, Terceira, and Saldanha, along with some moderates, controlled the government and tried to instill some order and inject some prosperity into a country utterly exhausted and still bleeding from its civil war. They had the full support of the foreign powers, who saw in them the warrants of a moderate, English-type constitutionalism, depending on loans from abroad and committed to pay them in time. They also managed to marry the queen to a German prince, Augustus of Leuchtenberg (January 1835) and when he suddenly died, two months later, to another German, Prince Ferdinand of Saxe-Coburg-Gotha (January

1836). The prince was given the title of Commander-in-Chief of the Portuguese Army. When his first son was born (1837), the queen had him proclaimed king-consort with the title of Fernando II.

The troubled situation of the country and the weakness of the several governments which succeeded each other made the conservatives unpopular, particularly in the large cities. The leftist opposition in the Chamber of Deputies, led by Manuel Passos (better known as Passos Manuel), kept the government under constant fire. Parliament was dissolved (June 1836), but in the following elections, the opposition won in several important places, among them Porto. When its representatives arrived in Lisbon, the city garrisons revolted with popular support, and forced the government to resign (September 1836). A new government, with Passos Manuel as the leading figure, assumed power, abolished the Constitutional Charter, and put in force the Constitution of 1822. The elections that followed gave him a majority that drafted a new constitution, more extreme than the Charter but far less than that of 1822.

"Septembrism," or the policies resulting from the September rebellion, quickly evolved toward a Center-Left compromise, where the moderate Viscount of Sá da Bandeira (i.e., the war hero Sá Nogueira) prevailed over the more leftist-oriented Passos Manuel. The 1836 rebellion had pretty much been a reaction of the urban industrial bourgeoisie, allied to middle-class traders (and both acclaimed by the lower classes), against the predominance of the rural landowners and upper business people. But it became clear that the new victors did not possess enough strength to carry on a radical program of their own. Moreover, although their interests were generally urban, they contradicted each other by opposing rich industrialists to petty traders and even to proletarians. Passos Manuel's kind of dictatorial government (actually the nominal premiership did not belong to him) brought about important and revolutionary measures but did not endure: eight months later he had to give up power to more moderate elements.

"Septembrism" lasted until 1842, but it tended to be less and less radical. Moreover, it had to fight constant attempts to restore the Charter: in November 1836, the queen and her advisers tried a coup d'état which failed; from July to September 1837, the Chartists revolted under the two prestigious marshals Saldanha and Terceira; other less important plots were discovered as well. On the other hand, the extreme leftists also rebelled in Lisbon against what they called the "betrayal" of the September revolution. As a consequence, the government tended to emphasize order and to lapse into authoritarianism. From 1839 on, the Secretary of Justice, Costa Cabral (a former radical), practically controlled things, being regarded by the Crown and the Right as the best warrant of order and prosperity.

The final step was taken in February 1842, when Costa Cabral himself restored the Charter at Porto in a bloodless coup d'état. He became the Secretary of the Interior in a new government, presided over by the Duke of Terceira but definitely controlled by himself. Power had returned again to the Right, but this time under an able and authoritarian leader, who knew how to rule and make himself obeyed.

"Cabralism" (from Cabral) emphasized order and economic development. As such, it set up in the country a regime of repression and violence, often comparable to Miguel's rule. But unlike Miguel, Costa Cabral did not want to go back to the past and to its obsolete structures; he rather fostered the development of Portugal in a progressive way, particularly in the fields of public works and administration. Many of his reforms endured, even when his name had become anathema for most people.

Costa Cabral's unashamed despotism, in contrast to his theoretical respect for the constitution and its liberties, together with his inability or unwillingness to carry violence to its limits and get rid of all opposition, brought about the most terrible and enduring civil war between liberals. Curiously enough, one of the main pretexts for a general rebellion was a highly progressive act that forbade burials in the churches and confined them to the cemeteries. Taxation increase also had its impact on the rebellion. A military uprising, early in 1844, had failed. Two years later, however, the common people in Minho rose in arms, with the actual participation of women. One of these, nicknamed Maria da Fonte, became a legendary figure and gave her name to the whole movement.

The Maria da Fonte revolution was a very complex affair. It put together several contradictory forces, encompassing old absolutists and partisans of Miguel, leftist radicals, moderates, and even right-wing Chartists annoyed with Costa Cabral's ruthlessness and shameless corruption. It included generals, aristocrats, clerics, bourgeois, proletarians. And it featured many interesting aspects of popular revolutionary organization in the form of local juntas which controlled local affairs and obeyed no central government.

The first phase of the Maria da Fonte movement lasted only a month (April–May 1846) and came to an end with the ousting of Costa Cabral from the government. He and his brother left the country while the Duke of Palmela headed a coalition cabinet formed by moderate Chartists and moderate Septembrists. This cabinet, however, pleased no one; on the contrary both Cabralists and leftists were against it, as well as the absolutists who aimed at the queen herself. A troubled situation lasted for some time, causing anxiety to the foreign powers and particularly Spain, where the fear of radical rebellions in union with the Portuguese was felt. To make things worse, Maria II and her advisers played politics too, forcing Palmela to resign (October 1846) and appointing Saldanha in his place to head a stronger government. This was the sign for the civil war: the Porto junta, which, like most others, had not been dissolved, rose in arms again carrying along all the North, part of Beira, Alentejo, and the Algarve. The guerrillas reappeared here and there. Many revolutionaries now planned the deposition of Maria II and her replacement by Prince Pedro, the heir to the throne, or even the proclamation of a Republic.

The war lasted for eight months and its results were generally favorable to the rebels. Their final victory, however, would bring about Maria's abdication and a government controlled by radicals. Neither England nor Spain could accept that. And concerning this, the two countries were eagerly supported by the Lisbon government itself. Saldanha asked for foreign intervention. A Spanish army entered Portugal, while the English fleet blockaded Porto. At Gramido, the rebels were forced to sign a treaty (June 1847) according to the terms of which they lay down arms with all honors.

The imposed peace of Gramido brought Costa Cabral and his partisans back. Saldanha still held power for a while in alliance with them, but palace intrigues and accusations of corruption led to his downfall in June 1849. Costa Cabral (made Count of Tomar) reassumed total power, this time as Prime Minister. Cabralism had returned, although in a more moderate, less violent form. Saldanha, personally offended with the government, the queen, and her advisers, became the main leader of the opposition. His enormous prestige and political naiveté made him welcomed by both the Left and the Center, despite his former associations with the extreme Right, including Cabral himself.

In April 1851 Saldanha revolted once again, and was supported by a military uprising in Porto. He called his movement the "regeneration of Portugal," his partisans becoming known henceforth as "Regenerators" (*Regeneradores*). Cabral's government fell, and Queen Maria II was forced to entrust Saldanha with the task of forming a new cabinet.

The rebellion had been in the making for a long time and rallied some of the best people in Portugal, including the great writer Alexander Herculano, who played a major role in its preparation and definition of goals. Saldanha's government gathered together some able and skilled personalities such as Rodrigo da Fonseca (Interior), Fontes Pereira de Melo (Finance and, later, Public Works, too), the poet and writer Almeida Garrett (Foreign Affairs), and several others. Politically, it began as a large and remarkable coalition of moderates, rightists, and leftists that deserved the acclaim of most people and was able to hold power for five years, albeit with several changes in its composition.

The country was tired of so much political turmoil, and desired peace. The bourgeoisie, particularly, required a strong yet flexible government, which could insure tranquillity and economic expansion. Saldanha's prestige accounted for the first; Fontes' plans for developing Portugal assured the second. Moreover, politically the liberal regime and the constitutional monarchy had reached maturity, which actually meant a maximum of freedom for a few, a docile and noninterfering monarch, a state of equilibrium among the several social classes and groups, and a clever manipulation of the political machine. The period of idealism was over. Economic and administrative problems replaced political doctrines as a program of government. The 1852 amendment to the constitution, along with the new electoral law, put an end to the division between Chartists and Septembrists and made the Charter acceptable to almost everyone. The industrial, financial, and trade expansion of Portugal attuned the interests of industrialists, financiers, traders, and rural landowners at the several levels, gathering together upper, middle, and petty bourgeoisie for a common goal. Between aristocrats and bourgeois the difference tended to fade away. From 1851 until the rise of the Republican Party in the 1880's and the 1890's one could say there was in Portugal no real "opposition" to the institutions, the ways of government, the economic and social policies or structures. From time to time there were some attempts to foster such opposition but always in vain. This firm hold on power by a united bourgeoisie would last for half a century and prevent any notions of rebellion from the lower classes. Summing up, one might say that 1851 saw the final adjustment of Portugal to the new conditions which had arisen with the loss of Brazil and the breakdown of the old regime.

Queen Maria II died in 1853, in childbirth. Although she was always respected as a mother and a person, her behavior as a constitutional queen often deserved bitter criticism. Obviously she liked to interfere in politics and leaned toward favorites in her choice of ministers. She listened too much to foreign advisers, including her husband, a German, and the envoys of countries like England and Belgium. She was probably primarily responsible for several political crises which shook Portugal from 1836 to 1851. King Fernando II, who in his youth liked to play politics too, became wiser with age and gained the esteem and respect of his subjects. Very talented and educated and with a disposition toward music and the arts, he had a major role in fostering the development of the arts in his new country and was responsible for the excellent education given to all his children. The heir to the throne, Pedro, was not of age, a regency being assumed by his nominal father King Fernando II. As king, Pedro V began ruling in 1855, but he died very young, of typhus, in 1861. He was remarkably intelligent and mature for his duties, and his death was deeply felt throughout the country. His brother Luis succeeded him on the throne. Not so much inclined toward public affairs as his older brother and his mother, Luis I passed into history as the model constitutional king. He preferred literature to politics and published several good translations of Shakespeare's plays in Portuguese. His marriage to Maria Pia, the daughter of Victor Emmanuel II of Italy, tightened the ties with that country and helped his popularity among the leftist anticlericals.

Portugal's internal policy during the reign of Pedro V and Luis I (1853–89) was one of relative quiet in the general framework of economic expansion and prosperity for the ruling classes. Regeneradores and Históricos (later called Progressistas) followed each other in power, both with a similar number of ruling years (the Regeneradores ruling in 1851–56; 1859-60; 1871–77; 1878–79; 1881–86; the Históricos, the Reformistas, and the Progressistas ruling in 1856–59; 1860–65; 1868–70; 1870–71; 1877–78; 1879–81 and 1886–90; and a coalition of the two parties, named Fusão, ruling in 1865–68), but the Regeneradores can be credited with greater achievements. Here and there, some minor crises shook the political order, but they were of no great significance. On January 1, 1868, for instance, there was some rioting in Lisbon in protest against new taxation. In 1870 old and proud Marshal Saldanha, because of a personal offense again, led an uprising against the government, ruled for some months with a group of talented people around him, and then stepped down. And in 1871 the famous lectures at the Lisbon *casino* formed the very beginnings of a true opposition to the institutions and the bourgeois order.

Portugal's external policy apparently was equally calm. Actually, however, the country had little autonomy, depending rather upon the general European order as decided by the Congress of Vienna (1815). England, France, Austria, and, to a certain extent, Spain controlled Portugal as they controlled most of the other small European countries. England acted as the main "protector" for economic reasons, and prevented a possible Spanish take-over. Yet, when some other important power interfered, England did little to enforce that protection. This happened, for instance, in 1831 when a French fleet paraded before Lisbon and threatened to bomb the city if some French demands were not answered. It happened, again, in 1857–58, when France violated Portugal's rights and imposed on her the payment of a heavy indemnity, because of the confiscation by the Portuguese authorities in Mozambique of a French slave ship (see chapter 11). Both English and French settled down in Portuguese or Portuguese-claimed territories in Africa (see chapter 11) with little respect for Portugal's rights there. Other countries' arbitration, when accepted by the great powers, generally gave credibility to Portugal's claims. And many other instances could be called upon to show this dependency. On the other hand, the Portuguese themselves asked for foreign protection and intervention in their home affairs: this happened in 1823, 1824, 1828–34 (both liberals and absolutists), 1836, and 1847. If such an interference was generally required by the conservative side, which was afraid of being displaced by radical movements, the leftists themselves were not entirely free from guilt. Whenever Spain, France, and England showed some sympathy for their principles, they would also ask for their support.

After 1848, the international order in Europe greatly changed. Foreign intervention in European countries became somewhat rarer, and the tendency was to let each nation solve her internal problems alone. For Portugal, the main problem which arose regarding foreign relations was that of Iberianism—the union between Portugal and Spain. This had been, of course, a centuries-old aspiration of both countries, but the Portuguese had given it up after 1640. Spain became the dangerous partner, and particularly during the nineteenth century her claims to an Iberian Union often endangered Portugal's independence. There were undoubtedly partisans of such a union in Portugal, but their number was small and their practical influence minimal. The unification of Italy (1859–61) and the trend toward the unification of Germany (effective in 1871) had an unquestionable impact on both Spain and Portugal. Spanish and Portuguese literature— including the press—debated the problem, either attacking or defending the union, and suggesting practical solutions. In 1868–70, the Spanish revolution and the two-year search for a king put the whole problem in a new light. Both Fernando II and Luis I of Portugal were thought of and invited as throne candidates, with the forethought that the two crowns might be united in the future. Both refused because of such a goal. Saldanha posed as a convinced partisan of Iberianism, and his seizure of power in 1870 probably had some Spanish influence behind it. The question was open again in 1873–75, until the Spanish throne solidified once more under Alfonso XII. For many Portuguese intellectuals, including a great number of Republicans, the dream of an Iberian Union had a strong appeal, as a remedy for the backwardness of both countries and the dawn of a new era for the united "Spaniards." They defended, of course, a sort of federation with Spain (or even a confederation of several states dismembered from Spain), which might preserve Portugal's cultural and political identity.

The stability of the 1870's and 1880's was followed by a deep political, economic, and financial crisis. The contradictions of the constitutional monarchy began to be evident to everyone. Its ideology no longer had any appeal to the younger generations. Instead, socialism and republicanism pointed a new way. The Spanish and French revolutions in the 1870's played a major role in the rise of a Portuguese political consciousness opposed to the cynical rotation of the parties and the enrichment of the bourgeoisie. The number of emigrants who left the country year after year suggested that the social problems of the lower classes were worsening instead of improving with the general economic expansion. Anticlericalism also played a major role in the shaping of an opposition.

Republican and socialist groups appeared in the 1870's. A decade later they had crystallized into two parties of some significance, particularly the Republican one. They were becoming more aggressive, more daring in their claims, more threatening in their work of subversion. The first Republican representative was elected to the *cortes* in 1878. King Luis I died in 1889, and the new monarch, Carlos I, intelligent but haughty and married to a very pious French princess, Amélie of Orléans, did not enjoy his father's popularity.

The crisis was provoked by the ultimatum that Great Britain sent to Portugal in January 1890, according to which the Portuguese had to give up their claims to a vast African territory connecting Angola with Mozambique, in what is now Zambia and Rhodesia (see chapter 11). This ultimatum caused a national wave of indignation against England and a widespread movement against the monarchy and the king himself, who was accused of neglecting the Overseas territories and of jeopardizing the nation's interests. There were some riots, and in January 1891 the first republican uprising took place in Porto. It failed, but for the first time it showed the existence of a real menace to the established institutions.

The events of 1890–91 took place in the context of an international economic and financial crisis. The Progressista government, headed by José Luciano de Castro, considered responsible for the ultimatum, fell. The king called the Regeneradores under António de Serpa Pimentel, who were unable to keep power and resigned some months later on account of the treaty to be signed with England. A national cabinet was then formed under a prestigious but aged figure, General João Crisóstomo (October 1890). It was followed by another coalition government under the economist José Dias Ferreira (January 1892), who included historian Oliveira Martins as Finance Minister. Dias Ferreira's cabinet was able to solve the financial crisis and smooth the situation again. As a consequence, the old party system came back to power. Regeneradores under Hintze Ribeiro and Progressistas under José Luciano succeeded each other up to 1906 (the Regeneradores ruling in 1893–97, 1900–4, and 1906; the Progressistas in 1897–1900 and 1904–6).

The political situation, however, was not entirely the same as before the ultimatum. New trends pointed either toward a stronger assertion of the royal power or toward a much more liberal conception of constitutionalism. Both could be ascertained in either party. In 1893, Hintze Ribeiro attempted a compromise with the liberal wing, which failed, the liberal ministers (Bernardino Machado and Augusto Fuschini) resigning some months later. It was the other wing that prevailed, with its main representative in João Franco, the Secretary of Interior. Hintze and Franco even tried a dictatorship in 1895. Party unity could not be enforced because of such trends, which were exacerbated by personal rivalries. In 1901, Franco seceded from the Regeneradores and formed (1902) a new party, the Regenerador-Liberal party, which stood for a new kind of monarchy, somewhat despotic but with social concerns (following closely the Bismarck pattern). On the other side, a small group of dissidents led by José Maria de Alpoim left the Progressistas (1905), clamoring for a more liberal regime, very close to a Republic. Yet the rising force, which more and more threatened and worried the constitutional monarchy, was the Republican Party, particularly after 1903 when Bernardino Machado, the former minister, became a Republican and threw all his influence and ability into reorganizing and strengthening the party.

Meanwhile, if the international position of Portugal had improved in regard to the Spanish menaces to her independence, the security of her Overseas territories was far from guaranteed. Germans and British kept an eye on Angola and Mozambique, and would not give up an opportunity to repeat the ultimatum of 1890. In 1898, both countries signed a treaty envisioning the partition of Angola, Mozambique, and Timor in case of Portuguese financial difficulties. The United States had some views on the Azores. In 1904 Germany planned to take all the Portuguese colonies. Well aware of this fact, the Portuguese governments did their best to appease the big powers' greediness and to a certain extent they succeeded. The secret Treaty of Windsor (1899), between Portugal and England, contradicted that of 1898. King Carlos himself acted as a good ambassador, with his frequent visits to the most important European countries and his playing the host to the rulers of England, Germany, France, and Spain. With his royal colleagues, King Carlos was as popular as he was unpopular with his fellow countrymen. Yet the main obstacle to a partition of the Portuguese colonies was the rivalry among the great powers themselves and the concern for maintaining the European equilibrium.

By 1906 the *cortes* had become an assembly for chicanery and personal debates. Obstruction to any government and filibustering were common practices. The two large parties did little to avoid the accusations of corruption, inefficiency, and uselessness laid upon them. The Republicans made the best use possible of internal monarchical dissensions to attack the regime. Behind them, a majority of urban middle- and lower-class people began successfully to sap the fundaments of the institutions. The king forced Hintze Ribeiro to resign and entrusted João Franco with the task of forming a new cabinet. The new premier first got the support of the Progressistas but soon lost it and decided to try the dictatorial way. The *cortes* were dissolved (1907) and no new elections set. The consequences were disastrous for the regime: Franco had against him the overwhelming majority of the organized forces in the country and could rely mostly on the royal support. It has been made public that the royal family owed the government (i.e., the nation) important sums of money in the form of successive loans, which brought about a campaign against the monarchy. Violence and repression featured Franco's second year in government. The students struck in Coimbra. In January 1908, an abortive rebellion rallied together Republicans and a good many monarchists too. Some of the main Republican leaders were arrested. On February 1, King Carlos and the heir to the throne, Prince Luis Filipe, were assassinated in Lisbon, while the second-born prince, Manuel, was slightly wounded.

Acclaimed as Manuel II, the new monarch, a youth of eighteen, dismissed Franco and called upon a coalition government headed by Admiral Ferreira do Amaral. The prevailing attitude was one of appeasement, in contrast to the fierceness of the fallen dictatorship. The Republicans were given more freedom than ever, and their influence among the people increased. In the municipal elections of 1908 they won in Lisbon. Porto had already a coalition of Republicans and liberal Monarchists in its municipal government since 1906. It became obvious to most people that the monarchy was coming to an end. This also derived from the weakness shown by all the monarchical groups and from governmental instability. From 1908 to 1910 there were six different cabinets, each one accounting for a new split within the two large parties. Behind the scenes, the old Progressista leader, José Luciano, controlled most of the political situation, his party backing all but the last of the six governments. In the general elections of August 1910, the Republicans triumphed in Lisbon and several other places. In a country like Portugal, where the weight of the capital is paramount in the nation's life, this meant the end for the constitutional monarchy. Indeed, on October 4, 1910, a military and popular revolution in Lisbon easily disbanded the last defenders of the throne, the Republic being proclaimed on the following day. King Manuel and his family left the country, never to return.

AFRICA

TRAVELS AND COLONIZATION

In the nineteenth century central and southern Africa began to be influenced by the growth of European settlement and expansion. Hunters, traders, missionaries, and concession-seekers began penetrating the mighty continent everywhere. The great explorations of David Livingstone (1852 to 1873) and H. M. Stanley (1874 to 1877) were only the best known of a long series in which the French, the British, the Germans, the Boers, the Belgians, and the Portuguese figured prominently as well.

Although not well known, the part played by the Portuguese was also a major one. From the late eighteenth century (see chapter 9) to the 1900's, one expedition after another left the coastal areas of Angola and Mozambique with varied purposes and dissimilar achievements. These explorations made known to the West vast territories between latitude 7° and 27° S., and were instrumental in promoting European settlement not only in Portuguese but also in British areas —in present-day Zambia and Rhodesia.

The first important expedition which the Portuguese carried on after 1820 took place in 1831–32. Major José Maria Correia Monteiro, with Captain António Pedroso Gamito as second in command, and a large force of 420 traders and porters left Tete (in Mozambique) in 1831, heading northwest and following the track which explorer Lacerda e Almeida had made known thirty years before. They went as far as Cazembe, near Lake Mweru (the border between present Zambia and Congo), for economic as well as geographic purposes. Robbed of most merchandise and gunpowder, they decided to return to Tete, where they arrived in 1832. Gamito wrote a report on the expedition.

In 1843, the governor of Angola entrusted Joaquim Rodrigues Graça with the mission of getting to the springs of the river Sena and the region known as Bié and establishing effective Portuguese sovereignty there. His was a long trip, up the Cuanza River and then, northeastward, down the Kasai to Mussumba between that river and the Lulua (in what is now Congo). He went back to Luanda, following the same route, in 1846.

From 1847 onward, to the 1850's, explorer Bernardino José Brochado went from Moçâmedes, in south Angola, to the Cunene River, in which area he traveled extensively, reporting very interesting findings on ethnography and geography. The precise knowledge of the Cunene, in its course, was a result of Brochado's trip.

In the 1840's and 1850's, the Portuguese settler and peddler Silva Porto (1817–90) undertook some of the most important expeditions in present-day Angola and Zambia. Settling down in central Angola, where no other Europeans were then living, he gained a tremendous prestige and influence among the local African rulers, which enabled him to implement a geographic and economic policy. He and his "envoys" got to Barotseland (where he met Livingstone), and regular contacts were established with that area. Besides other trips he also accompanied two Arab merchants (who had crossed Africa coming from Zanzibar) on their way back home almost to the Kafue River, in central Zambia (1853). There he stopped, but his African clients went on to the Indian Ocean (1854) and then back home by sea. Silva Porto's merits as an explorer and a defender of the Portuguese sovereignty in central Angola were rewarded with the office of Captain-Major of Bié. He later committed suicide when some local Bié tribes revolted against the Portuguese flag.

Still in the 1850's the Austrian naturalist Friedrich Welwitsch traveled widely in Angola under a commission of the Lisbon government. Caetano Ferreira departed from southeast Angola and traveled south, up the Cuando River, the springs of which he first saw in 1854. A year later, explorers Montanha and Teixeira left Inhambane, on the eastern coast of Africa, and headed west well into Transvaal (now Kruger National Park). Thus ended a first period of Portuguese geographical expansion.

After a twenty-year interval began a new period, marked by the most significant and the most daring of all the Portuguese expeditions. They were now better prepared and managed, by people with more expertise in all fields. The newly created Lisbon Geographical Society (1875) was instrumental in fostering, patronizing, and subsidizing the exploration movement.

Navy Commanders Hermenegildo Capelo (1841–1917) and Roberto Ivens (1850–98) left in 1877 for their first exploration. Departing from Benguela, they proceeded to Luanda, went up the Cuanza for awhile, then headed north to the Congo, looking for porters, then south again, in a sinuous line which took them to Silva Porto's headquarters, in Bié. They discovered the courses of the rivers Cubango, Luando, and Tohicapa, returning to Luanda in 1880. Their report, a fine piece of geographical knowledge, was widely publicized (*De Benguella ás Terras de Iacca*, Lisbon, 1888). A former companion of theirs, Captain Serpa Pinto (1846–1900), undertook the crossing of Africa, from west to east. From Silva Porto's headquarters (1877), Serpa Pinto went south, following the 1853 expedition tract to central Zambia. He continued further south via the Zambezi River, and then, accompanied by the French missionary Coillard, he proceeded all the way south to Pretoria (Transvaal) and Durban (1879), becoming the first Portuguese and one of the first Europeans to cross Africa. He wrote a famous account of his expedition, "How I Crossed Africa" (*Como eu atravessei a Africa*, 2 vols., Lisbon, 1880).

Within Mozambique, Navy Lieutenant António Maria Cardoso went from Inhambane to Sofala and back, following a wide detour west (1883). Again in Angola, Army officer Henrique de Carvalho traveled from Malange to the Kasai River (1884–86).

Capelo, Ivens, and Serpa Pinto undertook still a second voyage. The first two departed from Moçâmedes (South Angola) in 1884 and went all the way to Quelimane (Mozambique), where they arrived a year later, going as far north as Katanga, in Congo, and following the Zambezi down to its mouth. The report of their daring and successful trip was published in Lisbon in 1886, under the title *De Angola á*

Contra-Costa ("From Angola to the Other Coast"). Accompanied by Augusto Cardoso, Serpa Pinto also traveled in Mozambique in 1885–86, going from the town of Mozambique, on the coast, north to Ibo, and then west to Lake Nyassa.

These were simply the most renowned of all the expeditions, yet there were scores of others, undertaken by peddlers, officers, and scientists, within the present boundaries of Angola and Mozambique, which definitely helped make available better geographical knowledge of both colonies and formed the basis for the Portuguese political expansion in Africa. Indeed, the major motivation for the travels was the assertion of the Portuguese authority over historically claimed territories. Geographical and commercial motivations were also present. The elaborate maps of the late nineteenth and early twentieth centuries were their result, as well as the fostering of interest in trade projects among both blacks and whites. The Anglo-Portuguese treaty of 1890, defining the borderline between English and Portuguese Africa, pointed to the need for thorough and precise knowledge of at least the border region. Setting up the framework for modern Angola and Mozambique, it also stimulated the Portuguese to carry on an entire exploration of their territories, which they did throughout the last decade of the nineteenth and the first ten years of the twentieth centuries. Numerous map committees, geographical missions, and military operations completed the basic tasks started by the explorers of the mid-nineteenth century.

By 1830 or 1840 the Portuguese effective occupation of Angola was limited to a narrow strip of coastal territory, 50 to 80 miles wide, with no definite boundaries inland. In the north, occupation widened a little by encompassing part of the Congo River banks up to present-day Matadi, 171 km. (105 miles) inland where its navigability stops at the Livingstone Falls. In the south, southeast of what is now Benguela, Portuguese sovereignty reached Caconda, some 240 km. (150 miles) from the coast. The coastline itself was only thoroughly known as far as Benguela, before the reconnoitering expeditions of the 1830's and the 1840's, which mapped Angola's coast to the Bay of Tigres, 17° S.

In Mozambique, the Portuguese controlled even less territory than in Angola. From Cape Delgado to Lourenço Marques, occupation of the coastline was not even continuous: running north to south it stopped at Angoche, where the local ruler resisted the Portuguese; then it took over at Quelimane and proceeded to Delagoa Bay. From Cape Delgado to north of Angoche, the strip of land in the hands of the whites did not go beyond 40 km., or 25 miles; from Lourenço Marques to Sofala, it widened a little, mostly at the river valleys; yet only the Zambezi River corresponded to a deep penetration inland, for the Portuguese were well settled down to Tete and beyond, nearly 500 km. (320 miles) from the coast.

In Guinea, Portuguese authority had a mere coastal character and was limited to some fortresses and villages such as Bissau, Bolama (since 1828), Cacheu, Ziguinchor, Geba, Farim, and a few more, not necessarily connected by other than coastwise navigation. The situation in distant Timor was similar.

The reasons for this restricted occupation of the African continent were several. With the exception of Angola, in the late sixteenth and early seventeenth centuries, the Portuguese Crown had really never envisioned a substantial conquest of territory and was simply concerned about protecting the coastal settlements with a minimum hinterland, in the good tradition of the Asian "Empire." Secondly, Africa played a minor economic role for the Portuguese, compared with Brazil and the East, only slaves being of relevance. Thirdly, the African peoples generally offered fierce resistance to the European advance. And last but not least, the climate and the geographical features of the Continent posed insuperable hardships for white colonization. As a matter of fact, it is safe to say that the major stimulus to the Portuguese conquest of Angola, Mozambique, and Guinea was the foreign competition and the growing Portuguese fear of being "robbed" of what they regarded as parts of Portugal. This "uneconomic imperialism," to use Professor R. J. Hammond's words, must be emphasized to understand Portugal's position in Africa in the nineteenth century and attitude toward her colonies down to the present. Only in the twentieth century (in a few cases since the 1890's) did economic advantages clearly justify the Portuguese occupation of continental Africa. Until then, conquest, settlement, and reconnoitering were mostly planned and carried on by the government with political goals, but with very little interest from, and little capital invested by, private sources. Mobilization of a vast public opinion that supported the policy of imperialism—as it certainly did, to the extent of forcing the government to take better care of the colonies—had no other basis than national pride. To conquer Angola, Mozambique, and Guinea, to tell the world of the prowess of soldiers, sailors, and explorers over there, was for the Portuguese a way of balancing the frustrations felt at home and of lining up with the seven colonizing countries of the world: England, France, Germany, Italy, Belgium, Holland, and Spain (this last country being replaced by the United States after 1898).

The several attempts to officially promote colonization in Africa did not meet with great success. Emigrants preferred Brazil or the United States, where well-organized societies needed them and provided them promptly with jobs and high salaries, to Angola or Mozambique, where no one welcomed them and where profits seemed difficult to obtain. Statesmen like Sá da Bandeira tried to organize migration to Africa with poor results. In 1838 land was distributed in Mozambique to orphans and other former pupils of the Casa Pia of Lisbon, but with little success. In 1852 a special fund to promote emigration to the Overseas possessions had meagre results. In 1884 a more promising undertaking was carried on—the colonization of the Moçâmedes tableland by settlers from Madeira. Several companies and regulations to promote settlement failed too. As a matter of fact, deported outcasts and some soldiers were virtually the only ones the government could get to stay in Africa permanently. Because of this the society of Luanda or Lourenço Marques was not very appealing and lacked that minimum of respectability every emigrant wished for himself or for his family.

By the early nineteenth century there were throughout the Portuguese "Empire" less than 10,000 Europeans, and this figure did not change much up to the middle of the century. Cape Verde, Angola, and India absorbed the largest number, a great many of whom were banished outcasts and garrison men. The number of actual settlers was minimal, for most of the white Portuguese returned home after a time. Even the garrisons included a large majority of Africans and Asians under the command of white Portuguese officers. Half-breeds did exist but in small numbers, and they did not necessarily feel at home in the Overseas provinces. Many attempted to go to Portugal and settle down there, some successfully.

After the middle of the century, things started changing but not much. Although the white population of both Angola and Mozambique increased eight or nine times between 1850 and 1910, Angola housed only some 12,000 Europeans when the Republic was proclaimed, and Mozambique half of that number. Miscegenation occurred slowly, not only because of the relatively large number of white females, but also because of the high death rate among children. An analysis of the peacetime garrisons, which the Portuguese kept throughout the eight colonies at the end of the monarchy, showed a little more than 10,000 men controlling the empire, of which less than a third were whites: 5,000 in Angola, 2,800 in Mozambique, 1,000 in India, 500 in Macao, and the remainder distributed almost evenly in the other four colonies. The "Empire" was no demographic burden for Portugal nor did it solve her problems of migration. Manning those huge areas and keeping them peaceful proved a much easier task than keeping order in Lisbon (8,000 soldiers in Lisbon could not prevent the Republic from being proclaimed on October 5, 1910).

"Towns" were little more than small villages, with some few exceptions: Macao (78,000), Pangim (Goa), Luanda, and Lourenço Marques—none of the three exceeding 20,000 in 1910, all races included. This, however, happened to be true of most European cities south of the Sahara, and Luanda could still pose as a large metropolis on the West coast from Morocco to Cape Town.

Although the African peoples of Angola, Mozambique, and Guinea were many, subdivided into several language groups and tribes with different characteristics and traditions, they had some similar traits. Most of them spoke clearly related languages known collectively as Bantu, a sort of African "Latin" mother tongue. Their main activity was grain farming, leading to a rapid exhaustion of soils. As they had limited means of restoring fertility, there was often a shifting kind of cultivation. Many tribes combined grain farming with cattle raising. Culturally, most of the African peoples in contact with the Portuguese had reached a sort of prehistoric metal-age level. They used iron tools (hoes, for instance) but were not familiar with writing. Their religion, though combining fetishism with an often elaborate pantheon of gods, did not shun the existence of a Supreme Being. Their political organization generally lacked a traditional kingship, most of them forming independent or tributary chiefdoms under the control of paramount chiefs (*sobas*). In historical terms, they strikingly resembled the Germanic peoples in contact with the Roman Empire. This, however, varied from area to area. In certain parts of Guinea and of north-central Mozambique (mainly along the coast), centuries of Moslem influence had definitely raised the civilizational level of the Africans and changed many of their ways of life. They were Muslims in religion, many spoke languages (such as Swahili) or dialects with a strong Arabic content, and they were organized in petty Arab-like shiekates or even sultanates.

In Angola, by far the largest tribal group was that of the Ovimbundo (also called Ovampo), occupying a central position in the Benguela highlands. North of the Ovimbundos lived the Ambundos and the Congos, the latter stretching much beyond the frontiers of present-day Angola, well into the former Belgian Congo. South and east of the Ovimbundos there were several smaller tribal groups, among them the Ambo, covering a part of what is now Southwest Africa. They all spoke different Bantu languages.

In Mozambique the tribal groups and the languages spoken were still more numerous than in Portuguese West Africa. In the north there lived the Yao (not distinct from the people of present Malawi), the Makondas, and the Makwas (or Macuas), common to Mozambique and Tanzania and both often Islamized. Central Mozambique was occupied by the Basenega and the Baangoni, of Zulu origin. In the south, there were the Tsonga groups of the Baronga and Batonga, as well as the Bachopi and several other minor Zulu tribes.

In Portuguese Guinea, about a dozen peoples occupied most of the territory: the interior Islamized groups of the Fulani (Fulas), the Mandingo, and the Biafada or Biafar; and the non-Moslem Balanta, Manjaco, Papel, Fulup or Felupe, Bijagó, and Nalu.

Tribal differentiation, rivalries, and frequent warfare always prevented the African peoples in contact with the Portuguese (or with other European peoples) from uniting themselves against the common foe. Except in very brief periods of sporadic "empires," i.e., confederations of tribes under a prestigious leader (like the Zulu Tutsi or Watutsi Empire in South Mozambique), the Portuguese had relatively little trouble in imposing their sovereignty, whenever they were determined to do it. Usually, they preferred cunning to violence, exploiting tribal and subtribal petty rivalries, dividing the blacks, and often posing as protectors or defenders of one tribe against another. They also proclaimed Portugal's "might" and threatened unconvinced tribes with fierce revenge. Centuries-long contact with African peoples had taught the Portuguese how to be accepted as lords and how to rule with a minimum of force. As a counterpart, they usually required very little from the subdued peoples: a theoretical subjection to the Portuguese flag and authorities, and the payment of a tribute. Only the development of white settlement throughout the twentieth century changed this situation.

Whenever peaceful means were insufficient or proved useless, the so-called campaigns of submission took place. Again, the Portuguese were masters in "pacifying" a territory with a minimum of fighting. Few as they were, they often depended upon individual deeds, daring prowess, and the like, which had a deep impact on the minds of Africans. Despite the European superiority in weaponry and military organization, the blacks had many strengths of their own: they knew the ground, they were used to the climate and the insects, and they were overwhelmingly superior in number. From the mid-1800's on, most of the tribes fighting the Portuguese used rifles sold or given by other Europeans—who often wished to foster Portugal's defeat in Africa— or by the Portuguese themselves.

During almost all of the nineteenth century, colonization in Angola, Mozambique, and Guinea interfered little with African ownership of the land. Except in a few areas, such as the Zambezi Valley or along the coast, where Portuguese rule had been a matter of fact for centuries, the Africans were not dispossessed of their property, for the simple reason that settlers were very few and generally uninterested in agriculture. Still, when the Lisbon government and several private companies began systematically organizing and promoting white colonization, open appropriation of the African-owned lands was discouraged for fear of rebellion. It must be remembered that the population density in each of the three colonies was low: not more than 4 inhabitants per square mile in Angola, not more than 8 in Mozambique, about 20 in Guinea. Property demarcations were often vague or nonexistent; shifting agriculture fostered the movement of people, with vast areas belonging to nobody.

Moreover, Europeans preferred to live in towns rather than to scatter themselves about in the countryside. A form of settlement thus developed, similar to that in the South of Portugal, with huge areas of uninhabited land or land sparsely inhabited by Negroes separating relatively dense towns and villages. It was only well into the twentieth century that individual white farming based upon actual settlement could develop as the road network expanded and communications became easier, along with greater security and European familiarity with the environment.

The Portuguese system of colonization—whenever it existed—always aimed at converting the African into a Portuguese. As early as 1820, all natives of the Overseas provinces were considered Portuguese citizens, at least in theory. With such goals in mind, the Portuguese systematically rebuffed whatever might prevent that "Portugalization": teaching was to be in Portuguese and only Portuguese was accepted as the official language; religion and morals were to be Christian and, if possible, Roman Catholic; customs, traditions, and way of life were to relate to the Portuguese fatherland, not to the African past. Consequently, learning and preservation of African languages and cultures could only be envisioned from a strictly scientific standpoint or as a provisional bridge for communication between whites and blacks.

Between the Portuguese and the Africans cultural contacts were almost totally one-sided. The difference in technological advance was too great to make the Europeans permeable to any black influence. It must also be emphasized that the Portuguese always resisted influences from races and civilizations which they considered backward and therefore inferior. Considering the worldwide and centuries-long Portuguese expansion, amazingly few aspects of African, American, and even Asian origin are to be found in the Portuguese culture or way of life, in contrast to their often excessive permeability to European influences. A few words, some new plants, but little else was all that Africa gave Portugal at the time.

The question of slavery hovered over the entire Portuguese colonial administration to the twentieth century. In a disguised way, one could even say that it survived to the 1950's. In this, of course, Portugal was not alone; other colonial powers confronted the same problem.

The great industrial changes of the eighteenth and early nineteenth centuries made possible an anti-slavery movement with good chances of success. The French Revolution insisted on liberty and equality for mankind, instilling some freshness into the traditional but stagnant Christian doctrine of equality of all men before God. Slavery had already been abolished in most European countries during the eighteenth century, and fighting it became a sort of fashionable, enlightened attitude among intellectuals and aristocrats. A public opinion against slavery in general and the slave trade in particular developed throughout Europe in the early 1800's. England, where the industrial revolution had progressed most, could pose as the leading defender of liberty for the slaves and thus the leading enemy of slavery-indulging countries. During the nineteenth century, the British vessels (for they were everywhere in the world) acted as a kind of police body trying to stop the slave trade in Africa, Asia, and America. This, of course, had several other implications. Anti-slavery operations were often a disguise for political attitudes of imperialism. As warrants of freedom, the British felt a right to interfere anywhere—particularly in the subequatorial lands—and to meddle with the full sovereignty and liberty of action of other countries. It was often a pretext to extend Britain's "protection" to African areas and control their trade to the detriment of other countries.

Following the Treaty of Vienna (1815), England and Portugal signed an agreement to curb the slave trade in the Portuguese possessions. Portugal pledged to suppress it north of the equator, which meant her colonies of Cape Verde and Guinea. Septembrism (see chapter 10) generalized abolition, when Premier Sá da Bandeira decided to forbid all imports and exports of slaves south of the equator (1836). Sá da Bandeira also tried to put an end to compulsory labor, which often competed with and substituted for real slavery. Yet, easy as such measures seemed in theory, their practical application met with insuperable obstacles. Slave trade meant prosperity for many people, in fact the only source of prosperity for colonies like Guinea and Angola. The Brazilian demand for slaves was a temptation that few would resist. The acts of the Lisbon government, therefore, brought about widespread resistance and discontent. For a long time, enforcement of the anti-slavery policy appeared hopeless. Indeed, it succeeded only with the final abolition of slavery in Brazil in the 1880's (although the slave trade sharply declined after 1850).

The Treaty of 1842 between Portugal and Great Britain completely abolished all forms of slave trade in the Overseas possessions of both countries. Enlightened public opinion in Portugal pressured the government to carry out abolition, by declaring all slaves free. This, however, took a long time and required several intermediate steps. Slaves belonging to the state were first emancipated (1854), then those in possession of municipalities, charity brotherhoods (*misericórdias*), and churches (1856). In this same year, another act declared free all the children of a slave mother. The legislation of 1856 liberated all the slaves landing in Portugal, the Azores, Madeira, Portuguese India, and Macao, and abolished slavery altogether in some parts of northern Angola (Cabinda, Ambriz), in order to stop the British claims there. An act of 1858 foresaw total abolition with a twenty-year deadline, but the law of February 25, 1869, reduced it, by declaring an immediate end to slavery in every part of the Portuguese Empire.

There were no more slaves in theory, but some kind of replacement for labor demands had to be found. The act of 1869, like those from 1854 on, kept the old slaves in the condition of freed-men (*libertos*), compelled to give services to their former lords until 1878. This deadline was reduced to 1874 in the Cape Verde Islands and to 1876 in all the other Portuguese Overseas territories. The *libertos* disappeared, yet the *serviçais* (servants) came into existence according to the new code of native labor (1875), regulated three years later. Between slaves, freedmen, and servants differences did exist but in a minor degree. Clearly, total freedom for many Africans was still far away. Moreover, the labor code of 1875–78 (with a new version in 1899 and 1902) was applied to all Africans, following the principle that work civilizes and that in order to Europeanize the Africans one must start by accustoming them to work. A kind of disguised slavery thus appeared, with highly different aspects from area to area. As a matter of fact, the great majority of Africans in Angola, Mozambique, and Guinea continued to live free, forced only to pay a small tribute, but particularly conspicuous was the export of labor to the São Tomé plantations and to the South African mines.

The economic development of São Tomé in the second half of the nineteenth century required more and more handwork. When the condition of *liberto* disappeared, the planters hired free Africans from Sierra Leone, Dahomey, Liberia, Angola, and even China. Gradually, however, Angola's position rose, as the *serviçais* meekly replaced the former slaves and freedmen. Between 1885 and 1903, 56,189 *serviçais* entered São Tomé and Principe. At first they were free and, according to their hiring contract, they could go back home after a certain number of years. Later, the São Tomé planters made it more difficult for them to return and virtually imprisoned them within the limits of the islands. This fact worried both the authorities, who wanted to enforce the anti-slavery laws, and the Angolan settlers themselves, who complained of an increasing labor shortage. The situation of the Angola workers attracted the attention of countries like the United States, Great Britain, and Germany, where a campaign against Portugal was launched. The British planters of the West Indies and several other traders and industrialists, worried about the growing competition of São Tomé's cacao and coffee, operated behind the scenes, grossly exaggerating the violence allegedly inflicted upon the African workers. A British chocolate dealer, William Cadbury, was entrusted with investigating the matter. He went to Lisbon, then to São Tomé and Angola, and published a renowned report, attacking the existing forms of labor hiring and equating them with slavery. Cadbury was followed by several others, like J. Buret, all of them stirring public opinion for a while, leading to Parliamentary debates in London, and calling for a boycott of São Tomé's products.

The Portuguese administration tried to correct some of the abuses which it acknowledged: it promoted the hiring of Africans from other parts (namely from Mozambique) under improved and better controlled contracts; it corrected several injustices and published a new labor code (1909); it ordered an inquiry and a raise in salaries. On the Portuguese side several reports were also published—some by foreigners—contradicting Cadbury's conclusions and praising Portugal's labor policy.

The slave trade after its formal abolition continued to be carried on in Portuguese waters by other than Portuguese vessels. French, British, Brazilians, and some others were guilty of violating the trade ban and were often given chase by Portuguese and English cruising ships. An example of national interests and questions of pride prevailing over justice and international law happened in 1857. The French vessel *Charles et Georges,* indulging in slave trade from Mozambique to the French colony of Réunion, was confiscated by the Portuguese authorities and its captain sentenced to prison. Yet the French government of Napoleon III could not tolerate such on outrage to its flag. By a sort of ultimatum delivered to Portugal, France not only required the restitution of the ship but also the liberation of its captain and the payment of an indemnity. As Britain refused to interfere in a question that could jeopardize her relations with France, Portugal had to yield to the French demands.

The lack of a developed ecclesiastical organization and the shortage of clerics also hampered the Portuguese advance in Africa. To the end of the Monarchical period there were few signs of a missionary revival in the Overseas territories, which in fact simply continued a situation noticeable since the eighteenth century. The decadence of the Church was apparent in Africa or Asia, as in Europe.

There were practically no changes in the number or boundaries of the dioceses, which went back to the seventeenth and sixteenth centuries. On the contrary, the bishop of São Tomé and Principe virtually ceased to exist in 1816, although the diocese was never formally abolished. The extinction of the religious orders, in 1834, was behind the permanent lack of missionaries, in spite of the fact that the picture was already a dismaying one much before. The religious and political quarrels at home (see chapter 10) had their impact on the Overseas possessions too. In the East, the Portuguese rights of the Padroado were constantly violated by the Holy See through the Propaganda Fide organization, simply because the Portuguese were no longer able to promote an effective Christianization of India or China. In 1836–38, Pope Gregory XVI even dissolved several of the traditionally Portuguese-maintained sees in the East. The resistance of the local Christian communities, who stuck to their prelates and traditional organization and rebuffed the Propaganda Fide ministers, created a problem difficult of solution, often with chaotic aspects. It was only in 1857–59 that a Concordat signed between the Holy See and the Portuguese government somewhat eased the situation. The old dioceses were kept but their boundaries were considerably reduced. The Portuguese Patronage was maintained in Goa, Cranganore, Cochin, Meliapore, with jurisdiction over all British India, Malacca, and Macao. Yet the shortage of priests as well as the poor preparation of many of the existing

ones jeopardized the practical application of the Concordat and justified the action of the Propaganda Fide against Portugal. A new Concordat, signed in 1886, further restricted the Portuguese rights in India,
although granting the Archbishop of Goa the pompous but meaningless title of Patriarch of the East Indies.

Some measures to foster missionary activity in Africa had meanwhile been taken. A school for preparing priests to be sent to China
opened its doors in the 1840's at Bombarral. It simply revived an older
college founded in 1791 at Sernache do Bonjardim and closed in 1834.
In the 1850's the seminary of Bombarral was enlarged and granted
more funds, including the building of the ancient Sernache school.
In 1856 the government officially created the Royal College of Missions, aiming not only at China but also at Africa. This date marked
the beginning of a new missionary effort in the Portuguese Overseas
provinces. Gradually, the Royal College was given larger revenues and
its action could expand. Up to 1910 some 317 missionaries had been
educated there and sent to Africa and Asia.

ORGANIZATION

The Constitution of 1822 defined the Portuguese nation as "the union
of all the Portuguese of both hemispheres" (article 20), encompassing
Portugal proper, the Atlantic Islands, Brazil, and the African and
Asian possessions, which were clearly and carefully enumerated.
No distinction was made between whites and blacks, or between Portu-
guese from Portugal and Portuguese born in the Overseas territories.
The legislators of 1822 were obviously thinking of Brazil or India
rather than of Africa. Also, they could argue that most people living in
Angola and Mozambique under the Portuguese flag were indeed
Portuguese, for they were Europeans and a small number of more or
less Europeanized Africans (it must be remembered that only a narrow
strip of territory was then controlled by Portugal both in East and
West Africa). Yet the principle had been established and was repeated
again and again in the future, despite the growing annexation of
African peoples who were thoroughly strange to the Portuguese culture. Similar definitions and descriptions were included in the Con-

stitutional Charter of 1826, the Constitution of 1838, and the two Republican constitutions of 1911 and 1933. Unique in the constitutional history of the European colonizing powers was this indissoluble bond between Portugal and her Overseas provinces, for the nation was considered one and indivisible. Such premises, whatever their theoretical aspect, always have a deep impact on a country's policies and political attitudes. As a part of the constitutional law referring to the meaning of nations, they are most difficult to alter. They can be as sacred and unchangeable as religion itself. Incidentally, the Constitution of 1822 had not been revolutionary about the place granted to the Overseas in the shaping of Portugal. Many official acts and countless writings of the "Old Regime" referred to the provinces of America, Asia, and Africa as a part of Portugal. The absence of rigid constitutional texts, however, made it easier to adjust theory to practice and to shift colonial policies according to each case and to general circumstances.

The legislation of 1820–22 went still further. If all the people living under the Portuguese flag were Portuguese citizens, and if all the Overseas territories were simply provinces similar to those in Portugal, then there was no point in keeping a department to administer the Overseas as a whole. Consequently, all the matters relating to the colonies began to be dealt with by each of the departments of Portugal, together with the Portuguese affairs: Interior, Justice, Finance, War, and Foreign Affairs (Act of 1821). The absolutist reaction of 1823 reestablished the Department of the Navy and Overseas, but the final liberal victory, in 1834, again superseded it.

This utopia, which had brought about a considerable disorganization of the public services in Africa and Asia, came to an end in 1835 (Sá da Bandeira). The Secretariate of Navy and Overseas (*Marinha e Ultramar*) was revived, two "sections" being created within it, one for the Navy, the other for the Overseas (1838). In 1843, the Overseas section was divided into four bureaus (*repartições*)—one for Portuguese Asia; another one for Angola; the third one for Mozambique; and the fourth one for Cape Verde, Guinea, and São Tomé. Budgets were to be organized by the treasury bureau of the secretariate. In 1859, this system gave way to a classification by matters instead of by provinces. Four new bureaus replaced the four geographical ones: the first for general administration; the second for external affairs and colonization; a third for central administration; and a fourth for Public Works, Trade, and Industry. The number of these bureaus was later altered: three only from 1868 to 1878, six from 1878 to the Republic, but with no other structural changes. To assist the Secretariate of the Navy and Overseas the constitutional monarchy re-established in 1851 an Overseas Council (Conselho Ultramarino) which it had disbanded in 1833 (see chapter 8). This Council encompassed a body of experts in colonial affairs and had extensive powers. In 1868, its name was changed to Junta Consultiva do Ultramar, and its powers considerably reduced.

In legislation and its practical application to the Overseas, the nineteenth-century tendency could never get away from an excessive centralization. Laws for the African and Asian colonies would result from the decisions taken in *cortes*. The executive, however, had powers to legislate whenever urgency or the simple interruption of parliamentary sessions required it. Local governors were given emergency powers too (Constitution of 1838; First Amendment to the Charter, 1851), but later acts curbed them so much that Lisbon actually had to be consulted in every respect.

The Portuguese administrative, civil, and criminal codes, as well as other European-type legislation, were applied to Africa and Asia with few adjustments to the local usages and traditions. Similarly with the administrative organization. The acts of 1832 created "prefects" (*prefeitos*) for each of the Overseas "provinces," like those of Portugal, to replace the former captains or captains-general. In 1836, however, things were changed (Vieira de Castro): "general" and "particular" governments (*governos gerais; governos particulares*) were established for the Overseas "dominions," the former encompassing (1) Cape Verde and Guinea, (2) Angola, (3) Mozambique, and (4) India (called Estado da Índia, according to tradition), and the latter (1) São Tomé and Principe Islands (with Ajudá) and (2) Macao and Timor. Governors-general and governors, appointed by Lisbon, ruled them, with no interference in judicial affairs. A council (Conselho de Governo) was to assist each governor-general. This system lasted to 1869, when a new reform (Rebelo da Silva) somewhat increased decentralization by granting the governors larger powers and stimulating local initiatives through the newly created general juntas (*juntas gerais*). This reform mentioned "provinces" again, instead of "dominions," and abolished

UPPER LEFT: *Negro chieftains surrendering to the Portu-guese in the 1898 campaign, Mozambique.* BELOW: *Main Street, Beira (Mozambique), 1895.* ABOVE: *Portrait of Serpa Pinto.*

the general governments. Later changes separated Guinea from Cape Verde in 1879 (first called "province," then "autonomous district" in 1892, then "province" again after 1895), and Timor from Macao in 1863–66 (as "province") and in 1896 (as "autonomous district"). The governors-general were re-established in 1895 for Angola, Mozambique, and Portuguese India. Rebelo da Silva's decentralization policy led nowhere, because further legislation always prevented the governors from actually ruling with autonomy.

Moreover, the turnover in governors always plagued colonial administration during the constitutional monarchy, continuing in fact a very old tradition. In Angola for instance, there were thirty-seven governors from 1836 to 1910 (besides several interim juntas and councils of government), averaging less than two years each. The reasons for such instability were many: Portugal's unstable governments above all, but also the difficulties in ruling with all kinds of local quarrels and problems; the lack of preparation of many governors; conflicts with Lisbon; health and family motives; the slight appeal most colonial capitals had for a European; and so forth. The results were poor administration, lack of continuity, constant change of methods and manners.

The same concern for converting the African and Asian colonies into overseas Portugals caused the creation of "districts" (*distritos*) with several municipalities (*concelhos*) in each one, in the Portuguese manner, even in areas which had just been conquered and where the number of European settlers was minimal. Electoral representativeness existed from the very beginning of the constitutional regime: to the first Parliament, in 1821, seven representatives were elected by the African and Asian territories, one for Cape Verde and Guinea, one for São Tomé and Principe Islands, one for Angola, one for Mozambique, two for India, and one for Macao and Timor. This number of seven was roughly maintained to the end of the monarchy. Obviously, the electors were overwhelmingly white, not because of racial prejudice, but because only whites by and large fulfilled the qualifications for voting (see chapter 10). As a matter of fact, in most cases representatives were simply "appointed" by Lisbon, and often among people who had few connections with the electoral district, rather than being chosen by the white settlers. Yet some exceptions and real electoral struggle could occasionally be noted.

Colonial finance followed the same centralizing principles. Lisbon had the first and final word in allotting funds and collecting revenues. Yet the wish—which some formulated—that the colonies should pay for their own expenditures and even contribute to some of the mother-land's was almost never a reality. Local expenses always proved so huge —particularly when a greater concern with colonial administration and colonial development featured the Portuguese administrations— that, despite the growth in local revenues, there was usually a deficit, which the motherland had to pay. Military expenses, on the rise throughout the whole century, increased the deficit tendency.

Although the reform of 1836 had provided for local budgets for each colony, it was only after 1852 that colonial finance was organized on a regular basis. Finance juntas (juntas de fazenda) were restored in every Overseas province (1837), for the purpose of collecting revenues and paying expenses. In 1888 a new system came into force, which substituted finance bureaus (*repartições de fazenda*) for the juntas, under the control of finance inspectors. The bureaus were a part of the Secretariate of the Navy, and the whole new policy emphasized centralization in Lisbon. By 1898 centralization was further enforced when the finance courts (*tribunais de contas*), recently created in each colony to counterbalance excessive centralization, were discontinued. A General Inspection for the Overseas Finance Services, established in 1900, completed the Lisbon-oriented finance policy.

Analysis of the colonial budgets since the late 1830's leads to in-teresting and highly revealing conclusions. Up to the 1870's, Portu-guese India showed the largest revenues, and often a balanced budget. This was mainly a consequence of taxation of well-organized com-munities where trade played a major role. In India the Portuguese spent little on military affairs and had few internal or external ene-mies. The budget for 1874–75 first reveals the predominance of An-gola in the total revenues, but in 1885–86 India still took the lead. It was only in the 1890's and 1900's that Angola and then Mozambique definitely overtook India. Angola's revenues doubled in the 1870's (263 contos in 1867–68, 281 in 1870–71, 542 in 1874–75, 591 in 1882–83), then doubled again in the 1890's (594 contos in 1885–86, 1,374 in 1896–97), and again in the first decade of the twentieth century (1,677 contos in 1903–4, 2,528 in 1909–10). Mozambique's growth was still more astonishing. Until the 1880's, Mozambique definitely remained behind Angola, although her revenues had increased more than seven times since 1839 (70 contos in 1839, 100 in 1863, 248 in 1874–75, 462 in 1885–86). Afterward, however, and up to 1910, revenues more than decupled, doubling those of Angola when the Republic was proclaimed: 3,592 contos in 1896–97, 3,327 in 1903–4, 5,291 in 1909–10. This was mainly a result of the successful establishment of the "chartered companies," with their regular yearly payments to the treasury. Altogether, the revenues of the Portuguese colonies had increased from a total of 752 contos in 1852–53 to more than 11,000 in 1909–10. In proportion to the revenues of the motherland, the financial position of the Overseas had risen from some 7 per cent to almost 16 per cent, more than double.

As to expenditures, the rule was that they increased faster than revenues. Balanced budgets were only possible for a short time, in the 1870's, when a policy of economy prevailed, but even so neither Angola nor Mozambique ever experienced any surpluses. It was the colonies like India, Macao, São Tomé, or Cape Verde that in the end permitted a total surplus for purposes of political propaganda. Then, in the early 1900's, Mozambique was able to start paying for itself and for the usually huge Angolan deficits. Among the smaller territories, the interesting fact was that while India had increasing problems in balancing her budget from the early 1880's onward, Cape Verde, São Tomé, and Macao were in a satisfactory financial situation. Guinea and Timor were constantly in debt, as well as Angola. The 1909–10 colonial budget showed a deficit of 2,000 contos. Both in revenues and expenditures, Mozambique was in first place, followed by Angola, Portuguese India, São Tomé, Macao, Cape Verde, Guinea, and Timor. Mozambique, India, São Tomé, and Cape Verde could pay for themselves.

Up to the 1850's and even afterward, most of the Portuguese colonial economy rested upon slavery. Guinea supplied Cape Verde, Angola supplied São Tomé, and all of them supplied Brazil; Mozambique exported labor to Transvaal; even Macao derived huge profits from slave shipments to America and Australia. With few exceptions, the estimates of other exports showed poor agricultural or industrial development. This explains why the gradual decline of the slave trade, to its final extinction, jeopardized the development of most

Portuguese colonies and posed the difficult question of restructuring their economies.

Fontism (see chapter 10), and to a certain extent Cabralism before it, attempted in the Overseas dominions, albeit in a much more moderate way, what was being tried at home, i.e., the development of substructures as a means of promoting trade and agriculture. This policy was carried on almost without interruption up to the Revolution of 1910 and then continued by the Republican administrations. In the late 1860's and the early 1870's, however, a concern for economy slowed down state investments in the colonies. In any event, the growth of state expenditures Overseas always depended upon the economic and financial situation in Portugal proper.

Poor communications clearly hampered the economic development of the Portuguese Overseas provinces for a long time. Until the 1860's regular communications between Portugal and her colonies hardly existed. Only with Cape Verde (island of São Vicente) was there a permanent navigation line after 1851, served by the British ships going to Brazil. In the 1850's, the Portuguese government had signed a contract with a French company for the establishment of regular steamship lines between Lisbon and Angola, but with no further consequences. A short-lived Portuguese line (Companhia União Mercantil) did function between Lisbon and Luanda between 1858 and 1864, but failed. From 1864 on the Portuguese government subsidized a British navigation society to carry on ship connections between Lisbon and the West African colonies, which succeeded. The first regular communications with Mozambique and Portuguese India began eleven years later under the same circumstances, a British line being subsidized to take its ships from Lisbon to Mozambique and to Goa, via the Suez Canal. Later on, this same company called at Mozambique ports on its regular run from British India to Durban. In the 1890's, the government subsidized English and German societies to connect Lisbon and Mozambique, via Angola and Cape Town. Macao also began to be served by French and British lines connecting Europe with India and China. As to Timor, no direct connection existed with Lisbon before 1910. Passengers and cargo had to first reach Makassar (in Celebes) before a Dutch line took them to Dili, Timor's capital.

Successful Portuguese navigation companies began only in the

1880's. The Empresa Nacional de Navegação, founded in 1880, started a regular nonsubsidized service between Lisbon and Angola, via Cape Verde and São Tomé and Principe Islands. The same company, this time aided by a government subsidy, established regular connections among the Cape Verde Islands and between them and Portuguese Guinea. Between Lisbon and Mozambique, a regular Portuguese line proved more difficult. It was only after 1903 that the Empresa Nacional extended its navigation lines to Mozambique but depended upon a government subsidy. Two years later, a contract between this same company and the government provided several coastwise lines in all the Portuguese African provinces.

The development of maritime communications went along with better equipment of harbors and other facilities, the building of light-houses, the organization of the customs and the connection of the coast with the interior by means of roads and railways. The most relevant ports were those of Mindelo in São Vicente (Cape Verde), São Tomé, Luanda, Benguela and Lobito in Angola, Lourenço Marques (which gradually superseded Mozambique, up north), Mormugão (Portuguese India), and Macao. Mindelo (also called Porto Grande) was far ahead of all others, with total shipping of more than five million tons in 1908. It was one of the largest coal depots in West Africa called by the navigation lines between Europe and South America. Lourenço Marques came next, with more than two million tons (1910). Sao Tomé reached almost two million tons by the same time. The other harbors had much less, below one million tons.

Connections by submarine cable began in the 1870's, with a cable linking Lisbon to Goa, via Bombay. Contracts between the Portuguese government and British companies gradually connected Lisbon with all of Portugal's Overseas territories (except Timor) during the 1880's. Inside each of the colonies, too, telegraph communications improved much more rapidly than other means of communication.

Railroad building, involving huge capital, many laborors, skilled leadership, and military protection, took a long time to develop and never achieved a satisfactory level. The first rail tract attempted to connect Lourenço Marques with Transvaal, giving northern South Africa easy access to the sea. Begun in 1870, it took twenty-four years to reach Pretoria, although its Portuguese part had started functioning by 1887. It rapidly became one of the most significant railroads in all of Africa. The next railway was built in Goa, relating the port of Mormugão to British India (1881–87), but it could never overcome the competition of other Indian railways. In 1887 a new track began to be built in Mozambique—with the purpose of connecting Beira with present-day Rhodesia—as well as a first one in Angola, from Luanda inland. By the mid-1890's, the Beira railroad had reached the border (some 200 miles), while the Luanda one went as far as Ambaca, 220 miles east. Up to 1910, the Mozambique railway network advanced no further, but in Angola imposing enlargements were in the making. The Ambaca road was getting near Malange (310 miles east of Luanda), a new track from Lobito to Benguela and then east aimed at connecting Angola with the border (200 miles already built between 1902 and 1910), while a third one started at Moçâmedes, heading east too (80 miles constructed between 1905 and 1910). Most of these railroads were built by British firms and with British capital.

The development of internal communications, other than railroads or telegraph, proved a much harder task. Neither Angola nor Mozambique had any road network worth mentioning at the end of the Monarchical period. Whenever possible, rivers made up for the lack of highways. In most cases roads stopped at a short distance from the main towns, and only paths (if any) served as means of communication.

From an agricultural standpoint the great wonder was for a long time São Tomé and Príncipe. This tiny colony, less than 500 square miles in size, economically decadent to the mid-1860's, rapidly improved its status among the other colonies, its public revenues more than trebling from 1863 to 1867, then doubling to 1882, doubling again to 1896 and again in 1903, and nearly doubling again at the proclamation of the Republic. São Tomé's exports had risen from an estimated 18 contos (1842) to more than 8,000 contos (1910) with a positive balance of trade. By the early twentieth century, São Tomé was regarded as a model colony and was proudly displayed to the world as a proof of the Portuguese colonial capacities. This economic "miracle" was attributable to the well-managed coffee and cacao plantations (roças), served by cheap labor and relatively good trade facilities. Coffee (introduced from Brazil in 1800) had taken the lead to the 1890's, and replaced sugar cane as the colony's main product. Afterward, cacao (introduced in 1822) almost completely replaced coffee, reaching 95 per cent of São Tomé's total exports in 1910 and converting the islands into the world's greatest cacao producer. A sort of equatorial botanical garden, the two islands also nurtured many other exotic products like Peruvian bark, vanilla, rubber, cinnamon, clove, cola, tea, cotton, ginger, tobacco, and indigo, most of them introduced throughout the nineteenth century. The plantations and the islands' trade belonged mostly to Portuguese absentee landlords (both individuals and firms), but foreign capital was also well represented.

Agriculture was not equally successful in every other Portuguese colony. In Angola, for instance, despite all the efforts carried on to the beginning of the century, rubber, by far the most profitable export, reached only about one-third to one-half the value of São Tomé's cacao. Mozambique's agriculture, on the rise since the 1890's (oil seeds, rubber, sugar), could not compete with São Tomé's either. Often, the agricultural techniques were extremely primitive, lack of capital and resistance to new techniques preventing any improvements.

The long-standing Mozambique *prazos* (see chapters 7 and 9), thoroughly decadent during most of the nineteenth century, were revived in the 1890's and became productive to the state as well as to the colony itself. Regulations enacted in 1890 and 1896 curbed the exploitation of African labor by the *prazo*-holders and promoted a better use of the land.

Also in Mozambique, the need for a rapid development after 1890 brought about the establishment of chartered companies, some of which acted like states within the state. The example of the neighboring British East Africa Company and British South Africa Company (1888–89) was decisive for the Portuguese ones. In 1888, predominantly British and French capital (£1,000,000 pounds sterling) gave birth to the Mozambique Company (Companhia de Moçambique) chartered three years later. The Mozambique Company was granted extensive powers in central Mozambique, between the rivers Zambezi and Save (62,000 square miles), including administration and police authority. It had a monopoly in commerce, mining, construction, postal services, and the rights to transfer land and collect taxes. It promoted agriculture (rice, cotton, rubber, sugar cane, coffee), trade (5,500 contos in

1899, 8,000 contos in 1907), industry (textiles), and mining activities (salt, diamonds, gold), and was instrumental in developing central Mozambique for more than fifty years. The population of its "capital-city," Beira, rose from about 700 people (1891) to more than 3,400 (1910). The company also built roads and a railroad from Beira to Manica, and considerably improved its harbors. Several smaller companies depended upon it.

The Nyasa Company (Companhia do Niassa) appeared in 1894, with a similar capitalization, British and French in equal shares. It got a royal charter giving it sovereignty over a vast area in northern Mozambique, between the Rovuma and Lúrio rivers (100,000 square miles). With headquarters at Ibo, the Nyasa Company tried to develop its concessions, particularly in mining (iron, coal) but could never compete with its rival farther south. The land was far less developed by any previous European occupation or influence. Native rebellions required army and police activity before any economic progress could be achieved. As a result, the company's total trade did not exceed 1,200 contos in 1905, and declined to 1908, incurring a deficit in its accounts.

Much less privileged was the Zambezia Company (Companhia da Zambézia), founded in 1892 and devoted to the agricultural exploitation of the Lower Zambezi Valley (Quelimane and Tete areas, 60,000 sq. miles). Less wealthy (£600,000) and less independent (the Portuguese government owned one-tenth of the shares and received about 30/100 of the revenues), but also with a much lighter burden, the Companhia da Zambézia had a decisive impact on the development of the area where it ruled, building a railroad from Quelimane to Shire, opening canals and roads, erecting sanatoriums, and fostering mining activities.

Besides these three chartered companies (a fourth one, the Companhia de Inhambane, authorized in 1891, was never constituted), several other societies rose in Mozambique in the 1890's and early 1900's for agricultural (mainly sugar) and mining activities. Some failed but some prospered, and all together contributed to the quick upsurge of the colony's economy. In fact, Mozambique's exports surpassed those of Angola by far on the eve of the Republican movement, while her public revenues displayed the same amazing growth.

Another reason for Mozambique's rapid development after 1890 was the colony's increasing connection with Transvaal and Rhodesia, most of whose international trade made use of either Lourenço Marques or Beira. The international railroads definitely enhanced the position of the two Portuguese cities. In Lourenço Marques, commercial transactions rose from 1,020 contos in 1888 to 27,000 in 1908, of which 90 per cent concerned transit merchandise. By 1910, 57 per cent of the Transvaal external trade used Lourenço Marques, against 32 per cent for Durban and 2 per cent for Cape Town. Several agreements were signed between Mozambique and Transvaal (especially in 1875), then British South Africa (1901, 1904, 1909), for trade and railroad facilities, as well as for the export of African labor. Before the Boer War, an average of 25,000 Mozambique workers were employed annually in the Transvaal mines. By 1903, this figure reached 80,000–90,000.

Nothing of the sort existed in Angola. No developed hinterland made use of its ports and railroads. The colony had to depend on itself exclusively and an upsurge was hampered by a longer tradition of protectionism and old-fashioned economic policy. Shortage of labor (due to export of workers to São Tomé) was coupled with scarcity of capital. Foreign investments came less easily. A chartered company (Companhia de Moçâmedes), founded in 1894 with a predominantly French investment of £570,000, tried to follow in Angola the example of the Mozambique societies but with poor results to 1910. Deficits were registered year after year, and the company related its future success to the completion of the international Benguela railroad.

The economies of the smaller colonies also lagged. Portuguese India could not progress much, owing to the formidable competition of its only neighbor, British India, and it submitted to a situation of almost total dependency. Cape Verde and Guinea stagnated, while the development of Timor to 1910 was too small to be noticed. Only Macao revived after 1845, when the government declared it a free port. Its trade continued to grow (opium, silk, cotton, firecrackers, rice, sugar, tea, wood, tobacco), being larger than that of Angola and rivaling that of São Tomé. Being mostly Chinese and internationally oriented, however, Macao did not mean much either for the state or the Portuguese bourgeoisie.

In the economic and financial development of the Portuguese Overseas territories, the foundation of the Overseas Bank (Banco Nacional Ultramarino) in 1864 had a certain impact. Branches were established in Luanda, Cape Verde, and São Tomé to 1868, and then in Mozambique in 1877. The privileges granted by the government to the bank were several times enlarged, including the monopoly of banknote issues.

The cultural development of all the Portuguese Overseas provinces was slow throughout the nineteenth and early twentieth centuries. Lack of funds hampered all efforts at promoting education, both at the central and the local levels. But often the shortage of money was coupled with a lack of interest in developing the colonies from a cultural standpoint. After all, the number of white settlers was minimal and the concern for the black Africans was nil. And how could it have been otherwise, if the cultural advancement of Portugal itself progressed so slowly and so timidly?

Reforms of education in 1836, 1848, and 1868 tried to do something for the colonies. The act of 1836 even established schools of medicine in each administrative district of the Overseas provinces. Not one ever came into existence. The colonies needed primary schools first before any higher education.

Although statesman Sá da Bandeira—who ruled the Overseas as Navy Secretary in 1835-36, 1837, 1856-59, 1865, and 1870—commended the establishment of primary schools for all the sons of the African chiefs (sobas) and normal schools for the teaching of future African instructors, primary education gained only very slowly in the several provinces. The reform of 1848 provided the fundaments for public primary studies, which in the 1850's were introduced in most colonies.

Secondary education also started in the 1850's; in Goa the first liceu (high-school) was opened. In the other colonies, however, no liceus existed until the 1890's (Macao) and the 1900's. Technical schools appeared in the 1870's in Goa, Angola, and Mozambique, but much later (1900's) in places like Cape Verde and São Tomé. Some more specialized schools had been created in Goa (School of Pilots, 1871) and Macao (School of Pilots, 1862; Nautical School, 1881). In Goa, three normal schools were opened in the 1850's.

As to the university studies, only science and medicine could flourish, and only in Portuguese India. The old Pombaline School of Navy and School of Artillery were combined into a Military Academy, which was reorganized and renamed the Mathematical and Military School in 1841. The first School of Medicine and Surgery (1801) was re-formed twenty years later and then (1842–44) converted into a School of Medicine similar to those of Lisbon and Porto. Attempts to establish Schools of Medicine in Angola, Cape Verde, and Mozambique failed.

As a consequence, scores of young whites, along with some blacks and East Indians, came to Portugal to enroll in primary, high, and upper schools of education at the expense of the government. Many were indeed the sons of influential African and Goans, as Sá da Bandeira had advocated. It has been estimated that between 1834 and 1853 more than one hundred young students from the Overseas enrolled in Portuguese schools. Forty-eight came from Goa.

A printing press developed only very slowly in each of the Portuguese territories (with the exception of India and Macao) throughout the nineteenth century. The first local newspapers appeared, but with little continuity and poor editing. In every colony, the most important paper always was the administration gazette, called "Official Bulletin" (*Boletim Oficial*), which often included general news and even literary subjects. Curiously enough, a timid yet early Black (or Mulatto) African press began in this period: in 1882 a bilingual weekly (*O futuro de Angola*), printed in Portuguese and Quimbundu, made its appearance in Luanda. Local diocesan bulletins and other publications often had a wider readership and a longer endurance than privately owned newspapers and magazines. Up to the early twentieth century Portuguese India, Macao, and Cape Verde clearly led the way in press and literary activity.

In Lisbon, and elsewhere in Portugal, scientific interest in Africa developed considerably in the mid- and late-nineteenth century. In 1851 the government entrusted the Austrian botanist Dr. Friedrich Welwitsch with the mission of studying the flora of Angola, which he did in seven years of fruitful research (1852–59). His counterpart for the fauna of Angola was the Portuguese scientist José de Anchieta, who started his missions to Africa in 1864. The foundation of the Lisbon

Geographical Society (1875) had a decisive impact on the studies of tropical geography, ethnography, anthropology, history, botany, zoology, geology, and other related sciences. The Society fostered by every means an effective knowledge of Portuguese Africa. It helped prepare expeditions. It organized museums and a rich library. It published books, pamphlets, and articles on every aspect of African (and also Asian) science and life. Particularly under the leadership of men like Luciano Cordeiro (1844–1900), the Lisbon Geographical Society reached a remarkable level in the world's scientific associations.

By the late nineteenth and early twentieth centuries, several government-sponsored services were also established to carry on research and knowledge in the Overseas territories. They were particularly active in geology, meteorology, veterinary science, and hydrography. Scientific missions were dispatched to Africa, like those devoted to research and combat of sleeping sickness, where the Portuguese (under Dr. Aires Kopke's leadership) had a world priority. In 1902, an Institute for Tropical Medicine, including a school and a hospital, was opened in Lisbon, quickly ranking among the best in Europe. A school for colonial affairs also appeared in the nation's capital by the early twentieth century.

POLITICAL EVENTS

The political history of Portuguese Africa and Asia throughout the nineteenth and early twentieth centuries was marked by intense diplomatic activity to keep and enlarge the existing territories and no less intense warfare to occupy them permanently.

Up to 1885, no general European policy had been shaped for Africa. Each country with colonial ambitions—England, France, Germany—tried to subdue as much territory as it could, either in "vacant" lands or at the expense of the others. Historical rights, true or false, were often invoked to justify an act of conquest or its counter-defense. Among all the European countries, Portugal in particular followed a historically based policy, simply because Portugal was the weakest of the colonial powers in every respect: military force, manpower, and economic resources.

North of the equator, both the French and the British threatened the Portuguese claims and actual occupation of the coast of Guinea. The island of Bolama was a particular target. The English had landed there once, in the late eighteenth century, returning again in the 1830's. The Portuguese, who had established a small garrison there as early as 1828, resisted and refused to yield. There were several acts of violence from both sides, and in 1860 Britain decided to make Bolama a part of the Sierra Leone Crown Colony. The Portuguese continued to protest, until Great Britain accepted international arbitrage. The American President Ulysses Grant, chosen as arbiter, acknowledged Portugal's rights (1870), and Britain complied.

The French had gradually settled in the Guinea area, and by the late 1820's and the 1830's founded several trade ports along the Casamansa River, which the Portuguese had long considered their territory. An agreement could only be reached in 1886, according to which Portugal gave up her rights in the Casamansa basin (including part of Ziguinchor) in exchange for the French renunciation of the Cacine area.

In the Gulf of Guinea the Portuguese let the French and English advance with little opposition. The Portuguese had only São João Baptista de Ajudá, a useless fortress, and they made no efforts to claim any surrounding territory. In their turn, the French respected Ajudá's Portuguese flag and accepted its inclusion as a tiny enclave in their colony of Dahomey.

Along the coast of Angola, British and French pretensions also threatened the Portuguese interests and led to some loss of effective suzerainty, although Portugal succeeded in keeping most of her claimed territories. The British disputed the Portuguese sovereignty over Ambriz (a good harbor in North Angola) and especially over the mouth of the Congo, including Cabinda on its northern bank. The French had similar pretensions in the Congo area. More precisely, Portuguese rights were questioned between parallels 8° and 5°12' S. Ambriz was an important center for the slave trade, as well as for other commercial undertakings. When the "Septembrist" cabinets decided to occupy Ambriz permanently, after 1839, the British government protested. British ships active in the North Angolan area, under cover of preventing slave traffic, several times attempted to gain the local

Africans to their cause and make them revolt against the Portuguese. In 1855, however, an effective and permanent garrison hoisted the blue-and-white flag and established a firm Portuguese occupation, which the British gradually accepted. On the Congo River, however, the Portuguese were not so lucky, and if they managed to keep Cabinda (where their occupation could not be questioned), north of its mouth, they lost the right to the connection between Cabinda and Angola. Cabinda thus became an enclave in French and Congolese (later Belgian) areas, as it still is.

On the east coast, England and Germany posed the main threats. For a long time England tried very hard to oust the Portuguese from the Lourenço Marques area (Delagoa Bay), realizing the tremendous importance of that harbor for the economic development of interior Africa at the same latitude. The history of European settlement in Lourenço Marques is full of episodes. In the eighteenth century, the Dutch and the Austrians alternated with the Portuguese in sending trading vessels and small garrisons. International debates on Delagoa Bay ownership began in the 1820's: the Portuguese had built a new fortress there and were unwilling to yield to the British, who had replaced both Dutch and Austrians. Again, "diplomatic" activity with the local African chieftains played its role, in an attempt to change allegiances. To make things worse, the local Africans (Zulu Watutsi, called Vátuas by the Portuguese) fiercely opposed any permanent European occupation: they attacked the few Portuguese settlers again and again, beating them badly, killing many, destroying property, and forcing them to leave. Such occurrences made the Portuguese occupation of Delagoa Bay a precarious one and strengthened the British claims to the area. It was only in the 1870's that international arbitrage solved the question: in 1875 the French President, MacMahon, formally acknowledged Portugal's full ownership of Lourenço Marques and the surrounding areas.

In the extreme north of Mozambique the border settlement did not go unquestioned. The Germans had occupied present-day Tanzania (Tanganyika) and decided to hoist their flag on both banks of the Rovuma River. In 1894 they simply landed on its southern bank and replaced with Germans the few Portuguese authorities. Despite the protests of the Lisbon government, they extended their occupation to a sort of triangular area (generally called Kionga) which only World War I would restore to Portugal.

Yet the really big problem for Portugal, and the one where her efforts failed completely, concerned the interior of tropical Africa, connecting Angola and Mozambique.

In the 1870's Great Britain drafted a general plan of colonial expansion which, if carried on undisputed, would give her a foremost position in the world's affairs and destroy the European equilibrium. Germany (under Bismarck) and, to a lesser extent, France (much weakened after the Franco-Prussian war) attempted to check that boundless expansion and to replace it by an international agreement which might establish a new equilibrium in Africa too. For that purpose, an international conference had met in Brussels in 1876.

Officially called a Geographical Conference and summoned by King Leopold II of Belgium, it led to the foundation of an African International Association. This was theoretically a scientific and philanthropic association, organized to promote the exploration and civilization of Central Africa. Practically it implied political goals as well. King Leopold posed as a sort of arbiter of the big powers in conflicts stemming from their greed and competition, with Belgium as a sort of unthreatening competitor of England, Germany, and France. Portugal was not invited, and this corresponded to a deliberate policy of ignoring her pretensions as those of a small and backward country. The Conference of 1876 coincided with Stanley's great expedition to Central Africa. Two years later he became officially engaged by the International Congo Association (*Association Internationale du Congo*), sponsored by King Leopold, which all the European powers (including Portugal) recognized as an independent power with sovereign status in 1884–85.

By that time, the Belgian and French advance in the Congo areas favored a provisional bringing together of English and Portuguese. Under the circumstances, Great Britain acknowledged Portugal's sovereignty to both banks of the Congo River (Treaty of London, 1884), rather than having them fall into more unfriendly hands. Yet Germany, France, and Belgium promptly reacted, which prevented the treaty from being ratified. For the solving of this and other African problems, Bismarck summoned an international conference in Berlin

(1884–85), inviting Portugal to take part in it. On February 26, 1885, the conference drafted a "General Act," which defined "a new colonial public law." According to that General Act, occupation would require the existence of an authority strong enough to enforce any acquired rights as well as freedom of trade and passage. Therefore, effective occupation replaced historical rights. In this way the Berlin Conference invalidated the Treaty of 1884, and forced the Portuguese to display a quick and impossible effort in order to send troops and civil officials to all the areas which they claimed as theirs.

Yet the Portuguese did not give up that easily. From 1885 to 1890 they organized several expeditions and tried to promote the effective occupation of the territories between the two coasts. It was, of course, too late, and the government had neither the funds nor people nor persistence to carry on such a big enterprise. Instead, it became lost in theoretical dreams of establishing a large empire, which, by its very shape, conflicted with the British imperial plans. Cecil Rhodes, active in South Africa at the time, had coined the famous expression "British dominion from the Cape to Cairo," and was the inevitable bitter enemy of Portuguese plans. In 1887, the Portuguese foreign minister, Henrique Barros Gomes, presented to the House of Deputies a map of "Portuguese Meridional Africa" (dated 1886) in which Angola and Mozambique were connected. As the possessions were colored pink, this map became known as the "Pink Map" (*Mapa cor de rosa*).

The "Pink Map" opposed all the British plans, specifically those of Rhodes. Besides the traditional Angola, it designated as Portuguese all the territories south of parallel 11° S. (with a few exceptions) until parallel 18.5°. From meridian 26° (east of Greenwich) east, the Portuguese-claimed lands continued southeast to the Gaza district, in present Mozambique. In current language it gave Portugal almost all of Zambia, Malawi, and Rhodesia.

Meanwhile Portugal had signed (1886) with France and Germany two treaties that regulated the borders in Guinea and South Angola. According to the first one, Portugal lost several territories in the Casamansa River basin, partly compensated by France's recognition of the northern Cabinda border. According to the second one, the southern frontier of Angola was fixed on the Cunene River and the northern

0   600   1200 Km.

0   400   800   miles

Capelo
and Ivens I
(1877-80)

Serpa Pinto II
(1885-86)

Capelo
and Ivens II
(1884-85)

Serpa Pinto I
(1877-79)

frontier of Mozambique followed the course of the Rovuma River. Both borders sacrificed Portugal's interests and claims—namely, the western coast to Cape Frio—to Bismarck's aleatory support of Portuguese inland pretensions.

Throughout 1888 and 1889 the Portuguese made it clear that they intended to start the occupation of their claimed territories. Several expeditions were planned, and Major Serpa Pinto was entrusted with studying the area for a future railroad connecting Lake Nyasa and the eastern coast. Some skirmishes arose between the Portuguese and the Makololo tribes, who claimed allegiance to the British flag. This and other incidents roused in England a vigorous and aggressive press campaign against Portugal. As a matter of fact the British government had always rejected the Pink Map theory and warned the Portuguese cabinet about possible unpleasant consequences of its enforcement. Then too, Barros Gomes' pro-German foreign policy overestimated Germany's willingness to help Portugal against England, and he chose to follow a highly imprudent course. Relations between the two countries deteriorated quite rapidly, and on January 11, 1890, Lord Salisbury's government sent an ultimatum to Portugal requiring the immediate withdrawal of all Portuguese forces active in the Shire area (Nyasaland) and the lands of both Makololos and Mashonas (present-day Rhodesia). The alternative was a break in diplomatic relations, with use of force most probable.

Facing a threat of war, the Portuguese complied with the British demands, and withdrew. For months afterward they tried to have Great Britain accept some kind of international conference or arbitrage to decide the matter, but in vain. As neither Germany nor France showed any wish to decisively interfere, Portugal had to yield to all British requirements. Public opinion at home made things worse, by denouncing England and displaying all forms of resentment and anger. In Great Britain, too, feelings against the Portuguese were high. In Mozambique small incidents between English and Portuguese still embittered the situation.

A first treaty, signed by the governments of both countries in August 1890 (Hintze Ribeiro as Foreign Minister), was rejected by the Portuguese Parliament and by people in general. The government fell and the new Foreign Minister, Barbosa du Bocage, managed to negotiate a six-month *modus vivendi,* which confirmed the British occupation of Portuguese-claimed lands. Only in June 1891 was the final treaty ratified. Slightly worse for the Portuguese interests than the rejected one (which still granted Portugal a strip of land connecting the two provinces), it nonetheless gave Portugal some territories where the Portuguese had never set foot. In May another treaty, this time with the "Congo Free State," acknowledged as Portuguese a new and vast area in Angola, east of the Cuango River (present-day Lunda). Paradoxically, by replacing a well-defined country of nearly 800,000 square miles with a vague, unoccupied, and only historically claimed territory, the treaties of 1891 granted Portugal an empire almost as large as Brazil had ever been under effective Portuguese occupation. And, moreover, they granted it at a time when the number of white settlers and white soldiers did not reach 20,000. In Brazil, at the eve of independence, about 900,000 were whites with more than one million half-breed Europeanized settlers.

Some minor border areas were still disputed for a while. In south Angola, for instance, Barotseland was divided between Great Britain and Portugal by Italian arbitrage, in 1903. Much later, in the 1920's, other border adjustments came into force with the Belgian and the South African governments. The same happened in Guinea, where minor frontier changes took place in the 1890's and early 1900's. But, essentially, the map of Portuguese Africa had been drawn by 1891.

In the Far East, Portugal's problems could be solved more easily. In India, Britain recognized the borders of Goa, Damão, and Diu as defined in the eighteenth century (see chapter 9), never questioning the Portuguese presence there. In Macao, the Portuguese decided to profit from China's weakness during the nineteenth century to achieve full sovereignty over that small possession. A treaty with China, however, signed in 1862, was not ratified by the Chinese. Twenty-five years later, a new treaty met with the same resistance, which happened again and again in 1908 and in the 1920's. To the present, the Chinese have always refused to accept Portuguese full ownership of Macao, although for all practical purposes Portuguese sovereignty was complete from the mid-nineteenth century to the Communist takeover of China.

In Timor, financial difficulties led the local governor to sign a treaty with Holland in 1851 which sold the Portuguese rights to Solor and the island of Flores, located close-by. Although discovered by the Lisbon government, its practical clauses embodied a formal treaty between the two countries, definitely signed in 1859 and ratified a year later. This treaty defined the border between the Dutch and the Portuguese sides of Timor, acknowledging as Portuguese the enclave of Ocussi. Aside from some minor alterations introduced in 1902, Timor's territory has remained the same up to the present.

Border definition did not stop the greediness of the big powers concerning the Portuguese colonies. As shown before (see chapter 10), the Anglo-German convention of 1898 foresaw an economic partition of Angola, Mozambique, and Timor between the two countries in case of a Portuguese foreign loan based upon the revenues of the customs. A secret protocol to that convention mentioned the possibility of a political partition, "in the event Portugal might give up her rights of sovereignty over Mozambique, Angola and Timor, or by any other way lose those territories." Germany would keep Mozambique to the Zambezi River, the southern half of Angola, and Timor, and England the remaining parts of Angola and Mozambique.

However, the outbreak of the Boer War (1899) brought Great Britain and Portugal close together again. England needed Portuguese collaboration and the facilities Mozambique ports offered. By a secret treaty signed at Windsor in October of that year, Great Britain pledged to recognize and guarantee the territorial integrity of Portugal and her colonies, while Portugal undertook not to declare her neutrality and to allow the British troops to pass through Mozambique on their way to Transvaal. When the War came to an end in 1902, Portuguese Africa and Great Britain depended on each other more than ever. As long as Portugal accepted the all-pervasive British economic influence, Britain would guarantee the Angolan and Mozambican borders. Moreover, German imperialism was threatening the British interests increasingly, and obviously Britain would not welcome German growth in Africa at the expense of the Portuguese. Yet a new Anglo-German treaty about Portugal's colonies was signed in 1913, more as a provisional appeasing policy from the side of England than as a real menace to Portugal. Nonetheless, the Portuguese possessions were far from safe on the eve of World War I, the Germans openly uttering their imperialist designs over Angola, Mozambique, and other colonies. Portuguese diplomatic activity was of course never idle, and credit must be given to men like the Marquis of Soveral, foreign envoy to England during Carlos' and Manuel's reigns, or to his successor Manuel Teixeira Gomes after 1911. However, it was the outbreak of World War I and Portugal's intervention on the side of the Allies that definitely saved the African empire for the Portuguese.

The internal history of Angola, Mozambique, and Guinea up to the beginning of the twentieth century was one of constant warfare, marked by the successful, though difficult, Portuguese undertaking of subduing the African tribes. Financial problems at home always prevented a well-planned and well-executed policy of military subjugation. Expeditionary forces often arrived when it was too late, and their preparation and proper equipment were generally questionable. Thus, final victory depended on individual bravery and boldness, rather than on well-organized military action.

Nineteenth-century campaigns in Portuguese Guinea started in the 1840's, sometimes with eventual French help. More systematic operations began only in the 1880's, and from then on, to World War I, almost every year witnessed one or more campaigns against the fierce Papel, Balanta, Fula, Biafada, and Manjaco tribes. Some were sheer disasters, others quite successful, and the Portuguese authority gradually increased. The final conqueror of Portuguese Guinea was Major Teixeira Pinto (1876–1917), who died on the Mozambique front during World War I. Teixeira Pinto, whose score was already high as a soldier in Angola when he was sent to Guinea, directed four campaigns (1913 to 1915), where he cleverly combined field action with sea coverage and native collaboration.

In Angola a state of peace and obedience to the Portuguese flag was achieved for longer periods and with relatively less effort. After some scattered campaigns in the 1850's and 1870's, a major military campaign started in the mid-1880's under the intelligent command of Artur de Paiva (1858–1900). His main expeditions reached Caconda (1883), the Cubango River (1888), Bié (1890), the Cunene area (1892), and Humbe (1897), and were instrumental in achieving Portuguese sovereignty over most of Angola. As a major hero, Alves Roçadas (1865–1926) replaced him, campaigning in the Cuamato region (1904 to 1907). Pacification of the Angolan tribes was necessary again at the beginning of World War I, when the Germans fostered rebellion against the Portuguese. Alves Roçadas and then Pereira de Eça (1852–1917) enforced Portugal's sovereignty once more in 1914 and 1915.

Of the three, however, Mozambique proved, if not the most difficult to subdue, at least the one where military operations had a larger scope and where colonial heroes displayed their greatest deeds. In the south, the Portuguese faced a better-organized African state than anywhere else. The so-called Vátua empire controlled quite a large territory extending over the present south and central Mozambique and Rhodesia. The Vátua supreme and able leader, "emperor" Gungunhana, posed a permanent threat to the Portuguese sovereignty. The Vátuas were helped by the British and the South African settlers with weapons, money, and advice, as a possible means of weakening Portugal's authority and replacing it by the British one.

The Vátuas were not the only danger. To the north, the Islamized African peoples offered fierce resistance too, rebelling when the Portuguese tried to settle and frequently attacking the coastal villages and towns. The conquest of the Angoche sultanate, for instance, cost the Portuguese many lives, and was achieved only by the 1860's, to be lost again and reconquered in 1910. In Massangano, successive expeditions in 1867–69 met with constant disaster. There were destructive African rebellions and raids all over Mozambique up to the 1880's.

Vátua attacks on Lourenço Marques caused much fear in the 1890's. Former Minister of the Navy and Overseas, António Enes, was appointed Royal Commissioner for Mozambique, with extensive powers (1895). An able colonialist and statesman and aided by some first-class advisers, he prepared with great care a systematic campaign against the Vátuas. Under Major Caldas Xavier a first victory was attained at Marracuene. The Lisbon government sent reinforcements under the supreme command of Colonel Eduardo Galhardo (1845–1908). His troops, directed either by himself or by his seconds-in-command Freire de Andrade, Paiva Couceiro, and others, fought gallantly and achieved several much-celebrated victories (Magul; Coolela). A new military district was created at Gaza, and entrusted to Mousinho de Albuquerque (1855–1902). In a daring feat, Mousinho reached the Vátua capital, Chaimite, and arrested Gungunhana (1895), who was brought to Portugal where he died. Some months later, Mousinho de Albuquerque replaced António Enes as governor-general of

Mozambique and continued the military operations. His successors in government and command carried on Mozambique's subjugation in the late 1890's and early 1900's, to the eve of World War I.

In India some petty wars and rebellions also disturbed the Portuguese rule. There, however, rebellions assumed a much more political character, often reflecting the turmoil in Portugal. In the 1850's a new revolt opposed Hindus to Europeans, and only with difficulty could it be mastered. Early in 1870 there was a military rebellion against the newly created "India army," which, among other things, would bring about an increase in taxation. The uprising lingered on for several years and evolved into a sort of petty guerrilla warfare which lasted for awhile. Then, in 1895, a new anti-European movement exploded. The native Mahratta soldiers revolted and kept the colony in turmoil for months. Violent repression followed and only the tactful administration of Governor Joaquim José Machado (1897–1900) could re-establish order. All these rebellions had complex motivations and progressed for a variety of petty reasons. Racial tension came together with fiscal oppression, personal quarrels, and private economic questions.

In Macao, the only military trouble worth mentioning happened during Governor Ferreira do Amaral's administration (1846–49). The governor followed a violent policy which aimed at imposing full Portuguese control of the colony, both from the political and the economic standpoints. His authoritarian and repressive measures led to open rioting and finally to the killing of the governor himself who was assaulted and beheaded. Ferreira do Amaral's death meant the beginning of a general attack by the Chinese on Macao, which only the heroism of Lieutenant Mesquita—capturing with thirty-six men and one artillery field gun a fort manned by several hundred Chinese—could prevent.

In Timor there were several threats of native rebellion but the Portuguese military system was able to master them with few casualties. Governor Celestino da Silva, who ruled Timor for fourteen years (1894–1908), achieved full conquest of the Portuguese part of the island and maintained order with his skilled and progressive administration.

THE FIRST REPUBLIC

THE MAIN PROBLEMS TO BE SOLVED

About six million people were living in Portugal at the time the first Republic was established. The census of 1911 registered 5,960,056; that of 1920 almost the same, 6,032,991. In between, emigration to Brazil and to other American countries had deprived Portugal of nearly half a million inhabitants (not to mention the clandestine emigrants), the highest figure in all Portuguese history up to the 1960's. Moreover, epidemics and World War I took 80,000 lives. Once the war was over and restrictions on free immigration had been imposed by many countries of the New World, the growth rate went up again, with the census of 1930 registering 6,825,883 inhabitants.

This population, predominantly rural, was irregularly distributed from North to South. The agrarian laws of the late nineteenth century (see chapter 10) had improved settlement in regions like Alentejo, but the overwhelming majority of migrants still came from the North and the Northwest and also from Madeira and the Azores, where the density of population exceeded the means for decent survival. Altogether, three-fourths of the Portuguese population lived in the countryside; only one-fourth lived in the towns. And despite the general urban movement, more than half of that 25 per cent lived in two cities: Lisbon (435,000 in 1911, 486,000 in 1920, 594,390 in 1930) and Porto (194,000 in 1911, 203,000 in 1920, 232,000 in 1930). The rise of Lisbon in the 1920's was highly disproportionate to the general growth of

Portugal: 22 per cent against 13 per cent. As the preponderance of the capital did not diminish, the result was a tendency to reduce Portugal to Lisbon and to centralize there every lever of economic, social, political, and cultural life.

Porto's importance mainly derived from its industrial concentration, which was much greater than Lisbon's. The relative affluence and economic power of this northern city were disproportionate to its actual size. The small town of Coimbra was the only exception to the all-pervasive predominance of Lisbon and Porto. Coimbra continued to be a prestigious university city although this monopoly was lost in 1911. It had a greater cultural significance than Porto, although its demographic or economic rise appeared minimal.

The problems of emigration and of Lisbon's excessive growth could not be solved. It is true that, whereas the continuous flow of people to America created labor scarcity and angered social reformers, it also had a favorable side. Year after year emigrants sent back large sums of money, which helped make up the deficit in the balance of trade. Moreover, it acted as a relief valve, preventing widespread discontent, particularly in the rural areas. In those days, there was little hope of diverting emigration from America to Portuguese Africa, because conditions there were altogether unfavorable to a continuous settlement of people interested in rapidly improving their economic status. As to Lisbon's growth, it has continued unabated to the present, fostering an unhealthy centralization of services and economic functions.

Portugal's economic structure was based mainly on the land. Wine, cork, and fruit were the chief products and the chief exports, and the area devoted to the production of each expanded somewhat in the first quarter of the century. Grain, however, continued to be scarce. Therefore, the problem of wheat supply—particularly in Lisbon—absorbed much effort and concerned many governments in the period 1910–26. Both full protectionism and frank liberalism were tried for a while. Protectionism followed the trend which had started with the 1889–99 legislation (see chapter 10). It developed national production but made bread increasingly expensive because wheat prices had to be kept high in order to favor the landowner's interests. Imports from abroad were only permitted when no Portuguese grain was available. Yet the slight improvement in domestic grain production could not cope with the increase in population, countrywide and in Lisbon. More and more wheat had to be imported from foreign countries, and protective legislation was gradually relaxed. The outbreak of World War I disrupted the whole system of trade and revealed the impossibility of continuing the same grain policy. A more liberal import policy had to be adopted in order to provide cheap bread to the people. This, however, made the balance of trade increasingly in deficit. Domestic legislation reflected this situation, contradictory acts appearing from 1914 onward. Wheat imports rose from a yearly average of 70,000 tons, to 184,000 (1916), 200,000 (1921), 160,000 (1923), 150,000 (1925). In better years, these figures decreased, but rarely to less than 80,000 tons, i.e., consistently above the pre-1911 level.

The "bread question," as it was called at the time, was therefore a permanent one. In fact everybody wrote or talked about it. It was linked with many political and social crises, especially in 1917–23. The postwar governments tried to resolve the problem by importing grain directly from abroad and selling it to the mills at a price below its real cost. In this way bread could be provided quite cheaply for a while —the so-called "political bread."

Most of the economic problems—that of bread like so many others —were the result of poor organization of both landownership and commerce, together with a lack of industrialization in Portugal. Virtually no changes had been achieved in the division of property since the "agrarian reform" of the liberal period, except in the trend toward the parceling of units in the North, a result of the 1863–67 acts. It was these holdings, already too small, that hastened emigration. In the South, a small group of large landowners—absentees as a rule—held the best lands, caring little or nothing at all about yield ratio or increase in production through reclamation or technical improvement.

The problem of agrarian reform was of course posed with increasing urgency in a period so rich in discussion as the first Republic. A number of economists and essayists, partly dating from the monarchical era, recommended reforms in credit and taxation, along with widereaching irrigation projects. Among the workers, a socialist policy of property confiscation and redistribution also gained followers. After World War I, the impact of the Russian Revolution and of the social laws enacted all over the world brought about a more precise notion of what should be done in Portugal. The Secretary of Agriculture in 1924–25, Ezequiel de Campos, drafted a proposal for rural reorganization, including the parceling of private property, which he submitted to the Parliament. It got nowhere, because the left-wing government fell and its conservative successors quickly forgot Ezequiel de Campos' revolutionary measures. Some months later, a convention of Rural Workers' Unions met at Santarém and approved a program of complete land socialization. But the final triumph of the conservative forces in May 1926 prevented any practical results from all this debate.

Industry continued to lag much behind agriculture or commerce. It undoubtedly expanded during the sixteen years of the first Republic, but no essential changes were achieved. The country had little iron, little coal, and few other basic raw materials; these had to be imported in increasing quantities. World War I stimulated industrial activity, in Portugal as elsewhere in the world, particularly the production of canned fish (sardines), the exports of which almost doubled from 1910 to 1926. Chemical industries also developed, including soap, cement, and phosphate, the production of which, for example, increased tenfold from 1911 to 1916. In Barreiro, facing Lisbon on the southern bank of the Tagus, industrialist Alfredo da Silva started building up a remarkable industrial complex which in a few years became the largest in Portugal. In Maceira (district of Leiria), another industrial unit of vast proportions based upon cement rose in the 1920's due to industrialist Sommer's efforts. Yet the main Portuguese industry was still textiles, employing about a third of the workers and located mostly in the North. Industrial concentration also developed, for example in the milling industry which supplied Lisbon with bread and other doughs.

Most such industries aimed only at home consumption, including, of course, the colonies. In exports only the sardine industry was significant—actually occupying second place in the export figures for 1926. Except for some cotton, cork, and timber goods, there were practically no manufactured items in the Portuguese outgoing merchandise either in 1900 or in 1930. Iron and steel, industrial and agricultural machinery, coal, cotton and woolen textiles, mineral oils, railway rolling stock, automobiles, and paper ranked among the first twenty articles of Portugal's imports in 1923–25. Yet some signs of greater industrial expansion in the near future were shown by the growing imports of raw cotton (4,736 gold contos on the average for 1903–14, 6,962 in 1926), coal (4,377 to 6,691), machinery (6,613 to 13,522), and other fundamental industry materials. Also, the number of industrial societies and their capital showed an increase. Those whose livelihood depended on industrial activity of some sort (including craft workers) reached 25 per cent by 1930.

External trade thus had to depend heavily on the products of agriculture to assure a viable economy. The kind and the relative place of the main exports hardly changed up to 1930: wine first, three times the value of any other item before World War I and more than double that of the second-ranking item in 1926; then cork (declining in favor of sardines); sardines (rising to second place after the war); cheap textiles (mainly sent to the colonies); and fruit. The main imports, ranked by value, were wheat, textile fabrics (surpassed by machinery after World War I), machinery, raw cotton, coal, codfish (on the rise after World War I), sugar, steel and iron. The commercial balance showed a permanent deficit, which was partly compensated for by the money sent home by immigrants. According to the official statistics, imports generally were twice the value of exports. In any case, the balance of trade deficit appeared huge, particularly in the years 1919–21.

England was Portugal's main client, absorbing 70 per cent of her exports. In imports, however, the situation was more nearly balanced, England's share declining from 26 per cent (1913) to 23 per cent (1924). English ships entering the Lisbon and Porto harbors also carried a heavy share of Portugal's external trade: in 1924–25, more than one-fourth of the total tonnage was British, four to one over the Portuguese.

British, French, German, and Belgian investments in Portugal also controlled a large part of the industrial, trade, banking, and transport activities, as they had been doing for a long time (see chapter 10).

The communication and transport system was not always adequate to the country's needs, accounting for some of her economic difficulties. True, the railway network had increased since the early 1900's: 2,974 km. in 1912 and 3,282 km. in 1924, one-fourth of which were state-owned. Yet, judging by the standards of those days, railroads had not kept pace with progress. Only 300 km. were double-tracked, no electric lines existed, and the rolling stock was not in first-class condition, despite the government's efforts to acquire better materials. Roads had very much declined since Fontes' days, mainly because of the development of railways and the stress on trains rather than on carriages. The economic crisis of the 1890's further prevented the carrying on of Emídio Navarro's plans. When automobiles and—later on—trucks were first introduced in Portugal, roads were in poor condition, and they became worse up to the 1920's. The state of the roads, indeed, merited the bitterest protests, and pressure was put on the governments to do something toward their repair. An important plan, submitted to the Parliament in 1922, led nowhere. After 1924 more credits began to be voted, but very little had actually been achieved by 1926. Despite this, however, the road network increased from 11,000 km. in 1910 to 13,000 km. ten years later, mainly a result of municipal activity.

Motor cars and trucks were imported in increasing volume from Europe and the United States, particularly after World War I. There were some 6,500 automobiles in 1924 and double that number in 1927. Long-distance hauling by trucks could not develop properly because of the poor road system, but interurban bus transportation increased. In northern Portugal about eighty bus lines were in operation by 1926 out of such towns as Porto, Braga, Viana, Aveiro, and Coimbra. In southern Portugal about fifty lines were in operation, mainly for short distances. Inside Lisbon and Porto, however, the only passenger transportation continued to be the streetcar. A subway was planned for Lisbon, but never materialized. The telephone and telegraph networks also expanded greatly in the 1920's: the number of places served by phone lines in 1927 was four times that of 1924.

Even worse was the situation of the seaports. Portugal's main harbors—Lisbon, Porto, Leixões—lacked up-to-date accommodation for trading and for communications with the other European countries. This prevented a greater volume of traffic with America from being handled at Portuguese ports. The local "autonomous Juntas" (Juntas Autónomas), established after 1910 for the purpose of undertaking public works of several kinds, generally failed for lack of funds, which the state was also in no condition to provide. Yet some minor improvements, particularly in the Leixões port, could still be achieved. Coastal shipping partly compensated for the deficiency in internal means of communication.

The Portuguese merchant marine showed some signs of prosperity, particularly after 1916, when the taking over of seventy-one German and Austrian ships sheltered in Portuguese harbors suddenly increased the tonnage from 73,000 to 307,000. Of those ships, however, twenty were ceded to England while thirty others were lost because of the war. With the remaining twenty, the government created the state-owned merchant marine (Transportes Marítimos do Estado), which operated for a few years. The experiment, however, was premature. Poor organization and private pressure led to an almost complete failure. The ships were finally sold to capitalist societies in 1926.

These societies, including six large ones, continuously improved their services and the tonnage of their ships. All of the Portuguese Empire, to remote Timor, could be reached through them. Two acts of 1921 favored the Portuguese over foreign maritime vessels by establishing flag discrimination, rewards for shipbuilding, reduced taxation, and other advantages. In 1925, with similar measures, another government decree protected and stimulated Portuguese navigation between the Azores and Madeira Islands and the ports of northern Europe. By 1926 Portuguese ships from Lisbon reached a number of ports in Belgium, Holland, Germany, and France. In this way, new prospects for the country's merchant marine opened up, and the situation of 1920 (when 87.8 per cent of the total imports and 89.4 per cent of the exports were carried in foreign ships) gradually improved.

Financial equilibrium was a primary problem in the country's political life. Surplus in the public accounts had been impossible to achieve since the early nineteenth century (see chapter 10), and one of the Republican party's main goals in its attack on the Monarchy was balancing the budget. After 1910 public finance gradually improved, and the coveted aim was at last a reality under Afonso Costa's severe and able management of the state's moneys. Parliament voted the "brake-law" (lei-travão), according to which no deputy or government minister might propose any law that brought about a decrease in the public revenues or an increase in the public expenditure once the budget was being discussed. Final accounts for fiscal years 1912–13 and 1913–14 showed surpluses, respectively, of £117,000 and £1,257,000, a result of reducing expenditure considerably. Afonso Costa also attempted some fiscal reforms aiming at a rise in the public revenues, but in this he failed.

His immediate successors in government were not able to carry on his work. The outbreak of the war posed the whole problem again. Even before actually joining the Allies, Portugal had to send troops to Africa, which weighed heavily on the budget. Afonso Costa's return to the secretariate of finance (1915–17) did not result in new balanced budgets. War had been declared (March 1916), and total disaster for the public accounts was in the making. The years 1917–18 and 1918–19 were those of heaviest expenditure, although revenues substantially increased because of war taxation. The budgets of 1920–21 to 1922–23 saw a constant decrease in the public revenues, owing to the debasement of the currency. Receipts in 1922–23 reached only one-third of what they had been in 1919–20 and little more than a half of the prewar figures. A severe compression of expenditures brought the figures to less than they had been under Afonso Costa's strict control of finance.

From the standpoint of a balanced budget, the situation improved in 1923–24 to 1925–26. Premier António Maria da Silva had a taxation reform voted in Parliament (1922) which, first tentatively, then definitely after 1924–25, put up the state's revenues to a level comparable to that in the prewar period (£12,063,000). Debasement stopped altogether in 1924. Expenditure, too, after a year of severe contraction, in 1923–24 (£8,305,000), rose to more acceptable standards in 1924–25 and 1925–26. In this year the deficit was minor.

Regular public debt, on the other hand, hardly increased. In pounds sterling, the Republican governments were able to reduce the debt from £137,668,000 (1910) to £114,685,000 (1916). The war raised it again to £140,455,000 (1919); but the debasement of the currency, now acting as a deterrent, had lowered it to £68,344,000 (1924). In the following two years it rose again a little.

War debts, of course, followed another trend. They reached £22,-000,000 in 1925, all of it to England. The usual attempts by every allied country to make Germany pay led nowhere. It was only in the

1930's that the problem could be solved, but in an entirely different way (see chapter 13).

Regarding currency, the Republic started by making thorough reforms in an attempt to put the Portuguese unit on the same footing with other countries of Europe and avoid the disadvantages of too small a unit (the real). Thus, the escudo was introduced (1911), with the value of 1,000 old réis, subdivided into one hundred centavos. The act of 1911 established gold coins of 10, 5, 2, and 1 escudo (which were never minted); silver coins of 1 escudo; 50, 20, and 10 centavos; and bronze coins of 4, 2, 1 and $\frac{1}{2}$ centavo (the latter one never minted either).

Problems with the new currency started shortly afterward. The official value of 1 gold pound $= 4.5$ escudos could never be maintained (parity with the 1,000 réis had already dropped before the Republic) and debasements had reached 17 per cent when World War I began. The escudo went down to 6.34 to the pound (1915), 6.88 (1916), 7.37 (1917), 7.85 (1918), 7.54 (1919). Coins were short in the market, particularly in the smaller denominations, which led to many locally issued slips of paper and stubs. The lack of available metals brought about new coins with cheaper alloys, including iron. Silver coinage ceased altogether after 1916, with paper money becoming all-pervasive for many years.

The governments paid their rising budget deficits with bank notes, the circulation of which grew immensely, particularly in the 1920's. The amount of the Bank of Portugal notes in circulation early in 1926 was about £18,500,000, equivalent to the total sterling value of the currency of Portugal in 1914. In nominal values, fiduciary currency went up from 78,071 contos in 1910 to almost ten times that value in 1921, and to 1,820,899 contos in 1925. Yet, regarding the debasement of the escudo, the bank notes in circulation had actually risen from £17,349,000 (1910) to only £53,130,000 (1920), and then dropped to £25,236,000 (1921), £15,467,000 (1923) and £16,114,000 (1925), i.e., less than the prewar level. Thus the fall in the value of the currency was notably greater than the increase in the nominal value of the notes in circulation, in spite of the fact that prices had increased. This brought about a general decline in the internal and external purchasing power of the Portuguese people.

From 1919 to 1924 the value of the escudo dropped almost twenty times, its par to the pound going down from 7.54 (1919), to 11.54 (1920), 29.23 (1921), 45.78 (1922), 91.70 (1923) and 127.40 (1924). Several government acts put in circulation bronze and nickel coins which formerly had been in silver: 1 escudo, 50, 20 and 10 centavos, besides a new 5 centavos one. The smaller denominations disappeared altogether.

In 1924, Premier Álvaro de Castro was able to stop the ruin of the escudo. All over Europe a return to more normal times and stability permitted the gradual end of currency debasements. By a number of strict control measures and by the sale of vast amounts of silver which were kept in the National Bank, the government could fix the value of the escudo, which even improved in 1925 and 1926 (127.40 to the gold pound in 1924, 113.03 in 1925, 94.74 in 1926). The legislation of 1924 also reformed coinage by increasing alloy again and reducing the real value of the coins. Attempts were also made to get rid of paper bills for the smaller denominations.

One of the reasons for the inflationary tendency should also be looked for in the continuous transfer of capital abroad. After 1910, members of aristocratic or upper bourgeois families migrated or chose foreign banks (especially English) as a safe place for their deposits. This flight increased after the war. The amount of pounds sterling accumulated by Portuguese citizens abroad was estimated at about eight million, i.e., more than six times the total monetary circulation (mid-1920's). Besides, some one or two million pounds were in Spain for the smuggling of cattle, wheat, and salt. The large quantity of gold hoarded by the people—particularly in the countryside—should also be considered. Indeed, the Republic was never able to get support from the rich. It also did little to prevent the export of capital. It is not surprising, therefore, that the gold reserves of the National Bank constantly declined. Around 1925 they were among the lowest in Europe, but the worst period had already passed.

The world economic crises of course had their impact on Portugal too; however, the local crises often affected the country more than the general ones. Thus, the crisis of 1913–14 (that ended with the beginning of the war) was felt moderately in Portugal. Nonetheless, at least two banks closed their doors, while a rise in unemployment led to social disturbances, which were behind Afonso Costa's downfall early in 1914. World War I came along to solve the problems and bring about a general expansion of trade and industry after the first half of 1915. Yet it caused other and much worse economic and social dislocations, owing to the shortage of food, the inflation, the revolutionary activity, the state control of the economy, and so on.

In 1919–20, once the war was over, there was a boom in Portugal as almost everywhere else. The wine, cork, and sardine trade expanded. Excessive expenditures on luxuries were the inevitable result of the wartime scarcity. Imports increased. Eleven new banks opened their doors, a clear sign of capital affluence. When the boom came to an end, a new international crisis, that of 1920–22, soon spread throughout the country. As in Germany and elsewhere, it persisted through 1923, 1924, and even 1925, with a deep impact on Portugal's life. Money debasement and speculation characterized the first years. The discount rate of the National Bank rose from 5.5 per cent to 6 per cent (July 1920), then 6.5, 7, 8, and finally 9 per cent (September 1923), a rate which did not change for almost three years. The interest rate on treasury bonds also rose from $4\frac{3}{4}$ per cent to 5 per cent (July 1920), then successively up to 11 per cent (March 1924). Some fifteen banks went bankrupt. This severe depression, coupled with rising social and political disturbances, meant death for the Democratic Republic in May 1926.

The religious question hovered over Portugal during this whole period. At the beginning of the century, the Catholic Church had reorganized its forces in most countries after a long period of decay and had begun to launch a wide-reaching offensive against atheism and Christian apathy in their varied forms of expression (free-thinking, scientism, tolerance, republicanism, democracy, socialism). The first Vatican Council (1869–70) reasserted the traditional principles of the Church, underlined Papal centralization, and set up the bases for the struggle against "modernity" and its evils. A wave of piety led to the rapid spread of new devotions, new saints, and new religious orders primarily aiming at charity and education. It was this revival of the Catholic Church as a fighting body, not the contrary, that brought about a counteraction of violent anticlericalism, especially in France, Italy, and Portugal.

Despite the confiscation laws of 1820–34, the Portuguese Church persisted as a powerful force. The secular clergy had hardly been affected by the legislation against the orders. It continued to own property both in the towns and in the countryside. It had a part in commercial, industrial, and financial enterprises. Moreover, many religious orders had returned in a disguised way—see chapter 10—and joined forces with the secular clergy in restoring the Church's strength and influence. In the field of culture and education, the Church possessed the seminaries which provided free secondary education throughout the country, mainly to the poor. In 1910 there were in Portugal a dozen seminaries, with a total enrollment of several thousands. For the wealthier classes, the Church owned several schools (some of them excellent), which were highly fashionable among the middle classes and the aristocracy. It also controlled a few centers of research, and several newspapers and magazines. In charity, the Church influence was everywhere present through hospices for children and aged people, hospitals, and food distribution to the poor.

The Church revival of the late 1800's and early 1900's was particularly felt by the upper classes. In Portugal, the Church controlled the majority of the nobles, as well as the court, through the person of dowager-queen Amélia, who was deeply religious and devout.

Among the newly introduced religious orders, the Jesuits were predominant in influence (though exceeded in number of houses by the Franciscans, the Dominicans, and the Dorotheas; the latter, however, were under the Jesuits' control). By 1910 the Jesuits owned, both in Portugal and Overseas, more than twenty houses (eleven in Portugal alone) with 386 members. They had organized, and strictly controlled, a lay association with religious purposes called Apostolado da Oração, which in 1909 had 1,500 centers in Portugal with more than two million members. Operated by them or under their control were a dozen schools—among them the two foremost colleges of Campolide (in Lisbon) and São Fiel (in Beira Baixa)—with a total enrollment of more than 2,500 pupils. They directed a famous scientific and literary review called *Brotéria*. They had even helped organize a political party, the Nationalist Party, where their influence was all-pervasive; this party won some seats in Parliament after 1904.

Against the Church, the Republican Party organized a formidable offensive. By any and all means—including calumnies—it tried to convince the masses, as well as the élites, of the dangers of clericalism in a modern society. Books, newspapers, pamphlets, public speeches, and other methods were used to spread atheism (or at least a nonclerical Christianism), scientism, socialism, and other doctrines, along with well-chosen historical "facts" that denounced fanaticism, Jesuitism, the Inquisition. The Republicans also stressed the alliance between Church and ruling oligarchies, thereby managing to join together anticlericalism and antimonarchical feelings. In the towns, especially in Lisbon and Porto, this propaganda found fertile soil and became an effective combat weapon.

Once proclaimed, the Republic identified itself with the fight against the Church. All religious orders were again expelled (1910); the Jesuits particularly were humiliated and sometimes treated as criminals. In a few months all friars, brothers, nuns, and sisters had left the country or had been forced to disavow their habits. Religious houses, colleges, and charity centers were all closed down, their property passing to the state. This time, however, the anticlerical laws affected the secular Church too. Closely following the French legislation of 1905, an act of April 1911 separated Church and state in Portugal, declared religion altogether free (till then some restrictions affected the non-Catholic faiths), forbade the teaching of Christianity in all schools and teaching in general to the clerics, nationalized Church property (including churches, chapels, and their belongings), and strictly controlled every cult manifestation. All over the country, special committees in charge of the religious services were promoted. The wearing of long habits, which had no tradition in Portugal, was forbidden outside the churches, as well as any processions or other public religious displays which might provoke some disturbance. The state lent the Church for cult purposes all the temples. Bishops' and priests' dwellings were kept for their provisional use. Only five of the existing seminaries were left to the Church. All state expenses for religion were abolished both at the central and the municipal levels, but the law provided permanent allowances to the priests who asked for them. Papal bulls and similar documents could not be made public without the government's approval.

The Separation Law of 1911 had been preceded by some other

acts which clearly showed the anticlerical policy of the new regime. Thus, official religious oaths, including those taken in schools, were abolished; Catholic holidays were suppressed; and civil registry (Registo Civil), i.e., compulsory recording of births, marriages, and deaths by state officers instead of by priests in the churches, was decreed for all.

Along with a law introducing divorce for everyone, these measures caused general discontent within the Church ranks. Already, on Christmas Eve, 1910, the Portuguese bishops met together and issued a collective pastoral letter which was made public late in February 1911. They protested against the suppression of the religious oath, the abolition of church holidays, the expulsion of the orders, the law of divorce, the projected extinction of the School of Theology, the prohibition against teaching religion in the schools. The government promptly forbade the priests to read the pastoral letter in the churches. Many, however, defied the authorities, particularly in the North. The bishop of Porto was found guilty of encouraging disobedience among his subordinates, and was deposed.

Throughout 1911, 1912, and 1913 the religious struggle went on. Most priests gave up their right to state allowances, less than 20 per cent actually accepting them. The government charged the bishops with pressuring the priests to refuse those pensions and also to "strike" in their religious functions. All over the country, Catholics and anticlericals opposed each other, often to the point of violence. The patriarch archbishop of Lisbon, the bishops of Guarda and the Algarve, the new governor of the diocese of Porto, and finally all the remnant bishops were punished with a two-year banishment from their bishoprics. The bishop of Beja had to leave the country and was finally deposed too. Pope Pius X tried to interfere (bull *Jandudum in Lusitania,* 1911, confirmed 1912), but the government forbade the public reading or spreading about of his words. The legation in the Vatican was closed, and diplomatic relations with the Holy See were broken (1913). In October 1913 the International Congress of Free-Thinking solemnly met in Lisbon, with wide publicity.

It is true that the anticlerical laws displeased the majority of the people, particularly in the North. However, this meant little, for the majority were idle, passive, illiterate. Most of the active population, especially in the towns—and most particularly in Lisbon—welcomed the antireligious policy as theirs. They had made the Republic and they were supporting it. They justified the government's anticlericalism and made it popular among the town masses.

Yet the need for a smoother situation that would end the open war between the Church and the Republic was felt by everyone. Premier Bernardino Machado talked on behalf of it and acted in that direction by reinstating the bishop of Porto and granting an amnesty to all the priests found guilty of defying the government's orders, while the Separation Law began to be discussed in Parliament (1914). The Catholics, in turn, organized themselves better and realized the uselessness of a violent struggle as before. By 1912 the framework of a Catholic party was revived in Coimbra under the name Academic Center for a Christian Democracy (Centro Académico de Democracia Cristã), a group existing in the old days of the Monarchy but virtually inactive afterward. Its leaders were young and able students and scholars, among them the future statesman Oliveira Salazar. Other Catholic circles formed here and there, while the Catholic press acquired better management and a more clever combat attitude. The elections of 1915 brought the first Catholics to the Chambers. Some religious orders returned to Portugal in a very disguised way, the first ones being the Dorotheas, in 1916.

The outbreak of World War I and Portugal's intervention after 1916 made easier a revival of the Church influence. Public opinion forced the government to grant religious assistance to the soldiers. Bernardino Machado, elected President in 1915, tried to restore diplomatic relations with Rome. The Church also sought new weapons for achieving its goals: it allied with the most conservative Republican elements, as well as with the Monarchists, exploiting discontent aroused by less popular measures and by the economic crises. It strengthened and developed important contacts with the representatives of high finance, trade, and industry. And it sought new methods of stimulating faith and reconquering souls. In May 1917 the Church or some of its local elements possibly prepared—and certainly explored —the so-called Fátima apparitions, which soon had a great impact on the masses and caused an upsurge of devotion. In October of the same year, the last "apparition" took place, exactly at a time when the anticlerical elements were launching a new wave of persecution and punishment. The Church felt strong enough to defy the government once more. As a consequence, the bishops of Porto, Lisbon, Braga, and Évora were temporarily dismissed again.

The installation of a conservative and proclerical regime (December 1917) brought peace once more to the Portuguese Church. The deposed bishops were reinstalled, the Separation Law was finally revised, and diplomatic relations with the Vatican were re-established (1918). Five Catholic representatives entered Parliament. The return to power of the radicals in 1919 did not change things. The trend pointed now to a compromise between Church and state, just as the epoch pointed to a revival of Christianity and a decline of anticlericalism. President António José de Almeida even placed the cardinal biretta on the apostolic nuncio, in the manner of the old Portuguese kings (1923), while a radical Secretary of Education (Leonardo Coimbra) dared to propose to Parliament the reintroduction of religious teaching in the schools. More orders continued to return to Portugal —including the Jesuits—albeit always in a disguised way. Catholic representatives entered Parliament in every election. Things had obviously changed.

Among the essential points that the Republican Party had inscribed in its program was the relevant role of the family. It defended freedom for women and legal protection for children. It supported some of the most advanced principles being commended in speech and writing, if not in actual legislation, all over Europe and America.

In Portugal, as in most Mediterranean countries, women were in a backward condition; their rate of illiteracy (for those over seven) was 77.4 per cent, according to the 1911 census. Plunged into ignorance, women were an easy prey for fanatic priests, witches, clairvoyants, charlatans, and demagogues—a dangerous force acting behind the scenes in their influence on husbands and children and a permanent vehicle of resistance to progress. This fact was clearly realized by social and educational activists, who, by a slow yet persistent campaign, endeavored to promote the gradual emancipation of the female sex. A small group of clever and well-educated women helped them and strove for the same goal with still more determination and knowledge. The Republican League of the Portuguese Women, founded in

1909, played a remarkable role for that purpose, despite its small membership (less than five hundred in 1910). Its main leaders (Ana de Castro Osório, Adelaide Cabette, Maria Veleda) should not be forgotten in their efforts to create a new Portugal, open to modern ideas and closed to the traditional dictatorship of the male sex. According to its statutes, the League wanted new laws about the woman, the wife, and the child; it wanted equality of rights between husband and wife, economic autonomy for the wife, equal rights before the law, and the establishment of divorce, besides a whole program of education for the female sex. Once the Republic was proclaimed, the League fought for women's suffrage. Some women even wanted military service to be compulsory for both sexes.

The new regime brought about a number of interesting and highly progressive laws. The act of November 3, 1910, allowed divorce for all couples, regardless of the form of their wedding, and considered husband and wife as equal in respect to the causes and the results of divorce. Two acts published on Christmas Day, 1910 (which the Republic had renamed "Day of the Family") made civil marriage compulsory for all, granted equal rights to both sexes in marriage, and protected the legal rights of children (in cases of legitimacy, adoption, and illegitimacy). The first woman university professor—Carolina Michaëlis de Vasconcelos—was appointed in 1911. The electoral law of 1911 neither forbade nor permitted women voters, which enabled one female doctor to demand her enrollment and be accepted as a voter. Yet the new electoral law of 1913 promptly denied the vote to women; this was granted only in 1931 and then in a very limited way.

All over the world, the development of the industrial society was accompanied by social ferment. In Portugal, too, despite the moderate aspects which capitalism showed there, the first quarter of the twentieth century was a period of turmoil. The strike movement was on the rise when the Republic triumphed over its adversaries. The Republicans, who had succeeded in getting popular support by attacking capitalist exploitation and by defending a new order based upon work and justice, were now forced to fulfill some of their promises. Indeed the Provisional Government very soon proclaimed the right to strike (December 1910), albeit after the workers had already embarked on a strike movement without precedent. In the two last months of 1910 and throughout 1911, scores of strikes shook the country, involving workers of all kinds, both blue- and white-collar: railroad employees, telephone operators, masons, streetcar employees, stevedores, cork industry workers, bakers, shoemakers, salesclerks. A large percentage of the strikes affected rural workers. The motives for striking involved salaries (in about half the cases), but also sympathy with other strikers, working hours, etc. A majority succeeded in their objectives; many were solved by compromise; and a few had to accept defeat. Lisbon and her suburbs were of course the favorite areas, but the strike wave touched all of Portugal and even the islands of Madeira and the Azores.

This sudden social agitation caught most people by surprise, particularly the bourgeois elements. If it reflected, above all, the poor condition of most workers and their struggle for a better standard of living and more reasonable working-hours, it also suggested the rising force of the unions and their coordination with the workers' international movement. As time went by, it clearly revealed the divorce between the republican governments—controlled by the bourgeoisie—and the workers' aims.

As early as 1911, much of the sympathy previously accorded the blue-collar workers by the petty bourgeoisie was fading in view of the ever-increasing wave of strikes, which bourgeois public opinion regarded as untimely and favoring the enemies of the Republic. From then on, the gulf between the bourgeoisie and the proletariat continued to broaden, a fact that plunged the workers into a widespread opposition to the regime and led them to strange alliances with Monarchists and right-wing elements. And as the number of workers was relatively small—only some 100,000 real proletarians by 1910—in comparison with the bourgeois active population of Lisbon and Porto, one can easily understand why the workers' demands had little chance of full achievement and why the threat of a social revolution could never reach the level it did in other countries.

Yet the several administrations tried hard to solve or at least to lessen the social problem. In the framework of a noninterventionist, liberal state, the governments could do little, but they did what they could.

Secretary António José de Almeida (Interior) proposed, early in

1911, a law limiting the work week to six days and regulating the hours of work per day but only the former provision was enacted. Practically nothing else was achieved, and there was extreme violence throughout 1912 and 1913. Isolated strikes did lessen (35 in 1912, 19 in 1913); but organized labor action developed and managed to launch the first general strike (January 1912), which led to the declaration of a state of siege in Lisbon, the closing down of the workers' main seat (Casa Sindical), and the arrest of hundreds of people. Workers' conventions and Anarchist organization (paradoxical as it may seem) filled the years 1911 to 1914 with assertions of growing strength, social hatred, anti-government actions, and frequent bomb-throwing. Afonso Costa's government, while trying to appease discontent by enacting a quite progressive law on labor accidents (1913), repressed labor demands and persecuted many workers. The years that followed were relatively quiet, but had some important features. The workers of all Portugal, to start with, united in the National Workers Union (União Operária Nacional, 1914), in close contact with the international organizations. The Azevedo Coutinho Democratic government finally enacted a law (January 1915), which regulated the working hours: 7 for offices and banks, 8 to 10 for factories and workshops, 10 for commercial stores with a 2-hour break for lunch. In 1916 a Secretariate for Labor Affairs (Ministério do Trabalho e Previdência Social) came into existence.

Portugal's intervention in World War I signaled another period of social turmoil, which lasted to the end of the Democratic Republic. Opposition to the war and the rising cost of living set off a new wave of strikes in 1917, with a general strike in Lisbon, open fighting, arrests, and persecutions. Afonso Costa's third cabinet tried to get some support from the workers for his government's war effort. In a speech of July 1917 for instance, he showed his sympathy with the class struggle and his leaning toward Marxist theories. He also condemned the employers' exploitation of the workers and realized their need to strike. Yet there was little that either his government or his followers could do to solve the problem. Salary raises did not keep pace with the ever-rising cost of living and the debasement of currency. In real figures, for instance, civil servants were being paid in 1917 61.6 per cent of prewar wages, a percentage which declined further to 1920–21.

The governments of 1918 to 1920, threatened by the rising social disturbance, adopted several measures on behalf of the workers and lower civil servants, which, on the one hand, seemed too timid to appease discontent and, on the other, helped jeopardize the traditional support of the middle bourgeoisie to the regime. A series of laws in 1919 fixed a maximum of 48 working-hours per week for most blue- and white-collar workers and 42 for banks and offices, established compulsory social insurance for all employers (in case of illness, accident, old age) and established an Institute of Social Insurance. At the same time housing for workers was instituted on government initiative.

Wages, however, continued to be low. Middle civil servants saw their real salaries decline to 35.8 per cent (1918), 22.6 per cent (1920) and 22 per cent (1921) of the prewar level. Lower civil servants were in a somewhat better condition: 54.6 per cent (1918), 50.5 per cent (1919), 65.2 per cent (1920), 76.5 per cent (1921). Industry and trade workers, too, saw their efforts rewarded by improvements of the situation. This was the result of both the powerful organizations they had managed to build up and the permanent striking movement. Indeed, the strong Labor General Confederation (Confederação Geral do Trabalho) had replaced the U.O.N. after 1919, its control of the workers' movement being widely spread. As in Spain the Portuguese C.G.T. was anarchist in doctrine, repudiating political communism and subordination to Moscow. In 1924, by an overwhelming majority (104 syndicates out of 115), it voted its affiliation to the anarchist Workers' International Association.

Social agitation after 1919 appeared also in the form of bomb-throwing, individual clashes and killings, often with a political flavor. Despite the official workers' position of neutrality in the political struggle, considered a "bourgeois" affair, countless white-collar and blue-collar workers took part in the several revolutions that shook the country throughout the whole republican period.

The strike movement showed very few signs of abating. Although the actual figures fluctuated (21 strikes in 1919; 39 in 1920; 10 in 1921; 22 in 1922; 21 in 1923; 25 in 1924; 10 in 1925), strikes continued to be a permanent problem. General strikes were declared in 1919, 1920, and 1921, but only the first one met with some success. It is interesting to note that wage and working-hour objectives declined to only about

52 per cent of the cases (60 per cent in 1910–11), while sympathy strikes rose from 17 per cent to 24 per cent. These figures show that some of the workers' grievances had lessened, but also that their class consciousness had increased. Partly because of this, actual triumph could only be reached in 27 per cent of the strikes, whereas 44 per cent had succeeded in 1910–11. Compromise was the result for most others.

From the employers' side, things had also changed. In the beginning of the Republic, the employers were isolated and felt no need for union. Gradually, the rise of the workers' movement and the weak support employers received from the government (so they believed) led them into several forms of active organization. An Employers' Confederation (Confederação Patronal) appeared after World War I, its first leader being promptly killed by enemies of the organization. In 1924 a group of landowners, bankers, and other capitalists organized the Union of the Economic Interests (União dos Interesses Económicos), to fight what they called the "social subversion" and defend their capitalist interests.

Summing up, one could say that the labor movement succeeded in a good many objectives. A better standard of living had been achieved, despite the economic, social, and political troubles resulting from the strikes. The British consul in Lisbon could write in 1924 with some truth that "there is practically no unemployment and the manual worker was never so well off as he is today." The purchasing power statistics also show that the lower civil servants, although far from being overpaid, were nevertheless in 1926 in a slightly better situation than they were before the war (76.5 per cent in 1921, 137.5 per cent in 1922, 119.1 per cent in 1923, 94.4 per cent in 1924, 109.5 per cent in 1925).

Once the battle for the eight-hour day was won (the act of 1919 was being fulfilled only by 1922), the unions had immediately started another fight, for the six-hour day, which to most people looked thoroughly utopian.

Social problems had now shifted to another direction. It was the middle class and the upper civil servants who showed their dissatisfaction. True, many bankers and many capitalists had profited from the war and from the consequent speculations. True, a certain number of parvenus and carpetbaggers had risen in the social scale, forming a group of "nouveaux riches." The middle tradesman, the middle and upper civil servant—including the army and navy officers—the rural and urban owners, all those who in 1910 had been the pillars of the Republic, were now full of complaints against it. They complained about the fall in their real salaries (for the civil servants, 100 in 1914, 22 in 1921, 36.5 in 1922, 49.4 in 1923, 37.7 in 1924, 43.7 in 1925), about the small margin of profit in their business, about the tax increase, about the rise of labor unions and the labor movement.

The Republican propaganda before 1910 had insisted upon the urgent need to solve the cultural problem. The monarchical governments since 1820—and even before—had undoubtedly considered the question. Reforms of education, creation of schools and other institutions of culture, were of concern to several administrations, often with excellent results (see chapter 10). The rate of illiteracy for those over seven years of age had decreased 5.3 per cent in the last eleven years of the regime (1900–11), a quite remarkable achievement.

Yet results did not seem satisfactory to a great number of people. The Portuguese, always comparing their country with the most progressive and the wealthiest nations of the world, felt their cultural backwardness in relation to France, Belgium, and Switzerland. Indeed, by 1911, Portugal's total rate of illiteracy was 75.1 per cent with an actual 69.7 per cent for those older than seven. Moreover, the monarchical administrations were undoubtedly more concerned with railroads, trade, or banking than with education. Their emphasis rested more on the material than on the spiritual development of the country.

The Republican program was exactly the opposite, and this fact should be stressed in order to correctly appraise and understand the achievements of the Democratic Republic. Studies and discussions of culture, education, school teaching and methods of teaching interested a large public and most of the country's élite. In 1876 a famous poet, João de Deus (1830-96), had published a no less famous primer (*Cartilha Maternal*), where a quite revolutionary method of teaching how to read was introduced. Based upon the division of the word into its elements and reacting against the "learn by rote" tradition, this analytical and intuitive system deserved the approval of most progressive educators—despite its many opponents—and became a sort of banner for the Republican cultural propagandists. João de Deus' son, João de Deus Ramos (1878–1953), continued his father's struggle for a better education for children. He was the founder of child-centered experimental schools in Portugal, which he called "kinder-gartens" (*jardins-escolas*), and where the modern principles based upon the concept of the total development of the child, the individualizing of each pupil, and the effort to develop his creative ability and emo-tional maturity were carried on. The number of such kindergartens, however, did not increase very much, because of the lack of funds to build them. As a rule, the Republican governments gave their enthusi-astic support to the initiative, but no money. Consequently, progress was slow: the first kindergarten opened its doors in Coimbra in 1911, the second and the third in 1914; by 1927 only five had been estab-lished. The kindergartens provided education for young children (4 to 7), including elementary reading and writing.

The Republican reforms of primary education and the spirit be-hind them had an unquestionable impact on the quality of the edu-cation officially available to everyone. Their effects on mass education, however, were poor, because of the state's permanent poverty. The acts of 1911 established free, public education for all children—before and after reading age—and compulsory attendance at school from age 7 to 10. Methods and disciplines followed the most up-to-date sys-tems. The stress on decentralization as a general administrative prin-ciple had led the government to entrust the control of elementary education to the municipalities, a principle maintained to 1918 (when it returned to the central government again). Elementary teaching was classified as pre-primary (*infantil*) and primary, the latter still divided into three levels. Temporary or movable schools were also established, particularly for the teaching of adults. Salaries paid to the teachers were increased. The total number of primary official schools jumped from about 4,500 in 1910 to about 7,000 in 1927, while the number of teachers increased from some 6,000 to some 8,500. Parishes with no school were reduced by half: 702 in 1910 (i.e., 17.5 per cent of the total number of parishes), 345 in 1926 (8.6 per cent). There was one school for each 19.4 kilometers in 1911 and one for each 13.2 kilometers in 1927. Yet the rate of illiteracy decreased only slightly: 75.1 per cent in 1911, 70.5 per cent in 1920, 67.8 per cent in 1930. In almost twenty years, illiteracy had declined 7.3 per cent, certainly more than in any comparable period of the monarchical regime (3.8 per cent from 1878 to 1900, or 4.1 per cent from 1890 to 1911), but less than was expected from the new order. When the Democratic Republic came to an end, in the mid-1920's, more than half of the population was still illiterate, again posing the problem of mass education.

For the preparation of primary schoolteachers, official concern led to the creation of more normal schools, with improved methods and equipment.

Secondary teaching received comparatively less attention. The excellent reform of 1894–95 was kept and enforced with only a few changes. However, one new high school (*liceu*) was built and the number of teachers increased. Two normal schools were established in 1911. Much more important were the reforms in technical education. By an act of 1911 (António José de Almeida) the School of Industry and Commerce gave place to two, raised to university level: the School of Engineering (Instituto Superior Técnico) and the School of Commerce (Instituto Superior do Comércio), both with new plans of studies and up-to-date disciplines, methods, and equipment. The School of Agronomy and Veterinary Science was also divided in two: a School of Agronomy (Instituto Superior de Agronomia) and a School of Veterinary Science (Escola de Medicina Veterinária), both considered upper colleges of education too. The act of 1918 (Alfredo de Magalhães) reformed the lower technical schools and established a second upper school of commerce in Porto. All over the country several new schools for the teaching of agriculture, commerce, and industry opened their doors year after year. In 1923 there were 54 technical schools at the secondary level, a rate of one per 120,000 inhabitants. The number of pupils surpassed 8,000, which meant a school for each 150 students.

University education also received the attention of the Republican governments. As a basic principle, the Republic tried to put an end to Coimbra's centuries-long university monopoly. Toward this end the provisional government brought together the existing schools (see chapter 10)—which were renamed "colleges" (*faculdades*)—and created (1911, António José de Almeida) the University of Lisbon and the University of Porto. The only new schools set up by the new regime (1911) were a School of Law (Faculdade de Direito) in Lisbon—the most important step to enforce the above-mentioned principle—and a School of Arts (Faculdade de Letras) in Coimbra, replacing the School of Theology, which the prevailing anticlericalism had closed. Deep reforms of structure affected all the colleges, both in the number of disciplines and teachers and in the introduction of many up-to-date scientific devices and methods. Furthermore, the republican ideology abolished compulsory classes, the university tribunals, and decentralized upper education by making university presidents and other authorities elective and giving financial autonomy to the schools. Scholarships for needy students were also created. Under Afonso Costa a Secretariate for Education made its appearance (1913) and was kept afterward.

To promote research and postgraduate studies, the government established in 1924 a Junta Orientadora dos Estudos, where leading scientists and scholars met together. And in December of that year, the leftist government headed by José Domingues dos Santos even talked of making education totally free at every level.

Nevertheless, lack of material resources prevented the enforcement of many of these measures, at least at the rapid pace both governments and public opinion wished. If the great merit of the Republic was to provide the legislation and the general framework for a cultural revolution in Portugal, scarcity of funds prevented new schools from being opened rapidly enough and hindered the recruiting of instructors and the adequate equipment of libraries, laboratories, and other research centers.

A small part of this progressive legislation was later disavowed by some more conservative governments, or whenever political circumstances forced the state to interfere. Thus, centralization took the lead again after 1918–19, university presidents becoming government appointees once more. Political reasons, also, were instrumental in the failure of the attempt to deprive Coimbra of its School of Arts and to transfer it to Porto (1919). Compromise led to the maintenance of the Coimbra School and to the confirmation of Porto. Yet, when political events gave Coimbra a prominent role again, the School of Porto was closed down (1927).

Besides the official system of education, the Republican period witnessed a highly interesting cultural ferment, particularly in the fields of free learning and the popular spread of culture. Throughout the country, but especially in the cities, public and free classes of all kinds and at all levels burgeoned, often maintained by and through the initiative of cultural leagues and other associations. Among the most important ones, the so-called free universities (Universidades Livres, founded 1912) and the so-called popular universities (Universidades Populares founded 1913) should be mentioned. Set up in Lisbon and Porto, they provided permanent series of lectures and courses by voluntary specialists to a wide public, where the workers were often represented in large numbers. Many of those lectures were published as small booklets, distributed or sold cheaply to vast audiences. Along with them, several private publishers and associations undertook some interesting publishing programs, trying to spread culture to the masses by turning out international and Portuguese works of scientific, historical, or literary note. A literary association founded in Porto in 1912 (Renascença Portuguesa) had a major role in that field.

This same attitude of mass education as something urgent and vital for the country's survival and progress appeared in many other areas of culture, such as music (concerts for the people, opera shows in Lisbon transferred from a small and highly formal opera house to a 5,000-seat informal coliseum), art (exhibitions and museums all over Portugal), and literature. Archives and libraries were also very much reformed. Public archives were created in each capital of a district, and attempts were made to centralize in them the most valuable items still dispersed by local archives. Many important documents came to the National Archives in Lisbon. A number of libraries opened reading rooms for children. The National Library of Lisbon tried to lead the way in promoting higher culture, particularly from 1919 to 1927, when the writer (and later renowned historian) Jaime Cortesão was appointed its director. Through the initiatives of the Free Universities, open-air libraries were created in public gardens after 1922. An almost completely free press (despite some destructive raids on newspaper offices in revolutionary periods and some sporadic government confiscations), where every modern and "fashionable" subject could be debated, was behind the burgeoning of newspapers and magazines of all kinds. In 1919 there were in Portugal 337 daily and weekly papers, i.e., one per 18,500 persons. Political papers predominated, but there was no shortage of cultural magazines and even some good newspapers. They had a very wide circulation throughout the country despite the high illiteracy. In small towns and villages, the paper was often read aloud by some "intellectual," an amorphous mass of people gathering around to listen and to comment.

The political whirlwind (see chapter 10 and the present chapter), which heightened after 1910, was in a way harmful to the cultural development of the country. It engulfed some of the best authors, artists, and professors, draining their productive powers and enlisting them against each other. Everything was politicized. Literary and artistic movements always had a political side. Yet this stress on politics also had its benefits. It developed free discussion and free argument. It proved a good school for democracy. From the philosophical and the stylistic standpoints, it resulted in clear reasoning and in literary speech and writing. It was the final flourish of oratory (António José de Almeida, Alexandre Braga, Afonso Costa, Bernardino Machado, Cunha Leal). Yet it did not prevent the country from keeping up with the world's scientific, cultural, and artistic progress. Portugal's writers, doctors, lawyers, scientists, and artists were in close contact with their colleagues abroad, who respected and praised them.

In the fields of science and technology, the Portuguese made some contribution to the world's progress in those days. Tropical sciences (medicine, botany, and zoology) continued to be among their main research areas. Angola, Mozambique, and the other Portuguese colonies, along with the metropolitan area, had their flora and fauna carefully studied and inventoried by a small, competent group of scientists, which included some foreigners. In the 1920's Ricardo Jorge's work on epidemics was decisive for understanding pestilential disease and its transmission. Research on cancer was promoted with the creation of a Cancer Institute (1924), where some renowned doctors started working. Neurology, psychiatry, anatomy, and physiology also had their researchers, of world importance. Gomes Teixeira (1851–1933) published his major works on mathematics between 1904 and 1915. In astronomy, Campos Rodrigues (1836–1919) had his research rewarded by the Academy of Paris.

However, the greatest scientific achievements of Portugal during the Republican era took place in aviation. Closely studied and followed in Portugal from its very beginnings, aviation got a decisive push with World War I, the few Portuguese pilots ranking among the best aviators. After the war, the Portuguese attempted some wide-reaching air voyages: Gago Coutinho and Sacadura Cabral flew an uncharted course from Lisbon to Madeira in March 1921, with no ships to guide them, and then again in March–June 1922 without guidance they flew across the South Atlantic for the first time in a daring Lisbon–Rio de Janeiro hop, with stopovers in the Canary Islands, Cape Verde Islands, São Pedro and São Paulo rocks, Fernando de Noronha Island, Recife, Baía, Porto Seguro, and Vitória. Sacadura Cabral's death in 1924 prevented another scheduled air hop, this time around the world. But in the same year aviators Brito Pais and Sarmento de Beires flew from Lisbon to Macao (China), and in the next six years, several other air trips connected Portugal with her far-distant colonies. Gago Coutinho perfected a flying device (the sextant), which played a useful role in those days.

The literary movement should be studied by an analysis of groups and currents rather than by focusing on individual authors. The first third of the twentieth century showed the last reflection of a great epoch in literature (see chapter 10) and the small beginnings and experiments of a new literary era. Thus, it did not encompass many great writers (with one exception) but contained many genres. Essayists and journalists prevailed over novelists, poets, or playwrights, just as the short article, the newspaper serial, the lecture, the speech, and the interview prevailed over the long and deep novel, the sensitive poem, and the detailed monograph. On the other hand, the pervasive democratic concern of reaching a vast, popular audience instead of a small, sophisticated public often diverted authors from profound and subtle themes in pursuit of more superficial and vulgar, albeit educative or revolutionary, matters.

Good examples of such a tendency were Guerra Junqueiro (1850–1923) and Gomes Leal (1848–1921) in the field of poetry, two of the most beloved and cherished authors of their time, yet rather mediocre when considered objectively. Popular bourgeois drama and fiction were best represented by Júlio Dantas (1876–1962) and Henrique Lopes de Mendonça (1856–1931), both of whom wrote for an always attentive and responsive audience. Historical fiction, often presented in newspaper serials or sold in cheap fascicles, had a tremendous impact on the liberal public of the early twentieth century (Campos Júnior, 1850–1917, Rocha Martins, 1879–1952, Malheiro Dias, 1875–1941).

The most valid Portuguese literature of the time was generally characterized by a nationalist tendency, in a reaction against the cosmopolitan realism of the late 1800's. Such nationalism was expressed in the stress, for example, on historical themes and heroes; the cult for the "typical Portuguese" values, manners, and landscapes (the picturesque, the folklore, the countryside); the emphasis on tradition and religion. In form and style, symbolism set the tone. Authors like Teixeira de Pascoais (1877–1952), Afonso Lopes Vieira (1878–1947), and António Correia de Oliveira (1879–1960) were perhaps among the best representatives of that tendency in poetry. Less "nationalist" were António Feijó (1870–1917) and Eugénio de Castro (1869–1944), also poets. In prose, essayists António Patrício (1878–1930) and Raul Brandão (1867–1930) should be mentioned. Most authors started or developed their careers in a well-known magazine, where they published their works, which gathered together intellectuals with cultural affinities. An outstanding example was the Porto magazine *A Águia* (1910–30) and, in the field of history, the Lisbon *Revista de História* (1912–27), which reacted against positivism and materialism in history.

Narrow nationalism and excessive symbolism were strongly attacked by a much more cosmopolitan and French-influenced thought and style, rationalistically oriented and aiming at the development of a critical consciousness. Its best representatives were in the domain of politics and essay, with João Chagas (1863–1925) perhaps the leading exponent. After 1921 the weekly *Seara Nova* displayed a courageous effort in the same direction and rallied several of the best authors of twentieth-century Portugal: historian Jaime Cortesão (1884–1960), polemicist Raul Proença (1884–1941), philosopher and essayist António Sérgio (1883–1969), among others. Close to them in thought, although oriented more toward the aesthetic and sensualist in his novels and essays, was Manuel Teixeira Gomes (1860–1942), who was elected President of the Republic in 1923.

Modern currents got under way by 1915 but had little impact on the Portuguese society of the time. A series of periodicals (*Orpheu*, 1915; *Centauro*, 1916; *Portugal Futurista*, 1917; *Contemporanea*, 1922–

23; *Athena,* 1924–25) completely failed to effect a cultural revolution which would question the very bases of society. With their attacks on bourgeois morals and on common sense, their young founders and collaborators were considered lunatics by the great majority of the people. Mário de Sá Carneiro (1890–1916), Almada Negreiros (1893–1970), António Boto (1897–1959), and especially Fernando Pessoa (1888–1935) had no recognition at all in their generation, although they were among the most prominent. It is significant that Pessoa, the major Portuguese poet since Camões, was only "discovered" during and after World War II, most of his works being posthumously published (see chapter 13).

In the arts, the persistence of old forms and styles was felt still more than in literature. Naturalism and nationalism prevailed in painting, sculpture, and architecture, with the general approval of the public. The art exhibitions (which increased after 1910) clearly displayed the monotonous, yet ever-growing succession of neo-Romantic painters, indulging in the same themes, wherein the Portuguese farmer and the Portuguese landscape were beautifully and artistically exalted, with little concern for the city and its inhabitants. Historical or pseudo-historical facts were also very popular. Such a trend, despite the general quality of its representatives (Carlos Reis, Falcão Trigoso, António Saúde, Alves Cardoso, Alberto de Sousa, and the older masters previously mentioned), showed no innovations and did not reflect the great changes which were taking place in Portugal and abroad. The same situation prevailed in sculpture (where several "monumental" statues were constructed for the public squares and buildings of the country) and in architecture, where Neo-Gothic buildings were in great esteem, along with typical nineteenth-century public buildings and the so-called "Portuguese house" style, more or less inspired by traditional Portuguese models. The pavillions of Portugal in the several international exhibitions (Panama-Pacific, 1915: Rio de Janeiro, 1922; Seville, 1929) were good examples of traditionalism, albeit with some innovating traits—the systematic use of pictured tiles, for instance—and a fusion of elements resulting in a new aspect as a whole. Still stranger in their final display were the bourgeois dwellings in Lisbon that were yearly awarded the so-called "Valmor" prize.

"Modern" trends in the arts had only a few followers and met with little or no public support. The Salão dos Humoristas (Humorists Salon) of 1912 was the first to exhibit some innovating tendencies. The return to Portugal at the outbreak of World War I of painter Amadeu de Sousa Cardoso (1887–1918), who had studied in Paris, had some impact on the development of cubism and other "modernisms." Sousa Cardoso died quite young but left behind a remarkable and up-to-date collection of works. Painters Santa Rita (1889–1918) and Eduardo Viana (1881–1967) followed a similar trend.

Music flourished in this period compared with the nineteenth century. Composer Viana da Mota studied abroad and was later appointed director of the Lisbon Music Conservatory. He and his disciples produced some interesting concert and chamber music of high quality which placed him foremost in the history of Portuguese music.

National cinema also had an interesting phase of success and development. In the 1920's a few high-quality movies were produced, and a short-lived national school of cinema was even opened.

IDEOLOGIES AND POLITICAL STRUCTURE

Although a Republican ideology in Portugal can be traced back to 1820, it was only by the mid-century that it started to be clearly expressed and responded to. Costa Cabral's dictatorship and the general rebellion against him (see chapter 10) brought about much discontent and questioned the possibilities of a liberal monarchy. The French revolution of 1848 also had its impact on Portugal, where many of the younger generation showed their sympathy for democracy in demonstrations, pamphlets, and short-lived newspapers. From 1851 on, the economic expansion of Portugal, expressed by Fontism, meant compromise after compromise for the ruling groups. Monarchical ideologies had a smaller and smaller place in a country geared to business and practical considerations. Bourgeois prosperity did not favor widespread reactions against a moderate, tolerating, and all-embracing regime. Furthermore, King Pedro V (1853–61) and his successor Luis I (1861–89), at least in the beginning, were truly popular monarchs, arousing no hostility whatsoever. Nonetheless, a man like Henriques Nogueira (1825–58), one of the most active among the generation of 1848, was still able to write a sort of gospel of Portuguese Republicanism, emphasizing the principles of republicanism, municipalism, federalism, and association. He called for a decentralized republic (accepting historian Alexandre Herculano's idea of a renewed municipal organization), socialistic in Fourier's and Louis Blanc's terms, with a strong emphasis on voluntary association, and federalistic within a general federation of the Iberian peoples. This would bring happiness to Portugal and restore her glory and prestige.

It can be said that Portuguese Republicanism after 1858, with only one later addition, simply developed and made precise Henriques Nogueira's master ideas, which, after all, were common to other Republican ideologies throughout Europe.

The second great push to the growth of Republicanism in Portugal came with the generation of 1865–70 (see chapter 10). As they had twenty years before, a small group of young people proclaimed their faith in the Republican ideals and their hatred and contempt for the monarchical regime. But unlike their predecessors, the most active elements of the new generation (although not necessarily its best minds) did not die nor did they subscribe to the "establishment" when they grew older. Conditions in Europe had changed, and the prospect of a future Republican world seemed more hopeful. The Republic had triumphed in France (1870), was proclaimed in Spain (1873–74), and had found a fertile field in Italy. Also, Fontism had lost some of its early, all-pervasive, vigor, and economic crises were, from time to time, jolting the overconfident bourgeoisie.

Men like Teófilo Braga (1843–1924), Elias Garcia (1830–91), Basílio Teles (1856–1923), and Sampaio Bruno (1857–1915) were paramount in spreading the Republican ideals for more than thirty years, defining many of the vaguer points and enriching the contents with philosophical, political, and social elements. Scientism and positivism were preached with passion and accepted by most Republicans as an antidote to religion. Antireligiousness was indeed a newer addition to Republicanism, a reaction against the so-called Ultramontanism or excessive Papal centralization (the First Vatican Council, in 1869–70, had indeed defined the new dogma of Papal infallibility). As a counterpart, however, Portuguese Republicanism gradually lost the earlier socialist element. A social Republic began to be considered a utopia by many Republicans, who realized that actual conditions and possible achievements were very far from social equalitarian aspirations. In a country like Portugal, where industrial workers represented only an insignificant minority, to tie the dream of a Republic to their peculiar class goals would postpone an actual change of regime for several generations. It seemed more realistic, in order to appeal to the bourgeoisie, to give up "socialist" principles and carry on the political "democratic" ones. Yet social ideals were never forgotten, at least from a theoretical standpoint. To a certain extent, one could say that Portuguese Republicanism became "socialist" in principle but bourgeois in practice.

This solution proved to be the right one. The mid-1870's witnessed the creation of the Portuguese Socialist Party, divorced from the Republican orthodoxy, and with it the gradual expansion of the Republican Party. From the 1880's on, the Socialists always made a poor showing in contrast to the vigorous forward sweep of the Republicans.

Federalism was never completely forgotten, but the imperialist dreams of many Spaniards did not help its enforcement. Also, the deep trauma caused by the British ultimatum of 1890 renewed the spirit of nationalism, which carried along all the leading members of the generation of 1890.

From a strictly political standpoint, the Republicans followed the model of Swiss institutions. They defended universal suffrage—which they later abandoned—predominance of the legislative power over the executive, and minimal presidential power. They subscribed to the abolition of the compulsory military draft and of the diplomatic corps (only consuls were to continue). They were against several forms of taxation and fought for the development of cooperatives.

The rapid growth of Republicanism also had its disadvantages and weak points. To become an ideology of the masses, as it certainly did become (to the extent one could speak of "masses" in nineteenth-century Portugal), Republicanism lost in constructivism and consistency while gaining in destructivism and heterogeneity. To be a Republican, by 1890, 1900, or 1910, meant to be against the Monarchy, against the Church and the Jesuits, against political corruption and the monarchical parties, and against the oligarchical groups. But for what? The answers were vague and varied. Decentralization certainly remained a precise goal. As to the rest, and despite many exceptions, the tendency was rather to endow the word "Republic" with a mystical charisma, and to believe that its proclamation alone would liberate the country from all injustice and all evil. It is important to under-line this fact in order to understand the disillusionment and contra-diction of the Republicans when they finally triumphed, in 1910. In-deed, Republicanism ended as a sort of utopia too, in the sense that it implied a perfect regime "of the people, for the people," based upon complete equality, freedom, and "democratic justice." As a matter of fact, the Republican ideals in their last phase were little different from those of 1820 (i.e., those of the French Revolution), which the consti-tutional monarchy had tried to interpret and apply in a pragmatic way. The Republic was thereby deprived of a great many practical achievements, which had cemented and institutionalized the liberal monarchy, and almost reduced it to the difficult or impossible task of perfecting formulas already experimented with.

The Ultimatum of 1890 had humiliated the Portuguese and awakened interest in their colonies. The Republicans included in their program a full development of the Overseas provinces, which they carried on with vigor after 1910. Thus, colonialism, along with an exacerbated nationalism, also characterized the Republican ideals, evoking all kinds of romantic dreams for the future. Portugal was compared with Belgium or Holland in the potential for building up an empire. The national anthem adopted in 1910 was a symbol of such hopes and beliefs. "Oh sea heroes, oh noble people . . . raise again the splendor of Portugal; . . . may Europe claim to all the world that Portugal is not dead! . . . Hail the sun which dawns in the bright light of your sky; may it be the echo of an affront, the signal for resurge."

It would be wrong to state that Republicanism stopped with the proclamation of the Republic. If there were few or no changes in basic ideology, an actual policy of government was established and evolved, as reality opened the eyes of the Republicans and showed them the need for more precise goals. Many of the Swiss-based premises simply dissolved. Changes were also related to the history of party organiza-tion throughout the sixteen years of the Democratic Republic (1910 to 1926).

The basic structure of the Republican party system after 1910 encompassed a large and well-organized Center-Left party—the Democratic Party, officially sticking to the traditional designation of Portuguese Republican Party (P.R.P.)—and several marginal groups which grew up, declined, and faded away according to circumstances and to the personalities who led them. The P.R.P. held its strength and organization from the unified, thirty-five-year-old Republican Party, with a tradition of collective leadership, which made it highly malleable and capable of overcoming personal rivalries and quarrels. Although certain figures from time to time enjoyed enough prestige, political ability, and strength to impose a definite direction to the party—such as Elias Garcia and Bernardino Machado before 1910, Afonso Costa from 1911 to 1917, and António Maria da Silva in the 1920's—the P.R.P. never had a "boss." It was organized in parish, municipal, and district committees and ruled by a "Directory" elected every three (later two) years by the Party Convention, which also met for general policy supervision and discussion.

All the other parties were exactly the opposite. In 1911, the will to build up a strong conservative group that might check the pervasive influence of the P.R.P. broke before the stubbornness of two would-be bosses—António José de Almeida and Brito Camacho—who could not compromise with each other. Two conservative parties thus arose, the Evolutionist and the Unionist, with vague and little differentiated ideologies. In 1919, as the two "bosses" retired, a conservative party did come into existence, the Liberal Party, but too late to affect the positions acquired by the P.R.P. Moreover, the Liberal Party never overcame the same "boss" principle, but always lacked an able and undisputed boss. The result was poor organization, party indiscipline, and anarchical leadership. By 1923 the Liberal Party disbanded itself and tried to reorganize its forces under a new name and with the entrance of a relatively numerous group of dissidents from the P.R.P. This reshuffling led to the birth of the Nationalist Party, which proved no better and provoked two internal secessions in three years.

Dissident groups from either the P.R.P. or the other parties were still weaker and less organized. From the Evolutionists there sprang up in 1916 a small number who formed, a year later, the Center Party. Together with the so-called Decembrists—the revolutionaries who attained power in December 1917—they gave birth to the National Re-

UPPER LEFT: *Afonso Costa.* BELOW: *The first Normal School, built in Lisbon, 1916.* ABOVE: *A group of Republican revolutionaries, October 5, 1910.*

publican Party, a sort of loose popular front blindly following the President-Dictator Sidónio Pais. When he was shot (December 1918), the National Republican Party split up into several groups. Some joined the Liberals, some others decided to go on alone under the name of Republican Presidentialist Party. In 1925 they too joined the Nationalists. From the Nationalists seceded, early in 1926, the Liberal Union, headed by Cunha Leal.

In 1920 the Partido Reconstituinte, led by Álvaro de Castro, seceded from the P.R.P. The Reconstituintes, together with the former Liberals, gave birth to the Nationalists, three years later. But some months after this new party had come into existence, Álvaro de Castro and his people seceded again and started the Republican Action. Another dissension within the P.R.P. brought the Democratic Left Party into existence in 1925.

Finally, to finish the story of the splits in the once united Republican Party, one has to mention the Reformist Party (active 1911–18) and the Popular Party, which broke with the Evolutionists when the latter decided to fuse with the Unionists, in 1919. The Popular Party got together with the revolutionaries of October 1921 to form the Radical Party.

Summing up, when the Democratic Republic came to an end, there were six party branches, all deriving from the Republican Party: from the Left to the Right, these were the Radical Party, the Democratic Left Party, the P.R.P., the Republican Action, the Nationalist Party, and the Liberal Union.

This division did not exhaust all the Republicans. New groups had risen in opposition to and in no connection with the existing parties, although subscribing to the Republican form of government. These were the Portuguese Maximalist Federation (1919), later called Communist Party (1921), and the Seara Nova group (1921). There was still the old Socialist Party, always alone and always insignificant. The Anarchists also rose as the most important group among the workers.

The Seara Nova group was undoubtedly the most significant of all Republican and non-Republican groupings—with the exception of Integralismo Lusitano and the Socialist-Communist-Anarchist factions—in presenting a coherent ideology aiming at a thorough reform of the Portuguese mentality and politics. It was born as a reaction against the parties—as they were—and always claimed not to be a party but only a "group" willing to "help the parties to perfect themselves and to rule well." As such, Seara Nova posed as a defender of national interests against the exclusivisms of oligarchies, groupings, classes, and parties. Its goals and programs combined a rather vague assertion of the usual Republican slogans with some other more precise ideas: democratic socialism, non-Jacobin radicalism, internationalism, and pacifism. It strove for a national public opinion based upon truth and reason rather than upon pseudo-facts and emotion.

On the Right, political groupings had less of a "boss" orientation and a more ideological definition. In Coimbra, some active scholars under the leadership of Oliveira Salazar and Father Gonçalves Cerejeira revived and restructured the Centro Académico de Democracia Cristã (Academic Center for Christian Democracy, C.A.D.C.) by 1912. This was a student and teacher organization less concerned with the monarchy-republic dualism (although most of its membership leaned toward the monarchy) than with a Catholic-Social society based upon Leo XIII's encyclicals. Basically, the same people founded, in 1917, the Portuguese Catholic Center (Centro Católico Português) with similar goals but a wider-reaching organization. Both groups fought against the Republic as an atheist-oriented, anticlerical and individualistic regime.

Integralismo Lusitano, on the rise since 1914, had a more original and more radical program of future government and social organization, which opposed practically all the Republican ideologies (see chapter 13). A monarchical party, it accepted ex-King Manuel's rights up to 1919, but later (1920) subscribed to the anticonstitutional line.

After the suicide of the old monarchical parties, late in 1910, the orthodox monarchists started reorganizing by 1914 under Bernardino Machado's more tolerant government. Gathering together, they formed the so-called Causa Monárquica (Monarchical Cause), which, with few changes, subscribed to the regime dethroned in 1910. Causa Monárquica had ex-King Manuel's full support and was directed by a "lieutenant" appointed by him. As an "official" royalist party, it enjoyed great prestige and largely oriented or influenced most monarchical initiatives after 1914. Dissension, however, soon plagued its ranks, leading to an open party rebellion in 1923. A group of extreme Rightists, who subscribed to a new form of Monarchy close to the Integralist program, seceded and constituted its own group, the Acção Realista Portuguesa (Portuguese Royalist Action).

The fourth group of monarchists was the Legitimist party. It had virtually no ideology of its own except subscribing to Austrian-born Prince Miguel (whom they called Miguel II), a son of ex-King Miguel (see chapter 10), and rejecting Manuel's line. The Legitimists were very few in Portugal, until the Integralists joined them in 1920. Yet they started playing a role in active politics as early as 1912, siding with the Manuelists in the short-lived second "invasion" of Republican Portugal. They also succeeded in convincing Manuel to meet Miguel at Dover (1912) in an effort to reconcile the two branches. Later on (1922), Manuel declared he would, in the absence of a direct heir, accept the successor appointed in future *cortes*. "Miguel II" later "resigned" on behalf of his younger son, Duarte Nuno.

An interesting attempt to build up a consistent class party took place in 1924, when several large landowners, industrialists, financiers, and other businessmen founded the Union of the Economic Interests (União dos Interesses Económicos), as a defense against radical and socialist threats.

The secret societies were very active, particularly in the period immediately before and after 1910. One must be careful, however, in appraising their actual share of responsibilities and real political influence, because the usual tendency is to ascribe everything to the Freemasonry and the Carbonária and to impute all crimes to them. The truth is that we know very little about either society and that bibliography on the subject is nonexistent. The Carbonária, which may have counted some 40,000 members, declined very quickly after 1910, and practically disappeared, giving way to some sort of clubs or groupings which acted as private police bodies at the service of several parties (particularly the Democratic party) and the institutions themselves. Thus were born the Formiga Branca ("White Ant"), the Defensores da República ("Defenders of the Republic"), the Lacraus ("Scorpions"), the Grupo dos Treze ("Group of the Thirteen"), the Legião Vermelha ("Red Legion"), and others, where a clear line between political and criminal goals was often difficult to draw. The religious half-secret societies should also not be forgotten. The Freemasonry's role seems to have declined too, although believed by the Rightist public opinion generally to stand behind every revolution, assassination, public assault, or even rumor. In 1912 there were probably no more than 2,887 Portuguese Masons, with 148 lodges. Yet it survived the Republican period under the able leadership of Magalhães Lima (to 1928), posing as a sort of wordly club to which every Republican would be proud to be admitted.

The Republican Constitution of 1911 largely followed the Brazilian Constitution of 1891, as well as the Swiss, French, and monarchical-Portuguese constitutional laws. Based upon democratic-liberal premises, it emphasized the rights and warrants of the individual. In this, formulas adopted in the nineteenth century (such as freedom, individual security, and property) were combined with proper Republican principles, such as social equality (defined as the rejection of all privileges depending upon birth, nobility titles, and even honorary orders) and laicism (expressed by equality and freedom for all religions, secularization of public cemeteries, religious neutrality in teaching in public schools, prohibition to all religious orders to establish themselves in Portugal, and compulsory and exclusive civil registry). Paragraph 37 of article 3 granted the right of resistance to any orders which might violate the individual guarantees.

The Constitution of 1911 went back to the three-power doctrine, stressing the legislative power, which in fact became the relevant one for most purposes. Parliament (officially named Congress) encompassed a Chamber of Deputies, composed of representatives aged 25 or over elected every three years, and a Senate, composed of representatives aged 35 or over of the districts and the Overseas provinces, elected every six years (half of the Senate would be elected every three years). Both Chambers were directly elected by the people. The President of the Republic was elected by the Congress every four years and could not be reelected for the following term. He appointed the Prime Minister and the cabinet ministers, who were to attend the Congress meetings and whose maintenance in power became practically (although not constitutionally) dependent upon Congressional majorities.

The Constitution of 1911 was twice revised, in 1916 and in 1919–21. A product of war circumstances, the First Amendment simply restored decorations and authorized the death penalty only for cases of treason or defeatism on the battlefield. The Second Amendment gave the President the right to dissolve Congress, created a Parliamentary Council to advise the President, and provided the bases for colonial decentralization. In March 1918 and in 1928 (see chapter 13), dictatorial laws altered some articles of the Constitution, namely the manner of electing the President, which was to be by popular ballot. However, election by the Congress was again restored in December 1918.

The Republican emphasis on democracy and popular representation enhanced the importance of the electoral body and underlined the meaning of elections. Yet the concern in preparing a conscious body of citizens by means of education and in avoiding traditional bossism prevented a substantial enlargement of the number of electors and rejected universal suffrage. The electoral law of 1911 enforced the voting restrictions of the monarchical era by granting the right to vote only to those aged 21 and over who could read and write or were heads of family. The taxation basis disappeared altogether. From the resulting 850,000 electors, only some 60 per cent actually went to the polls to elect the all-Republican nominees. Two hundred and thirty-four representatives composed the first provisional Parliament. Thus, excluding the colonies, representatives roughly corresponded to one deputy for 27,000 people, a number far above that of the monarchical era (one/40,000). However, when the Constitution was adopted, representatives dropped to 1/36,000, because the 71 Senators—i.e., three for each of the 21 administrative districts of Portugal, Azores, and Madeira, and one for each of the 8 colonies—were chosen among the 234 representatives. In the following elections, representativeness was kept at 1/36,000 (163 representatives since 1915) and went down to 1/39,000 in 1918 (155 representatives). The electoral codes of 1913 and 1915 restricted voting to literate males only. Electors dropped to 471,000. The electoral law of 1918 established suffrage for all males, irrespective of literacy. As a result, the electoral body jumped to some 900,000. However, the law of 1919 brought back the former state. In 1925 there were 574,260 electors registered.

The electoral history of the Democratic Republic was far from peaceful. In sixteen years there were seven general Parliament elections—in 1911, 1915, 1918, 1919, 1921, 1922, and 1925 (besides supplementary ones)—and eight presidential elections—in 1911, 1915 (twice), 1918 (twice), 1919, 1923, and 1925—not to mention elections for the municipalities. Part of them were featured by violent acts here and there, as well as by questionable results in some districts. Yet there has been too much exaggeration in speech and writing about the elections of the Republican period. As a rule, they were more free than any of those held before 1910, and control by opposition groups to the government was much more effective than ever before. Also, complaints against alleged irregularities were duly accepted by the electoral tribunals and careful inquiries were frequently carried on. It seems beyond doubt that some progress toward a legitimate popular representation had been achieved and continued to improve. Therefore, studies of electoral geography in terms of party representation are much more meaningful than for the monarchical period. Again, towns had a greater significance than rural areas in legitimate and conscious balloting.

The Republican governments, however, were never able to mobilize a vast body of electors, as they became less and less interested in the too frequent visits to the polls and were gradually disillusioned with the Republican achievements. In 1911, at the peak of enthusiasm, only 60 per cent of the electors voted. It may be assumed that most of the remaining 40 per cent were monarchists, and that the elections were thus genuinely free. The percentage of abstentions always went up, despite the several campaigns carried on by the parties to convince people to vote: more than 50 per cent in Lisbon, both in 1913 and 1915; 64 per cent also in Lisbon in 1918; and similar or still higher figures afterward. The presidential elections of 1918 had 40 per cent abstentions despite all of Sidónio Pais's charisma. These facts made popular support of the Democratic Republic increasingly questionable and helped explain many of the events after 1926. Nonetheless, abstentions should not be interpreted only as a rejection of the Republican regime, especially when Monarchist and Catholic candidacies were available. They often stood for apathy, depolitization, negligence, and other customary attitudes in democratic countries.

The electoral laws of the Republican period always provided for incomplete ballots giving a proportional representation to minorities. How large this representation should be was a matter of much dispute.

Before 1910, the legislation in force granted the minorities more than 22 per cent of the seats in the Chamber of Deputies (35 out of 155). Such a proportion was roughly maintained by the 1911 and 1913 electoral laws. Increasing complaints from the opposition parties (particularly after the nearly complete Democratic victory in 1913) raised the minority allotment to almost 27 per cent after 1915 (44 in 163). Also debated was the electoral division of the country into districts (generally coinciding with groups of counties) and the allotment of Parliamentary seats to some key districts such as Lisbon and Porto. The study of its changes, which has not been done, may bring some highly revealing conclusions on the predominance of the capital and the reactions against it.

A general characteristic of the Portuguese political life after 1910 was doubtless the parliamentary, presidential, and governmental instability. In sixteen years there were seven general parliamentary elections, eight presidential elections, and forty-five governments. This situation had certainly begun much before, during the monarchical period, and the Republic was simply the climax. Actually, parliamentary stability improved a little, for in seventy-six years of constitutional monarchy there had been forty-three elections and as many Chambers with a different party composition, i.e., an average of one year and eight months per legislature. With the Republic, however, governmental instability grew worse and presidential instability was introduced. With cabinets having an average duration of four months, the Portuguese Republic was ahead of all Europe in instability, exceeding France (both the Third and Fourth Republics) and Spain (Second Republic).

The reasons for this were manifold. Undoubtedly, the excessive weight of Parliament in the political life of the country accounted for much instability. In 1923, Parliament met eleven months throughout the year. In eleven other years, it convened from seven to ten months a year. In all, the average number of months in which Parliament met each year was seven. This system, if it had some advantages in preventing large-scale corruption and forcing a constant dialogue between rulers and popular representatives, also had tremendous disadvantages. Parliament meddled with every aspect of governmental life, constantly demanding explanations to the cabinet members, filibustering on the side of the minorities, attacking just for the sake of personal and party effects, insulting and posing more as an assembly for chicanery than for the care of national interests. Governments entirely depended upon Parliamentary majorities: they often fell because of petty questions, personal dislikes, or whimsical actions. About twenty cabinets had to resign because of parliamentary distrust.

Loose party discipline also accounted for political instability. Even when the Democratic party had majorities in both Houses, stability did not necessarily result. The inability to build up a strong opposition party which might rotate in power with the Democrats and win substantial gains in the electoral race brought about permanent frustration, hatred, and impatience among the opposition. Unable to gain the electorate and displace the all-pervasive Democratic machine, the opposition parties sought a refuge in illusory arguments such as defective electoral laws, fake elections, political corruption, and the like. The growing feeling (whatever its actual veracity) that Portugal was dictatorially and corruptly governed by the Democratic party and that freedom was at stake as long as the Democrats kept power, led to the conviction that only violent methods could displace them and improve the situation. The Democrats, of course, retaliated with more violence. A general climate of mutual suspicion poisoned the relationships between government and opposition throughout the sixteen years of the First Republic. The results were revolution after revolution, another motive for political instability: eight cabinets and four presidents fell because of uprisings or murders. Practically each year saw a successful, unsuccessful, or abortive plot to overthrow the existing order. Some years there was even more than one.

Obviously, violence could not have developed if a strong authority had prevailed. Indeed, government weakness was another feature of the Republic. Neither the Armed Forces nor the National Guard nor the Police Corps were disciplined enough to obey the government all the way. On the other hand, they had no internal cohesion of their own to force the government to accept their orders. The Republic, unable to reach an equilibrium, seesawed between the civilians (generally in command of administration and government) and the military (reflected not only in actual force but also in ideals and ways of life).

Finally, one should not forget the maneuvers, still little known, of anti-Republicans, Catholics, and foreigners (especially Spaniards), all aimed at subverting and discrediting the regime. There was civil war thrice, always promoted by the monarchists. Clerical and international participation in conspiracies and uprisings still awaits its historian.

THE EVENTS

Once in power, the Republican party set up a provisional government symbolically headed by the aged and respected professor Teófilo Braga; the actual leaders, however, were the secretaries of the Interior (António José de Almeida), Justice (Afonso Costa), Foreign Affairs (Bernardino Machado), and Public Works (Brito Camacho). In less than one year, this government achieved some of the main objectives of the republican program, as well as tranquility inside the country and foreign recognition for the new regime.

Among the alterations which almost immediately took place, some symbolic acts must be emphasized, because they helped dissociate the new generations from the old, monarchical ones: the flag, which changed from white and blue to green and red; the national anthem, which was the *Portuguesa* instead of the *Hino da Carta;* the currency, which adopted the escudo instead of the real; and the ortographical reform, which simplified spelling. Although regarded by many as minor, these changes succeeded in building up a psychological distinction between the old days and the new ones. World War I, in which the Portuguese intervened, definitely imposed the green and red colors as the symbol of the fatherland, preventing later emotional rallies around the white and blue flag.

To the general elections of May 1911, only the Republican party presented candidates, plus a small number of independents. The so-called Constituent National Assembly, where the middle-class bourgeois including army and navy officers and civil servants had a majority, drafted and approved a parliamentary constitution. Rivalries among the cabinet members led to a very quick split of the Republican Party into three branches, Afonso Costa leading the bulkiest and

most radical faction (Democratic Party), António José de Almeida a
hodgepodge of Center, Right, and even some Left-wing elements (Evolutionist Party), and Brito Camacho the smallest, most conservative
group (Unionist Party). Such a division was further enhanced by the
rise of a small, yet aggressive faction of angered Republicans, headed
by Machado Santos (Reformist Party), who thought they should play
a role in politics too.

These dissensions first became evident to everybody in the presidential elections (August 1911), which followed the approval of the
Constitution. The partisans of António José de Almeida and Brito
Camacho, who together had a majority in Parliament, succeeded in
electing their candidate, lawyer Manuel de Arriaga, instead of Afonso
Costa's nominee, former university professor Bernardino Machado.
The new president, who wanted to prevent Afonso Costa's rising control of the country, stuck to the rule of not appointing any ministers
who had taken part in the Provisional government. He also defended
the principle of national nonpartisan governments. Therefore, to
January 1913, coalition cabinets ruled the country, with a plurality
of Evolutionists and Unionists. Such governments were weak, met with
little popular support, and had no possibility of carrying on any definite program of their own. In a short time, Parliament ceased to represent the political reality of the country, for its members reflected
only the situation of May 1911, when the Republican Party was still
united.

In spite of this, the new regime increasingly got the support of
the nation. Several monarchical plots and attempts to foster civil war
and the return of the king failed. The old monarchical parties had disbanded; no organized force opposed the Republicans. A majority of
the Army sided with the Republic, and the Navy almost entirely. The
only real danger to the regime was the Church, and therefore against
the Church an almost continuous fight took place from 1910 on.

By late 1912 it became evident that the Democratic Party had
enough strength to govern alone. It had gained an immense popularity
among the townspeople, while the other parties were losing it. Quite
unwillingly, President Arriaga was forced to entrust Afonso Costa
with the task of organizing a new cabinet (January 1913). With the
support of the Unionists in Parliament, Afonso Costa and his group

legislated intensely, balanced the budget, strengthened the government's authority and raised his popularity among the bourgeoisie. He lost it, however, within the lower classes by ruthlessly suppressing street demonstrations, discouraging strikes, and sending to jail numerous workers. He also roused the hatred of the monarchists, the Church, and the upper classes by repressing their plots and imprisoning their leaders. Elections held for many vacant seats in Parliament gave the Democrats an overwhelming victory and a majority in the House of Deputies.

Petty parliamentary quarrels and Arriaga's undiminished dislike of Afonso Costa brought about Costa's downfall a year later. The president called upon Bernardino Machado, who organized another cabinet, less Democratic, yet supported by them. Up to January 1915, the Democratic Party ruled Portugal for all practical purposes.

Meanwhile World War I had started. It became clear to most responsible people that Portugal's national interest was to join the allies. There had been much talk of a 1913 secret treaty between England and Germany for the partition of the Portuguese colonies, similar to that of 1898. If Portugal helped England and France to win the war, that danger might be considered over. Also, Spain's foreseen neutrality (quite sympathetic to the German cause) would contrast with Portugal's share of international responsibilities and help reassert Portugal's prestige and independence in the Europe of the future.

Both Democrats and Evolutionists agreed to that. The Unionists, however, thought the contrary, and wanted to wait for a clearer picture of the war outcome. Many among them sympathized with the German cause and the German conception of government. A good number of monarchists, army officers, and Church people felt the same way. After all, to side with the allies was to side with atheistic France, protestant England, and schismatic Russia. And moreover, it was to side with Afonso Costa, the symbol of all evil.

Bernardino Machado did not entirely commit Portugal to the allied cause. His government made clear the intention of intervening in the struggle, but only if and when England required it. Yet a strong wing within the Democratic Party felt that Portugal should join the allies without any further waiting, in order to force England to accept her collaboration on the same footing as the other countries. This point of view was supported by the several German border violations and attacks in Portuguese Africa.

Alarmed with the bitter political struggle and the gradual taking over by the Democrats, President Arriaga staged a coup d'état in January 1915 and entrusted a personal friend of his, aged General Pimenta de Castro, with the difficult task of pacifying the country and presiding over impartial elections. Behind him stood the Evolutionists (because of their opposition to the Democrats), the Unionists (because of the same, plus the war policy), a part of the army, the monarchists, and the Church. Pimenta de Castro gave seven of the nine portfolios to the military and tried to appease discontent. The war policy was practically forgotten, persecutions against the monarchists and the Church stopped altogether (with many dismissed officers and civil servants being reinstated), and discrimination against the Democrats started. In March army troops prevented Parliament from meeting.

It was too early, however, for a Right-wing government in Portugal. The Democrats, along with others who also resented the old general's dictatorship, had behind them the bourgeois support of the major cities. Most people saw in Pimenta de Castro's measures a disguised way of restoring the monarchists to power. In May 1915 a violent rebellion in Lisbon, backed by some army corps, the navy, and popular elements, threw the government out and reinstated the Democrats. President Arriaga resigned, old Teófilo Braga being sworn in as provisional head-of-state. General elections gave the Democrats a majority in both houses of Parliament. In August, regular presidential elections put Bernardino Machado in control of the situation. Nothing now prevented Afonso Costa from getting back the premiership (November 1915).

Early in 1916, increasing problems in sea transportation led Great Britain to ask Portugal to seize a number of German and Austrian merchant ships, which had sought shelter in Portuguese harbors since the beginning of the war. When Portugal did seize these ships, Germany declared war upon her (in March 1916). The Democrats and the Evolutionists got together in a so-called Sacred Union (União Sagrada), shaped in the French way, Afonso Costa stepping down from the premiership on behalf of his old foe, António José de Almeida. The Unionists also backed the new government. For all practical purposes, however, the Democrats kept control of the situation, and Afonso Costa, as Finance Minister, had the final word in most important decisions. Later on, a cabinet reshuffling gave him the premiership again (April 1917).

This war government undertook the difficult task of organizing an expeditionary force to fight in France, besides the several expeditions sent to Angola and Mozambique. The Portuguese army was in poor shape, lacking modern equipment, training, and even discipline. The War Minister, Norton de Matos, achieved what people then called a "miracle" by preparing an army corps in a remarkably short time. The first Portuguese troops arrived in France early in 1917 and, if not the best in the struggle, they did not discredit their flag either.

At home, however, the war effort and the world's situation in general brought about disastrous results. There was a shortage of food and even hunger among the lower urban classes. Many things were rationed. The increasing number of troops who had to leave Portugal to participate in the struggle aroused widespread discontent and reaction against the government. For many, the war was unpopular and the need for Portuguese intervention highly questionable.

Moreover, throughout 1917 and into the summer of 1918, the fear of a German victory haunted many people and made them wish for a Portuguese pullout as soon as possible.

Afonso Costa's conduct of the war and the general administration was good, but his popularity sank from day to day. Social unrest plagued the country, forcing the government to adopt severe measures of repression. On the other hand, the cabinet and its leader seemed to try an approach with the workers and supported many of their demands, producing uneasiness among the bourgeoisie. The Church and the monarchists profited by all this by intriguing and plotting against the regime.

In December 1917, with most of the army fighting in France and Africa and the head of the government abroad, some Lisbon garrisons revolted with popular support, under the leadership of the former envoy to Germany, Major Sidónio Pais. The government surrendered, President Bernardino Machado was forced to leave the country, and Sidónio Pais set up a military dictatorship. He changed the Constitution, introduced a presidential regime in the American style, and had himself elected as President in April 1918. General elections held at the same time, but in which the three main parties refused to participate, gave birth to a House of Deputies and a Senate, where the new government party had the majority but where the Monarchists and the Catholics were strongly represented too.

Sidónio Pais' regime (called the "New Republic"—República Nova) was one of increasing confusion and terror. Though well-intentioned and skilled, enjoying an immense popularity because of his gallant presence, boldness, and demagogical attributes, Sidónio always lacked cadres to help him in complex tasks of administration and warfare. The Unionists (who were fellow party members) backed him at first but soon refused to go along with his dictatorial schemes. The small group headed by Machado Santos supported him too, but it lacked able people itself. Therefore, Sidónio had to rely more and more on the extreme Right (monarchists, Clericals, upper bourgeois groups), whose support pushed him away from the Republican public opinion. He had to change minister after minister, with the result that political instability worsened and administration became chaotic. The consequences of the war were deeply felt, and the problems that fomented the revolution of 1917, far from being solved, increased. The influence of pacifists and Germanophiles, the presence of the military who did not want to fight, all this accounted for a lessening of the war effort. Troops were not relieved, some army corps were called home, the main defenders of Portugal's intervention were calumniated, tried, or arrested. Social unrest went on undiminished. Many workers, who had trusted Sidónio Pais, now realized that his policies were the same, or worse, than those pursued by the Democrats. Repression was the consequence of all this. Thousands were arrested and often tortured or badly beaten, a good many fled the country, censorship increased.

The liberal opposition revived, strengthened by Sidónio Pais' successive failures. There were several plots against the "New Republic" and one effective uprising. In December 1918 the President was assassinated and Portugal was plunged into the worst political crisis of her modern history.

Even before Sidónio's death, the government was losing control of the situation in several parts of the country. Military juntas had risen in the North and the South, with the alleged purpose of defending

Portugal against subversion, but in fact with monarchical goals. The
War Minister himself was a confessed Monarchist. After Sidónio's
murder, the juntas increased their power, particularly in the North.
The cabinet hastily had its dean, Admiral Canto e Castro, elected
President by the two Houses of Parliament (according to the 1911 system
and revoking Sidónio's act of 1918), and tried to compromise with the
Left and the Right at the same time. Its weakness became increasingly
obvious to everyone. The monarchists prepared the restoration of the
regime deposed in 1910, calling upon ex-King Manuel's approval.
Alarmed by such a prospect, the Republicans attempted to get full
control of the situation. They revolted in January 1919, but failed. Almost at the same time, the military juntas proclaimed the Monarchy
in Porto and in Lisbon, and hoisted the white-and-blue flag again.

It was relatively easy to master the uprising in the South. Most
of the capital's garrisons remained faithful to the government. Helped
by the Navy and by tens of thousands of voluntary civilians who
rushed to save "their" Republic, the rebels had to lay down arms and
accept defeat. In the North, however, the situation was not so easy to
handle. For a month the monarchists held on, controlling all of
Minho, Douro Litoral, Trás-os-Montes and part of the Beiras, with
headquarters in Porto. Major Paiva Couceiro, a former hero of the
African campaigns, headed a provisional junta of the government.
From England, ex-King Manuel II, without formally denying his support to the insurgents (as he did later), waited for the results. They
were a semblance of civil war, which ousted the monarchists and reinstated the Republican authorities.

In Lisbon, a coalition cabinet of "old" Republicans and Sidonists
had, in the meantime, been organized. It even included a Socialist as
Labor Minister. It was followed (March 1919) by another coalition
but where the Sidonists no longer participated. This meant that the
"New Republic" had come to an end and that the "Old Republic" was
back in power. Indeed, the June general elections gave a plurality to
the Democrats and installed an all-Democrat government presided
over by Coronel Sá Cardoso. For the Presidency, old party leader
António José de Almeida, who had given up the direction of his
Evolutionists, was chosen (August 1919). Most Evolutionists and
Unionists fused into a new party, the Liberal Party, which tried to

oppose the all-pervasive Democrat influence in government, administration, and popular trust.

Meanwhile, the Allies were meeting together at the Peace Conference. Portugal's prestige had sunk greatly because of Sidónio's rule and the country's general instability, and therefore Portugal's representatives at the conference (Egas Moniz and later Afonso Costa played a fundamental role in all this) had a hard time securing equal representation with the other belligerents. In the end, they managed to get back Kionga from the Germans (in north Mozambique), to obtain a share in the German war payments, and to get integrity of the colonies guaranteed.

The new "Old Republic" was not the same as before. To start with, international and national circumstances had very much changed because of the war: inflation, currency debasement, economic and social problems, generation conflicts, were shaping a new order. Communism and Fascism were on the rise. Political murders occurred frequently. All over Europe, anarchy and instability marked the years 1919 to 1923.

The old politicians were gone. Afonso Costa retired to Paris and, while accepting commissions from his government such as representative at the Peace Conference and the League of Nations (he even presided over the League of Nations General Assembly convened to approve Germany's entrance in 1926), never returned home. António José de Almeida, prematurely old and ill, had been elected President of the Republic, which put him in the role of an arbiter rather than an active politician. Brito Camacho accepted the office of governor of Mozambique and then faded from the political scene. Others had retired, lost interest in politics, or preferred to act as observers rather than participants. The leading positions in government fell to second-rate personalities, unskilled or unprepared to cope with the rising problems of postwar Europe. The results were incompetence, chaos in administration, widespread discontent. Moreover, high-level military officers coming back from the war, with prestige and popularity, thought they should play politics and be the best warrants of Portugal's entry into a new era. Yet their ability for administration was often poor, their political intelligence questionable, their preparation incomplete. Tired of anarchy and social unrest, people of all classes saw in them the saviors of the country and eagerly supported them against the civilians.

From 1918 on, the number of army and navy cabinet ministers steadily increased. Up to 1926, twelve out of twenty-six cabinets (46 per cent) were presided over by military men (before Sidónio Pais, the figure had been only 15 per cent). In Parliament a similar situation was taking place. It is true that the military in the government acted as individuals, not as representatives of the army or navy. Nonetheless, many people realized that it would not take long for an active participation of the armed forces themselves as a conscious body.

One of the main reasons for political instability was the failure of the Democrats to obtain a majority that allowed them to rule by themselves. They always had to depend upon the other parties, which made and unmade alliances as they pleased. Petty questions brought down cabinets and prevented any continuity in administration. Coalition governments had few bases for enduring, because party interests clashed. Governments lasted three to six months on the average; but there were even one-month and ten-day governments! Instability went along with periodical revolutionary attempts, plots and coups d'état. In 1919, for a better defense of the Republic, the Democrats had armed the National Guard with artillery and granted it extensive powers. As a result, the National Guard practically made and unmade governments for two years.

The year 1921, in Portugal as in many other countries of Europe, was a terrible one. Corruption, political crime, and lack of authority were more rampant than ever. Lt. Col. Liberato Pinto, chief of staff of the National Guard, Prime Minister for three months, was accused of embezzlement by the cabinet succeeding him (a coalition presided over by the former President, Bernardino Machado), and was tried and convicted. This brought about a strong reaction in the ranks of the National Guard, which ousted Bernardino Machado by violent means and accepted an all-Liberal regime under businessman Barros Queirós (May 1921). The general elections which followed gave a plurality to the Liberals, although the Democrats won in Lisbon, as always. Another Liberal Cabinet replaced it, headed by António Granjo, one of the most honest and prestigious statesmen of the time. Yet passions had risen too high for the moderate-conservatives to hold power for long. The trend pointed to the Left, to radical and extremist situations. A radical rebellion brought down the cabinet (October). One night several well-known politicians, including Granjo himself and Machado Santos, were murdered. It seems that the crimes were not directly related to the rebellion but to a mixture of elements where personal issues predominated but where Rightist influences were present (the monarchists, the Church, even Spain behind the scenes). The Radicals could not endure, and early in 1922 new general elections put the Democrats in power once more. The National Guard was extensively disarmed and ceased to present any danger. Only the Army now showed a certain cohesion and prestige.

Political fatigue made the years 1922 and 1923 somewhat calmer, António Maria da Silva being able to head an all-Democratic cabinet for twenty-one months. The general ambience tended to improve, along with the gradual fading away of the war problems. In August 1923 Parliament elected the Democrat nominee, Manuel Teixeira Gomes, a writer and ambassador to London, as President. On the political scene, the Liberal Party, with a reshuffling of its elements, became the Nationalist Party, where the Right-wing trend predominated. In the Democratic ranks, the Left-wing aggressively clamored for reforms and for a clear social policy. It was backed by an influential group of intellectuals, the Seara Nova group previously mentioned. Seara Nova people entered the government in 1923–24, then again in 1924–25, when the Left Democrat José Domingues dos Santos presided over a three-month government. This "Leftist" tendency collided with most of the Army which showed its sympathies toward authoritarian regimes like Mussolini's in Italy and Primo de Rivera's in Spain. Two suppressed Army uprisings during 1925 clearly showed such sympathies.

The general elections of 1925 gave another victory to the Democrats, but not a complete one. António Maria da Silva organized what would be the last government of the First Republic. President Teixeira Gomes, constantly attacked by the Nationalists, resigned, and old Bernardino Machado stepped in for his second term as President.

The general situation of Portugal had undoubtedly improved since 1923. The budget tended to be balanced, public debt went down, the currency became stable again. The concern for public works, reforms, and social welfare was in the minds of most statesmen and expressed itself in some timid acts. It seemed possible for the Republic to adjust with the country and start a new era, comparable to the constitutional monarchy after 1851.

But it was too late for that. Dissatisfaction was general. Everybody complained about the regime, even some of the Democrats themselves. All the other parties conspired against the supremacy of the Democrats and strove for power. Also, the Republic was logically tending toward radicalism in the socialist way. Agrarian reform, increase of taxation of the wealthy, nationalization, development of social welfare, improvement in the living standard of the lower classes, all these subjects were under discussion if not in operation. Such an evolution, however, if it seemed too slow to some people—the intellectuals and workers—seemed, on the contrary, too rapid to others—the rural landowners, the capitalists, part of the middle class, the Church. The upper and the middle ranks of the Army, as well as the upper and middle civil servants, had their purchasing power reduced to a half of what it had been in 1910. The bankers, top traders, and industrialists felt burdened with taxes (or threatened by them) and with the economic crisis, and were frightened by the rise of socialism and anarchism. The clergy wanted to regain its lost influence. Some of the workers were made impatient by their social grievances. Part of the intelligentsia (including many young people) were disenchanted with republicanism and enraptured by the novelty of fascism.

The middle- and lower-class people of Lisbon, who had been the best supporters of the Republic, were tired of the constant revolutions, street agitation, and interruption of normal life which were always taking place, resented anarchism in its daily violent manifestations, longed for a strong government that might restore order and tranquility. And like a huge backdrop were the agrarian, conservative, and feminine elements, the majority of the country, reacting against the progressive minority in the two leading towns—Lisbon above all. It must also be emphasized that, unlike nineteenth-century liberalism, the Democratic Republic was not the beginning of something structurally new but was rather the last phase of something which had started much before, in 1820. The Republic meant the climax of a process, the natural result of the evolution of monarchical liberalism.

To a certain extent, it might be compared to enlightened despotism as the end of an historical period. Thus, it had no future. It must die and be replaced by something totally different. That something was Fascism.

On May 28, 1926, General Gomes da Costa, one of the most prestigious war heroes, rebelled in the North (Braga) and marched on the South. Most of the army joined him or accepted the coup. In Lisbon, the government resigned (May 30), and the President entrusted one of the revolutionary leaders, Navy Commander Cabeçadas, with the task of organizing a new cabinet. On May 31, Bernardino Machado himself resigned. Early in June, Parliament was dissolved. The revolution had won.

THE "NEW STATE"

PORTUGUESE FASCISM

A well-defined, Right-oriented ideology arose in Portugal after 1914. This was Integralismo Lusitano (Lusitanian Integralism), a political trend primarily patterned after French Maurrassism (Action Française) but also with highly original views of its own. Integralismo Lusitano combined a body of radical objections to current political doctrines with a system of relatively precise views on how to organize a future new regime. Against liberalism, both political and economic, it was also against most doctrines which originated in or resulted from the French Revolution. Therefore, Integralists violently denounced individualism and popular sovereignty, with their practical political forms of constitutional monarchy or republic. They denied almost completely the nineteenth-century *en bloc* with its "fallacious" belief in progress and liberty. They pointed out the dangers of ill-interpreted scientism, leading to atheism, positivism, and other doctrines which tended to deny God, religion, and absolute virtues. Naturally, they most strongly condemned what they called the corollaries of "demo-liberalism": collectivism, with its forms of socialism, and (since 1917) communism. From Maurras, Integralists also took over a dislike of Semitism, both in its racial and religious aspects, but they never carried on anti-Semitism to the extent that other pre-Fascist and Fascist ideologies did. They regarded Semitism in the same way as the Reformation and the whole Protestant movement, as something that threatened the all-pervasive influence of both the Church and tradition.

Integralismo Lusitano gradually presented a full program of beliefs and policies. It stood for unbreakable tradition and for the cult of the past as the best teacher of the present. Consequently, it defended a pre-constitutional monarchy, based upon religion, authority, and corporatism. It accepted the social organization as defined by the Church, namely by Leo XIII's encyclicals (*Rerum Novarum,* 1891). It emphasized nationalism and the perpetuity of the "nation," against cosmopolitanism and international doctrines. It also stood for decentralization as it had existed in medieval times, with extensive municipal, provincial, and regional autonomies. Integralists were at first willing to accept ex-King Manuel II, provided that he yielded to their doctrines and complied with their program of a "total remodelling of Portuguese society." But when Manuel refused to do so, sticking to his constitutional oath and to the parliamentary institutions, they withdrew their support and chose the Legitimist cause instead. In 1920, they formally acknowledged as their monarch King Miguel's grandson, young Prince Duarte Nuno, who was living in Austria, as well as the legitimacy of his branch. In doing so, they were certainly being consistent with their beliefs, by rejecting the constitutional line on behalf of the absolutist.

As time went by, Integralismo Lusitano found its leaders, its apostles, and even its martyrs. It also defined some important points in its doctrine concerning real problems of the time, such as the agrarian question, the structure of the future "Parliament," the financial problem. António Sardinha (1888–1925) was the main philosopher of Integralism, José Pequito Rebelo its greatest economist, President Sidónio Pais—who was never an Integralist himself, but who welcomed Integralists as his advisers and cabinet ministers—its martyr and sole (partial) executor.

But Integralismo Lusitano meant also a generation gap, a rebellion of young people (most of them belonging to the generation of 1910–14) against the "establishment" of their time. In this sense it was extremely fashionable (like Fascism in general) and appealed to many youngsters, who cared less about ideologies than about fighting something they abhorred because it stood for their parents' convictions.

The romanticism of physical violence, which Integralists preached and sometimes put into action, added to that appeal. For many, Integralism was the doctrine of an elite in opposition to the vulgar "demo-liberal" principles shared by a majority of mediocrities. Indeed, Integralists rarely sprang from the lower class; they were recruited from upper and middle-class aristocrats, landowners, and bourgeois.

Portuguese Fascism had other origins too, although with much less impact than Integralism. There were the pure Catholic groups, such as the CADC (Centro Académico de Democracia Cristã) of which future President Salazar was the general secretary; the Catholic Center (Centro Católico), which was neutral on the monarchist-republican issue and of which Salazar, too, was a leading figure; and even certain Right-wing political groups within the parliamentary Republic (the Nationalists, for instance).

Italian Fascism (since 1922) and General Primo de Rivera's authoritarian regime in Spain (1923–30) also had a strong impact on the building up of Portuguese Fascism. Both President Carmona and Premier Salazar were great admirers of the two dictators and undoubtedly learned some lessons from Mussolini's and Primo de Rivera's experiments and experiences. By 1926 Fascism was becoming increasingly popular in Portugal among the intelligentsia, its solutions being pointed to as "the solution" for the Portuguese case. This worried intellectuals of the Left and Center very much, particularly the Seara Nova people, who launched a "week against Fascism" two months before the revolution of May 28, denouncing the dangers of authoritarian regimes, emphasizing the negative sides of Fascism, and warning the country against Fascist demagogy.

It would be hard to call the army rebellion of 1926 a Fascist movement. Action had been taken against the "corruption" and "degradation" of the parliamentary republic rather than against the parliamentary institutions as such. The demo-liberal Constitution of 1911 was not abrogated or repealed until 1933. Many leading Army officers stood for a democratic republic and for a return to "constitutional normality," which might imply some changes in the constitution and some purges against the "bad" politicians, but nothing else. This actually was the hope of all parties but the Democratic, which had supported or welcomed the movement as a means of breaking the electoral machine and the all-pervasive influence of the Democrats. The "program" of the Revolution encompassed a long series of vague aspirations which everybody in the country wished to realize, from the Left Democrats to the Right Conservatives: inquiry into the public services, suspicious civil servants, and the "great fortunes"; economies and good administration; valorization of the escudo and decrease in the cost of living; road repair; an end to nationalization and return to private companies of the nationalized services; reforms of the army and the navy; increase in the number of schools; reforms in justice; better administration of the colonies. There was little or no ideology in all this, a fact which permitted a general rally in support of the revolution and explained the difficult task of carrying it on.

The military dictatorship of 1926–28 carefully avoided any action that might be interpreted as aiming at a restoration of the monarchy. Not only were the majority of the ruling officers republicans, but the government felt that it needed the support of the nation, which certainly was against the king. Quite wisely, the monarchist elements decided to wait for a better opportunity. In 1932, however, ex-King Manuel's death inflicted a blow to any monarchical hopes. It substituted an unknown, foreign young pretender, related to the still-hated Miguelist faction, for the beloved, respected, and unhappy last king of Portugal. With Manuel's death, all serious chances of a monarchical restoration died too. Most Monarchists, including Salazar himself, realized this, and supported the Republic. A good many Integralists, waiting for Duarte Nuno's being of age, were not hostile to Republican institutions.

By 1928 the first steps in shaping a new order were being undertaken, but rather slowly. In the fall of 1929, Salazar described the future constitutional reorganization as one based upon a "solid, prudent and conciliatory nationalism"; emphasized the roles of the family, the moral and economic corporation, the parish and the municipality; and uttered the slogan which would become famous: "Nothing against the Nation, all for the Nation." This emphasis on nationalism was to recur in Salazar's and his partisans' speeches and writings as a leitmotiv for the regime. Quite artificially, the new order seized upon nationalism as something new, something typical of itself and in contrast to the former antinational or at least a-national policy.

By repeating it again and again, a method probably learned from Italian Fascist practices, Salazar managed to convince a great part of the population, and perhaps himself too, of the truth of such an assertion. In 1931 he defined the goals of the government as the setting up of a "well understood political, economic and social nationalism, controlled by the unquestionable sovereignty of the strong state."

This doctrine of a strong state, another of the regime's slogans, appealed to a bourgeoisie tired of political instability. With his usual exaggeration when appraising the immediate past, Salazar opposed the old "disorder" to the new order. Thus in 1930 he said: "One single word—*disorder*—defined in every field the Portuguese situation," and further, "we all know where we come from—one of the greatest disorganizations which may ever have existed in Portugal, in economy, finance, politics, public administration; . . . the same spectacle of permanent disorder . . . we can say that seriousness and justice had disappeared from Portuguese life: thus, indiscipline was general" (1932). Such a strong state should rise by strengthening the Executive Power, abolishing the parties and class unions, enforcing censorship, and reorganizing the Army, the Navy, and the Police. Yet Salazar always spoke against totalitarian regimes and criticized both the Italian Fascist and the German Nazi systems. He clearly distinguished between authoritarianism and totalitarianism.

The New State—the word was coined by 1930 and never dropped since—should be social and corporate. Its fundamental cell was the family, its basic elements the moral and economic corporations, where the interests of both employers and employees would together aim at a common "national" interest. Following the Integralist doctrine, Salazar rejected the class struggle as inevitable and regarded it as thoroughly opposed to the principles of the New State. Therefore, the National Labor Statute (Estatuto do Trabalho Nacional), enacted in 1933 and very much like the Italian Labor Charter, followed by a complex number of other laws and regulations, defined a corporate organization for the industrial sector and for agricultural employers. The so-called "Primary Elements" encompassed (1) the national syndicates, composed of employees or members of liberal professions; (2) the *grémios*, gathering together individual employers or firms and extended to the farmers too (casas da lavoura, grémios da lavoura);

(3) the *casas do povo*, rural unions of both employers and workers; and (4) the *casas dos pescadores*, associations of fishermen and their employers. The so-called "Intermediate" or "Secondary Elements" encompassed the National Federations or Regional Federations, i.e., associations of identical syndicates or *grémios*, and the unions, or associations of similar syndicates or *grémios* having common interests. Finally, the "Corporations" proper would constitute, according to the law that created them, "the unitary organization of the production forces, completely representing their interests."

It took a long time to achieve a thorough regulation for all these bodies and make them all operative. Besides the general resistance and indifference to them, it soon became clear that real economic benefits deriving from the corporative organization were few (other than employment of some thousands of new civil servants) and that, on the contrary, many of the Primary and Secondary elements only hampered production and trade. The labor organizations quickly became instruments of government policy which dictated the timing and terms of labor contracts. Most of the labor associations were made compulsory, while internal regulations restricted freedom of self-government and closely defined their powers in dealing with the *grémios*. The working agricultural population was only partly encompassed by this scheme (in the 1960's, only one-fifth of the rurals belonged to the *casas do povo*). The initial enthusiasm with which some had welcomed the birth of the corporative system rapidly faded, and it was only in 1956 that the government, more for reasons of consistency than for anything else, decreed the basic rules for the setting up of the corporations. Down to 1974, only the economic ones had been established: agriculture (1957), industry (1958), trade (1958), transports and tourism (1957), credit and insurance (1957), fishing and fish-canning 1957), press and graphic arts (1959), and show business (1959).

Besides these three orders of "Elements," the government also instituted the so-called "organs for economic coordination," sort of precorporative bodies aiming at relating the state to the corporations. They were the "regulating committees" (*comissões reguladoras*) to control imports, the "national juntas" (*juntas nacionais*) to develop and control exports, and the "institutes" to supervise and officially guarantee the quality of exports. Several other organs appeared to direct and orient professional and corporative activities.

The real consequences for the country of all this complex system are still to be appraised, and its final destiny remains questionable. But it seems beyond doubt that the corporative state shaped a new Portugal, very much in the socialist way, which will be hard to destroy. Regardless of its faults and poor results in production and standard of living, the corporate system built up an economically organized country, an interventionist state essentially different from the liberal, "laissez-faire" Republican order. Almost forty years of actual performance have made the Portuguese accustomed to, and more and more dependent upon, the state. To contrast this new "order" to the one before 1930 would be as legitimate as to contrast the liberal order to the one before 1820. In this sense, the corporate system brought about a true revolution for Portugal, for it changed some of the country's basic structures. This fact must be emphasized to understand the continuity of a regime for more than forty years.

The anti-democratic characteristics of the New State should also be mentioned. In his key speeches of 1930, Salazar clearly put aside the concepts of individual freedom and party organization, although emphasizing the "legitimate individual and collective freedoms." The party—which he regarded as a fiction—must be replaced by the association—which he called a "reality." And in 1934 he went on to say that the 1926 movement "tended to proscribe definitely liberalism, individualism, and partisan or social struggles." Therefore, all political parties and secret societies were finally disbanded when the new constitution was put into effect in 1933, and only a "union of all the Portuguese," typically christened as "National Union" (*União Nacional*), allegedly nonpartisan, was tolerated. It was only after the allied victory of 1945 that a new and vague wording, "organic democracy," came into existence, a term invented by the regime to keep up with the needs of the present.

After 1936, the trend toward a fascistization of the New State intensified. The old Integralist element received the growing influx of the Portuguese Fascist groups, namely the National Syndicalists (very active in 1932–34, which later blended with the National Union), and obviously that of the Fascist experiments all over Europe. The outbreak of the Spanish Civil War led to the birth of the regime's militia, the Legião Portuguesa (Portuguese Legion), a paramilitary organization, which, in its beginnings, had much of a spontaneous movement

of volunteers. Its purposes were to participate in the "anti-bolshevik crusade" and to defend "the spiritual patrimony of the Nation" as well as the corporate order. It is said to have reached some 20,000 members in the late 1930's and early 1940's, membership becoming virtually compulsory in certain public employments, but it quickly faded away and ceased to be taken seriously, as generally happens in Portugal after awhile.

Another Fascist paramilitary group, very much modeled along the Italian and the German patterns, was the Mocidade Portuguesa (Portuguese Youth), a compulsory organization destined to embrace the entire school and university population, but later restricted (in its compulsory form) to the ages of eleven to fourteen. The Mocidade blended some interesting aspects of scouting with political and religious indoctrination. Also established in 1936 (with a precedent in the Associação Escolar Vanguarda, existing since 1934), it rapidly declined and became a subject of contempt or ironical comment for most adolescents.

Both organizations stuck to the typical Fascist uniforms (green shirts), the Roman salute (with the hand position slightly different from the Italian and German ones), the terminology, the internal structure, certain slogans, and so on. Much of this was discontinued from 1945 on, yet it was still possible to watch the Minister of Education raising his arm in the Roman salute by the late 1950's. Regardless of the criticisms against both Legião and Mocidade, they were able to survive until 1974, being given new and more up-to-date tasks (for instance, civil defense for the Legion, student welfare for the youth), in an attempt to revive them and instill new enthusiasm into them. Quoting H. Martins, these two examples "illustrate a characteristic behaviour pattern of the régime: the tenacity with which it holds on to its key symbols and the resilience with which it revives dormant organizations after periods of international discredit."

The other totalitarian institutions of the New State were the repressive mechanisms: censorship, the Police Corps, and several more less obvious devices.

Censorship of periodicals was instituted shortly after the revolution of May 1926, and maintained ever since. It was gradually extended to other media, such as theater, cinema, radio, and television.

In every case, no word could be published, uttered, or broadcast without the censors' prior approval. Of all the repressive mechanisms, censorship can be regarded as the most efficient, the one that certainly has done more to keep things little changed for forty years. It maintained a check not only on political or military matters but also on morals, patterns of behavior, religion, and every news item or address susceptible of influencing the people in a "dangerous" way. Thus, censorship might ban the description of a revolutionary plot at home against the government, as well as the news of some social grievance abroad, or even the tale of a scandalous orgy somewhere. As censors varied greatly both in ferocity and in culture (not to mention intelligence), it happened that their action might reach absurd limits, and sometimes let pass important materials. Also, censorship was rarely centralized, each district or each town having its own body of censors. As a consequence, harshness of censorship varied with geography too. Yet censors were far from free in the use of their "blue pencil." Besides being trained on the "subversive" matters they must ban, they were constantly receiving fresh instructions from their superiors (who ultimately depended upon the Prime Minister). Yet there is no doubt that a part of their activity depended on the censors themselves.

The ultimate consequences of a censorship extended for so long a period were to self-discipline authors, journalists, impresarios, and all those concerned with public media, and to force upon them a self-censorship, in order to avoid having their production constantly harassed and mutilated. This self-censorship has often led to extremes of caution with little real justification. It has also led to the rise of a highly original crypto-writing on the part of authors and to a sharp understanding on the part of readers and listeners. Another obvious result for the public was a hypercriticism of everything and a widespread doubt of what was read and said.

Although censorship was never extended to books, they could be and were frequently withdrawn on police orders. In this case, authors and publishers may be punished. Again, this included both political and nonpolitical material. Foreign periodicals and books might be confiscated or prevented from entering the country, although the latter form of control almost never succeeded.

The political police, which went back to some timid forms in the pre-1926 days, was reorganized in the 1930's, apparently with the advice and training of German and Italian experts. First called P.V.D.E. (Polícia de Vigilância e Defesa do Estado), it had its name shortened into P.I.D.E. (Polícia Internacional e de Defesa do Estado) after 1945, a year in which the powers of the organization were considerably increased.

Although less violent—and especially less well organized—than the German Gestapo or the Soviet Secret Police, the P.V.D.E.-P.I.D.E. record was good enough to make us think of the Inquisition in its golden days. As with the Inquisition the Portuguese Secret Police reached such extremes of power and pervasiveness under Salazar that it defied the authority of the state itself—including that of the Armed Forces—and gradually became a state within the state. And like the Inquisition, it had to justify its own existence and powers by often "inventing" nonexistent threats to the regime's security and "making" Communists and other opponents to the New State out of tenuous presumptions or hearsay. It is, of course, too early to analyze objectively an institution on which so many partisan views have been expressed. But it may be said that neither P.V.D.E. nor P.I.D.E. belong in a civilized world and partake rather of pre-liberal prejudices and methods. The insistence of the Secret Police on the most sophisticated forms of torture, as well as other physical and psychological pressures (written and non-written testimonies on this subject are endless); their use of dismal civilian prisons and concentration camps (a major one was in operation in the Cape Verde Islands from 1936 to 1956, its name, Tarrafal, becoming a symbol of the New State methods of terror); their breaking into residences and seizure of personal belongings; their presence everywhere (so people believe and what people believe does make the general ambience)—all this cemented Salazar's power over the decades and helped explain the famous "order in the streets" he was so proud in claiming. It seems beyond doubt that the Secret Police killed hundreds (if not thousands), while keeping many others in jail for years and years. In 1956 a governmental act introduced the so-called "security measures," which enabled the Ministry of Justice under proposal of the Police to keep indefinitely under arrest (by three-year renewals of the term of sentence) all those who were believed to be dangerous to "society." It is true that such measures have rarely been applied; yet they created a dangerous principle, by overcoming the concept of individual rights and equating political prisoners with the worst delinquents. Also, the act of 1956 implicitly gave the Police the power of unilaterally deciding on how "dangerous" or "regenerated" a political prisoner was.

The main targets of the P.V.D.E.-P.I.D.E. were always the Communists or Communist sympathizers, whose martyrs far surpassed any other oppositionists. It also seems a fact that lower-class elements were generally treated worse than the middle or upper class. Nevertheless, all currents of opinion, including the Catholics and the Integralists, were victims of police persecutions.

Other police corps that acted as instruments of repression were the National Guard (Guarda Nacional Republicana), particularly active in rural areas, the ordinary Police Force (Polícia de Segurança Pública), used to break up meetings and demonstrations, and even the Fiscal Guard (Guarda Fiscal). None of them, however, was specifically related to the New State; their activities were traceable to the past when they sometimes had more strength and influence (as, for instance, the National Guard in the early 1920's).

The repressive mechanism did not stop here. On the contrary, other, less evident, forces were often more relevant in achieving the goals of the regime than the obvious censorship and police authority. This was true of the political pressures on civil servants, which lead to a complete taming of most elements, including instructors and army and navy forces. From time to time, selective purges got rid of the most dangerous and acted as examples to the others. Also, in a small country like Portugal, highly centralized, political pressures affected many "independent" professions, other than the civil servants. Sometimes, the real political reasons for persecution were carefully omitted, professional or moral motivations being invoked instead. Pressure was also put on firms to dismiss or deny admission to politically unreliable people. And a whole climate of "moderate" terror has been shrewdly established. Quoting Hermínio Martins,

The Portuguese case provides an object lesson in the economy of terror. There can be an optimum coefficient of terror comprehensive in impact, embracing the totality of the population, without the extermination of large numbers, but with maximum visibility or publicity as well as cruelty. The

Portuguese régime has achieved such an optimum: with a small number of political murders and arrests (between 1948 and 1959 the annual rate of political "cases" registered by the P.I.D.E. with the political tribunals fluctuated between 700 and 2,000) it has succeeded in politically atomizing the underlying population and paralyzing the élite opposition. Part of its success lies in the unremitting character of the repression, with no wide swings between "excesses" and "liberalizations."

According to Salazar himself (speech of May 26, 1934), the "gospel" of the New State encompassed the Constitution, the Colonial Act, the Organic Charter of the Empire, the Statute of National Labor, and the program of the National Union. To this, the Concordat of 1940 should be added. Leaving the colonial texts to another chapter, and having already mentioned one of the other documents, let us now briefly analyze the Constitution of 1933.

Influenced by the Republican Constitution of 1911, the Constitutional Charter of the Monarchy, and the German Constitution of 1919, the new constitutional text reflected a clear compromise between the "demo-liberal" principles (which Salazar so sharply attacked) and the Integralist-Fascist tendencies, both theoretically and practically expressed in many governmental acts since 1926. It meant a further compromise between republic and monarchy. Because of this, it met with little real approval and actual enforcement, being an object of derision for most oppositionists and one of slight concern for the regime itself.

The Constitution defined the state as unitary and corporative. It classified power in four branches: the President of the Republic, the National Assembly, the government, and the tribunals. It gave the President extensive powers, comparable to those which the Constitutional Charter granted the king; moreover, it provided for the President to be elected by popular vote. A presidential regime might have resulted, yet Salazar's thirty-six-year-old premiership transferred power to the government and reduced the President to almost nothing.

The National Assembly (Assembleia Nacional) was formed by ninety representatives (*deputados*) elected by the people for a four-year term. Its functions were to supervise administration, and to vote the acts proposed by the government or the representatives. In practice, the latter rarely happened, most laws coming from the government, and the role of the National Assembly has always been minimal.

A Corporative Chamber (Câmara Corporativa), composed of representatives (*procuradores*) of the corporations, the municipalities, the Church, the universities, the institutes of charity, and the bodies of administration, assists the National Assembly and the government in lawmaking. Its role has generally been negligible.

The government became the real source of power, and its head (President of the Council of Ministers) the true and sole leader of the country. Quoting Marcelo Caetano, one could define the Portuguese system as a "presidentialism of the prime-minister."

The Constitution of 1933 also registered all kinds of freedoms for the citizen (including freedom of speech, association, the right to habeas corpus, etc.) but made the citizen dependent upon "special laws" which must regulate him. In practice, such "special laws" often overruled the Constitution itself and became the actual law of the country.

Several amendments changed the Constitution now and then but generally in secondary points only. Thus, the number of representatives to the National Assembly went up to 120 (1945), then to 130 (1959). The Colonial Act, considered a part of the Constitution, was substantially altered in 1951. The only major change took place in 1959, by making the election of the President dependent upon an electoral college (composed of the National Assembly, the Corporative Chamber and representatives of the municipalities and the Overseas provinces) rather than upon direct suffrage.

Despite the few practical implications of the electoral system, mention should be made of its functioning. The size of the electorate, to start with, did not significantly increase in forty years, although college-graduated women and female heads of family were given voting rights in the early 1930's: 1,300,000 in 1933, about 1,500,000 in the 1960's. In the same period, however, the population grew by two million and the illiteracy rate declined by 50 per cent. This means that a considerable part of the people qualified to vote (and illiterates were not) never did register, or rather that a good many others were written off the balloting rolls. Both things did happen, maintenance on the voting lists generally (but not consistently) depending upon actual vote-casting in the previous election. Electoral registration was never encouraged, a symptom of both governmental fear before a wide-reaching election and doctrinal scorn of elections as such. As a rule, a high level of abstentions featured the electoral "farces" (as oppositionists called them), although the official figures almost always gave over 80 or 90 per cent victory results.

Up to 1945, only the National Union might nominate the candidates to the National Assembly and the Presidency. Conceived by Salazar as a sort of "anti-party," uniting every Portuguese to a common goal, the National Union virtually became a government party from its very beginning. Indeed the New State differed in such a revolutionary way from demo-liberal or socialist tendencies that a real national union in tune with its principles was utterly impossible. Also, Salazar deliberately closed the door to any possible union when saying: "We have a doctrine and are a force . . . under these circumstances there are no possible agreements, nor transitions, nor compromise" (speech of November 1932). Again, in 1940, he repeated words of condemnation to all his political foes and talked of them as having been "spurned" by the "Fatherland's justice." Thus, the National Union only encompassed the Right-wing, Fascist, or Integralist-oriented side of the nation. In terms of pre-1926 political currents, it gathered together most of the Constitutional Monarchists, Integralists, Legitimists, Catholics (namely the C.A.D.C. and the Catholic Center people), members of the Union of the Economic Interests, along with some "Liberals" (of Cunha Leal's party) and "Nationalists." All the others stayed outside, with a few exceptions, their more than forty-year uncompromising opposition to what they always called "the Dictatorship" featuring a rare and exemplary, albeit useless, attitude in Portuguese history. The regime was never able to "integrate" that opposition (although neutralizing it completely); it has remained a sort of permanent ghost haunting the regime's achievements and victories. Unlike Spain and even Italy, where a significant part of the intelligentsia subscribed to Fascism, the great majority of the Portuguese intellectuals chose the hard road of opposing an authoritarian regime. (This was particularly true since the 1930's. Previously, an older generation of intellectuals was somewhat more sympathetic to the dictatorship. Fernando Pessoa, the greatest Portuguese author of the twentieth century, openly applauded the revolution of May 1926 and its further steps, but he died in 1935.) Despite the several amnesties granted—incidentally never complete and often tricky—scores of distinguished writers, scientists, professors, politicians, as well as thousands of gifted persons, lived in forced exile a great part of their lives and died abroad. Others chose a voluntary exile rather than compromise or be persecuted at home. This happened, to cite a few instances, to men like old President Bernardino Machado (in exile from 1926 to 1940), former Premiers Afonso Costa (who died in Paris in 1937) and José Domingues dos Santos (1927 to the 1950's), essayist António Sérgio (1927 to 1936), and historian Jaime Cortesão (1927 to 1956). Professor Egas Moniz, Portugal's sole Nobel Prize winner (1949), was often harassed too.

The Catholic feature of the New State must be emphasized but not exaggerated, for Salazar's regime (unlike Franco's) never posed as an "apostolic" system engaged in some kind of crusade against anti-Catholic elements. The Premier's few public remarks on Catholicism and religion in general were always strikingly moderate and tolerant, in contrast to his strong beliefs and extremist attitudes on other subjects. His speech of 1940, when the Concordat with Rome was signed, showed a remarkably middle-of-the-way position, uncommitted to any all-pervasive Church influence and definitely opposed to Church meddling with politics. In this sense, one might conclude that the Maurrassist political standpoint prevailed over Salazar's own religious beliefs, and that the traditional Portuguese anticlerical policy did not entirely disappear from his handling of state affairs. His masters had probably been the clever bourgeois statesmen of the constitutional period prior to 1910, when the Church was more controlled by the state than in control of it.

Thus, no attempt was made to reunite Church and state. No one was ever persecuted or even discriminated against because of his religious faith or atheist principles. And the Concordat, while yielding to some Catholic requirements such as the abolition of divorce for couples married in church or the teaching of religion in schools, neither put an end to civil marriage and civil divorce nor gave back to the Church all the property confiscated since 1910. Cemeteries were not sacralized. Religious orders were accepted providing they indulged in some kind of charitable or educational work. Religious oaths were not reestablished. Classes on religion were not compulsory and no passing exams were required. Official schools of theology could never be reestablished at the universities. In short, if the Concordat meant a sort of compromise between the pre-1910 situation and the lay attitude of the Republican regime, it leaned more to the latter than to the former.

It is true that no anti-Catholic propaganda or writings were permitted and that the propagation of other religions was generally discouraged. This, however, derived more from subscribing to tradition and to the advantages of religious homogeneity than from intolerance. In the 1950's a certain revival of religious fanaticism led to the constitutional definition of the Catholic religion as the "religion of the Portuguese Nation," which the original text of the 1933 Constitution had carefully avoided.

More than any definite clerical attitude, Salazar rather emphasized his stand in defense of "Christian civilization" and the creating of a state well equipped for that purpose. Such a belief could be traced back to his speeches in the early 1930's and became a sort of obsession in his later years as premier. He often posed as a prophet of the world's tragedies because of the Western leaders' relinquishment of the true values of Western civilization, which he had always underlined, and because of their surrender to the forces of evil. Such forces were of course Communism, another of Salazar's and his regime's obsessions to the end. Salazar's public mention of Communism and its threats became more frequent after 1936 (because of the Spanish Civil War) and a favorite topic after the end of World War II. Neither the Soviet Union nor any of the Communist countries were ever recognized by the Portuguese government with the exception of Cuba (because with Cuba diplomatic relations were never broken). The foreign attacks on the Portuguese Overseas policy in the 1950's and 1960's gave Salazar and the regime a further reason to stress this anti-Communist attitude and discover a Communist conspiracy against the West.

PORTUGAL BY THE MIDDLE OF THE TWENTIETH CENTURY

When Salazar took power, in 1928, Portugal was obsessed with financial crisis. Balancing the budget was the top priority in every party program. Most countries of Europe (though by no means all) had balanced theirs a decade after the war, and Portugal wanted to be among them. Salazar's first budget, that of 1928–29, accomplished the miracle: revenues reached 2,175,000 contos, while expenditures were kept to 1,900,000 contos, i.e., a surplus of 275,000 contos. To achieve such a result, Salazar's policy had consisted in cutting back expenditures (by 270,000 contos) through strict economies, and in slightly increasing revenues (by 207,000 contos) by introducing some new taxes and better management of public monies (the so-called finance reforms).

From 1928–29 up through 1974, Portuguese budgets were balanced. This had become a sort of fetish of the New State and a cornerstone of its administration, a symbol of good management and continuous progress. To World War II revenues were practically stagnant, the 1939 figure showing not more than 50,000 contos over the 1928–29 figure. Expenditures declined a little, with the result that surpluses never went beyond the level of Salazar's first year in government. In 1936 a finance reform changed the fiscal year and made it coincide with the civil year.

World War II brought some prosperity to the country. Being neutral, Portugal could sell her products quite favorably without greatly disturbing expenditures for war material. Exports of wolfram made many people wealthy and helped the state too. By 1946 revenues had nearly doubled (in relation to the 1939 level), while currency debasement did not go beyond 10 per cent. Gold reserves reached high levels, creating monetary stability.

This trend continued after the war. In the late 1940's revenues surpassed 5 million contos, reaching 9 million in the following decade. The amazing increase of the 1960's brought revenues to almost 13 million in 1966, 20 million in 1967 and 22 million in 1968, double 1960 and ten times those of the prewar era. The taxation reforms of 1958–65 altered the basic rules followed until then, improving efficiency on behalf of the state. New taxes were created, particularly in 1965 (surplus value tax) and 1966 (transactions tax). Expenditures, of course, increased similarly. From the end of the war onward, the tendency was to reduce surpluses more and more, with only a few exceptional years. In the same period the escudo was debased only once (1949) by about 12 per cent.

The world's economic crises did affect Portugal but only moderately. The depression of 1929 had its impact on public revenues, which slightly decreased from 1929–30 to 1932–33, recovering slowly afterward. Prices went down (index 2272 in 1929, index 1960 in 1932), bank rates fell, and unemployment increased slightly. Yet Portugal's overwhelming economic dependency upon countries like England and France rather than the United States, as well as her small degree of industrialization, slowed down any catastrophic results. The public work policy actively carried on by the administration prevented generalized unemployment. Currency was tied to the British pound up to the 1930's: in June 1931 Salazar had completed his first finance reform and publicly announced the return to a gold standard (which England had done as early as 1925). Yet, when the gold standard was abandoned by Britain in September 1931, Portugal had to do likewise, with a few months between a return to gold and the final farewell to gold. With the outbreak of World War II (1939) Portugal tied her currency to both the dollar and the pound in order to keep its value with a minimum of change. The cost of living started increasing again, 1941 reaching the level of 1929. Only in the late 1940's was it possible to slow down the rise in prices. Inflation began again with the African rebellions (1961–64) and economic expansion. In 1968 the cost of living had gone up 31 per cent over that of 1958.

Comparable in so many ways to mid-nineteenth-century Fontism (see chapter 10), the New State embarked on an extensive program of public works. Beyond all the propaganda effects—constantly heralded at home and abroad—this policy aimed at a development and betterment of substructures considered instrumental in the shaping of the country's new economy. Public works became a sort of leitmotiv, a subject that revealed the new Portugal on the move, and indeed one of the great achievements of Salazar's administration. But while Fontism had mostly relied on private investments and private initiatives—a liberal state would not permit it otherwise—public works under the New State were fundamentally a government undertaking, and a way to avoid unemployment in epochs of economic depression or stagnation.

The railroads changed little. The railroad network of 3,300 km. of the mid-1920's increased only slightly, to 3,500 km. in 1935 and 3,600 km. in the 1940's, but then stopped increasing altogether as roads and motor cars developed instead. Rolling stock, however, improved, as well as service in general. Electrified railroads started in 1926, but for more than thirty years only 25 km. of railways were electrified. In the 1950's and 1960's electrification and equipment with Diesel locomotives speeded up (almost 900 km. were electrified in 1968). In 1951 the government granted a railroad monopoly to the largest operating private company (Companhia Portuguesa de Caminhos de Ferro), giving up its share in railroad ownership. Another important novelty was the opening of the Lisbon subway in 1959.

Road building and road repairing were for many years the proud symbol of a new administration. The total road network doubled in twenty-five years (13,000 km. in the mid-1920's, 26,000 by 1950) and surpassed 30,000 km. in 1968. The first—and for a long time the only —expressway was opened to traffic in the 1940's, modeled after Germany's. Road repairing was still more important, particularly in the late 1920's and the 1930's, large sums being allotted yearly for that purpose. To the late 1950's Portuguese roads could be regarded as good by European patterns. Yet traffic increase—particularly of trucks—and a gradual lack of concern with highway repair brought about a considerable deterioration in the 1960's and the obvious need for radically changing the entire road structure of the country. Road building was accompanied by bridge building, several outstanding and spectacular bridges being erected from the 1930's to the present (the arch-bridge over the Douro at Oporto, opened in 1963; the bridge over the Tagus in Lisbon, the longest suspension bridge in Europe, opened in 1966).

Telegraph and telephone networks expanded remarkably too (8,000 km. of cables by 1930, 100,000 in 1968; 300 km. of phone wires in 1930, nearly 60,000 in 1968), phones being totally nationalized in the mid-1960's.

Port facilities were considerably improved. In Lisbon, Leixões (the port of Oporto), and other places extensive works were carried on for the purpose of enlarging piers, deepening bottoms, erecting protective walls, and equipping harbors with modern facilities. The same happened with airports, although to a lesser degree.

A policy of land irrigation and electrification led to the building of numerous dams scattered all over the country (Castelo do Bode, Cabril, Paradela), a field in which Portuguese engineers excelled and became known worldwide. Yet Portugal was far from being totally electrified in the 1960's.

Public works encompassed many other aspects of life such as housing (houses for workers), health (hospitals), sports (stadiums), justice (courthouses and prisons), administration (government buildings), army and navy (barracks, shipyards), tourism and history (state-owned inns and restoration of monuments). State participation in most works undertaken by private initiative or by the municipalities became a matter of fact, a natural and indispensable condition, increasing everyone's dependency upon the administration.

The public works policy bore fruit, making possible—along with the general expansion of Europe—the rapid economic development of Portugal in the 1950's and the 1960's. In the balance of trade, for instance, exports rose ten times between 1926 and 1951 (mostly after World War II), then doubled to 1964, and reached more than twenty-eight times their former level in 1967 (722,000 contos in 1926; 7,563,000 contos in 1951; 14,814,000 contos in 1964; 19,685,000 contos in 1967). As imports increased only twelve times (2,342,000 contos in 1926; 29,135,000 contos in 1967), the usual deficit of the balance of trade—only avoided in 1941–43 because of the war—declined in relation to the trade volume. Exports, which were generally below the deficit level, showed a surplus for the first time in 1936–46, and then permanently after 1950 (with an exception only in 1961). The remaining deficit was largely made up with money sent by emigrants and with the profits of tourism, particularly since the 1950's.

The development of exports was a result of industrialization mainly, yet some agriculture and mining products (like cork, wine, fruit, and stone) also expanded or obtained better prices. Textiles constituted one-fourth of all exports in the mid-1960's, but only one-fifth in 1961, 5 per cent in 1934, and 6 per cent in 1926. Chemical products doubled in five years (1961–65) for export purposes, reaching 7 per cent of all exports in 1965. Paper machinery also doubled in the same period. The steel industry was introduced in the 1950's. Canned fish maintained its place as an important item in foreign markets. Altogether, the role of industry in exports rose from one-third (1926) to almost two-thirds by the late 1960's. Imports hardly changed in character. Portugal continued to order all kinds of manufactured items, like machinery and transport equipment, textiles, plastics, rubber, oil and coal, metals, grain, and the like.

Highly revealing for the political situation of Portugal in the world were the changes in export-import markets. To the 1920's Great Britain had by far the leading place in both. In the early 1930's one-third to one-fourth of all imports came from Britain. Germany, the United States, Belgium-Luxemburg, and France were far behind. The Overseas provinces were as important as Germany, with about one-ninth of imports. Exports went first to the colonial empire (one-fifth to one-fourth), followed closely by Great Britain. Much behind was Germany, France, Spain, and the United States.

World War II and world changes afterward modified this picture. The dependency upon the Overseas provinces constantly increased; they reached first place both in imports (17 per cent in 1954, 14.2 per cent in 1967) and exports (25.3 per cent in 1954, 24.3 per cent in 1967). The second place was irregularly held by Britain (imports—15 per cent in 1954, 13.7 per cent in 1967; exports—15 per cent in 1954, 21.5 per cent in 1967), closely followed by Germany (imports—13.7 per cent in 1954, 15 per cent in 1967; exports—6.9 per cent in 1954, 5.3 per cent in 1967) and the United States (imports—8.3 per cent in 1954, 6.9 per cent in 1967; exports—10.3 per cent in 1954, 10 per cent in 1967).

Despite the great changes and accomplishments which took place in most economic fields, particularly after World War II, the New State could not transform Portugal into a well-developed country. The main reason was that in other underdeveloped countries of Europe the rate of economic growth was faster than in Portugal, and was coupled with a wise policy of cultural development which Portugal lacked. In the 1950's the administration launched extensive plans of combined national development including the Overseas provinces, the Portuguese equivalent of the famous Soviet Five-Year Plans. A first Plano de Fomento covering the years 1953–58 was followed by a second (1959–64), then by a complementary one (Plano Intercalar, 1965–67) and finally by a third one (1968–73). It is still too early to appraise the value and impact of these plans but it seems beyond doubt that their contribution to the shaping of a developed country, halfway between capitalism and socialism, was a major one. In the mid-1960's Portugal's gross national product provided a yearly per capita revenue of $408.00 (Sweden—$2,740.00; Turkey—$275.00), placing her among the lowest-ranking European countries. The number of emigrants leaving Portugal in search of better salaries was a clear proof of poor conditions at home. The war in Africa, if it provided a stimulus for economic development and migration, also hampered prospects of a faster rate of growth at home, with 50 per cent of the national budget being applied to military expenses. Portugal's increasing dependency upon the Overseas provinces (see chapter 14) was another obstacle to a full development in the framework of a united Europe.

In the field of agriculture, one of the main concerns for many years was to achieve self-sufficiency in grain production. A direct result of the pre-1926 situation, this goal also reflected a general European tendency in the 1930's. Mussolini had launched his widely advertised "battle of wheat" or campaign for wheat production; it had a strong impact on Portugal. In 1929 the *campanha do trigo* (wheat campaign) was started, and throughout the thirties a vast effort was aimed at enlarging harvest areas, particularly in the South. Results looked promising at the beginning: wheat areas increased and wheat production grew from 284,000 tons to a maximum of 771,000 tons (1935). In 1934 and 1935 harvests were so bountiful that wheat was stored for export purposes. Final results, however, were poor. Most soils had not been conditioned for grain cultivation and became quickly exhausted. Problems arose as how to place wheat surpluses in international markets at a compensating price. Overproduction proved as harmful as underproduction had once been. Moreover, the population increase completely destroyed any prospects of making Portugal self-sufficient in grain. Despite some sporadic attitudes to the contrary, the wheat campaign was over by World War II, and wheat imports had to be resumed once more. Nonetheless, some of the early results remained, both harvest lands and wheat production (along with maize and other crops) continuing to increase to the 1960's.

Much more successful and useful was the tree-planting policy, which converted barren fields and mountain soil into green and productive lands. The total forest area increased from 23.1 per cent in 1920 to 27.8 per cent in 1939, and to 28.2 per cent in 1957. Irrigation also developed, with a growing number of dams and artificial lakes scattered over the country. A general campaign for agrarian production, launched in the 1930's and the 1940's, was coupled with a somewhat more successful effort for rational colonization inside Portugal (Junta de Colonização Interna), something being done in the field of land reclamation with enduring results.

Among the traditional cultures vineyards somewhat expanded to the 1940's, wine production increasing from 5 million to 14 million hectoliters but declining later on. Olive oil, cork, and fruit had their production substantially enlarged too. Fishing also developed, with important results for the canning industry, one of the most relevant in Portugal.

From 1930 to 1968 the population of Portugal increased more than one-third. The rate of growth was particularly high from 1930 to 1940. Figures, as shown by decennial censuses, were 6,825,883 in 1930, 7,722,152 in 1940, 8,441,312 in 1950, and 8,889,392 in 1960. By the late 1960's the number of Portuguese exceeded 9.5 million. The death rate declined by 50 per cent from 1926 (20.43 per thousand) to 1965 (10.72 per thousand) although child mortality was still high: 64.9 per thousand in 1965 (it was 126.1 per thousand in 1940). The birthrate declined too (32.82 per thousand in 1926; 23.74 per thousand in 1965).

An important factor explaining demographic changes was emigration. After the high figures of the post-1919 period, emigration declined during the 1930's and the 1940's because of restrictions adopted by American countries and because of the war. The return to normality brought about a new and ever-increasing wave of emigration to Brazil (1945 to 1963), the United States and Canada (in the late 1960's), and Europe (also in the 1960's). Official figures registered 20,000 emigrants in 1950, 30,000 in 1951, nearly 50,000 in 1952, a 30,000 average in 1953–63, 55,000 in 1964, 89,000 in 1965, 120,000 in 1966, and 95,000 in 1967. The last three figures surpassed the high levels of 1912–13 (see chapter 12) in absolute figures but not in proportion to the population. In the 1960's most emigrants went to France and Germany where they were offered salaries far higher than those at home. Regardless of the human aspects of the problem, emigration brought about a number of advantages, such as important amounts of foreign exchange credits regularly mailed to Portugal, as well as the need for a higher mechanization of agriculture, and the raising of rural salaries at home. Yet it deprived the country of hundreds of thousands of able men and women, posing difficult labor problems.

Urban growth continued, the areas of Lisbon and Oporto attracting a great influx from the rural and the more backward hinterland. In 1960, 25.1 per cent of all Portuguese lived in those two areas. Total urban population, however, did not go beyond 22.8 per cent. This means that a large percentage (49 per cent in 1950, 44 per cent in 1960, 40 per cent in the late 1960's) still depended upon agriculture, with less than a third (34 per cent in 1950, 29 per cent in 1960, 30 per cent in the late 1960's) occupied in industrial jobs.

Reforms in administration stand out among the main achievements of the New State governments. Concerned with "order" above all, Salazar and his ministers tried their best to improve public services in general. In all ministries internal reforms were carried on, particularly in the early 1930's, aiming at a more efficient and economic organization. Public services, such as the Post Office, also experienced important changes. The army and navy were several times reorganized. Extensive reforms took place in the field of justice too.

The number of ministers was successively increased, according to a higher specialization of functions: ten in 1926 (Interior, Justice, Finance, War, Navy, Foreign Affairs, Commerce and Communications, Colonies, Education, Agriculture; in 1932 Agriculture was put together with Commerce, but a Ministry for Public Works was created); eleven from 1933 to 1940 (Agriculture autonomous again); ten from 1940 to 1947 (Agriculture and Commerce reunited under the general title of Economy); eleven from 1947 to 1950 (Communications added); thirteen from 1950 to 1955 (National Defense and Presidency, a sort of Vice-Premiership, added); fourteen from 1955 to 1958 (a new Ministry of Health); fifteen from 1958 to 1965 (Corporations created); fourteen again from 1965 to 1969 (Presidency abolished). Many undersecretaries were also created, which increased the total figure of government members to nearly thirty in the mid-1960's.

Salazar also changed traditional methods of governing. Cabinet meetings were reduced to a minimum and replaced by frequent two- or three-person meetings between the Prime Minister and his ministers. Total Cabinet reshufflings came to an end in 1932. Up to his forced retirement, thirty-six years later, Salazar changed 50 per cent or more of his cabinet members all at once only five times: in 1936, 1944, 1947, 1958, and 1968. Periodic changes of ministers (once a year to 1936, once each three or four years afterward with few exceptions) generally affected no more than a third of his people. This practice brought about continuity in administration and perfect control by the Prime Minister, who never met a complete set of new faces at once. The average number of years in power for cabinet ministers from 1932 to 1968 reached four and a half. Yet there were much longer ministries, stretching for ten or more years: Navy Minister Américo Tomás (later elected President) ruled from 1944 to 1958; his successor, Fernando Quintanilha de Mendonça Dias, in 1958–68; Justice Minister João Antunes Varela was in power from 1954 to 1967 and his predecessor, Manuel Cavaleiro Ferreira, from 1944 to 1954; Finance Minister António Pinto Barbosa ruled in 1955–65; Public Works Minister Eduardo Arantes e Oliveira in 1954–67; Communications Ministers Manuel Gomes de Araújo and Carlos Ribeiro held power in 1947–58 and 1958–68. Permanence in power increased after the end of World War II, as Salazar grew older and less inclined to change.

The two administrative codes of 1936 and 1940 stressed centralization for all practical purposes. Yet the general administrative division of Portugal was basically unaltered. Besides the parishes (*freguesias*), municipalities (*concelhos*), and districts (*distritos*), the Constitution of 1933 officially reintroduced the provinces as units of administration. Eleven in number (Minho, Trás-os-Montes e Alto Douro, Douro Litoral, Beira Alta, Beira Baixa, Beira Litoral, Estremadura, Ribatejo, Alto Alentejo, Baixo Alentejo, and the Algarve), they were later eliminated again, according to the reform of 1959. A new district was also created in Setúbal (1926). The number of both *concelhos* and *freguesias* considerably increased after 1926, a result of the population growth. The ecclesiastical division was improved with the setting up of a new bishopric in Aveiro (1940). With the publication of a new Civil Code in 1966, the New State achieved one of its coveted aims. Most of the country's legislation from top to bottom was now its own.

A policy of mass education was never a top priority for the New State, despite periodical claims to the contrary by officials. The total rate of illiteracy went down slowly to the 1950's: 67.8 per cent in 1930, 55 per cent in 1940, 45 per cent in 1950. Primary schools numbered some 7,000 in 1927, 10,000 in 1940, and 10,800 in 1950, with corresponding figures for teachers of 8,500 in 1927, 13,400 in 1940, and 14,000 in 1950. Plans for school building and effective erection of schools were a feature of the New State era, yet they brought about a replacement of the new for the old, rather than a significant increase in total number. After 1950 some further steps were taken to promote literacy: widespread campaigns for adult teaching and mass education with considerable propaganda aims but also some real impact on illiteracy were conducted in 1953 and 1956. Primary schools reached 11,500 in 1960 and 18,000 in 1968. Illiteracy declined to 38.1 per cent in 1960 but was still 30 per cent in 1968, which placed Portugal below all other European countries. Elementary teaching, abolished in 1936, again got some official support after the 1950's. Compulsory school years increased from three to four in 1960 and then to six in 1967. Yet the percentage of the national product applied to education was only 1.9 per cent in 1963, indeed more than in Spain but less than in countries like Cuba (5.8 per cent), Mexico (3 per cent) or Greece (2.1 per cent).

Secondary and technical education received comparatively more attention from government. New high schools and technical schools rose everywhere, school population increasing from 32,000 in 1926, 74,000 in 1940, 95,000 in 1950, 217,000 in 1960, and 350,000 in 1968, ten times over. The number of teachers, however, did not grow proportionately, with the result that classes became larger and education deteriorated. Nonetheless, Portuguese secondary education did retain quality, despite the heavy political indoctrination in subjects like history, philosophy, and "political and administrative organization of the nation." The highly centralized education system led to the so-called "sole books" (*livros únicos*), officially approved by the government and imposed on all schools as the only authorized textbooks. The *livro único* policy was also adopted in primary schools. Several reforms in secondary education, generally influenced by French methods, were introduced to improve techniques and update the system with relative success (1929–32, 1936, 1947–48, etc.).

Higher education generally declined, a result of political harassment and mistrust of instructors and students alike. Periodic purges deprived the universities of some of their best talents, while political reasons prevented recruiting of qualified staff, hindered promotions and shoved up mediocre but politically reliable people. In 1930 a government act created a Technical University in Lisbon encompassing the existing schools of Engineering, Business Administration, Agronomy, and Veterinary Science, but no new schools were ever established. On the contrary, the government closed down the School of Arts in Porto (1928) and the School of Pharmacy in Coimbra (1928, restored 1932), and envisioned doing the same for the Schools of Law and Arts of Lisbon. In 1933 the School of Commerce of Porto was also closed. It was only after the 1950's that the university system progressed a little, benefiting from the country's economic expansion and the enrollment of larger and larger numbers of young people (6,000 students in 1926; 9,000 in 1940; 14,000 in 1950; 20,000 in 1960; 35,000 in 1968). The School of Arts of Porto was reopened (1961), and a new School of Economics also in Porto, made its appearance (1953).

Successive reforms in each group of upper schools enhanced centralization but had very little impact on quality of education. Basically, and with a few exceptions in colleges of science and engineering, methods and subjects remained the same as before 1926, often with unchanged staffs and endowments. The public works policy led to the building of a new campus at Coimbra (started in 1948), then to the beginning of another one in Lisbon (started in 1953). In the fields of medicine and engineering, however, some real progress was achieved, with the creation of several excellent laboratories and other centers of research (Institute of Stomatology, Institutes of Climatology and Hydrology, etc.) and the development of existing ones (like the Cancer Institute). The National Laboratory for Civil Engineering, founded in 1946, quickly ranked among the best in the world.

Student organizations were either disbanded or strictly controlled by government acts. Contacts with international groups were forbidden. Official policies of enhancing the role of the Mocidade Portuguesa in the universities, however, failed utterly, and students always represented the most untamed and active focus of rebellion against the regime, particularly after 1960.

Government control of research activities led to the strengthening of the junta founded in 1924 (see chapter 12), which gradually became the only source of grants and the sole framework for post-graduate studies. Renamed Junta de Educação Nacional (1929), then Instituto para (later de) a Alta Cultura (1936), it evolved toward a highly bureaucratic organism, politically oriented and discriminatory.

Competition with the all-pervasive government control of education started only in the 1950's, with the establishment of the wealthy Gulbenkian Foundation and several other less important private groups with cultural and scientific purposes. The Church also managed to create a rudimentary Catholic University (1960's); and several private schools for less formal and more practical matters (business management, foreign languages, hotel management, tourism) opened their doors to a large audience.

Outside regular education the general development of culture was jeopardized by the growing interference of the government and its mistrust of progressive currents of thought. In the world of letters censorship operated again and again, erasing or mutilating articles, bringing periodicals to an abrupt end and preventing others from appearing. Countless book manuscripts could never be published because of editors' fears of possible consequences. Many others were confiscated shortly after publication. Similar things happened with theater plays and movies, as well as with radio and television broadcasts. Very few international movements of cultural renovation could enter Portugal on a wide basis or entered only when they were no longer new. Portuguese authors and other interested people had to travel abroad or depend upon foreign publications in order to get acquainted with the current world of culture and overcome the prevalent stagnation and backwardness at home. To their credit it must be emphasized that they always managed to keep up with what was going on in the world. Yet, curbed in their possibilities of addressing a broad audience, they had to hoard that knowledge or transmit it in a superficial and crippled way only. As a consequence, the up-to-date cultural elite contracted more and more, and became a sort of closed aristocracy whose contacts with the people tended to be narrower and narrower.

Major prose and poetry writers to the 1950's were Aquilino Ribeiro (1885–1963) and Miguel Torga (born in 1907), both Nobel prize candidates; Ferreira de Castro (1898–1974) most of whose works were translated into numerous languages; José Régio (1901–69); Alves

Redol (1911–69), the greatest exponent of neo-realism; and António Sérgio (1883–1969), the philosopher and essayist.

One of the great moments in the Portuguese cultural life in modern times was undoubtedly the "discovery" of Fernando Pessoa's work (see chapter 12). Unknown to most people up to the 1940's, Pessoa quickly became one of the top Portuguese and world writers, ranging immediately after Camões according to many critics. His major books were all published in the 1940's and 1950's (since 1943), and his strong impact on Portuguese literature is still hard to measure. His works are currently being translated into English and French.

Journalism declined with the establishment of censorship and the systematic harassment of the publication of new periodicals. The number of periodicals (some 500 in 1926) increased to 702 in 1933, then went down to 497 in 1944. Although it went up again later (1,111 in 1967), it could never reach its former level in proportion to the literate population of the country and in relation to its impact on public opinion. Political reasons again were instrumental in discouraging all kinds of literary activity, from poetry (the least hindered) to playwriting, or in preventing the rise and development of new themes (generally regarded as subversive). Nonetheless, the Portuguese were able to survive and even to try some competition with foreign countries. By the mid-1960's Portugal ranked fourteenth in Europe in the number of books published yearly (it had ranked eleventh in 1960), which roughly corresponded to her demographic place in the continent—irrespective of her illiteracy rate—and seventeenth in the world. In proportion to her total population this put her above countries like the United States. Translations from foreign books reached one-fifth of the total number of books published altogether.

Political ideologies had a lesser impact on the arts, yet the trend toward centralization in every field did influence the development of architecture, sculpture, painting, and the other arts. Many artists were forced into permanent exile or residence for long periods outside Portugal. The foundation of the National Secretariate of Propaganda—later called National Secretariate for Information—in 1933 was instrumental in creating a fascist "national" style (very much influenced by "traditional" forms), which pervaded the arts at least to the 1950's. Under the direction of António Ferro (1895–1956), the S.N.P.-S.N.I.

undertook multiple efforts in every artistic field, mostly perhaps with typical political goals but some others with highly interesting features of art development. New trends, more liberated from official control, asserted themselves after World War II, accompanied by a younger generation of remarkable painters, sculptors, and architects. On the world scene, however, only painter Maria Helena Vieira da Silva (born 1908), who lived abroad after 1928, should be mentioned.

The Cinema declined after a brief period of timid flourishment in the thirties and early forties, when the vogue of musicals or song-based films was general throughout the world. Official insistence on old-fashioned or propaganda themes and discouragement of innovation harassed neorealism and other modern trends, leading to the gradual vanishing of Portuguese cinema.

Science and technology developed unevenly. In some fields, such as medicine, Portugal's contribution was a major one. Professor Egas Moniz (1874–1955) received the Nobel prize in 1949 for his discoveries in brain angiography and leucothomy. He founded an important school of research in those and other fields. Tropical medicine, too, had a remarkable development in Portugal. Another good example of progress was civil engineering. Many sciences, however, stagnated or declined, for lack of funds devoted to equipment and research or because of political discrimination.

THE EVENTS

Cabeçadas' government, a compromise between the Republican public opinion and the Fascist-oriented army groups, had no basis to endure. It tried to conciliate what, by its very ideological principles, was irreconcilable. Backed by most of the Army, General Gomes da Costa staged a coup d'état (June 17) and imposed his full authority on the new cabinet. Yet his dubious reliability as a Rightist (he had belonged to the Radical Party) and his thorough ineptitude at political maneuvering led to his quick downfall. On July 9, 1926, another Army coup, directed by monarchist General Sinel de Cordes, ousted Gomes da Costa (who was arrested and deported to the Azores; he was later awarded the title of field marshal and allowed to return) and replaced him with General Oscar Carmona, a Rightist and a former war minister in a short-lived Nationalist government, who had little military prestige.

Up to 1928, Sinel de Cordes and Carmona ruled Portugal in a typical military dictatorship. Carmona kept the presidency but Cordes was the Finance Minister and the strong man of the new regime. He tried to reorganize finance and to balance the budget, as well as stimulate Portugal's economy. But he had no preparation for such an undertaking, and the results were disastrous. The deficit rose to an unheard-of amount and the government had to ask the League of Nations for a loan.

The dictatorship was obviously backed by a large number of people, at least in the beginning. As they were dissatisfied and united against the "status quo," they applauded the revolution, many because they were unable to understand it and many others because they thought they could take advantage of it. This was clearly true of the parties in opposition to the Democrats. But, as the Rightist elements began to take the lead and the Fascist and Monarchist trends began to assert themselves, more and more people began to regard the new regime with concern, even within the armed forces. Several groups claimed that Sinel de Cordes and Carmona had betrayed the revolution and its goals, that the Republic was in danger and the democratic institutions threatened. Indeed, the regime had established censorship of the press at the outset, along with several other repressive measures.

The growing opposition expressed itself in the usual way: force. In February 1927 a violent revolution broke out in Porto and in Lisbon, gathering together Army and Navy corps and thousands of civilians. It failed, with several hundreds dead or wounded. In July 1928 another though less serious army and civilian uprising took place in Lisbon, Setúbal, and elsewhere. This one also failed. In 1931 there were two revolts, the first one in Madeira, the Azores, and Portuguese Guinea (led by deported politicians and holding out for nearly a month); the second one in Lisbon. The government always won. Some abortive coups d'état within the leading elements themselves also took place but no essential change occurred in the regime except that it became increasingly Right-oriented. The consequences of such uprisings and conspiracies were the development and improvement of the re-

pressive machine. Censorship was tightened up, thousands were arrested (many being deported to the Overseas), the secret police interfered more and more in everyone's daily life. Civil servants, army and
navy officers, and schoolteachers were dismissed because of their hostility (or even suspicion of hostility) to the regime. Thousands fled the
country and lived in exile. In this way, the dictatorship gradually got
rid of its worst enemies, including most of the professional revolutionaries or conspiracy-trained elements, and was able to impose on
the country a state of "peace and tranquility."

Late in 1927 it had become clear that Sinel de Cordes' financial
policy led nowhere but to catastrophe. The government formally requested help from the League of Nations. Previously, it had tried to
get money from foreign banks. But in Paris the main exiles, including
ex-President Bernardino Machado, Afonso Costa, and several others,
had warned the foreign governments that only Parliament might ask
for loans of any kind, and that they would not acknowledge any loans
if they ever returned to power. The League sent to Lisbon a committee
of experts, who studied the Portuguese situation and set up a number
of conditions for the loan involving practically international control
of Portugal's finances. This the regime thought offensive to the country's independence, and the loan was rejected. It also meant the end
for Sinel de Cordes. His prestige sunk to nothing; and he and his
clique had to step back and be replaced by new and younger people.

Meanwhile, some dictatorial acts had changed the Constitution
(which theoretically remained in force), providing for a popular presidential election. Carmona was the only candidate and was therefore
elected President of the Republic. He entrusted Coronel Vicente de
Freitas with the task of forming a new government (April 1928). This
cabinet, totally different from the former one (the Foreign Minister
excepted), included Professor Oliveira Salazar as its Finance Minister.

Less of a politician than his predecessor, Vicente de Freitas
seemed to point toward a national conciliation policy within a Republican framework. Only three of the cabinet members were military,
and emphasis was placed on technicians with little or no definite
political affiliation. Carmona ceased to play any major role in politics.
But this trend did not continue. A cabinet reshuffling in November
opened the door to extreme Rightist elements in the portfolios of

Justice and Education. In July 1929 the Right wing obtained a victory on a minor religious issue, which led to Vicente de Freitas' resignation and to the appointment of another moderate, General Ivens Ferraz, as premier. His intent to carry on a moderate policy of national union failed too. In January 1930 Carmona accepted General Domingos de Oliveira, a more Right-oriented personality, as Prime Minister. This meant Professor Salazar's nearly complete triumph.

Oliveira Salazar, a thirty-nine-year-old professor of economics at the University of Coimbra (School of Law), was deeply involved in politics when he accepted the Finance portfolio. He had organized and developed the Catholic Party and had been proposed as Catholic representative to Parliament several times, being elected once. In 1919, he was suspected of plotting against the Republic, and dismissed from his teaching position for several months. Far from being unknown, he was regarded as a good deputy of the Right-wing, Catholic interests, sympathetic to the Monarchy. Moreover, his books and articles on economic and financial problems had made him praised and respected by friends and foes. Cabeçadas accepted him as Finance Minister in 1926, but Gomes da Costa's coup d'état ousted him after some days in office. In 1928 he accepted Vicente de Freitas' invitation on condition that he would control all the private budgets of the ministries and have the right of *veto* on every increase of expenditure.

His successful policy gained him immense prestige and made of him the "saviour" of the country. The budget for 1928–29 envisaged a surplus, the first one in fifteen years. His concise and quiet speech, elegant and simple, in contrast to the usual vain rhetoric of politicians, was pleasing to, and could be understood by, everybody. In June 1928, for instance, he told the nation that a good policy of administration must be "so clear and simple as any good housekeeper can make it— a plain and modest policy, which consists in spending well what one possesses and in not spending more than one's own resources."

Gradually, Salazar's control of the government reached the political and military. Already in 1929 he was addressing the nation on nonfinancial problems and suggesting slogans of government in which Right-wing nationalism was emphasized ("Nothing against the Nation, all for the Nation"). In 1930 he made two famous speeches in which the main points of the future organization of Portugal were clearly defined. Behind Salazar, of course, were powerful forces: capital and banking, which wanted a free hand to expand without restrictions, protected from social claims, strikes and continuous unrest; the Church, proclaiming a new victory of the Christian ideals and morals over the Republican demo-liberal atheism, and exploiting the Fátima apparitions; the majority of the Army, constantly praised by Salazar himself, respected and granted increasing privileges; the Right-wing intellectuals with a high percentage of professors from Coimbra; and most Monarchists, firmly believing that Salazar's full control of power would give them back their king (Manuel II himself uttered explicit praise of Salazar).

The so-called "New State," as well as the National Union, or government party, were also defined throughout 1930 and 1931. The dictatorship policy regarding the Overseas also had a written expression, in a sort of code called the "Colonial Act" (see chapter 14). Opposing the regime in a legal way, a number of democrats, socialists, former 1926 revolutionaries (including Cabeçadas himself), and many others tried to organize a Republican Socialist Alliance, under the main leadership of General Norton de Matos. But the dictatorship would not tolerate it. As to the other parties, they were either disbanded or inactive. The growing repressive machine prevented every political activity outside the leading groups.

In July 1932 Domingos de Oliveira peacefully stepped down, and President Carmona formally entrusted Salazar with forming a government of his own. It included a number of young civilians, mostly belonging to Salazar's own generation or still younger, and devout admirers of his. The most promising personalities were Armindo Monteiro, a law professor and Minister of the Colonies; Duarte Pacheco, an engineer, Minister of the Public Works.

Throughout 1932 and 1933, the final steps toward a Fascist state took place. Ex-king Manuel had died in England with no direct successors, and Salazar made it clear that he considered the monarchical question closed. He also proposed the dissolution of the Catholic Party, dismissed any agreements or compromises with the opposition groups, and called upon a national rally with the National Union, of which he became the leader. The draft of a new Constitution was published in February 1933 and a vote was held on March 19. According to the official figures, only 6,190 people dared to vote "No"; there were some 800,000 "Yes" and about 500,000 abstentions, which the government regarded as approving ballots according to the terms of a previously announced declaration. The Statute of the National Labor followed, along with other forms of the new corporate organization of the country. All political parties, secret societies, and labor unions were disbanded. Late in 1934 the first general elections brought to the new Parliament an all-National Union representativeness (no other candidates could be nominated). In 1935 Carmona was reelected President without opposition. Throughout 1936, two typically Fascist organizations, the Portuguese Legion, a body of volunteers for the defense of the regime, and the Portuguese Youth, a compulsory paramilitary framework for the young, made their appearance, rousing much enthusiasm and response. The "New State" seemed firmly established.

Yet dissension continued to assert itself, even within the ranks of the "Nationalists," as the partisans of the new order liked to be called. Former Premier Vicente de Freitas, the man who had called Salazar to the government, denounced the National Union as a totalitarian party and criticized the new Constitution; he was promptly dismissed from his office as President of the Lisbon municipality (1933). Reacting against the new labor organization, thousands of workers launched a general strike, partially successful (1934). In the same year, the National-Syndicalists, or Blue Shirts, a fascist group which had supported Salazar, tried a plot against his "non-revolutionary" trend. In 1935, some Right-wing and Monarchist elements were planning a military uprising in Lisbon, which was uncovered by the Secret Police. In 1936, the Spanish Civil War encouraged two battleships to revolt in Lisbon and led to a certain social unrest. The "last" effective attempt to knock out the regime happened a year later when a bomb, designed to kill the Prime Minister, failed to explode.

It was not too difficult for the dictatorship and the New State to be at ease with the foreign powers and to be accepted among them. England was very relieved to see the end of the political and social turmoil which might have endangered her economic interests and the security of the peninsula. As early as 1931 the Prince of Wales and his brother, the Duke of Kent, paid an official visit to Portugal. In France, the pressure of the exiles strained good relationships for a while but not for long. Italy, of course, had only praise for the new order. Spain, where General Primo de Rivera ruled, was the first country to welcome the new Portuguese order, modeled after that of Spain, Carmona visiting Madrid and other places in 1929, and meeting King Alfonso XIII with all his government. The proclamation of the Spanish Republic (1931) worried the Portuguese cabinet, particularly when many exiles moved from France to Spain and started benefiting from the Spanish system of freedom to organize conspiracies against the dictatorship. Yet the Spanish Republic quickly moved to the Right, and it was possible for Salazar to keep good diplomatic contacts. The Portuguese Foreign Minister, Armindo Monteiro, even paid an official visit to Madrid during 1935. The victory of the Popular Front and the outbreak of the Spanish Civil War undoubtedly worried Salazar and his partisans for some months. But as the Spanish Nationalists quickly took control of their country all along the Portuguese border, the regime felt safe again. Actually, Portugal had been a center of conspiracy against the Spanish Republic for some time, and was among the Nationalists' best friends immediately after the insurrection. During the fierce battles close to the border, Republican fugitives in Portugal were promptly turned over to the Nationalists. A privately owned broadcasting company in Portugal, fully supported by the government, decisively helped the Spanish insurgents with all kinds of information. Portuguese Fascist volunteers soon joined Franco in his struggle for Spain, estimated at 20,000 *viriatos* (volunteers), of whom 8,000 died. In October 1936 Salazar broke diplomatic relations with the Republican government, recognizing Franco as early as May 1938. Because of weapon deliveries to Nationalist Spain, Portugal even severed her diplomatic relations with weapon-producer Czechoslovakia, when that country demanded assurance that the weapons delivered to Portugal would not be sold to Spain. It should also be mentioned that within the League of Nations, Portugal always backed Italy in the Ethiopian affair.

What should be emphasized—and that to Salazar's credit—is that a new foreign policy for Portugal was in the making. While never rejecting the traditional alliance with England, the New State tried a more independent and nationalist tack, which accounted for Portugal's political sympathies. The rise of Nazi Germany, Fascist Italy, and Nationalist Spain undoubtedly favored and conditioned that policy. Economically, too, Salazar was trying to make Portugal less dependent upon one country and more dependent upon several. The economic features of the world in the 1930's and 1940's—World War II forcing all neutral or non-occupied nations to face new choices—helped him in that direction.

At home, Salazar's control of the regime increased as time passed. He himself realized that a new era of consolidation had started by 1936. Besides the direction of the government, and the portfolio of Finance, he took for himself those of War (after 1936) and Foreign Affairs (after 1936), all of which he kept until World War II. He considered himself the guide of the nation, believed that there were things which only he could do ("unfortunately there are a lot of things that seemingly only I can do"—official note published in September 1935), and convinced more and more of his countrymen of that too. His all-pervasive interference in every field of administration even extended to programs of celebration and festivities. In 1938, for instance, he drafted a full program of the 1939 and 1940 commemorations of Portugal's eight hundred years of autonomy and three hundred years of restoration of independence, down to the details of the kinds of books to be officially published and the pageantry to be organized. He became more and more of a dictator, more and more inclined to deify himself and to trust others less. As a result, his choice of able collaborators started to shrink, his grant of autonomy to his fellow-ministers declined, and he relied more and more upon favorites and upon a system of repression.

The outbreak of World War II gave him some five years of truce at home. Most of his enemies agreed to stop any subversive action until the end of the war. Portugal declared her neutrality from the very beginning, and was able to enforce it because of a complex group of motives. Salazar's cunning should not be dismissed, but Mussolini's awkwardness in attacking Greece in the fall of 1940 and inability to win that war without German help (the attack in the Balkans, April 1941), was the main factor that prevented Hitler from invading the

Iberian Peninsula and occupying Portugal at the right time. Franco's unwillingness to commit Spain to another war slowed down the German plans of capturing Gibraltar and later postponed them indefinitely.

Salazar's neutrality, however, had its price, and a heavy one. He swallowed his pride and tolerated the national humiliation of watching Portuguese Timor (in Indonesia) being invaded by Australia (1941), then by Japanese troops (1942), and fully occupied for three years with tens of thousands of lives lost and extensive destruction, without any response on his part, not even a break in diplomatic relations with Japan. He was also compelled to allow the Allies (Great Britain and the United States) to establish military bases in the Azores (1943) with little or no compensation. Despite a romantic eulogy to Poland, early in October 1939, Salazar's sympathies obviously were much more with Germany and Italy (so much of whose regimes he had copied at home) than with democratic Great Britain or the United States, allied to his obsessive foe, Soviet Russia. But luckily for him and the political situation he had built up in Portugal, Franco Spain remained neutral and survived the allied victory. With Franco, Salazar had signed a treaty of nonaggression and friendship as early as March 1939. Such a treaty was confirmed by a joint declaration of both countries in May 1940, followed by a protocol in July and by a meeting of Franco and Salazar in Seville, in February 1942. The so-called "Iberian Bloc" thus came into existence. This new bulwark of Portugal's external policy (a clear innovation in the country's external tradition) counterbalanced the alliance with England, which Salazar always carefully emphasized.

The year 1940 represented for the New State in all its purity the peak of glory. To commemorate the tricentennial of independence the regime organized a full set of ceremonies, expositions, congresses, and publications, of which the "Exposition of the Portuguese World" was the best example. Carefully prepared and brilliantly presented by some of the most competent architects, artists, and decorators of Portugal, the Exposition was in itself a typical Fascist display in its manner of interpreting the past and abusing it to herald the present. It could be regarded as a personal success for Salazar and for António Ferro, the able head of the National Secretariate of Propaganda, directly depending upon him.

Troubles started again with the end of the war. The allied victory in Europe (May 1945) was a pretext for pro-democratic and pro-socialist demonstrations throughout the country. For most people, and particularly for the opponents of the regime, the triumph of the democracies heralded drastic changes within the New State, if not the return to a fully democratic system. This conviction created widespread public opinion in the main cities, which questioned Salazar's achievements and continuance in power. Great Britain and the United States were also favorable to a political change in Portugal (as in Spain) and pressured Salazar about it. In September, the National Assembly was dissolved, and the government announced free elections for the coming November. Such an announcement aroused great agitation, both within and outside the regime. Tens of thousands gave their adherence to the newly created M.U.D. (Movimento de Unidade Democrática or Movement of Democratic Unity), a sort of Popular Front against the "New State." Censorship of the press was lifted during the electoral campaign, revealing widespread discontent and a wish for revolutionary changes.

The opposition soon realized, however, that the freedom granted was a very relative one, and that it had no time to promote a political organization of its own which could fight the regime at the polls. It asked for a postponement of the elections. When Salazar answered in the negative, it gave up and refused to participate. All of the National Union nominees were therefore elected without question, as before (in 1934, 1938, 1942). Shortly afterward, a vast purge aiming at those who had subscribed to the M.U.D. jailed several hundreds, dismissed many civil servants (including army and navy officials), and placed under surveillance a large number. The Secret Police was reorganized and its methods perfected; it even got a new name—P.I.D.E. (Polícia Internacional e de Defesa do Estado). All the repressive machinery was improved. Obviously, Salazar had not counted upon such a widespread movement against the regime and was both angered and worried. The same may be said of the major social and economic forces which backed him: the upper class, the Army, the Church. On the other hand, revolutionary action by the M.U.D. was discouraged by England and the United States, increasingly concerned about a Communist take-over of Europe.

From 1945 on, the existence of an opposition cannot be denied. It has expressed itself in many different ways, but it has existed as a permanent bogey to the government. In 1946, a military uprising took place in the North (from Porto to Mealhada, north of Coimbra), the first one in ten years. Although the regime put it down easily, it opened a new era of abortive plots and conspiracies. In 1947 one of the most important of these showed wide military participation, with the possible backing of President Carmona himself, who wished greater freedom of action and was tired of Salazar's leadership. The main reflex of the anti-Salazar movement, however, was shown every four years, when general elections took place, or whenever presidential elections called upon the popular vote. During the one-month electoral campaign, the government would reduce censorship to a minimum, allow open attacks on the institutions and enable the opposition to display its force and ability. Yet, as no changes took place in the electoral law and as no warrants of free balloting ever occurred, the opposition nominees either withdrew on the eve of election day or accepted competition on the uneven governmental terms and lost. This happened again and again, in 1949, 1953, 1957, 1961, and 1965. It became a matter of general strategy for the opposition and its very raison d'être; but it also became a clever safety valve for Salazar's control of the country, and a good propaganda weapon to tell the foreign countries that the Portuguese regime was not Fascist and depended upon popular support. It also hampered the opposition's legality and divided it as to the best methods for overthrowing the New State.

Until 1949 the regime undoubtedly faced a serious crisis. Many people expected the victorious Allies to adopt, in regard to Portugal, the boycott policy they were using in regard to Spain. The United Nations opposed Portugal's admission. At home there was uneasiness, many rumors, aborted conspiracies, and increasing repression. Schoolteachers and university professors were being fired. The concentration camp of Tarrafal (Cape Verde Islands) reopened its gates for the first political prisoners, most of them Communists or Communist-sympathizers. In the presidential elections of 1949 (Carmona had been reelected again in 1942, without opposition), the M.U.D. nominated aged General Norton de Matos, the former War Minister in Afonso Costa's time, and twice governor of Angola. Contrary to all forecasts,

Norton de Matos campaigned vigorously with the help of a remarkable group of advisers. He denounced all the failures and contradictions of Salazarism, pointed out the evils of repression and continuous censorship, and announced his intentions of restoring democracy to the country. Many Portuguese believed in Norton's possible victory, and Salazar may have feared it too. No guarantees of free elections were given, and when the M.U.D. nominee realized the unchanging situation, he withdrew from the race. The almost senile Carmona, despite his growing dislike of Salazar, was therefore reelected once again. Yet, in several parts of Angola, a province in which Norton de Matos enjoyed great popularity, and where electoral competition went on to the end, he won a majority.

The year 1949 was the high point for a united front against Salazar. Internal dissension, which had existed since 1945, became more and more threatening. Communists, socialists, moderates, and old democrats fought one another for preeminence, strategy, and goals. The memories of the "good old days" before 1926, and the fact that the old personalities, active in politics twenty-five years before, were the ones with prestige and political authority, plagued the Portuguese opposition with personal bitterness, rivalries, and old-fashioned ideals. This prevented the opposition from adjusting to modern times and proposing to the nation something definite, clear, and appealing. For many, to throw down the regime would mean to erase all of the Fascist legislation since 1926. But for many, benefits of all kinds had resulted from that legislation and from its practical achievements. It also became clear that the clandestine Communist Party, being the only opposition group with some cohesion and organization, tended to prove itself to the others and instill its doctrines. This further contributed to the split in the M.U.D. and provided excellent material for clever Fascist propaganda.

When President Carmona died, in April 1951, elections presented little danger to the government. The moderates nominated old Admiral Quintão Meireles, a former minister of the Vicente de Freitas' cabinet (1928–29), one of those who felt that Salazar and his partisans had betrayed the revolution. The Left campaigned for Rui Luis Gomes, a renowned mathematician and university professor. The Supreme Court denied its placet to him, on the accusation of Communism; Quintão Meireles withdrew as usual; and Salazar's candidate, General Craveiro Lopes, was elected without question.

By that time, the regime had undoubtedly overcome its first serious crisis and was gradually strengthening its position. Fearing a Communist takeover and not wanting to take risks, the Western Allies were now definitely backing Salazar. Portugal became a member of NATO from its very beginning (1949) and posed as a defender of the free world. To appease international public opinion and rising criticism of colonialism, an amendment to the Constitution repealed the Colonial Act of 1930 and introduced some changes in the status of the "natives" as well as in the official name for the colonies (from then on called "Overseas provinces"). The Soviet Union allowed Portugal to enter the United Nations, along with several other countries in 1955. At home, public works were intensified, industrialization fostered, and salaries raised. Governmental stability increased. Several foreign heads of state and cabinet members visited the country. At the same time, repression was the rule and repressive methods improved. Salazar's ivory tower had become more impregnable as he grew older; and contacts with the lower ranks of administration, as well as the people in general, altogether ceased, particularly after he dropped the ministries of Finance (1940), War (1944), and Foreign Affairs (1947), and simply remained as the head of the government. Thus, it became easier for a group of protégés and more clever advisers to surround him and make him listen to them almost exclusively. As a consequence, too, corruption within the administration seems to have grown. Coronel Fernando dos Santos Costa, the War Minister since 1944 and for a long time considered the "strong man" of the regime, gradually stood out as one of the premier's favorites and a possible successor. An extreme Rightist and Monarchist, he probably influenced Salazar to open the monarchical question again by calling to Portugal the pretender to the throne, Duarte Nuno (a grandson of King Miguel), allowing him and his family to dwell in the country, tolerating open monarchical organization and propaganda (in contrast to the Republican opposition groups), and even mentioning the possibility of a "monarchical solution" in one of his speeches. The tension between President Carmona and Salazar may have been one of the reasons behind the premier's decision to support the monarchists again.

In 1958 the second great political crisis for the regime began. Salazar's growing insensibility and unawareness of the world he was living in provoked extensive reaction, not only within the opposition ranks but among the regime's supporters. In the National Union a "liberal" wing had risen, which demanded a progressive opening up of the political structure to a larger group of persons. They required a change, or reform, in methods of administration, government policies (both at home and abroad, including the Overseas problem), and attitude toward the opposition. A younger generation of technicians and intellectuals had also matured, with no responsibilities or connections with the earlier times of the Salazar administration. They were willing to share government tasks and jobs, but they wanted up-to-date changes. Yet they deeply respected and admired Salazar, having little historical knowledge of the past and not questioning most of the regime statements in regard to the Democratic or pre-Republican period.

This "left"-wing group had been represented in government now and then. By the late 1950's, one of its leaders was Marcelo Caetano, a professor of law in Lisbon, a historian, and one of the ablest and most enlightened supporters of the regime. A former monarchist and extreme Fascist in his youth, he had gradually evolved toward a more moderate and "Center-Left" position within the National Union. He had worked with Salazar several times and been a part of his cabinet, as Minister of the Colonies in 1944–47. He returned to power in 1955 as Minister of the Presidency, a sort of vice-premiership.

The presidential elections of 1958 showed unmistakably the dissensions within the regime. President Craveiro Lopes, who had tried to be other than a puppet in Salazar's hands, was not renominated by the National Union. Instead, Admiral Américo Tomás, the Minister of Marine since 1944 and a docile admirer of the premier's, was chosen. The moderate opposition accepted Air Force General Humberto Delgado, a hot-blooded top civil servant and former partisan of Salazar's, as its leader. The extreme Left nominated Arlindo Vicente, a well-known lawyer.

Delgado proved to be the man fit for the situation. A demagogue, he easily got in close contact with the people and aroused widespread enthusiasm throughout Portugal, as never before. The Left soon re-

alized Delgado's charisma and dropped its separate candidacy, rally-
ing behind him. As in 1949 the regime feared for its survival and prepared military action in case of a possible takeover by the opposition.
Although no guarantees of electoral freedom were granted, and no
poll control by the opposition was accepted, Delgado decided to fight
to the end. Official figures gave him one-fourth of the votes (he won
in several places, including a number of towns in Mozambique), but
he always claimed to be the real winner.

Once the election was over, repression was intensified again. General Delgado was dismissed from his position, then forced to ask for
political asylum at the Brazilian Embassy. He later left Portugal for
Brazil and Algeria. Many of his partisans were fired, arrested, and
tried. The bishop of Porto, who wrote a letter to Salazar insisting
on a change of government methods and policies, had to leave the
country too. A cabinet reshuffling (August 1958), if it sacrificed Santos
Costa—who was becoming too much for the premier himself, also got
rid of Marcelo Caetano.

Political turmoil continued. A group of liberal Catholics were
now actively engaging in political activities and fighting against the
regime which, so they claimed, was jeopardizing the Church's position
with the people. In March 1959, a rebellion in Lisbon was uncovered
with the Catholics having a major role. In 1961 the general situation
worsened with the capture of the liner Santa Maria by political exiles,
in connection with the Angolan uprising in February (see chapter 14).
In April of the same year, the Minister of Defense, General Botelho
Moniz, attempted a coup d'état against Salazar, but failed. In December, the Portuguese possessions in India were invaded and lost, an
event that very much shook the prestige of the regime. All this led to
a new military uprising, on January 1, 1962, in Beja (Alentejo) where
the Under-Secretary of the Army lost his life. Finally, a widespread
student and faculty movement broke out in March (mostly in Lisbon)
and lasted through May. It included strikes, demonstrations, protests,
and massive arrests. At the beginning, Marcelo Caetano, who was then
the President of the University of Lisbon, resigned in a quarrel with
the government on university autonomy.

Yet it was still possible for Salazar to emerge victorious from this
crisis and start another period of stabilization (albeit short, and the

last one). Repressive measures hit both students and instructors. Many were expelled from the university and prevented from studying for several periods of time or altogether. Hundreds were arrested, tried, and condemned. Some teachers were dismissed and others forced to resign under several pretexts. The students did continue their fight for university autonomy and political freedom, but with much less vigor than before. Utterly divided, the opposition posed no great problems to the regime. The years after 1962 were marked by the rise of several petty groups of Chinese-oriented Communists, independent Communists, or other Marxists with different tendencies.

In 1965, Admiral Américo Tomás was reelected President. Deciding to run no more risks, Salazar had caused the Constitution to be amended (1959), providing for an election by a body of electors instead of by the people.

The main question had now shifted from Portugal to the Overseas where the African revolts, acts of terrorism, and foreign participation were worrying everyone. Guerrilla wars broke out in Portuguese Guinea (1963) and in Mozambique (1964). In Macao, the Communists imposed their authority (1966), while tolerating a theoretical Portuguese rule. The military draft was intensified and the number of years of conscription increased. Most draftees spent two years in one of the threatened Overseas provinces. Many never came back. The colonial problem helped to isolate Portugal from the other countries, particularly in the United Nations. Yet, once more the Portuguese foreign policy triumphed, by carefully exploring any dissensions among the Western powers and the African countries, granting economic privileges and interests to foreign initiatives and capital at home, as well as military bases to NATO fellow-members (Germany, France). At the same time, much more attention began to be paid to the colonies by increasingly investing money, developing local resources, and fostering economy and education. The Minister of the Overseas, Adriano Moreira, a former Leftist, played a relevant role in all this, and for a while (1961–62) he was regarded as a possible successor to Salazar. Emigration from Portugal to Angola and Mozambique soared in the 1960's, the number of white settlers doubling or trebling.

By the late 1960's, and despite the apparent maintenance of order and quiet, the regime was no longer what it had been. Division plagued its ranks; Salazar's obvious senility and inflexibility endangered administration and general policy. Control had almost completely passed on to the censorship services and the Secret Police. In February 1965, General Humberto Delgado was assassinated when trying to cross the Spanish-Portuguese border secretly. Most people attributed responsibility for this murder to the P.I.D.E. in complicity with the Spanish Secret Service (many also claimed that some Communist groups had played a part in preparing a trap for Delgado, who was threatening Communist control among the exiles). In 1968, opposition leader Mário Soares was deported to the Overseas, a fact without precedent since the 1930's. Repression haunted the late 1960's as in the days of triumphant Fascism. To many people, it became clear that something had to change in a short time.

The change came in a most unexpected way. Early in September 1968, a chair collapsed under Salazar, whose head hit the ground. The result was a blood clot in his brain. Following an operation to remove it, the premier suffered a brain hemorrhage (September 16), and his condition was soon considered hopeless for purposes of practical recovery. On September 26, President Américo Tomás, quite unwillingly, had to replace the seventy-nine-year-old head of the government and to appoint Marcelo Caetano instead. If the regime was not over, at least forty years of continuous, personal rule were.

THE OVERSEAS EMPIRE IN THE TWENTIETH CENTURY

POLICIES

As early as 1911 the Republic established a new ministry in the cabinet, that of "Colonies" (*Colónias*). It was a sign of the growing concern with the Overseas territories, the fulfillment of Republican promises, and a good beginning for more thorough development of Portuguese Africa and Asia. The word "colonies" meant little—a result of French influence (in France, a *ministère des colonies* existed since 1894) rather than any new doctrine in administration. From a constitutional standpoint the "colonies" were considered part of the nation as before, and the first Republican Foreign Minister, Bernardino Machado (1910–11), had clearly stated that the new government regarded the Portuguese Overseas dominions as a patrimony as sacred as the territory of the motherland itself. In the Constitution of 1911, as well as in many other official texts, the word "colony" appeared along with the word "province" with obviously the same meaning.

Nonetheless, the Republic did introduce essential changes in the Overseas administration. For at least a decade new principles of colonial government were employed to shape a more progressive Portuguese Africa and to foster its development decisively.

The "new look" was based on extensive decentralization, a trend quite characteristic of the Republican ideology since the old propaganda days (see chapter 12). Early in 1914 the Afonso Costa government (Almeida Ribeiro, Minister of Colonies) presented to Congress some basic rules of administration (Leis Orgânicas), sort of constitutional texts, which were approved in general (1914) and then in particular (1917) for each of the Overseas territories. They set up the bases for financial and administrative decentralization. They also established basic principles on how to deal with the indigenous populations. Accepting in general the doctrine espoused by António Enes and his followers (see chapter 11), the acts of 1914–17 set forth a sort of native law, totally different from the Portuguese one, and applicable to the African (and Timoran) stage of civilization. In each colony natives were to be tutored and protected by the governor and his subordinates under special legislation. Private law would follow their usages and traditions. No political rights were acknowledged to them except within their own tribal life.

The abnormal circumstances caused by Sidónio Pais' uprising (late 1917) and World War I prevented a complete enforcement of those acts. But as soon as victory came, along with the Democrats' return to power (1919), the Portuguese administration decided to carry on decentralization on a wide basis and to regulate the laws on native policy. The Constitution had to be amended to make room for the new principles. After a lengthy parliamentary debate, the bills of August 1920 introduced six new articles in the constitutional text and changed a seventh one. According to the adopted wording, the Portuguese colonies would have financial autonomy and decentralization (under supervision of the mother country), compatible with the development of each one. Special organic laws would apply to them. Functions of administration would belong to the governor of each colony, assisted by an executive council and supervised by the Portuguese Executive. When the latter thought it convenient, executive powers could be temporarily delegated to High Commissioners (a practice sporadically followed in the past), whose functions would be merged with those of governor. Indeed, the government appointed former Cabinet ministers Norton de Matos and Brito Camacho as the first High Commissioners to Angola and Mozambique. They left Portugal early in 1921.

The policy of colonial autonomy, better defined and corrected in the years following, came to an end with the gradual definition of the

New State (see chapter 13). The trend toward decentralization was reversed, and a more centralized system, similar to the one before 1914, restored. Successive laws enhanced control by Lisbon with the intent of curbing abuses and dictatorial tendencies (1926). Governors-general replaced High Commissioners again (1930). A new word, "Portuguese Colonial Empire" (Império Colonial Português), made its appearance in the official terminology. The acts of 1926 (João Belo) underlined the political unity of the colonial territories, although theoretically maintaining an administrative and financial autonomy for each of them. The policy regarding the natives changed little. In 1926 a Political, Civil, and Criminal Statute for the noncivilized Africans of Angola and Mozambique was enacted, regulating a number of principles already set forth and applied before. It was later (1927) extended to Portuguese Guinea too. Altered in 1929, the Native Statute underwent further changes a year later.

The "Colonial Act" (Acto Colonial) of 1930, in the conception and writing of which Salazar played a major role, enforced the basic principles of 1926. Conceived as a sort of Constitution for the Overseas territories (and therefore broader in scope than the Native Statute that was not suppressed by it), later appended to the Constitution of 1933, it introduced some ultra-nationalist tendencies, so dear to Salazar. Thus, its article 2 declared to belong "to the organic essence of the Portuguese Nation the historical mission of possessing and colonizing overseas dominions, as well as civilizing the native populations encompassed by them." Article 5 considered the Portuguese Colonial Empire as interdependent in its several parts and with the mother country. Article 12 forbade chartered companies but allowed the existing ones to subsist to the deadline of their contracts. Article 13 defended national interests against foreign capital. A number of other articles protected and defended the "natives of the colonies"—though no clear definition of "native" was given—with full guarantee to their property, free labor, and freedom of conscience. Yet article 20 gave the state the right to compel natives to work "in public works of general interest for the community, in occupations the result of which belongs to them, in execution of penal judiciary decisions, or for the fulfillment of fiscal obligations." Article 22 spoke of "special statutes" for the natives, according to their stage of evolution, and pledged to respect (temporarily, one assumes) their current usages "which may not be incompatible with morals and the admonitions of humanity."

As time passed, centralization was more and more enforced, to the extent of condemning the pre-1926 regime as a-national. Writing in the late 1930's, former Colonial Minister Armindo Monteiro sharply accused the past Portuguese administrations of "renouncing its duties to the Overseas territories" and High Commissioner Norton de Matos of usurping powers belonging to Congress. In Armindo Monteiro's words, "the idea of national solidarity was erased from Angola's law."

The principles of the New State concerning colonial administration were also embodied in the "Organic Charter of the Colonial Empire" and the Overseas administrative reform, both enacted in 1933. A conference of all the colonial governors met in Lisbon in 1935 to reinforce the premise of solidarity. President Carmona paid a first visit to São Tomé and Angola (1938), then to Cape Verde and Mozambique (1939). His successors Craveiro Lopes and Américo Tomás visited all the Overseas territories again and again. Other frequent visitors were the Colonial Ministers.

All the legislation concerning natives defended principles traditional in Portuguese history. Its final purpose consisted in bringing the "non-civilized" Africans and Timorans up into the European civilization and the Portuguese nation, by means of a gradual change in their usages and their moral and social values. Local cultures, social organization, and law should be respected and maintained, but only on a transitional basis. As soon as the natives were regarded as Europeanized—by learning Portuguese, going to school and becoming Christians—they received the status of "assimilated" (assimilados) and were granted rights like any Portuguese citizen. The condition of native was never imposed on Cape Verde, India, or Macao, where every inhabitant held the status of citizen.

The assimilado policy was logical from a European standpoint, but it also had a number of dangers. It might tend to circumscribe the native in a vast ghetto and make it hard for him to leave it. To state when someone became "assimilated" was largely arbitrary and uncontrollable. Moreover, most of the assimilado practice took place in the 1930's and the 1940's, which were periods of stagnation for Portuguese Africa. As a result, the number of "assimilated" increased only very slowly: some 30,000 in Angola and a little more than 4,000 in Mozambique in 1950. It is true that these figures are much behind the actuality, for thousands of "civilized" Africans refused, in their turn, to apply for an *assimilado* condition, which would force them to pay higher taxes. But it is also true that *assimilados* hardly became first-class citizens, being discriminated against both economically and socially.

After the end of World War II, anticolonialism gained a new dimension. Critics of the Portuguese colonial system arose, denouncing the serfdom of most Africans and the economic stagnation of the colonies. To appease this first wave of attacks, Salazar approved some changes in the early 1950's. The Constitution was amended, with the essence of the "Colonial Act" being inserted in its text as title 7, under the heading "On the Portuguese Overseas." The words "colony" and "colonial" altogether disappeared, giving way to "overseas province" and "overseas." The official designation of "Empire" faded away. The condition of "natives" was officially defined as transitory (1951). A new "Organic Law" (Lei Orgânica do Ultramar Português) appeared in 1953, followed by a more enlightened Statute of the Portuguese Natives of the Provinces of Guinea, Angola, and Mozambique (1954).

In this way, the Portuguese government could evade the Charter of the United Nations with all of its clauses on the responsibility and the duties of colonial countries regarding dependent territories. Portugal simply ignored resolutions like the one of November 1960, requiring her to report on her colonial management without delay. Similar resolutions would be passed again and again until 1974, with the same fate. Addressing the National Press Club at Washington, in November 1967, the Portuguese Foreign Minister, A. Franco Nogueira, claimed that "we (the Portuguese) consider ourselves to be an African nation as well, through integration and multiracialism."

In 1961 the Statute of the Portuguese Natives came to an end, and all the inhabitants of Angola, Mozambique, and Guinea became full Portuguese citizens. The *assimilado* condition disappeared, and African populations were given "wider possibilities of looking after their interests and participating in the administration of their affairs." Colonial Minister Adriano Moreira (1961–62) tried to reintroduce administrative and economic decentralization by establishing municipal assemblies, commissions, and local committees, recognizing village councils as local administrative bodies, granting land concessions, etc. Although basic principles of converting the African into a European did not change, greater attention was paid to tribal cultures and traditions, and to studying, analyzing, and even preserving traditional practices and institutions.

The international campaign against the Portuguese colonial labor system (see chapter 11) led to a new effort to change European-African relationships, particularly in Angola and São Tomé. The Republican ethic proclaimed liberty and equality for all. Republican propagandists had denounced all kinds of abuses practiced both at home and in the Overseas provinces. No wonder that, once victorious, they tried very hard to correct every fault in colonial administration and to introduce a new spirit of governing. On the other hand, the European attitude toward the Africans at the time defended work as a moral and legal obligation, a civilizing factor which every colonial power should impose on the natives to make citizens out of them. From such a contradiction a narrow and difficult solution resulted, urging the indigenous populations to work with a minimum of force.

Governor Norton de Matos was the best-known exponent of the Republican "new look" toward the Africans. As he clearly stated, he found slavery in Angola "hidden, disguised, deceitful." This was indeed the situation in several other non-Portuguese colonies too, where some form of slavery had been maintained because of labor shortages and powerful world economic forces.

Norton de Matos curbed, as much as he could, the compulsory recruitment of African labor. The labor code of 1911 was suspended during his governorship. He forbade corporal punishment, published an abundant set of decrees providing official protection to the African, curbed alcoholism, and instituted committees for assistance to the natives. He also tried, and often succeeded, in repatriating Angolan workers living in São Tomé. At the same time, a plan to convert many Africans into permanent farmers was drafted and partly executed. Norton de Matos' idea was to grant each African farmer full ownership of his plot, and to organize land cadaster, where every inhabitant, or community, could have his name permanently registered. In this way, he argued, a new Angola would be built, and the African need for offering their labor to the white planters would, if not altogether disappear, at least be considerably reduced.

Norton de Matos' first period as governor (1912–15) virtually changed the traditional methods of labor hiring. Free hiring contracts replaced the disguised forms of slavery. Salaries were fixed and often raised, while official surveyors inspected native conditions of life, particularly in nourishment, housing, dressing, and medical assistance. From 1915 to 1921 administrative control of these and other matters somewhat slackened, mostly because of government instability (nine governors in six years), but Norton de Matos' return with higher powers confirmed the Republican policy to the late 1920's, even after his second resignation (1924).

The 1930's and the 1940's were regressive or stagnant periods in regard to protection for the African. The Republican program required a permanent struggle against tradition, prejudice, and vested interests. Many acts had never been enforced or were just starting to be. With the change of policies in Lisbon, however, the white settlers were given a much freer hand than before. The fight against capitalist interests and their consequent exploitation of native labor slowed down. Much progressive legislation of Norton de Matos (and other governors) was forgotten or neglected. Disguised forms of slavery reappeared. A number of decrees further restricted freedom of Africans to choose where to work. Only the assistance provided by missionaries increased because of the New State's open protection of the Church.

In more recent times Mozambique, rather than Angola, became the main target of all attacks regarding forced labor hiring. Indeed, the development of South Africa as a major economic power required cheap workers from the neighboring countries, Mozambique being the obvious and easiest place to find them. The long-established emigration to the South African mines became better organized and regulated with the passage of time. An annual contingent of 50,000 African workers was regularly supplied by the Portuguese government to Transvaal throughout the whole Republican period. Many others passed the border clandestinely. An agreement signed in 1928 allowed for the recruitment of at least 65,000 and at most 100,000 Mozambicans by the Transvaal mining corporation, but such figures have rarely been reached. Export of labor, also to Rhodesia, accounted for a considerable sum in the colony's receipts. Despite an increasing concern with health assistance, and the repatriation of most workers after a period of two to three years, hiring conditions were never perfect and death rates were often high among such emigrants (4 per cent to 5 per cent in the 1920's).

Several laws (1953, 1960, 1961, 1962) have forbidden all forms of nonremunerated work and obligatory labor. Although labor conditions considerably improved between 1910 and 1974 (particularly after 1961), exploitation of the Africans went on, because of economic needs and long-established traditions. One form or another of compulsory labor was always present, because of "economic ills," "emergency," or similar arguments.

What must be emphasized is that economic motivations, rather than racial attitudes, generally were behind the Portuguese-African relationships. Only in Mozambique, and by no means consistently, was there some racist bias against the blacks, by Rhodesian or South African influence, and despite official efforts to the contrary. Exploitation of the native, actual (and illegal) discrimination, negligence in fostering literacy, and most other signs of a typical "colonial" regime could also be found in Portugal, where the lower classes were similarly exploited, discriminated against, and neglected in their illiteracy. The history of the Portuguese Overseas territories and the policy of Portugal in Africa in the twentieth century have to be understood as a magnified replica of the history of Portugal, with all of her slow economic development, defects in social structure, and cultural backwardness. Failure to recognize this has led to all kinds of misunderstandings and erroneous interpretations.

FROM PACIFICATION TO THE PROSPECTS OF INDEPENDENCE

By 1910 Portuguese authority was more or less respected by the native populations of Angola, Mozambique, Guinea, and Timor. The Republican administration, putting its emphasis on the civilian rather than the military, tried to avoid as much as possible "subjugation" campaigns in the traditional manner. Instead, governors were instructed to devote their energies to peaceful, yet firm and consistent, contacts with the indigenous peoples that might substitute a useful, paternalistic, and appealing image of the Portuguese for the destructive, authoritarian, and hateful image of the conqueror. Even when military force was found necessary, methods and practices of pacification were to have less violence and hero worship than before.

Military campaigns did occur in North Mozambique to 1913, in West Timor in 1912–13, in Northwest Angola to 1914, and especially in Guinea (see chapter 11) to 1915. World War I fostered some rebellions against the Portuguese by German influence, both in Angola and in Mozambique. German forces raided the border of the two Portuguese colonies as early as 1914, inflicting some casualties on the local garrisons. Lisbon sent two expeditions to Angola (1914–15) and four to Mozambique (1914–17). In Angola the fight with the Germans did not last long and was limited to border skirmishes, marches, and countermarches. South African and British troops completely occupied German Southwest Africa by the summer of 1915, which put an end to the war. Yet an African rebellion south of the Cunene River (southern Angola) late in 1914 forced the Portuguese to a lengthy and extensive campaign of subjugation to the summer of 1915 against three main tribes (the Cuanhamas, the Cuamatos, and the Evales) under the command of Lieutenant-Colonel Alves Roçadas, then of General Pereira de Eça. In Mozambique war brought about worse results. After a brief period of success (spring-summer 1916), when the Portuguese troops reoccupied Kionga and invaded Tanganyika, German counteroffensives under Von Lettow-Vorbeck pushed the Portuguese south nearly to Quelimane (summer 1918) and then retreated peacefully north again.

Summing up, World War I cost Portugal in Africa about 15,000 casualties, with some 5,000 dead and more than 10,000 wounded, among Europeans and Africans. Total effectives had reached 57,000 (32,000 Europeans and 25,000 African troops).

A few native uprisings still happened here and there in the 1920's, but with minor participation of tribes and still less impact on the colonies' general life. In the 1930's Guinea registered some agitation too. Police operations were enough to put them down. Later, urban rioting and protests did occur, as in Portugal, for economic reasons, but without involving any sort of resistance to the Portuguese rule.

World War II meant a fight in Timor only. Late in 1941, Australian troops landed on the island and occupied it, despite the official protests of Lisbon. The Japanese came next to oust the Australians, and occupied the island in their turn, this time with open violence and intensive destruction. Guerrilla warfare between them and small groups of Australians and Portuguese Timorans did last to the end of the war. When the Japanese left, in 1945, thousands of Timorans and Portuguese had died in combat and in concentration camps, Dili and other towns had been burned out, and crops were destroyed.

Although independence movements in Portuguese Africa began only in the 1960's, their roots can be traced back to the time of the first Republic. Unrestricted freedom of press and association encouraged several groups of Europeanized blacks and half-breeds, living both in the colonies and in Portugal proper, to form societies and start newspapers where they denounced the abuses of the administration. In 1920 an African League (*Liga Africana*), established in Lisbon, tried to gather together the blacks and mulattoes who were studying in Portugal. The League participated in the third Pan African Conference held in London and organized the second session of the Conference in Lisbon (1923). Other societies arose in Angola and Mozambique, all demanding more rapid development of the colonies and equal rights for the Africans. But by the early 1930's authoritarian repression spreading from Portugal to the Overseas muzzled open protests and confined the African societies and newspapers to more harmless activities. From then on, African consciousness, revolt against Portugal, or resistance to the assimilation policy could only be expressed in literature—poetry and short stories.

After World War II the general awakening of Africa and the widespread independence movements had their impact on the Portuguese colonies too. Several more or less clandestine groups appeared both in Africa and in Portugal uniting Africans. By 1950, some black and mulatto students of the University of Lisbon met and drafted a precise program of independence under an African framework. Among them were men like Eduardo Mondlane from Mozambique and Mário de Andrade from Angola. Harassed by the police, they had to leave Portugal and went into exile. Later they returned to Africa and started organizing rebellions in Angola, Mozambique, and Guinea.

Theirs was a typical intellectual movement with very few contacts with the local populations. Submerged in a primitive, tribal way of life, the overwhelming majority of the Africans did not respond to intellectual activists and could not understand their goals. They had no national feeling whatsoever for "Angola" or "Mozambique," artificial creations of the late nineteenth century, which could only have meaning for the Portuguese settlers or the few Europeanized blacks and mulattoes. The peoples of Portuguese Africa, thoroughly divided by tribal (and language) differences, could hardly reach beyond their narrow horizons of local agriculture and cattle raising. Therefore, the only possible way of promoting rebellion was to foster racial hatred (black versus white) and/or to exploit discontent against physical violence on the part of the settlers.

Another possibility was to join forces with the anti-Salazar movement, launching a general rebellion against Fascism as a first step toward a subsequent revolt against colonialism. This seems to have been accepted by some Portuguese opposition groups—particularly among exiles—although one wonders to what extent they thought of it just as a political strategy to overthrow the New State. In any case, a former adviser and protégé of Salazar's, exiled Captain Henrique Galvão, was instrumental in organizing a timed revolution of both anti-Fascist and black independent activists in Angola. His plans were still broader, for they included a Portuguese-Spanish union of anti-Fascists, who would raise the banner of free Spain and free Portugal in the Spanish colonies of Fernando Po and Rio Muni (equatorial Africa) and thence proceed to Angola. For this purpose the liner Santa Maria was hijacked in Caribbean waters in the extraordinary adventure of January 1961.

Yet, if Galvão's plans failed, the Angolan uprising did not. In February 1961 some hundreds of members of the M.P.L.A. (Movimento Popular de Libertação de Angola), headed by Mário de Andrade, attacked several prisons, barracks, and the broadcasting station of Luanda. The government, however, was aware of potential rebellion and had sent troops to Angola beforehand (besides arresting hundreds of suspects and indulging in other acts of precaution), and could control the situation and rout the attackers. A widespread feeling of fear among the settlers led to the slaughtering of scores of blacks and the flight of hundreds of others, many of whom joined the insurgents. In March, tribes in northern Angola rebelled with Congolese backing and massacred several hundred settlers (including children) in a most savage way. All this brought about increasing repression from the side of authorities and whites alike, with the support of many natives as well. Hundreds were killed and retaliation was drastic, with African villages entirely wiped out and blacks hastily fleeing Angola toward the Congo. It seems the Northern uprising was organized mainly by another Angolan group, the U.P.A. (União das Populações de Angola, later F.N.L.A., Frente Nacional de Libertação de Angola), headed by Holden Roberto, a rival of Mário de Andrade's.

The rebellions of 1961 made many people, inside and outside Portugal, think that the days of Portuguese colonialism were numbered and that the granting of independence to all or most of Portugal's colonies would happen in the near future. A guerrilla war started in northern Angola, with some territory actually occupied throughout 1961. Reports of alleged Portuguese atrocities were widely publicized, and international focus on the Portuguese case attracted world attention. Yet the insurgents, like the foreign countries in general, underestimated Portugal's tenacity and capacity to deal with the war by military and other means. Relatively well-trained and well-equipped troops were sent in larger and larger numbers. The P.I.D.E. displayed no less activity, their agents in Africa outnumbering those active in Portugal. Force and terror controlled Angola in the times after the first uprising. The administration realized, however, that other means were necessary. The government's funds poured in as never before. Attention was finally paid to long-lasting claims. Africans were granted all rights, better jobs, and higher salaries. Public education and welfare were improved. Public works were intensified. In less than ten years more was done to foster the development of the colonies than in the three decades before. Quoting Douglas Wheeler, "the atmosphere of 1966–67 in Luanda is reflected in half-serious proposals that Portugal should erect a monument to the *catana*, the African field machete used as a weapon in the 1961 attacks, to honor the instrument of what many consider an economic 'miracle' in Angola." At the same time, Salazar's foreign policy aimed at getting NATO support for the Portuguese position—which could be obtained only indirectly—convincing the Western world of the advantages of Portuguese survival in Africa, welcoming foreign capital, and tightening relations with south and central African countries. Salazar succeeded remarkably well in most points. South Africa and Rhodesia became Portugal's best allies in the South, but some new black states, like Malawi and even Zambia, also accepted collaboration with Portugal because of economic advantages and technical assistance. A major power in Africa, with the second highest number of whites south of the Sahara, Portugal developed a cunning foreign policy which prevented much help to the independence cause.

Nonetheless, guerrilla warfare did not fade away. On the contrary, it increased with the outbreak of rebellions in Guinea (1963) and north Mozambique (1964). Unlike Angola, where internal dissension plagued the rebels (five major groups could be counted in 1967, subdivided in more than a dozen party units), both Guinea and Mozambique held on under nearly unified organizations. In Guinea the P.A.I.G.C. (Partido Africano da Independência da Guiné e Cabo Verde), with Amílcar Cabral as secretary-general and headquarters in Conacry (Republic of Guinea) controlled the situation on the side of the insurgents. Partly because of this, partly because of sparse European settlement, the guerrillas progressed rapidly and claimed effective control of one-third to one-half of the colony (but of no cities) by the late 1960's. In Mozambique, unity was achieved under the able leadership of Eduardo Mondlane and his FRELIMO (Frente de Libertação de Moçambique), with headquarters in Dar-es-Salaam (Tanzania). FRELIMO developed its activity in the north, claiming effective control of a small area between the rivers Rovuma and Lúrio (just where the Portuguese occupation was more reduced). Mondlane's assassination in 1969 was a great blow to the independence cause, but his successor, Samora Machel, proved an able leader as well.

By 1968 more than 100,000 Portuguese troops were active in the three territories, yet actual confrontation only rarely happened and the great majority of soldiers went back home without having ever seen or heard the enemy. The result was that casualties were relatively few: 1,653 dead in combat to December 31, 1968. Casualties by accidents were perhaps twice as high, which raised total figures to about 5,000, i.e., as many in eight years as during World War I in Portuguese Africa. Thus the impact from actual fighting in both colonies (Guinea excepted) and in Portugal was slight, except as a source of political agitation. On the contrary, war brought about prosperity and a better way of life for thousands of soldiers, who got a higher payment than in their daily jobs at home. Coupled with an intensive nationalist propaganda carried on by the government and with brain washing at the barracks, this fact made the war, if not popular, at least not thoroughly abhorred.

The smaller colonies were not free from agitation. In São Tomé an uprising of African workers (1953), because of labor conditions, led to violent repression but also to some attempts at meeting the demands of labor. On the Gulf of Guinea coast armed forces of the newly created Republic of Dahomey ousted the few Portuguese officials from the fortress of Ajudá, after a romantic gesture on the part of their commander of setting fire to the building before surrendering (1961). In India, Nehru's administration vainly tried for years to induce a voluntary withdrawal of the Portuguese from Goa, Damão, and Diu, as the French had done with their smaller enclaves. Lisbon, however, stuck to the doctrine that such territories were part of the fatherland and could not be surrendered. Several peaceful "invasions" of the three districts by Indian volunteers began in the 1950's. The Portuguese responded by shooting and by putting many in jail. In 1954 two tiny enclaves near Damão were permanently occupied by India. Portugal filed a complaint to the United Nations (1955). At last Nehru realized that only force could make the Portuguese leave. In December 1961 Indian troops invaded Goa, Damão, and Diu. Greatly outnumbered, the Portuguese offered a symbolic resistance only, Governor-General Vassalo e Silva surrendering without further question. After a few months, all the Portuguese and thousands of Goans were repatriated. Once in Lisbon, Vassalo e Silva and his military staff were court-martialed and expelled from the army.

In Macao, the political opposition between Fascist Portugal and Communist China led to intervention by China and quasi-occupation of the town. Chinese pressures began in the early 1950's; in 1955–57 they prevented official celebrations of four hundred years of "Portuguese" Macao, alleging that Macao had always been a part of China.

In the 1960's, Maoist propaganda flooded the tiny colony. When the authorities tried to resist, China fostered an uprising (1966) that compelled the governor and Lisbon to yield to every demand the Chinese made. From then on, Macao virtually came under Communist control.

Summing up, the Portuguese Empire faced serious problems in the 1960's, with the loss of one colony, the acceptance of a sort of protectorate of another, and a guerrilla war in three more. Yet the Portuguese survived, and by 1968 controlled the situation better than they had since 1961. If in the 1970's the military situation deteriorated in some ways, nevertheless the war could go on for years with no decisive result. It was the Portuguese army that stopped fighting, thus permitting the triumph of all independence movements in 1974.

THE "EMPIRE" BY THE MIDDLE OF THE CENTURY

A history of Portuguese Africa in the twentieth century should consider three principal periods: one, from the end of the military campaigns to about 1930, featured by decentralization and unbalanced development; a second one, from 1930 to the 1950's, characterized by stagnation or little growth; and a third period to the present, displaying an immense leap forward. This three-period theory more or less applies to the several aspects one might envisage.

The demographic analysis shows it clearly. In Angola the number of white settlers increased from less than 10,000 in 1910 to about 50,000 in 1930, a 500 per cent growth; after a decade of stagnation or even decline (44,000 in 1940), the white population reached some 100,000 in the mid-1950's, double the 1930 figure; yet, by the end of the 1960's, there were more than 300,000 whites, treble the preceding decade. In Mozambique white population jumped from a little more than 5,000 at the time of the proclamation of the Republic to nearly 28,000 in 1930; in 1945 it barely passed 31,000, in 1950 nearly 50,000, but it doubled in 1960 and doubled again at the end of the decade. This was the result of canalizing to both territories a part of the usually high Portuguese emigration, particularly after 1960, when the economic expansion of Angola and Mozambique started offering emigrants conditions and facilities similar to those they expected to find in foreign countries.

Changes in the number of blacks showed a possible decline in Angola, from about 4 million in 1910 to about 3 million in 1930, although statistics are not reliable for this period. By 1950, however, they had reached the level of 1910 again, were near 5 million ten years later and surpassed that number by the late 1960's. In Mozambique, black population evolved from a little more than 3 million in 1910 to 3.5 million in 1920, 4 million in 1930, 5 million in 1940, then 5,600,000 in 1950, 6,600,000 in 1960, and over 7 million at the end of the decade.

White settlers and native blacks were not the only population groups of Portuguese Africa. Mulattoes were an important category at the beginning of the century, their number matching or even surpassing that of whites in either Angola or Mozambique. As time went by, the percentage of mulattoes declined because of increasing white immigration from Europe. There were about 15,000 in Angola in 1930, and only 30,000 in the mid-1950's. In East Africa they increased from some 12,000 in 1930 to double that number in 1950. Nearly as important was the group of Indians and Orientals in Mozambique (15,000 in 1950), a result of emigration from Goa, Macao, and other Asian countries.

Opposition of cities and countryside increased both in Angola and in Mozambique. While most whites, mulattoes, Asians and Europeanized blacks lived in towns, the overwhelming majority of non-Europeanized Africans continued to dwell in the countryside, devoted to their traditional agricultural way of life. As in the motherland, cities totally controlled the rest of the country, Luanda and Lourenço Marques (to the 1950's) containing at least half of the Europeanized population and centralizing the colony's life, exactly like Lisbon in Portugal. The development of the Portuguese white settlement led to the foundation of new towns or the quick growth of many others. Thus, in Angola, Lobito rose from nothing in 1910 to the second most important town, immediately after Luanda (50,000 inhabitants) in 1960; Nova Lisboa (formerly Huambo), practically founded by Norton de Matos in 1912 and officially nominated as capital of Angola (act of 1928), was the second city of the colony in 1950 and the third ten years later (40,000 people); Malanje, Sá da Bandeira, and Carmona, almost nonexistent at the beginning of the century, had risen to fifth, sixth, and seventh places in the 1960's. Luanda, however, became the great metropolis of

Portuguese West Africa, the second Portuguese town immediately after Lisbon and a large city on the continent: 15,000 inhabitants in 1910, 30,000 in 1923, 60,000 in 1940, 140,000 in 1950, 225,000 in 1960, nearly 500,000 in 1968, with an ever-increasing proportion of whites. In Mozambique the urban structure was somewhat different; Lourenço Marques being located too far south, there was a quick development of other towns scattered all over the country, the growth pace of which it was unable to match. Thus, being five times larger than the second city in 1910 (some 15,000 people against 3,000 for Beira), Lourenço Marques' lead declined to less than double in 1928 (37,000 and 20,000 for Beira), and it was narrowed considerably by Quelimane in 1960 (64,000 against 78,000 for Lourenço Marques), closely followed by João Belo (49,000), Beira (45,000), Tete (38,000), Vila Cabral (28,000), and Porto Amélia (21,000). João Belo and Vila Cabral were insignificant villages at the end of World War II.

The government tried to attract Portuguese colonization to the countryside by fostering rural settlement in several places such as Cela in Angola, where settlers were forbidden to hire African labor. Mixed settlements also appeared (Cunene in Angola, Médio Limpopo in Mozambique) as well as a few for African families only (Caconda in Angola, Inhamissa in Mozambique). At the time massive emigration from Portugal was eased after the end of World War II, with the result that thousands of families started leaving Portugal for Africa year after year. Emigration of non-Portuguese to Portuguese Africa as a rule was not encouraged.

In the late 1960's, areas of higher density of population in both Angola and Mozambique encompassed the traditional coast line and plateau regions plus a number of new lands where railroad tracks passed or highways had been built. The spreading of guerrilla warfare and the consequent setting up of Portuguese garrisons all over the vast territories of the two colonies have contributed to a better knowledge of remote zones and the opening of new roads in recent years.

In the smaller colonies population patterns followed entirely different trends. Continuous growth occurred only in Guinea (343,000 in 1926, 350,000 in 1940, 510,000 in 1950, 544,000 in 1960) but at a very low rate. In the other provinces the number of people varied. In Cape Verde there were almost as many inhabitants in 1950 as fifty years before (less than 150,000) with fluctuations in the intervening years. The 1960 census registered a little more than 200,000· people. Overpopulated for its resources, Cape Verde sent emigrants in large numbers to the United States, Brazil, and other countries. In São Tomé, population declined to the 1950's (68,000 in 1910, 56,000 in 1950), then went up a little (63,000 in 1960). Again, the two small islands had reached their demographic limit. Portuguese India's population declined, then went up (like all of India) to the 1950's: 550,000 by 1910, 432,000 in 1926, 580,000 in 1930, 624,000 in 1940, 637,000 in 1950; the troubled political situation afterward led to a decline again, thousands having migrated to the Indian Union as well as to Mozambique and British East Africa (a traditional trend). On the eve of its loss by Portugal, Goa. had only 626,000 inhabitants. Macao's population varied widely, due to immigrants from neighboring China. During World War II it may have reached 400,000 or more. Again, the Communist takeover flooded Macao with fleeing Chinese. The 1950 census registered 188,000 inhabitants, that of 1960 only 169,000, a figure already too high for the small size of the colony (16 square kilometers). In Timor the population grew up to the war, then declined because of killings and migrations: 440,000 in 1926, 460,000 in 1940, 442,000 in 1950, 517,000 in 1960. Consequently, and with the exception of Macao, no large towns have risen in any of these territories, where urbanism has been slow to develop. Provincial capitals varied between a few thousand (Dili in Timor) and the 20,000 reached by Pangim (Portuguese India) and Bissau (Guinea) in modern times. The latter gradually surpassed Bolama, Portuguese Guinea's former capital, and became the seat of administration.

Percentages of whites and half-breeds did not undergo essential changes. In Cape Verde mulattoes always predominated, in Portuguese India and Macao there were considerable numbers of mixed natives. In Guinea, São Tomé, and Timor the overwhelming majority were pure natives. In all cases (Cape Verde excepted) whites and half-breeds lived in towns, engaging in trade and administration rather than agriculture.

An important step in the regular organization of Angola, Mozambique, and Guinea consisted in substituting the civil for the military administration. At the time of the proclamation of the Republic, each of the two big colonies was generally divided in a certain number of districts (*distritos*), subdivided into captaincies-major (*capitanias-mores*), which further comprised administrative posts (*postos administrativos*). In Guinea there were no districts, and captaincies-major were called residencies (*residências*). There were also a few municipalities (*concelhos*) in some districts where European density was greater. In every case the military prevailed over the civilian, and military organization characterized the three levels of the administrative system.

In 1911 a first attempt was made in Mozambique to introduce civil units in some areas. But it was in Angola that Governor-General Norton de Matos systematically fostered the new principle by creating in 1912 thirty-five administrative circumscriptions (*circunscrições administrativas*) at the second level, coexisting with the captaincies-major (twenty-five), the number of which significantly decreased. Eleven municipalities also came into existence. Gradually, the new civil units prevailed over the military, which altogether disappeared in 1921. The Angolan administrative reform of that year (Norton de Matos' second government) created eleven districts, sixty-five circumscriptions and 287 posts, besides thirteen municipalities. Progress in Angola's occupation had increased the number of districts to fourteen and the circumscriptions to eighty-two when Norton de Matos quit, in 1924. There were no significant changes to 1936 (though the number of circumscriptions declined), when a new administrative reform introduced larger units known as provinces (as in Portugal) and increased the municipalities to thirty, facing thirty-six circumscriptions. The reform of 1954 abolished the provinces, reduced the districts to thirteen, and registered fifty-five municipalities against only twenty circumscriptions, a step forward in the Europeanization of Angola's administrative system. In Mozambique the trend toward civil circumscriptions, later replaced by municipalities, followed a similar, if slower, pace. From the beginning of the century to 1936, there were five districts (a military territory, still existing in 1910, was shortly afterward annexed to Lourenço Marques), plus the areas administered by the two chartered companies. After 1935 the district of Mozambique absorbed the Nyasa Company territory. The reform of 1936 created three provinces, six districts—a fourth province and a seventh district appeared in 1941 with the territory of the Mozambique Company (the

UPPER LEFT: *Norton de Matos*. LOWER LEFT: *Marcelo Caetano*. BELOW: *Cambambe Dam, Angola*.

company charter ended in that year)—sixty-six circumscriptions and twelve municipalities. Districts were later increased to nine. In 1963 provinces disappeared, districts remained the same, but the number of municipalities increased to thirty-two against sixty-one circumscriptions. The greater backwardness of Mozambique in contrast to Angola is easily perceived by comparing such figures.

In Guinea, São Tomé, Macao, and Timor no districts or provinces were ever created. Guinea had two full municipalities in 1910, the same two in the 1920's and the 1930's, three in the late 1950's and nine in 1968. Timor kept its sole *concelho* to the present. Both colonies also had circumscriptions. In São Tomé, Macao, Cape Verde, and India full municipal organization was achieved very soon, no circumscriptions having ever been established. Two districts were set up for Cape Verde (1963) and three for Portuguese India, which dated from monarchical times.

General administration in each colony included local organs, such as the Legislative Council created in 1920 and several times reformed, an Economic and Social Council for Angola and Mozambique; and a Council of Government for the smaller colonies. Their powers varied according to circumstances but generally had little impact on the highly centralized colonial system.

The economic development of all the Portuguese Overseas provinces, but particularly Angola and Mozambique, was irregular and uneven. In most of the period 1910–68 the colonies—Guinea excepted—depended upon foreign markets and foreign capital more than on Portugal's. The wide fluctuations in the demand for tropical and equatorial products have had tragic consequences for colonial economies.

But the development of backward territories is also an outcome of good administration and of able statesmen. An exceptional leader like Norton de Matos (1912–15; 1921–24) followed, to a certain extent, by Vicente Ferreira (1926–28), was able to give Angola the impetus to put her ahead of Mozambique in European penetration and (later) economic development. Yet, by 1910 Mozambique's revenues and expenditures were double those of the West Coast colony, and its total volume of trade was also double Angolan trade. It was only in the late twenties and the thirties that Mozambique began to lag.

Until the first years of the twentieth century, rubber was the chief product exported by Angola and the main source of its revenues. Wax, coffee, fish, and hides followed, but at a great distance. This was still the situation in 1910, although the decline in demand for rubber—a consequence of the world's rubber crisis—was noticeable. From 1911 on, rubber exports fell sharply and Angola faced a difficult period of adjustment till World War I. Governor Norton de Matos succeeded in developing a number of cultures, namely those related to improved European settlement and traditional African agriculture: maize and beans, for example. He also fostered cotton, coffee, and sugar production. In the 1920's both coffee and cotton were on their way up, while coconut, palm oil, and wax provided important revenues too. Sugar faced a general crisis. After 1921 diamonds started giving Angola a new source of wealth.

Norton de Matos' second government, which elevated Angola and made of it the most important Portuguese colony up to 1974, brought about a difficult crisis (economic and financial) further aggravated by the High Commissioner's forced resignation in 1924. His successors were unable to slow down the crisis, which worsened with the beginnings of the world depression. Angola's development came to an end and stagnated up to World War II.

In the 1930's coffee had become number one in the colony's exports, followed by diamonds, fish meal, maize, cotton, and sisal. When coffee went down, again because of the world crisis, diamonds replaced it, maize took second place, and sugar and cotton came next. By the late 1940's coffee was back as Angola's main wealth, and so it has remained to the present. Diamonds, sisal (a prosperous culture because of World War II, the Korea war, the Vietnam war and all wars in general), maize, sugar, and cotton followed. In the 1950's iron ore was discovered and quickly ranked among Angola's sources of income. So did oil, actively explored in the 1960's.

Foreign investments were encouraged, and extensive economic concessions were granted to a few powerful companies. The *Diamang* (Angola Diamond Company), with Portuguese, Belgian, French, English, and American capital, founded in 1917 and given the first important privileges under Norton de Matos in 1921, saw its concessions further enlarged and confirmed. It became a true state within Angola, a sort of new Mozambique-type company, with exclusive rights to diamond extraction all over the colony and extensive authority over several thousand square miles. It organized its own police system, built its own road system, and created its own towns (e.g., Henrique de Carvalho, Portugália). It also patronized some interesting cultural activities shown by the establishment of a museum and the annual publication of monographs on African ethnography, geology, botany, zoology, and history.

Figures for external trade clearly show the several periods of Angola's economic development. To the early 1920's, the colony progressed little. Exports and imports displayed few variations and even indicated some decline during World War II if one recalls the debasement of the escudo. Yet surpluses in the balance of trade happened now and then, and deficits were generally small. In the 1920's both imports and exports increased, a result of Norton de Matos' policy. Angola's crisis and the depression put them down again. In 1936 Angola exported scarcely more than in 1924 and imported far less. World War II unleashed a continuous leap forward in both exports and imports: export figures for 1945 were almost double those of 1938, but figures for 1948 were more than double those of 1945. Expansion slowed down from 1954 to 1961 but from then on it reached levels unheard of, export figures for 1967 doubling those of ten years before. As to the balance of trade, it was consistently positive from the early 1930's on, to the 1950's. Portugal always was Angola's main partner, both for imports and exports, yet her position as a buyer generally declined to the late 1950's, as colonial trade with foreign countries developed. Exports to Portugal declined from 90 per cent (by 1910), to 77 per cent (1913), 53 per cent (1923), 57 per cent (1933), 39 per cent (1943), 21 per cent (1953), 25 per cent (1963), and 36 per cent (1967). As to imports, the figures were about 90 per cent (1910), 77 per cent (1920), 54 per cent (1922), 51 per cent (1933), 74 per cent (1943), 48 per cent (1953), 48 per cent (1963), and 38 per cent (1967).

Government plans for general economic development began in Angola prior to those in the motherland. A first Plano de Fomento started in 1938, followed by a second in 1945 and a third in 1951. In 1953 the launching of the first of such plans in Portugal brought the Angolan ones to an end, because it encompassed all the Portuguese economic area, including the Overseas provinces.

A public works policy, actively carried on since 1912 (initiated by Norton de Matos), helped in the development of Angola. There were at the time 100 km. of roads and less than 1,000 km. of railways. Twelve years later the road network reached 25,000 km. (nine-tenths of which were built in 1912–15 and 1921–23), while railroads covered more than 1,500 km. Afterward the growth slowed down: to 1933, 10,000 km. more of roads were built, but from then on, to 1960, the road network stagnated. A new leap forward only began in the 1960's: 35,500 km. in 1960, 72,000 in 1967. Railroads progressed to the late 1920's: the Moçâmedes line was continued to Sá da Bandeira (1923); the Benguela line reached Huambo (now Nova Lisboa) in 1912, then Silva Porto (1922), and finally the border with Congo (1929), more than half of its whole course being built in 1926–29; a new track was built from Porto Amboim inland (1923–25) in central Angola. The total network exceeded 2,000 km. at the time of World War II. Since then several small branches of the main lines have been opened to traffic, while the Amboim and the Moçâmedes ones progressed a little longer. The total network encompassed 3,200 km. in 1965–67. Air transport services came into existence in 1938, planes reaching most of Angola during the 1950's and enlarging their flights afterward. Sea communications with Portugal and other countries improved considerably, as more and better ships were acquired by Portuguese maritime companies, and port facilities were improved. Lobito became the first port of Angola after the extensive works carried on since 1922 and the completion of the Benguela railroad. Luanda came second, then Moçâmedes and many others. As in Portugal several big dams were begun, particularly in the 1940's and the 1950's, with the main purpose of supplying electric power and irrigating vast areas.

The economic development of Mozambique followed a different pattern. More than half of the colony belonged to three private companies (see chapter 11), two of which were chartered. Their lands were among the oldest colonized by the Portuguese and where European settlement was most developed. This means that the Lisbon government had to invest much less in Mozambique than in Angola to obtain similar results but also that sheer economic problems, such as international economic conjunctures, would have a much greater impact than in Angola.

Up to the 1960's public revenues of the colony were consistently higher than in Angola. So was external trade, if one added the values of exports (or imports) from the Lourenço Marques–administered part to those from the chartered companies. Yet Mozambique had fewer Europeans, a more irregular distribution of white population, and a smaller road and railroad network.

Altogether, Mozambique's main production and sources of wealth did not change much in fifty years. As in Angola rubber played a major role at the beginning of the century, but not so exclusively as on the West Coast. Oleaginous products (copra, sesame, peanuts) actually held first place, and kept it to the present. Sugar came third. When rubber declined and finally disappeared, sugar held second place, followed by sisal and cotton. Such was the situation in the mid-1920's and the mid-1960's the only difference being that cotton and sugar changed places. Tea also became a major source of wealth.

The Mozambique Company prospered and contributed to the colony's development to the mid-1920's. Its exports generally surpassed those of the rest of the province (Nyasa Company included), despite the fact that it encompassed only one-sixth of Mozambique's territory and one-tenth of the colony's population. The Beira railroad and the Beira port permitted an ever-increasing international traffic. Beira had become the second town of Mozambique (20,000 in 1928), much ahead of any other. The Company had proportionally opened more schools and could register a higher attendance than the government-administered sector (1930: 6,402 grammar-school pupils against 42,868; 1940: 8,408 against 72,154). It built new railroads, opened a substantial road network, and made several other improvements.

An economic and financial crisis began to affect the Mozambique Company by 1923–24 with dramatic results. Exports went down sharply (figures for 1927 were one-third of 1922). A slight recovery in 1928 was negated by the outbreak of the depression, which thoroughly ruined the Company's external trade and main source of prosperity. In 1933 exports had declined to 0.7 thousand gold contos in contrast to 2.6 thousand in 1927 and the peak of 8.7 thousand in 1922. Although the situation improved in the following years, exports were still at the 1.3 thousand level by 1940, the eve of the Company's last days.

Completely different was the Nyasa Company's troubled existence. It never had the means, nor perhaps the able administration, to carry on the development of a vast region with little European penetration and settlement. It never built any railroads, and only a few roads resulted from its action. Its capital cities, Ibo, then Porto Amélia, never went beyond the level of tiny villages (Porto Amélia had 1,633 inhabitants in 1928, of which only 67 were whites). It suffered from World War I, being invaded by the German forces from Tanganyika, which ravaged a part of the territory and were expelled only in 1918. Its trade movement was relatively small, stagnant, or in decline, with a few years of prosperity (1911–12; 1926–29). When it ended its days, in 1929, exports reached one-fourteenth of the colony's and one-fourth of the Mozambique Company's. Yet it encompassed one-fourth of Portuguese East Africa, with one-eighth of its total population. For the Lisbon government the inheritance of the Nyasa Company was a heavy burden.

The Republican decentralization system and the High Commissioner regime failed to foster Mozambique's development as it did Angola's. Governor Alvaro de Castro (1915–18) and High Commissioner Brito Camacho (1921–23), probably the two most energetic leaders appointed by Lisbon, were in no way comparable to Norton de Matos. Mozambique somewhat stagnated to the late 1930's, when public revenues started increasing. From 1935 to 1945 revenues doubled, then doubled again in five years, and again to 1955. From 1955 to 1967 they doubled once more, yet the pace of growth was lagging behind that of Angola. From 1965 on, Mozambique's revenues were below those of the West Coast. In trade, World War II again was a major stimulating factor, but surpluses were lacking and the total trade volume was below that of the other coast. The balance of trade showed a consistent deficit, although exports very much increased; in 1967 they were double the value of ten years before. However, receipts from transit trade, migrant earnings, and tourism resulted in a satisfactory balance of payments. All this means that Mozambique paid more to the government (because it possessed a tighter and more developed capitalist structure and a larger population) but was actually poorer in economic resources.

The Republican period meant for Mozambique a considerable development of substructures, namely port equipment and railroads. Lourenço Marques and Beira, due to their international importance, were equipped with modern facilities and therefore attracted most of Transvaal's and Rhodesia's traffic. New railroads were built in the South (Goba line, reaching the border with Swaziland, opened 1912; Limpopo line, connecting Lourenço Marques with Rhodesia, opened 1914; and other smaller ones); the Center (Tete and Quelimane lines); and the North (Mozambique line connecting the coast with Vila Cabral, started 1924). Therefore, the railroad network jumped from 500 km. in 1910, to almost 1,000 in 1920, and 2,000 in 1925. Growth continued in the 1930's, with 2,500 km. in 1935. A period of stagnation followed, but enlargement of the railway network was resumed from the 1950's onward: 2,700 km. in 1955, 3,200 in 1960, more than 3,500 in 1967.

Other public works included roads: 14,000 km. in 1928, 24,000 in 1940, 37,000 in 1955, 38,000 in 1967; dams; schools; and the usual public works also displayed in the mother country as a token of the New State administration.

Industrial development in both colonies drew comparatively much less attention. To the 1960's Portugal followed a typical colonial policy of fostering the production of raw materials but discouraging industrial activities in the Overseas provinces. Only the rubber and textile industries had some significance by the late 1950's. The outbreak of the guerrilla war changed the whole picture and brought about a quick industrial rise, which it is still too early to appraise from a historical standpoint.

The existence of the smaller colonies, Macao excepted, was not an easy one. Efforts to develop Angola and Mozambique often led the Lisbon administration to forget or neglect the other ones. Their economies and financial situation were far from brilliant, despite the fact that they frequently displayed surpluses in the balance of trade and the budget. The usual deficits found in Portugal or in Angola and Mozambique, up to the time of the New State, did not often exist in the smaller Overseas territories. In Cape Verde, for instance, budgets were balanced in difficult years such as 1916, 1917, 1919, and 1920. São Tomé's relative importance declined, yet the colony continued to be the largest or one of the largest producers of cacao and to prosper economically. Since the 1930's, the policy of "solidarity" among the mother country and all the colonies, coupled with the absolute requirement of presenting balanced budgets every year (not always accomplished), has meant that the most prosperous territories paid for the least prosperous ones, and all "re-paid" the mother country her "loans."

In general one can say that the smaller colonies stagnated to the 1950's, when their economic expansion followed world prosperity, Portugal's, and that of their two big partners, Angola and Mozambique. Public revenues doubled or more than doubled in Cape Verde, Guinea, Macao, and Timor in 1958–67, while in São Tomé revenues increased more than 50 per cent. In Portuguese India public revenues had expanded six times since the late 1940's when Indian soldiers cut it off from the Portuguese. In Guinea, exports sharply declined after the beginning of the guerrilla war and the occupation of vast areas by independence supporters.

From the 1950's onward, the New State administration envisaged a common market (escudo zone) area for Portugal and the Overseas territories. For that purpose tariffs were to be gradually reduced to complete extinction over a ten-year period starting with 1962. The partial execution of such an ambitious plan brought about closer contacts between Portugal and all of her colonies.

Well aware of the importance of Catholic missions to Europeanize the Africans, the first Republic did not impose on the Overseas the anticlerical policy followed at home (see chapter 12). Nonetheless the Separation Law of 1911 foresaw a complete withdrawal of all religious orders and their replacement by secular clerics. At the same time it provided for the establishment of lay missions (called "civilization missions") with teaching purposes void of any religious ideology. Their missionaries (male and female) were to be properly educated at home and possess a minimum training as instructors in Portugal. Eventually the lay missions would entirely replace the Christian ones.

None of these projects could be fully enforced. Few missionaries belonging to orders ever left because of the Republican legislation. Local circumstances justified their permanence and required a provisional suspension of the law. Persecutions were few and did not last. Yet, as Catholic missions were not encouraged by the authorities, competition by Protestant and even Moslem centers developed, arousing some protest and fear of "denationalization." After 1919 the Lisbon government decided to interfere and curb the free establishment of foreign or non-Catholic missions, forcing them to comply with a certain number of rules. Catholic missions recovered some support in the early 1920's. On the other hand, the lay missions had little time to develop and prosper, notwithstanding the important subsidies which the law granted them. Only nine had been created in Angola and five in Mozambique, when they were abolished in 1926 after the Rightist takeover in Portugal. Full protection to the Catholic missionaries was restored again.

The new Organic Statute of the Portuguese Catholic Missions (1926) enforced the nationalist spirit so dear to the "new order." It repressed foreign and non-Catholic missions, increased subsidies, and openly favored the Catholic priests. The Church was given a free hand to operate in all Portuguese colonies under a highly privileged situation. The Concordat of 1940 (see chapter 13) and the Missionary Agreement of the same year, both signed with the Vatican, further enhanced the possibilities of the Church in Christianizing and civilizing the natives.

The number and equipment of missions, however, always failed to meet the requirements of mass evangelization. In Angola, statistics showed only 24 missions in 1910, 49 in the mid-1930's, 93 in the 1950's, and more than 200 by the early 1960's; in Mozambique there were some 25 missions in 1910, 30 in 1930, 60 in 1940, double that number in the 1950's and double again in the 1960's. Religious missions also maintained rudimentary and elementary schools. But with so few effectives, their action had to be a limited one. Both in evangelization and education, results were far from brilliant. In the mid-1950's the official number of Catholics (an estimate many considered too optimistic) slightly surpassed one million in Angola (i.e., one-fourth of the total population, facing more than half a million Protestants), 350,000 in Mozambique (one-fifteenth of the population against 500,000 Muslims), 66,000 in Timor, and 19,000 in Guinea.

An important result of the agreements between Church and state after 1940 was the thorough reorganization of the ecclesiastical structure in the Portuguese Empire. In that year Angola and Mozambique were raised to archbishoprics (with seats in each colony's capital), two other dioceses being created in Angola—Nova Lisboa and Silva Porto

—and two in Mozambique—Beira and Nampula. Guinea was also separated from Cape Verde in 1940 and in 1955 it was made an apostolic prefecture. In Timor another diocese came into existence (1940). In this way ecclesiastical organization did coincide with the political shape of the Portuguese Empire, as in the sixteenth through the eighteenth centuries. Later development of both Angola and Mozambique led to new dioceses: Sá da Bandeira (1956), Malanje (1957), and Luso (1963) in West Africa, and Quelimane (1954), Porto Amélia (1957), Inhambane (1962), and Tete (1963) in East Africa. Ecclesiastical and civil districts were made almost coincident. In the East, the relative decline of the Portuguese influence put an end to the right of Patronage, which the Holy See practically abolished under agreement with the government of Portugal (1950), after considerable limitations since 1928.

Cultural development lagged much behind the economic. For many years, only Cape Verde, Macao, and Portuguese India had some educational framework worth mentioning. At the time of the proclamation of the Republic there was no secondary teaching whatsoever in the remaining five Overseas provinces.

Primary schools were ridiculously few for the total population. Angola had some fifty of them only in 1910, Mozambique perhaps double that number. For Guinea, São Tomé and Timor the figures were proportionately lower. In contrast, Cape Verde could boast ninety grammar schools, with Macao and India not too far behind. Aside from these three colonies school attendance was overwhelmingly restricted to the European or half-breed population.

Emigration increase and the Republican policy of fostering education brought about the need for more primary schools and the beginnings of a somewhat higher education. In Angola, grammar schools rose to eighty-four in 1923 plus half a dozen technical schools. The first *liceu* (high school) opened its doors in Luanda in 1918. Most of the rise had taken place during Norton de Matos' two administrations. In Mozambique education developed at a more rapid pace: 129 grammar schools in 1918 and 225 in 1926 (of which more than a half belonged to Catholic missions). High school teaching was carried on in two different places and there were several technical schools as well.

To the end of World War II education stagnated, or advanced

very slowly. In 1945 Angola had 129 primary schools with 8,000 pupils, Mozambique 822 with 120,000 (statistics in this case follow a different method, for they refer to the pre-primary teaching of African students as well), Guinea 44 with 870, São Tomé 14 with 1,700. Timor, just emerging from a destructive Japanese occupation, was reorganizing its educational system. The better-developed colonies displayed 100 schools with almost 6,000 pupils (Cape Verde), still surpassed by India (more than 10,000), and Macao. Secondary teaching showed higher figures in proportion, with 32 high schools and technical schools in Angola and 45 in Mozambique.

The great leap forward happened in the 1950's and the 1960's in all the Overseas provinces but especially in Angola and Mozambique. Figures for the school year 1966–67 showed 3,171 primary schools in Angola with an enrollment of 264,836. Mozambique's growth was still larger, both in schools (3,667) and pupils (468,983). Educational reforms in the 1960's created a unified governmental system for both rural and Europeanized Africans (together with the children of white settlers), all mission schools being officialized and instructed to offer the same kind of instruction everywhere. Methods of teaching Portuguese to the African pupils ranged among the most advanced in Africa. Textbooks—illustrated with pictures and stories from Angolan and Mozambican life—were of higher quality than those used in Portugal. Secondary education revealed a smaller, yet important, increase: 95 high schools in Portuguese West Africa, 84 in East Africa with student contingents more than ten times higher (Angola) and nearly four times higher (Mozambique) than in 1945. The need to respond to autonomist tendencies led the government to create universities in both colonies (1963), which developed rapidly.

In the other territories growth was less spectacular yet thoroughly positive. Secondary education was introduced in Guinea, São Tomé, and Timor. By the late 1960's the educational system in the Portuguese Overseas provinces, although far from being the best in Africa, showed an undeniable capacity for quick growth and could compare favorably with many others on the Continent.

The great question, undoubtedly, was how to provide mass education to the African rural populations. Christian missions had been making remarkable efforts in that direction, but they were never enough. Rates of illiteracy were still over 90 per cent in Guinea, Mozambique, and Angola (in 1950 they were, respectively, 98.85 per cent, 97.8 per cent and 96.4 per cent), over 80 per cent in São Tomé, and over 70 per cent in Cape Verde. In Angola and Mozambique hundreds of thousands, even millions, of remote Africans had no contact whatsoever with the Portuguese culture and were unable to speak Portuguese. In Macao constant migrations and countermigrations made percentages meaningless. In India, when the Portuguese left in 1961, the rate of illiteracy was above 70 per cent (78.3 per cent in 1950).

CONCLUSION

The appointment of Marcelo Caetano as Prime Minister was received with a mixture of hope, skepticism, and fear. Many people naively expected a radical change in policies, a practical end to the New State, with a gradual return to a regime of freedom and democracy. Others, who saw in both Salazar and his successor only symbols, thought the well-woven fabric of government had not been destroyed or even touched. Consequently, they expected little or no change. Many others were afraid of a troubled period following Salazar's retirement—either a Leftist takeover or the seizure of power by ultra-Rightist elements.

Marcelo Caetano's policy was extremely cautious. Well aware of the difficult situation he had inherited, he tried to keep things stable, making only slight and barely perceptible changes. He knew that powerful forces (the Army, the Navy, the police bodies, the top capitalists and bureaucrats, and a part of the Church hierarchy) were watching him closely and that he would have their support only if they were sure that "stability" and their vested interests would prevail. On the other hand, being in close contact with many opposition intellectuals and an intellectual himself, and fully realizing that times had changed, he felt he could not entirely shun a policy based upon some opening to the left and some appeal to the various opposition groups. Thus, as people said jokingly and as he himself quipped, he signaled "Left" and turned "Right."

To signal "Left" meant that he compromised on some minor, harmless points. He recalled opposition leader Mário Soares from his São Tomé exile and welcomed back many others, including the bishop of Porto, who had been forced to leave in 1958. He curbed the activities of the P.I.D.E., and he eased press censorship. He allowed a congress of opposition elements to meet in Aveiro under cover of being a historical "Republican Congress." Bookstores started to display all kinds of "subversive" works, which would have been immediately confiscated before. Theaters exhibited much more daring movies and plays. In public places people felt they breathed easier and talked more freely.

The turn "Right" was tò maintain the New State structure. Salazar-appointed cabinet ministers were replaced only gradually by Marcelo Caetano's men, four of the Salazar men still ruling by the summer of 1970. Portuguese troops continued to be sent to Africa to fight the rebels. Political parties were not allowed. No amnesty was granted. Freedom of association was denied. There were no changes in foreign policy. The corporative framework was not touched. No press law appeared. Nothing in essence had really changed two years after Salazar's downfall.

The general elections of November 1969 may have been a turning point in Portugal's political life. For the first time in forty-four years the opposition went to the polls in almost all the districts of Portugal. And for the first time, too, free elections were held in several places though by no means in all. Women were allowed to vote. Opposition candidates belonged to several groups, officially designated as "electoral committees." In most of Portugal unity of opposition forces could be achieved, but in Lisbon and Porto the Communist-oriented and the Socialist-oriented factions broke apart. There were also Monarchists and even dissidents from the National Union. Yet, as no political parties were permitted and as electoral activity could only develop in the month prior to the elections, the opposition had no chance to break through the National Union's powerful machine. Many of the eligible voters had not registered and many others had been removed from the balloting lists. Trusting neither government nor opposition many people decided to stay home and await the outcome, with the result that the number of abstentions, particularly in large towns, surpassed the number of votes. Moreover, the law provided for election only if a candidate obtained 50 per cent of the ballots. With no representation allotted to minorities, the opposition lost everywhere, and once more the National Assembly was composed of one-party representatives. Nonetheless, dissent within the official party became somewhat more common. A group of young people believed in opposing the regime within its own framework. In the new National Assembly one-fourth to one-third of the representatives displayed some "heretic" tendencies and angry voices rose against the "immobility" of the administration. The official party itself changed its name to Popular National Action (Acção Nacional Popular).

With the electoral period coming to an end, the honeymoon between Marcelo Caetano and the opposition came to an end too. Bitter reproaches came from both sides, and opposition leaders started denouncing the Prime Minister's alleged hypocrisy and contradictions. The war in Africa was the main point of dissent, the government tolerating no questions whatsoever about Portugal's permanence in the Overseas or how it was dealing with these affairs. By the spring of 1970 Mário Soares was forced into exile again, while several other opposition leaders were arrested or persecuted.

Hostility of college students toward the regime and demands for thorough reforms in education prevented regular instruction in both 1969 and 1970. Early in 1970 the Premier appointed a new Education Minister, who made some compromises on student demands, possibly heralding fundamental changes in the system of instruction.

EPILOG

In 1972 and 1973 the situation of the country grew worse, as a long period of its history was drawing to a close. From a military standpoint the situation Overseas was almost static. Its cost, however, kept increasing, and the weight fell heavily upon every aspect of Portuguese life. The Army felt a loss of prestige for not having achieved a victory in a guerrilla war that could go on indefinitely. Its middle and upper ranks were tired of more than ten years of war with no foreseeable outcome. The government showed no signs of changing its intransigent attitude and permitting any talks with the enemy or any solution but a military one. Desertions increased, the number of young men living in exile reaching several thousands.

Politically, the New State proved incapable of any renewal or opening up. Its structures were rigid and obsolete, with a group of extremists influencing them strongly and allowing no changes whatsoever. The leader of this group was none other than President Américo Tomás himself, who for the first time in the life of the regime was trying to use his extensive constitutional powers. Pressured by this group, Marcelo Caetano kept intact all of Salazar's machinery for repression, which he had lightened in the first years of his rule but intensified again in his last ones. Because of the timidity and the ambiguity of his policy he had lost all support from the Left. The liberal group formed in the Assembly in 1969 quickly evolved into sheer opposition or was tamed by the government's despotism. Opposition members, of course, were not reelected. The general elections of 1973 differed little from those of Salazar's days.

Economically, the world's crisis and the consequences of the war overshadowed the country. Inflation, above all, frightened many people and made them abandon a neutral line. Discontent grew all over the country. In this area, as in most others, the government was utterly incapable of acting with decision and efficiency.

Social tensions also grew worse. An elite segment of the bourgeoisie controlled some important monopolies, too large and too affluent for Portugal's size and resources. They pocketed most of the war profits as well as the main fruits of the country's gradual development. Opposed to them was an ever-growing middle class eager to get its share of the power and profits. A large proportion of the workers had a middle-class standard of living and formed a natural alliance with this latter group.

In 1973 the Governor of Portuguese Guinea (now Guiné-Bissau), General António de Spínola, a man who had attained great military and political prestige Overseas, was relieved of his command for advocating a new policy in Africa. Early in 1974 he was appointed Vice-Commander of the Armed Forces General Staff. The Commander was General Costa Gomes, another prestigious military leader who also disagreed with government policies.

At the same time, a conspiracy by a group of Army captains was in progress. It had started as a protest against some minor points regarding promotions in the ranks, but it quickly evolved into a broader movement against the regime.

In February 1974 Spínola, with Costa Gomes' approval, published a famous book, *Portugal and the Future,* where he openly criticized foreign and domestic Portuguese policies, favored a federalist solution for the Overseas problem, and suggested a sort of military coup d'état to save the country.

On March 14 the two commanders were dismissed from their posts. Two days later a first military uprising took place in Caldas da Rainha, sixty miles north of Lisbon. Owing to lack of organization and coordination, it was quickly put down by the government. But it led to a second uprising, on April 25, 1974. The overwhelming majority of the armed forces were now together and acted in concert. In about twelve hours they put an end to the regime. The government surrendered; Marcelo Caetano, Américo Tomás, and several cabinet ministers were arrested and deported to Madeira; and a Junta of National Salvation (Junta de Salvação Nacional) assumed leadership of the country. Its head was General Spínola, with Costa Gomes second in command. With practically no bloodshed the New State had come to an end.

The military movement of April 25, 1974 had little of the ideological in its roots. It had been, above all, a rebellion against the situation of the armed forces and the endless colonial war. In the background, undoubtedly, were all the other reasons, economic, social, and political in character. But awareness of them among the authors of the movement arose only gradually. The same could be said of their ideology in terms of a political philosophy and a coherent set of goals.

The program of the Armed Forces Movement (M.F.A.), known the day after the revolution, encompassed a set of measures that all social groups, with the possible exception of the higher-class bourgeoisie, would approve: removal of all top fascist authorities; extinction of the Secret Police, the Portuguese Legion, and political organizations among the youth; imprisonment of those mainly responsible for the regime and its crimes; economic and financial control; amnesty to those arrested for political reasons; an end to the censorship; purgation of the armed and militarized forces; and little else. In a short time, a new President of the Republic and a provisional government would be chosen, though the Junta of National Salvation would be kept in force. All freedoms would be restored, including the freedom to create political associations. The provisional government would set the basic principles for a new economic policy, "having as immediate concern the fight against inflation and the excessive rise of the cost of living, which necessarily will lead to an anti-monopolistic strategy." It would also establish a new social policy whose basic purpose was "the defense of the workers' interests." It would follow a foreign policy of respect for all international commitments then in force and a colonial policy "assuming that the wars in the Overseas have to be solved by political and not military means" in order to achieve peace. No reference was made either to socialism or to an immediate grant of independence to the colonies. Within a year, at most, a National Assembly would be elected in order to prepare the new Constitution.

One hundred per cent military, rejecting any civilian collaboration, the uprising installed in power, as in 1926, a military caste convinced of its legitimate right to govern the country. Yet the people quickly showed their intention of taking part in the movement, not only by their enthusiastic, spontaneous support from the north to the south of Portugal (the huge demonstrations on May 1, 1974 were a clear proof of this) but also in the form of political party organization and other groupings. Communists of several tendencies were particularly active, attempting to take control of power levers at the local and professional levels. They also launched a vast offensive aiming at the introduction of socialist programs into M.F.A. planning and a victory at the polls. Álvaro Cunhal, the well-known Secretary-General of the Portuguese Communist Party (Moscow-oriented) returned to Portugal early in May. So did the Socialist Leader Mário Soares and gradually thousands of exiles who had been scattered all over the world.

The first provisional government established in May was an attempt at a national, non-fascist coalition government. It was headed by a civilian, the Center Democrat Adelino da Palma Carlos, a well-known lawyer with a long record of fighting fascism, and included Communists and their kindred (Álvaro Cunhal and several others), Socialists (Mário Soares, among others), Social-Democrats, and even Monarchists. The key ministries, with the exception of Labor (which was Communist), were in Socialist hands. A few days earlier General Spínola had taken office as President of the Republic.

The political conflicts within both the government and the armed forces—which reflected, though to a different degree, the divisions among the Portuguese people—prevented the first provisional government from carrying out the majority of the huge tasks necessary to build a new Portugal. The same would happen to all incoming governments for more than a year. Palma Carlos was obliged to resign in July 1974, giving way to a second provisional government, presided over by Colonel (later Brigadier-General and then General) Vasco Gonçalves, that turned over half the ministries to the military. A third (September 1974), a fourth (March 1975), and a fifth (August 1975) provisional government followed, all headed by Vasco Gonçalves but showing progressively heavier Left-Communist influence and military power. Late in September 1974, after an attempt at a coup d'état, General Spínola resigned and was replaced by Costa Gomes. In March 1975, some Center and right-wing military led another unsuccessful uprising which resulted in the arrest and exile of hundreds, among them Spínola himself. Because of all this, the Junta of National Salvation was replaced with an enlarged Revolutionary Council (Conselho da Revolução), and the Armed Forces Movement was set up as an organized institution.

On April 25, 1975, a year after the revolution, elections were held, the first free ones in fifty years. The number of voters surpassed 90 per cent of those registered. Well aware of the political and economic options, after a year of intensive party propaganda, the Portuguese gave a clear victory (72.5 per cent) to the non-Communist parties (Socialists, Social-Democrats, Center Democrats). The Socialists got 37.9 per cent of the vote and the Social-Democrats 26.4 per cent. The Communist Party received only 12.5 per cent.

After this electoral result, the victorious parties tried to force the military to hand them their proportional share of power. But the Communists and their allies stopped them for a while. From April to September 1975 Portugal was torn apart by political struggle between Communist and non-Communist groups. North of the Tagus the struggle often broke into violence. In July the Socialists and the Social-Democrats left the (fourth) coalition government and passed on to become the opposition. It was then that Vasco Gonçalves, with the support of the Portuguese Communist Party, organized his last ministry.

The economic, financial, social, and political situation of the country had reached such grave proportions by then that widespread opposition to both the government and the armed forces was general. Among the military, divisions became deeper and deeper. The Western European countries and the United States of America intensified their pressure for a change. During August, the Army and the Air Force both made it clear they would not support the government for long. In September, President Costa Gomes forced Vasco Gonçalves to resign and called on Admiral Pinheiro de Azevedo to be Prime Minister. A sixth provisional government was constituted, with a Socialist and Social-Democratic majority and a promise of change in the country's policy. In November the Communists staged their coup d'état, which failed, and the government gathered a new strength, while the general situation of the country slowly tended to improve.

After almost two years of rule, the second Portuguese Republic had to its credit an impressive number of achievements: freedoms and fundamental rights had been thoroughly restored; the colonial wars had come to an end and soldiers had returned home from all the former colonies; independence had been granted to the new republics of Guiné-Bissau, Moçambique, São Tomé e Príncipe, Cape Verde, and Angola; the big economic monopolies had been broken and numerous basic firms nationalized; an agrarian reform was being carried out; citizens all over the country had gained a much stronger political awareness and were active in all kinds of organizations; diplomatic relations had been established with almost all countries; the standard of living was considerably higher than before the revolution among the middle and lower social groups; and so on.

But the negative aspects of the new Republic were also impressive: an extremely difficult economic and financial situation; unemployment reaching over 300,000 persons (5 per cent of all the active population); uncontrolled inflation; a breakdown of authority and discipline; chaotic situations in the former colonies of Angola and Timor; increased political hatreds at home; the flight of technical cadres abroad; the existence of thousands of political prisoners; the problematic return of 200,000 Portuguese from the former colonies; and so on. A long period for rebuilding the country was ahead.

BIBLIOGRAPHY

Note: This bibliography covers publications up to 1972.

Chapter Ten: Constitutional Monarchy

Old Structures and New Order, pages 1–41

Among the general histories, only the *História de Portugal,* directed by Damião Peres, vol. VII, Barcelos, Portucalense Editora, 1935, is relevant for the analysis of structures. There is a school handbook by Fortunato de Almeida, *História das Instituições em Portugal,* 2nd ed., Porto, Magalhães e Moniz, 1903, which is quite useful as a survey. The *Dicionário de História de Portugal* once again deserves serious attention.

On the general economic—as well as social—aspects, see Armando Castro, *Introdução ao Estudo da Economia Portuguesa (Fins do séc. XVIII a princípios do séc. XX),* Lisbon, Cosmos, 1947; Vitorino Magalhães Godinho, *Prix et Monnaies au Portugal, 1750–1850,* Paris, SEVPEN, 1955; and Ezequiel de Campos, *O Enquadramento Geo-Económico da População Portuguesa através dos séculos,* 2nd ed., Lisbon, Ocidente, 1943. Joel Serrão provides some useful material on more specific subjects (including cultural matters) in his *Temas Oitocentistas, Para a História de Portugal no Século Passado,* vol. I, Lisbon, Ática, 1959, and vol. II, Lisbon, Portugália, 1962.

On currency see A. C. Teixeira de Aragão, *Descrição Geral e Histórica das Moedas cunhadas em nome dos Reis, Regentes e Governadores de Portugal,* vol. II, 2nd ed., Porto, Fernando Machado, n.d. The budget was studied by Armindo Monteiro, *Do Orçamento Português,* vol. I, Lisbon, 1921.

On the Church, see Fortunato de Almeida, *História da Igreja em Portugal,* vols. III and IV, 2nd ed., Porto, Civilização, 1970–72.

On cultural aspects see António José Saraiva and Óscar Lopes, *História da Literatura Portuguesa,* 2nd ed., Porto, Porto Editora, n.d., as well as José Tengarrinha, *História da Imprensa Periódica Portuguesa,* Lisbon, Portugália, 1965. On the arts there is a comprehensive monograph by José Augusto

França, *A Arte em Portugal no século XIX*, vols. I and II, Lisbon, Bertrand, 1966.

Among the nineteenth-century authors who wrote on contemporary history, Alexandre Herculano and Oliveira Martins are indispensable for today's historian, particularly Oliveira Martins' *Portugal Contemporâneo* (covering the period 1826–68), 3 vols., 7th ed., Lisbon, Guimarães, 1953.

The Political Life, pages 41–53

On the Liberal ideology and its early introduction in Portugal, there are good articles in the *Dicionário de História de Portugal*, directed by Joel Serrão, vol. II ("Liberalismo," "Maçonaria," "Imprensa," etc.). See also Joel Serrão's recent work, *Do Sebastianismo ao Socialismo em Portugal*, Lisbon, Livros Horizonte, 1969. All these articles and books include good bibliographies.

The Constitutions were studied by Marcelo Caetano, in a short, clear book, *História Breve das Constituições Portuguesas*, 2nd ed., Lisbon, Verbo, 1968.

There is no general work on the elections and the electoral systems. Marcelo Caetano gives some indications in the aforementioned book. A good source continues to be the *Manual Parlamentar para uso dos Senhores Deputados da Nação Portugueza*, edited by José Marcelino de Almeida Bessa, Lisbon, Imprensa Nacional, 1901.

On the parties and the party system, see the articles on each party and its leaders in the *Dicionário*, as well as M. Caetano's work, and the short article by A. H. de Oliveira Marques, "Revolution and Counterrevolution in Portugal—Problems of Portuguese History, 1900–1930," offprint of *Studien über die Revolution*, Berlin, Akademie-Verlag, 1969, pp. 403–418.

The general histories of Portugal also give information on the political life of the country in this period.

Main Events, pages 54–75

Damião Peres' edition of *História de Portugal*, vol. VII, Barcelos, Portucalense Editora, 1935, gives the best account of the facts. The *Dicionário de História de Portugal*, edited by Joel Serrão, includes, as usual, several excellent articles on persons and events. Joaquim Pedro de Oliveira Martins' *Portugal Contemporâneo*, 7th ed., 3 vols., Lisbon, Guimarães ed., 1953, covers the period to 1868, but should be used with extreme caution, for the author tends to adopt a too pessimistic view of his country's history.

Fortunato de Almeida's *História de Portugal,* vol. VI, Coimbra, 1929, is of little use except for the religious problems. It includes, however, good bibliographical references.

Chapter Eleven: Africa

Travels and Colonization, pages 77–91

On travels in Portuguese Africa, the best accounts are still the explorers' own reports, most of which were published in Lisbon throughout the nineteenth century. Gamito, Brochado, Silva Porto, Welwitsch, Serpa Pinto, Capelo, Ivens, Henrique de Carvalho, and others left complete descriptions of their deeds of which no English translations are available. There is no good history of the Portuguese expeditions in general, but accurate references can be found in the general works on Portugal and on Portuguese Africa, namely the *História da Expansão Portuguesa no Mundo,* edited by António Baião, Hernâni Cidade, and Manuel Múrias, vol. III, Lisbon, Ática, 1940, as well as under each explorer's entry in the *Dicionário de História de Portugal,* edited by Joel Serrão. Both works contain bibliographies. Another first-rate source for the scientific study of nineteenth-century Portuguese Africa is the *Boletim da Sociedade de Geografia de Lisboa,* published since the 1870's.

On other aspects see the general works mentioned, which provide much of the extremely scattered bibliography. On slavery see, among other sources, Sá da Bandeira's *O Trabalho Rural Africano e a Administração Colonial,* Lisbon, 1873, and Luciano Cordeiro's *Questões Histórico-Coloniais,* Lisbon, 1936. James Duffy's *A Question of Slavery,* Cambridge, Mass., 1967, must be used with caution because of the author's anti-Portuguese bias.

On the Christian missions and the Church policy see, besides the general histories and Fortunato de Almeida's *História da Igreja em Portugal,* Eduardo dos Santos, *L'Etat Portugais et le Problème Missionaire,* Lisbon, 1964.

Organization, pages 91–107

Besides the general works already mentioned (particularly the *História da Expansão Portuguesa no Mundo,* vol. III), Angel Marvaud's report on Portugal and her colonies (*Le Portugal et ses Colonies: Etude politique et économique,* Paris, Félix Alcan, 1912) is of immense value, especially for the economic and financial questions. The classic book by Pinheiro Chagas,

As Colonias Portuguezas no seculo XIX (1811 a 1890), Lisbon, A. M. Pereira, 1890, still renders good service. The chaotic *Historia das Colonias Portuguesas,* by Rocha Martins, Lisbon, Empresa Nacional de Publicidade, 1933, is useful but must be used with caution. A good general history restricted to the Overseas affairs is clearly lacking.

Political Events, pages 107–118

Although the bibliography on the political and military history of the Portuguese Overseas during the nineteenth century is a vast one, there is hardly a good, recommended, general survey. The best works available are the *História de Portugal,* edited by Damião Peres, vol. VII, Barcelos, Portucalense, 1935, and the *História da Expansão Portuguesa no Mundo,* edited by António Baião, Hernâni Cidade and Manuel Múrias, Vol. III, Lisbon, Ática, 1940.

In English there are at least two good and up-to-date monographs which cover the international aspects of the Portuguese African policy: Richard J. Hammond, *Portugal and Africa, 1815–1910: A Study in Uneconomic Imperialism,* Stanford, Calif., Stanford University Press, 1966, and Eric Axelson, *Portugal and the Scramble for Africa, 1875–1891,* Johannesburg, Witwatersrand University Press, 1967. See also Mabel V. Jackson Haight, *European Powers and South-East Africa: A Study of International Relations on the South-East Coast of Africa, 1796–1856,* New York and Washington, Praeger, 1967, and Philip R. Warhurst, *Anglo-Portuguese Relations in South-Central Africa, 1890–1900,* London, Longmans, 1962.

Chapter Twelve: The First Republic

The Main Problems to Be Solved, pages 119–149

There are extremely few syntheses on this period and on its special aspects that can be recommended. Damião Peres' *História de Portugal,* vol. VII, Barcelos, Portucalense, 1935, and "Suplemento," Porto, Portucalense, 1954, do cover the whole period but emphasize the factual and political elements. For a short survey see A. H. de Oliveira Marques, *Portugal no século XX: Problemas de história portuguesa 1900–1930,* offprint of *Ocidente,* vol. LXXVI, Lisbon, 1969, pp. 253–272 and especially his *A 1ª República Portuguesa (para uma visão estrutural),* Lisbon, Livros Horizonte, n.d. [1971]. The *Dicionário de História de Portugal,* directed by Joel Serrão, contains some useful and up-to-date studies, all with bibliography.

There is more for literature and the arts: António José Saraiva and Óscar Lopes (*História da Literatura Portuguesa*, 2nd ed., Porto, Porto Editora, n.d.) explain the literary currents, while José Augusto França (*A Arte em Portugal no século XIX*, vol. II, Lisbon, Bertrand, 1966) gives a clear picture of the trends followed in the arts to the 1920's. For music, see João de Freitas Branco, *História da Música Portuguesa*, Lisbon, Europa-América, 1959.

There is nothing in English to recommend.

Ideologies and Political Structure, pages 149–164

On the Republican general ideology, the best account is from Joel Serrão (J.S.) in his article "Republicanismo," in the *Dicionário de História de Portugal*, III, 587–595, which also gives the most important bibliographical references. The party system has not been studied yet: see some remarks in Marcelo Caetano, *História Breve das Constituições Portuguesas*, 2nd ed., Lisbon, Verbo, 1968, in A. H. de Oliveira Marques, "Revolution and Counterrevolution in Portugal—Problems of Portuguese History, 1900–1930," offprint of *Studien über die Revolution*, Berlin, Akademie-Verlag, 1969, pp. 403–418, and especially in Damião Peres, *História de Portugal, Suplemento*, Porto, Portucalense, 1954. On the role played by Seara Nova there is a good article by Gerald Moser, "The Campaign of *Seara Nova* and Its Impact on Portuguese Literature, 1921–61" in *Luso-Brazilian Review*, II, 1 (June, 1965), 15–42, besides the survey by David Ferreira, "Seara Nova" in *Dicionário de História de Portugal*, III, Lisbon, 1968, 805–810. See also the articles included in this same Dictionary on each party and secret association.

The Constitution of 1911 was studied by several authors, as for instance, M. Caetano in the aforementioned book. There is no work on elections or electoral geography.

The Events, pages 164–175

The only work that gives a factual account of the Republican period is the *História de Portugal*, directed by Damião Peres, vol. VII, Barcelos, Portucalense, 1935 (chapters written by Ângelo Ribeiro and Hernâni Cidade), and particularly its *Suplemento*, Barcelos, Portucalense, 1954, written by Damião Peres himself. It covers the period to 1933. In English see A. H. de Oliveira Marques, "Revolution and Counterrevolution in Portugal—Problems of Portuguese History, 1900–1930," offprint of *Studien über die Revolution*, Berlin, Akademie-Verlag, 1969, pp. 403–418.

Chapter Thirteen: The "New State"

Portuguese Fascism, pages 177–194

The only recommended study of the New State is Hermínio Martins' outstanding, if short, analysis, *Portugal,* an offprint from *European Fascism,* edited by S. J. Woolf, London, Weidenfeld and Nicolson, 1968, pp. 302–336 (American edition, New York, Random House, 1969).

On Integralism, besides H. Martins, see Raul Proença, *Páginas de Política,* vols. I and II, Lisbon, Seara Nova, 1938–39; Carlos Ferrão, *O Integralismo e a República (Autópsia de um mito),* 3 vols., Lisbon, Século, 1964–66; David Ferreira's (D.F.) article "Integralismo Lusitano," in *Dicionário de História de Portugal,* edited by Joel Serrão, II, 556–560; and *A Questão Ibérica* (collection of lectures by leading Integralists), Lisbon, 1916.

On Italian and other foreign influences on the Portuguese regime, see the long-forgotten, yet useful, small book, *Origine e caratteri dello "Stato Nuovo" Portoghese,* edited by Aldo Bigarri, Milan, Instituto per gli studi di Politica Internazionale, 1941.

The best source for the study of the essential New State principles and evolution, as well as Salazar's thought, is of course Salazar himself: see his *Discursos e Notas Políticas,* 5 vols., Coimbra, Coimbra Editora, 1935–68. António Ferro's classic, *Salazar: Portugal and Her Leader,* Lisbon, 1939, continues to be the best study on the Dictator, done by one of his followers. Recommended biographies by non-Portuguese authors are Hugh Kay's *Salazar and Modern Portugal,* London, Eyre & Spottiswoode, 1970, and particularly Christian Rudel, *Salazar,* Paris, Mercure de France, 1969. On Corporatism see Marcelo Caetano, *O sistema corporativo,* Lisbon, 1937. His short, excellent *História Breve das Constituições Portuguesas,* 2nd ed. (important because of the author's rise to premiership and his authoritative remarks on Salazar's rule), Lisbon, Verbo, 1968, gives a summary of the regime's constitutional framework.

I strongly advise anyone interested in the Portuguese political and economic structure to consult any of the *liceu* (high-school) "political organization" textbooks for the upper grades, as for instance, A. Martins Afonso, *Princípios Fundamentais de Organização Política e Administrativa da Nação,* 14th ed., Lisbon, Papelaria Fernandes, n.d. [1966].

On repression see, for instance, among scores of passionate, yet valid, testimonies, Fernando Queiroga, *Portugal Oprimido (Subsídios para a história do fascismo em Portugal),* Rio de Janeiro, Editora Germinal, 1958, or

P. Fryer and P. MacGowan Pinheiro, *Oldest Ally: A Portrait of Salazar's Portugal,* London, 1961, or the judiciary proceedings edited by lawyer Francisco Salgado Zenha, *Quatro Causas,* Lisbon, 1969.

Hermínio Martins is also the author of a short but penetrating analysis of the Portuguese opposition: *Opposition in Portugal,* reprint from *Government and Opposition,* vol. IV, No. 2 (Spring, 1969), pp. 250–263.

Portugal by the Middle of the Twentieth Century, pages 194–208

The use of yearly books such as the *Encyclopaedia Britannica Book of the Year,* the United Nations publications, and the Portuguese annual statistics (*Anuário Estatístico*) must make up for the lack of general histories or even detailed monographs on the New State as a whole. Ezequiel de Campos, *O Enquadramento Geo-Económico da População Portuguesa através dos Séculos,* 2nd ed., Lisbon, Ocidente, 1943, and Orlando Ribeiro, *Portugal,* vol. V of Manuel de Terán's *Geografía de España y Portugal,* Barcelona, Montaner y Simón, 1955, give interesting surveys on economic and demographic questions to the 1950's.

On Salazar's financial reforms, see Salazar himself, *A reorganização financeira, Dois anos no Ministério das Finanças, 1928–1930,* Coimbra, Coimbra Editora, 1930, followed by several of his speeches and notes, namely in *Discursos e Notas Políticas,* vol. II, *1935–1937,* Coimbra, Coimbra, Editora, 1937 ("Questões Financeiras," pp. 351–395). José Joaquim Teixeira Ribeiro in his textbook *Introdução ao Estudo da Moeda,* Coimbra, Atlântida, 1949, devotes one chapter to the Portuguese monetary evolution to 1948. See also Marcelo Caetano, *A obra financeira de Salazar,* Lisbon, 1934.

On public works there is an official publication called *Quinze Anos de Obras Públicas (1932–1947),* Comissão Executiva da Exposição de Obras Públicas, 2 vols., Lisbon, 1949, covering the period to 1947. Among the many books and pamphlets on economic subjects, see Araújo Correia, *Portugal Económico e Financeiro,* Lisbon, 1938; Ezequiel de Campos, *Problemas Fundamentais Portugueses,* Lisbon, 1946; Pereira de Moura and Luis Maria Teixeira Pinto, *Problemas do crescimento económico português,* Lisbon, 1958; V. Xavier Pintado, *Structure and Growth of the Portuguese Economy,* Geneva, 1964; and Vitorino Magalhães Godinho, *O Socialismo e o Futuro da Península,* Lisbon, Horizonte, 1969. There is a good summary report on internal colonization by Henrique de Barros, *Economia Agrária,* vol. III, Lisbon, Sá da Costa, 1954. On other aspects of agriculture, see

Mário de Azevedo Gomes, Henrique de Barros, and Eugénio de Castro Caldas, "Traços principais da evolução da agricultura portuguesa entre as duas guerras mundiais," in *Revista do Centro de Estudos Económicos,* nos. 1 and 2 (1945), pp. 21–203 and 49–86; Álvaro Cunhal, *A Questão Agrária em Portugal,* Rio de Janeiro, Ed. Civilização Brasileira, 1968 (the communist standpoint), and others.

Population changes were studied by J. T. Montalvão Machado, *Como nascem e morrem os Portugueses,* Lisbon, Gomes e Rodrigues, n.d., and more recently, by Alberto de Alarcão, *Mobilidade Geográfica da População de Portugal (Continente e Ilhas Adjacentes): Migrações internas 1921– 1960,* Lisbon, Fundação Calouste Gulbenkian, 1969.

On administration, the best report is Marcelo Caetano's textbook, *Manual de Direito Administrativo,* 8th ed., 2 vols., Lisbon, Coimbra Editora, 1969. Educational problems were studied by scores of people. See, for instance, Rogério Fernandes, *Ensino: Sector em Crise,* Lisbon, Prelo, 1967; *Análise Quantitativa da Estrutura Escolar Portuguesa, 1950–1959,* Lisbon, Centro de Estudos de Estatística Económica do Instituto de Alta Cultura, 1960; or the two volumes of periodical *Análise Social,* vol. V and VI, 1967–68, devoted to "A Universidade na Vida Portuguesa."

For the general panorama of literature, see António José Saraiva and Óscar Lopes, *História da Literatura Portuguesa,* Porto, Porto Editora, n.d.

The Events, pages 208–224

Damião Peres' *História de Portugal: Suplemento,* Porto, Portucalense, 1954, stops in 1934. To 1945 there is a list of the main events (from the government standpoint) in the *Anais da Revolução Nacional,* ed. by João Ameal and Domingos Mascarenhas, 5 vols., Lisbon, 1948–56. For later times, as for the whole period, see the *Encyclopaedia Britannica Book of the Year* or any other good Encyclopedia.

Chapter Fourteen: The Overseas Empire in the Twentieth Century
Policies, pages 225–232

Damião Peres' *História de Portugal: Suplemento,* Porto, Portucalense, 1954, provides the main information for the period 1914–33. Further elements are contained in the António Baião, Hernâni Cidade, and Manuel Múrias edition of *História da Expansão Portuguesa no Mundo,* vol. III, Lisbon, Ática, 1940. See also Henrique Galvão and Carlos Selvagem, *Im-*

pério Ultramarino Português, 4 vols., Lisbon, Empresa Nacional de Publicidade, 1950–53.

For the period after 1945 the bibliography is large but scattered and uneven in objectivity. There are acceptable historical data in Ronald H. Chilcote, *Portuguese Africa,* Englewood Cliffs, Prentice Hall, Inc., 1967, and in Eduardo Mondlane's *The Struggle for Mozambique,* Penguin Books, 1969. From the other side see, for instance, Adriano Moreira's *Portugal's Stand in Africa,* New York, 1962, and *The Road for the Future,* Lisbon, 1963, along with many of his speeches and interviews translated into English. See also Marcelo Caetano, *Portugal e a internacionalização dos problemas africanos,* Lisbon, 1963, and A. Franco Nogueira, *The United Nations and Portugal: A Study of Anti-Colonialism,* London, 1963.

On specific labor problems and the Portuguese labor policy, see José Norton de Matos, *Memórias e Trabalhos da Minha Vida,* 4 vols., Lisbon, 1945–46 (particularly vol. 3), and his *A Província de Angola,* Porto, Maranus, 1926. For a general survey, see Joaquim M. da Silva Cunha, *O sistema português de política indígena: Princípios gerais,* Lisbon, Agência Geral do Ultramar, 1952, and his *O trabalho indígena: estudo de direito colonial,* Lisbon, 1954. On the problem to 1920, see James Duffy, *A Question of Slavery,* Oxford, Clarendon Press, 1967.

From Pacification to the Prospects of Independence, pages 232–239

On the last pacification campaigns and World War I in Portuguese Africa the bibliography is vast. See general surveys in *História da Expansão Portuguesa no Mundo,* edited by António Baião, Hernâni Cidade, and Manuel Múrias, vol. III, Lisbon, Ática, 1940, and in *História de Portugal,* edited by Damião Peres, vol. VII, and *Suplemento,* Barcelos and Porto, Portucalense, 1935 and 1954. See also the authoritative monograph by General M. Gomes da Costa, *A Guerra nas Colonias, 1914–1918,* Lisbon Portugal/Brasil, n.d.

Bibliography on the African uprisings is also vast. Most of it is unreliable because of partisanship.

On the side of the independence movements, see, among many others:
(a) General works—James Duffy, *Portugal in Africa,* Penguin Books, 1963; Ronald H. Chilcote, *Portuguese Africa,* Prentice-Hall, Englewood Cliffs, N.J., 1967; "Three Revolutions," special issue of *Africa Report* on Portuguese Africa, vol. 12, No. 8 (November, 1967).
(b) On Angola: *Angola: A Symposium: Views of a Revolt,* Ox-

ford University Press, 1962; *Les Angolais,* edited by Robert Davezies, Paris, Editions de Minuit, 1965; Pierre Moser, *La Révolution Angolaise,* Tunis, Société d'Action, d'Édition et de Presse, 1966; John Marcum, *The Angolan Revolution,* vol. I, *The Anatomy of an Explosion (1950– 1962),* M.I.T. Press, Cambridge, Mass., 1969.

(c) On Mozambique: Eduardo Mondlane, *The Struggle for Mozambique,* Penguin Books, 1969.

(d) On Guinea: Gérard Chaliand, *Lutte armée en Afrique,* Paris, François Maspéro, 1967.

On the side of the Portuguese Government:

Angola: Curso de extensão universitária, Lisbon, 1963; Amândio César, *Angola 1961,* Lisbon, Verbo, 1962; Artur Maciel, *Angola Heroica,* Lisbon, Bertrand, 1963.

The "Empire" by the Middle of the Century, pages 239–257

There is no recommendable history of the Portuguese Empire in the twentieth century. Henrique Galvão's and Carlos Selvagem's four-volume work, *O Império Ultramarino Português,* Lisbon, Empresa Nacional de Publicidade, 1950–53, contains much useful information. Official statistics appear in *Anuário Estatístico do Império Colonial Português* (later called *Anuário Estatístico do Ultramar*), Lisbon, 1943–59 and in the general *Anuário Estatístico* for all of Portugal after 1960. Portuguese and general encyclopaedias must also be consulted. There are local *Anuários* in each colony. In English there is nothing really commendable, but both James Duffy's works (*Portuguese Africa,* Cambridge, Mass. and London, 1959; and *Portugal in Africa,* Penguin Books, 1963) and Ronald Chilcote's (*Portuguese Africa,* Englewood Cliffs, 1967) may be useful, if used with caution.

Bibliography on specific problems is endless. Chilcote gives a quite extensive and reliable list of books which can be used for the study of the Portuguese twentieth-century Empire.